MW00809595

INTERPRETING THE
NEW TESTAMENT TEXT

INTERPRETING THE NEW TESTAMENT TEXT

Introduction to the Art and Science of Exegesis

**DARRELL L. BOCK
AND BUIST M. FANNING**

EDITORS

:: CROSSWAY®

WHEATON, ILLINOIS

With the exception of the Scripture quotations in chapter 9, unless otherwise noted, all Scripture quotations are the authors' translations.

Scripture references marked NIV are from *The Holy Bible: New International Version.*® Copyright © 1973, 1978, 1984 by International Bible Society. Used by permission of Zondervan Publishing House. All rights reserved.

The "NIV" and "New International Version" trademarks are registered in the United States Patent and Trademark Office by International Bible Society. Use of either trademark requires the permission of International Bible Society.

Scripture quotations marked ESV are from the ESV® Bible (*The Holy Bible, English Standard Version*®), copyright © 2001 by Crossway. Used by permission. All rights reserved.

Scripture quotations marked NASB are from *The New American Standard Bible.*® Copyright © The Lockman Foundation 1960, 1962, 1963, 1968, 1971, 1972, 1973, 1975, 1977, 1995. Used by permission.

Scripture references marked RSV are from *The Revised Standard Version.* Copyright © 1946, 1952, 1971, 1973 by the Division of Christian Education of the National Council of the Churches of Christ in the U.S.A.

Scripture references marked NRSV are from *The New Revised Standard Version.* Copyright © 1989 by the Division of Christian Education of the National Council of the Churches of Christ in the U.S.A. Published by Thomas Nelson, Inc. Used by permission of the National Council of the Churches of Christ in the U.S.A.

Scripture quotations marked NET are from *The NET Bible*® copyright © 2003 by Biblical Studies Press, L.L.C. www.netbible.com. All rights reserved. Quoted by permission.

Scripture references marked NLT are from *The Holy Bible, New Living Translation,* copyright © 1996. Used by permission of Tyndale House Publishers, Inc., Wheaton, Ill., 60189. All rights reserved.

Scripture references marked JB are from *The Jerusalem Bible.* Copyright © 1966, 1967, 1968 by Darton, Longman & Todd Ltd. and Doubleday & Co., Inc.

Scripture references marked NEB are from *The New English Bible* © The Delegates of the Oxford University Press and The Syndics of the Cambridge University Press, 1961, 1970.

Scripture quotations marked KJV are from the King James Version of the Bible.

All emphases in Scripture quotations have been added by the authors.

ISBN-13: 978-1-58134-408-0
ISBN-10: 1-58134-408-2
ePub ISBN: 978-1-4335-1922-2
PDF ISBN: 978-1-4335-1812-6
Mobipocket ISBN: 978-1-4335-0824-0

Library of Congress Cataloging-in-Publication Data

Interpreting the New Testament text : introduction to the art and science of exegesis / Darrell L. Bock and Buist M. Fanning, editors.
    p. cm.
    Includes indexes.
    ISBN 13: 978-1-58134-408-0 (hc : alk. paper)
    ISBN 10: 1-58134-408-2
    1. Bible. N.T.—Hermeneutics. 2. Bible. N.T.—Criticism, interpretation, etc. I. Bock, Darrell L. II. Fanning, Buist M.
    BS2331.I58 2006
    225.601—dc22   2006024375

Crossway is a publishing ministry of Good News Publishers.

SH   26 25 24 23 22 21 20 19 18 17 16
16 15 14 13 12 11 10 9 8 7 6 5 4

Contents

Preface

I (Fanning) recall the conversation well, even though thirty-five years have passed between then and now (as this is written in Spring 2006). Picture a group of first-year seminarians complaining over lunch about whether we could survive "New Testament Introduction" and whether it was worth the effort! Our young professor, Harold Hoehner, had been taking us through the intricacies of intertestamental history and culture, textual criticism, the Synoptic problem, NT authorship issues, and other NT questions that we never knew existed. Our heads were spinning. But somehow, in spite of ourselves, at least some of us found it fascinating and saw the connection to the primary passion that had brought us to that class, that is, a hunger to know the Scriptures, to live by them, and to see others' lives transformed as ours had been. There was something about our professor's own fervor for ministry as well as scholarship that helped us to find our way.

Experiences like that are shared by all of us who have contributed to Part One of this book (Harold's colleagues at Dallas Theological Seminary) as well as by the "former student" contributors in Part Two. So it gives us great delight to present this book as a tribute to our teacher, mentor, colleague, and friend, Harold W. Hoehner! Together with the other friends and colleagues who have joined us in Part Two, we offer this volume to Harold as a token of our profound appreciation, esteem, and affection.

Many others have benefited as well from Harold's personal and professional gifts. He has had a fruitful and significant career teaching and giving leadership to the academic work of Dallas Theological Seminary (serving on faculty from 1968 to the present, as Department Chair of New Testament 1977-2001, and as Director of Ph.D. studies 1975-2002). Directly and indirectly he has influenced thousands of students who now serve all over the world. As a teacher Harold has always pushed his students toward excellence, careful study of Scripture, and engagement with the wider world of NT scholarship. Starting in the early 1970s he revolutionized the way exegesis was taught at DTS, and this book is the expression of what we have learned from him and hammered out together over many years of teaching and serving together as coworkers in the Word.

What can be said about Harold as a person! He is a man of integrity, energy, frugality, strong opinions, and hard work, but always coupled with a genial sense of humor, humility, and a loyal and collegial spirit. Those of us who have served with him at DTS have had the rare favor of genuine mentoring: he guided us as students, recruited us as neophyte faculty, defended us and challenged us when necessary, and all along modeled for us what scholarship in the service of Christ can be. His loving and robust family life with Gini, their children, and now grandchildren has pictured what we want for our own families. Most of all Harold has shown us what it means to be a man of God, committed to Christ and his gospel, and reflecting the fruit of the Spirit over a lifetime of faithful service.

—The Editors

Contributors

Part One (faculty at Dallas Theological Seminary)

Darrell L. Bock (Ph.D., Aberdeen)
Michael H. Burer (Ph.D., Dallas)
Buist M. Fanning (D.Phil., Oxford)
Joseph D. Fantin (Ph.D., Dallas; Ph.D., Sheffield)
John D. Grassmick (Ph.D., Glasgow)
W. Hall Harris III (Ph.D., Sheffield)
J. William Johnston (Ph.D., Dallas)
David K. Lowery (Ph.D., Aberdeen)
Timothy J. Ralston (Ph.D., Dallas)
Jay E. Smith (Ph.D., Trinity)
Daniel B. Wallace (Ph.D., Dallas)

Part Two

Herbert W. Bateman IV, Moody Bible Institute, Chicago
David Catchpole, Sarum College, Salisbury, England
Scott S. Cunningham, Accrediting Council for Theological Education in Africa and Jos ECWA Theological Seminary (Nigeria)
E. Earle Ellis, Southwestern Baptist Theological Seminary, Fort Worth, Tex.
W. Edward Glenny, Northwestern College, St. Paul, Minn.

Don N. Howell, Jr., Columbia Biblical Seminary, Columbia, S.C.

I. Howard Marshall, University of Aberdeen, Scotland

Narry F. Santos, Greenhills Christian Fellowship–South Metro and International School of Theology–Asia, Manila, Philippines

Timothy B. Savage, Camelback Bible Church, Paradise Valley, Ariz.

Helge Stadelmann, German Theological Seminary, Giessen, Germany; and Evangelische Theologische Faculteit of Leuven, Belgium

Donald J. Verseput (d.), Bethel Theological Seminary, St. Paul, Minn.

Joel F. Williams, Columbia International University, Columbia, S.C.

Edwin M. Yamauchi, Miami University, Oxford, Ohio

Abbreviations

AB	Anchor Bible
ABD	*Anchor Bible Dictionary,* ed. David Noel Freedman et al., 6 vols. (New York: Doubleday, 1992)
Amplified	Amplified Bible
AnBib	Analecta biblica
ANRW	*Aufstieg und Niedergang der Römischen Welt,* ed. Wolfgang Haase and Hildegaard Temporini (Berlin: de Gruyter, 1972-)
ANTC	Abingdon New Testament Commentaries
AÖAW	*Anzeiger des Österreichischen Akademie der Wissenschaft*
ASV	American Standard Version
BAGD	Walter Bauer, *A Greek-English Lexicon of the New Testament and Other Early Christian Literature,* trans. and adapted by William F. Arndt and F. Wilbur Gingrich, rev. and augmented by F. Wilbur Gingrich and Frederick Danker, 2nd ed. (Chicago: University of Chicago Press, 1979)
BDAG	Walter Bauer, *A Greek-English Lexicon of the New Testament and Other Early Christian Literature,* rev. and ed. Frederick Danker, 3rd ed. (Chicago: University of Chicago Press, 2000)
BDF	Friedrich Blass and Albert Debrunner, *A Greek Grammar of the New Testament and Other Early Christian Literature,* trans. Robert W. Funk (Chicago: University of Chicago Press, 1961)
BDR	Friedrich Blass and Albert Debrunner, *Grammatik des neutestamentlichen Griechish,* ed. Friedrich Rehkopf, 15th ed. (Göttingen: Vandenhoeck & Ruprecht, 1979)
BECNT	Baker Exegetical Commentary on the New Testament
BJRL	*Bulletin of the John Rylands Library*
BNTC	Black's New Testament Commentaries
BSac	*Bibliotheca Sacra*

CBQ	*Catholic Biblical Quarterly*
CBQMS	Catholic Biblical Quarterly Monograph Series
CEV	Contemporary English Version
CGTC	Cambridge Greek Testament Commentary
DJG	*Dictionary of Jesus and the Gospels,* ed. Joel B. Green, Scot McKnight, and I. Howard Marshall (Downers Grove, Ill.: InterVarsity Press, 1992)
DLNT	*Dictionary of the Later New Testament and Its Developments,* ed. Ralph P. Martin and Peter H. Davids (Downers Grove, Ill.: InterVarsity Press, 1997)
DM	H. E. Dana and Julius R. Mantey, *A Manual Grammar of the Greek New Testament* (Toronto: Macmillan, 1927)
DPL	*Dictionary of Paul and His Letters,* ed. Gerald F. Hawthorne and Ralph P. Martin (Downers Grove, Ill.: InterVarsity Press, 1993)
ECB	*Eerdmans Commentary on the Bible*
EDNT	*Exegetical Dictionary of the New Testament,* ed. Horst Balz and Gerhard Schneider, 3 vols. (Grand Rapids, Mich.: Eerdmans, 1990-93)
EKKNT	Evangelisch-katholischer Kommentar zum Neuen Testament
ESV	English Standard Version
ExSyn	*Greek Grammar Beyond the Basics: An Exegetical Syntax of New Testament Greek,* Daniel B. Wallace (Grand Rapids, Mich.: Zondervan, 1996)
GT	German text
HCSB	Holman Christian Standard Bible
HNT	Handbuch zum Neuen Testament
HNTC	Harper's New Testament Commentaries
HTKNT	Herders theologischer Kommentar zum Neuen Testament
HTR	*Harvard Theological Review*
ICC	International Critical Commentary
IDB	*The Interpreter's Dictionary of the Bible,* ed. George Arthur Buttrick, 5 vols. (New York: Abingdon, 1962)
ISBE	*The International Standard Bible Encyclopedia,* ed. Geoffrey W. Bromiley, 4 vols. (Grand Rapids, Mich.: Eerdmans, 1979)
JAAR	*Journal of the American Academy of Religion*
JB	Jerusalem Bible
JBL	*Journal of Biblical Literature*
JECS	*Journal of Early Christian Studies*
JETS	*Journal of the Evangelical Theological Society*
JR	*Journal of Religion*
JSJ	*Journal for the Study of Judaism*
JSNT	*Journal for the Study of the New Testament*
JSNTSup	Journal for the Study of the New Testament Supplement Series

JSS	*Journal of Semitic Studies*
JTS	*Journal of Theological Studies*
KJV	King James Version
L&N	Johannes P. Louw and Eugene A. Nida, *Greek-English Lexicon of the New Testament: Based on Semantic Domains,* 2 vols. (New York: United Bible Societies, 1988)
LSJ	Henry George Liddell and Robert Scott, *A Greek-English Lexicon,* 9th ed., rev. and aug. Henry Stuart Jones and Roderick McKenzie (Oxford: Clarendon, 1940; revised supplement, 1996)
LXX	Septuagint
MHT	James Hope Moulton, *A Grammar of New Testament Greek,* vol. 3., *Syntax,* by Nigel Turner (Edinburgh: Clark, 1963)
MM	James Hope Moulton and George Milligan, *The Vocabulary of the Greek Testament* (London: Hodder & Stoughton, 1930)
MNTC	Moffatt New Testament Commentary
MS(S)	manuscript(s)
NA[27]	*Novum Testamentum Graece,* 27th ed., ed. B. Aland et al. (Stuttgart: Deutsche Bibelgesellschaft, 1993)
NAC	New American Commentary
NASB	New American Standard Bible
NCB	New Century Bible
NCV	New Century Version
NEB	New English Bible
NET	*NET Bible, New English Translation,* First Edition (Dallas: Biblical Studies Press, 2005)
NET-Nestle	*New English Translation*—Novum Testamentum Graece *New Testament* (Stuttgart: Deutsche Bibelgesellschaft; Dallas: NET Bible Press, 2004)
NIBC	New International Biblical Commentary
NICNT	New International Commentary on the New Testament
NIDNTT	*New International Dictionary of New Testament Theology,* ed. Colin Brown, 3 vols. (Grand Rapids, Mich.: Zondervan, 1975-78)
NIGTC	New International Greek Testament Commentary
NIV	New International Version
NIVAC	NIV Application Commentary
NJB	New Jerusalem Bible
NKJV	New King James Version
NLT	New Living Translation
NovT	*Novum Testamentum*
NovTSup	Supplements to Novum Testamentum
NRSV	New Revised Standard Version

NT	New Testament
NTC	New Testament Commentary
NTS	*New Testament Studies*
NTTS	New Testament Texts and Studies
OT	Old Testament
ÖTK	Ökumenischer Taschenbuchkommentar zum Neuen Testament
OTP	*Old Testament Pseudepigrapha,* ed. James H. Charlesworth, 2 vols. (Garden City, N.Y.: Doubleday, 1983-85)
REB	Revised English Bible
RevExp	*Review and Expositor*
RSV	Revised Standard Version
RTR	*Reformed Theological Review*
SBLDS	Society of Biblical Literature Dissertation Series
SBT	Studies in Biblical Theology
SNTSMS	Society for New Testament Studies Monograph Series
SP	Sacra pagina
TDNT	*Theological Dictionary of the New Testament,* ed. Gerhard Kittel and Gerhard Friedrich, trans. Geoffrey W. Bromiley, 10 vols. (Grand Rapids, Mich.: Eerdmans, 1964-76)
TEV	Today's English Version
THKNT	Theologischer Handkommentar zum Neuen Testament
TLZ	*Theologische Lituraturzeitung*
TNIV	Today's NIV
TNTC	Tyndale New Testament Commentary
UBS[4]	*The Greek New Testament,* 4th ed., ed. K. Aland et al. (Stuttgart: Deutsche Bibelgesellschaft/United Bible Societies, 1993)
WBC	Word Biblical Commentary
Weymouth	*The New Testament in Modern English,* R. F. Weymouth
WTJ	*Westminster Theological Journal*
WUNT	Wissenschaftliche Untersuchungen zum Neuen Testament
ZBK	Züricher Bibelkommentare
ZNW	*Zeitschrift für die neutestamentliche Wissenschaft*
ZPEB	*Zondervan Pictorial Encyclopedia of the Bible,* ed. Merrill C. Tenney, 5 vols. (Grand Rapids, Mich.: Zondervan, 1975-76)

Introduction

Exegesis is not only a word that people rarely use; it is a course that is falling on hard times in many seminary programs. Once taken as a given for pastors and teachers of the Word, the interpretation and exposition of the NT rooted in a firsthand encounter with the original Greek has become rare in a world where languages can be translated by a computer and where high-quality English translations abound. Such realities raise questions like why exegete and why produce a textbook on NT exegesis.

The answer is simple. We exegete the Scripture because working with a text firsthand is the best way to get to know it. That does not mean the interpreter is not interested in the study others bring to the text. A good exegete is not an interpreter functioning alone on the island of his or her own thoughts. A good exegete, as we hope to show, engages others who study the text. A solid exegete has developed the science and art of assessing how the text is being handled, not just what it says. A competent exegete can explain the interpretive choices that have been made, as well as the options from which the choice emerged. All of this requires interaction with the Greek text and with the discussion that text has generated from others.

An exegete is able to have a conversation with the Bible where the very wording, structure, and presentation of the Bible directs the dialogue. The exegete can see and develop nuances that otherwise get lost in the move from Greek to the student's native language. To use a modern metaphor, exegesis is a high-definition form of reading and studying the Bible. The detailed pixels give color and depth to the message that the Bible contains. So a textbook on exegesis is a form of high-tech Bible study, where options and nuances are weighed and appreciated. What emerges is one of the most fundamental skills for a teacher of Scripture, the ability to understand the Word *and* sort out the various views people affirm about its meaning.

In addition, exegesis takes more than simply "just doing it." There are basic steps in doing exegesis. The more conscious one is of method, the more likely one will avoid the pitfalls that can come when one simply just does it. Often the most difficult aspect of interpreting is working carefully through the steps and articulating the rationale for why taking those steps is important to reading and interpreting, especially when it is a second language that is being studied.

This textbook is rooted in almost thirty years of teaching exegetical method at Dallas Theological Seminary, a post-graduate school of theology that has established a reputation for preparing students to study the Bible in the original languages. All the writers in the first section on exegetical method have taught the course on exegesis, many of them for over twenty years. The topics have been "field tested" in the classroom for that period and reflect a genuine team effort where the syllabus was shared as were lecture materials. Working hard on how to articulate this process to beginning students and trying to do it with clarity have been among the key goals of the class. The value of these team roots means that this text is not the reflection of a single person's strengths or weaknesses (or hobby horses). Each topic was hammered out through departmental interaction and input. We believe the team character of the input has strengthened the results. The chapters reflect the work of the entire team, evidencing a cooperation in ministry and method that has made us all better for the effort.

Taking the chapters in Part One in isolation, however, obscures the kind of interconnected relationship these procedures have when one actually does exegesis. Some measure of artificial separation of the units here is required when teaching an introduction to exegesis, but these units coalesce more tightly as one gains experience with the method. As with learning any skill, practice brings improvement when accompanied by a desire to grow. This textbook is a little like participating in spring training. The basics are gone through in detail, step by step. Which steps and how much detail to apply becomes clear as one gains experience and begins to sense what a particular text requires. Thus, while exegesis is a science—that is, a skill to be learned—there also is an art to it. The art involves gaining a feel or possessing an instinct for what needs to be done with a particular text, that is, what procedures best fit that passage and what questions need to be answered. In the game that is exegesis, one does not follow the same pattern all the time, but draws on the basic skills worked on in spring training that are necessary to get to the goal, namely, a better understanding of the text's message.

This text is designed to facilitate that process through carefully presented introductory essays on key elements of exegetical method in Part One, as well as through examples gathered from exegetes around the world in Part Two. The samples in Part Two give vivid illustrations of key elements of method or in some cases combinations of those elements. One can survey the brief summaries included with the chapters in Part Two to see which procedures are being illustrated in that essay in development of ideas presented in Part One.

We are all students. Students gather to learn. Just as we have taught each other and myriads of students working side by side to encourage each other in serious study of God's Word, so it is our hope and prayer that other equally motivated students will be introduced to the fascinating world of exegesis through the introduction this textbook provides. So open your Greek texts, and let's begin. May we see God's face and message as we interact with the inspired Word of God in Greek.

PART ONE

Exegetical Methods and Procedures

Opening Questions

1

Definition and Philosophy of Exegesis

DARRELL L. BOCK

For many students, taking an exegesis course is walking into a foreign world. Not only is the language of study not their own but even the word exegesis gives the feel of entering an alien land. However, when it comes to biblical study, there are few courses more fundamental than exegesis. Working firsthand with an ancient text in its original language gives a kind of direct access to the message of the New Testament that nothing else does. So in this chapter we hope to introduce you to the concept of exegesis, why it is important, the philosophy that stands behind it, and its relationship to the disciplines of theology and hermeneutics.

1.1 Definition of Exegesis

The term *exegesis* has its roots in the Greek term ἐξηγέομαι, which means "to lead out of" and so it means to "read out" the meaning of the text. It is to explain or interpret a text. It has two senses: (1) exegesis is a product, such as a technical commentary, and (2) it is a method of study. In this second sense, one "exegetes" a text through the use of various methods this book will explore in an initial way. It is both an art and a science. Some elements of the exegetical process are as instinctive as an artist's work. The artistic exegete is able to ask the text the right set of questions and discern a passage's inherent conceptual unity with a clarity that also reveals a passage's depth. Exegesis also is a science, in that there are methods that can be applied to the text. These methods help the interpreter discover the information a text possesses. This volume hopes to discuss the methods of exegesis that make it a skill that can be taught, while also giving samples of exegesis that reveal what exegesis looks like in the hands of mature practitioners.

If we wanted to express the meaning of exegesis more precisely, we would define it as setting forth the authors'/text's meaning by interaction with the original language through the use of sound hermeneutics with a view to applying the text to the contemporary church and the world.

This definition has four key parts. First, the basic point in exegesis is to set forth the author's meaning as expressed in his text. The ambiguity of the definition in terms of the author/text makes the point that exegesis is not concerned with an author's state of mind or why he writes, as much as it is concerned with what he has said in the text he produced. Authorial intent has fallen on hard times in recent hermeneutical discussion for a variety of reasons, most of which relate to the difficulty of establishing what a standard of authorial intent means and discussion over how one can overcome the historical distance between an author and readers. Nonetheless, once one realizes that the pursuit of authorial intent is a function of validating or justifying between competing understandings and involves judgment as opposed to an airtight hermeneutical approach, much of the rationale for challenging the importance of pursuing the author evaporates. For it is a fact that we have a text because we had an author(s) who produced a text for us to seek to understand. Interpretation then very naturally should be concerned, at least initially, with what the author who produced the text sought to communicate through it.

Although the reader has to construe what the text affirms—and much attention in recent hermeneutical study is given to how a reader reads[1]—the

---

1. One can think here of a series of technical hermeneutical texts where readers are a major concern: Hans-Georg Gadamer, *Truth and Method*, 2nd rev. ed., trans. rev. Joel Weinsheimer and Donald G. Marshall (New York: Continuum, 1994); Anthony Thiselton, *The Two Horizons: New Testament Hermeneutics and Philosophical Description with Special Reference to Heidegger, Bultmann, Gadamer and Wittgenstein* (Grand Rapids, Mich.: Eerdmans, 1980); idem, *New Horizons in Hermeneutics: The Theory and Practice of Transforming Biblical Reading* (Grand Rapids, Mich.: Zondervan, 1992); Kevin J. Vanhoozer, *Is There a Meaning in This Text? The Bible, the Reader, and the Morality of Literary Knowledge* (Grand Rapids, Mich.: Zondervan, 1998). In contrast to this stands a hermeneutical work that has been influential on much conservative evangelical hermeneutics, where the author and his intended meaning is the primary concern: E. D. Hirsch, Jr., *Validity in Interpretation* (New Haven, Conn.: Yale University Press, 1967). Hirsch has also more recently discussed the role of the reader and issues

purpose of exegesis is to articulate what the author expressed, since the text is the "voiceprint" of an author. Even when we do not know an author's exact identity, as is the case in a book like Hebrews, we can still examine his text for his meaning. One other element in this first portion of the definition is worth noting. It is the fact that the location of the apostrophe in "authors" follows the "s," so we speak of the authors' meaning. Here we allude to the fact that the New Testament ultimately is seen theologically to have two authors, the human author and the divine author who inspired the text. Often the importance of this distinction is not significant to exegesis, but what it does affirm is that there is an ultimate unity to the New Testament—its theology—and that the theological task ultimately moves in a canonical direction. An appreciation of the dual authorship of Scripture often is excluded in more confined definitions of exegesis, where only the historical setting of the human author is the concern. Such an appreciation of the complexity of biblical authorship raises its own unique problems in reading Scripture and makes it quite unlike reading any other book. There is a unity that exists among its human authors that the divine authorship provides. In addition, God knows where Scripture is going as a whole in a way that the Bible's human authors did not appreciate. All of this means that good exegesis pays attention not only to the meaning of a passage in its "book" context but in its "canonical" context as well, where the correlation of texts across authors becomes an important concern.

The second key portion of the definition is the specification that exegesis involves work with the text's original language. In the case of the New Testament, this means the Koine Greek of the text. Whereas those who interpret the Bible may work with the English or their own primary language, exegesis has generally been reserved for those who can interact directly with Greek. Knowledge of the language allows one a direct access to the expressions of the text and its lexical, grammatical, syntactical roots that working through a translation does not permit. Though it requires much labor to learn a language, the "payoff" is in gaining a level of access to the text and the way it structures itself that a mere use of one's native language cannot attain.

The third element of the definition appeals to the use of sound hermeneutics. Here we read a text with sensitivity to its vocabulary, its grammatical expression, its historical setting, its literary genre and expression, its sociocultural context, and its theological scope. Much of this book discusses the methods that help one read with such sensitivities. Sound hermeneutics

---

of application in a way that represents a slight but important shift in his position, in "Meaning and Significance," *Critical Inquiry* 11 (1984): 202-25, and "Transhistorical Intentions and the Persistence of Allegory," *New Literary History* 25 (1994): 549-67.

means making well-considered judgments about the text. In a world of competing interpretations, appreciating the process of validating a reading is one of the most important of exegetical skills to develop. Here learning how to ask the right questions of the text and how to pursue the answers, as well as being aware of what the text is not addressing or answering, is part of both the skill and the art of exegesis. Sound hermeneutics and careful interpretation involve a series of judgments. The careful exegete appreciates that dimension of exegesis and what the process of judgment means for the decisions made about how the text reads.

The final element of the definition states the ultimate goal of exegesis. In one sense, this movement to application is not part of the more technical definitions of exegesis, which focus only on explaining the text.[2] However, the character of the Bible itself is not merely to inform us about the past or even about God's work in the past, but to move its readers to be responsive to God and to live well and wisely as a result (2 Tim 3:16-17). So a more complete definition of exegesis, at least in terms of its function in the church, is to lay solid groundwork for application that is biblically informed. Therefore we shall have a chapter that discusses the movement to application that grows out of exegesis. Such movement to application is not always as easy or straightforward as some think. Exegesis is a good way to be sure we are not engaged in reading into the text (eisegesis) what is not there by being sensitive to the scope and setting of a given text. By carefully reflecting on the meaning of a text and the scope of what it addresses, we are in a better place to apply the text in ways that do not go beyond its intention.

As we have already suggested, exegesis deals with the terms of the text and presupposes the work of textual criticism in determining what the actual wording of the text is. Then the message of the text is pursued by working with the lexical terms and their usage through the examination of the terms in word study and through attention to the grammar expressed in the text. The contexts of how this expression appears in its historical, literary, and theological concerns are also important features to examine within exegesis. So we will have chapters examining these various levels of study and the process of making judgments about which of the possible meanings of a text is most likely its meaning. For the goal of validating the text exegetically is to set forth why one of the many possible ways to construe the text is in fact most likely the meaning that the author desired to convey. Once

---

2. For another work desiring to broaden the definition of exegesis and with a nice treatment of how the term has been defined in the last several centuries, see Stanley E. Porter and Kent D. Clarke, "What Is Exegesis? An Analysis of Various Definitions," in *Handbook to Exegesis of the New Testament,* ed. Stanley E. Porter (Leiden: Brill, 1997), 3-21, esp. 9-18.

this exegetical meaning is in place, then the move to exposition and application can be made.

In sum, exegesis as a process has three basic outcomes: (1) to understand the message of the text, (2) to articulate why one thinks that is the text's message—both as a whole and in its particular details—(validation), and (3) to prepare for application(s) rooted in that biblical message.

The tools of exegesis include the Greek text, multiple translations (to surface options and exegetical disputes), a concordance (for word study), grammars and grammatical aids, extrabiblical texts (to help gain an understanding of the historical and cultural setting), lexicons and theological word books (to help with terms), and commentaries, especially technical commentaries (to serve as discussion partners about what the text means). Subsequent chapters will go into more detail about how each of these areas and the tools that go with them contribute to the exegetical process.

1.2 Why Exegesis Is Important

For those in Christian ministry, it is perhaps transparent that exegesis is important because understanding the meaning of the biblical text is one of the central responsibilities of someone who ministers and preaches the Word of God. Teachers in the church have a stewardship that makes exegesis a central element of ministry in seeking to serve God faithfully (2 Tim 2:15; Jas 3:1). There are several other reasons why exegesis is important.

There is a recognition even within the biblical text that some of the other texts written by biblical authors are not easy to understand. 2 Pet 3:16 calls some of Paul's writings difficult to understand. This difficulty means that sometimes effort and reflection need to be given to the text in order to ascertain its meaning.

Interaction within the Christian community and with those outside of it requires that the interpreter appreciate not only what is believed but how one determines that this understanding of a text is more adequate than another reading of it. A corollary to this is that the existence of false teaching also requires that one consider how to read the text accurately. The ability to explain how readings that undermine the text actually fail to represent the meaning well is an important skill for one who teaches in the church or gives instruction about its most sacred text (Tit 1:9).

The goal of the Spirit in inspiring the text is to lead the child of God into an adequate walk with God (2 Tim 3:15-17). Such a spiritual understanding of fellowship with God is supported by a serious engagement with the meaning of the inspired text. In a sense, one can well say that the Spirit works with the Word as a significant element of how he forms us spiritually, and a proper understanding of the text is a key tool used to get us there.

1.3 A Philosophy of Exegesis: Appreciating How to Read Texts, Readers, and the Role of Communities

A proper philosophy of exegesis involves more than applying a bunch of rules to how we read the text. There needs to be an appreciation for what the writer of a text gives us and how the way a reader reads impacts what is seen in the text. In other words, the hermeneutics that goes into understanding a text involves reflection on the procedures one applies to the text, what we often understand as hermeneutics. However, a full appreciation of exegesis also considers how we as readers approach texts and how that impacts our reading. This aspect of hermeneutics considers the process of how and from what social, ideological, and/or ethnic location one reads and engages texts—the more philosophical side of hermeneutics. Both aspects of the hermeneutical process, what the text yields and what the reader sees and why, need attention by the careful exegete.

The beginning and most fundamental point for exegesis is a serious and careful consideration of the text and what the author sought to communicate through it. The author is the communicative agent most central to the interpretive task. The author produced the text, and articulating the meaning that author produced is the basic goal of the exegete. Such a view is not naïve or unaware of recent philosophical discussion. Rather, it is a recognition that an author deserves respect for having produced a text for readers to understand. Although many who work in hermeneutics today have banished the author from a central role in exegesis and have given a primary place to readers, such a move is not the most effective way to approach exegesis.[3] A text is the recorded product of an author so that even if the author's identity is not known or the author is dead and unavailable, the text gives access to the author's expression and thought. This goal of determining the author's meaning through the text is the pursuit of a *what.* It is what the author seeks to affirm that is the goal of

---

3. A diverse set of theorists argue that the author and pursuit of authorial meaning are important. See, for example, Vanhoozer, *Is There a Meaning in This Text?* 201-80; G. B. Caird, *The Language and Imagery of the Bible* (Philadelphia: Westminster, 1980), 39; and Gary B. Madison, *The Hermeneutics of Postmodernity: Figures and Themes* (Bloomington: Indiana University Press, 1988), 25-39. Madison is a postmodern interpreter of the Anglo-American type (not a deconstructionist postmodern). He argues texts have meaning that can be determined and even gives ten criteria to use in finding it. These are: coherence, comprehensiveness, penetration, thoroughness, appropriateness, contextuality, agreement with language of author, agreement with (or better, sensitivity to) traditional readings of the author, suggestiveness, and potential.

the exegete, not a reproduction of a state of mind, as some who criticize authorial intent characterize the view. The reasons why the author speaks are also important, but only to the extent that they help us determine the scope, context, and content of what is said. Expressed in this way, the fundamental and indivisible linkage between the author and the text the author produced receives recognition as the most basic element of interpretation. In this way, even though we may not know the identity of the author, we still meet his presence and message in the text.

In making this affirmation, however, the reader is not banished to irrelevance in the interpretive process. Nor does the affirming of such a goal for exegesis mean there is a lack of recognition that getting to the author's meaning can be difficult and often is a matter for genuine discussion and debate. Exegesis is fundamentally a process that involves multiple judgments. A change of mind here and there can result in a very different reading of the text. However, it is important as we exegete that we are agreed as interpreters that the starting place for our dialogue is what the author of the text initially affirmed, because without such agreement it is difficult to know what we are discussing when it comes to treating issues of what the Bible meant and means.

On the other hand, readers read and are responsible for construing meaning. Interpretation is always a dialogue between interpreter and text. What a reader sees and how a reader reads is determined not only by what is in the text but by how the reader is prepared to read by his or her culture, theological perspective, personal background, and appreciation of the text's setting. As much as we may wish to try, we cannot make ourselves blank slates as readers when approaching a text. We are better off appreciating how this influences our reading than to pretend we can entirely neutralize these factors. Modern hermeneutical discussions have highlighted this feature of hermeneutics, maybe even exaggerated it. However, the role of readers was underappreciated previously and also needs attention as one thinks theoretically about the process of interpretation. Readings of the Bible in a pre-Copernican world would inevitably read texts on creation differently than we do. The amount of background we bring to the reading impacts how well we read. Many of the chapters in this book are designed to make the exegete more sensitive to the many levels in which one can get a better grasp of background, whether it be how Greek words are used, how customs worked, what the values of the first-century culture were, or how the author presents the argument. The goal of such methods is to make us better readers as we seek to recover the author's meaning.

One creative role the reader has as an exegete is when the move is made to set up application, because only the reader lives in the world in which the text is to be applied. This means that as one seeks how to apply the

Bible to modern questions about how one deals, for example, with television, movies, stem cell research, and other more modern questions, it is the reader's appreciation of how a text works and how it relates canonically to other texts on the theme that pulls the reader into a reflective yet creative theological process of seeking out the full theological perspective of Scripture. The issue of distinct cultural settings and contexts also enters into the reflective process at this point. So a reader is another important part of the process.

One way to check the undisciplined reading of a text is to appreciate that the Bible functions within communities of readers. We speak of communities because readers do not all share the same presuppositions in reading the Bible and often read it with their own ideological or theological concerns at the forefront. Such concerns may well skew the reading, but they may also open up fresh questions or angles from which the text in question should be read. So engaging the text with an awareness of these other positions is important not only to affirm the text but also to be in a position to explain where other readings may not reflect the text's meaning well.

From a historical point of view, the Bible has been read and studied for centuries. As such, some grasp of the history of its interpretation and of the interpretive history of given passages is helpful in acknowledging the centuries-long impact of Scripture. In addition, the dialogue about meaning carried out in a commentary tradition that also has a rich history is an important conversation partner in the process. In the chapters to follow, we shall indicate some of the more beneficial resources to surface this aspect of the process. Although the goal of exegesis is to make a student competent in making exegetical judgments, this goal is not reached by a kind of solitary exegesis in isolation from the discussion that has swirled around texts. These discussions often surface issues and questions that the exegete working alone never would have considered. They also serve as a check on the exegete's own biases in reading. There is a community dimension to exegesis that also deserves to be a part of the exegete's method.

So we have author-text, reader, and community to consider in the process of exegesis. The author establishes the meaning in the text, but the reader is left with the responsibility of construing that meaning and applying it in fresh contexts. By interacting with the various communities that read the text, the exegete gets a look at a variety of textual perspectives and may gain insight into questions the text raises that otherwise would have been ignored or missed. He or she may also be in a better position to discuss and evaluate readings that do not reflect what the author said.

1.4 Exegesis and Its Relationship to the Theological Disciplines

For people in the church there is a nagging question about exegesis. It is whether all this "academic" effort is required, since reading the Bible is a spiritual exercise that comes with the promised illuminating work of the Holy Spirit. Put crassly, one might ask, "Why exegete when the Holy Spirit is going to teach me anyway?" The reply is equally direct. It is that the Spirit's work has less to do with understanding words and what language means than with appreciating, discerning, and accepting what is coming from God. The Spirit gives an "internal witness" to the Word so that we receive it as God's Word as it convicts us of its basic content. This is what is stressed in Jesus' remarks about the Spirit's convicting work in John 16:8-11. In fact, the key passage on the Spirit's illuminating work to give believers the mind of Christ speaks of actions like receiving (δέχεται) the word (here referring to the apostolic preaching) and discerning (ἀνακρίνει) its content so that it is not foolishness to them (1 Cor 2:14-16). A consideration of the Jewish leadership shows that they understood Jesus' claims cognitively, but never received them or discerned them to be true. So illumination has more to do with correlating God's truth to the whole of Scripture and having a heart open to receive its content. In addition, a claim of illumination cannot be a guarantee that one has the content correct, because one can be wrong about whether one is illumined. Illumination, when it takes place, helps us get to meaning, but it also involves more than merely giving us the meaning. God used language to give us access to meaning. In that sense, the meaning of Scripture is available to any careful reader as a matter of comprehension. However, illumination allows us to hear that Word as promise, assertion, warning, command, or exhortation and then to be responsive to it from within. The Spirit works with the Word and opens our eyes and heart so we can more fully appreciate the text's meaning and import. As such, exegesis is simply another way of saying we will carefully study and engage God's Word. Our prayer is that the Spirit comes alongside to impress its content on our mind, heart, soul, and spirit.

Seen in this light, exegetical method then becomes the building blocks for interpretive, biblical, and theological work. Exegetical results are the raw elements that go into understanding a book or a biblical author and developing a biblical theology that appreciates the contribution of a specific biblical author. Exegesis also supplies the basic material for theological study as one correlates texts on topics and across books and authors into a systematic theology. Exegesis serves as the hub of pastoral reflection, standing at the base of sermons and spiritual development by shaping our thoughts and minds in directions God has given. Though hermeneutics is a broader discipline than exegesis, a major goal of hermeneutical understanding is that we be better prepared to be sensitive exegetes as we appreciate what both the author and the reader bring to the engagement of a text and what is required of the reader who construes that text.

1.5 Conclusion

Exegesis gives the student the unique opportunity to engage Scripture directly through the original language. It also enables the student to appreciate in a deeper way the nature of the debate and judgment that goes into construing a passage's meaning. Such careful study can deepen one's understanding of theology and God's message. Not only does the exegete gain an appreciation for what the text says, but also there is comprehension of the roads of debate and dialogue that surround the text and its details. In a sense, the exegete experiences the meaning of Scripture in all its colors and hues, more like a high-definition television portrait than a black-and-white image. In sum, the careful exegete can articulate what the text means and why. He or she can also explain why others may see it differently. Such are the skills and artistry of the mature theologian-exegete. May their tribe increase.

1.6 For Further Reading

Gadamer, Hans-Georg. *Truth and Method*. 2nd rev. ed. Translation revised by Joel Weinsheimer and Donald G. Marshall. New York: Continuum, 1994.

Hirsch, E. D., Jr. *Validity in Interpretation*. New Haven, Conn.: Yale University Press, 1967.

Osborne, Grant R. *The Hermeneutical Spiral: A Comprehensive Introduction to Biblical Interpretation*. Downers Grove, Ill.: InterVarsity Press, 1991.

Thiselton, Anthony. *New Horizons in Hermeneutics: The Theory and Practice of Transforming Biblical Reading*. Grand Rapids, Mich.: Zondervan, 1992.

Vanhoozer, Kevin J. *Is There a Meaning in This Text? The Bible, the Reader, and the Morality of Literary Knowledge*. Grand Rapids, Mich.: Zondervan, 1998.

Laying a Foundation

2

New Testament Textual Criticism

DANIEL B. WALLACE

Before we can know what a particular text means we must know what it says. This foundational endeavor is the goal of textual criticism. More formally, the goal—and definition—of textual criticism is the study of the copies of any written document whose autograph (the original) is unknown or nonexistent, for the primary purpose of determining the exact wording of the original.[1]

Textual criticism is necessary for most ancient literature. The NT is no exception, because the originals no longer exist and because the extant

---

1. Recently, David Parker, Bart Ehrman, and Eldon Epp have advocated that the primary goal of NT textual criticism should be other than seeking to determine the wording of the original (see David C. Parker, *The Living Text of the Gospels* [Cambridge: Cambridge University Press, 1997], 1, 3, 6, 7, 211; Bart D. Ehrman, "The Neglect of the Firstborn in New Testament Studies," Society of Biblical Literature southeastern regional section presidential address delivered on March 14, 1997, in Macon, Ga.; idem, *The Orthodox Corruption of Scripture: The Effect of Early Christological Controversies on the Text of the New Testament* [Oxford: Oxford University Press, 1993], xi; Eldon J. Epp, "Issues in New Testament Textual Criticism: Moving from the Nineteenth Century to the Twenty-First Century," in *Rethinking New Testament Textual Criticism,* ed. David Alan Black [Grand Rapids, Mich.: Baker, 2002], 55-61). This is a shift from the objective that has held sway for centuries. For a critique, see Moisés Silva, "Response," in Black, ed., *Rethinking New Testament Textual Criticism,* 149.

(remaining) copies disagree with one another.[2] In fact, there are several disagreements per chapter between even the two closest early MSS.

2.1 The Quantity and Quality of Textual Variants

On the one hand, when one considers all of the witnesses to the text of the NT, the variations number in the tens of thousands. For the 138,000 words, give or take a few, in the Greek NT, there are between 300,000 and 400,000 textual variants. A large part of the reason for this number of variants is the abundance of NT MSS that we have today. The textual problems listed in the apparatus of NA[27] are just the tip of the iceberg.

On the other hand, the text of the NT has been surprisingly stable through the centuries. This can be measured by the differences between the Greek text behind the KJV (known as the *Textus Receptus* or *TR*) and the one behind modern translations of the NT. Although the KJV is a four-hundred-year-old translation, it is based on significantly later MSS than modern translations are. It represents a text that had grown over the centuries. Yet there are only about five thousand differences between the *TR* and NA[27]. In other words, they agree more than 96 percent of the time.

Another way to look at this is to consider the nature of textual variants. All textual variants can be broken down into three groups: insignificant for the meaning of the text, significant (or meaningful) but not viable, meaningful and viable. (By "viable" we mean a variant that has a plausible claim on authenticity.) The vast majority of textual variants belong to the first two categories.

The largest group of textual variants are spelling changes, most of which cannot even be translated. Consider the following examples. "John" is spelled either as Ἰωάννης or Ἰωάνης in the MSS. Every movable *nu* in the NT moves away in some MSS, stays put in others. It affects nothing. The scribes were creative spellers when it came to diphthongs, especially those that involve an *iota*. But it almost never affects one *iota* of meaning. Such spelling differences belong to the insignificant category.

Several of the spelling differences are nonsense readings. These can come about when a scribe is fatigued, inattentive, or perhaps does not know Greek very well. One might think that scribes who made such errors could have a serious impact on the copies of the text. In reality, nonsense readings are almost never duplicated by the next scribe. Further, nonsense readings tell us a great deal about how a scribe went about his work. For

---

2. Bruce M. Metzger and Bart D. Ehrman, *The Text of the New Testament: Its Transmission, Corruption, and Restoration,* 4th ed. (Oxford: Oxford University Press, 2005), xv.

example, an early MS of Luke and John, known as P[75], has some interesting nonsense readings. But they involve one or two letters each time, suggesting that the scribe copied the text one or two letters at a time.[3] Indeed, this scribe was very careful. He or she[4] was a detail person!

Included in the insignificant variants would be many of the instances of transpositions among the MSS, synonyms, use or absence of articles with proper names, and the like. As an illustration, consider the ways in which one could say "Jesus loves Paul" in Greek. Although each may involve a slightly different emphasis, the essential meaning is the same:

1. Ἰησοῦς ἀγαπᾷ Παῦλον
2. Ἰησοῦς ἀγαπᾷ τὸν Παῦλον
3. ὁ Ἰησοῦς ἀγαπᾷ Παῦλον
4. ὁ Ἰησοῦς ἀγαπᾷ τὸν Παῦλον
5. Παῦλον Ἰησοῦς ἀγαπᾷ
6. τὸν Παῦλον Ἰησοῦς ἀγαπᾷ
7. Παῦλον ὁ Ἰησοῦς ἀγαπᾷ
8. τὸν Παῦλον ὁ Ἰησοῦς ἀγαπᾷ
9. ἀγαπᾷ Ἰησοῦς Παῦλον
10. ἀγαπᾷ Ἰησοῦς τὸν Παῦλον
11. ἀγαπᾷ ὁ Ἰησοῦς Παῦλον
12. ἀγαπᾷ ὁ Ἰησοῦς τὸν Παῦλον
13. ἀγαπᾷ Παῦλον Ἰησοῦς
14. ἀγαπᾷ τὸν Παῦλον Ἰησοῦς
15. ἀγαπᾷ Παῦλον ὁ Ἰησοῦς
16. ἀγαπᾷ τὸν Παῦλον ὁ Ἰησοῦς

These variations represent only a small fraction of the possibilities. If the sentence used φιλεῖ instead of ἀγαπᾷ, for example, or if it began with a conjunction such as δέ, καί, or μέν, the potential variations would grow exponentially. Factor in synonyms (such as κύριος for Ἰησοῦς), spelling differences, and additional words (such as Χριστός, or ἅγιος with Παῦλος) and the list of potential variants that do not affect the essence of the statement increases to the hundreds. If such a simple sentence as "Jesus loves Paul" could have so many insignificant variants, a mere three to four hundred thousand variants among the NT MSS seems trivial.

3. E. C. Colwell, "Method in Evaluating Scribal Habits: A Study of P45, P66, P75," in *Studies in Methodology in Textual Criticism of the New Testament*, NTTS 9, ed. Bruce M. Metzger (Leiden: Brill, 1969), 115-16.

4. On female scribes, see Kim Haines-Eitzen, "Girls Trained in Beautiful Writing: Female Scribes in Roman Antiquity and Early Christianity," *JECS* 6, no. 4 (Winter 1998): 629-46; idem, *Women and Early Christian Literature: Gender, Asceticism, and the Transmission of Texts* (Oxford: Oxford University Press, 2006).

A fair number of significant variants are not viable. They are readings found in a single MS or group of MSS that, by themselves, have little likelihood of going back to the wording of the original text. For example, Mark's Gospel opens with Ἀρχὴ τοῦ εὐαγγελίου Ἰησοῦ Χριστοῦ υἱοῦ θεοῦ. Whether υἱοῦ θεοῦ is authentic is disputed, since a few early and important MSS lack the words. This is a significant and viable variant. But in the same textual problem there are two significant variants that are not viable. One MS (codex 1241) instead of υἱοῦ θεοῦ has υἱοῦ κυρίου, while five late MSS read simply τοῦ θεοῦ (thus, "Jesus Christ of God"). Both readings are significant but neither is likely to be authentic. In Romans 8:1, the earliest and best witnesses read simply Οὐδὲν ἄρα νῦν κατάκριμα τοῖς ἐν Χριστῷ Ἰησοῦ, although most—especially later—MSS add μὴ κατὰ σάρκα περιπατοῦσιν ἀλλὰ κατὰ πνεῦμα. As we will see, it is not the number of MSS that matters, but their weight. One MS (1501) agrees with the majority except in one word: it has νόμον instead of σάρκα, suggesting perhaps the scribe's interpretation that living according to the flesh is the same thing as living according to the law. A meaningful variant, but not at all viable.

Another group of illustrations of meaningful variants would be the many harmonizations in the Gospel MSS. Scribes had a tendency to harmonize parallel passages in Mark, Matthew, and Luke. Two groups of MSS, known as the Western text and the Byzantine text, especially displayed this tendency. Indeed, one of the ways that we can tell whether a particular variant is authentic or not is whether it harmonizes. If it does, it isn't. Since it is a known scribal practice to harmonize the wording between two Gospels,[5] the reading that does not harmonize is typically considered to be authentic. Especially when such *non*-harmonizations are found in earlier MSS, the evidence is generally convincing that these readings are authentic. An example of harmonization in the Gospel MSS can be found on any page of the Gospels. One will have to suffice for our purposes. In Matthew 9, Jesus is eating with some unsavory people. (This story is also found in Mark 2 and Luke 5.) This offends the Pharisees. In v. 11 they ask Jesus' disciples, "Why does your teacher eat with tax collectors and sinners?" A handful of Greek MSS and other early versions add "and drink" after "eat" to conform the wording to what is found in Luke 5:30. Meanwhile, in Mark 2:16, the wording is similar to Matthew's, but here the *majority*

---

5. See Gordon D. Fee, "Modern Textual Criticism and the Synoptic Problem: On the Problem of Harmonization in the Gospels," in *Studies in the Theory and Method of New Testament Textual Criticism,* ed. Eldon Jay Epp and Gordon D. Fee, Studies and Documents 45 (Grand Rapids, Mich.: Eerdmans, 1993), 174-82. Even some advocates of the Majority Text acknowledge that there are harmonizations in their preferred text-form. See Willem Franciscus Wisselink, *Assimilation as a Criterion for the Establishment of the Text: A Comparative Study on the Basis of Passages from Matthew, Mark and Luke* (Kampen: Kok, 1989), 87-90.

of later MSS add the words "and drink." As for Luke 5:30, there is only one known MS that omits "and drink," thus bringing it into conformity with the wording in Matthew and Mark. This textual problem illustrates a couple of things. First, scribes were prone to harmonize the Gospel accounts, even when there was no real discrepancy between them. Second, when it came to harmonization, the scribes tended to add material to one Gospel rather than take away material from another.

The last category—meaningful and viable—involves only about 1 percent of all textual variants. But even here the situation can be overstated. By *meaningful* we mean that the variant changes the meaning of the text *to some degree*. If the variant affects one's understanding of the passage then it is considered meaningful. For example, one of the most notorious textual problems in the NT is found in Rom 5:1. Does Paul say, "We *have* peace" (ἔχομεν) or *"let us have* peace" (ἔχωμεν)? The difference between the indicative and subjunctive is a single letter. The omicron and omega were most likely pronounced alike in Hellenistic Greek (as they are in later Greek), leaving the decision even more difficult. Indeed, scholars are split on this textual problem.[6]

In 1 Thess 2:7, Paul describes himself and his colleagues as either "gentle" or "little children." The difference between the variants in Greek is but one letter—either νήπιοι or ἤπιοι. If "little children" (νήπιοι) is the correct reading, then Paul has mixed his metaphors (though he is prone to do this from time to time[7]), for he follows this up by declaring that he has loved the Christians in Thessalonica "like a nursing mother." In one breath, he calls himself a little child, then a nursing mother. The violent switch has caused many scholars to judge this variant as too hard and due to scribal oversight, hearing error, or fatigue. Others see it as authentic, and point out that it would be a great temptation for a scribe who also thought the metaphor switch was awkward to simply drop the *nu*, turning "little children" into "gentle."[8]

2.2 The Problems of NT Textual Criticism

The problems of NT textual criticism can be succinctly discussed under two broad labels: materials and methods.

6. For a helpful discussion of the issues, see the "tc" note at Rom 5:1 in NET-Nestle. Although UBS[4] gives the indicative verb an "A" rating (which indicates the highest level of confidence in its authenticity), several scholars have made a case for the subjunctive reading. In the least, the indicative is most likely what Paul originally wrote, although the A rating is a bit too generous.

7. E.g., Gal 4:19.

8. See the "tc" note in NET-Nestle for discussion.

2.2.1 *The Materials*

It is an understatement to say that the materials used for determining the wording of the Greek NT are overwhelming. What adjectives can truly describe the situation? While scholars of other ancient literature suffer from a lack of data, those who work with NT MSS suffer from an embarrassment of riches. These witnesses to the text of the NT fall under three subcategories: Greek MSS, ancient translations or versions, and quotations from the NT in the writings of the church fathers.

2.2.1.1 GREEK MANUSCRIPTS

The Greek MSS are the principal documents used to determine the wording of the NT. They are broken down into four groups: papyri, majuscules, minuscules, and lectionaries. These are designated as follows:

- papyri: $P^{1, 2, 46, 75,}$ etc.
- majuscules: $\aleph$, A, B, W, Γ, Ξ, 0278, etc.[9]
- minuscules: 1, 2, 33, 1506, 2813, etc.[10]
- lectionaries: *l*213, *l*1707, etc.[11]

The first group—papyri—derive their name from the material that the MS is made of. The second and third groups—majuscules and minuscules—are so named because of the writing style (either capital letters or cursive hand) of the MSS. And the designation of the last group—lectionaries—refers to the fact that these MSS are not continuous texts from the Gospels, epistles, etc., but are various portions of text that were assigned reading for particular days. Most of the NT MSS are written on parchment or vellum, with the exception of the papyri and some of the later MSS, which were written on paper. Generally speaking, the papyri are the earliest of these four groups of MSS, and certainly the rarest (owing to the fragile writing material), while the majuscules are next, followed by the minuscules and lectionaries.

9. All majuscule MSS are designated with an Arabic number that begins with a zero. The earliest of these to be catalogued also are referred to with a capital letter from the Latin alphabet or the Greek alphabet. One MS uses a letter from the Hebrew alphabet.

10. These numbers refer to individual minuscules. The minuscules are also referred to in groups such as f^1, f^{13} (family 1, family 13), *Byz* (the majority of Byzantine minuscules, a designation found in UBS[4]), and 𝔐 (a designation found in NA[27] for the majority of Byzantine minuscules and other MSS that are grouped with the Byzantine minuscules to save space in the apparatus).

11. As a group the lectionaries are designated *Lect* in UBS[4].

As of March 2006, the statistics on the Greek MSS of the NT are as follows[12]:

Papyri	Majuscules	Minuscules	Lectionaries	Total
118	317	2877	2433	5745[13]

These MSS date, for the most part, from the second to the sixteenth century.[14] The earliest fragment is most likely from the first half of the second century (ca. AD 100-150), known as Papyrus 52 or P^{52}. In recent years, a cache of several more papyri was discovered at Oxford University, bringing the number to ten to fifteen that are as early as the second century.[15] Two of these papyri ($P^{46, 66}$) are quite substantial. Beginning in the third century, there is a steady stream of witnesses to the text of the NT. The most important papyri are the Chester Beatty papyri ($P^{45, 46}$) and the Bodmer papyri ($P^{66, 75}$). Of these, P^{45} belongs at times to the Alexandrian text-type, at times to the Western, and at times to the Caesarean; the other papyri are Alexandrian. (For an explanation of the term "text-type," see section 2.3.2.2, below.)

By the fourth century, the great majuscule MSS were produced, including what is now the earliest complete NT, codex Sinaiticus. Equally important but not as complete is codex Vaticanus, probably from the early fourth century. Sinaiticus (a.k.a. ℵ, or 01) and Vaticanus (a.k.a. B, or 03) both belong to what is called the Alexandrian text-type. However,

---

12. The official clearinghouse of Greek NT MS identifications, the *Institut für neutestamentliche Textforschung* (Institute for New Testament Textual Research, or INTF) in Münster, Germany, catalogs the MSS, assigning them each a new number. The updated catalog can be downloaded from the Institute's website as a pdf file: www.uni-muenster.de/NTTextforschung/ KgL_Aktualisierung.pdf.

13. This number is a bit deceiving, however. Some of the MS fragments have been identified as belonging to another MS that was already catalogued under a different number. Thus, P^{64} and P^{67} are actually part of the same MS, even though they have different identifying numbers. The totals are thus somewhat less than 5745.

14. A few more MSS will be added soon, discovered by the Center for the Study of New Testament Manuscripts (www.csntm.org).

15. These MSS include P^{52} (AD 100-150), $P^{90, 104}$ (second century), P^{66} (ca. AD 175-225), $P^{46, 64+67}$ (ca. AD 200), P^{77}, 0189 (second or third century), P^{98} (second century?).

These nine MSS are the extent of those that the INTF has identified as possibly or definitely from the second century. Philip W. Comfort and David P. Barrett, *The Text of the Earliest New Testament Greek Manuscripts* (Wheaton, Ill.: Tyndale, 2001) argue for at least half a dozen other MSS as possibly from the second century. Comfort and Barrett's method, however, is generally to take the earliest date possible. Nevertheless, the dates they suggest for P^4 (second century) and P^{32} (late second century) are likely. In addition, renowned papyrologist Herbert Hunger considered P^{66} to be from no later than the middle of the second century ("Zur Datierung des Papyrus Bodmer II (P^{66})," *AÖAW* 4 [1960]: 12-33). The original editors of P^{75} also thought this MS should be dated late second to early third century (see Metzger and Ehrman, *Text*, 58).

they are not as closely related as has sometimes been suggested. There are thousands of differences between them. Their common ancestor must be quite ancient since they are relatively closely related to each other yet there are numerous and substantial differences. This suggests that there were several intermediary ancestors between the common archetype and these two majuscule documents. This is similar, to some degree, to relatives at a family reunion. Some members may be tall, thin, blue-eyed, blond, while others are short, thick-boned, brown-eyed, with black hair. Others are in between. Those who look substantially like each other could well be more closely related.[16] Following this analogy, ℵ and B are virtually distant cousins whose common ancestor must go back several generations. Indeed, when they agree, their common reading usually is from the early second century.[17]

The importance of B cannot be overestimated. Its text is very much like that of P[75] (B and P[75] are much closer to each other than B is to ℵ). Yet the papyrus is at least a century older than Vaticanus. When P[75] was discovered, some entertained the possibility that Vaticanus could have been a copy of P[75], but this view is no longer acceptable: in several places, the wording of Vaticanus is certainly more primitive than that of P[75].[18] They both must go back to a still earlier common ancestor, one that is deep in the second century. The combination with ℵ is a powerful witness to the earliest form of the text.

Other important majuscule MSS include A (02), C (04), D (05), D (06), F (010), G (012), and W (032).

Some of the later MSS show evidence of being copied from a much earlier source. For example, MS 1739, a tenth-century minuscule MS, was most likely copied from a late-fourth-century MS.[19] Although the

16. The analogy breaks down, however, at a crucial point: in each new generation of a family, there is always a 50 percent mixture from a foreign element—the marriage partner. Although MSS showed mixture, they did not have this kind of rapid and significant mixture every new generation.

17. See B. F. Westcott and F. J. A. Hort, *Introduction [and] Appendix*, vol. 2 of *The New Testament in the Original Greek* (Cambridge: Macmillan, 1882), 212-50. "With the discovery . . . of p[66] and p[75], both dating from about the end of the second or the beginning of the third century, proof became available that Hort's Neutral text goes back to an archetype that must be put early in the second century" (Metzger and Ehrman, *Text*, 312).

18. See Gordon D. Fee, "P[66], P[75] and Origen: The Myth of Early Textual Recension in Alexandria," in *New Dimensions in New Testament Study*, ed. Richard N. Longenecker and Merrill C. Tenney (Grand Rapids, Mich.: Zondervan, 1974), 19-45; C. L. Porter, "An Evaluation of the Textual Variation Between Pap75 and Codex Vaticanus in the Text of John," in *Studies in the History and Text of the New Testament in Honor of Kenneth Willis Clark*, Studies and Documents 29, ed. Boyd L. Daniels and M. Jack Suggs (Salt Lake City: University of Utah Press, 1967), 71-80.

19. Metzger and Ehrman, *Text*, 91.

majority of minuscules are of the Byzantine text-type, a good number are not Byzantine. Among the most important minuscules are 33, 81, 1739, and 2053.

The lectionaries are MSS that are organized by assigned Scripture reading for appointed days. They are not continuous texts of whole books, but select passages. On the one hand, lectionaries exerted something of a liturgical influence on the later MSS, causing the text to grow over time. On the other hand, they resisted updating, preserving archaic readings due to their constant use in worship services.

2.2.1.2 VERSIONS

The second most important kinds of witnesses to the NT text are known as versions. A version is technically a translation. The value of a version depends on its date, the translation technique and care, and the quality of the text it is translated from. But the textual basis and technique are not always easy to determine, hampering scholars' assessment of various versions. For example, Latin has no definite article, while Greek does. When a textual problem involves an article in Greek, the Latin witnesses have no voice in the matter.[20] However, *major* differences in the text can easily be detected (such as adding or dropping whole phrases). The versions are important for another reason. By comparing the text-forms of the various versions with NT quotations in patristic writers, it is possible to determine when the various versions came into existence. Except in rare and controlled instances, once a version was completed it did not interact with the Greek MSS again. This means that when a particular version consistently has one reading in its remaining copies, one may usually regard that reading as going back to that version's origin.[21] The three most important versions are the Latin, Coptic, and Syriac. Other versions of relative value are the Gothic and Armenian, followed by the Georgian and Ethiopic.

Through a rich and complex history, the Latin MSS of the NT have come to dominate this field—in terms of quantity. There are roughly twice as many Latin MSS of the NT as there are Greek (over 10,000 compared

---

20. See, for example, the apparatus of UBS[4] or NA[27] at Eph 2:21 for πᾶσα οἰκοδομή. The variant reading is πᾶσα ἡ οἰκοδομή, but the Latin MSS are not listed here since Latin cannot fairly represent the textual problem.

21. For example, in 1 Tim 3:16, the original Greek text almost surely read, "who was manifest in the flesh." All but one of the Latin MSS have "which" for "who." Later Greek MSS have "*God* was manifest in the flesh," a difference from "who" of but two horizontal strokes in the letters in the Greek MSS (OC vs. $\overline{\Theta C}$). But the Latin "which" (*quod*) and Latin "God" (*Deus*) are quite different. It is evident that the Latin MSS originated by copying a Greek text that had "who" instead of "God," for there is no other way to account for "which" in the Latin MSS.

to about 5700).[22] They date from the third century to the sixteenth, but their origins probably go back deep into the second century.[23]

The most important Coptic dialects are the Sahidic and the Bohairic. The Sahidic NT origins reach back to the beginning of the third century. They are representatives of the Alexandrian text-type.

The Syriac church finds its origins in the second century. Although no extant Syriac NT MSS are that early, it is certain that the NT was translated into Syriac no later than the early third century.[24] The earliest form, the Old Syriac, is a representative of the Western text.

All told, the ancient versions of the NT still in existence are probably between fifteen and twenty thousand. Exact numbers are difficult to come by because not all the MSS have been catalogued.

2.2.1.3 QUOTATIONS (COMMENTARIES) BY CHURCH FATHERS

Quotations of the NT by the church fathers number well over a million—and counting![25] "Indeed, so extensive are these citations that if all other sources for our knowledge of the text of the New Testament were destroyed, they would be sufficient alone for the reconstruction of practically the entire New Testament."[26] The Fathers are as early as the late first century, with a steady stream through the thirteenth, making their value for determining the wording of the NT text extraordinary.

There are problems in citing Fathers, however. First, the Fathers' writings are found only in copies, not originals. Second, some Fathers are notorious for quoting the same passage in different ways—because of lapses in memory, use of different MSS, allusions rather than quotations, lack of care in citation, etc.

But there are ways to determine on many occasions, with a great deal of certainty, what form of the NT text a particular Father was quoting from. In particular, when a Father is quoting from a long passage, it is likely that he is not quoting from memory but is using a MS to transcribe from. There are other ways to gain certainty about a Father's text of the NT.[27] Not only this, but sometimes a Father discusses textual variants,

---

22. Bruce M. Metzger, *The Early Versions of the New Testament: Their Origin, Transmission and Limitations* (Oxford: Clarendon, 1977), 293, 334.

23. Metzger and Ehrman, *Text*, 276-77.

24. Ibid., 96-98.

25. See J. Lionel North, "The Use of the Latin Fathers for New Testament Textual Criticism," in *The Text of the New Testament in Contemporary Research: Essays on the* Status Quaestionis *(A Volume in Honor of Bruce M. Metzger)*, ed. Bart D. Ehrman and Michael W. Holmes, Studies and Documents 46 (Grand Rapids, Mich.: Eerdmans, 1994), 210 n. 6.

26. Jacobus H. Petzer, "The Latin Version of the New Testament," in *Contemporary Research*, 126.

27. See the essays by Fee in *Theory and Method*, 299-359; idem, "The Use of the Greek Fathers for New Testament Textual Criticism," in *Contemporary Research*, 191-207.

noting MSS that have one wording or another.[28] "When properly evaluated . . . , patristic evidence is of primary importance . . . in contrast to the early Greek manuscripts, the Fathers have the potential of offering datable and geographically certain evidence."[29]

2.2.1.4 SUMMARY: AN EMBARRASSMENT OF RICHES

The wealth of material available for determining the wording of the original NT is staggering: about 5700 Greek NT MSS, as many as 20,000 versional MSS, and more than one million quotations by patristic writers. In comparison with the average ancient Greek author, the NT copies are well over a thousand times more plentiful. To put this another way, if the average-sized MS were two-and-a-half inches thick, all of the copies of the average Greek author would stack up four feet high, while the copies of the NT would stack up over a *mile* high. This is indeed an embarrassment of riches.

These thousands of MSS, versions, and patristic quotations have produced hundreds of thousands of textual variants. These two considerations—the number of MSS and the number of variants—lead to our next consideration: How should we sift through all this material? What methods should we use to determine exactly what the original wording of the NT is?

2.2.2 The Methods

There are different schools of thought about how best to get back to the original wording of the NT text. These schools can be organized by how much they focus on the two broad databases of textual criticism—external evidence and internal evidence. External evidence has to do with the materials—the MSS, versions, Fathers. Internal evidence has to do with the wording of the text in these various witnesses and why it has undergone changes. In other words, external evidence looks at the variety of witnesses, while internal evidence looks at the variety of variants.

Under these two umbrellas are different emphases. On one extreme are those who believe the internal evidence is our only sure guide to recovering the wording of the original. Some would go so far as to say that internal evidence is objective. On the other extreme are those who view the external evidence as the only certain window on the autographs, viewing the MSS themselves as objective. In the middle are the majority of textual critics

---

28. See two essys in Bruce M. Metzger, *New Testament Studies: Philological, Versional, and Patristic*, NTTS 10 (Leiden; Brill, 1980): "The Practice of Textual Criticism Among the Church Fathers," 189-97; "St. Jerome's Explicit References to Variant Readings in Manuscripts of the New Testament," 199-210.

29. Fee, "Use of the Fathers," in *Contemporary Research*, 191.

today: they argue that both internal and external evidence are subjective in varying degrees, and that the skillful wrestling with both considerations is the surest way to recover the wording of the original text.

In broad strokes, the methods used in NT textual criticism can be placed on a grid as follows:

School	Rigorous Eclecticism	Reasoned Eclecticism	Majority Text View
Emphasis	Internal priority	Roughly equal emphasis on internal and external	External priority
Advocates	G. D. Kilpatrick, J. K. Elliott	Bruce Metzger, Gordon Fee, Michael Holmes, and most textual critics	Zane Hodges, Maurice Robinson, only conservatives

The problem with rigorous eclecticism is that history seems to take a backseat in the drive to accessing the wording of the autographs. Since rigorous eclecticism sees all MSS as corrupt (rightfully so), it tends to view them as all equally corrupt. But the confluence of early versions, patristic comments, and Greek MSS shows that all MSS are not created equal. In particular, the discovery of the early papyri in the last century has strongly confirmed that the great majuscule MSS of the fourth century followed a relatively stable line of transmission. Looking at this from another perspective, rigorous eclecticism's neglect of history is also seen in its textual decisions that are made without regard for the MSS that are opposed to these decisions. A medieval MS may have the wording that the rigorist thinks belongs in the text. How it is possible that a single late MS could contain the original wording against the rest of the testimony is not answered. This view also leads logically to conjectural emendation. Although rigorous eclectics denounce conjectural emendation,[30] their position inevitably leads to such, because the chance of having the correct wording preserved in a single late MS is not much more likely than that the correct reading is not to be found in any MS. And what today has a MS basis, dubious though it may be, a few decades ago often had no external support at all.[31]

The problem with the Majority Text view is that it, too, disregards history. Although 80-90 percent of the MSS usually agree with each other and belong to the Byzantine text-type, the Byzantine text did not become the majority until the ninth century. The majority of MSS through

30. G. D. Kilpatrick, "Conjectural Emendation in the New Testament," in *New Testament Textual Criticism: Its Significance for Exegesis: Essays in Honour of Bruce M. Metzger*, ed. E. J. Epp and G. D. Fee (Oxford: Clarendon, 1981), 349-60.

31. For the best critique of rigorous eclecticism, see Fee, "Rigorous or Reasoned Eclecticism—Which?" in *Theory and Method*, 124-40.

the first eight centuries, as far as the extant data reveal, belonged to the Alexandrian text. Thus, an important question to ask is, *When* do we count? Further, there are no Byzantine MSS, versions, or Fathers prior to the late fourth century. Several patristic writers comment on variants, and show that what is often a majority in later centuries is a minority in earlier centuries. It will not do to assume that all early Byzantine MSS wore out due to frequent use. Such a simplistic explanation for the lack of early Byzantine MSS is a desperate expedient based on philosophical presupposition rather than historical inquiry.[32]

Long ago, Hort argued that the Byzantine text (what he called the Syrian text) was inferior. His arguments are still essentially valid today: (1) conflations (i.e., a new reading combined from two earlier readings) show that the Byzantine text is *secondary,* because the Byzantine text is the only text-type to conflate (cf. Luke 9:10; 24:53); (2) no ante-Nicene fathers seem to quote distinctive Byzantine readings, demonstrating that the Byzantine text is *late*[33]; (3) internal evidence reveals that the Byzantine text is *inferior.*[34] Although Hort's argument was not airtight, the few small leaks are not enough to sink his boat.

The most balanced approach to the textual criticism of the NT is that of reasoned eclecticism. Although there are problems with this view, too, no theory has replaced it. In essence, it treats external and internal evidence equally, giving no mandatory preference to either aspect, no mandatory preference to any text-type or group of MSS. It recognizes that even though all MSS are corrupt, they are not all equally corrupt, and although all internal evidence is subjective, it is not all equally subjective. Most of all, reasoned eclecticism attempts to take into account the historical processes in which the variants arose. If there is a mantra that describes this method it is this: *choose the reading that best explains the rise of the others.* As we examine the practice of NT textual criticism, we will do so from the perspective of reasoned eclecticism.

2.3 The Practice of NT Textual Criticism

The two aspects of textual criticism, external evidence and internal evidence, need to be handled separately at first. Then, the results are compared. When the external and internal evidence point in the same direction, one can have great confidence that the wording of the original text has been deter-

---

32. For a critique of the Byzantine text-type, see Daniel B. Wallace, "The Majority Text Theory: History, Methods and Critique," in *Contemporary Research,* 297-320.

33. See M. H. Heuer, "An Evaluation of John W. Burgon's Use of Patristic Evidence," *JETS* 38 (1995): 519-30.

34. Westcott-Hort, *Introduction [and] Appendix,* 93-119.

mined. Internal evidence is often in conflict with external evidence, however, requiring more probing to determine the wording of the autographs.

2.3.1 Examination of the Internal Evidence

Internal evidence is an examination of the *wording* of the variants in order to determine which reading gave rise to the other(s) and is, therefore, most probably original.

2.3.1.1 THE CANONS OF INTERNAL EVIDENCE

The basic guideline of internal criticism is: *Choose the reading that best explains the rise of the others.* As one will no doubt observe, this is the same rule for all of textual criticism, whether it is external or internal. Although at times judging internal evidence is quite subjective, it can be a very objective approach. Indeed, everyone practices this sort of textual criticism every day. David Parker ingeniously illustrates this in *The Living Text of the Gospels:*

> Everybody who reads the newspaper is expert in textual criticism, in coping with those distctive errors of omssion and displaced lines, and jumbling of letrset. This sophisticated process of recognizing nonsense and picking up the sense is so natural to us the classical scholars of ancient Alexandria or the Benedictines of that we perform it without thinking, unaware of our kinship with St Maur. Textual criticism is not an arcane science. It belongs to all human communication.[35]

Although some of the errors in the above paragraph may take a little while to figure out, one should be able to determine exactly what they are. No other MSS are needed to compare the statement to; what the author meant to say can be deduced by an examination of the wording with a view toward detecting known errors. This is internal evidence.

There are numerous guidelines under the broad umbrella of choosing the reading that best explains the rise of the others, but two stand out: the shorter reading is to be preferred and the harder reading is to be preferred.[36]

---

35. Parker, *Living Text of the Gospels,* 1. The errors in the text and the displaced lines were intentional on Parker's part.

36. These guidelines are not applied mechanically. That is, other considerations are brought to bear on the problem. In particular, if a reading could have been created *unintentionally,* the canons of shorter and harder generally do not apply. The reason this is the case is that the vast bulk of unintentional readings will be harder (to the point that many are nonsense readings!), and many shorter readings are also due to writing once what should have been written twice (known as haplography), fatigue, etc. Thus, unintentional possibilities need to be dispensed with before any level of certainty can be offered on behalf of shorter or harder readings.

1. The harder reading is to be preferred.

The harder reading is the reading that is more awkward, more ambiguous, more cumbersome. Harder readings also use rarer words, or involve wording that could be perceived as a discrepancy. The canon of preferring harder readings is important because scribes tended to smooth out difficulties in the text rather than create difficulties. For example, for the space of eighty-nine consecutive verses (Mark 6:31–8:26), Jesus is *never* identified by name or title. He is not called "Jesus," "the Lord," "teacher," "rabbi," etc. The pronouns and verb endings are the only indications that he is in view. Because of the influence from the lectionaries, most MSS add nouns here and there to identify the person in view. In this instance, "Jesus" is added in the Byzantine MSS in Mark 6:34; 7:27; 8:1, and 17. Here, the original reading is both shorter and harder.

This sort of thing happens with Gospel parallels (the smoother reading is the one that harmonizes the wording of one Gospel to another), with grammar, with style, and with theology. Yes, theology. Scribes tended to change the wording of the text to conform it more explicitly to their theological convictions.[37] This does not mean that the original text was not orthodox; rather, it is not always as *explicitly* orthodox as the scribes would like, or its orthodoxy is slightly different from what the scribes believed.

To understand this process, an analogy regarding the rough texture of the original text may help. In Tolkien's *Lord of the Rings,* when the beleaguered hobbits meet the dark stranger, Strider, at the Prancing Pony Inn, they are relieved to learn that he is on their side. He announces that he is Aragorn, and that if he had been their enemy he could have killed them some time ago:

> There was a long silence. At last Frodo spoke with hesitation, "I believed that you were a friend before the letter came," he said, "or at least I wished to. You have frightened me several times tonight, but never in the way that servants of the Enemy would, or so I imagine. I think one of his spies would—well, seem fairer and feel fouler, if you understand."[38]

Likewise, the original text has a stubborn way of making some students of Scripture nervous, but in the end it is something that we can both discern and trust.

---

37. See discussion of 1 Tim 3:16 in note 21 for an example of a theologically motivated variant.

38. J. R. R. Tolkien, *The Lord of the Rings,* Part 1: *The Fellowship of the Ring* (New York: Ballantine, 1954), 233.

2. The shorter reading is to be preferred.

Scribes had a strong tendency to add words or phrases rather than omit. The text tended to grow in time rather than shrink (although, it grew only about 2 percent over the span of fourteen hundred years). Only on rare occasions did scribes *intentionally* omit anything.[39] Thus, as long as an unintentional omission is not likely, the shorter reading is usually to be preferred.

At the end of every book of the NT the word ἀμήν appears in at least some of the MSS. Such a conclusion was routinely added by scribes to NT books because a few of these books originally had such an ending (Rom 16:27; Gal 6:18; Jude 25). A majority of Greek witnesses have the concluding ἀμήν in every NT book except Acts, James, and 3 John (and even in these books, ἀμήν is found in some MSS). It is thus a predictable variant and a longer reading.

Scribes also added more substantial things. For example, in Rom 8:1, the external evidence points conclusively to the wording Οὐδὲν ἄρα νῦν κατάκριμα τοῖς ἐν Χριστῷ Ἰησοῦ. Two principal variants compete with this wording. Some MSS add μὴ κατὰ σάρκα περιπατοῦσιν. Still later MSS add ἀλλὰ κατὰ πνεῦμα. Scribes had a tendency to add to grace, to qualify absolute statements. In this instance it is obvious that the third reading originated from the second (otherwise, if it arose without the second reading in place, the verse would make no sense at all: "There is therefore now no condemnation for those who are in Christ Jesus, but who walk according to the Spirit"!). In this instance, the shortest reading gave rise to the intermediate reading, which then gave rise to the longest reading.

In sum, these two rules are very helpful in determining the wording of the original text. At the same time, they must not be applied in isolation from other considerations. Some MSS, especially of the Western text, were prone to omit whole verses. Although the Western text is early, it also was produced in a somewhat carefree manner. Here is where external evidence weighs in and exercises some quality control over internal evidence.

2.3.1.2 THE DIVISIONS OF INTERNAL EVIDENCE

1. Transcriptional Probability

Transcriptional probability has to do with what a *scribe* (copyist) would be likely to do. There are two types of changes to the text that scribes made—intentional and unintentional.[40]

---

39. For an exception to this rule, see Matt 27:16-17 and the "tc" note in NET-Nestle on "Jesus Barabbas."

40. For a detailed discussion of the kinds of changes scribes made to the text, see Metzger and Ehrman, *Text,* 250-71.

A. INTENTIONAL CHANGES

Often scribes intended to alter the text—for grammatical, theological, or explanatory reasons. It is here especially that the two canons of shorter and harder reading are helpful. (See discussion above for illustrations.)

B. UNINTENTIONAL CHANGES

Due to problems of sight, hearing, fatigue, or judgment, scribes often changed the text unwittingly. A common mistake of the scribes was to write once what should have been written twice (haplography). It especially occurred when a scribe's eye skipped a second word that ended the same way as the word before it. But it also occurred when two lines ended the same way. For example, in 1 John 2:23 we read, "Everyone who denies the Son does not have the Father either. The person who confesses the Son has the Father also." In Greek these two clauses both end with "has the Father." A slavishly literal rendering would be, "Everyone who denies the Son neither *has the Father;* everyone who confesses the Son also *has the Father.*" By writing the Greek in sense-lines, the parallels are even more similar:

$$\pi\hat{\alpha}\varsigma\ \acute{o}\ \acute{\alpha}\rho\nuο\acute{\upsilon}\mu\epsilon\nuο\varsigma\ \tau\grave{o}\nu\ \upsilon\acute{\iota}\grave{o}\nu\ ο\grave{\upsilon}\delta\grave{\epsilon}\ \underline{\tau\grave{o}\nu\ \pi\alpha\tau\acute{\epsilon}\rho\alpha\ \check{\epsilon}\chi\epsilon\iota},$$
$$\acute{o}\ \acute{o}\mu\omega\lambda\omega\gamma\hat{\omega}\nu\ \tau\grave{o}\nu\ \upsilon\acute{\iota}\grave{o}\nu\ \kappa\alpha\grave{\iota}\ \underline{\tau\grave{o}\nu\ \pi\alpha\tau\acute{\epsilon}\rho\alpha\ \check{\epsilon}\chi\epsilon\iota}.$$

The Byzantine text-type lacks the second clause of this verse. Although shorter readings are usually preferred, if an unintentional error is likely, shorter readings are generally considered secondary. This is a classic example of such an unintentional omission: The τὸν πατέρα ἔχει of the preceding clause occasioned the haplography.

2. Intrinsic Probability

This examines what the biblical *author* was likely to have written. Again, two key issues are involved (though there are others as well): context and style.

A. CONTEXT

Which variant best fits the context? For example, in John 14, Jesus is speaking to his disciples on the night before he was crucified. In v. 17 he tells them about the Holy Spirit: "But you know him, because he resides with you and will be in you." Instead of "will be" (ἔσται) some early and important MSS have "is" (ἐστιν). When one considers what the author would have written, the future tense is on much stronger ground. The immediate context (both in 14:16 and in the chapter as a whole) points to the future, and John's Gospel overall regards the advent of the Spirit as a decidedly future event. The future tense thus has better credentials in terms of the context.[41]

B. STYLE

Which variant better fits the author's style? Here the question concerns what an author normally does, how he normally expresses himself, what his motifs and language usually involve. One of the reasons that most scholars do not regard Mark 16:9-20 to be authentic is that the vocabulary and grammar are quite unlike what the rest of the Gospel of Mark has. When this observation is coupled with the strong likelihood that scribes could hardly resist adding to Mark's abrupt ending ("for they were afraid" [v. 8]), and with the fact that the earliest and best MSS lack these twelve verses, the evidence is overwhelming in favor of seeing Mark 16:9-20 as added later.

Stylistic considerations also weigh in on one-word variants. Thus, in John 4:1, the MSS vary between "Now when *Jesus* knew that the Pharisees had heard that he was winning and baptizing more disciples than John" and "Now when *the Lord* knew that the Pharisees had heard that he was winning and baptizing more disciples than John." Indeed, many of the better and earlier MSS have "the Lord" here instead of "Jesus." However, the narratives of John rarely call Jesus "Lord" prior to the resurrection, at most only twice (6:23; 11:2). Meanwhile, "Jesus" is used scores of times. Thus, the stylistic consideration is in support of "Jesus" instead of "the Lord."

3. Conclusions of Internal Evidence

Once the internal evidence has been examined, one usually has a sense as to which reading likely gave rise to the others. To the degree that the intrinsic and transcriptional probabilities confirm each other, one can have confidence that that reading is most likely correct. The final step in internal evidence is to rate the preferred reading with a letter grade (A, B, C, or D). If the evidence seems conclusive (leaving no doubt in one's mind) for a particular reading, it deserves an A. If the evidence is very difficult to determine, almost to the point where one has to flip a coin to make a decision, the preferred reading deserves a D. It is crucial to note that *only* the preferred reading, rather than all the readings, gets a letter grade. Attaching a grade to one variant indicates that that wording is preferred; the letter itself indicates how certain is the preference.

One other comment about internal evidence is in order. So as not to prejudice oneself in making text-critical decisions, we recommend that

---

41. See James M. Hamilton, Jr., "He Is with You and He Will Be in You" (Ph.D. dissertation, Southern Baptist Theological Seminary, 2003), 213-20.

the internal evidence be examined first. Too often, students see the great majuscules or some early papyri on the side of one of the readings and assume that the textual problem is already solved. Doing textual criticism properly requires one not to let his left hand of external evidence know what his right hand of internal evidence is doing. Instead, one should notice the diacritical marks in NA[27], and see if he can predict what the variant is in that place. And if he can successfully predict the variant, it is highly likely that such wording could have been produced by various scribes who have no connection with one another. Predictable variants are motivated readings: if we can predict it, some scribe was probably tempted to write it.

2.3.2 Examination of the External Evidence

There are three external criteria used to judge which variant is more likely to be the wording of the original: date and character, genealogical solidarity, and geographical distribution.

2.3.2.1 DATE AND CHARACTER

The preferred variant or reading is the one found in the earliest MSS. This is because there is less time between them and the originals and thus less time for intermediary copies. The more direct pipeline a MS has to the original, the better are its chances of getting the wording right. Also, the MSS which elsewhere prove themselves to be the most reliable are given preference. A meticulous scribe working on a fifth-century MS may produce a more reliable text than a third-century scribe who is more interested in getting the job done quickly.

Also regarding character, it is usually considered more important to see if a given MS is a good witness to its text-form rather than to the original text, because the route to the wording of the original text is through the various text-types. This is an important distinction, but one that must be maintained in doing textual criticism.

2.3.2.2 GENEALOGICAL SOLIDARITY

Most of the MSS were written in locales in which certain traditional variants were copied repeatedly. That is to say, most MSS find their roots in a local ancestor (or what we might call a regional archetype) that influenced the various descendants in this locale. Thus, various patterns of readings emerged in each locale, giving that locale a distinctive type of text. When all or almost all of the MSS that are identified as belonging to a certain text-type agree on a certain reading, one could say that the local ancestor of that text-type probably contained that reading (and the reading is considered genealogically solid).[42]

What exactly is a text-type? A modern analogy may help. All translations take on a certain pattern of readings. Thus, the KJV sounds archaic, though elegant; the NIV sounds almost conversational; the Message sounds lively. Now, suppose that the printing press had not yet been invented, and each pastor had to spend the first year of his seminary training writing out his own copy of the Scriptures. At each seminary, a different version of the Scriptures would be utilized and the students would be expected to learn that version well. Students in Chicago might write out a copy of the NIV; those in Los Angeles, the NASB; those in Dallas, the NET. None of the handwritten copies of the various versions would be exactly like the "local original." But they would be close, and a comparison of them to each other would help one to see what the original archetype looked like. Suppose, too, that hundreds of years have gone by and all that remains of the NIV, NASB, or NET are a dozen or so copies from each "text-type." But one of the NIV copies is found in Dallas and it has several NET-like readings in it. One would say that that MS has some mixture. And even if it were early, the mixture would make it less important than a purer NIV copy that came later. This is how the "character" of a MS can be assessed: is it close to the wording of the local original, or does it have a lot of mixture from other text-types? The former is better than the latter for the purposes of trying to get back to the wording of the local archetype.

The text of the NT is similar to this. There are three major text-types: the Alexandrian, the Western, and the Byzantine. The Alexandrian was produced especially in Egypt, the Western in Rome and the West (though also elsewhere), and the Byzantine mostly in the East. Most scholars agree that the Alexandrian text-type began in the second century, as did the Western. The Byzantine text, however, was a later development, based largely on Western and Alexandrian MSS.[43] The best Alexandrian MSS are those that do not have mixture from Western or Byzantine readings. And when one looks at all the Alexandrian MSS, a pattern emerges for a given reading. When the better Alexandrian MSS have the same reading, there is a high degree of confidence that the Alexandrian local original had that reading. This is true even though that local original no longer exists. It is a simple deduction from the available evidence. Thus, by genealogical

---

42. For a discussion of which MSS belong to which text-types, see Bruce M. Metzger, *A Textual Commentary on the Greek New Testament*, 2nd ed. (Stuttgart: Deutsche Bibelgesellschaft, 1994), 14*-16*; and Michael W. Holmes, "New Testament Textual Criticism," in *Introducing New Testament Interpretation*, ed. Scot McKnight (Grand Rapids, Mich.: Baker, 1989), 59-60.

43. For a discussion of the Byzantine text-type and its place in textual criticism, see Wallace, "Majority Text," 297-320.

solidarity, one can push back the date of a reading *within* a text-type to its local original. (This is similar to the deduction one would make if he were to meet an extended family of fifty blue-eyed Swedes: the ancestors also most likely had blue eyes.) Since the Alexandrian and Western texts have roots that go deep into the second century (which can be confirmed by patristic quotations from certain geographical locations in the second century), when each of these text-types has genealogical solidarity, their readings are said to be second-century readings.

By way of illustration, consider two families whose ancestors immigrated to the United States in the early 1800s. In one family (let's call them the Dodd family), the story of where they came from, what year they arrived, and where they landed, is consistent: Wales, 1833, New York. Virtually all the sources agree. Some of these sources are living voices, some are diaries or letters from previous generations. To be sure, some later sources have different information, but there is very little disagreement. One letter, written by a twelve-year-old, says that her ancestors arrived in 1883; the diary of a person who married into the family said they came from England. Thus, although not all the records agree entirely, the best witnesses agree and the deviating ones don't deviate too much. Further, the deviations are clearly understandable. In one case, the difference is due to accident (1883 vs. 1833), while in the other case it may be due to the tendency to replace the less familiar with the more familiar. The other family (let's call them the Wallace family) has a different tale: some say that the ancestors came to the U.S. in 1819, others in 1847; some say the ancestors came from Scotland, others from Germany; some say the ancestors landed in Boston, others in Rhode Island. When there are discrepancies of this sort for the second family, there is no genealogical solidarity. The truth needs to be determined by some other means. But the Dodd family has a consistent story, and genealogical solidarity suggests that this story reaches all the way back to 1833. By itself, genealogical solidarity is not enough to prove that a reading is authentic, but it does demonstrate that it is older than any of the remaining MSS of that text-type.

As well, even when the MSS of the Alexandrian text-type are not completely solid, one can often suggest a date for *two streams* of tradition that antedate the extant witnesses. This is because the Alexandrian text most likely had two branches: the primary and secondary Alexandrian. Both of these are ancient streams of transmission, with the primary Alexandrian being more carefully produced. Thus, even though the various regional archetypes have disappeared, it is possible to suggest a date for a variant that antedates any of the MSS in which it is found.

2.3.2.3 GEOGRAPHICAL DISTRIBUTION

The variant that is found in geographically widespread locations in the first few centuries of the Christian era is more likely to be original than the one that is found in only one location. Collusion of witnesses is much less probable when these witnesses are distributed in Rome and Alexandria and Caesarea than when they are all located in just Jerusalem or Antioch. Thus, if a third-century MS in Egypt, a third-century version in Rome, and a third-century Father in Gaul all agree on the wording of a passage, chances are that they all are reproducing an earlier source. The geographical spread of sources that agree with each other is a very important factor in determining the wording of the original text. Not only does this demonstrate that the particular reading was not produced by some sort of collaboration, it also shows that the reading is much earlier than any of the extant sources. By this method, one can legitimately "push back" the date of a reading behind the time of the sources that attest it.

Consider again our analogy with the Dodd and Wallace families. If another family, unrelated to either of these families, were to confirm some of the statements in the family records of the Dodds or Wallaces, that would be similar to geographical distribution. There is no relation between this other family and the Dodds or Wallaces, yet they offer an independent witness as a confirmation of the truth of an event recorded in the Dodd or Wallace family records. This kind of "multiple attestation" strengthens the likelihood that the event really happened. By itself, it does not prove it, for there could be independent reasons for both sets of records to say the same thing. (See the concluding thoughts on internal evidence on pages 50-51, above.) Nevertheless, geographical distribution is an important factor in determining the wording of the original NT.

It should be noted that after the first four centuries geographical distribution is no longer nearly as helpful, since by this time there would be extensive cross-pollination (mixture) among the MSS, due to the freedom of exchange of information once Christianity became a legal religion.

Geographical distribution can also be imperfectly illustrated by a variation of the "telephone game." This is a game every child knows. It involves a line of people, with the first one whispering some statement into the ear of the second. As this statement goes down the line, it gets garbled. The whole point of the telephone game, in fact, is to see how garbled the statement becomes. There is no motivation to "get it right." Now suppose instead of one line there were three. And the last person in the line was not the only one who was asked to repeat the statement for all to hear; others in the line could do that as well. One may well be able to construct much of the original utterance by comparing the three lines and finding the things they had in common. This is geographical distribution.

Taking this one step further, suppose it were determined that one of the lines was far more conservative than the other two in conveying the utterance. This could be tested by hearing what someone "up the stream" said compared with someone further down the line. If there was very little change from person to person, that line would be deemed superior to the other lines. (Of course, to actually determine what the original message was, internal evidence would need to be brought in.)

In sum, date and character, genealogical solidarity, and geographical distribution are three ways of looking at the external data and deciding which reading is most likely earlier than the other. These need to be compared to each other, with the objective of determining which reading is the earliest, which reading gives rise to the others. In places where the early MSS disagree, or where there is minimal geographical distribution, or where one of the readings is predictable (i.e., is the kind of wording a scribe would be likely to create), internal evidence may be far more important.

As with internal evidence, a letter grade needs to be given to the preferred reading.

2.3.3 Conclusions

Once external evidence and internal evidence are compared, we can come to a conclusion as to which reading is the original. The textual variant that has the greatest claim to authenticity will be found in the earliest, best, and most geographically widespread witnesses; will fit the context and the author's style; and will be the obvious originator of its rival reading(s) on a literary level. For the vast majority of textual problems, this is a no-brainer.

However, there are many occasions in which the external evidence seems to point one way, while the internal evidence points another. How do we decide in such instances? Frankly, this is the kind of conundrum that fills theological journals! If a particular variant is found only in non-Greek MSS, or is found only in a few late MSS, even if its internal credentials are excellent, it must be rejected. When we are dealing with as many thousands of MSS as we are, unpredictable accidents and unknowable motives may be the cause of a stray reading here or there that internally may have good credentials. On the other hand, on a rare occasion, the external evidence is solidly on the side of one reading but there are sufficiently important MSS for an alternate reading, and the internal evidence is completely on the side of the second reading. In such instances, the second reading is most likely original.[44] Some problems cannot yet be

44. Thanks are due to Kregel Publications for permission to exploit my chapters on NT textual criticism in *Reinventing Jesus*, by J. Ed Komoszewski, M. James Sawyer, and Daniel B. Wallace (Grand Rapids, Mich.: Kregel, 2006).

solved with our present state of knowledge. Others can only be solved by repeated examination, patient reflection, and deep probing—characteristics that reflect the scholarship of the man to whom this chapter is dedicated, Harold Hoehner.

2.4 For Further Reading

Aland, Kurt, and Barbara Aland. *The Text of the New Testament: An Introduction to the Critical Editions and to the Theory and Practice of Modern Textual Criticism*. 2nd ed. Grand Rapids, Mich.: Eerdmans, 1989.

Ehrman, Bart D., and Michael W. Holmes, eds. *The Text of the New Testament in Contemporary Research: Essays on the Status Quaestionis (A Volume in Honor of Bruce M. Metzger)*, Studies and Documents 46. Grand Rapids, Mich.: Eerdmans, 1994.

Epp, Eldon J., and Gordon D. Fee, *Studies in the Theory and Method of New Testament Textual Criticism,* Studies and Documents 45. Grand Rapids, Mich.: Eerdmans, 1993.

Metzger, Bruce M. *A Textual Commentary on the Greek New Testament*. 2nd ed. Stuttgart: Deutsche Bibelgesellschaft, 1994.

Metzger, Bruce M., and Bart D. Ehrman. *The Text of the New Testament: Its Transmission, Corruption, and Restoration*. 4th ed. Oxford: Oxford University Press, 2005.

New English Translation—Novum Testamentum Graece *New Testament*. Stuttgart: Deutsche Bibelgesellschaft; Dallas: NET Bible Press, 2004.

The text-critical notes are helpful to guide the student in the discussions of the major textual problems in the NT.

Grammatical Analysis 3

Making Connections

J. WILLIAM JOHNSTON

Anyone who has undertaken the labor of learning to read NT Greek may feel a sense of accomplishment once the initial joys and pains of the learning experience are over. But the study of Greek, though rewarding, is certainly no end in itself. With exegesis as our goal, we are not so much students of a language as we are students of the exegetical process. That process is modeled in the teaching and writing of Harold Hoehner, and particularly embodied in his indispensable commentary on Ephesians. This chapter offers practical advice for intermediate students to integrate Greek grammar with exegesis.

We often use the term *grammar* to refer to the study of the constituents of a language such as its parts of speech and morphology (such as declensions and conjugations). Analysis at this level covers subjects such as case usage, tense, voice, mood, and the like. We use the term *syntax* to talk about principles of how clauses and sentences are arranged, and what patterns of arrangement mean. Such descriptions are not mathematically precise but establish the framework of semantic probability.[1] The study of syntax touches virtually every area of NT interpretation.

---

1. A. T. Robertson, *A Grammar of the Greek New Testament in the Light of Historical Research,* 4th ed. (Nashville: Broadman, 1923), 384-87.

Understanding syntax is vital to making appropriate judgments about internal evidence in text-critical problems. Syntax forms the basis for decision making about clausal layouts and diagramming. It can even be important for word study. Its contribution is most keenly felt at the level of exegetical problem solving and validation because much of the carefully fashioned argumentation in the commentaries is about the relationship of the parts of a clause.

Grammatical analysis, particularly selecting the right category from among a list of possible meanings, is both science and art. Your sense of frustration as a student probably runs high as you make the transition from grammatical neophyte to experienced novice. You pore over a list of categories with each phrase in the Greek text. Any category is *possible*, but which one is *right?* The situation is not unlike a group of initiates to bird watching turned loose for the first time on the nature trail, equipped with enthusiasm, binoculars, and a field manual. A bird lights in a nearby tree, pages in the manual turn, someone calls out a name. But that identification is unlikely, the guide gently corrects, because the bird suggested by the novice does not typically range into this part of the country.

You may have experienced something like this in an intermediate Greek course: λέγει flutters by in the text. "Gnomic present," says one student. "Progressive present," declares another. "The context is historical narrative," offers the professor, "so historical present is most likely." This is part of the process of learning: repeated exposure to examples is necessary to be able to recognize commonly occurring features.[2] Like bird watching, syntactical analysis requires patience, practice, and knowledgeable guides. To borrow the words of the writer of Hebrews, "perceptions are trained by practice to discern" one syntactical category from another (Heb 5:14, NET).

3.1 Where to Begin

Since ability to read and translate Greek is only preliminary, the next step is acquisition of a working set of syntactical categories. You can find an essential library of reference grammars and good guides to syntactical study at the end of this chapter. A look at the table of contents of any of these reference grammars reveals the most general outline of Greek syntax. The areas are: (1) noun system, (2) verb system, and (3) clauses. A corresponding understanding of *English* syntax is also needed. Of course, this simple list belies the complexity of the language. Commit the

---

2. Nor should you be disappointed when you encounter an ordinary usage, because even sparrows are important (Matt 10:29).

most important or most frequent categories to memory.[3] Keep in mind that speed and confidence in your analysis will improve with practice, and you will begin to develop a "feel" for syntax. Syntax is not the *only* method for studying the Greek text of the NT, but it certainly is vital. As A. T. Robertson put it, "Exegesis is not syntax, but syntax comes before real exegesis."[4]

It is often difficult to prioritize what to study, since it is tempting to study *everything* in detail. A working knowledge of ordinary usage allows you to recognize extraordinary use of language in the NT text. The unusual or debated categories of usage will require more validation. Thus, you will know when more detailed study is necessary. It remains to be said, however, that two other major sources for grammatical help are available. One source is the dictionary. Lexical tools such as BDAG often present important grammatical peculiarities and usage examples for particular words. The other source of grammatical help is the vast array of commentaries, particularly exegetical-critical commentaries (those that deal directly with the Greek text).

The following general roadmap to grammatical/syntactical analysis may be useful to the intermediate student.[5] These steps are not intended to be mechanical, but to be used as a guide to discovering what is most important. In general, with the noun system, case is of primary concern. In the verb system, tense/aspect[6] and voice dominate the field of exegetical importance. Now to the process of grammatical observation: beginning with your clausal layout[7] of the passage, parse and classify the tense, voice, and mood of the finite verbs attached to the structural markers; they are backbones of their respective clauses. Next, work on the adverbial participles (commonly identified by the lack of an article, though not all anarthrous participles are adverbial). Participles offer the

---

3. *ExSyn* helpfully marks the most common categories with arrows and the frequently misunderstood categories with daggers in each section's table of contents. Bear in mind, too, that terminology differs from grammar to grammar.

4. Robertson, *Grammar,* 389.

5. For the step-by-step suggestions in this section, I am especially indebted to John D. Grassmick, *Principles and Practice of Greek Exegesis: A Classroom Manual,* rev. ed. (Dallas: Dallas Theological Seminary, 1976), 139-40.

6. While *tense* for English grammar often indicates little more than time, for Greek grammar *tense* represents aspect (kind of action or state) and time. One hesitates to attempt a definition in view of the fierce debate that has raged over this topic (mostly over whether time is essentially encoded in the verb form). For key bibliography see especially *ExSyn,* 495.

7. See chapter 4, "Sentence Diagramming, Clausal Layouts, and Exegetical Outlining: Tracing the Argument" for detailed instructions on how to construct a clausal layout. I sometimes find it useful to record syntactical information directly on the clausal layout. You might wish to use "hidden" text (if your word processor supports the feature) so that you can print versions of your layout with and without the grammatical observations.

most reward—and the greatest challenge—in the study of syntax. Indeed, "mastery of the syntax of participles is mastery of Greek syntax."[8] Next, classify the tense and voice of the adverbial infinitives. One of the most common adverbial uses of the infinitive is complementary (following a very narrow list of verbs),[9] and can be passed over as exegetically insignificant. For nouns and adjectives, classify significant uses of case. Unusual or non-standard uses of case are significant. There is hardly anything surprising, for instance, about a noun in the nominative case acting as the subject of a finite verb. Pay close attention to the genitive case, since it is the most flexible of the cases. Particularly when the head noun is a verbal noun, check to see whether the genitive might be subjective or objective in function, although these are not the only two possibilities.[10] Next, identify and classify the relative pronouns and their antecedents. Occasionally, prepositional phrases also prove to be noteworthy, particularly when it is difficult to tell what they modify.

One good way to surface grammatical/syntactical problems is by comparing English translations (other languages, too—the more, the better), which will differ slightly in just about every passage. The differences of no concern are the use of synonyms for specific terms. But *real* disagreements of meaning between translations usually indicate exegetical disputes. Eliminate translation differences arising from divergent textual readings (e.g., Rom 5:1, "let us be at peace," BBE[11] [ἔχωμεν] vs. "we have peace," NET [ἔχομεν]), English style, vocabulary, or the like. Then determine what syntactical decision making went into the translator's choice. In comparison with the formal-equivalent variety (e.g., NASB, NIV), translations that tend toward the dynamic-equivalent range (e.g., NET, NLT) will usually reflect grammatical categorizations more specifically. This kind of comparison will reap considerable benefits for exegesis. For instance, NASB renders the participle ἀκούσας in Eph 1:15 "having heard," while NIV translates "ever since I heard," and NET reads, "because I have heard." In this instance, NASB translates without making any indication of the value of the participle, NIV prefers a temporal sense, while NET makes a causal force explicit.[12]

---

8. *ExSyn*, 613.

9. See ibid., 598-99.

10. A verbal noun (in the lexical, not syntactical sense) is a noun that implies an action. See ibid., 112-21. One quick (though not infallible) way to check for this property is to use a lexicon to see if the noun has a verbal cognate. For instance, for the noun ἀγάπη there is the verb ἀγαπάω. So genitives dependent on some form of ἀγάπη are candidates for this identification (e.g., Rom 5:5).

11. S. H. Hooke, ed., *The Basic Bible, Containing the Old and New Testaments in Basic English* (Cambridge: Cambridge University Press, 1949).

12. In other passages, the issue may involve not just the *force* of the participle but also which *main verb* it modifies. Consider ἐπέχοντες (from ἐπέχω) in Phil 2:16, which means "hold fast" (BDAG, 362 s.v. 1) if it modifies γένησθε ("you will prove yourselves blameless . . . holding

Differences between English translations may help you discover the most important exegetical issues.

Now that you have done some preliminary work to uncover exegetical options, the next place to look is the index of each reference grammar you have available. Start with the Scripture index and check to see if the verse is treated in the grammar. Some of the "hits" in the index for the verse may not be useful (because the grammar does not treat the desired part of the verse). If the verse itself is not listed in the index, check the subject index or table of contents for the construction you are studying. Use what you find in the reference grammars as a starting point for your own inquiry.

3.2 Making Sense of Syntax

Making an observation about the syntax of a Greek text does not magically provide the right interpretation. Statements that begin "In the Greek, it really says . . ." do not provide ample evidence for a view. Nor is using Greek a means of picking the category label that achieves a desired interpretation. The proper use of Greek syntax involves testing grammatical identifications by careful, contextual exegetical validation. When an interpretive difficulty involves a grammatical issue, statements about the nature and meaning of a construction must be based on sound method.

These are the most important imperatives to keep in mind[13]: (1) Validate using as many clear (as distinct from disputed) examples of the same construction as possible; it is unwise to be dogmatic about conclusions that are based on only a few examples. (2) Use examples from the Hellenistic period (330 BC to AD 330) as distinct from the earlier or later periods.[14] (3) Decide based on what is *likely* given the context rather than what is merely *possible*. There is more to context than just the words spoken because context can involve factors like body language, tone, previous shared experience of the writer/speaker and the audience/reader, "cultural scripts" (see chapter 5, on word study) and other clues that syntax alone cannot measure. In short, much like sound word study method, *sound*

---

fast" [NASB]) or "hold out" (LSJ, 619 s.v. II. [but note most of the examples cited come from the Classical period rather than the Hellenistic period]) if it modifies φαίνεσθε ("you shine . . . as you hold out" [NIV]). Either one could be supported by various details of the context, so it is easy to see why the versions disagree.

13. For this section on grammatical method, I am drawing on *ExSyn*, 1-11, which I advise the student to read carefully. There are other deeper considerations addressed there about philosophy of language that we do not have space to discuss.

14. In the case of some rare constructions, you may have to consider examples from earlier Greek.

grammatical method must be based upon examination of actual usage in an appropriate historical time frame.

It has become somewhat easier to find specific examples of usage in the NT with the availability of computerized search engines such as Accordance, BibleWorks, Gramcord, and Libronix. This kind of software allows the user to search the Greek NT (and other corpora of ancient literature such as the LXX, Philo, and Josephus) for syntactical patterns. Though each of these programs has its own advantages and disadvantages, spending the time to learn the more advanced features (especially specification of parameters like word order and morphological agreement) can pay some rich dividends for inductive study. Specialized software tools have become all but indispensable to the interpretive task. However, despite these great advances in technology, it is still necessary to learn syntax. Computer programs can help us to find the raw material quickly, but they are not sophisticated enough to do exegesis for us.

Having offered some advice about grammatical observation, I want to devote our remaining space to two examples in which grammar helps exegesis. Let us use Eph 2:1-10 as an example of the grammatical/syntactical issues to consider. Then we will move to a specific example: the force of the phrase ἐν πνεύματι (Eph 5:18).

3.3 Grammatical Observations

The structural markers from a clausal layout of Eph 2:1-10 illustrate what grammatical problems confront us. Of course, we could turn to the commentaries first, but this would short-circuit the inductive process. By way of preliminary observation we can point out two interesting and potentially tricky constructions: (1) ὑμᾶς ὄντας νεκρούς[15] in v. 1 is repeated in v. 5 (with a change from ὑμᾶς to ἡμᾶς), and should be understood as the object of the finite verbs in vv. 5-6 (see below); (2) χάριτί ἐστε σεσῳσμένοι in v. 5 anticipates the same expression in v. 8.[16] The fact that the phrase occurs in v. 5 makes the syntax ambiguous, because these words fit logically in the latter position. Please note that the following are only grammatical observations and would not pass for commentary by any stretch of the imagination.

Verse 1. The participle ὄντας with its predicate adjective νεκρούς ("you were dead") must be understood in relation to the finite verbs of

---

15. To make for smoother reading of the Greek text, I may quote from part of a verse or omit words from verses without indication of ellipsis.

16. Something to be regarded as a "parenthetical outburst" (Harold W. Hoehner, *Commentary on Ephesians* [Grand Rapids, Mich.: Baker, 2002], 331).

vv. 5-6 (see below). We would normally expect the present participle to present action contemporaneous to the verb, or, better, because εἰμί is a stative verb, a state or condition that existed at the time of the action of the aorist main verbs.[17] The participle is modified by the datives τοῖς παραπτώμασιν and καὶ ταῖς ἁμαρτίαις. The options may be exegetically significant: these might be datives of cause ("because of trespasses and sins") or sphere ("in trespasses and sins").[18]

  Verse 2. The phrase ἐν αἷς (consisting of a preposition and a relative pronoun) introduces the next clause. The antecedent is ἁμαρτίαις in the previous verse, but notice also the parallel to the relative clause in the next verse. The verb περιεπατήσατε is the main verb of this clause. The tense (aorist) deserves attention—probably a constative aorist summarizing the pre-salvation lifestyle of the audience. The fact the verb is modified by the enclitic adverb ποτε may emphasize a then/now contrast (cf. 2:13, νυνί). The verb περιεπατήσατε is also modified by two parallel prepositional phrases: κατὰ τὸν αἰῶνα ("according to the age") and κατὰ τὸν ἄρχοντα ("according to the ruler"), each with dependent genitive phrases. Each κατά prepositional phrase reveals something about the standards by which the audience formerly conducted their lives.[19] The second prepositional phrase, κατὰ τὸν ἄρχοντα, is modified by τῆς ἐξουσίας τοῦ ἀέρος, both seemingly genitives of rulership: the ruler has authority over the "air." The next genitive phrase, τοῦ πνεύματος, is somewhat more problematic because of (1) its lexical value and (2) its syntactical value. This is a fine example in which the lexical and syntactical are intertwined. Put simply, πνεῦμα may be taken personally, as a spirit-being, or impersonally, as a frame of mind or attitude.[20] As to syntactical value, τοῦ πνεύματος could (1) be dependent on or in apposition to ἀέρος (the "air" is the same thing as, or characterized by the spirit at work in the "sons of disobedience"), (2) be in apposition to ἄρχοντα (the ruler *is* this evil spirit), or (3) be dependent upon ἄρχοντα, so that the prince rules over both the air and the spirit (influence) at work in the "sons of disobedience." Wallace prefers view (3) since a genitive of apposition does not occur where both head noun and dependent genitive are personal nouns.[21] So the most likely construal is "[the ruler] over the spirit."

  Verse 3. Like v. 2, v. 3 begins with a relative clause. This time the pronoun is masculine, with its antecedent υἱοῖς, emphasizing the environment of

---

  17. BDF §339 (3), p. 175 would label this as "representing the imperfect."

  18. For dative of *cause* see *ExSyn,* 167; for *sphere* and the distinction from *reference* see *ExSyn,* 153-54.

  19. BDAG, 512 s.v. κατά B.5.a.

  20. Cf. "spirit" BDAG, 833-36 s.v. πνεῦμα 4 or 5; "disposition" or "spiritual state" BDAG, 833 s.v. 3c.

  21. *ExSyn,* 95-100; 104 and n. 86.

their former lifestyle. The readers were dead because of sin (v. 2) among people who were sinners (v. 3). The verb of the clause (ἀνεστράφημεν) is again aorist tense, and in view of the syntactical parallel (including repetition of the adverb), its semantics for the aorist tense are probably parallel too (so also a constative aorist). However, one important change should be noted: the shift from second person to first person, showing that even the author was in the same situation as the readers.[22] The main verb is qualified by the adverbial participle ποιοῦντες, which must be classified.[23] Manner ("we lived out our lives . . . indulging the desires of the flesh" [NET]) seems most likely, describing *how* the readers conducted their lives. A second finite verb, ἤμεθα ("we were"), joined by καί to the first must also be classified. The imperfect tense of the verb joined with its generally stative nuance is also revealing. Furthermore, combined with the adverb ποτε, ἤμεθα hints that there is a radical transformation in store between vv. 1-3 and vv. 4-7.

The last clause of v. 3, ὡς καὶ οἱ λοιποί, illustrates that Greek can sometimes be elliptical. Because the conjunction ὡς typically invites comparison, we must supply a verb. Note also the parallelism between καὶ ἡμεῖς and καὶ οἱ λοιποί, so the comparison is probably we "were by nature children of wrath even as the rest [were/are children of wrath]." The comparison is to τέκνα φύσει ὀργῆς, in which the genitive ὀργῆς is understood as dependent on τέκνα and the dative φύσει is probably a dative of reference ("in our natural condition").[24] The genitive presents, again, some options: (1) an attributive genitive "wrathful children [= people]" or (2) a genitive of destination "people destined for [the] wrath [of God]."[25] The latter fits better with the context because the thrust emphasizes that sinfulness ends in divine punishment (cf. Eph 5:6) rather than further emphasizing a particular kind of human sinfulness.

Verse 4. The conjunction δέ becomes a major structural marker, contrasting "you" and "we" on the one side and "God" on the other. Put another way, it contrasts the spiritual death of people in vv. 1-3 with God's gracious remedy in vv. 4-10. The participle ὤν is adverbial, modifying

22. Care must be taken, however, not to be wooden in interpreting first person plurals. See *ExSyn,* 393-99 for a discussion of the scope of "we." In the present context, the addition of πάντες to the pronoun allows for an all-inclusive sense. The fact, too, that the pronoun ἡμεῖς is explicitly stated and emphasized by an ascensive καί ("even" BDAG, 495-96 s.v. 2.b.), makes it all but certain that the author includes himself in the subject of the verb.

23. The most common adverbial participle categories are: temporal, conditional, concession, causal, means, purpose, manner, and result. Arranging them this way allows for the mnemonic device: "The crucified Christ's cross means people marvelously redeemed." Special thanks for an earlier form go to my former student David Tang.

24. *ExSyn,* 144-45; BDAG, 1069 s.v. φύσις 1.

25. *ExSyn,* 101; the similar expression σκεύη ὀργῆς ("vessels of wrath") in Rom 9:22 almost certainly involves a genitive of destination; see also the NET Bible note.

the finite verbs in vv. 5-6. Although concession ("although God is rich in mercy") is possible in a rhetorical structure like this, cause ("because God is rich in mercy") is the better category label. This is further confirmed by the causal sense of the phrase διὰ τὴν πολλὴν ἀγάπην αὐτοῦ ("on account of his great love"). Together these expressions modify the following three finite verbs in vv. 5-6. The relative clause modifying ἀγάπην also has a verb (ἠγάπησεν) whose aorist tense merits some comment: the time of the verb possibly points to the past action of Christ's sacrificial death on the cross. The constative aorist aspect summarizes this sacrifice without exploring its action.

Verses 5-6. Three aorist tense main verbs convey the heart of the action of this passage (συνήγειρεν, "he raised us together"; συνεκάθισεν, "he seated us together"; and συνεζωοποίησεν, "he made us alive together"; all to be taken with the dative of association τῷ Χριστῷ, "with the Messiah"). The aorist tense once again deserves attention. The tense of the verbs specifies a past time, and the indicative mood is declarative. A very real change in the state of the readers' relationship to God has taken place—even though there are aspects of that relationship that have yet to be fully experienced (cf. Eph 1:14). The accusative construction that opens v. 5 also deserves notice for its parallel and for its difference from the opening of v. 1. The expression ὄντας ἡμᾶς νεκροὺς in v. 5 parallels ὑμᾶς ὄντας νεκρούς, but a first person pronoun replaces the second person pronoun (cf. καὶ ἡμεῖς in v. 3), again emphasizing the unity of author and readers in the transforming power of God's remedy for spiritual death.

Verse 7. The next major structural marker is the subordinating conjunction ἵνα with its subjunctive verb ἐνδείξηται. Together these form the purpose (or result) of the three finite verbs in vv. 5-6. It may also be that the time frame implied by the adjectival participle ἐπερχομένοις ("coming") modifying τοῖς αἰῶσιν ("ages") is exegetically significant too. But grammar alone cannot provide *all* the important data for consideration: the participle brings to mind biblical theological themes like the so-called "apocalyptic" worldview in which the unfolding of the plan of God is seen as both "already" and "not yet" (cf. Matt 12:32; Mark 10:30).

Verse 8. The next clause begins with the conjunction γάρ, connecting vv. 8-10 to vv. 4-7, but the nature of that connection should be explored. It probably does not indicate the *cause* of vv. 4-7, but demonstrates the grounds upon which Paul can say God provided the remedy for sin.[26] Thus, salvation by grace is the ground or evidence upon which Paul makes the assertion that the readers are seated with Christ. The main

---

26. BDAG, 189 s.v. γάρ 2, "marker of clarification, *for, you see.*"

verb of the clause is ἐστε σεσωσμένοι, a periphrastic construction consisting of the verb εἰμί and the perfect passive participle (an especially common occurrence in the perfect tense[27]). The aspect of the verb in modern English translations ("you have been saved") could give a wrong impression: the assumption a modern English reader could make is that the past-ness of the action is more in view than its present results. But the force of the aspect here is probably intensive (resultative) rather than extensive. The emphasis is thus on the saved state of the readers.[28] The dative case χάριτι is of some importance, too—is it means ("by grace") or cause ("because of grace")? The article τῇ preceding χάριτι is probably anaphoric[29] to the same word in v. 7 ("by the grace that I have been talking about" in vv. 4-7). The phrase διὰ πίστεως also modifies the main verb, and presents the more immediate means of the verb ("through faith"). More important, the sense of the demonstrative pronoun in the expression καὶ τοῦτο is vitally important. Commentators disagree on whether τοῦτο refers to χάριτι alone (meaning that *grace* is the gift of God) or πίστεως alone (meaning that *faith* is the gift of God), or to both in a general sense (the *whole package* of salvation is the gift of God).[30] The latter of these, if τοῦτο has its demonstrative force, seems most likely in view of the gender of the pronoun (neuter) compared with the gender of its possible antecedents (feminine). But perhaps καὶ τοῦτο is not intended to refer to either, because it is possible that the phrase simply adds an emphatic point ("and especially"). If this is the case, Paul intends no specific antecedent for the demonstrative.[31] The next three clauses, one here, two in the next verse, have an elided verb, ἐστιν, "it is," all of which clarify the true source of salvation. The first negative οὐκ ἐξ ὑμῶν ("[it is] not from you") is paralleled by οὐκ ἐξ ἔργων ("[it is] not from works") in v. 9. Both emphasize that the source or cause of the salvation experience resides neither in the readers nor in their accomplishments.

Verse 9. The negatives "not from you . . . not from works" bracket a positive θεοῦ τὸ δῶρον ("[it is] the gift of God"). The clause ἵνα μή τις καυχήσηται ("so that someone might not boast" or "so that no one might boast") gives the negative purpose or result of the elided verbs in the previous clauses ("[it is] not . . . [but it is]"). The result (or purpose) of the fact that the matter of salvation is *not* (μή) a result of human effort is that no one would be able to take credit for salvation.

---

27. BDF §352, p. 179; DM 231; MHT 3:88; *ExSyn,* 647.
28. See *ExSyn,* 575. The KJV "are ye saved" is more on target here.
29. *ExSyn,* 217.
30. Andrew T. Lincoln, *Ephesians,* WBC 42 (Dallas: Word, 1990), 111-12.
31. BDAG, 741 s.v. οὗτος 1.b.γ.

Verse 10. Like v. 8, v. 10 begins with the conjunction γάρ that connects vv. 8-9 to v. 10. This conjunction probably adds a further point to vv. 8-9 rather than introducing the grounds on which the statements of those verses are made.[32] The word order of v. 10 is likewise potentially important. The fact that αὐτοῦ is positioned forward in the clause (i.e., before the noun ποίημα) makes the word order emphatic. It is not enough to declare the word order emphatic—what is being emphasized should be explored: the fact that the whole operation of salvation is God's work as opposed to our own. The aorist passive participle κτισθέντες agrees in number with the embedded subject of ἐσμεν, and the relation between the participle and main verb needs explanation. It most likely is causal to the verb ἐσμεν, giving the very reason why believers are *God's* creation alone ("we are *his* workmanship because we were created for good works"). The participle's passive voice also clarifies that believers are the recipients of the action of the verb "created." The aorist tense is again constative, emphasizing the summary aspect of salvation as new creation (cf. the use of κτίζω in Eph 2:15).

Occasionally the sense of a prepositional phrase, such as ἐπὶ ἔργοις ἀγαθοῖς, may become exegetically significant. Here ἐπί with the dative case indicates the purpose[33] for which believers were created. The presence of the adjective ἀγαθοῖς also contrasts mere *human* works (the unqualified ἔργων of v. 8) to God's accomplishments and his plans for the believers he created. The following structural marker is the relative pronoun οἷς (not accusative case, but attracted[34] into the dative case by its immediately preceding antecedent ἔργοις ἀγαθοῖς) with the verb προητοίμασεν. The aorist tense is significant, denoting God's previous (the προ- prefix also contributing to the idea) action of preparation.[35] The final structural marker of the passage is ἵνα περιπατήσωμεν ("so that we should walk") which shows the purpose or result of προητοίμασεν in the preceding clause.

The observations we made above provide the groundwork for further research. Now each option should be carefully validated using numerous examples of similar constructions and context (in both the narrow and the broad senses). Chapter 6, "Validation: Exegetical Problem Solving," will explain the process of reasoning and the proper use of secondary literature.

32. It is difficult to decide between BDAG, 190-91 s.v. γάρ 2 "marker of clarification, *for, you see*" and s.v. 3 "marker of inference, *certainly, by all means, so, then.*"

33. BDAG, 366 s.v. ἐπί 16.

34. BDF §294, p. 153.

35. BDAG, 869 s.v. προετοιμάζω notes "used in our lit. only of God."

3.4 Grammatical Problem Solving

Now that we have demonstrated the process of making grammatical observations, let us turn to a different passage to investigate a single problem in more detail: what does πληροῦσθε ἐν πνεύματι, "be filled with the Spirit" (Eph 5:18), mean? The key grammatical/syntactical issues for the construction are: (1) the force of the dative case in the phrase ἐν πνεύματι, which may influence the identification of (2) the referent of πνεύματι, and the force of the (3) present tense, (4) imperative mood, and (5) passive voice for the verb πληροῦσθε. These issues are discovered by comparing English translations, consulting grammars and lexica, and by using other tools, especially exegetical commentaries. We will focus here only on what ἐν πνεύματι means in relationship to πληροῦσθε. But exegetical issues hardly ever occur in isolation.

Most English versions read "be filled with the Spirit" (e.g., KJV, NASB, NIV, RSV, ESV). The word *with* is vague, for it could mean that the command is to be full *of* the Spirit (content), or to be filled *by* the Spirit (means or instrument). BBE reflects the *content* option: "be full of the Spirit," while NET opts for *instrument*: "be filled by the Spirit."

One would think that the grammatical inquiry should begin with reference grammars, but in this situation, it should begin with the lexicon's entries on ἐν and πληρόω. Another important factor for our method in this situation is a proper distinction between uses of a case *following* a preposition and uses of a case *without* a preposition because, although there are often overlapping senses between case usage with and without prepositions, they are simply not the same. As Wallace puts it, "you would err if you shut yourself up to the categorical *possibilities* of the naked case."[36]

An array of possible helpful meanings from among BDAG's entry on ἐν present themselves (each is rendered in italic type using our text ἐν πνεύματι): "1. marker of a position defined as being in a location"[37] *in the s/Spirit;* "4. marker of close association within a limit,"[38] *within the limits of the s/Spirit;* "6. marker of agency"[39] *by the agency of the Spirit;* "11. marker denoting kind and manner,"[40] *be filled spiritually;* "12. marker of specification or substance"[41] *with regard to the s/Spirit.*

Of course, identifying the sense of πνεῦμα influences judgments about the sense of the prepositional phrase, but we do not have space to consider

36. *ExSyn*, 361. See especially the discussion on 360-64.
37. E.g., ἐν τῇ ἐρήμῳ "in the desert," Matt 3:1.
38. E.g., ἐν αὐτῷ κατοικεῖ πᾶν τὸ πλήρωμα "all the fullness dwells in him," Col 2:9.
39. E.g., δικαιωθέντες ἐν τῷ αἵματι αὐτοῦ "justified by his blood," Rom 5:9.
40. E.g., ἐν χάριτι "graciously," Gal 1:6.
41. E.g., πλούσιος ὢν ἐν ἐλέει "being rich in mercy," Eph 2:4.

this factor in detail. If the sense of πνεῦμα is the *human* spirit, then the sense of the prepositional phrase is more likely to be sphere or location—*be filled in your spirit*. If the referent of πνεῦμα is the Holy Spirit (which on the whole is more likely[42]), then the sense of ἐν πνεύματι is more likely to be instrumental—*be filled by means of the Spirit*. Our passage, then, seems to fit definition 5 best: "marker introducing means or instrument." The preposition ἐν was already used in this sense in classical Greek, but BDAG suggests the instrumental sense became more common in the NT under the influence of LXX usage and a parallel use of the preposition בְּ in the native Hebrew or Aramaic of most NT writers.[43]

But when we consider the lexicon entry for πληρόω,[44] we find Eph 5:18 listed "W. ἐν and dat. of thing ἐν πνεύματι *with the Spirit*" with an additional note that Col 4:12, if the variant reading πεπληρωμένοι (read by P⁴⁶ D² Ψ 075. 0278 𝔐 sy) is adopted, fits under this category.[45] But this category of dative usage for ἐν πνεύματι has no other examples of its kind.

To summarize the more important options for the meaning of the dative case with πληροῦσθε ἐν πνεύματι: (1) location (*be filled in spirit*), in which case the idea of πνεῦμα would be more along the lines of "human spirit," (2) close association (*be filled within the limits of the s/Spirit*), (3) agency/instrument (*be filled by the Spirit*), (4) kind or manner (*be filled spiritually*), and (5) substance (*be filled/full with regard to the S/spirit*).

But which one is most likely? At this point, in keeping with the method articulated earlier, it is important to consider evidence that is as closely parallel as possible to the construction πληροῦσθε ἐν πνεύματι in our verse. It is readily evident that means/instrument is an attested sense for ἐν with the dative. But the examples often cited involve *active* voice verbs (e.g., Rev 6:8 ἀποκτεῖναι ἐν ῥομφαίᾳ, "to kill with [a] sword"). We need to examine the use of the dative case with *passive* voice verbs.

At this point, the most useful resource is a software concordance. There are two lines of inquiry to pursue with this tool: (1) to find ample examples of similar syntactical situations which will help generally illuminate the particular instance we are studying, and (2) to find examples that use the specific vocabulary in similar syntactical situations. Although grammarians of ages past operated quite adequately without computers, software can help remove some of the more tedious aspects of grammatical inquiry. When using a search engine to look for examples, check to see if the verse

---

42. The majority of the occurrences of πνεῦμα in Eph (1:13, 17; 2:2, 18, 22; 3:5, 16; 4:3, 4, 23, 30; 5:18; 6:17, 18) refer to the Holy Spirit.

43. BDAG, 328 s.v. ἐν 5.

44. BDAG, 827-29.

45. BDF lists Eph 5:18 under both dative of content (§172, p. 95) and dative of instrument (§195, pp. 104-5).

under study appears in the results. This is a general way to check the logic of your search. Of course, this criterion is a rather blunt instrument, so use it with only the most general error correction in mind.

A general query for our problem looks for instances of a passive voice verb with the dative case. Keep in mind that Eph 5:18 has a passive voice verb with the preposition ἐν and the dative case. The results will need to be narrowed down, of course, since we are looking for instances in which the verb is *modified by* a substantive in the dative case. Since the concept *modified by* is a semantic category, most grammatical search engines are not yet able to detect such a relationship. The purpose of this search is to find examples of usage that would help us evaluate the semantic range of πληροῦσθε ἐν πνεύματι.

A search for a passive voice verb and a noun in the dative case produces literally hundreds of examples. For instance, one of the first hits, Matt 1:18 εὑρέθη ἐν γαστρί ("she was found in the belly"), has a passive voice verb with a dative (ἐν occurs, so it is interesting so far), but the example must be rejected because the prepositional phrase modifies the following participle ἔχουσα ("having [it] in the belly"—an idiom for pregnancy). So carefully examine each example a grammatical search engine finds. But there are good examples of a dative of means with a passive voice verb. For instance, Mark 9:49, πᾶς γὰρ πυρὶ ἁλισθήσεται ("for everyone will be salted with/by fire"). Yet this example does not use ἐν.

One of the best examples of the kind of construction we are searching for is Acts 1:5: ᾽Ιωάννης μὲν ἐβάπτισεν ὕδατι, ὑμεῖς δὲ ἐν πνεύματι βαπτισθήσεσθε ἁγίῳ, "John baptized by water, but you will be baptized by the Holy Spirit" (same wording as in 11:16).[46] Notice the parallel instrumental dative in the μέν clause (although the verb ἐβάπτισεν is active voice, unlike the parallel μὴ μεθύσκεσθε οἴνῳ ["do not become intoxicated by wine"] in Eph 5:18). The syntactical parallelism of Acts 1:5 implies (although it does not guarantee) semantic parallelism. Thus it is natural that ἐν πνεύματι here is also instrumental in sense ("you will be baptized by the Holy Spirit"). Several more examples can be mentioned (Rom 5:9, 10; 1 Cor 3:13; Eph 6:10; 1 Tim 3:16 [ἐδικαιώθη ἐν πνεύματι, "justified by the Spirit"]; Heb 9:22 [ἐν αἵματι πάντα καθαρίζεται, "everything is cleansed by blood"]; Rev 18:8), some other examples are somewhat debatable (John 9:3 [φανερωθῇ ἐν αὐτῷ, "displayed in/by him"]; John 17:10 [δεδόξασμαι ἐν αὐτοῖς, "I have been glorified in/by them"]; 1 Cor 6:2 [ἐν ὑμῖν κρίνεται ὁ κόσμος, "the world is judged among/by you"]; Eph 3:5 [ἀπεκαλύφθη ἐν πνεύματι, "revealed by the Spirit"]; Col 1:9; 1:16). The expression in Eph 1:13, ἐσφραγίσθητε τῷ πνεύματι, "you

---

46. While there is a theological connection between the filling of and the baptism of the Holy Spirit, the warrant for citing this passage comes from the *grammatical* parallel.

were sealed by the Spirit" occurs again at 4:30, where ἐν ᾧ ("by whom") is used in the same sense. These examples indicate that an instrumental sense for ἐν in general in the NT is common, and that the same sense for ἐν πνεύματι is possible in Eph 5:18.

A search for the verb πληρόω, its cognate adjective πλήρης, and the synonymous verb πίμπλημι, especially with πνεῦμα in the same verse, produces very important results.[47] Luke–Acts describes various kinds of content for filling (e.g., leprosy [Luke 5:12], wisdom and/or faith [Acts 6:3, 5], anger [Acts 19:28]), and describes Satan (Acts 5:3) as an agent of at least one instance of filling. Other than Eph 5:18, πληρ-roots (or πίμπλημι) and πνεῦμα occur only in Luke–Acts.[48] What is clearly different between Paul and Luke is that the Lukan examples all involve the *genitive*, while in our passage the *dative* is used. So it is all but certain that the *content* of the filling in Luke–Acts *is* the Spirit, but it is far from likely that the content of the filling in Eph 5:18 is the Spirit, and more probable that the Spirit is the *means* or *instrument* of the filling. To this the context of Ephesians and its "filling" language can be added (Eph 1:10, 23; 3:19; 4:10, 13; 5:18). The *what* of the filling has already been explained in 3:19 as τὸ πλήρωμα τοῦ θεοῦ, the *how* and *who* of the filling is explained in 5:18 as the Spirit.[49] As noted earlier, there are several other related syntactical issues and lexical identifications that ought to be made to provide a more comprehensive interpretation of Eph 5:18.

While there are many experts in biblical studies on whose books we all depend, we must not use their conclusions uncritically. A judicious use of Greek grammar and syntax can aid us in confirming for ourselves what we find in the exegetical tools. If the Bereans were commended for "examining the scriptures" after hearing the apostle Paul (Acts 17:11), how much more then should we who have labored at learning Greek consider carefully what we read?

3.5 Intermediate and Reference Grammars

Blass, Friedrich, and Albert Debrunner. *A Greek Grammar of the New Testament and Other Early Christian Literature.* Translated by Robert W. Funk.

47. These kinds of connections are often hard to think of or find, but the semantic domain approach of L&N gives some help here.

48. Luke 1:15, 41, 67; 4:1; Acts 2:4; 4:8, 31; 6:3, 5; 7:55; 9:17; 11:24; 13:9, 52. Very frequently the qualification of πνεῦμα by the adjective ἅγιος is explicit.

49. See *ExSyn*, 375; and Ernest Best, *A Critical and Exegetical Commentary on Ephesians,* ICC (Edinburgh: Clark, 1998), 508; Hoehner, *Ephesians,* 702-4; Lincoln, *Ephesians,* 344; Peter T. O'Brien, *The Letter to the Ephesians,* Pillar New Testament Commentary (Grand Rapids, Mich.: Eerdmans, 1999), 386.

Rev. and trans. of the 9th-10th German ed. Chicago: University of Chicago Press, 1961.

Burton, Ernest DeWitt. *Syntax of the Moods and Tenses in New Testament Greek*. 3rd ed. Chicago: University of Chicago Press, 1898.

Moule, C. F. D. *An Idiom Book of New Testament Greek*. 2nd ed. Cambridge: Cambridge University Press, 1959.

Moulton, James Hope *A Grammar of New Testament Greek*. Vol. 1, *Prolegomena*. 3rd ed. Edinburgh: Clark, 1908.

Moulton, James Hope *A Grammar of New Testament Greek*. Vol. 2, *Accidence and Word Formation*, by Wilbert Francis Howard. Edinburgh: Clark, 1929.

Moulton, James Hope *A Grammar of New Testament Greek*. Vol. 3, *Syntax*, by Nigel Turner. Edinburgh: Clark, 1963.

Moulton, James H. *A Grammar of New Testament Greek*. Vol. 4, *Style*, by Nigel Turner. Edinburgh: Clark, 1979.

Porter, Stanley E. *Idioms of the Greek New Testament*. 2nd ed. Biblical Languages: Greek, vol. 2. Sheffield: Sheffield Academic Press, 1995.

Robertson, A. T. *A Grammar of the Greek New Testament in the Light of Historical Research*. 4th ed. Nashville: Broadman, 1923.

Smyth, Herbert W. *Greek Grammar*. 2nd ed. Rev. Gordon M. Messing. Cambridge, Mass.: Harvard University Press, 1956.

Wallace, Daniel B. *Greek Grammar Beyond the Basics: An Exegetical Syntax of the New Testament*. Grand Rapids, Mich.: Zondervan, 1996.

Young, Richard A. *Intermediate New Testament Greek: A Linguistic and Exegetical Approach*. Nashville: Broadman & Holman, 1994.

Zerwick, Maximillian. *Biblical Greek: Illustrated by Examples*. Rome: Pontifical Biblical Institute, 1963.

Sentence Diagramming, Clausal Layouts, and Exegetical Outlining
4

Tracing the Argument

4.0 Introduction

4.0.1 The Elusive Goal: Tracing the Argument

PowerPoint, sound bites, bullet points, television commercials that fire a barrage of images. It might be nice if the NT epistles had been written in a similar style. Unfortunately, they were not. Rather, the epistles and in particular Paul's letters consist of or at least contain sustained, logical arguments.[1] They are letters, but they are letters with an argument. They move progressively and logically in a sustained direction. In this way, they are more like a suspense thriller than an automobile commercial with its rapid-fire images. Miss ten minutes of the mystery-suspense movie and you are lost. It is much the same with the argumentation in Paul's letters. He is developing an argument, pursuing a line of thought. Everything is connected. It is difficult to jump in midstream and catch the drift of what

---

1. Although the principles and procedures that we set forth in this chapter will apply in some measure to all NT authors, and especially to those employing the epistolary genre, we will use Paul and his letters as our primary illustration.

he is saying. The epistolary genre is not a collection of proverbs or a set of classic one-liners. Rather it consists of a series of paragraphs, each of which contains an argument that, in succession, contributes to the author's overall developing argument.

We, however, prefer the random, the proverbial, or the stream-of-consciousness approach. It is easier for our flabby minds, which prefer not to think deeply in ways necessary to follow a sustained, logical argument. And sadly, our culture reinforces the mentality that says, "I'll give you my focused attention for two to three seconds, but you had better 'wow' me with some special effects or otherwise titillate my senses." Itemized lists and cutesy graphics are "in"; sustained logical discourse is passé.

Paul, however, refuses to be domesticated. He does not conform to our standards. His writings are complicated, and his logic is often difficult to follow.[2] And sadly, we have not been taught to read such discourse, and nearly everything in our culture entices us away from this invaluable but hard-won skill. Perhaps most important, Paul, not you or I, sets the agenda. If we want to understand Paul as he wanted to be understood, as he must be understood, then we must seek to follow, to engage, to unpack Paul's argument, his train of thought.[3] We are not trying to disclose isolated facts, ideas, or even themes. We are trying to trace the argument—the plot, the story line, if you will. We want to see how Paul's ideas are developed, explained, substantiated, and applied. We are not merely trying "to think Paul's thoughts after him" but to think Paul's thoughts after him and see *the connections between* those thoughts.

4.0.2 The Threefold Strategy

Creating what we will call a *structural layout of Greek clauses* will help us trace Paul's line of thought. These clausal layouts indicate where the action takes place—where ideas are presented, developed, clarified, and applied. However, before we take a detailed look at clausal layouts and how they work, we will review a skill that forces us to make the syntactical decisions necessary to exploit the value of the structural layout of Greek clauses. This preliminary step is *sentence diagramming*. Since the particulars of this skill are complex, and since it involves a fairly complicated set of abilities that take time and practice to master, we can provide only a brief survey to this useful tool.

2. Needless to say, Paul did not produce a set of *Cliffs Notes* or a bulleted list in *USA Today*!

3. The teacher or preacher is faced with the double difficulty of unpacking Paul's argument and then repackaging it for an audience that is usually not prepared to follow all the complexities therein. Yet, the substance and *ramifications* of what Paul argues should and can be placed within the audience's reach—"Put the cookies on the lowest shelf." Admittedly, this is not an easy task, but the more precisely we understand Paul, the easier the process.

As helpful as diagramming and clausal layouts are, they are not an end in themselves. They are valuable tools, but only that—tools to help us achieve our goals of understanding accurately the argument that Paul develops within a given paragraph and then representing that line of thought in clear, meaningful English. Therefore, after surveying diagramming and after explaining clausal layouts in some detail, we will take a final step and convert or "translate" our clausal layout into a formal *exegetical outline*. Again, this is a demanding skill that takes practice and patience to develop. Nevertheless, it is critical if we hope to unpack Paul's thoughts, to trace out his argument, and to think his thoughts after him.

This chapter, then, will address the principles and procedures behind three basic tools of the NT exegete: (1) *sentence diagrams,* (2) *structural layouts of Greek clauses,* and (3) *exegetical outlines.*[4] Individually, these are useful tools for analyzing and interpreting the NT text. When used together, their value for understanding the message of the text is difficult to overestimate. Together they form a powerful alliance for tracing an author's line of thought and unpacking his argument in precise detail. More specifically, diagramming is especially useful in analyzing structure (syntactical relationships) *within* clauses. Clausal layouts excel in analyzing structure (syntactical and/or conceptual relationships) *between* clauses. And exegetical outlining is helpful for converting this surface structure into a meaningful "semantic structure" that expresses in clear English the meaning intended by the author *within* a given paragraph.

4.1 Sentence Diagramming

4.1.1 Definition and Illustration

Alonzo Reed and Brainerd Kellogg, English grammarians at what is now Brooklyn's Polytechnic University and pioneers in the basic procedures of sentence diagramming, describe the sentence diagram as "a picture of the offices and relations of the different parts of a sentence."[5]

---

4. This sequence orders our presentation and parallels the level of detail involved in each skill. Thus, we will progress from the most detailed to the least, from micro-analysis (diagramming), to analysis (clausal layouts), to synthesis (outlining). This order also represents the generally recommended sequence for employing these tools. In this way, the exegete progressively builds on each prior step in an inductive fashion—from the specific details to a broader synthesis.

5. Alonzo Reed and Brainerd Kellogg, *Graded Lessons in English: An Elementary English Grammar* (New York: Clark & Maynard, 1889), 16. Reed and Kellogg's system, which has remained essentially unchanged since it was introduced in 1875, is the standard for diagramming English sentences. The specific system used in this essay follows that developed by John D.

Although Reed and Kellogg's definition is quite serviceable, clarity and precision can be added by expanding it into a detailed description: *A sentence diagram is a visual schematic that organizes every element of a sentence according to a predetermined set of rules into a standardized framework of lines, branches, and terraces so that the syntactical relationships within the sentence are clearly revealed.*

In short, a sentence diagram is a "grammatical visual aid" that reveals the syntactical structure of a sentence.[6]

Illustration: Eph 1:4

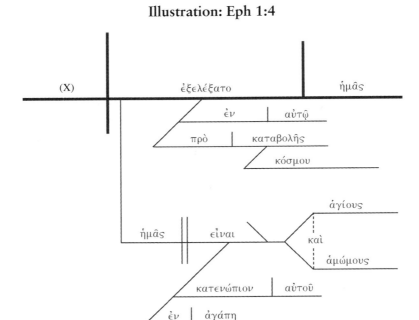

<hr />

Grassmick in his *Principles and Practice of Greek Exegesis,* rev. ed. (Dallas: Dallas Theological Seminary, 1976) and is quite similar to that of Reed and Kellogg. The method presented by Grassmick (or its core) seems to be the dominant approach among NT scholars from North America (see, for example, Donald A. Hagner, *New Testament Exegesis and Research: A Guide for Seminarians* [Pasadena, Calif.: Fuller Seminary Press, 1999], 25-28; and Thomas R. Schreiner, *Interpreting the Pauline Epistles,* Guides to New Testament Exegesis [Grand Rapids, Mich.: Baker, 1990], 77-96). It is perhaps worth noting with H. A. Gleason that, "British school grammar is similar in many ways to American, differing mostly in the total absence of Reed and Kellogg diagramming" (*Linguistics and English Grammar* [New York: Holt, Rinehart & Winston, 1966], vi).

6. Although linguists have developed other "visual aids," e.g., immediate constituent (IC) analysis and phrase structure tree diagrams, classic Reed-Kellogg diagrams continue to be a staple of NT study. Of all the "visual aids" that have been developed, only diagramming will concern us here.

4.1.2 Use and Value

Reed and Kellogg admirably describe the use and value of a diagram: the diagram "will enable the pupil to present directly and vividly to the eye the exact function of every clause in the sentence, of every phrase in the clause, and of every word in the phrase—to picture the complete analysis of the sentence, with principal and subordinate parts in their proper relations."[7] Then, in a stroke of genius, they add, "The diagram drives the pupil to a most searching examination of the sentence, brings him face to face with every difficulty, and compels a decision on every point."[8] Pay dirt! The exegete is "brought face to face with every difficulty," is "compelled to a decision on every point," and thus is "driven to a most searching examination of the sentence." Therein lies the value of diagramming.[9]

The implications of Reed and Kellogg's work can be briefly summarized:

- Diagramming is both comprehensive and precise, i.e., it forces the exegete to account for the syntactical connection of every element in the sentence.

> Corollary 1: The exacting analysis that is demanded by diagramming enhances accuracy, precision, and clarity in exegesis.[10]
>
> Corollary 2: Diagramming is thoroughly at home with a high view of Scripture. In other words, a verbal, plenary view of inspiration, which extends to the very words of the text,

---

7. Alonzo Reed and Brainerd Kellogg, *Higher Lessons in English: A Work on English Grammar and Composition* (New York: Charles E. Merrill, 1913), 8. Thomas R. Schreiner, in describing his own experience, reaches similar conclusions: "I began to see that diagramming forced me to think through the syntactical relationship of every word, phrase, and clause in the sentence" (*Interpreting the Pauline Epistles*, 77).

8. Reed and Kellogg, *Higher Lessons in English*, 9. Similarly, Martha Kolln and Robert Funk, *Understanding English Grammar*, 6th ed. (New York: Longman, 2002), 52.

9. As Schreiner points out, "One of the great values of diagramming, then, is that it compels the interpreter to slow down and to think carefully through every decision of the text" (*Interpreting the Pauline Epistles*, 77-78). Many relationships (or ambiguities inherent in the text) are not readily apparent apart from diagramming. Moreover, we have, in many cases, become desensitized to the details of the text because we are so familiar with it. Few things overcome this dullness like the time and effort spent in diagramming sentences.

10. Grassmick teases out this fundamental point into a helpful and detailed list of seven "uses of diagramming" (*Principles and Practice*, 82). See also John A. McLean, *A Handbook for Grammatical Diagramming Based on Philippians* (Vancouver, Wash.: The Gramcord Institute, 1993), iii.

demands "a most searching examination of the sentence" and compels "a decision on every point."[11]

- Diagramming is only a means to an end, not an end in itself. Its primary goal is a "searching examination of the sentence" so that the exegete might better understand the meaning/content of Scripture.

Additionally, a sentence diagram can serve as a very helpful exegetical worksheet, on which key grammatical, syntactical, and lexical notes can be recorded.

Illustration: Eph 1:4

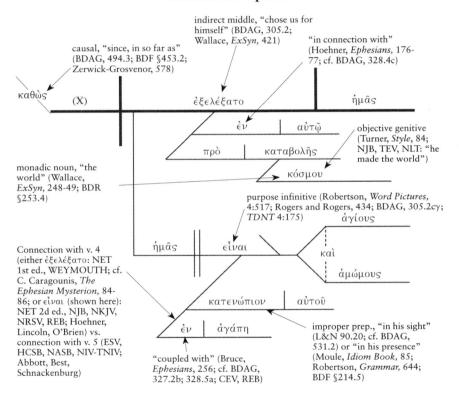

11. For a similar assessment, see F. Furman Kearley, "Diagramming and Sentence Analysis," in *Biblical Interpretation, Principles and Practices: Studies in Honor of Jack Pearl Lewis,* ed. F. Furman Kearley, Edward P. Myers, and Timothy D. Hadley (Grand Rapids, Mich.: Baker, 1986), 83; George J. Zemek, "Grammatical Analysis and Expository Preaching," in *Rediscovering Expository Preaching,* ed. Richard L. Mayhue and Robert L. Thomas (Dallas: Word, 1992), 154-55.

4.1.3 Limitations and Cautions

Diagramming is indeed a very powerful tool, but it is just that, a tool—and an imperfect one at that. It brings with it inherent drawbacks and liabilities:

- By rearranging the sentence to show the syntactical relationships that exist among its words, diagramming does not maintain the original word order of the sentence.
- By conforming to a predetermined set of rules and a standardized framework, diagramming may not represent all sentence structures clearly.[12]
- By focusing exclusively on syntactical structure, "it ignores possible skewing between form and meaning."[13] In other words, by adhering strictly to the surface structure of grammar and syntax, diagramming often fails to recognize the deeper structure or semantic relationships between elements.[14]
- By focusing on every syntactical connection within every sentence, the broader units or structures that carry forward the argument or plot in narrative or apocalyptic sections of the NT tend to fall outside of the purview of diagramming.[15] Therefore, its value for these genres is lessened.

These limitations are indeed a concern. However, one must remember that diagramming is simply a tool at the exegete's disposal—and not the only one at that. We have yet to explore two additional tools: (1) structural

---

12. See Gleason, *Linguistics and English Grammar*, 302, and #1 at §4.1.8 below.

13. Richard A. Young, *Intermediate New Testament Greek: A Linguistic and Exegetical Approach* (Nashville: Broadman & Holman, 1994), 267; similarly Peter Cotterell and Max Turner, *Linguistics and Biblical Interpretation* (Downers Grove, Ill.: InterVarsity Press, 1989), 200.

14. For helpful discussions on this point, see John Beekman and John Callow, *Translating the Word of God* (Grand Rapids, Mich.: Zondervan, 1974), 268-71; Cotterell and Turner, *Linguistics*, 199-200; Daniel B. Wallace, *Greek Grammar Beyond the Basics* (Grand Rapids, Mich.: Zondervan, 1996), 667 n. 2; and further Kolln and Funk, *English Grammar*, 367-77; J. P. Louw, *Semantics of New Testament Greek*, SBL Semeia Studies (Atlanta: Scholars, 1982), 73-89; Grant R. Osborne, *The Hermeneutical Spiral* (Downers Grove, Ill.: InterVarsity Press, 1991), 32, 80-81. The substantival participle ὁ εὐλογήσας in Eph 1:3 illustrates this phenomenon. Syntactically, the participle stands in apposition to θεός, but semantically it functions causally to introduce the reason that God is worthy of praise (so Harold W. Hoehner, *Ephesians: An Exegetical Commentary* [Grand Rapids, Mich.: Baker, 2002], 166).

15. Even within epistolary literature, diagramming can lure the exegete into an atomistic reading in which he or she fixates on an individual sentence, clause, or word to the neglect of the broader context.

layouts of Greek clauses and (2) exegetical outlining, both of which will mitigate these drawbacks.

4.1.4 Overview

We can neither develop nor review all of the procedures involved in diagramming (let alone cover rare or exceptional cases). This has been done elsewhere and requires a far more extensive presentation than is possible here.[16] Instead, we offer a basic review of the most important features.

- The nucleus or core of the sentence (subject + verb) is placed on a horizontal line known as the baseline.[17]
- Words, phrases, or clauses that modify this nucleus are written beneath the baseline even though some of these modifiers may precede the nucleus in word order. Thus, the nucleus of the sentence is always placed first on the page and any subordinate clause or modifier is placed beneath it.
- These modifiers are connected to the baseline by a series of lines, branches, or terraces.
- The resulting schematic becomes a visual aid or grammatical blueprint that identifies the syntactical relationships within the sentence. In short, the diagram is to grammar and syntax what the map is to geography.

4.1.5 General Procedures

1. Place the nucleus of the independent clause on the horizontal baseline and identify its component parts by the use of vertical or slanted lines.[18]

---

16. Grassmick provides the single best treatment (*Principles and Practice*, 81-138). For other treatments, see Richard P. Belcher, *Diagramming the Greek New Testament* (Columbia, S.C.: Richbury, 1985); Lee L. Kantenwein, *Diagrammatical Analysis*, 3rd rev. ed. (Winona Lake, Ind.: BMH, 1991); McLean, *Handbook for Grammatical Diagramming*; Schreiner, *Interpreting the Pauline Epistles*, 77-96.

17. For a more precise definition of "nucleus" or "core," see note 19.

18. For more on clauses, especially independent clauses, see "General Procedures" under our discussion of structural layouts of Greek clauses below. At this point, the exegete should decide whether he or she will construct the diagrams freehand or with the aid of computer software. A number of Bible software programs facilitate this by providing templates for the various lines, branches, and terraces that are needed (see the suggestions for further reading below). They have a number of advantages over drawing diagrams freehand, not the least of which is the ability to revise previously constructed diagrams with relative ease. In addition to

The precise makeup of the nucleus depends upon the specific type of clause pattern in question. The nuclei of the three major independent clause patterns (commonly known as sentence patterns), as well as several subtypes, are shown below[19]:

a. Transitive clauses

Normal: S-V-DO (with or without Indirect Object)

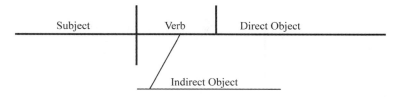

Double Direct Object: S-V-DO person–DO thing

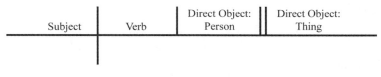

Object Complement: S-V-DO-OC

Bible software, a number of general drawing programs can be used to create the various lines that are needed to construct a diagram.

19. It needs to be emphasized that we are not referring to the four forms that a sentence can take (simple, compound, complex, or compound-complex) nor to the four functions it can have (declarative, imperative, interrogative, or exclamatory). Rather, we are referring to the three patterns of independent clauses. See further, David A. Black, *Linguistics for Students of New Testament Greek: A Survey of Basic Concepts and Applications,* 2nd ed. (Grand Rapids, Mich.: Baker, 1995), 102-6; Eugene Van Ness Goetchius, *The Language of the New Testament* (New York: Scribner, 1965), §§50-56 (pp. 39-45); §§178-88 (pp. 140-46). From these clause patterns, it can be seen that the nucleus of an independent clause consists of the simple subject + simple predicate + direct object or complement (if either are present). Complements include both object complements and subject complements (predicate nouns and predicate adjectives). For a brief treatment of these clause patterns from an English-language perspective, see John C. Hodges et al., *Hodges' Harbrace Handbook,* 15th ed. (Boston: Thomson Heinle, 2004), 21-22; cf. 3, 43-45; Thomas P. Klammer, Muriel R. Shulz, and Angela Della Volpe, *Analyzing English Grammar,* 4th ed. (New York: Pearson Longman, 2004), 195-224; Kolln and Funk, *English Grammar,* 24-51 (esp. 27-28).

b. Intransitive clauses

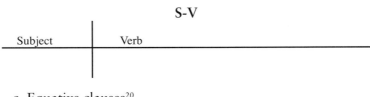

c. Equative clauses[20]

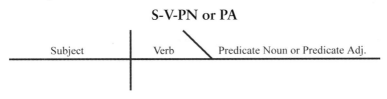

2. Terrace modifiers beneath the horizontal baseline using left-slant (acute angle) terraces, right-slant (obtuse angle) terraces, or vertical (right angle) terraces.

a. Left-slant terraces hold modifiers containing no verbal element (e.g., adjectives, adverbs, prepositional phrases, and genitive, dative, or accusative constructions).

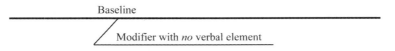

b. Vertical terraces hold clauses containing non-finite verbs (i.e., participles and infinitives).

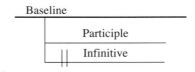

20. This type of sentence contains an equative (linking) verb. In Greek, the most common equative verbs are: εἰμί, γίνομαι, and ὑπάρχω. English grammarians prefer the term *linking* verbs, and these include: *appear, be, become,* and *seem.* In English, sensory verbs (e.g., *feel, look, smell, sound,* and *taste*) often function as linking verbs. Note that the verb εἰμί (or γίνο-μαι, for that matter) does not have to have a complement. "I am" (ἐγὼ εἰμί, John 8:58) is a perfectly acceptable clause/sentence. In such cases, however, εἰμί functions as an intransitive verb (see BDAG, 282.1-2, who refer to "a pred. use" as opposed to an "equative function"). For similar intransitive uses but with adverbs of time or place, see BDAG, 284.3 and cf. 1 Cor 6:18: "Every sin is (ἐστίν) outside the body." See further Black, *Linguistics,* 103; Donald W. Emery, John M. Kierzek, and Peter Lindblom, *English Fundamentals: Form C,* 12th ed. (New York: Longman, 2003), 23-24.

    c. Right-slant terraces hold clauses containing a finite verb (e.g., subordinate clauses introduced by subordinating conjunctions).[21]

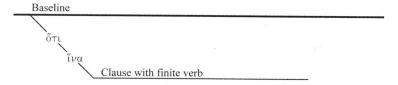

3. Stack terraces, which hold words, phrases, or clauses modifying the same word, beneath one another.

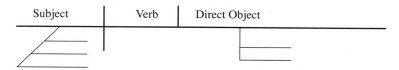

4. Branch (a) the baseline or (b) a terrace into upper and lower (or more as needed) branches to accommodate a compound grammatical unit.[22]

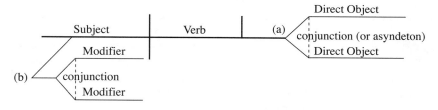

5. Shelve on a horizontal line, which is drawn independently of the baseline or a terrace, grammatical units such as (a) appositives, (b) relative clauses, (c) grammatically coordinate words in an extended list, (d) vocatives, (e) signpost connectives,[23] (f) clauses supported by a standard (for "standard," see #6 below), or (g) grammatically independent units such as a genitive absolute.

21. A finite verb is one that "has" or indicates person, i.e., first person ("I/we"), second person ("you"), and third person ("he, she, it, they"), as opposed to non-finite verbs (participles and infinitives) that do not specify person.

22. The difference between stacking and branching is generally the presence of one or more coordinating conjunctions.

23. "Signpost connectives" are connective words (including particles, conjunctions, and prepositional phrases) like ἄρα, γάρ, διὰ τοῦτο, οὖν, etc. They are so named because, like signposts, they stand at major intersections within the overall argument (at the seams between paragraphs, sections, or other thought-units) and connect them like literary street signs.

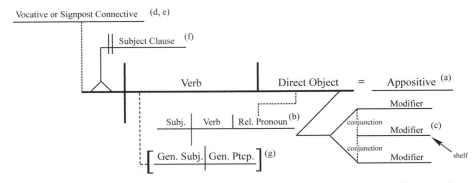

6. Insert with a "standard" (a "pedestal, stilt," i.e., a vertical line with two legs that rests on or is suspended from a baseline, terrace, or shelf) a group of words or a clause that is used *as a unit* in the place of another element of the sentence. Such units are commonly substantival clauses—either participial, infinitival, or those introduced by ἵνα or ὅτι.[24]

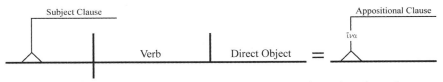

7. Connect coordinate clauses, phrases, or words with a dotted "connective" line. Relative pronouns are connected to their antecedent with a similar line, and vocatives, "signpost connectives," and absolute constructions (e.g., genitive or nominative absolute) are likewise connected to the baseline.

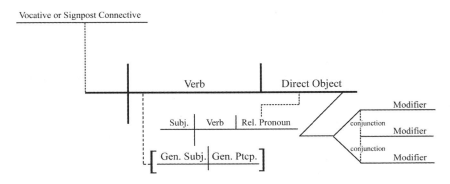

24. The "standard" functions much like the caret (^) used to insert omitted text within a document. Similarly, the standard allows a group of words functioning as a unit to be "squeezed" into a single syntactical "slot."

8. Shift the position of the diagram with a dashed horizontal "spacer" line. This line will shift the diagram to the left or right to accommodate space limitations of the page.

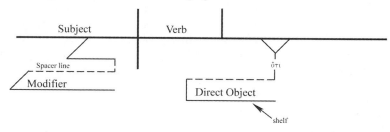

4.1.6 Specific Strategy

1. Identify the independent clause (or clauses) in the sentence.

   a. Isolate the nucleus and place it on the baseline.
   b. Determine the relationships of the other words in the independent clause to its nucleus and place these on appropriate lines, terraces, branches, shelves, or standards (for clauses that are placed on standards, see 3a and 3b below).

2. Identify any dependent (subordinate) clause or clauses in the sentence. Note that dependent clauses are commonly introduced by or structured around one of *four forms or structures:* participles, infinitives, subordinating conjunctions with their verbs, and relative pronouns (or relative adjectives and relative adverbs) with their verbs.[25]

   a. Isolate the nucleus of the dependent clause and place it on a baseline beneath the independent clause.
   b. Determine the relationships of the other words in the dependent clause to its nucleus and place these on appropriate lines, terraces, branches, shelves, or standards.

3. Connect the baseline of the dependent clause to the baseline of the independent clause.[26] To do this, one should (1) remember that dependent clauses have one of three syntactical *functions:* adver-

---

25. For a helpful review of Greek clauses, both their form and their function, see Wallace, *ExSyn,* 656–65. See also Kendell H. Easley, who, in identifying these four structures, notes that "in Greek, only four formats exist for dependent clauses" (*User-Friendly Greek: A Common Sense Approach to the Greek New Testament* [Nashville: Broadman & Holman, 1994], 8).

26. Dependent clauses may modify not the independent clause but another dependent clause. We present a simplified example for pedagogical reasons.

bial, adjectival, or substantival, and (2) note that the function of a particular dependent clause determines the exact point of union with the independent clause. Adverbial clauses are connected to the verb, adjectival clauses are connected to a noun, and substantival clauses are connected to and fill a noun "slot," e.g., the subject or direct object. The following procedures (listed below as a, b, c, d) combine the *four forms or structures* that introduce dependent clauses with their *three functions* into meaningful diagrams:

a. Participles

Dependent clauses that contain a participle are commonly of three types (functions): adverbial, adjectival, and substantival.

Adverbial and adjectival clauses containing a participle are placed on a vertical terrace, i.e., a terrace with a perpendicular connection to the baseline of the independent clause. Adverbial clauses are normally connected to the main verb. Adjectival clauses are tied to the noun they modify.

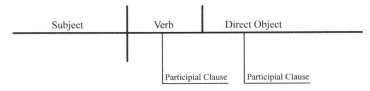

Substantival clauses containing a participle are placed on a standard that rests on the baseline of the independent clause.

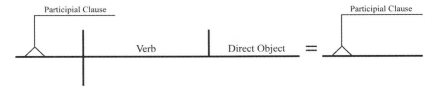

b. Infinitives

Dependent clauses that contain an infinitive are commonly of two types (functions): adverbial and substantival.

Adverbial clauses containing an infinitive are placed on a vertical terrace, i.e., a terrace with a perpendicular connection to the baseline of the independent clause. Adverbial clauses are normally connected to the main verb.

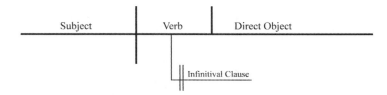

Substantival clauses containing an infinitive are placed on a standard that rests on the baseline of the independent clause.

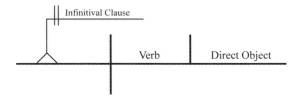

c. Subordinating conjunctions and their finite verbs

Dependent clauses that contain a subordinating conjunction and contain a finite verb are commonly of two types (functions): adverbial and substantival.

Adverbial clauses containing a finite verb and introduced by a subordinating conjunction are placed on a right-slant terrace with the subordinating conjunction (e.g., ὅτι and ἵνα) suspended midway on the connecting line between the baseline of the dependent clause and the baseline of the independent clause. Adverbial clauses are normally connected to the main verb.

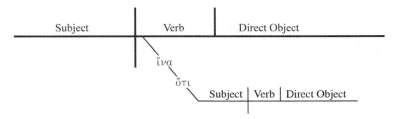

Substantival clauses containing a finite verb and introduced by a subordinating conjunction are placed on a standard with the subordinating conjunction (commonly ὅτι and ἵνα) suspended midway on the connecting line between the baseline of the dependent clause and the baseline of the independent clause.

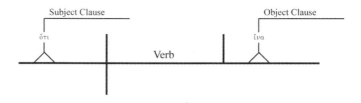

d. Relative pronouns

Dependent clauses that contain a relative pronoun are commonly
adjectival. These adjectival clauses are placed on a shelf, and
the relative pronoun is connected to its antecedent (usually a
noun or some other substantive in the independent clause) by a
dashed or broken connective line.[27]

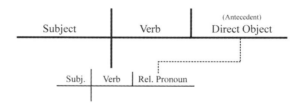

4.1.7 Summary of the Strategy

The basic strategy is one of DIVIDE AND CONQUER. Divide the sentence
into its component independent and dependent clauses. Analyze and diagram each separately.[28] Then connect the individual clauses. If needed, the
same "divide and conquer" strategy can be used within a single clause to
break it up into more manageable sections.

Dependent clauses, whether adverbial, adjectival, or substantival, are
structured around four *major forms or structures:* participles, infinitives,
subordinating conjunctions with their verbs, and relative pronouns (or
relative adjectives and relative adverbs) with their verbs. The following
diagram shows how these *structures* are to be connected to the baseline
containing the independent clause:

27. Relative clauses introduced by relative pronouns and functioning as adjectives are the
simplest and most common type of relative clause. Relative adjectives (e.g., ὅσος, "as much as";
οἷος, "such as, as") and adverbs (e.g., ὅπου, "where"; ὅτε, "when") that have, respectively,
adjectives and adverbs as their antecedents also occur (relative adverbs also frequently have nouns
as antecedents). They are diagrammed much like relative pronouns. See further, Goetchius, *The
Language of the New Testament,* §317 (pp. 239-40); Wallace, *ExSyn,* 659.

28. In my classes, I have developed a slogan: "Have a clause? Draw a baseline!"

DEPENDENT CLAUSES
Four Major Forms (Structures)

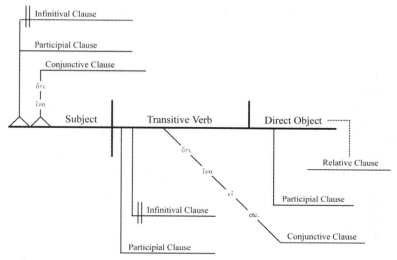

These four major forms (structures) introduce the three major functional categories of dependent clauses: adverbial, adjectival, and substantival. A "conjunctive" clause is a clause introduced by or structured around a subordinating conjunction.

4.1.8 Additional Points

1. Direct and indirect questions are diagrammed as statements. The exegete must recognize these, not from the diagram per se, but from the formal structures (e.g., the interrogative pronouns τίς or τί) used to introduce them in the Greek text. However, in the case of direct questions, the exegete may want to add punctuation to his or her diagram.
2. Dependent clauses may modify a dependent clause rather than an independent clause.
3. If there are two or more parallel independent clauses with an accompanying coordinating conjunction, suspend the conjunction midway on a dotted connective line drawn between the two baselines of the independent clauses.

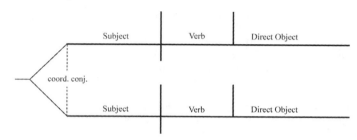

4. Redrawing complicated diagrams is often advisable.[29] Diagramming is much like negotiating a maze and thus may involve a number of missteps and subsequent corrections. Although perfectly accurate, such working drafts can be cluttered and confusing. A simple redrawing can give them greater clarity and utility.

5. Although technically the definite article should be diagrammed beneath the word it modifies (much like an adjective), such placement seems to clutter the diagram unnecessarily. Therefore, it is advisable to place the definite article on the same line and adjacent to the word it modifies.

6. Elided elements in the Greek text should be supplied from the immediate context whenever possible and enclosed within parentheses (alternately, English equivalents can be supplied—especially when the student is unsure what Greek word or form provides the sense necessary—or actual ellipses [. . .] enclosed within parentheses can be used). In some cases, such as a finite verb without an expressed subject, a simple "X," enclosed within parentheses, can be supplied.

7. Diagramming is most valuable in tightly argued epistolary literature where there is considerable syntactical as well as logical subordination. However, it can prove quite helpful in other genres in those passages that require careful syntactical analysis.[30] Furthermore, in that diagramming requires the exegete to read the text of the NT more carefully, it has value for all literary genres.[31] See Fig. 4.3 (page 134) for a "Master List" of symbols commonly used in diagramming.

4.2 The Structural Layout of Greek Clauses

4.2.1 Definition and Illustration

The structural layout of Greek clauses is a visual representation of the Greek text that shows how individual clauses are related to one another.[32]

---

29. Here we are assuming that the diagrams are being drawn by hand rather than with computer software.

30. See Grassmick, *Principles and Practice*, 82, whose wording we have adapted.

31. Care must be exercised so that the broader context is not ignored. Diagramming need not (and should not) force an atomistic reading of the NT so that any given sentence or clause is cut loose from either the immediate context or the developing themes, motifs, and argument of the author.

32. It also shows, to a lesser degree, how other grammatical features are related to one another. Although somewhat similar, a structural layout of Greek clauses should not be confused with arcing (see Osborne, *Hermeneutical Spiral*, 34-35; John Piper, *Biblical Exegesis:*

Illustration: Eph 1:4-5

⁴ . . . ἐξελέξατο ἡμᾶς ἐν αὐτῷ πρὸ καταβολῆς κόσμου

εἶναι ἡμᾶς ἁγίους καὶ ἀμώμους κατενώπιον αὐτοῦ ἐν ἀγάπῃ,

⁵ προορίσας ἡμᾶς εἰς υἱοθεσίαν διὰ Ἰησοῦ Χριστοῦ εἰς αὐτόν, κατὰ τὴν εὐδοκίαν τοῦ θελήματος αὐτοῦ . . .

4.2.2 Primary Purpose

The primary purpose of the structural layout is to make the central and supporting ideas of the text evident. Specifically, it reveals, through textual rearrangement, independent and dependent clauses and shows how they are related to one another. In short, the structural layout isolates a paragraph's major units of thought.

4.2.3 Overview

Each clause, whether an independent clause or a dependent clause, is placed on a separate line to isolate it from every other clause.[33] In short, every clause begins a new line.[34]

4.2.4 General Procedures

1. Identify the major structural markers or "argument bearers" that significantly advance (set forth and develop) the author's argument.

Discovering the Original Meaning of Scriptural Texts [Minneapolis: Desiring God Ministries, 1999], 15-48; Schreiner, *Interpreting the Pauline Epistles,* 97-126) or semantic structure analysis (Cotterell and Turner, *Linguistics,* 188-229; George H. Guthrie and J. Scott Duvall, *Biblical Greek Exegesis: A Graded Approach to Learning Intermediate and Advanced Greek* [Grand Rapids, Mich.: Zondervan, 1998], 39-53; Young, *Intermediate NT Greek,* 255-62, 274-80). What we refer to as "structural layouts of Greek clauses" has more in common with the methods that other scholars variously label: "structural analysis" (David A. Black); "paragraph flow" (Kendell H. Easley); "sentence flow" (Gordon D. Fee); "syntactical display" or "block diagram" (Walter C. Kaiser); "textual transcription" (William G. MacDonald); "phrasing" (William D. Mounce); "mechanical layout" (Merrill C. Tenney); or "thought-flow diagramming" (Richard A. Young).

33. With the term *clause,* we follow a traditional understanding and use the term to designate something very specific: a clause is a group of related words containing a subject and a predicate (verb) and is not to be confused with a phrase, which "contains less than the minimum subject-verb sequence essential for a clause" (Frank X. Braun, *English Grammar for Language Students* [Ann Arbor: Ulrich's Books, 1947], 14).

34. This is a rather broad operational procedure that we will narrow as we proceed. In my classes, I have developed a second slogan: "Have a clause? Need a new line!"

There are two major classes of structural markers: (1) grammatical elements that introduce independent clauses and (2) grammatical elements that introduce dependent adverbial clauses. This focus on clauses is absolutely central since they are the smallest grammatical units that assert something or make a statement.[35] Without the subject-verb sequence of a clause, no determinate meaning is conveyed.[36] In short, clauses form propositions, which are the building blocks of the author's argument. In this way they are the key to the author setting forth his argument and to our tracing it.

With regard to dependent clauses, it must be emphasized that, as a rule, *only adverbial clauses are of concern.* This is because adverbial clauses, by modifying verbal ideas, advance the argument of the paragraph. They are "where the action takes place"—where ideas are presented, developed, clarified, or defended.[37] On the other hand, adjectival and substantival clauses merely identify or describe individual items rather than push the thought of the paragraph forward in significant ways.[38]

In terms of form or structure, independent clauses are usually introduced by or structured around finite verbs (often indicatives but other forms as well, e.g., imperatives and subjunctives). Dependent *adverbial* clauses are most often introduced by or structured around the following: (a) adverbial participles, (b) adverbial infinitives, and (c) subordinating conjunctions and their verbs.[39]

2. Place every structural marker on its own separate line, i.e., every structural marker triggers a new line of text. In other words, place

---

35. For those who recognize the centrality of clauses vis-à-vis smaller grammatical units, see, for example, David A. Black, *Learn to Read New Testament Greek,* 2nd ed. (Nashville: Broadman & Holman, 1994), 185-86; idem, *Using New Testament Greek in Ministry* (Grand Rapids, Mich.: Baker, 1993), 101-2; Easley, *User-Friendly Greek,* 19-30; William W. Klein, Craig L. Blomberg, Robert L. Hubbard, Jr., *Introduction to Biblical Interpretation,* 2nd ed. (Nashville: Nelson, 2003), 265; Osborne, *Hermeneutical Spiral,* 29; Schreiner, *Interpreting the Pauline Epistles,* 98-99.

36. The wording here is Daniel P. Fuller's (*Hermeneutics,* 5th ed. [Pasadena, Calif.: by the author, 1973], 3.1) and is echoed by Piper (*Biblical Exegesis,* 17). See further Beekman and Callow, *Translating the Word of God,* 267-77; and also Louw, *Semantics of New Testament Greek,* 91-117. Philip Gucker puts it plainly: "A subject or a predicate by itself doesn't say anything" (*Essential English Grammar* [New York: Dover, 1966], 3).

37. Cf. Easley, *User-Friendly Greek,* 21.

38. In short, they are merely modifiers adding "color" to the propositions (clauses). See further, Schreiner, *Interpreting the Pauline Epistles,* 109-11; and also Piper, *Biblical Exegesis,* 39-43; Louw, *Semantics of New Testament Greek,* 101, 107-9. Although we may have overstated our case, what we have affirmed is generally true and has pedagogical utility at this point in the discussion.

39. Again, for a helpful review of Greek clauses, both their form and their function, see Wallace, *Greek Grammar,* 656-65; and also Easley, *User-Friendly Greek,* 8, 24, 30.

each structural marker with the clause that it introduces on its own separate line.

  a. Begin independent clauses at the left margin of the page.
  b. Indent dependent adverbial clauses under the clauses they modify to indicate subordination.

3. Consider elevating other grammatical elements to the status of a structural marker. Occasionally other grammatical elements—even though they do not introduce or constitute a complete clause—may, in the exegete's opinion, significantly advance the author's argument, i.e., they serve as major "argument bearers." In such cases they can be treated like full-fledged clauses and given or placed on their own line. Such elements might, for example, include the following: adverbs, prepositional phrases, relative clauses, and substantival clauses. For simplicity, we might refer to this catchall class of structural markers as "wild cards."[40]

4.2.5 Specific Strategy

1. Import the section (paragraph) of the Greek text to be studied into a standard word processing program.[41]

2. Reformat the paragraph so that the beginning of each verse, with its reference, is placed at the left margin of the page.

Illustration: Eph 1:3-6

³ Εὐλογητὸς ὁ θεὸς καὶ πατὴρ τοῦ κυρίου ἡμῶν ᾽Ιησοῦ Χριστοῦ, ὁ εὐλογήσας ἡμᾶς ἐν πάσῃ εὐλογίᾳ πνευματικῇ ἐν τοῖς ἐπουρανίοις ἐν Χριστῷ,
⁴ καθὼς ἐξελέξατο ἡμᾶς ἐν αὐτῷ πρὸ καταβολῆς κόσμου εἶναι ἡμᾶς ἁγίους καὶ ἀμώμους κατενώπιον αὐτοῦ ἐν ἀγάπῃ,

---

40. Experience suggests that expanding the criteria for structural markers beyond those that explicitly introduce clauses should be done very judiciously. Yet, certain non-clausal elements represent such interpretive significance that they justify being treated as full-fledged structural markers (see further §4.2.5 # 6).

41. For specific help on determining the limits or boundaries of a paragraph, see Beekman and Callow, *Translating the Word of God*, 279-81; Richard J. Erickson, *A Beginner's Guide to New Testament Exegesis* (Downers Grove, Ill.: InterVarsity Press, 2005), 62-67, 80-93; Guthrie and Duvall, *Biblical Greek Exegesis*, 113-14; Stephen H. Levinsohn, *Discourse Features of New Testament Greek*, 2nd ed. (Dallas: SIL International, 2000), 271-84; Stanley E. Porter, *Idioms of the Greek New Testament*, 2nd ed., Biblical Languages: Greek 2 (Sheffield: JSOT Press, 1994), 301-2.

⁵ προορίσας ἡμᾶς εἰς υἱοθεσίαν διὰ Ἰησοῦ Χριστοῦ εἰς αὐτόν,
κατὰ τὴν εὐδοκίαν τοῦ θελήματος αὐτοῦ,
⁶ εἰς ἔπαινον δόξης τῆς χάριτος αὐτοῦ ἧς ἐχαρίτωσεν ἡμᾶς ἐν
τῷ ἠγαπημένῳ.

3. Place each independent clause and each dependent *adverbial* clause
on its own line beginning *at* the left margin of the page.

    a. Do not rearrange the order of the clauses; proceed in the order
of the text.

    b. Do not indent any clauses yet.

    c. Underline the structural markers for easy identification.

4. Single-space each clause and double-space between clauses. This is
a very important consideration since some lines of text (i.e., long
clauses) will inevitably wrap to the next line. Single-spacing will
then indicate the continuation of a given clause. Double-spacing
will separate clauses.[42]

5. Place dependent adverbial clauses under the clauses they modify[43]
and indent them one-half inch.[44] If the line of text wraps on to the
next line, be sure that this wrapped portion is likewise indented
one-half inch. Indent each successive level of subordination an additional one-half inch (note that two successive lines indented to the
same position, as in vv. 3b and 4a in the illustration below, modify
the same clause).

    Our directive to place the dependent clause under the clause that
it modifies assumes that the dependent clause follows what it modifies—an assumption that, of course, does not always hold true. In cases
where dependent clauses precede main clauses, we prefer to adhere
to the original order of the text and place the dependent clause above
the main clause. This should not cause confusion, for the exegete will
have already worked with the text in some detail, and by this stage of

---

42. Note that most word processing programs have features that allow one to create "white
space" that mimics double-spacing without actually resorting to double-spacing (via the return
key) between clauses. Using such a feature is recommended since it allows for simpler and cleaner
revisions. For this same reason, use of the tab key or space bar to align text is especially discour-
aged. Instead, use the "indent" feature of your word processor to control indentation.

43. This step reflects a good deal of prior syntactical analysis, for which a sentence diagram
is a useful tool!

44. To place the structural marker directly under the precise grammatical element it modifies unnecessarily complicates the layout because of the flexibility of Greek word order. This
added complication often severely hampers the layout's clarity and usefulness. Furthermore, it
unnecessarily replicates much of the information expressed by a sentence diagram.

the exegetical process the connection should be transparent (of course, this might confuse someone unfamiliar with this text).

Although structural layouts normally should reproduce the order of the text, occasionally the relative placement of independent and dependent clauses can be compromised by this guideline. However, with a simple textual rearrangement, the exegete can often circumvent the problem. The English text of 1 Cor 8:7b provides an illustration: "Their conscience since it is weak is defiled." In this case, the dependent clause can be placed beneath the independent clause and yet its original word order can be shown by an ellipsis and an arrow:

Their conscience . . . is defiled.

↑

since it is weak

6. Account for any "wild card" structural markers that you have isolated. In the example below we have identified the substantival participle ὁ εὐλογήσας as a structural marker, as we have explained above.[45] Also, the prepositional phrase in v. 6 serves as a structural marker because this phrase is repeated two additional times (vv. 12, 14). In this way, it forms a "refrain" in this hymnic/poetic passage (1:3-14).

Illustration

3 Εὐλογητὸς [ἐστιν] ὁ θεὸς καὶ πατὴρ τοῦ κυρίου ἡμῶν Ἰησοῦ Χριστοῦ,

ὁ εὐλογήσας ἡμᾶς ἐν πάσῃ εὐλογίᾳ πνευματικῇ ἐν τοῖς ἐπουρανίοις ἐν Χριστῷ,

4 καθὼς ἐξελέξατο ἡμᾶς ἐν αὐτῷ πρὸ καταβολῆς κόσμου

εἶναι ἡμᾶς ἁγίους καὶ ἀμώμους κατενώπιον αὐτοῦ ἐν ἀγάπῃ,

5 προορίσας ἡμᾶς εἰς υἱοθεσίαν διὰ Ἰησοῦ Χριστοῦ εἰς αὐτόν, κατὰ τὴν εὐδοκίαν τοῦ θελήματος αὐτοῦ,

6 εἰς ἔπαινον δόξης τῆς χάριτος αὐτοῦ ἧς ἐχαρίτωσεν ἡμᾶς ἐν τῷ ἠγαπημένῳ.

7. Position coordinating conjunctions (e.g., ἀλλά, δέ, καί) so that they reflect their function as links or bridges that connect coordinate clauses (or other elements).

45. See note 14.

Illustration (Eph 1:20)

<u>ἐνήργησεν</u> ἐν τῷ Χριστῷ

    <u>ἐγείρας</u> αὐτὸν ἐκ νεκρῶν

    καὶ

    <u>καθίσας</u> [αὐτον] ἐν δεξιᾷ [χειρι] αὐτοῦ . . .

8. Supply any ellipses needed to complete the sense of the Greek text. These should be placed within brackets and italicized to distinguish them from the text of the printed editions of the Greek New Testament.[46]

Illustration: Eph 1:3

Εὐλογητὸς [<u>*ἐστιν*</u>] ὁ θεὸς καὶ πατὴρ τοῦ κυρίου ἡμῶν Ἰησοῦ Χριστοῦ,

9. Place verse references *in* the left-hand margin for easy reference.[47]

10. Consider whether to orient the page layout to landscape or to portrait. Each has advantages and disadvantages. Landscape will reduce the number of times that a line of text will wrap to the next line, producing a cleaner appearance, with minimal word/line wraps. Conversely, portrait can create a densely packed, even cluttered layout. Yet, it has the benefit of displaying more text per page and thus facilitating the observation of various elements and relationships within a given paragraph.

11. Use the structural layout as a worksheet to observe the details of the text. For example,

    a. Add shading or boxes to highlight repeated or parallel terms and ideas.

    b. Add arrows to identify the antecedents of relative pronouns.

    c. List references to OT quotes.

---

46. I recommend using unaccented Greek words suggested by the context. (Since accenting adds unnecessary problems, we dispense with it, as does the Nestle-Aland apparatus.) However, some may want to use an asterisk [*] or an actual ellipsis [. . .]. In our illustration (Eph 1:3), some prefer to supply other forms of the copula such as the optative εἴη, "May God be blessed . . ." The indicative, ἐστίν, is favored by both Hoehner (*Ephesians,* 163) and Peter T. O'Brien (*The Letter to the Ephesians,* Pillar New Testament Commentary [Grand Rapids, Mich.: Eerdmans, 1999], 94 n. 39).

47. This is my preference. Others may prefer a different position.

    d. Note punctuation differences, especially as they are shown in the various English translations.

    e. Add signs or symbols to denote chiasms, inclusios, anacolutha, rearrangements in word order, apposition, examples of grammatical attraction, etc.

12. Improvise. The structural layout is your servant, not your master. Develop a style and system that allows you to exploit the power of the structural layout for unfolding the message of the text. See Figs. 4.1 and 4.2 for two illustrations of a "finished" structural layout.

4.2.6 Use and Value

Although clausal layouts are still subject to some of the same liabilities or deficiencies as sentence diagramming, a well-constructed structural layout has a number of benefits and practical uses.[48]

1. It reveals basic syntactical relationships. It does not reveal all syntactical relationships within a sentence, which is properly the domain of diagramming, but it does show the syntactical relationships that exist between clauses, i.e., it reveals how the clauses are tied together.[49] Thus,

    a. It discloses the author's main points within a paragraph, as well as the supporting ideas he uses to develop these main points.[50]

    b. In disclosing these main points and supporting ideas, the layout reveals the basic flow of thought in a passage. Thus, the lay-

---

48. Clausal layouts are still prone to neglecting broader units of thought and structure (as found especially in narrative and apocalyptic material) and to the skewing of grammatical form and intended meaning. For several additional advantages, see Gordon D. Fee, *New Testament Exegesis: A Handbook for Students and Pastors*, 3rd ed. (Louisville: Westminster/John Knox, 2002), 13, 139; William D. Mounce, *A Graded Reader of Biblical Greek* (Grand Rapids, Mich.: Zondervan, 1996), xv.

49. On the significance of this, cf. Black, *Using New Testament Greek in Ministry*, 101-2; Klein, Blomberg, and Hubbard, *Introduction to Biblical Interpretation*, 267; Mounce, *Graded Reader*, xv.

50. A word of clarification or caution is necessary. As we have pointed out above (note 14), there is often a skewing between form and function so that the logical or semantic importance of a clause far outweighs its grammatically subordinate position. In short, main ideas can come from subordinate clauses. Osborne is correct: "What is subordinate grammatically at times can have equal or greater stress than the main clause in the writer's actual thought development" (*Hermeneutical Spiral*, 32). See further Walter L. Liefeld, *New Testament Exposition: From Text to Sermon* (Grand Rapids, Mich.: Zondervan, 1984), 45-56, and §4.3.2.5 below. With our treatment of exegetical outlining below, we will try to ameliorate this difficulty.

Fig. 4.1: Illustration, Eph 1:3-6

3 Εὐλογητὸς [ἐστιν] ὁ θεὸς καὶ πατὴρ τοῦ κυρίου ἡμῶν Ἰησοῦ Χριστοῦ,

   <u>ὁ εὐλογήσας ἡμᾶς ἐν πάσῃ εὐλογίᾳ πνευματικῇ</u>
      ἐν τοῖς ἐπουρανίοις
      ἐν Χριστῷ,

4 <u>καθὼς ἐξελέξατο ἡμᾶς ἐν αὐτῷ πρὸ καταβολῆς κόσμου</u>

   <u>εἶναι</u> ἡμᾶς ἁγίους καὶ ἀμώμους κατενώπιον αὐτοῦ ἐν ἀγάπῃ, [←NET, NRSV] [ESV, NASB→]

5 <u>προορίσας</u> ἡμᾶς εἰς υἱοθεσίαν διὰ Ἰησοῦ Χριστοῦ εἰς αὐτόν, κατὰ τὴν εὐδοκίαν τοῦ
   θελήματος αὐτοῦ,

6 <u>εἰς ἔπαινον δόξης τῆς χάριτος αὐτοῦ ἧς [= ᾗ] ἐχαρίτωσεν ἡμᾶς ἐν τῷ ἠγαπημένῳ.</u>

Note three simple changes. We have: (1) aligned the second and third ἐν phrases in v. 3 with the first to highlight the parallel constructions, (2) added references to several English translations in v. 4 to indicate the problem over the punctuation and placement of ἐν ἀγάπῃ, and (3) indicated in v. 4 the relative pronoun's antecedent and the fact that it involves a case of attraction.

Fig. 4.2: Illustration, Eph 1:20-23

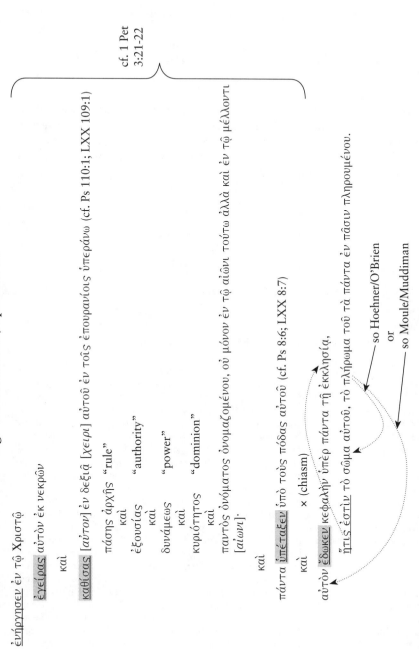

20 ἐνήργησεν ἐν τῷ Χριστῷ

   ἐγείρας αὐτὸν ἐκ νεκρῶν

     καὶ

   καθίσας [αὐτον] ἐν δεξιᾷ [χειρι] αὐτοῦ ἐν τοῖς ἐπουρανίοις ὑπεράνω (cf. Ps 110:1; LXX 109:1)

21   πάσης ἀρχῆς "rule"
          καὶ
       ἐξουσίας "authority"
          καὶ
       δυνάμεως "power"
          καὶ
       κυριότητος "dominion"
          καὶ
       παντὸς ὀνόματος ὀνομαζομένου, οὐ μόνον ἐν τῷ αἰῶνι τούτῳ ἀλλὰ καὶ ἐν τῷ μέλλοντι [αἰωνι]·

cf. 1 Pet 3:21-22

22   καὶ

   πάντα ὑπέταξεν ὑπὸ τοὺς πόδας αὐτοῦ (cf. Ps 8:6; LXX 8:7)

     καὶ   x (chiasm)

23   αὐτὸν ἔδωκεν κεφαλὴν ὑπὲρ πάντα τῇ ἐκκλησίᾳ,

   ἥτις ἐστὶν τὸ σῶμα αὐτοῦ, τὸ πλήρωμα τοῦ τὰ πάντα ἐν πᾶσιν πληρουμένου.

so Hoehner/O'Brien
or
so Moule/Muddiman

Observe several notations. We have: (1) cited an important NT parallel from 1 Peter, (2) shaded four parallel aorist tenses, (3) listed allusions to OT texts, (4) supplied several English glosses, (5) marked a chiasm (A πάντα, B ὑπό, C πόδας—C΄ κεφαλήν, B΄ ὑπέρ, A΄ πάντα) with an x, and (6) identified the antecedent of ἥτις, along with different options (Hoehner/O'Brien vs. Moule/Muddiman) for the antecedent of πλήρωμα.

out reveals the structure, direction, and emphasis of the author's argument.

c. By revealing the basic flow of thought in a paragraph, the layout forms an *initial* "objective" textual basis for constructing an exegetical outline that traces the argument of the author.[51]

2. By exposing main, subordinate, parallel, repeated, emphatic, introductory, and concluding points within a paragraph, it can serve as a very effective worksheet for (a) observing the particulars of the text and (b) recording these observations and other important exegetical notes. As a worksheet, the structural layout maintains a provisional character that is subject to continual review and revision.

4.3 Exegetical Outlining of Epistolary Literature[52]

4.3.1 Fundamentals of Formal Outlining

4.3.1.1 GENERAL CONSIDERATIONS

A formal outline indicates the various levels of subordination that exist among the major points/ideas and subpoints/ideas of a passage. To show the relationships that exist between these points or ideas, a formal

---

51. See further on exegetical outlining below. Rather than outlining a paragraph from only an intuitive or impressionistic basis, the clausal layout provides some level of initial "objective" control. *Clausal* layouts, in particular, have an objective basis, namely the Greek clause, which is introduced by a regular set of structures or forms, has a standard set of functions, and is the smallest grammatical unit that can assert something or make a statement. In contrast, many *structural* layout schemes have a more subjective and intuitive basis—whatever grammatical element grabs the exegete's attention. However, this assessment should not be understood as negatively as it might at first seem. "Objective" structure is not the end-all, as the preceding note makes clear. Moreover, what grabs the "experienced" exegete's attention is not to be dismissed lightly.

52. Exegetical outlining, as we will present it, is best suited for tightly argued logical discourse, like that typically found in epistolary literature—especially but not exclusively Pauline literature, which we will again refer to by way of illustration. Outlining other types of literature, such as narrative, is more dependent on features less prominent in epistolary literature, e.g., stages of plot (exposition, rising action, climax, falling action, and denouement—as they are categorized in classic fashion by Freytag's "pyramid") or certain literary forms with conventional patterns (e.g., pronouncement story, miracle story, or farewell address) (for Freytag's pyramid, see Gustav Freytag, *Technique of the Drama: An Exposition of Dramatic Composition and Art,* trans. Elias J. MacEwan [1863; reprint, New York: Benjamin Blom, 1968], 114-40). When outlining narrative, the exegete is well advised to note, among other things, chronology (including issues of frequency, timing, and duration), geography, arrangement of material (topical/thematic or chronological), degree of detail and length of presentation, the sequence of events and their causal connections (whether cultural, historical, personal, etc.), the interaction among characters (actors), and the structure and thematic development of the surrounding context or book as a whole.

outline uses a consistent series of indentations and symbols (numbers and letters). In this way, it functions as a kind of picture of the logical development of the passage. The main ideas form the major headings and the subordinate and supporting ideas form subheadings, with each succeeding level containing more specific information than the preceding one.[53] Although formal outlines follow general conventions for content and format, some variability exists. The following basic scheme is commonly used[54]:

Central Idea / Thesis Statement

I. First main idea
  A. First subordinate idea
    1. First supporting idea
    2. Second supporting idea
      a) First supporting detail
      b) Second supporting detail
  B. Second subordinate idea
    1. First supporting idea
    2. Second supporting idea
II. Second main idea
  A. First subordinate idea
    1. First supporting idea
    2. Second supporting idea
    3. Third supporting idea
  B. Second subordinate idea
    1. First supporting idea
      a) First supporting detail
      b) Second supporting detail
        (1) etc.[55]
        (2) etc.
          (a) etc.
          (b) etc.
            i) etc.
            ii) etc.
      c) Third supporting detail

---

53. For the substance of this description of a formal outline, see Hodges et al., *Harbrace Handbook*, 433.

54. So *The Chicago Manual of Style*, 15th ed. (Chicago: University of Chicago Press, 2003), §6.130 (p. 275); and also Kate L. Turabian, *A Manual for Writers of Term Papers, Theses, and Dissertations*, 6th ed. (Chicago: University of Chicago Press, 1996), §2.73 (p. 38).

55. Most exegetical outlines, as summaries of the argument, will probably not extend to this level of subordination, let alone go beyond it.

2. Second supporting idea

The beauty of an outline is that it clearly distinguishes *main, subordinate,* and *coordinate* ideas from each other. In other words, in a properly constructed outline the relationships between headings and subheadings reflect the coordination and subordination of thought. Thus:

- *Main ideas* incorporate their subpoints. That is to say, main points should summarize the content and cover all the elements (and verses!) of their subordinate points.
- *Subordinate ideas* support another, more comprehensive point. In other words, each subordinate point should relate (amplify, explain, illustrate, apply, etc.) directly and logically to the larger heading beneath which it stands.
- *Coordinate ideas* are ideas of equal weight, force, or importance that appear in parallel headings and support the same larger heading.

These points can be illustrated from this portion of a larger topic outline:

  I. Wars of the Nineteenth Century
  II. Wars of the Twentieth Century
   A. U.S. Wars
    1. WW I
    2. WW II
    3. Korean
    4. Vietnam
    5. Desert Storm
   B. European Wars
   C. etc.
  III. Wars of the Twenty-First Century

Points 1, 2, 3, 4, 5 are parallel and of the same level of specificity and thus represent coordinate ideas. However, as examples of "U.S. Wars," they also represent subordinate ideas that serve to define the larger subheading A, "U.S. Wars." Similarly, points A, B, and C are coordinate to each other but represent subordinate ideas that amplify the larger heading II, "Wars of the Twentieth Century." Finally, heading II represents a main point that incorporates all of its subpoints (A, B, C, as well as 1, 2, 3, 4, 5).

It is important to note that headings and subheadings stand for or summarize a group or division of some kind (e.g., point A, "U.S. Wars," summarizes various military conflicts, namely WW I, WW II, the Korean Conflict, the Vietnam War, etc.). Since such a group or division denotes at least two elements, subordinate points or ideas that support a larger heading must logically come in at least pairs. Ultimately, this means that each outline should have at least two main headings—a I and a II that are summarized by or support a larger, central thesis.

Moreover, if heading "I" has a subheading marked "A," it should also have a subheading marked "B." If subheading "A" has a "1," it should also have a "2" and so on. In other words, an "A" must always have a corresponding "B," and a "1" must always have a corresponding "2." Logically, a subdivided heading must break into at least two parts—it cannot be divided into only one part. If a heading seems to have only one subpoint, the subpoint should be absorbed into the larger heading or rechecked for its relevance to the heading.[56]

Note the following examples, showing proper and improper subordination and coordination in the outline of a hypothetical biblical text.

Correct Subordination and Coordination

When correct subordination and coordination are observed, each heading incorporates all its subpoints, and related subpoints are of the same level of specificity and support their larger heading:

```
 I. . . . . . . . . . . . . .vv. 5-10
   A. . . . . . . . . . .vv. 5-7
      1. . . . . . . . .v. 5
      2. . . . . . . . .vv. 6-7
         a) . . . . . . .v. 6
         b) . . . . . . .v. 7
   B. . . . . . . . . . .vv. 8-10
      1. . . . . . . . .vv. 8-9
      2. . . . . . . . .v. 10
 II. . . . . . . . . . . . .vv. 11-15
```

Incorrect Subordination and Coordination

In the example below, some subheadings (A and B) fail to incorporate all their subpoints and conversely some subpoints (both 1s) fail to support their larger headings. Some subheadings (A and B) are subdivided into only one part (1). Finally, the main heading I covers vv. 5-10, but

---

56. An outline can be developed inductively, i.e., from the specific subpoints to the general headings (this is the typical process that one performs when outlining a biblical text—one typically builds general headings from the specific details) or deductively, i.e., moving from the general headings to the specific subpoints (as in drafting an essay). The point still stands: subdivided headings break into at least two parts since a given heading cannot logically be divided into one part.

the subpoints omit v. 10 (note that every verse in the passage must be reflected in the outline).

    I. . . . . .vv. 5-10
      A. . . . . .v. 5
        1. . . . . .v. 6
      B. . . . . .v. 7
        1. . . . . .vv. 8-9
    II. . . . . .vv. 11-15

4.3.1.2 TOPIC AND SENTENCE OUTLINES: SUGGESTING STRUCTURE VS. CAPTURING THE ARGUMENT

The most commonly used types of outlines are (1) the topic or phrase outline and (2) the sentence outline. A topic outline expresses headings and subheadings in grammatically parallel phrases (often a noun + modifiers). A sentence outline expresses headings and subheadings in complete and parallel (usually) sentences.[57]

The advantage of a sentence outline is that full sentences enable the exegete to express complete thoughts (rather than fragments and generalizations) about the specific contents of a paragraph of Scripture. The advantage of the topic outline, besides its brevity, is the clarity with which it can suggest the structure of a passage. Its major disadvantage is that it often communicates very little specific content.[58] Consider, for example, the following section of a hypothetical outline:

    I. God's call
      A. The focus
      B. The cause
      C. The purpose

This section gives us some idea of the structure of the passage, but reveals virtually nothing about the focus, cause, or purpose of God's call.

Consider the same section presented as a sentence outline:

    I. God calls sinners because of his grace so that they might be saved.

57. Hodges et al., *Harbrace Handbook*, 433-36. Hodges provides several helpful examples, as does Lynn Q. Troyka, *Simon and Schuster Handbook for Writers*, 6th ed. (Upper Saddle River, N.J.: Pearson Education, 2002), 44-45.

58. Cf. Charles H. Vivian and Bernetta M. Jackson, *English Composition: Fundamental Principles of Effective Writing*, College Outline Series (New York: Barnes & Noble, 1961), 46.

    A. God calls sinners.

    B. God calls because of his grace.

    C. God calls so that sinners might be saved.

Here is specific, meaningful content. Consequently, sentence outlines are particularly helpful in summarizing the message of a NT text.[59]

4.3.1.3 SUMMARY: GUIDING PRINCIPLES OF FORMAL OUTLINES[60]

- Indentations and symbols denote groupings and indicate their relative importance (i.e., they distinguish between main points and subpoints).

- Sections and subsections reflect logical relationships (i.e., they distinguish between main, subordinate, and coordinate ideas).

- Coordinate ideas of equal weight or importance appear in parallel headings.

- Each subdivision has at least two parts (i.e., an "a" must have a "b").

- Parallel headings and subheadings indicate the same level of generality/specificity and are expressed in parallel grammatical form if possible.

4.3.2 Exegetical Outlining

4.3.2.1 GENERAL CONSIDERATIONS

1. Each statement or point in the outline is a complete declarative sentence.

2. Each statement in the outline clarifies the essential point as briefly as possible (in approximately 30 words or less).[61]

---

59. It is often possible to combine topic outlines with sentence outlines in very helpful ways. For example, we might present point B as: The Cause: God calls because of his grace.

60. Adapted from H. Ramsey Fowler and Jane E. Aaron, *The Little, Brown Handbook,* 8th ed. (New York: Longman, 2001), 41, with help from Troyka, *Simon and Schuster Handbook,* 41-46. Many others affirm these principles; see esp. Vivian and Jackson, *English Composition,* 45-51, and also Charles C. Ryrie, *Ryrie's Practical Guide to Communicating Bible Doctrine* (Nashville: Broadman & Holman, 2005), 83-84.

61. The suggestion of 30 words or less is somewhat arbitrary. However, it reflects the conviction that the outline should be briefer than the text itself, as well as a desire to capture clearly the essential point being made. Our aim is to be strategic, not exhaustive. In the finished outline illustrated §4.3.2.7, page 131 below, our longest statement is 24 words (excluding the central idea of 33 words).

3. Each statement has a subject—what the author is talking about, i.e., the topic about which something is said or asserted.[62]

4. This subject is usually derived from and represents the syntactical force (or the semantic/conceptual force)[63] of the structural marker that introduces a dependent adverbial clause plus what that marker modifies (usually the preceding clause or verbal element). In this way, the subject is not left up to the exegete's subjective opinion, but falls under the purview of syntactical and contextual controls.

5. Each statement has a complement—what the author is saying about what he is talking about.[64]

6. This complement is usually derived from and represents the substance or "content" of the dependent adverbial clause introduced by the structural marker.[65] This "content" completes the statement begun by the subject by indicating what is said about the subject. In short, the complement "completes" the subject by providing its content (below we will illustrate and explain more fully the construction of subject-complement statements). Therefore,

7. The wording of each of these subject-complement statements is tied to the syntactical, semantic, or conceptual force of each line of the structural layout of Greek clauses.

8. Each statement (point in the outline) contributes to the central or main idea of the passage.

9. This central idea summarizes the major points of the outline (and thus captures the thrust or argument of the passage) and is expressed with a complete sentence in a subject-complement format.

4.3.2.2 CONSTRUCTING SUBJECT-COMPLEMENT STATEMENTS

1. Gather the appropriate tools: your diagram (with syntactical classifications), your structural layout of Greek clauses, and the other results of your exegetical study (e.g., lexical data or background information). Although one can construct a preliminary exegetical outline early in the exegetical process, the finished outline,

---

62. Here the term *subject* is used more broadly than as the simple, grammatical subject of a sentence.

63. We are referring to such categories as cause, time, purpose, result, manner, means/instrument, condition, concession, etc. For these syntactical or semantic/logical functions, see, for example, H. E. Dana and Julius R. Mantey, *A Manual Grammar of the Greek New Testament* (New York: Macmillan, 1927), §§243-90 (pp. 268-303); Porter, *Idioms,* 204-17; 230-43; Wallace, *ExSyn,* 656-78.

64. For more on subjects and complements, see Haddon W. Robinson, *Biblical Preaching: The Development and Delivery of Expository Messages,* 2nd ed. (Grand Rapids, Mich.: Baker, 2001), 41-50.

65. In other words, the complement is *what is affirmed by the dependent adverbial clause.*

as a reflection of one's exegesis, represents one of the final steps in the exegetical process. It is the product of intensive exegetical analysis.

Illustration: The Structural Layout of Greek Clauses for Eph 1:3-6

3 Εὐλογητὸς [ἐστιν] ὁ θεὸς καὶ πατὴρ τοῦ κυρίου ἡμῶν 'Ιησοῦ Χριστοῦ,

> ὁ εὐλογήσας ἡμᾶς ἐν πάσῃ εὐλογίᾳ πνευματικῇ ἐν τοῖς ἐπουρανίοις ἐν Χριστῷ,

4 > > καθὼς ἐξελέξατο ἡμᾶς ἐν αὐτῷ πρὸ καταβολῆς κόσμου

> > > εἶναι ἡμᾶς ἁγίους καὶ ἀμώμους κατενώπιον αὐτοῦ ἐν ἀγάπῃ,

5 > > > προορίσας ἡμᾶς εἰς υἱοθεσίαν διὰ 'Ιησοῦ Χριστοῦ εἰς αὐτόν, κατὰ τὴν εὐδοκίαν τοῦ θελήματος αὐτοῦ,

6 > > > > εἰς ἔπαινον δόξης τῆς χάριτος αὐτοῦ ἧς ἐχαρίτωσεν ἡμᾶς ἐν τῷ ἠγαπημένῳ.

2. Working from your structural layout, list the structural markers and their verse references.

Here are the structural markers for Eph 1:3-6 that were gleaned from the structural layout:

> [ἐστιν] (v. 3a)
> ὁ εὐλογήσας (v. 3b)
> καθὼς ἐξελέξατο (v. 4a)
> εἶναι (v. 4b)
> προορίσας (v. 5)
> εἰς (v. 6)

3. Create a subject-complement statement for the first structural marker.[66]

For pedagogical reasons, we will deviate a bit and begin with the third structural marker, καθὼς ἐξελέξατο, in v. 4a. (We will eventually cover all the structural markers.)

---

66. In essence, we are following Merrill C. Tenney, who constructed an outline that followed his version of a structural layout (*Galatians: The Charter of Christian Liberty*, rev. ed. [Grand Rapids, Mich.: Eerdmans, 1957], 168-73).

The subordinating conjunction καθώς with its verb ἐξελέξατο expresses a causal relationship ("since / insofar as he chose") and is dependent on the elided verb ἐστίν ("is") in v. 3.[67] Thus it gives a reason that God is blessed. In other words, "The God and Father of our Lord Jesus Christ is blessed . . . since / insofar as he chose us in him before the foundation of the world."

To create a subject-complement statement for καθὼς ἐξελέξατο (actually, for the dependent clause introduced by this subordinating conjunction and its verb):

- Isolate the subject, which is the structural marker's syntactical force (causal in this case) plus what the marker modifies (usually the verbal element of the preceding clause):

  "The reason the God and Father of our Lord Jesus Christ is blessed"

- Isolate the complement, which is the "content" of the dependent adverbial clause introduced by the structural marker:

  "because he chose us in him before the foundation of the world"

- Link the subject and complement with an equative verb:

  "The reason the God and Father of our Lord Jesus Christ is blessed *is* because he chose us in him before the foundation of the world."

- A little synthesis (reflecting some exegetical decision making!) and some rewording to conform the thought and language to the original context and setting produces:

  The reason God was worthy of praise was because he chose the Ephesians in eternity past.[68]

  or alternately:

---

67. BDAG, 494.4.

68. Technically, "us" (ἡμᾶς) refers to Paul (with his companions?) and to the saints at Ephesus (v. 1). We restrict it here and throughout to the Ephesians for the sake of simplicity (pedagogical reasons).

> *The reason God was worthy of praise was his choice of the Ephesians in eternity past.*
>
> or:
>
> *The reason for God's praise was his election of Ephesian believers.*

Note that the subject—what Paul is talking about—is not God, praise, or election. Rather, the subject is the REASON that God is worthy of praise. Subjects such as this one are called adverbial subjects since they clearly reflect the relationship (often adverbial in force) that exists between related clauses. Such adverbial subjects are preferred over those found in simple descriptive statements (e.g., *God is worthy of praise. God chose us.*) since the latter merely summarize or express the content of clauses without indicating the nature and direction of Paul's argument (i.e., they do not reveal relationships between clauses or ideas).[69]

Also remember that a subject-complement statement has two parts: a subject and a complement.

The subject
- is what the author is talking about, i.e., the topic
- is usually derived from and represents the syntactical force (or the semantic/conceptual force) of the structural marker plus what that marker modifies
- is usually adverbial in force, e.g., "The *reason* God was worthy of praise . . ."

Thus, the subject is not simply the main characters or even the key theological concepts but is the how, when, where, or why these main characters and concepts move, develop, and change. In other words, the subject concerns the argument, or in the imagery of the theater, the plot—how and why the story line develops. Thus, the subject will rarely, if ever, be "Paul," "believers," "Christ," "redemption," "prayer," etc.

---

69. This is the ideal insofar as it is warranted by the biblical text. Of course not all clauses express an adverbial relationship or have adverbial force. Also note the redundancy in our first statement: "The *reason* . . . was *because* . . . ." Notice too that we tidied it up, without losing the adverbial force of the relationship, so that it reads: "The reason God was worthy of praise was his choice of the Ephesians in eternity past." Redundancy, while not elegant, is acceptable and certainly preferable to omitting, neglecting, or overlooking the adverbial force of subjects.

Instead, good subjects tend to represent or reflect the questions posed by the interrogative adverbs: Why? How? When? Where?, not simply those of the interrogative pronouns: Who? Whose? Whom? Which? What?[70] The following have potential to be good subjects:

- The reason Gentiles were joined . . .
- The time of the Ephesians' sealing . . .
- The means by which death is abolished . . .
- The place where unity was achieved . . .
- The condition on which reconciliation depended . . .
- The purpose/aim/goal (or result) of election . . .
- The standard by which the Galatians lived . . .
- The content of Paul's prayer . . .

The following subject-complement statements contain examples of poor subjects, which are to be avoided:

Example 1:

> *God chose the Ephesians in eternity past.*

This is a classic descriptive statement for Eph 1:4a. It contains a poor subject ("God") because it makes simply "God's election" the focus of the statement. However, in Eph 1:4a this is *not* what Paul is talking about. Rather, the subject—what Paul is talking about—is *the reason God was worthy of praise.*[71] The following, as we have seen above, contains a much better adverbial subject:

> *The reason God was worthy of praise was because he chose the Ephesians in eternity past.*

Example 2:

> *The Ephesians were to be holy and blameless.*

70. See the helpful chart in Klein, Blomberg, and Hubbard, *Introduction to Biblical Interpretation,* 267. Also note that the subject is not the answer to these questions but reflects or represents these questions (to which the text supplies the answers). For example, in the first illustration, the question is, "Why were the Gentiles joined?" The answer is given in the complement: "The reason the Gentiles were joined *was* . . ."

71. In addition to accurately identifying the true subject, note that adverbial subjects also narrow subjects that are vague or general. For example, the descriptive subject "God" in the statement, "God was worthy of praise," would become "The *reason* God was worthy of praise . . ."

This too is a classic descriptive statement, but this time for Eph 1:4b. It too contains a poor subject ("the Ephesians") because it makes "the Ephesians and their behavior" the focus of the statement. Again, this is not what Paul is talking about. Instead, he is talking about the purpose for which God chose the Ephesians. The following contains a much better adverbial subject (we will explain it more fully below):

> The purpose for which God chose the Ephesians was to make them holy and blameless.

In brief, good subjects are usually adverbial (whenever possible), not simply descriptive of their content.

The complement
- is what the author is saying about what he is talking about
- is usually derived from and represents the substance or "content" of the dependent adverbial clause introduced by the structural marker
- provides the "content" necessary to complete the subject, e.g., "because he chose the Ephesians in eternity past"

The subject-complement statement
- links the subject and the complement with an equative verb, e.g., "The reason God was worthy of praise *was* because he chose the Ephesians in eternity past."

4. Create a subject-complement statement for the next structural marker.

Work with the next (fourth) structural marker, εἶναι, in v. 4b.

- The subject is usually the structural marker's syntactical force (εἶναι is a purpose infinitive) plus what the structural marker (εἶναι) modifies (ἐξελέξατο in this case).[72] Thus our subject is "The purpose for which God chose the Ephesians . . ."
- The complement is the "content" of the clause introduced by the structural marker (εἶναι). Thus our complement is ". . . in order that they might be holy and blameless before him in love."
- After rewording this to reflect the original setting, our whole subject-complement statement is: "The purpose for which God

---

72. For these details, see Hoehner, *Ephesians*, 178.

chose the Ephesians *was* so that they would be holy and blameless before him in love."

A little synthesis and some rewording produces:

The purpose of God's election of the Ephesians was that they might be morally pure.[73]

- Our finished subject-complement statement should be a complete sentence of 30 words or less.

5. Create a subject-complement statement for the next structural marker.

Our next structural marker is προορίσας ("predestining") and it too modifies ἐξελέξατο ("chose").

- The subject is the structural marker's syntactical force (προορίσας is a causal participle) plus what the marker (προορίσας) modifies (ἐξελέξατο).[74] Thus our subject is "The reason God chose the Ephesians . . ."
- The complement is the "content" of the clause introduced by the structural marker, προορίσας. Thus our complement is ". . . because he predestined the Ephesians to adoption . . ."
- So our next subject-complement statement is: "The reason God chose the Ephesians *was* because he predestined them to adoption through Jesus Christ according to the good pleasure of his will."
- A little rewording produces:

The reason for God's election of the Ephesians was his predestination of them to adoption through Christ because this pleased him.

or alternately:

The reason for God's election of the Ephesians was his predestination of them to salvation.

or:

---

73. This statement reflects some exegetical decision making and follows our "additional suggestions" below. Even more concisely, we might have, "The goal of election was moral purity."
74. The force of the participle is debated. Here, we follow Hoehner, *Ephesians,* 194.

The reason for God's election of the Ephesians was his prior determination of those who were to be saved through Christ.

6. Follow this basic procedure for all the structural markers.

The next structural marker, εἰς, yields:

The purpose of God's predestination of the Ephesians was so that he might be praised for the glorious display of his grace shown in Christ.[75]

Picking up ὁ εὐλογήσας in v. 3b gives:

The reason God was worthy of praise was his bestowal on the Ephesians of every spiritual blessing in Christ.[76]

This brings us to the elided ἐστίν in v. 3:

God was worthy of praise.

Here we should note that some structural markers, especially finite verbs that begin a new paragraph or section, might not explicitly modify a preceding element or clause. In such cases, we might ask "What question is Paul answering?" Here it seems to be something like: "What was the proper response to God?" or "What was God worthy of?" Thus we can word our subject to reflect this question, and our complement to answer it: "The proper response to God was praise," or more simply "God was worthy of praise."

Through the use of the so-called signpost connectives (ἄρα, γάρ, διὰ τοῦτο, οὖν, etc.), many finite verbs that begin a new paragraph will explicitly express some relationship to the previous material.[77] Although these connectives tie paragraphs together and thus provide especially important clues to the development of the author's overall argument, they only indirectly contribute to the idea *within* a paragraph. For this reason they can often be ignored in the outline of the paragraph itself, provided that the

---

75. For εἰς as a structural marker, see #6 at §4.2.5 above. The line introduced by εἰς forms part of a refrain that is repeated three times in 1:3-14 (vv. 6, 12, 14). This reveals its importance to Paul's argument.

76. For ὁ εὐλογήσας as a structural marker, see note 14 above.

77. When an explicit connection to the previous material is lacking, as in the case of Eph 1:3, the exegete must ask and answer the question: "What is the implicit connection between the previous discussion and the material introduced by this seemingly isolated structural marker?"

exegete uses some means (e.g., a brief note, introductory heading, etc.) for making explicit the connection between paragraphs.[78]

Reproducing our subject-complement statements in textual order gives us (do not subordinate any statements yet):

God was worthy of praise (v. 3a).

The reason God was worthy of praise was his bestowal on the Ephesians of every spiritual blessing in Christ (v. 3b).

The reason God was worthy of praise was his choice (election) of the Ephesians in eternity past (v. 4a).

The purpose of God's election of the Ephesians was that they might be morally pure (v. 4b).

The reason for God's election of the Ephesians was his predestination of them to salvation (v. 5).

The purpose of God's predestination of the Ephesians was that he might be praised for the glorious display of his grace shown in Christ (v. 6).

7. Avoid poor subject-complement statements.

Although we have already alluded to poor subject-complement statements, the issue needs to be developed further. It reaches to the very heart of the matter at hand.

We might be tempted to create the following three statements for the structural markers καθὼς ἐξελέξατο, εἶναι, and προορίσας:

God chose the Ephesians (v. 4a).

The Ephesians were to be holy and blameless (v. 4b).

God predestined the Ephesians to adoption (v. 5).

78. A passage must "never" be cut loose from its surrounding context. Here, in Eph 1:3-14, we would probably want to indicate in a separate note or heading the fact that this paragraph is (1) modeled after the OT *berekah* (see, for example, Ps 41:13; 66:20; 72:18) and functions as an introductory blessing or expression of praise, and that it is (2) inserted, contrary to Paul's typical practice, between his salutation (1:1-2) and his introductory thanksgiving (1:15-23).

These statements are true, but they are unrelated, isolated statements. In Eph 1:4-5, however, these ideas are not unrelated fragments. They are related to one another, and the exegete's job is to disclose the relationships that exist between them. This is the key to tracing the author's argument, his line of thinking.

The argument of a passage turns on the relationships that exist between the statements found within the text, and this is where the structural markers come into play. They are the key to tracking these relationships.

In this regard, it cannot be emphasized too strongly that a given paragraph from one of Paul's letters is not a random collection of theological thoughts merely placed side by side. Paul's letters are neither a cluster of proverbs nor the stream-of-consciousness musings of a religious mystic. Quite the contrary, Paul has crafted a well-structured and coordinated case. It progresses logically and relentlessly, point by point, toward its conclusion. It is not a random or haphazard collection of facts, evidence, and testimony. In short, Paul is not wandering aimlessly. He has an agenda and is pursuing it vigorously. The exegete's job is to track with that agenda, to trace Paul's argument.[79]

The direction of thought is usually indicated by these structural markers. It is this line of thought, this course of reasoning (i.e., argument) that we are trying to disclose. We are not trying to discover isolated facts, concepts, or even themes. We are trying to follow the plot, the story line, the argument. The structural markers help us to do this. They are where the action takes place—where *ideas* are established, developed, explained, and applied.

Another example of a poor subject-complement statement using the marker καθὼς ἐξελέξατο (v. 4a) may further clarify the process:

Paul gave the reason that God was worthy of praise.

---

79. See Schreiner, *Interpreting the Pauline Epistles*, 97-99; and also Beekman and Callow, *Translating the Word of God*, 268, 287-312; Guthrie and Duvall, *Biblical Greek Exegesis*, 39; Klein, Blomberg, and Hubbard, *Introduction to Biblical Interpretation*, 264-67; Louw, *Semantics of New Testament Greek*, 95-96. However, note J. Christiaan Beker's warning against imposing an "architectonic structure" on Romans or conceiving "of any Pauline letter as an exercise in thought without concrete historical mooring" (*Paul the Apostle: The Triumph of God in Life and Thought* [Philadelphia: Fortress, 1980], 64-69). The temptation to impose neat structures, with extreme logical precision, on Paul's letters must be tempered, for it implies that he was writing in a historical vacuum and was engaged in thought only with himself.

This is true, but it merely identifies Paul's subject—"the reason God was worthy of praise"—without specifying that reason. In the end, the statement expresses little, if any, meaningful content about the subject. Remember, Paul was not merely asking the question, "Why is God worthy of praise?" but also answering it. The following statement is much better for it specifies or identifies the reason God was worthy of praise (i.e., answers the question that was posed) and reveals the precise relationship between v. 3a (praise) and v. 4a (election) that is clearly expressed in the text through the structural marker, καθὼς ἐξελέξατο:

The reason God was worthy of praise was his choice (election) of the Ephesians in eternity past.

Again, statements such as this one are said to contain adverbial subjects since they (the statements) clearly reflect the relationships (commonly adverbial in force) that exist between related clauses.

8. Consider these additional suggestions:

    a. Be clear and accurate, but avoid complex or cumbersome statements. By definition a subject-complement statement should be a single declarative sentence containing a single subject and its corresponding complement. Do not overload these sentences with every last detail given by the modifiers—"isolated abstractions of individual words or phrases"—in the text.[80] Summarize! Synthesize! Major on the majors. Minor on the minors.

    b. In general, use the past tense (unless it is inappropriate for the context, e.g., when timeless theological truths are being expounded).[81] It gives a better historical perspective and forces us to think (for the time being) about the biblical author's intended meaning rather than timeless principles or present-day applications. Similarly, make sure that your statements reflect

---

80. The wording is Walter Kaiser's (*Toward an Exegetical Theology: Biblical Exegesis for Preaching and Teaching* [Grand Rapids, Mich.: Baker, 1981], 100). In this approach, the details that are lost are more than made up for in clarity and in prioritization (distinguishing between the central and the peripheral). And yet the details are not lost, for they surface in another place—one's commentary on the text. To overload the outline is to misunderstand its function and to usurp the role of [the] commentary. In short, modifiers are important, and very much so, but they are generally not critical to the major point (argument) being made.

81. See further, Richard Marius, *A Short Guide to Writing About History*, 3rd ed. (New York: Longman, 1999), 159-60.

the original setting. For example, be sure to indicate that Paul encourages *the Ephesians* and not *us,* or that *Paul prayed* and not that *you or we should pray.*[82]

c. Subject-complement statements should reflect syntactical relationships and should explain the text. In other words, syntactical choices must be reflected,[83] obscure wording clarified, figures of speech unpacked, and ambiguous referents specified. In brief, your statements must reflect your exegetical decisions.

d. Each subject-complement statement should be a statement, not a question or a command.[84]

e. Not all statements are explicitly adverbial, and so they should not necessarily be expressed in that way. Numerous imperatives provide a classic example of this and can be expressed as follows: "The content of Paul's exhortation . . ." Prayers and benedictions can be displayed similarly.

f. Each subject-complement statement should be as specific and as unique as the text warrants. Each portion of the NT makes a more-or-less distinct contribution, so rarely will two subject-complement statements be identical.

4.3.2.3 GROUPING S-C STATEMENTS AND ORGANIZING THE OUTLINE: GENERAL GUIDELINES

1. Based on conceptual breaks in the passage, group the subject-complement statements into larger conceptual units and construct new subject-complement statements for each of these new units.[85] These new subject-complement statements should capture the *thrust* of these new, more comprehensive units. The new statements are not merely a conglomeration of the previous set of subject-complement statements but reflect a true synthesis of these previous statements. In other words,

---

82. For pedagogical reasons (i.e., to make explicit the link between our subject-complement statements and the biblical text), we have not always followed this principle in our discussion.

83. This is usually true with hypotactic structure (i.e., subordinating clauses). With paratactic structures (i.e., coordinate structures) the "deep" structure might be different and would need to be inferred. See note 14, and §4.3.2.5 for a further discussion.

84. A question tells us what the author is talking about, but does not tell us what he is saying about what he is talking about. A command, exhortation, or appeal rightly belongs to a homiletical outline.

85. To make these breaks, look for, among other things, new, common, or repeated ideas/concepts, as well as structural clues (e.g., chiasm, inclusio, repeated and concentrated use of the same words or grammatical features) or syntactical breaks (e.g., shifts in grammatical person, tense, or mood). For additional suggestions, see Beekman and Callow, *Translating the Word of God,* 279-81; Erickson, *Guide to New Testament Exegesis,* 62-67, 80-93. Good exegetical commentaries can often provide help at this stage.

not all of the details should be put into a new "summary" statement. You must prioritize; you must discriminate between the thrust of the passage and the peripheral details. In a word, you must be synthetic and so capture the overriding thrust or focus of the subsection.[86]

Such synthetic thinking is demanding and perhaps more art than science, but it is at this point that the major movements in the author's argument begin to emerge from the details.

As an example, consider this hypothetical set of subject-complement statements for non-theological material[87]:

1. Apples are nutritious.
2. Oranges are nutritious.
3. Peaches are nutritious.
4. Plums are nutritious.
5. Carrots are nutritious.
6. Celery is nutritious.
7. Radishes are nutritious.
8. Potato chips are not nutritious.
9. Cheetos are not nutritious.[88]
10. Jelly beans are not nutritious.
11. Jawbreakers are not nutritious.

We might group our subject-complement statements into larger units as follows:

A. Fruits are nutritious.
    1. Apples are nutritious.
    2. Oranges are nutritious.
    3. Peaches are nutritious.
    4. Plums are nutritious.
B. Vegetables are nutritious.

86. It is a mistake to label this approach as a compromise between specificity and detailed analysis, on the one hand, and generality and broad synthesis, on the other, especially if one thinks of a compromise as finding the lowest common denominator in which the details become casualties in the process. Rather, this approach is a marriage between analysis and synthesis in which the result is a genuine unity that shows how the details are the building blocks of a larger whole.

87. We have eliminated the adverbial force of these subject-complement statements for the sake of simplicity. Our concern is in illustrating how to build an outline from the subject-complement statements.

88. A Hoehner favorite!

1. Carrots are nutritious.
2. Celery is nutritious.
3. Radishes are nutritious.
C. Salty snacks are not nutritious.
   1. Potato chips are not nutritious.
   2. Cheetos are not nutritious.
D. Candy is not nutritious.
   1. Jelly beans are not nutritious.
   2. Jawbreakers are not nutritious.

Note that these new summary statements (A, B, C, D) do not reflect a single structural marker but summarize (capture the thrust of) several structural markers that are conceptually related to one another.[89]

2. Group these larger conceptual units (i.e., this new level of coordination—the A, B, C, and D in our illustration) according to common ideas or constructions to form into still more comprehensive conceptual units, and construct new, summary statements for these new conceptual units (where necessary).

Continuing our illustration, we might group our summary statements into larger units as follows:

I. Produce is nutritious.
  A. Fruits are nutritious.
    1. Apples are nutritious.
    2. Oranges are nutritious.
    3. Peaches are nutritious.
    4. Plums are nutritious.
  B. Vegetables are nutritious.
    1. Carrots are nutritious.
    2. Celery is nutritious.
    3. Radishes are nutritious.
II. Junk food is not nutritious.
  A. Salty snacks are not nutritious.
    1. Potato chips are not nutritious.
    2. Cheetos are not nutritious.
  B. Candy is not nutritious.
    1. Jelly beans are not nutritious.
    2. Jawbreakers are not nutritious.

89. Also note that the original subject-complement statements persist throughout the outline. This is not unusual.

3. If it is necessary, group these new, larger conceptual units to form still larger conceptual units, and construct summary statements for these new more comprehensive units.
4. Continue to group conceptual units into larger units and to construct new summary statements until you construct one, final, central idea that captures the thrust or main idea of the entire passage in a single sentence.[90]

Again, this central idea is made of two parts: a subject and a complement. The subject is what the biblical author is writing about (i.e., the topic), and the complement is what he is saying about the subject. For our illustration we might have:

The identification of nutritious food is associated with / linked to produce, not junk food.[91]

Limiting the central idea to one sentence rather than a paragraph forces you not only to be concise but also to think synthetically, to capture the overriding message of the passage. In short, it requires you to determine the subject of the passage and what is said about the subject. The outline itself will reveal how the individual verses, sentences, and clauses develop this, the central idea.

4.3.2.4 GROUPING S-C STATEMENTS AND ORGANIZING THE OUTLINE: SPECIFIC PROCEDURES, BUT NO MAGIC FORMULA

1. Group subject-complement statements into larger conceptual units.

   a. Use your judgment and push yourself to think synthetically. Think carefully (and prayerfully) about textual relationships and the flow of thought.
   b. Look for changes in subject matter and for syntactical/structural seams or breaks to make these groupings. Repeated observation and careful reflection are invaluable.
   c. Consult good exegetical commentaries for help (note the section headings and the outlines they contain).[92]
   d. Make sure that your division of the material is consistent with (reflects, coheres with) your exegesis.

---

90. See Beekman and Callow, *Translating the Word of God,* 272.
91. The subject—what we are talking about—is something along the lines of "the identification of nutritious food." Our subject asks the question: "Which foods are nutritious?" The complement provides the answer: "produce, not junk food." If we simplify the subject-complement format, our central idea is: "Nutritious food includes produce, not junk food."
92. For a helpful example, see Hoehner, *Ephesians,* 61-69.

e. Realize that there is not necessarily a single, automatic division of the material, although there are probably at most two or three ways to group the material into an outline without doing violence to the author's intended meaning.

2. Construct new subject-complement statements for these units. These new "second-tier" subject-complement statements:

   a. Summarize (capture the thrust of) each new unit.
   b. Allow the author's argument to emerge.[93]
   c. Begin to organize the outline (these statements provide initial direction for the outline and represent various levels of subordination in the final outline—however, each of these statements will probably not represent a Roman numeral).

3. Group these "second-tier" subject-complement statements into larger conceptual units (if possible and/or necessary) and construct new, "third-tier" subject-complement statements for these units.

4. Repeat this process until you have disclosed the major movements within the passage—the pivotal anchors of the argument (Roman numerals I, II, III, etc.)—and have a clear picture of the overall message (the central idea).

5. Organize the major ideas and the minor, supporting ideas that have been disclosed into a balanced (properly coordinated and subordinated) formal outline.[94]

6. Employ a whole-part-whole method throughout the process.

   If one progressively builds each successive tier of subject-complement statements from the preceding tier, the exegete runs the risk of "building a house of cards." Change one subject-complement statement and the entire structure might collapse. In other words, if one of the initial subject-complement statements is "wrong," it has the potential to skew the entire outline. Its contribution can ripple through the entire structure.[95]

---

93. Note that we do not want to impose *our* outline on the author. Instead we want *his* outline to emerge from the details.

94. Review the suggestions in point 1 immediately above.

95. Since the outline emerges from the details of the pericope being studied, the contents of that section will determine the shape of the outline. Therefore, if the paragraph boundaries that serve to delimit the pericope are misplaced, the outline can be skewed. Guard against this by ensuring that the section of Scripture being studied forms a clear unit of thought before attempting to outline it. In other words, carefully review the placement of paragraph breaks so that you are working with a "self-contained" unit of thought. For help with this, see note 41.

Although our fundamental principle is to build the outline from the bottom up (from the subpoints to the main points), repeatedly take a "top down" view to guard against this "ripple effect." That is, repeatedly observe the details of the passage and reflect on it as a whole rather than *just* reflecting on the subject-complement statements you have constructed. Ask yourself: Does this new second-tier or third-tier subject-complement statement capture Paul's thought?[96] Is it fair to the text and the argument it presents? In short, do not take a strictly linear path from subject-complement statements to one central idea. Rather take a circular route. Begin with the initial subject-complement statements and build upward, but constantly check your construction from a top-down perspective, i.e., from the text itself and the movement, direction, and focus within the text as a whole. Ask yourself what are the major movements (Roman numerals I, II, III)? What is the burden or message of the passage (the central idea)? Is my emerging outline moving in that direction? Is a seamless merger developing? Why or why not? Have I misunderstood something? Am I reading into the text? Or misreading the text? The outline, we suggest, is often a merger between a purely bottom-up approach and a more subjective top-down approach that is very cautious about imposing one's ideas on the author.[97] Admittedly, this is not an entirely objective process. Building an outline is both a science and an art, and the emphasis between these two may fall on the latter. Careful and reasoned judgment is needed. Subjectivity is inevitable but should not be wild and unrestrained. At this point, the mature reflection of respected commentators is often helpful.

In short, we are arguing for a whole-part-whole method in which we are constantly checking the details (each subject-complement statement) against the whole and checking the whole against the details. Thus outlining is not linear—moving straight from the details to the major ideas. Nor is it eisegesis—letting the major ideas predetermine what the details must say. The process is cyclical and repetitive: examining the whole, then the parts, then the whole again, then parts again, in an ever tightening spiral.[98]

7. Balance the difficulties of outlining with its benefits.

---

96. It must be emphasized that subject-complement statements, no matter how accurate and helpful, are one step removed from the explicit statements of Scripture.

97. A merger, not a compromise that does not satisfy the demands of either approach.

98. Cf. Osborne's metaphor of the spiral, which is getting tighter and tighter with each successive turn or cycle (*Hermeneutical Spiral*, 6). See also Guthrie and Duvall, *Biblical Greek Exegesis*, 127; and Timothy S. Warren, "The Theological Process in Sermon Preparation," *BSac* 156 (1999): 343-44.

a. Realize that exegetical outlining is a challenging task, for

- The NT documents are punctuated with features that can play havoc with formal outlines, e.g., digressions, variations in standard or set literary patterns, chiasms, diatribal features, and hymnic or poetic material.

- Despite our best efforts, many of our exegetical decisions are fragile and subject to revision.

- We are grappling with "things that are hard to understand" (2 Pet 3:16; cf. Rom 6:19). The concepts are often obscure and difficult to understand, making synthesis especially demanding.

b. Yet, realize that exegetical outlining is of genuine value, for

- It forces us out of our comfort zone of endless, hair-splitting analysis and demands that we think synthetically—that we organize individual exegetical fragments, exegetical minutiae, into a meaningful and coherent whole. Only then does the passage as a whole make sense, for only when the pieces of a puzzle are assembled do they convey a clear, distinct image of the whole.[99] Now both the trees and the forest are seen.

- It is built from the "bottom up," i.e., the outline emerges from the details of the text and is not imposed upon them. This characteristic, which is the opposite of the "top down" process—beginning with main points and then developing subpoints—helps ensure that we reveal the author's argument rather than imposing our own on his details.[100]

- It brings clarity both by giving structure and order to the passage and by bringing "to the fore matters of priority and relationships within the material."[101]

99. Cf. our reference below to Claude Monet's impressionism.

100. An accountant, who is preparing an overall statement of an institution's financial health, examines the details in order to make his or her summary statements. He or she can give an assessment of the whole only after examining the individual departments (i.e., details). Similarly, we can structure the whole only after examining the individual details.

101. Ryrie, *Communicating Bible Doctrine*, 86. In the words of Tenney, "The outline affords a clue to [the passage's] organization" (*Galatians*, 174).

- And perhaps most important, it forces us to think deeply in sustained ways about the message of Scripture and about *how* the author presented that message (i.e., his argument).

4.3.2.5 SYNTAX AND THE OUTLINE: AN IMPORTANT CLARIFICATION ON THE RELATIONSHIP BETWEEN SYNTAX AND MEANING (I.E., THE SKEWING BETWEEN FORM AND FUNCTION)

Merrill Tenney suggested the following system for outlining a passage: (1) the main topics of the passage form the outline's principal divisions (e.g., I, II, III, etc.); (2) the main clauses form the next subheads (e.g., A, B, C, etc.); (3) the subordinate clauses form the smaller subpoints (e.g., 1, 2, 3, etc.).[102] This is a very helpful way of approaching the problem of outlining. Yet, Greek syntax is often too flexible to allow an outline, as a summary of the developing logic of a passage, to be read like a transcript from the main and dependent clauses. The outline is not necessarily a mirror image of the syntactical structure, and grammatically subordinate points often form Paul's main points.[103] These are critical points that are often misunderstood—they warrant brief expansion.

First, Paul's main points or ideas are often represented by grammatically subordinate structures. Osborne provides a helpful example from Phil 2:2: "Make my joy complete by being like-minded, having the same love, being one in spirit and of one mind." He notes, "Obviously the primary emphasis is not the completion of Paul's joy but the harmony of the Philippian church, developed in four successive subordinate phrases telling the means for bringing Paul greater joy."[104]

Second, the syntactical structure of a passage does not necessarily follow the parameters of a formal outline. In other words, the syntactical structure of a passage often cannot be converted *directly* into a formal, logical outline. Instead of slavishly following the syntax, we must see how the syntax contributes to the develop-

102. Tenney, *Galatians*, 168.

103. Cf. notes 13, 14, 50.

104. Osborne, *Hermeneutical Spiral*, 32. For additional examples, see Liefeld, *New Testament Exposition*, 45-56; Cotterell and Turner, *Linguistics*, 199-200; and note 110. Also note Eph 3:2-6, where Paul's main concern (v. 6) is "buried" under multiple layers of subordination. Note too that the converse can be true: main clauses often serve subordinate roles in supporting other affirmations (see, for example, Eph 4:27, 30 with Hoehner, *Ephesians*, 614, 622; O'Brien, *Ephesians*, 334-35, 340, 345; and esp. Andrew T. Lincoln, *Ephesians*, WBC 42 [Dallas: Word, 1990], 293, 302, 308; cf. also Wallace, *ExSyn*, 667 n. 2).

ment of the ideas and concepts that Paul is trying to communicate. These ideas and concepts are what the outline tries to capture and express. It is not intended to mirror the syntax of the passage, as if one were trying to use the syntax as mere template for constructing the outline. Syntax is merely a tool, a vehicle, to help us unpack the progression of Paul's thought as it unfolds the thesis he is seeking to defend, explain, or develop. In short, syntax is a means to an end, not an end in and of itself.

Note the following hypothetical examples:

Paul might inform us that "God loves us" and follow this with two ὅτι clauses that give the reasons for this. In this case, the syntax is quite amenable to a formal outline:

> I. God loves us.
>   A. Reason
>   B. Reason
> II. etc.

However, what is perhaps more typical of Paul is that he tells us that "God loves us" and then follows this with one reason (ὅτι) for that love. Then he gives one purpose (ἵνα) for that reason. Such syntax cannot be transferred *directly* into a properly structured (formal) outline:

> I. God loves us
>   A. Reason
>   1. Purpose
> II. etc.

In the end, our approach tries to adapt Tenney's so that it makes allowances for the flexibility and subtlety of Greek syntax and for syntactical structure that cannot be transferred *directly* into a formal outline. Thus our approach seeks to be more faithful to the author's intended meaning.

All of this raises the question of the appropriateness of trying to reduce a NT author's argument to a formal outline. Do formal outlines do violence to the grammar and syntax of the passage and impose an alien, Western way of thinking on the author? Is not outlining like trying to squeeze the proverbial square peg into a round whole? Perhaps! Yet, on the one hand, we must remember that exegetical outlining is only a tool—and an imperfect one at that. On the other hand, we must acknowledge that it is still a powerful and effective tool, for it forces us to think deeply about synthesis and coherence and helps give some sense of priority and order to material. In other words, it forces the exegete to analyze how the individual ideas in a given passage are related to one another and what overall message or argument is being forged. In a word, the exegetical outline demands *synthesis*. The question that repeatedly confronts us is this: "How do these ideas link together to form a unified message?" Relationships—how ideas are related—not isolated thoughts or fragments are the ticket.

Additionally, it would seem that we need a structured summary to gain some semblance of order from the seeming "chaos" and "confusion" that make up the detail of Paul's discourses. We need to structure, summarize, synthesize, and integrate the details of the text somehow in order to be able to grasp them mentally, to get our "cognitive arms" around the passage. We need and want to see the big picture.

Moreover, we must see the whole to make good sense of the individual pieces. In minute detail, Monet's impressionism looks like a random set of smears on canvas. If one steps back and surveys the whole, the beauty of his work reveals itself. So it is with outlining.

Much like the translator, we are attempting to represent the NT message accurately and clearly. Yet, translation is risky business. Something always gets lost in the process. As the Italian proverb (*traduttore, traditore*) indicates, the translator is after all a traitor to the original, betraying it every time he or she cannot capture the exact nuance of the original. Yet, the rewards are priceless—God's Word made clear and understandable. So it is with outlining, and the risk is indeed worth the reward.

4.3.2.6 SUMMARY-REVIEW

The goal of exegetical outlining is to identify and to summarize the development or progression of an author's thought in a clear and meaningful format. In short, exegetical outlining tries to summarize the main ideas of a given paragraph in a brief and readily accessible form.[105] The outline should bring clarity to a sea of details—bring order to "chaos"—by summarizing the specific details (individual clauses and phrases) into larger and meaningful wholes. The mass of detail expressed by an author in a given paragraph must be

---

105. Cf. John C. Hodges et al. in the classic *Harbrace Handbook:* "Outlines are . . . useful for summarizing the main ideas of . . . reading material when you want to communicate ideas to other people in a brief, readily accessible form" (*Hodges' Harbrace Handbook*, 13th ed. [Fort Worth: Harcourt Brace, 1998], 360-1).

analyzed and then "repackaged" or displayed in a clear, consistent fashion.

The exegetical outline is:

- a sentence outline in which each point is expressed as a complete, declarative sentence (since it trades in ideas, the outline consists of complete sentences);
- a blueprint or map of the author's argument and flow of thought;
- a succinct yet accurate summary of the passage that strategically discriminates between the central and the peripheral;
- an explanation in which figures of speech are cleared and "Christianese" (parroting biblical language) is interpreted;
- a bold restatement that clearly reveals the interpretation (reflects exegetical decisions) and argument of the passage.

The exegetical outline is not:

- a topic or phrase outline, which conveys little specific content;
- a homiletical or theological outline, which moves the passage out of its original, first-century setting and is ultimately designed for preaching or teaching;
- a mere description of the contents of the paragraph, i.e., a list of statements in which the contents of individual verses or even half-verses are merely described via restatement or paraphrase without disclosing the relationships that exist between these verses or half-verses. *The exegetical outline is not a mere collection of isolated fragments. Rather, it is a series of statements that reveals the relationships and connections within the paragraph and so traces the author's line of thought, his argument;*
- a vague statement that is heavily dependent on the biblical language of the paragraph ("Christianese");
- a cautious, uninterpreted (and therefore safe) recounting of the paragraph.

The benefits/value of exegetical outlining:

- Presents the argument of the passage in a clear and formal way.
- Summarizes the details of the text and integrates them into a clear and meaningful "package."[106] In other words, it forces us

---

106. As Sheridan Baker points out, "An outline lays out the plan of [the passage] as no other can, giving the fullest statement of the ideas, and showing clearly and explicitly the logical relation of parts. . . . Making a sentence outline really masters [a passage] for you" (*The Complete*

to "major on the majors and minor on the minors" and not to fall prey to the reverse.

- Forces synthesis upon us and does not allow us to be content with a fragmented or atomistic reading of the text. It will help us see the "forest" (main message) and the "trees" (important details) despite the branches ("incidental" details).

- Demands repeated observation of and careful reflection on the text. This, of course, is a benefit in and of itself, but it also encourages the reevaluation of important exegetical decisions.

- Lays the foundation upon which to build a teaching or homiletical outline.

4.3.2.7 ILLUSTRATION OF EXEGETICAL OUTLINING USING EPH 1:3-6

Picking up the subject-complement statements that we have already constructed for Eph 1:3-6, we will use this passage to illustrate the process of constructing an exegetical outline.

List the initial subject-complement statements in textual order:

1. God was worthy of praise (v. 3a).
2. The reason God was worthy of praise was his bestowal on the Ephesians of every spiritual blessing in Christ (v. 3b).
3. The reason God was worthy of praise was his choice (election) of the Ephesians in eternity past (v. 4a).
4. The purpose of God's election of the Ephesians was that they might be morally pure (v. 4b).
5. The reason for God's election of the Ephesians was his predestination of them to salvation (v. 5).
6. The purpose of God's predestination of the Ephesians was that he might be praised for the glorious display of his grace shown in Christ (v. 6).

Group these initial subject-complement statements and construct new second-tier statements[107]:

1. God was worthy of praise (v. 3a).

Stylist and Handbook, 3rd ed. [New York: Harper & Row, 1984], 137). See also Mortimer J. Adler and Charles Van Doren, *How to Read a Book,* rev. ed. (New York: Simon & Schuster, 1972), 75-95. Baker was commenting on the value of sentence outlining both for crafting an essay and for reading one. Interestingly, Baker (1918–2000) was not a biblical scholar but an English professor at the University of Michigan and the author of *The Practical Stylist,* a widely used college text on composition.

107. Cf. the schematic offered by Beekman and Callow, *Translating the Word of God,* 276-77.

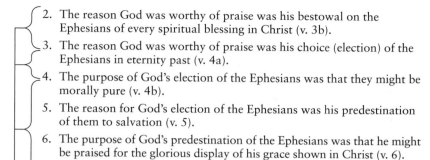

2. The reason God was worthy of praise was his bestowal on the Ephesians of every spiritual blessing in Christ (v. 3b).

3. The reason God was worthy of praise was his choice (election) of the Ephesians in eternity past (v. 4a).

4. The purpose of God's election of the Ephesians was that they might be morally pure (v. 4b).

5. The reason for God's election of the Ephesians was his predestination of them to salvation (v. 5).

6. The purpose of God's predestination of the Ephesians was that he might be praised for the glorious display of his grace shown in Christ (v. 6).

Second-tier Statements:

The reason God was worthy of praise was his bestowal on the Ephesians of every spiritual blessing in Christ (v. 3).

The reason God was worthy of praise was his choice (election) of the Ephesians in eternity past (v. 4a).

The goal of God's election of the Ephesians was their good and his glory (vv. 4b-6).

Rationale for these second-tier statements:

If we consider the larger context of vv. 3-14, v. 3 appears to be a heading (God was to be praised because of his blessings), and vv. 4-14 is the amplification of this, i.e., it specifies these spiritual blessings. Election is the first such blessing (vv. 4-6). It is followed by redemption (vv. 7-12) and sealing with the Spirit (vv. 13-14).[108] Our first two, second-tier statements reflect, most importantly, this understanding of the larger context and highlight the parallel between subject-complement statement #2 (v. 3b) and #3 (v. 4a). Our third new statement tries to do several things: (1) show that subject-complement statements #4-6 are ultimately tied to and expound on the concept of election, (2) reflect that subject-complement statements #4-6 are dominated by the idea of purpose or goal, and (3) summarize the thrust of vv. 4b-6, namely, election is for the Ephesians' good/godliness (moral purity) and God's glory. Finally, note that we have not tried to pack everything into the outline. Instead we have tried to capture the thrust of the argument. Summary and synthesis demand that some details be subsumed under/into more comprehensive concepts.

Group these second-tier subject-complement statements, and construct new third-tier statements:

108. So Hoehner, *Ephesians,* 64, 153-245.

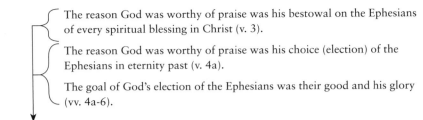

The reason God was worthy of praise was his bestowal on the Ephesians of every spiritual blessing in Christ (v. 3).

The reason God was worthy of praise was his choice (election) of the Ephesians in eternity past (v. 4a).

The goal of God's election of the Ephesians was their good and his glory (vv. 4a-6).

Third-tier Statements:

The reason God was worthy of praise was his bestowal on the Ephesians of every spiritual blessing in Christ (v. 3).

The reason God was worthy of praise was his choice (election) of the Ephesians, which was for their good and his glory (vv. 4-6).

Rationale for these third-tier statements:

We have combined our second and third statements into a new subject-complement statement, in which the goal or purpose of God's election (vv. 4a-6) has been transformed into a prepositional phrase ("*for* their good and his glory"). The subject of this statement concerns "the reason God . . ." because the larger context (vv. 3-14) is dominated by the reasons that God was worthy of praise.

Assemble the outline and isolate (disclose) the central idea:

Central Idea: The reason God was worthy of praise was his bestowal on the Ephesians of every spiritual blessing, but especially election with its goal of their good and his glory.

I.   The reason God was worthy of praise was his bestowal on the Ephesians of every spiritual blessing in Christ (v. 3).

II. The reason God was worthy of praise was his choice (election) of the Ephesians, which was for their good and his glory (vv. 4-6).
   A. The reason God was worthy of praise was his choice (election) of the Ephesians in eternity past (v. 4a).
   B. The goal of God's choice (election) of the Ephesians was their good and his glory (vv. 4a-6).
      1. The purpose of God's choice (election) of the Ephesians was that they might be morally pure (v. 4b).
      2. The reason for God's choice (election) of the Ephesians was his predestination of them to salvation (v. 5).
      3. The purpose of God's predestination of the Ephesians was that he might be praised for the glorious display of his grace shown in Christ (v. 6).

"Tweak" the outline for clarity (esp. in light of the larger context of vv. 3-14)[109]:

Central Idea: The reason God was worthy of praise was his bestowal on the Ephesians of every spiritual blessing, but especially election, redemption, and sealing with the Spirit, which had as their goal God's glory.

I.   The reason God was worthy of praise was his bestowal on the Ephesians of every spiritual blessing in Christ (v. 3).

II. The *first* reason God was worthy of praise was his choice (election) of the Ephesians, which was for their good and his glory (vv. 4-6).

   A. The reason God was worthy of praise was his choice (election) of the Ephesians in eternity past (v. 4a).

   B. The goal of God's choice (election) of the Ephesians was their good and *ultimately* his glory (vv. 4a-6).

      1. The purpose of God's choice (election) of the Ephesians was that they might be morally pure (v. 4b).

      2. The reason for God's choice (election) of the Ephesians was his predestination of them to salvation (v. 5).

      3. The purpose of God's predestination of the Ephesians was that he might be praised for the glorious display of his grace shown in Christ (v. 6).[110]

III. The *second* reason God was worthy of praise was redemption . . . (vv. 7-12).

IV. The *third* reason God was worthy of praise was the sealing of the Spirit . . . (vv. 13-14).

4.4 Conclusion

We have surveyed three exegetical tools that focus on the paragraph and the relationships *within* the paragraph:

- Diagramming focuses on relationships (syntactical) *within* clauses and displays them in a set framework of lines, branches, and terraces.
- Clausal layouts focus on relationships (syntactical and/or conceptual) *between* clauses and display them in a rewritten form of the text.
- Outlining focuses on the logical or conceptual priority of these relationships and displays them in a series of English statements that capture the author's flow of thought / intended meaning.

109. We have briefly expanded the outline's coverage to include all of vv. 3-14. The italicized words in the outline itself are intended to reflect this larger context.

110. The repetition of the phrase "to the praise of his glory" in 1:6, 12, 14 suggests that it functions at a higher level in the structure/thought of the passage than the syntax alone would suggest (in this hymnic section of 1:3-14 it functions essentially as a refrain). We have tried to reflect this with the addition of the expression "ultimately" in point B and in our wording of the central idea.

However, once our vision expands beyond the paragraph, these tools begin to fail us. This is true not only in tightly argued epistolary literature but even more so in narrative and apocalyptic literature. Not only do relationships *within* paragraphs need attention but relationships *between* paragraphs demand attention as well, and thus the exegete needs a heightened resolve to exploit diagramming, layouts, and outlining beyond the boundaries of the paragraph, where they function so effectively. But more than that, the exegete needs a specialized set of tools that focuses on the broader structural and thematic development that occurs not only *between* paragraphs but also *between* still larger units of discourse.[111]

4.5 For Further Reading

4.5.1 Diagramming

Grassmick, John D. *Principles and Practice of Greek Exegesis*. Rev. ed. Dallas: Dallas Theological Seminary, 1976. Pages 81-142.

Schreiner, Thomas R. *Interpreting the Pauline Epistles*. Guides to the New Testament. Grand Rapids, Mich.: Baker, 1990. Pages 77-96.

4.5.2 Diagramming Software

Although they do not teach diagramming, several software programs enable exegetes to construct diagrams by providing templates for the various lines, branches, and terraces that are needed. In addition to producing a clean, professional appearance, these diagrams, once created, can be printed, saved for future use, exported to word-processing programs, and revised easily (a major advantage over hand-written diagrams!). Three of the best-known programs are the following:

Accordance Bible Software. OakTree Software, Altamonte Springs, Fla. http://www.accordancebible.com.

BibleWorks. BibleWorks, Norfolk, Va. http://www.bibleworks.com.

Logos Bible Software. Logos Research Systems, Bellingham, Wash. http://www.logos.com.

4.5.3 Structural Layouts of Greek Clauses

There are numerous methods for creating "structural layouts." Most are not based exclusively on Greek clauses and so lack the objective controls that

---

111. See the accompanying chapters on the different genres present within the NT. These chapters will explore more fully the dynamics of interpreting narrative and apocalyptic literature.

come with a clause-based system. They call for a more intuitive approach to structure (much like our "wild cards"). Gordon Fee, who routinely uses structural layouts to great advantage in his commentaries on 1 Corinthians and Philippians, provides a good starting point for further investigation into structural layouts—an incipient form of discourse analysis.

Fee, Gordon D. *New Testament Exegesis: A Handbook for Students and Pastors.* 3rd ed. Louisville: Westminster/John Knox, 2002. Pages 12-14, 41-58, 138-39.

4.5.4 Exegetical Outlining

Kaiser, Walter C., Jr. *Toward an Exegetical Theology: Biblical Exegesis for Teaching and Preaching.* Grand Rapids, Mich.: Baker, 1981. Pages 99-104, 149-63.

Liefeld, Walter L. *New Testament Exposition: From Text to Sermon.* Grand Rapids, Mich.: Zondervan, 1984. Pages 45-56.

Exegetical outlining, as we have presented it, has not been the subject of extensive discussion. However, other complementary means of tracing the author's argument have been developed, and these should be noted:

4.5.4.1 ARCING

Daniel Fuller has developed a technique known as arcing. Many of its goals and procedures overlap with exegetical outlining.

Schreiner, Thomas R. *Interpreting the Pauline Epistles.* Guides to the New Testament. Grand Rapids, Mich.: Baker, 1990. Pages 97-126.

Schreiner provides an excellent presentation of the technique pioneered by Fuller, whose material is not widely available since it is contained in his unpublished class notes (see n. 36 above).

4.5.4.2 SEMANTIC STRUCTURE ANALYSIS

Arcing also overlaps with semantic structure analysis, and it too is focused on the development of the author's argument.

Cotterell, Peter, and Max Turner. *Linguistics and Biblical Interpretation.* Downers Grove, Ill. InterVarsity Press, 1989. Pages 188-229.

Guthrie, George H., and J. Scott Duvall. *Biblical Greek Exegesis: A Graded Approach to Learning Intermediate and Advanced Greek.* Grand Rapids, Mich.: Zondervan, 1998. Pages 39-53, 125-28.

Fig. 4.3: Master List of Common Symbols

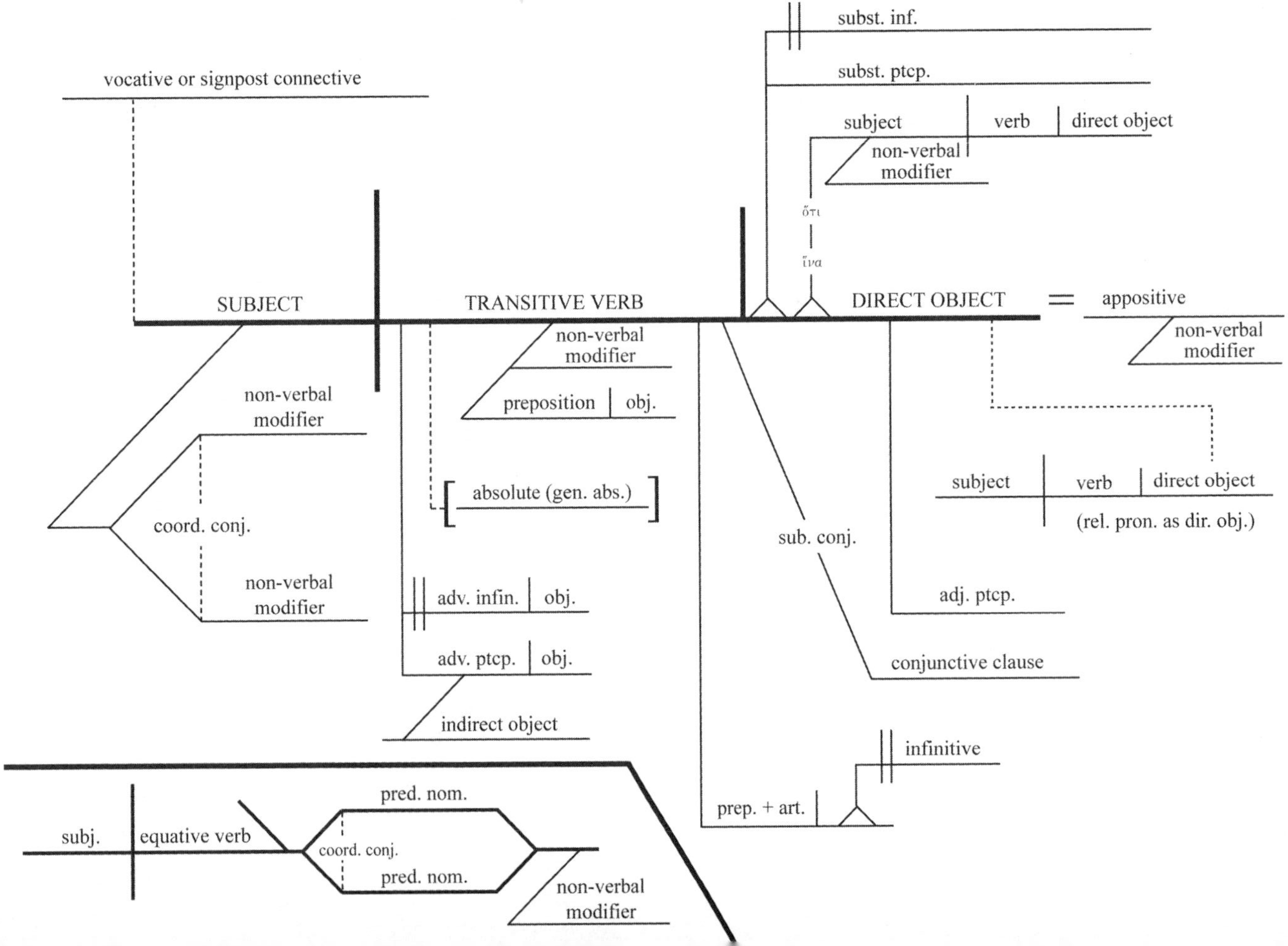

Lexical Analysis 5

Studies in Words

DARRELL L. BOCK

5.0 Introduction[1]

Watching a building under construction fascinates people. After the edifice has been constructed piece by piece, it eventually reveals a master plan. Similarly, words—the building blocks of Scripture—reveal mind-changing concepts about God and his world. The construction of words determines not only the meaning of the parts but also shapes the concepts of the whole. Studying the words of the NT involves investigating the most basic components that lead to exegetical and theological discovery. When one examines the words in the NT, one is looking at the units that form the starting point for exegetical and theological meaning. There is something exciting not only about understanding what is before the student of Scripture but also in determining how that understanding is present.

However, words are tricky things, because there is a flexibility in their usage that the exegete must remain sensitive to as he seeks precisely to define a term's usage in a given context or when she examines how a term

1. This chapter is an updated version of my "New Testament Word Analysis," in *Introducing New Testament Interpretation,* ed. Scot McKnight (Grand Rapids, Mich.: Baker, 1989), 97-113. Used by permission.

is used across several contexts. This means we must appreciate how words work and the various questions an interpreter must raise in order to study a term, both in context and with an eye to its overall usage. So our next section overviews the structure of this chapter and introduces important preliminary questions about words and method in word study.

5.1 Overview of the Chapter and of Method in Word Study

Anyone who studies the Bible for very long knows that interpretation is often not a straightforward matter of immediate agreement about what the Bible teaches. Like any other deep and complex work, disagreement about what a text exactly teaches can emerge. Obviously, the words of Scripture are an important part of such discussions. What can get in the way of agreement about a term's meaning? How is the interpreter to hurdle the obstacles that lead to such disagreement? How do we proceed through the possibilities of what the biblical text might and does mean? How sensitive should we be to the types of disagreements that arise? Are some differences of opinion more important than other differences? The rest of this chapter will attempt to explain what hinders our understanding of the meaning of words and how words should be handled. In thinking through word analysis, one should first consider several fundamental questions: What are the basic rules of word study? What obstacles about the meaning and makeup of words impede an understanding of their meaning? These two questions drive the rest of this section of the chapter.

In this chapter's next section we will overview the two important approaches to word study, the diachronic approach (or "through time," comprehensive word study) and the synchronic approach (or "at a given time," more focused word study). A fourth section will detail a list of common errors that often accompany the study of words, while the fifth and final section will take the results of our example study and compare them to some of the basic lexical tools we have. A proper method may not remove all the ambiguity and debate—after all, humans are finite creatures—but it should allow exegetes to understand why a passage speaks as it does and to articulate clearly their own understanding to others so that together they can discuss and benefit from each other's insights and observations on the Scriptures.

5.1.1 Fundamental Rules of Word Study

In thinking about words and interpretation, there are three fundamental rules that should have general assent:

1. *The exegete must initially pursue the meaning intended by the author for his original audience.*[2] Communication fundamentally involves the transfer of an idea from one mind to another. In biblical study the interpreter's goal is to understand what the original author meant through the terms he used. One needs to recognize that words do not automatically have meaning. They receive their meaning from the author who wrote the words.

Another point emerges from this consideration. To communicate, the message must be potentially shareable with the audience. It must relate to a category of meaning that the writer's audience can perceive—or else the message is incomprehensible. This observation does not deny that an author can communicate new sense in the words that he uses. It does suggest, however, that when the author intends new meaning, he will signal it so that the audience can grasp the new force of the term.[3]

2. This point is treated in the first chapter in this book. Authorial intent is the *initial* goal of the exegete. The exegete is preoccupied with the message of the human author. Initially the goal is to understand the message as set forth in the setting in which the author operated. The process of correlating that message with other biblical texts, either earlier or later ones, is the task of a subsequent theological process. In this latter phase one wrestles with concepts like the "progress of revelation," the "fuller sense" that God intended, the use and application of the OT in the NT, and the personal application of the text. All of these involve subsequent reflection beyond the initial exegetical concern with the message of a given document in a given setting. E. D. Hirsch presents a fine discussion and defense of authorial intention in *Validity in Interpretation* (New Haven, Conn.: Yale University Press, 1967); see also Kevin J. Vanhoozer, *Is There a Meaning in This Text? The Bible, the Reader, and the Morality of Literary Knowledge* (Grand Rapids, Mich.: Zondervan, 1998), 201-90, for a well-developed defense of authorial intent that is conversant with recent critiques of this view and that also stresses the goal that response to the author's meaning plays in meaning, so that meaning is more than propositional restatement. For a fine caveat in regard to authorial intention, see J. P. Louw, *Semantics of New Testament Greek* (Philadelphia: Fortress; Chico, Calif.: Scholars, 1982), 48. The complex issue of *sensus plenior* is handled nicely by Douglas J. Moo, "The Problem of *Sensus Plenior*," in *Hermeneutics, Authority, and Canon*, ed. D. A. Carson and John D. Woodbridge (Grand Rapids, Mich.: Zondervan, 1986), 179-211, 397-405.

In speaking of authorial intention, one does not try to reproduce what the author must have been thinking at a given point or why he wrote. Rather, the interpreter's goal is to ascertain what the writer wanted to communicate through the terms he chose for his message. Speaking about an author's intention is more appropriate than speaking about the meaning of the text, since words do not carry meaning autonomously and their meaning can be variously construed when detached from their original setting. The concern of the exegete is the meaning that emerged from the author's choice of expression, the sense he gave to the words in presenting them.

3. This means that in historically sensitive interpretation one will not use later NT passages to determine the referents of OT passages. Since meaning can emerge in a variety of ways when one introduces the factor of the passage of time, going to later revelation at this stage of the exegetical-interpretive process would possibly cloud the force of the original message, if not obscure it altogether. For this complex area see Darrell L. Bock, "Evangelicals and the Use of the Old Testament in the New," *BSac* 142 (1985): 209-23, 306-18, which surveys and evaluates four models offered by evangelicals to deal with this particularly difficult issue. See also the chapter in this book on the use of the OT in the NT.

2. *To establish the precise meaning of a word, one must recognize its possible range of meanings.* Often an interpreter simply assumes that a word has a certain meaning. However, the meaning of terms can change—from situation to situation, from person to person, and most important, from context to context. Therefore, the exegete must exercise care to be most sensitive to the context of a given usage. Words do not have an "automatic" general meaning. They have a range of meanings, which yields a specific sense in a specific context.

3. *Words operate in a context and receive meaning from that context.* This point is crucial. Words as separate, isolated entities do not provide the key to the meaning of Scripture. Instead, words *in relationship* to other words form the basis of the concepts that represent the text's message. Thus the interpreter's major concern in determining the meaning of a word is the setting of the word in its verse, paragraph, and book. In other words, words are like chess pieces on a chess board. Their importance and force are determined by their relationship to other pieces in the sentence and paragraph.

These three fundamentals provide a solid foundation for lexical analysis—a crucial discipline that the interpreter must appreciate in order to interpret the Word of God correctly.

5.1.2 The Complexities of Meaning

5.1.2.1 THE MEANINGS OF MEANING

Part of what makes meaning so difficult to ascertain is its very complexity. Most of us do not think about how many levels of meaning we interact with in dealing with words and trying to interpret them. Formally speaking, meaning and the study of words are bound together with the formal and broader academic discipline called semantics.[4] Semantics is the study of "signification" or "meaning." It can offer to the interpreter many insights regarding the issue of method in studying words. The goal

---

4. See James Barr, *The Semantics of Biblical Language* (Oxford: Oxford University Press, 1961), 1; Anthony C. Thiselton, "Semantics and New Testament Interpretation," in *New Testament Interpretation*, ed. I. Howard Marshall (Grand Rapids, Mich.: Eerdmans, 1977), 75-104, esp. 75; Moisés Silva, *Biblical Words and Their Meaning: An Introduction to Lexical Semantics* (Grand Rapids, Mich.: Zondervan, 1983); and Peter Cotterell and Max Turner, eds., *Linguistics and Biblical Interpretation* (London: SPCK, 1989), 106-87. For an excellent study of all aspects of semantics as it applies to NT word studies, see Louw, *Semantics of New Testament Greek*. This study addresses meaning as it is related to words, sentences, and paragraphs. For the broader discipline of semantics, see Stephen Ullmann, *The Principles of Semantics*, 2nd ed. (Oxford: Blackwell, 1957), 1-137, 197-258; idem, *Semantics: An Introduction to the Science of Meaning* (Oxford: Blackwell, 1962); and John Lyons, *Semantics*, 2 vols. (Cambridge: Cambridge University Press, 1977).

of this discipline at the lexical level is to examine how meaning is communicated through words.

In semantics one of the problems of lexical meaning is, in fact, determining what one means by speaking about a word's meaning![5] Semanticists have produced as many as twenty-five possible senses for meaning; but a few distinctions are extremely significant for exegesis and indicate the need for careful analysis. A list of these distinctions follows.

1. *Entailment meaning* pertains to a word or idea that implies some type of conclusion or implication not explicit in the term or context. For example, a passage that shows Jesus engaged in an activity that only God can perform entails the idea that Jesus is divine, even though the specific theological assertion that Jesus is God is not explicitly made in the text (e.g., Mark 2:1-12).

2. *Emotive meaning* applies to the use of a term that carries emotional force. So when James calls his readers adulteresses for their poor behavior (4:4), he is picking a term with emotive meaning to purposely shame them. A sensitive interpreter will note this emotive force to the term.

3. *Significance meaning* refers to a term or concept that takes on new meaning when brought into a context different from the original one (e.g., the NT use of the OT may bring additional force or emphasis to an earlier text). So when Jews were seen as enemies of Messiah in Acts 4:25-27 using an appeal to Psalm 2, the category of enemy expanded in terms of referent. It went from the general expectation of a Psalm that used to be read by Israel about the nations who opposed God's chosen regal ruler to include also Jews who opposed the Lord and his chosen. The switch in who is referred to shows how much things have changed with Jesus' coming and the rejection of him by many Jews. A text that once expressed Jewish hope now reveals their potential opposition to the gospel.

4. *Encyclopedic meaning* denotes all the possible meaning that a term may have. One generates such a full list from a dictionary, lexicon, or exhaustive word study tool.[6] This range of possible meanings allows for

5. G. B. Caird, *The Language and Imagery of the Bible* (Philadelphia: Westminster, 1980), 37-61.

6. In a normal lexicon the meanings of a word are simply listed along with passages that reflect a particular meaning. They can also be charted semantically in relation to the term's "field of meaning," where the senses are charted as categories of meaning that a word may have and are placed alongside other terms that can be associated with that category of meaning (see Thiselton, "Semantics," 91, where he charts out the word πνεῦμα; see also Louw, *Semantics of New Testament Greek*, 60-66). Words that address the same conceptual area are said to share the same semantic domain. A semantic domain lexicon examines words according to these conceptual groupings. See Johannes P. Louw and Eugene A. Nida, eds., *Greek-English Lexicon of the New Testament Based on Semantic Domains,* 2 vols. (New York: United Bible Societies, 1988). For another excellent treatment of the various relationships among words, see Silva, *Biblical Words*, 118-35.

a variety of interpretations, as well as misinterpretation. The goal of an interpreter is to take these possibilities for meaning and determine which particular meaning fits in a given context.

5. *Grammatical meaning* refers to the grammatical role of a term, such as the categories that one learns in an intermediate Greek grammar course. Some interpreters use this limited area of grammatical or syntactical classification to secure meaning, when in fact all these categories often do is limit the array of possible meanings. Just as words have possible meanings, so grammatical categories often have a variety of possible forces or uses, with the exact force being determined by contextual factors.

6. *Figurative meaning* indicates the use of a term because of the association it makes, not because the term's sense and referent are directly applied to what the term describes. For example, when Jesus speaks of faith that can "move mountains," he is not referring to the use of earth-moving equipment but to faith that can do marvelous things. Many exegetical debates turn on whether a term is literal or figurative, which is always an appropriate question to consider. Usually an understanding of genre, idiom, a judgment about whether a literal meaning makes "good" sense, and authorial style help in interpreting figures.

These senses of meaning can be significant in assessing the force of a given term, and must receive attention in thinking through the study of a term. However, they are not as central to the study of a term as the three basic elements of a word.

5.1.2.2 The Three Elements of a Word

Considered most abstractly, words are made up of three basic elements that contribute most directly to their intended meaning: *sign, sense, and referent.* In reality a word is a symbol that communicates meaning within a given culture or subculture.[7] A word does not *have* meaning; it is *assigned* meaning through cultural convention and usage.

The first element of a word is the *sign,* the collection of symbols that comprise a word. For example, the English word "p-a-r-a-c-l-e-t-e" is made up of nine alphabetic symbols. These symbols allow us to identify and pronounce the word. If we know the symbols and the coding patterns of the language, then we can understand the meaning. Sometimes a word is obscure because we do not know the symbols that comprise it. For example the term παράκλητος makes no sense to someone who does not know Greek, because the symbols of the word make no sense. If one went to Israel and tried to read Hebrew without having studied the language, that person could not begin to work with meaning because he or she would not

---

7. This point is illustrated by the existence of different languages and alphabets, which are simply different symbolic systems for representing concepts in words.

be able to read the symbols that make up the word. Without translation or explanation, the reader would be unable to work with the text.

The second element of a word is *sense*, which is the content associated with the symbol.[8] The sense of a word is closely related to one of the lexical "definitions" of the word, with the exact sense being a function of the word's use in context. However, the concept referred to by the sense of the term need not precisely identify what a text is actually referring to with a given term. For example, the Greek term for "paraclete" means "comforter," which by itself is ambiguous in English, since it could refer specifically either to an object similar to a quilt or to a sympathetic encourager. The ambiguity results in part from an ambiguity in the "receptor" language (in this case English). In addition, one must identify who or what exactly is referred to as a comforter. In this case, the sense of the term is really a description of an attribute as opposed to making an identification of what exactly is being described. So the sense often gets one closer to the meaning of a text, but it does not always specify or identify clearly what exactly is being referred to by the term in question. Interpretation requires that we inquire into what exactly is being described. The context in which the word appears will help us not only to determine the term's sense, but also, hopefully, its referent (what it actually refers to). Nonetheless, once the term's general content is clear, one begins to know the passage's general direction in terms of its meaning.

The third element of a word is the *referent*. The referent is the actual thing denoted by the term in a specific context. In John 14–16, for example, the referent of "paraclete" is clearly neither a human sympathetic figure nor a blanket; rather the term refers to the one Jesus will send after his resurrection to be with believers. This is specifically a reference to the Holy Spirit. The identification of the referent, where possible, produces specificity and clarity in interpretation. Thus, specifying referents, where possible, is an important goal in exegesis.

The complex nature of a word's meaning and its various elements requires that the interpreter exercise great care in approaching the study of words. Once the biblical student has grasped the fundamentals of word study, the meaning of meaning, and the basic elements of a word, then he or she can proceed with care and precision in the actual procedure of word analysis.

5.2 Diachronic and Synchronic Word Analysis

Word meanings can be examined in two ways. First, words can be studied historically by examining how they have been used in the past and

---

8. Silva, *Biblical Words*, 101-3.

how they have changed in meaning through time. This is called *diachronic word analysis*, and it is the approach of the technical word study tools like *TDNT* and *NIDNTT*.[9] These two reference tools examine a word's use beginning with the classical Greek period and continuing through the NT or even the patristic period. Examining words in this way indicates the possible senses that a term may have.

Second, words can also be studied within a given period (e.g., the intertestamental period, or pre–AD 70), or within the writings of a specific author (e.g., Paul, John, Matthew, Philo, or Josephus). This is called *synchronic word analysis*. This is perhaps the most crucial phase of lexical analysis since the meaning of a word in its specific context, either temporal or literary, is the interpreter's major concern.

The following sections present an example of both the diachronic and synchronic processes used for NT word analysis. They also name the key tools one can use for each phase of the lexical study.

5.2.1 Basic Procedure for NT Word Analysis: Getting Ready

Getting ready to examine words and their usage on our own requires various tools. These tools come in two forms, book resources and computer tools. Basic book resources include major lexicons, like Liddell-Scott-Jones (LSJ) for general Greek usage or Moulton and Milligan (MM) for Koine Greek Usage and Bauer-Danker-Arndt-Gingrich (BDAG) for NT and early Christian usage. They might include concordances like Hatch-Redpath for the Greek Old Testament (LXX) or a solid concordance of the Greek New Testament or secondarily of a solid NT translation.

Computer programs can help accomplish the same thing as a concordance. In fact, a computer concordance may be the most effective tool to use, if the program uses an up-to-date edition of the text in question. For the Windows operating system, we have found the *Logos/Libronix*, *BibleWorks*, or *Gramcord for Windows* programs to be most helpful for such study, while *Accordance* has proven most helpful for the Macintosh platform. These come with individual modules of selected key ancient works in their "scholarly" collections that allow you to search a range

9. *Theological Dictionary of the New Testament*, ed. Gerhard Kittel and Gerhard Friedrich, trans. Geoffrey W. Bromiley, 10 vols. (Grand Rapids, Mich.: Eerdmans, 1964-76), abbrev. *TDNT*; and *The New International Dictionary of New Testament Theology*, ed. Colin Brown, 4 vols. (Grand Rapids, Mich.: Zondervan, 1975-85), abbrev. *NIDNTT*. The difference in these tools is that *TDNT* lists individual lexical terms tied to a specific root form, while *NIDNTT* organizes words according to concepts, groups of similar lexical terms, or synonyms that may not necessarily share the same root form. While *TDNT* provides fuller historical information, *NIDNTT* traces concepts better since it explicitly associates related terms. For a critique of *TDNT*, see Barr, *Semantics*, 21-45, 206-62.

of ancient materials for information. For computer help with classical Greek, there is the *Thesaurus Linguae Graecae* (*TLG*) and online there is the *Perseus* project (www.perseus.tufts.edu). These last two tools require a detailed acquaintance with Greek.

Other tools that can be used for reference by advanced students include the ten-volume *Theological Dictionary of the New Testament* (*TDNT*), the four-volume *New International Dictionary of New Testament Theology* (*NIDNTT*), and the three-volume *Exegetical Dictionary of the New Testament* (*EDNT*).[10] For firsthand diachronic word study, the above noted tools are part of a basic resource library.

Several options exist as to which terms to select for closer analysis. First, one could choose to study any words whose English definition is unclear. Second, words that have apparent synonyms and antonyms in the context make good candidates. Third, words that are used rarely or only once (*hapax legomena*) are also good candidates, especially if they appear to carry conceptual weight in a passage. Fourth, words used figuratively make a good choice, since their precise meaning is often not transparent. The most crucial words, however, are those terms that are either repeated or that appear to bear a passage's conceptual weight. One must understand these key words to ascertain the passage's meaning.

An expositor should learn how to spot the key terms in a given passage. If a personal reading of the text does not reveal these key terms, then the use of lexically sensitive commentaries on the Greek text or solid commentaries working from an interaction with the Greek behind an English translation can often help to locate them. Another way to discover these key terms is by comparing different English translations. If the translations render the original Greek text with clearly non-synonymous English terms, then perhaps the term behind the differences merits closer examination.

5.2.2 Lexical Method: Stages of Diachronic and Synchronic Study

5.2.2.1 DIACHRONIC STAGE 1: CLASSICAL USES

A diachronic word study includes four distinct stages, each of which utilizes a certain tool or set of tools. We first overview these four stages.[11]

10. These tools are for advanced students because sometimes these tools make critical assumptions about date and authorship of biblical works or about issues tied to historical background that require significant historical knowledge by the student who uses these tools. Key bibliographic information for these tools follows in the discussion of the individual subsections to which the tool applies.

11. A fifth step could be added that studies the use of NT terms in Christian patristic literature. For this latter step, use G. W. H. Lampe, *A Patristic Greek Lexicon* (Oxford: Clarendon, 1961-68), which gives one access to the use of terms in the writings of the church fathers. The most complete collection of Greek patristic texts is J.-P. Migne, *Patrologia Graeca*, 161 vols.

The examination of terms used during the classical Greek period (900-330 BC) requires the use of the Liddell-Scott-Jones lexicon and comprises the first stage of study.[12] Next one enters the Hellenistic or Koine period (330 BC–AD 330). Here one will consider three groups of material: the LXX, popular nonbiblical sources, and the NT. A study of the Septuagint (LXX) will involve the use of the concordance of Hatch and Redpath or an equivalent concordance to the LXX and is the second stage of the diachronic study.[13] An examination of terms in nonbiblical sources of the Koine period involves using both LSJ and the volume of Moulton and Milligan and is both the third stage of the diachronic study and the first stage of a synchronic study.[14] The fourth and final stage involves the study of terms in the NT through the use of a NT concordance, the most up-to-date being the work produced by Bachmann and Slaby or computer programs tied to the Nestle-Aland 27th edition or the UBS 4th edition of the Greek New Testament.[15]

[Practically speaking, the best way to proceed is to use sheets of paper and record the results of the study in these four areas of study.]The information recorded on these sheets or on note cards will ultimately help to organize one's thoughts and formulate one's conclusions about the data. Such study can also be recorded in a computer word processing format. For exegesis, the most significant results will emerge as one moves closer

---

(Paris: Migne, 1857-66). Many of these texts have been translated and can be located in other series. A possible sixth step could examine the use of related terms in Jewish or rabbinic literature (e.g., Hebrew or Aramaic equivalents). For this step, judiciously use Hermann L. Strack and Paul Billerbeck, *Kommentar zum Neuen Testament aus Talmud und Midrasch*, 6 vols. (Munich: Beck, 1926; 6th unrevised ed. 1974). See also Marcus Jastrow, *A Dictionary of the Targumim, the Talmud Babli and Yerushalmi, and the Midrashic Literature* (London: Judaica, 1971) and the series of original language concordances by B. Kivsosky from the nineteenth century.

12. Henry George Liddell and Robert Scott, *A Greek-English Lexicon*, rev. and aug. Henry Stuart Jones and Roderick McKenzie, 9th ed. (Oxford: Clarendon, 1940; revised supplement, 1996). Hereafter abbreviated as LSJ. The intermediate lexicon by Liddell-Scott is abbreviated as LS.

13. Edwin Hatch and Henry A. Redpath, *A Concordance to the Septuagint and the Other Greek Versions of the Old Testament (Including the Apocryphal Books)*, 2 vols. (Oxford: Clarendon, 1897; available in various reprint editions).

14. James Hope Moulton and George Milligan, *The Vocabulary of the Greek Testament* (London: Hodder & Stoughton, 1930; available in various reprint editions).

15. Horst Bachmann and Wolfgang A. Slaby, eds., *Concordance to the Novum Testamentum Graece*, 3rd ed. (Berlin: de Gruyter, 1987). Another concordance that could be used is that by W. F. Moulton and A. S. Geden, *A Concordance to the Greek Testament*, 6th ed., rev. I. Howard Marshall (Edinburgh: Clark, 2002), a work originally based on the 1881 text of Westcott and Hort but now reflecting the UBS 4th ed. Major advantages of the Bachmann and Slaby *Concordance* include not only its use of the most recent Greek text but also the larger context it provides for each word it cites. Advanced students will profit by using Kurt Aland, ed., *Vollständige Konkordanz zum griechischen Neuen Testament*, 2 vols. (Berlin: de Gruyter, 1975-83), a multivolume tool that offers complete word statistics.

to the text in question, with primary consideration being given to context and authorial intention.[16]

The following sections illustrate the four stages of a word study, using the Greek noun ἀρραβών (transliterated and pronounced *arrabōn*). In regard to the classical period the basic definitions for this term as found in the lexicon are: (1) earnest-money, caution-money; (2) pledge, earnest; and (3) present, bribe.[17] Examples in the writings of Isaeus[18] and Aristotle show that ἀρραβών is a commercial term that refers to the initial payment in a series of payments. For classical usage we are looking for works dated before 300 BC. Dates can be checked in Index I of LSJ (Authors and Works). Classical sources to which LSJ refers may be checked in the Loeb Classical Library (LCL) or online through the Perseus Project (www. perseus.tufts.edu).[19]

The study of a word's usage in the classical period yields a base from which to draw possible meanings. Only in the case of rarely used words, however, does it have significant importance, because later uses are often far more contextually appropriate. However, the examples may illustrate the term's force.

5.2.2.2 DIACHRONIC STAGE 2: HELLENISTIC BIBLICAL USES (LXX)

In this particular step, one studies the use of Greek terms in the LXX, the Greek translation of the Hebrew Old Testament.[20] Here the study becomes more interesting and complicated: more interesting, because one of the objectives of this step is to determine possible religious or theological meaning for terms in the LXX; more complicated, because this step involves a knowledge of Hebrew.

---

16. It should be stressed that in lexical matters evidence for usage is weighed, not counted. Thus a word whose meaning is uncertain will not necessarily reflect the most commonly occurring sense. Context is always the most important factor: the sense that fits the context best is the most likely sense.

17. LSJ, 246. Ideally, in this stage one would look up all uses of a word, something only rarely done because of lack of access to materials. The TLG collection can yield more examples than the lexicon.

18. LSJ cites Isaeus 8.20; however, the term of the entry is not found in this section but in 8.23. This example illustrates the value of looking up references, for then errors and typos can be discovered and removed.

19. The Loeb Classical Library (Cambridge, Mass.: Harvard University Press) is an extensive collection (approx. 450 vols.) of both Greek and Latin texts with English translations.

20. For a helpful presentation on the value of the LXX for biblical studies, see Frederick W. Danker, "The Use of the Septuagint," in his *Multipurpose Tools for Bible Study,* rev. and expanded ed. (Minneapolis: Fortress, 1993), 77-88; and Karen H. Jobes and Moisés Silva, *Invitation to the Septuagint* (Grand Rapids, Mich.: Baker, 2000).

This particular step, however, is not free from potential errors. One common error is simply to discover the Hebrew word behind the Greek translation in the LXX, and then determine the translation of the Hebrew word to get the Greek idea. This procedure ignores three important facts. First, words in languages do not overlap exactly in meaning.[21] Second, the LXX is often a paraphrase and not a word-for-word rendering of the Hebrew.[22] In fact, in some places the exact wording behind the LXX is very uncertain. Third, often a particular Greek term was chosen not because the translator was attempting to render a specific Hebrew term but because of the way the passage had been traditionally read and translated. These facts should warn the exegete against hastily concluding that a term has picked up its Greek sense from the Hebrew or that a term indicates technical Hebraic usage. The words may be used in a similar manner, but that does not mean they carry exactly the same sense.

Once the exegete has generated a list of Hebrew words that the Greek LXX terms translate, then he should study the meanings of those Hebrew terms in a Hebrew lexicon and, if possible, a theological dictionary for biblical Hebrew words.[23]

Looking up ἀρραβών in the LXX reveals that this term occurs only in Genesis 38:17, 18, and 20,[24] the passage about Tamar and Judah. In these verses the meaning of ἀρραβών clearly is "pledge," since an object was given to Tamar as a guarantee. The term as used here indicates a "business" deal; though no money was exchanged, a family seal, cord, and staff were. A glance at the Hebrew term עֵרָבוֹן, which is translated "pledge" (NIV), shows that the LXX term is merely a transliteration of the Hebrew term. It is a "loanword," that is, a borrowed word. For example, the term Christ for "anointed one" came to English directly from Greek Christos.

21. For example, English has one word for "history," while German has two, "Geschichte" and "Historie." To equate either of the German words with the English is to lose some of the precision in the German terminology. The problems in this area are detailed by Silva, *Biblical Words*, 52-73.

22. In fact, the translation quality of the LXX varies from book to book. For details, see Bleddyn J. Roberts, *The Old Testament Text and Versions: The Hebrew Text in Transmission and the History of the Ancient Versions* (Cardiff: University of Wales Press, 1951), 172-87. For an overview of Septuagintal studies, see Emmanuel Tov, "Jewish Greek Scriptures," in *Early Judaism and Its Modern Interpreters,* ed. Robert Kraft and George W. E. Nickelsburg (Philadelphia: Fortress, 1986), 223-37; and Jobes and Silva, *Invitation to the Septuagint.*

23. Francis Brown, S. R. Driver, and Charles A. Briggs, eds., *A Hebrew and English Lexicon of the Old Testament* (Oxford: Clarendon, 1907); or Ludwig Koehler and Walter Baumgartner et al., eds., *The Hebrew and Aramaic Lexicon of the Old Testament,* 5 vols. (Leiden: Brill, 1994). The student should also consult G. Johannes Botterweck, Helmer Ringgren, and Heinz-Josef Fabry, eds., *Theological Dictionary of the Old Testament,* 14 vols. (Grand Rapids, Mich.: Eerdmans, 1974-2003).

24. Hatch and Redpath, *Concordance to the Septuagint,* 160.

For lexical method it is more important to study the use of the Greek word in its LXX context regardless of the Hebrew term it renders. Look for the contextual clues that show the nuance of meaning it carries (as here in Genesis 38).

5.2.2.3 DIACHRONIC STAGE 3 AND SYNCHRONIC STAGE 1: HELLENISTIC NONBIBLICAL (OR KOINE) USES

When we move to this period, we begin to cross from diachronic analysis to synchronic analysis. The objective in this phase of study is to trace the variety of meanings a given term has within the time period of 330 BC to AD 100. Actually, the Koine period extends beyond this later date, but when studying NT usage the student need not move beyond the period of the NT writings.

A significant resource for the study of Hellenistic Greek words in nonbiblical sources is the volume by Moulton and Milligan.[25] This tool illustrates the use of Koine Greek words as found in papyri and epigraphical remains. Some examples are left untranslated, but fortunately, most examples are translated or summarized, as well as dated. Some examples postdate the NT period and should be evaluated closely (how late are they; do they illustrate only later developments?). However, many excellent examples occur that vividly illustrate the everyday usage of many terms from the NT period.[26]

A quick look at ἀρραβών in Moulton and Milligan discloses several important items.[27] First, the entry notes that the term is a Semitic loanword, an observation we made earlier after comparing the LXX term with the Hebrew term that it translated. Second, the entry gives alternate spellings of the term. Third, according to several helpful examples, ἀρραβών is used for a deposit of 1000 drachmae for the purchase of a cow, a deposit of 160 drachmae for a land purchase, and a down payment of 8 drachmae

25. See note 14. This work is somewhat dated (1930); however, it is in the process of being updated, though it is uncertain when the update will be produced (for information see G. H. R. Horsley and John A. L. Lee, "A Lexicon of the New Testament with Documentary Parallels: Some Intermediate Entries," *Filologia Neotestamentaria* 10 [1997]: 55-84; and 11 [1998]: 57-84). For selective studies, see the series *New Documents Illustrating Early Christianity*. This is currently up to nine volumes (1981-2002), originally edited by G. H. R. Horsley and later by S. R. Llewelyn, published by The Ancient History Documentary Research Centre, Macquarie University, Australia, and (later) by Eerdmans in Grand Rapids. These are papyri collections that update and supplement information available in Moulton and Milligan.

26. Moulton and Milligan contains only a small sampling of all of the occurrences of a given word, so it should not be regarded as providing an exhaustive treatment of terms in this period. Exhaustive treatments of this material do not exist in a single collected form. However, some papyri updates are available online on the Perseus project site at www.perseus.tufts.edu or in the *New Documents* series noted above. Remarks in note 17 about ideal method also apply here.

27. Moulton and Milligan, *Vocabulary,* 79.

for the services of a mouse catcher. These examples clearly indicate the use of ἀρραβών as a commercial term. A note to the entry says, "The above vernacular usage amply confirms the NT sense of an 'earnest,' or a part given in advance of what will be bestowed fully afterwards, in 2 Cor 1:22, 5:5, Eph 1:14."[28] In this entry, they have not only defined the NT term with "earnest" but have also paraphrased it with "a part given in advance of what will be bestowed fully afterwards."[29]

In some cases, the study of terms in the Koine period will surface new meanings. Usually, however, the Koine sources will supply information about the common understanding of terms in the period contemporary to the NT writings or provide vivid illustrations of usage.

5.2.2.4 DIACHRONIC STAGE 4 AND SYNCHRONIC STAGE 2: BIBLICAL USES (NT)

The objective of this phase of word study is to determine the meaning of a term in the NT. There are a variety of ways to do this. First, one can study the use of a term author by author, creating lists for each writer of the NT material. This approach allows the student to make valuable biblical-theological observations by observing each author's distinctive treatment of terms. Second, the use of a term can be studied within a specific genre (i.e., within the Gospels, Pauline Epistles, Apocalypse, etc.). The value of this division is that one can examine how genre may affect the use of certain terms and images. Third, one can also study the use of a term by proceeding through the text in chronological order. This process is perhaps less helpful in the Gospels, since these documents in their final written form portray events that occurred considerably earlier. But in Paul or in the General Epistles this third approach can help trace the development of a writer's theology or the theology of the early church. (Here, "development" may simply mean the introduction of a new topic that naturally produced new associations.)

Now what does one find about ἀρραβών?[30] It occurs only three times in the NT, all in Pauline letters. Its uses in 2 Cor 1:22; 5:5; and Eph 1:14 show that it is related both to the Holy Spirit and to the idea of sealing. According to 2 Cor 1:22, God "put his Spirit in our hearts as a deposit [ἀρραβών], guaranteeing what is to come." In 2 Cor 5:5 Paul states that God "has given us the Spirit as a deposit [ἀρραβών], guaranteeing what is to come." Eph 1:13-14 says that believers "were marked in him with a

---

28. Ibid.

29. The entry includes several intriguing later examples. One example relates ἀρραβών to "purchasing a wife." A second example speaks of the engagement ring as an ἀρραβών. Again, the picture of an object as a pledge is very clear here.

30. Bachmann and Slaby, *Concordance*, 222.

seal, the promised Holy Spirit, who is a deposit [ἀρραβών] guaranteeing our inheritance until the redemption of those who are God's possession. . . ." Thus the gift of God's Spirit to believers not only indicates God's ownership (seal) of them, but also a pledge of his future inheritance for them. Clearly, for Paul the Spirit is a pledge, a promise of more to come.

Sometimes time prevents one from doing a full diachronic study. Often the most crucial step is the NT study using a concordance. This step is almost always valuable to pursue.

This concludes the basic four-step process. A question that the exegete might now ask, however, is "Which tools should I own?" Ideally, all the tools that have been mentioned should be owned. But at a minimum, one should own the Bauer lexicon, a Greek NT concordance, and either *TDNT* or *NIDNTT*. The advantages of *TDNT* are that its articles offer a full array of ancient references; they often cite portions of the pertinent ancient texts; and they frequently include notes about the exegetical possibilities in a given passage. *NIDNTT* has the advantage of examining concepts, of being more up-to-date in its discussion and method, and of being more succinct. Also, the one-volume abridgement of *TDNT*, called "little Kittel," is helpful as a quick reference guide and gateway to the larger *TDNT*.[31] Another helpful tool that presents compact discussion of key data is the *Exegetical Dictionary of the New Testament (EDNT)*.[32] All such tools also need to be evaluated for their own method and approach, especially as they relate to certain historical judgments about the date and authorship of NT books or the relevance of issues tied to debates about relevant historical background to certain key terms. Thus such tools are for advanced students who understand how they work and are aware of the limitations and suppositions.

5.3 Avoiding Errors: Common Fallacies Made in Word Analysis

Before turning to the final step of the procedure, one additional issue needs attention: to note the common fallacies made in the word study process.[33] Several of the most common fallacies are listed in the following paragraphs.

31. *Theological Dictionary of the New Testament*, ed. Gerhard Kittel and Gerhard Friedrich, trans. Geoffrey W. Bromiley, abridged in one volume by Geoffrey W. Bromiley (Grand Rapids, Mich.: Eerdmans, 1985).

32. Horst Balz and Gerhard Schneider, eds. *Exegetical Dictionary of the New Testament*, 3 vols. (Grand Rapids, Mich.: Eerdmans, 1990-93). Another word tool, Ceslas Spicq, *Theological Lexicon of the New Testament*, 3 vols. (Peabody, Mass.: Hendrickson, 1994), is helpful but very selective in the words it covers.

33. For a more comprehensive discussion of fallacies, see D. A. Carson, *Exegetical Fallacies*, 2nd ed. (Grand Rapids, Mich.: Baker, 1996), 27-64. He notes sixteen such fallacies. This chapter shall note only the more common errors.

The *etymological fallacy*, also known as the "root fallacy," assumes that the meaning of a word is governed by the meaning of its root or roots.[34] Also, it may assume that what a word originally meant is what a later author meant by the term. Though the sense may be related, it is not certain that an author cites a term with a knowledge of the meaning of its component parts. Thus it is best not to appeal to etymology unless contextual factors make it clear the author is aware of this meaning.

Illegitimate totality transfer assumes that a word carries all of its senses in any one passage. It could be called "meaning overload." However, linguists agree that the "correct meaning of any term is that which contributes the least to the total context."[35] One of the implications of this error is that technical meanings or unusual meanings for terms need to be determined contextually rather than imported from other contexts. It is best not to give a term a multiple nuance in a given context unless double entendre is clearly signaled by context, authorial style, or genre.

Another error is the problem of *semantic anachronism*, in which a late meaning of a word is read back into an earlier term. What often contributes to this error is the way that the church today uses biblical terminology. Often a technical meaning will develop for a term that is more specific than ancient usage. A simple example of this is the term *salvation*, which in the popular modern church often means justification or "getting saved." Yet in the NT its Greek equivalent (σωτηρία) can refer to justification, sanctification, glorification, or to all of these together. Another example of this problem is when appeal is made to later Jewish or Greek materials to support a first-century meaning for a term that lacks attestation for that sense in earlier sources. Obviously keeping a careful eye on the dates of sources guards against this error.

Semantic obsolescence is when one assigns to a term an early meaning that is no longer used. In NT word study this would be the same as giving a classical Greek meaning to a first-century Koine Greek term. An English illustration can suffice. One reason why the KJV is difficult to read in places is because the meanings of some of its terms have fallen out of use since 1611 (e.g., "conversation" in Phil 3:20; the term still exists but its meaning has shifted).

---

34. See Louw, *Semantics of New Testament Greek,* 23-31; Silva, *Biblical Words,* 35-51; Barr, *Semantics,* 107-60. An English example may suffice. The suffix "-gate" means scandal, but it has nothing to do with the lexical meaning of the term but rather is tied to a historical event, "Watergate," that led to the creation of the suffix. Etymology of the root "gate" is meaningless for the resultant meaning!

35. E. A. Nida, "The Implications of Contemporary Linguistics for Biblical Scholarship," *JBL* 91 (1972): 86; Louw, *Semantics of New Testament Greek,* 51-52.

The *prescriptive fallacy* argues that a word has only one meaning and means the same thing in every passage. For example, if a word has the meaning "X" in 13 out of 14 occurrences, then it must mean "X" in the disputed case. But word meanings are determined by context, not word counts.[36]

The *word-idea fallacy* assumes that the study of a term is the study of an idea. But the study of a concept is broader than word study, and many terms can be related to a single concept. For example, if one studies the concept of Jesus as King, one is not limited to those texts where the term *king* (Gk. βασιλεύς) appears. Other relevant terms for study might include *rule, reign, kingdom,* and the like.

The *referential fallacy* limits meaning to only a specific referent. However, in contexts where principles are given, where commands are offered, where figures are used, or where abstractions are expressed, it is faulty to limit the meaning to a single referent. In such cases, the specific referent of a term is not the only object to which the passage can be related.[37]

When the OT prophets, for example, spoke of the return from exile with language suggesting a "new exodus," they applied an earlier image of the OT to their own experience (Isa 40:1-5; 44:27; Mal 3:1-2). When the NT authors cited OT passages that originally referred to Yahweh and applied them to Jesus, they avoided the referential fallacy by interpreting the OT in the light of activities that Jesus performed (Rom 10:11-13). It should be noted, however, that as an interpreter today moves beyond the original referents to which an author refers, he or she is moving beyond the technical realm of exegesis, whose goal is to recover the author's original intention, toward application, how and what the text addresses in the present.

Verbal parallelomania refers to the practice of some biblical exegetes who claim that the presence of the same term in several different, often extrabiblical, contexts automatically indicates conceptual parallelism, borrowing of terms, or literary dependency. Admittedly, many ancient cultures used similar terms in vaguely similar contexts, and the Greek religious world used terms that also appear in the NT. However, Philo's use of the term *logos* does not mean that it has the same sense for him

---

36. This raises a key issue that often complicates exegesis, especially for the beginning student. One does not establish a meaning merely by showing that a term's sense is contextually possible. Often commentators think their work is done when they have shown that a context could support the defended sense. However, the sense that should be chosen is the one that is the most likely among the options. Often a context can support a variety of senses, but the meaning is the one that fits the context the most naturally and with the least amount of contextual strain.

37. This fallacy is the most abstract of the ones mentioned and is difficult to explain briefly. For a more detailed discussion, see Silva, *Biblical Words*, 103-8.

as it does for the apostle John. Only careful, comparative study of all relevant texts will establish the veracity of possible parallels, borrowings, or literary dependencies.

Perhaps the most serious error is the *selective evidence fallacy* wherein one cites only the evidence that favors the interpretation one wants to defend. Certainly, unintentional errors in judgment do occur sometimes. However, the intentional avoidance of certain facts will always result in inaccurate and biased conclusions.

These nine fallacies present a cross section of some of the obstacles that can hinder the exegete in determining the meaning of words. At one time or another every exegete trips over one or more of these obstacles while engaged in the enterprise of interpretation. This is why dialogue with other reference works is an essential part of the process. Thus, we include one final step in the analysis of words: comparing the results of our study with the results obtained by other biblical scholars.

5.4 Checking Other Authorities: BDAG, *TDNT, NIDNTT*

A check of these sources shows that our analysis of ἀρραβών agrees with that of others. For example, the *TDNT* article says that ἀρραβών "always implies an act which engages to something bigger."[38] Thus the Spirit is "the guarantee of their full future possession of salvation,"[39] an excellent description of the contextual force of the term ἀρραβών. *NIDNTT* agrees with this description but also notes that since the Spirit is a gracious gift from God, one should not speak of God as our debtor.[40] This is one instance in which the image differs from its daily use. BDAG defines ἀρραβών as a "first installment," "deposit," "down payment," or "pledge." It is a commercial or legal term that denotes "payment of part of a purchase price in advance," and so it "secures a legal claim to the article in question, or makes a contract valid."[41]

This concludes the final step of the process of word analysis whose focus is a NT term.[42] Thus the use of a term has been traced through various periods (diachronic word analysis), as well as the NT period (synchronic word analysis).

38. *TDNT,* 1:475.
39. Ibid.
40. *NIDNTT,* 2:39-40.
41. BDAG, 134.
42. For possible fifth and sixth stages of a full diachronic process involving the church fathers' usage and Jewish usage, see note 11 above.

5.5 Conclusion

Lexical analysis is demanding but necessary. Through lexical study the barriers that hinder one's understanding of the meaning of terms are often overcome or significantly lowered. The exegete who strives to understand the basic rules of word study and grasps the complexities of meaning is in a better place to work with biblical terms. The student who appropriates and implements sound methodology, and who avoids the common fallacies made in word study will be able to achieve a high level of accuracy in interpreting words, the building blocks of Scripture. The result will be more precise and accurate exegesis. The student also will build up his or her knowledge about how Scripture or its individual authors use terms, all worthy goals of biblical study. With a careful consideration of how words are being used, the student is also better prepared to expound the Word, either in a passage or thematically.

5.6 For Further Reading

Barr, James. *The Semantics of Biblical Language*. Oxford: Oxford University Press, 1961.

Caird, G. B. *The Language and Imagery of the Bible*. Philadelphia: Westminster, 1980.

Cotterell, Peter and Max Turner, *Linguistics and Biblical Interpretation*. Downers Grove, Ill.: InterVarsity Press, 1989.

Louw, J. P. *Semantics of New Testament Greek*. Philadelphia: Fortress; Chico, Calif.: Scholars, 1982.

Silva, Moisés. *Biblical Words and Their Meaning: An Introduction to Lexical Semantics*. Grand Rapids, Mich.: Zondervan, 1983.

Validation

6

Exegetical Problem Solving

DAVID K. LOWERY

The part of the process of exegesis that evaluates various points of view in order to arrive at the most probable meaning of the subject under investigation is called validation.[1] It requires a willingness on the part of the interpreter to follow the data to the most likely conclusion. It is an inductive process that interacts with the history of interpretation as comprehensively as possible and discounts no relevant information in the evaluation of various points of view, arriving finally at a conclusion that is the most probable (or the least problematic) in terms of all available data.[2]

1. This essay incorporates some of the notes prepared in outline form by Darrell L. Bock for the Dallas Seminary class NT104, *Introduction to NT Exegesis*. These notes were subsequently turned into a CD course supplement produced by W. Hall Harris (Garland, Tex.: Exegetica Software, 2004). Any statements that seem intemperate or immoderate are my own, however (unless otherwise noted), and do not reflect the more sober reserve of these colleagues.

2. The person who taught me exegetical method was Harold W. Hoehner (he said facetiously the W stood for "wonderful"). I remember well his repeated emphasis on following the facts of the text to the most likely conclusion. Harold later became my adviser in the NT track and my thesis supervisor. He had a pastoral concern for all his advisees, and we spent many hours in his home. We appreciated the combination of academic rigor and the emphasis on humility and spiritual vitality that he modeled for us. Some years later when I became his colleague I saw another dimension of Harold, his skill at any number of manual tasks, a legacy of growing

This process may be better understood by clarifying what it is not. It is not a matter of coming to a conclusion about the interpretation in question at the beginning of the process and then arguing the case for that point of view by citing the data that seem supportive of it. In other words, an exegete is not an advocate, like a lawyer representing a client. A good lawyer will try to put his client and his case in the best possible light. He knows what conclusion he wants to reach before the trial begins and will seek to discount (or exclude) the relevance of any data that may prove problematic for winning agreement on the point of view he is putting forward.

Most of us would welcome a lawyer like this arguing our case in a trial. However, many biblical interpreters are confused about their proper role, and function for all practical purposes like lawyers arguing a point of view. They decide at the beginning of the process what view they regard as most compatible with their theological or ecclesiastical or personal conviction and then work to demonstrate the reasonableness of this interpretation against all competing interpretations. If certain data are problematic for their interpretation, they are ignored or discounted. It is a regrettable fact that many sincere (though misguided) people carry out research and writing as theological lawyers rather than biblical interpreters. Please do not be one of them.

I hesitate to belabor this point but want to say as clearly as possible that manipulating the data of the text to support a particular point of view is not authentic exegesis or interpretation, and it is not validation that has any integrity of method associated with it. When you as a researcher detect this bogus approach to exegesis in the writing you are reading (or the lecture you are hearing), regard it as the wishful thinking of its author that it is. If you own writing of this sort, the only reason to read it is as an example of what not to do (libraries, by virtue of their role, routinely find shelf space for work of this sort and must be excused). Let no one say of you that you made up your mind about your conclusion before you started the process of validation. Instead, aim to follow the data to the most probable conclusion. Practice integrity of method. Your conclusion may be unsettling to you and may create more than a little personal tension (a circumstance that may never be resolved for some issues: welcome to life in an imperfect world). But you (and those you minister to) will be better for it if you treat the data with integrity (and you will not be a phony exegete).

---

up on a farm. Whenever I had a question about household or automotive work, Harold had an answer or lent a hand to get it done. His neighbors knew this too. I remember calling him one summer to ask about progress on a commentary he was writing. He was helping a neighbor with a project at the time and, as his wife, Gini, observed, Harold's problem was he knew how to do too many things! All who know him appreciate his love for God and for people. And we in turn find that to know Harold is to love him as well.

6.1 Getting Started

Since validation aims to arrive at the most probable interpretation of a text, it usually requires sorting through a variety of possible meanings. Some of these alternatives can emerge through a process of self-discovery. Using an array of basic reference tools like lexicons, concordances, or grammars, a thoughtful exegete can surface a variety of possible interpretations. The joy of discovery that accompanies this process has much to commend it but requires considerably more time (and at least for the beginner, greater expertise) than most people are able to devote to this phase of exegesis. For this reason the history of interpretation that can be assembled from reading periodicals, monographs, or commentaries is a vital source of information. The best writers will point out the important issues to be considered in the text under consideration, review the significant points of view in the history of interpretation, and assess the strengths and weaknesses of the alternative proposals. Obviously a commentary that offers this kind of detailed information will be of formidable size. But even commentaries of modest length can be useful in discussing the issue to be considered and presenting an interpretation that can be evaluated along with competing alternatives. As Charles Spurgeon advised novice preachers (in his straightforward style) more than a century ago:

> In order to be able to expound the Scriptures, and as an aid to your pulpit studies, you will need to be familiar with the commentators: a glorious army, let me tell you, whose acquaintance will be your delight and profit. Of course, you are not such wiseacres as to think or say that you can expound Scripture without assistance from the works of divines and learned men who have laboured before you in the field of exposition. . . . A respectable acquaintance with the opinions of the giants of the past might have saved many an erratic thinker from wild interpretations and outrageous inferences. Usually, we have found the despisers of commentaries men who have no sort of acquaintance with them; in their case it is the opposite of familiarity which has bred contempt.[3]

The current trend seems to be for commentators to discuss the history of interpretation without necessarily settling on a particular point of view. While this may be appropriate for certain reference commentaries, those who preach and teach (and write papers for professors) should come to conclusions about debatable issues, explaining their reasoning for preferring one interpretation over another. Preachers and teachers should express their conclusions with due humility. For those who hold to the authority of the Bible, it is important for them to distinguish their role as interpreters

---

3. C. H. Spurgeon, *Commenting and Commentaries* (New York: Sheldon, 1876; reprint, London: Banner of Truth, 1969), 1.

of the Bible from the authority of the Bible itself. By that I mean to say it is constructive for preachers and teachers to occasionally say about a debated issue, "I think this is the best solution to this issue but I could be wrong," in order to help their congregation or class see the importance of personally engaging the process of reading and interpreting the Bible for themselves. More than one preacher (and teacher) has been confused on this point, to the detriment of himself and the congregation he claims to serve (authoritarian preachers and teachers seem frequently to serve their own concerns).

6.2 Identifying the Problem

A text may have a variety of debatable issues to consider, so it is important to determine the nature of the question at hand. For example, if the debate revolves around the meaning of a particular word then reference works such as lexicons, concordances, and theological word dictionaries will be essential resources to use in forming a conclusion about the most reasonable interpretation.[4] In a similar way, grammatical or syntactical questions will involve grammars, lexicons (particularly helpful for questions about the function of particles, conjunctions, pronouns, and adverbs), and concordances in dealing with issues to be considered. Specialized dictionaries and encyclopedias will help with questions about social manners, customs, and history (even if only to suggest more detailed works by way of bibliography) that may be essential to understanding and resolving a debated point. Any commentator worth his salt will also use these tools, so commentaries should also be consulted. But a commentary should always be used as a secondary source in the resolution of a debate (in other words, if you are working on a lexical or grammatical issue, do not cite a commentator as the primary support for the conclusion you regard as most probable). This is because few commentators are also specialists in these foundational disciplines.

6.3 Steps in the Process

If you have not already done so (as discussed preliminarily in the preceding paragraph) the first step in solving a debated point is defining the nature of the problem. This can be a challenge for the novice interpreter who is developing skill in NT exegesis since many things in Greek may

---

4. The method used in some articles in the *Theological Dictionary of the New Testament*, ed. Gerhard Kittel and Gerhard Friedrich, trans. Geoffrey W. Bromiley, 10 vols. (Grand Rapids, Mich.: Eerdmans, 1964-76) has been faulted (notably by James Barr, *The Semantics of Biblical Language* [Oxford: Oxford University Press, 1961]), but it remains a gold mine of primary source information and should not be ignored.

pose a problem of one sort or another. Here the commentators can be a great help in identifying debated issues in a particular text. Here too examining a variety of translations may target a point of debate.[5]

Next, sort out the proposed interpretations and attempt to identify the reasons in support of the different points of view. The particulars of the text and its immediate context are more important at this point than arguments based on theological systems or logical extrapolations. If the debated issue concerns the meaning of a word or phrase, lexicons and concordances should be consulted as primary aids in the evaluation process. If the debate involves a matter of grammar and syntax, check to see if the interpretation is supported by treatments in the standard grammars. Older commentators (writing a hundred years ago, for example) are usually strong in matters of grammar and syntax because they often came to NT study with considerable facility in reading and writing Greek and Latin (in contrast to the deficiency of some modern commentators on matters of Greek grammar). But advances in lexicography based on the increased availability of manuscript evidence in the ensuing years may make their discussion of word meaning less sound. That is why consulting a wide variety of sources in this phase of the process is important. Ideally, read until you find the viewpoints becoming repetitive and are satisfied you have exposed the significant variants in the debate as well as the evidence set forth in support of the respective interpretations.

When you have assembled the basic points of view along with supporting arguments, you are ready to ask a few questions of yourself and your sources. First, is all the relevant evidence being considered? (Remember, you are trying to function as an interpreter, not as a theological advocate.) Second, do I understand the arguments both for and against the various interpretive options set out? Third, do the respective arguments follow the evidence to the most probable conclusion? Here it is important to avoid being attracted to a possible interpretation that is agreeable to you for a variety of reasons other than the compelling nature of the data at hand. The aim of this process is to arrive at the most probable interpretation based on the available evidence. Fourth, are the competing views mutually exclusive? While the answer to this is almost always affirmative, it is possible that an occasional issue may not be an "either/or" but a "both/and." Fifth, do I understand clearly the view(s) I am rejecting and why I am doing so? Finally, does the view adopted make the most sense in terms of the immediate context? Correlation with a wider context has a place in the interpretive process but allowance must be made for the

---

5. Volumes that put several translations in columns for easy comparison are particularly helpful, e.g., *The Contemporary Parallel New Testament*, ed. John R. Kohlenberger III (New York: Oxford University Press, 1997).

fact that a writer may qualify in one passage what was stated without qualification in another. To demand that one text control the meaning of another may lead to a misinterpretation of the text under consideration. Let each passage speak. Whatever nuancing may be required or discussion of how this text may qualify another can be addressed later.

6.4 Stating a Conclusion

To a certain extent the time and space available to you to deal with a particular subject will dictate the length and detail of your statement that concludes the validation process. However, at the very least you should take the time to cite specific reasons in support of the view you think most probable (and, if possible, the reasons against any alternatives). Here it should be stressed that names of particular adherents of the view adopted are no substitute for the evidence. It may be interesting to know that certain commentators, for example, also maintain the interpretation you are putting forward (if, on the other hand, no one holds the view you regard as most likely you should probably go through the process again), but names alone do not make a case. Even compilers of lexicons or authors of grammars may draw wrong conclusions (though disagreeing with a specialist should give you pause), so evidence and reasons must be stated (rather than an array of compelling personalities simply noted).

It is usually helpful to prioritize your evidence. To the degree that it is relevant (and in most cases it is crucial) cite specific data from the immediate context. Finally, state the significance of the interpretation adopted for the meaning of the text or passage being studied.

Although you aim to arrive at the most probable conclusion, it remains to be said that every conclusion involves relative degrees of certainty. The Greek New Testament of the United Bible Societies uses letters from A through D in the textual apparatus to indicate the committee's level of certainty regarding a particular text-critical decision, with A being "certain" and D indicating "great difficulty in arriving at a conclusion."[6] Without necessarily adopting this system, it is helpful to communicate a level of certainty about a decision, particularly when an issue is more than a little problematic. Commentators will occasionally acknowledge ambivalence on knotty problems, and preachers and teachers would do well to routinely register reservations about interpretive points also. Some problems are like jigsaw puzzles with missing pieces. If you are missing too many pieces, the finished product may appear more than

6. *The Greek New Testament*, 4th rev. ed., ed. Barbara Aland, Kurt Aland et al. (Stuttgart: Deutsche Bibelgesellschaft/United Bible Societies, 1993), 3*.

a little indistinct. Some interpretive puzzles are like that, and it is okay to say so.

Here a word of warning may be appropriate concerning preachers, teachers, or interpreters who seem remarkably confident about everything they assert. Watch out for people who seem to be absolutely sure about everything they affirm. Their confidence is often in inverse proportion to the actual strength of the case. People like this should come with a warning label: "Often wrong but never in doubt." The fact that they have earned numerous degrees may mean nothing more than that they have made education a career. Do not be bowled over by personalities. Look at the facts. State what you can and cannot know. And do not be self-deluded about the certainty of your own conclusion. If the evidence is weak, admit the limitations of your conclusion. Do not just pay lip service to the virtue of humility, practice a little of it occasionally.

6.5 Do the Hard Work

Good validation is not easy, but it is a key to good exegesis. It attempts to follow the data of the text to the most probable conclusion. Doing research can be tedious. It almost always takes more time than you think it should. It will probably involve following some intriguing lines of thought that turn out to be more or less irrelevant for solving the problem at hand. Count on not being able to incorporate in your discussion all the reading and research you have done. Please! Nobody wants to read or listen to details irrelevant to the issue at hand. Even if you end up with notes that cannot be immediately put to use, your reading and research is not wasted time. You are building a foundation on which good preaching and teaching is built. Persevere. It is work worth doing.

6.6 Two Illustrations

The discussion of the two illustrations that follows is intended to reaffirm the importance of thinking carefully about the context in arriving at a most probable interpretation. If an interpretation is at odds with details in the context, it is more than likely wrong and should be rejected. The first illustration also is intended to be a reminder to guard against concerns such as correlation dictating at the outset the interpretation of a particular passage. The interpreter should always ask the question, What does the passage say? (rather than, What would I like it to say or think it should say?).

6.6.1 Matthew 19:1-12

The question of divorce and remarriage has been a problematic issue from earliest times (as the narrative of this passage shows) and remains a debated subject. This passage is an important part of that debate because it includes a phrase introducing an exception ("except for immorality," v. 9) in contrast to the absolute statements precluding divorce found elsewhere in the Gospel accounts (Mark 10:1-12; Luke 16:18). If correlation (or harmonization) of Matthew's account with Mark and Luke is the constraining factor at the outset of the process in the interpretation of this passage, the focus of discussion will become an attempt to minimize the application of the exception in some way. For example, based on the account of Joseph and Mary described earlier in the Gospel, it could be argued that the words of exception in Matthew refer to the breaking of the marriage contract during the time of betrothal, when divorce could take place (Matt 1:19) even though the marriage had not yet been formalized and consummated. The problem with limiting the exception in this passage to the betrothal period is the fact that the Old Testament texts cited by the Pharisees (Deut 24:1 in Matt 19:7) and Jesus (Gen 2:24 in Matt 19:5) refer to an established marriage. This is clearly the case with the Genesis citation, which refers to the marriage relationship as "one flesh," that is, the establishment of a distinct family unit, something that does not exist until after the marriage ceremony and the consummation of the relationship have taken place. Here the wider context shows that the limitation of the exception to the betrothal period does not fit the subject of the texts being discussed and is therefore a very problematic interpretation.

Another attempt at showing that the exception to divorce given in this passage does not apply to marriage in general focuses on the meaning of the word "immorality" (v. 9). Some have sought to define the word in light of the Old Testament kinship laws prohibiting particular sexual relations (Leviticus 18, 20), maintaining that Matthew's exception applies only to marriages that correspond to these prohibitions.[7] In effect, marriages of this sort would be regarded as null and void because they are a violation of these kinship boundaries and would not constitute a legitimate marriage in the normal sense of the term. In this way Jesus' words are understood to not stand as a qualification to the prohibition of divorce in Mark and Luke.

Commentators on Matthew's Gospel for the most part find this technical narrowing of the meaning of "immorality"[8] unlikely since the debate

7. BDAG, 854.
8. Ibid.

in the passage concerns the meaning of Deut 24:1, where kinship factors are not in question. Here is an illustration where consideration of these two OT texts discussed in the passage clarifies the subject of Jesus' teaching in Matthew's Gospel: it is marriage as normally understood. Understanding this point is but one part of the process of interpreting this exception but enables the question about what the passage means to go forward without having a conclusion dictated by the question of how this meaning may be reconciled with statements elsewhere in the other Gospels. The tension between the Synoptic accounts remains. Mark and Luke show Jesus affirming the ideal: no divorce. Matthew additionally shows Jesus addressing the issue of marital sin as a factor frustrating the attainment of the ideal.

Since this appears to be a debate among Jewish interpreters of the OT, any information from contemporary Jews like Josephus, Philo, the tradition preserved in the Mishnah (a document from around AD 200 containing sayings from first-century rabbis), the Qumran literature, or other evidence (obtained from archaeology, inscriptions or papyrus fragments) is also relevant in helping to clarify the various points of view about the question of divorce and remarriage in Jesus' day. Since sorting through this evidence would be a daunting task for a beginning student, it is helpful to have available secondary sources that assemble the relevant data. Two monographs with information about the subject of marriage and divorce in biblical times are by Craig Keener and David Instone-Brewer.[9] These works illustrate the importance of considering evidence from history and culture in the process of interpretation, evidence that may be too extensive for a commentary to detail. All of this to say, sometimes primary evidence is most easily accessed by means of secondary sources. Be thankful for these secondary works, but use them with discretion since they are engaging in the process of interpretation just as you are.

6.6.2 Ephesians 1:4

The process may also be illustrated by looking at a syntactical issue in Eph 1:4. The question concerns the function of the last two words in the text of this verse: "in love." This prepositional phrase can modify words in three different parts of an unusually long and complex sentence in Greek that begins in v. 3 and finally ends in v. 14. The alternatives in a question like this are often illustrated by a comparison of English translations.

---

9. Craig S. Keener, . . . And Marries Another: Divorce and Remarriage in the Teaching of the New Testament (Peabody, Mass.: Hendrickson, 1991); and David Instone-Brewer, Divorce and Remarriage in the Bible: The Social and Literary Context (Grand Rapids, Mich.: Eerdmans, 2002).

Although the phrase occurs at the end of the Greek text of v. 4, the New Living Translation links it to the verb "chose" at the beginning of the verse with the translation, "God loved us and chose us." The New International Version (retained in the TNIV) illustrates a second option by linking the phrase to the participle that begins v. 5 with the translation, "In love he predestined us."[10] The third alternative is illustrated by the translation in the King James Version (retained in the NKJV). In this version the phrase is linked to the immediately preceding phrase in v. 4, "that we should be holy and without blame before him in love."[11] Volumes that arrange translations in parallel form for easy comparison are helpful tools for a study like this. In that regard it may also be helpful to enumerate the translations that reflect one or the other of these alternatives. Although a decision should never be made on the basis of counting proponents and following the majority, a comparison may suggest the likelihood of a particular option if a majority of translations adopt it.

In this case, for example, the first option appears in only one translation (in our limited sample). That is probably because the verb "he chose" appears at the beginning of the verse in the Greek text and the phrase "in love" is at the end. Phrases are usually placed closer than this to the words they modify, although alterations in word order can be a means of emphasis. God's love is a significant theme in Ephesians so the first option is certainly possible, but the second option makes the same point by associating God's love with the participle "predestined" (which immediately follows the phrase "in love" in the Greek text and so avoids the question of separation of word and modifier).

The second option is preferred by the standard lexicon (BDAG), accompanied by this comment: "the rhythm of the passage suggests the believers as agents for [love] in vs. 4 (cp. vs. 15) but 2:4 favors God; s. the comm."[12] The phrase following the semicolon is the lexicographer's way of acknowledging that more could be said about these alternatives and the reader is advised to consult the commentaries for more discussion. If a grammar had addressed the function of this particular phrase the lexicographer would probably have referred to it, but none apparently does, so he refers you to the commentaries.[13]

---

10. The RSV, NASB, ESV, NCV, and CEV have a similar translation.

11. The NRSV and NET also have this translation.

12. BDAG, 6.

13. Do not be put off by older works. Commentaries written a century or more ago are particularly helpful on matters of Greek grammar and syntax, including works by T. K. Abbott (1897), H. Alford (1871), J. Eadie (1883), C. J. Ellicott (1884), H. A. W. Meyer (1843), J. A. Robinson (1903), and S. D. F. Salmond (1903), to name a few on Ephesians. When your training has included reading and writing classical Greek, as was the case for many of these older commentators, your comments about grammar and syntax are worth considering.

Notice that BDAG discusses the alternatives in light of both the immediate context (the references to believers in v. 4 and v. 15) and the wider context of the letter (the reference to God's love in 2:4). If you followed up this comment by looking at the references to "love" in the letter, both as a noun and as a verb (using a concordance), you would find that by a margin of two to one human love is mentioned more frequently than divine love, suggesting that BDAG's reference to God's love at 2:4 is hardly decisive. Coupled with the fact that nowhere else in the immediate context (vv. 3-14) is a prepositional phrase placed before the word it modifies, one can see why some of the translations adopted the third option.

What makes the third option somewhat problematic is the fact that the phrase "in love" is read as a modifier of two nouns ("holy and blameless"). Prepositional phrases usually function like adverbs rather than like adjectives, making options one and two more likely on this ground. The result is that options one and two are reasonable translations and possibly correct. The fact that BDAG suggested option two probably accounts for the fact that many translations adopted it. However, since human love is a significant theme in this letter, option three might be regarded as slightly more probable. Were we to assign a letter indicating degree of certainty concerning this conclusion, with "A" being most certain and "D" being least, this would probably be a "D."[14]

Although we have affirmed the value of using commentaries in the validation process, we have not examined one in any detail. In conclusion, it may be instructive to do so. We choose a commentary of some detail on Ephesians (authored by Harold Hoehner). Even though it is a relatively recent publication (2002) it will probably have something to say about the issue we have been considering, given its breadth (Ephesians is a letter of six chapters; the commentary is nearly 900 pages). In fact, discussion of the syntax and meaning of the phrase "in love" (1:4) occupies five pages.[15] After surveying the strengths and weaknesses of the three options mentioned previously, Hoehner finds the third option most likely and provides several reasons in support. Significantly, of the five times this phrase occurs in the letter (in addition to 1:4) it follows the words it modifies in four (4:2, 15, 16; 5:2) and refers in each case to human rather than divine love.[16] In sum, Hoehner suggests the meaning of this option is that "the purpose of God's work in believers today is to produce holiness within them and love toward one another."[17]

14. In this case, both human and divine love will be addressed frequently in this letter so this decision does not preclude consideration of the alternative.

15. Harold W. Hoehner, *Ephesians: An Exegetical Commentary* (Grand Rapids, Mich.: Baker, 2002), 180-85.

16. Ibid., 184.

17. Ibid.

6.7 The Value of Validation

Research and writing are often tedious (and always seem to take longer than you think they should) but understanding the options and weighing the evidence are essential parts of any interpretation that has integrity. Going through the process will enable you to state the reasons why you think a particular interpretation is to be preferred over competing options, with reasons based on the text and the context. This in turn should temper your writing, teaching, and preaching with a measure of humility as you realize how difficult some of these decisions are while at the same time giving you a sense of confidence in stating the meaning of the passage, knowing you have considered the relevant options. In truth, coming to a conclusion about the meaning of a passage is usually the easy part compared to putting that message into practice. As in all things related to the life of faith, God help us!

6.8 For Further Reading

Carson, Donald A. *Exegetical Fallacies*. 2nd ed. Grand Rapids, Mich.: Baker, 1996.

Countryman, L. William. *Interpreting the Truth: Changing the Paradigm of Biblical Studies*. Harrisburg, Pa.: Trinity Press International, 2003.

Erickson, Richard J. *A Beginner's Guide to New Testament Exegesis: Taking the Fear out of Critical Method*. Downers Grove, Ill.: InterVarsity Press, 2005.

Stein, Robert. *Interpreting Puzzling Texts in the New Testament*. Grand Rapids, Mich.: Baker Books, 1996.

Trueman, Carl R., et al., eds. *Solid Ground: 25 Years of Evangelical Theology*. Leicester: Apollos, 2000.

Background Studies

Grounding the Text in Reality

7

JOSEPH D. FANTIN

The opportunity to contribute an article on the use of background material in a volume dedicated to Harold Hoehner is a great honor. Not only do I have a great respect for him as a teacher and man of God, but he is also responsible for much of my early interest in this area.[1] My memory of his New Testament Introduction class in the Spring of 1993 remains one of my fondest from seminary. Although the course was demanding and despite persistent rumors to the contrary, I can confirm that his claim that he does *not* quiz from footnotes is accurate.

The exegete has a multitude of tools in his tool belt. Preparation and training are necessary in order for the tools to be used properly. Failure to invest this time may result in damage to the final product.[2] Each tool needs to remain sharp through continual use and refinement. For

---

1. For the content of this article I must acknowledge my debt not only to Harold Hoehner but also to the faculty of the Biblical Studies Division at Dallas Theological Seminary who have taught in the NT Backgrounds Ph.D. seminar as well as my supervisor at the University of Sheffield, Loveday Alexander. Also, I thank my intern John Pulliam for his careful reading of this article and for helpful suggestions.

2. I apologize for this unfortunate label for the results of the exegetical process. However, it continues the metaphor already established.

maximum benefit, each must be used for the purpose for which it was designed. Some problems will demand more use from certain tools than from others. This is the case with background material as a means of illuminating the biblical text.

In order for a student to understand most passages in the NT, every exegetical skill discussed in this book will be necessary. However, each passage will demand certain emphases. For example, some tasks will demand comprehensive word studies and others detailed syntactical analysis. Many projects will demand an in-depth understanding of the historical and cultural context to bring out the intended meaning of the author.

When an author produces a text, there are many aspects of the context shared by both the author and the original readers. These do not need to be made explicit. A problem arises when readers who do not share these same contextual aspects read the text. For example, in John 4, the reader is confronted with a midday encounter between Jesus and a Samaritan woman. The woman is introduced in v. 7: ἔρχεται γυνὴ ἐκ τῆς Σαμαρείας ἀντλῆσαι ὕδωρ. Although not unimportant, syntactically classifying the tense and mood of the verb ἔρχεται, doing a word study on ἀντλῆσαι, determining whether the prepositional phrase ἐκ τῆς Σαμαρείας modifies the noun γυνή or the verb ἔρχεται, and syntactically classifying the prepositional phrase in that relationship will not yield much benefit to understanding the passage beyond what a simple translation makes clear, "A woman from Samaria came to draw water." For this particular passage, understanding certain background information will be much more helpful. Interestingly, John makes explicit one aspect of the social context which is important: οὐ γὰρ συγχρῶνται Ἰουδαῖοι Σαμαρίταις (John 4:9, "for Jews do not associate [share food items] with Samaritans"). Apparently he thought that his readers would be unfamiliar with local ethnic rivalries in early first-century Palestine. However, there are many other contextual issues not made explicit that he assumed would be understood. For example, women normally came to draw water early or late to avoid the heat of the day, women did not usually come alone, and women did not usually speak to unfamiliar men. The woman's actions were in conflict with all of these norms. All of these violations of socially acceptable behavior would suggest that this woman was not a socially accepted individual within her community.[3] This familiar example serves to demonstrate the importance of background material for understanding a particular passage. What about passages with contexts that are not so well known?

The goal of the use of background material is to help the modern reader place himself or herself into the shoes (or sandals) of the original

---

3. See the helpful discussion in Craig S. Keener, *The Gospel of John: A Commentary*, 2 vols. (Peabody, Mass.: Hendrickson, 2003), 1:591-601.

readers (in some sense this is a goal of the entire exegetical process). It is an attempt to recreate as much of the shared environment between the writer and original readers as possible. Modern readers are too distant in both time and culture to do this thoroughly. Nevertheless, we should attempt to grow continually in our understanding of the ancient context in order to become better interpreters of the text.

Given the overall goal of background studies, one can attempt to understand the text and world of the NT in a number of ways. In addition to gaining an overall familiarity with the era, one may wish to focus on certain areas in his or her research. First, relevant practices or customs reflected in the text may be studied. Second, historical matters may be researched to understand the context of a passage. Finally, one may desire to study literature that may have influenced the NT's composition. Other areas will also be evident below.

The purpose of this brief article is fourfold: to help the reader appreciate the value of background studies, to help him or her identify aspects of passages that may benefit from background analysis, to familiarize the student with some of the vast resources available, and to provide a starting point for using these resources to contribute to better understanding of the biblical text. These goals will be accomplished in four primary ways. First, the *raw materials* of background studies (sources) will be described and their uses explained. Second, types of background studies will be distinguished. Third, some methodological principles will be described for the student's use. Finally, a specific example will be presented illustrating how background material can be used to provide further insight into the meaning of the text.

7.1 Preliminary Matters: Understanding the Sources

The study of any historical matter could not take place without sources. For the ancient world, sources are *remains*, literary or otherwise, that were produced in the period under investigation. Additionally, literary productions written about an earlier period serve as sources for later students of this same period. Essentially, anything used to recreate the past is a source. Sources are diverse and must be used appropriately. The responsible use of sources begins with an understanding of the differences between them.

7.1.1 Primary and Secondary Sources

Arthur Marwick, in the revision of his classic work on history, identifies sources from the period of investigation as *primary sources* and those written later as *secondary sources*.[4] Secondary sources range from scholarly monographs and articles to popular books on a subject.[5] For the exegete, the best secondary sources are those that interact responsibly with primary sources. They help the reader understand and appreciate the important primary sources.

Marwick's distinction is helpful but needs refinement for the study of the ancient world.[6] This is clear when one considers ancient sources. Both Augustus's *Res gestae divi Augusti* and Cassius Dio's *Roman History* provide information about Augustus's reign. Both are ancient sources from approximately 2000 years ago. However, Cassius Dio is 200 years removed from the reign of Augustus. He is certainly closer to the events than the modern historian, and he had access to sources not available to us. Nevertheless, he was as distant from the reign of Augustus as we are from the presidency of George Washington. He is a secondary source. However, he is clearly a different type of source than a modern biography of the emperor. Thus, I propose a distinction be made between *ancient* secondary sources and *modern* secondary sources.

The distinction between primary and secondary sources is really dependent upon the subject of inquiry. For example, if one is interested in Paul's thought, his letters are primary sources and the book of Acts is an important secondary source. However, if it is first-century Christianity that is the subject of interest, both Paul's letters and Acts are primary sources.

7.1.2 Jewish and Hellenistic Sources: Two Opposing Influences?

It is a common practice to classify NT background sources as either "Jewish" or "Hellenistic" (or "Greco-Roman").[7] If this distinction referred strictly to religious writings produced by Jews and non-Jews, it would be somewhat helpful. However, it is usually much broader than this and suggests a fundamental division between Jewish and Greco-Roman culture. This division is presented as well defined and often implies little cross-pollination. Most strikingly, it suggests that the Jewish writings were produced in somewhat isolated circumstances. They are Jewish sources over and against Hellenistic ones.

---

4. Arthur Marwick, *The New Nature of History: Knowledge, Evidence, Language* (Chicago: Lyceum, 2001), 26-28, 155-57.

5. Ibid., 27.

6. Marwick is aware of problems with this classification (ibid., 27-28, 157). However, his emphases do not demand he make further distinction.

7. The titles of works often reflect this categorization. See, for example, J. Julius Scott, Jr., *Jewish Backgrounds of the New Testament* (Grand Rapids, Mich.: Baker, 1995); and Arthur Darby Nock, "Early Gentile Christianity and Its Hellenistic Background," in *Essays on the Trinity and the Incarnation,* ed. A. E. J. Rawlinson (London: Longmans, Green, 1933).

This distinction is both false and misleading. Unlike the Hebrew OT, a source of vital importance, most extant sources produced in the period between the Old and New Testaments (and those of the NT period) bear some mark of Hellenism. Hellenism and Judaism are not two concepts of the same class. Hellenism is much broader. Troels Engberg-Pedersen defines Greco-Roman Hellenism as:

> . . . the comprehensive cultural melting pot that one finds in the lands first conquered and held by Alexander the Great and his successors and then by the Romans. This mixture was sufficiently similar across times and places for the culture to count as a single, comprehensive entity. Within the mixture there certainly were differences in different times and places, reflecting the use of different languages. Such differences might also result from different traditions with roots before the Hellenistic period proper.[8]

The "different traditions" mentioned include Judaism as well as other local cultures such as Lydian, Celtic, and the like. In other words, Judaism in this period is a specific culture within Hellenism. It maintains its cultural identity but yet has incorporated Hellenistic elements that help it to relate to other Hellenistic peoples.

This observation is clear when one considers Jewish writings such as the First and Second books of Maccabees. These books strongly argue against Hellenistic powers attempting to impose Hellenism on the Jewish race. However, they include a positive view of (a somewhat Hellenized) Rome with whom Israel makes an alliance (1 Macc 8:1-32), and 2 Maccabees was actually written in Greek![9] Clearly some Hellenistic influence is embedded into the Jewish culture that existed within a Hellenized area of the world. The strong reaction against Hellenism in these books is not against all Hellenism but only against those aspects that explicitly conflict with the deep-seated Jewish beliefs and traditions that cause them to maintain their identity within a Hellenistic world. Additionally, the work quoted most often in the NT is a Greek translation of the OT. This is a product of Hellenistic Jews intended to make the OT understandable to those who have lost touch with the language of their ancestors.

8. Troels Engberg-Pedersen, "Introduction: Paul Beyond the Judaism/Hellenism Divide," in *Paul Beyond the Judaism/Hellenism Divide,* ed. Troels Engberg-Pedersen (Louisville: Westminster/John Knox, 2001), 2. See also the earlier work by Martin Hengel, *Judaism and Hellenism: Studies in Their Encounter in Palestine During the Early Hellenistic Period,* trans. John Bowden (London: SCM, 1974; reprint, London: Xpress Reprints [SCM], 1996).

9. First Maccabees is extant in Greek; however, many believe it was originally written in Hebrew.

Therefore, in this article when specific sources are described as Jewish, Roman, and so forth, it is implied that these are all Hellenistic writings. Nevertheless, this should not minimize important differences between sources.

7.1.3 Types of Sources

Two further distinctions among sources need to be drawn. Sources may broadly be classified by the nature of their content and the type of material on which they are deposited or produced. As to content, literary sources are what most consider when they think of background materials. These are sources that communicate through the use of writing. Most prominent are literary works such as Josephus, the Apocrypha, and so forth. These tend to have a *literary* character. In other words, they are often considered culturally important and are valued as such. These often are the products of and written for the higher, more educated classes in society. However, other literary sources exist such as personal letters, public inscriptions, and so on. In addition to literary sources, there are background materials that do not use explicit language. These include art, architecture, and the nonlinguistic findings of archaeology (unrelated to other noted materials).

In addition to content classification, some background materials are distinguished by type of material. Thus, there are inscriptions (usually carved in stone), papyri (a paper-like substance made from the papyrus plant), and ostraca (pieces of broken pottery used as writing surfaces).

These classification systems can cause confusion. For example, a literary work such as Homer's *Iliad* may be found written on papyri. Here I will suggest a means of classifying these materials that combine both systems and allow for some flexibility. First, the distinctions between *literary* and *nonliterary* and between *linguistic* and *nonlinguistic* will be maintained. Second, background sources often classified by material will represent the general type of nonliterary content the extant material often has written upon it. For example, literature such as Homer or Hesiod, written on papyri will be considered "literature." The label *papyri* is reserved for the common linguistic but nonliterary content such as lists, receipts, personal letters, and the like.[10] There is a gradual spectrum between literary and nonliterary. At one end of the spectrum is full-blown literature and at the other end is completely nonlinguistic material remains. Our description of sources will begin with the most literary.

10. It is acknowledged that the presence of literature in the papyri is significant. In addition to contributing to determining the original text of a work, one may get a general idea of how popular a literary work was based on the amount of examples in the extant papyri.

Before we discuss the sources themselves, a few words about format are in order. In many cases, editions of the sources described below can be found in both print and computer (digital) format. Here I will note only print sources, for three reasons. First, at this time, the primary format of these sources is print. Computer sources are released either after or with the print form. Second, since print is the main format, all can be found in this form. Computer resources are quickly growing but are still far behind the print forms. A work not in digital form at the time of writing this article may be in that form by the time of publication. If a digital form exists for a specific resource, it can be found with the print bibliographic information or an Internet search. Third, not all computers can use every digital format. For these reasons, print editions will be mentioned without comment on whether a digital form exists.

I will conclude with a caution. Because of copyright issues, it is easy to release older material for computer. If one desires to work with the more acceptable editions of sources, be sure to look not only for the source but also the edition. For example, a collection of OT Pseudepigrapha is available digitally; however, the standard edition (i.e., Charlesworth's edition [see below]) is not yet (as of early 2006) in digital form for all platforms. Serious work must use Charlesworth's edition. It is likely that in the future this situation will change, and unique reference works will appear exclusively in digital form.[11]

7.1.4 Description of Sources

Familiarity with the most important sources is an essential first step in using background material. Our purpose here is to give the reader an introduction to various sources usually considered important in background studies. Familiarity with these sources in a general manner will facilitate the use of secondary sources which often refer to them. It is also hoped that students will feel confident to use some of these ancient sources for themselves. Our discussion will necessarily be brief. The student is encouraged to consult the referenced material in the footnotes for further information and especially to become familiar with the ancient sources themselves.[12]

---

11. To some extent this is already happening. For example, Logos Bible Software (www.logos.com) plans to release a morphologically tagged Greek edition of 70 Pseudepigrapha works (81 works are claimed, but they are counting the 12 Patriarchs as twelve works). This edition will include introductions and an English translation (it should be noted that not all of these works were originally written in Greek). It is unlikely that this will replace Charlesworth as an English translation, and its usefulness for research is yet to be determined.

12. In addition to the bibliography in this section, introductions to all of the materials here can be found in the standard dictionary-type sources that I will mention in the methodology section below.

7.1.4.1 LITERATURE

Literature records the history, stories, and anything else that a specific people wishes to preserve. When one contributes a work of literature to a culture he or she is adding to the ever growing context. Works in existence at the time someone sets out to write may influence the new work and/or reflect shared cultural experience with it. This reflects any contribution to society whether written or otherwise. However, because of the nature of literature, its influence has the potential to be far-reaching. It can be transferred easily in either written or oral form. It can even be summarized or changed and still impact the culture. Additionally, one must recognize that literature has biases. In order to maximize the value of literature, this must be considered (see below).

Literature for background studies of the NT can be divided into five functional categories (although some sources can fit more than one category). First, there are historical works that can be used to provide the basic chronology of peoples, events, and the like, of the NT period. Such literature is usually later than the NT.[13] Second, works written before the NT may have been known or used by the NT writers. Third, literature from around the time of the NT can be used to help recreate the worldview of the NT period because of a measure of shared experience. Fourth, later literature not specifically related to the NT can often include traditions reaching back into the first century and can contribute to the reconstruction of the history and the conceptual world (i.e., the ideas and thoughts circulating at the time). Finally, literature written after the NT often reveals how the NT was understood by the earliest readers of this material. Literature classified in groups two and three above may actually have influenced the NT writers.

The NT was produced in the midst of a vibrant literary context. It is saturated with quotations and allusions from many sources. The most important source without question is the **Old Testament**.[14] The NT writers quote and allude to the OT extensively. A strong knowledge of the OT is probably the best preparation for NT interpretation. One striking feature of the NT's use of the OT is that most quotations are clearly taken from a Greek translation of the OT, often called the **Septuagint**[15]

---

13. The best resource for the history of the first centuries BC and AD for the purposes of NT studies is probably Emil Schürer, *The History of the Jewish People in the Age of Jesus Christ (175 B.C.–A.D. 135),* a new English version revised and edited by Geza Vermes and Fergus Millar, vol. 1 (Edinburgh: Clark, 1973).

14. The standard Hebrew OT is *Biblica Hebraica Stuttgartensia,* ed. K. Elliger and W. Rudolf (Stuttgart: Deutsche Bibelgesellschaft, 1984).

15. There are problems with this label. The Septuagint was produced over time and exhibits different types and quality of translation. There probably is no such thing as *the* Septuagint. For our purposes this label is intended only to refer to the general Greek translation used by Jews

(LXX).[16] Little is known about the origins of this translation.[17] It began in the middle of the third century BC with a rather literal translation of the Torah. The remainder was translated over the next 200 years or so. Given the extensive use of the LXX, it is also helpful to be aware of important differences that might exist between the Hebrew and Greek versions of the OT. Good NT commentaries (see below) will usually discuss these issues in detail when they affect the NT. A new translation of the Septuagint is being produced called, A New English Translation of the Septuagint.[18] This promises to be a helpful means of getting acquainted with the Septuagint.

In addition to understanding the OT, it is crucial to understand what intertestamental and especially first-century Jewish communities believed about the OT. This should not be confused with the OT itself. There is a large body of extant literature that helps us understand first-century Jewish views of the content of the OT. In addition, this material also contributes to our knowledge of Jewish society and culture that is not directly tied to biblical texts.

Much of the material that will be described here (and the later Jewish and post-NT Christian-influenced material mentioned below) is briefly described in Craig Evans's Ancient Texts for New Testament Studies: A Guide to the Background Literature.[19] This helpful volume briefly clas-

---

and Christians around the time the NT was composed. For an introduction to the Septuagint, see Jennifer M. Dines, The Septuagint, Understanding the Bible and Its World (London: Clark, 2004); and Karen H. Jobes and Moisés Silva, Invitation to the Septuagint (Grand Rapids, Mich.: Baker, 2000). For the Septuagint's use in NT studies, see R. Tim McLay, The Use of the Septuagint in New Testament Research (Grand Rapids, Mich.: Eerdmans, 2003).

16. The most accessible edition of the Septuagint is that of Alfred Rahlfs, Septuaginta: Id est Vetus Testamentum graece iuxta LXX interpretes (Stuttgart: Deutsche Bibelgesellschaft, 1935; reprint, 2 vols. in 1, 1979). Rahlfs's edition is not a critical text (it is essentially based on a few manuscripts). Serious work in the LXX should consult one of two critical editions: Septuaginta, Vetus Testamentum Graecum Auctoritate Academiae Scientiarum Gottingensis editum (Göttingen: Vandenhoeck & Ruprecht, 1931-); or The Old Testament in Greek According to the Text of Vaticanus, Supplemented from Other Uncial Manuscripts, with Critical Apparatus Containing Variants of the Chief Ancient Authorities for the Text of the Septuagint, ed. Alan E. Brooke, Norman McLean, and Henry St. John Thackeray (Cambridge: Cambridge University Press, 1906-40). Neither edition is complete. The Cambridge edition contains the Pentateuch and the historical books and is now discontinued. The Göttingen edition is in process, with most OT books complete.

17. The Letter of Aristeas is a work from the OT Pseudepigrapha (see below) which presents a fanciful description of the origins of this translation. This source describes the translation as being completed by seventy-two translators in seventy-two days. There is little if any historical reliability to the description provided by this book.

18. Only Albert Pietersma's translation of Psalms is presently available (New York: Oxford University Press, 2000).

19. Peabody, Mass.: Hendrickson, 2005. This is a revised and expanded edition of Evans's Noncanonical Writings and New Testament Interpretation (Peabody, Mass.: Hendrickson, 1992).

sifies and describes the content of most of the literature described here. The exception to this is the Greco-Roman literature. Evans's discussion is minimal and provides only a very brief summary of many of the relevant authors. Nevertheless, this summary is a helpful resource to familiarize oneself with the authors. Additionally, Evans includes abbreviations to the ancient literature, making this a handy reference volume both for using the ancient material and for identifying it in modern secondary sources.[20]

The collections of most value are the OT Apocrypha and OT Pseudepigrapha. The Apocrypha was completed before the first century AD. The Pseudepigrapha books date from the intertestamental period well into the Christian era. In addition to a clear quotation of *1 Enoch* 1:9 in Jude 14 and the source for Jude 9 likely being a lost ending of the *Testament of Moses*[21] (both Pseudepigrapha), the current standard critical edition of the Greek NT (Nestle-Aland 27th ed.) includes over five pages of possible allusions to these works.[22] The **Apocrypha** is well known and is included in many manuscripts of the Septuagint. It is also bound with many modern Catholic and Orthodox Bibles. It is a collection of 13 books.[23] Although all are very important, *Sirach* (also called *Ecclesiasticus*) and the *Psalms of Solomon* are especially helpful. *First Maccabees* is an important source for our knowledge of intertestamental history. The **Pseudepigrapha** is a loose collection of writings including apocalypses, testaments, wisdom literature, and the like, many of which are written under the name of a

---

Also helpful for much of the Jewish literature (excluding most of the later material) is Richard Bauckham, "The Relevance of Extracanonical Jewish Texts to New Testament Study," in *Hearing the New Testament: Strategies for Interpretation*, ed. Joel B. Green (Grand Rapids, Mich.: Eerdmans, 1995), 90-108; and Larry R. Helyer, *Exploring Jewish Literature of the Second Temple Period: A Guide for New Testament Students* (Downers Grove, Ill.: InterVarsity Press, 2002). Finally, a more detailed presentation of much of the information covered by Evans is found in two volumes of the Compendia Rerum Iudaicarum ad Novum Testamentum series: Michael E. Stone, ed., *Jewish Writings of the Second Temple Period: Apocrypha, Pseudepigrapha, Qumran Sectarian Writings, Philo, Josephus*, Compendia Rerum Iudaicarum ad Novum Testamentum 2.2 (Philadelphia: Fortress, 1984); Shmuel Safrai, ed., *The Literature of the Sages: First Part: Oral Tora, Halakha, Mishna, Tosefta, Talmud, External Tractates*, Compendia Rerum Iudaicarum ad Novum Testamentum 2.3.1 (Philadelphia: Fortress, 1987).

20. More comprehensive lists of abbreviations are included with collections themselves, good commentaries, and many dictionary-type sources. Many such works are referenced below.

21. The *Testament of Moses* is also called the *Assumption of Moses*.

22. *Novum Testamentum Graece*, ed. Barbara Aland, Kurt Aland, Johannes Karavidopoulos, Carlo M. Martini, and Bruce M. Metzger, 27th rev. ed. (Stuttgart: Deutsche Bibelgesellschaft, 1993), 800-806.

23. The *Prayer of Manasseh* is often classified as Apocrypha; however, it is best included with the Pseudepigrapha (James H. Charlesworth, "Apocrypha," *ABD*, 1:293). The number of Apocrypha books may vary slightly among traditions. For an introduction to the Apocrypha, see Daniel J. Harrington, *Invitation to the Apocrypha* (Grand Rapids, Mich.: Eerdmans, 1999); and David A. deSilva, *Introducing the Apocrypha: Message, Context, and Significance* (Grand Rapids, Mich.: Baker, 2002).

famous OT figure. There is no specific "pseudepigrapha canon" as such; rather, it is roughly defined by James H. Charlesworth's (ed.) two-volume collection entitled, *Old Testament Pseudepigrapha*.[24] This collection lists 85 works and includes 65. Most important is *1 Enoch,* which appears to have been an important book during the NT period.

The **Dead Sea Scrolls** provide an interesting contribution to NT studies. Unlike the Apocrypha, Pseudepigrapha, and most other groups of sources mentioned here, this is a collection of writings classified by the location in which they were discovered. Most were found at Qumran, which is near the Dead Sea in modern Israel. This material is probably a portion of a library from a strict religious sect called the Essenes. This group apparently was stricter than the Pharisees and seemed to reject the main religious organizations and practices of the time (including the temple). The community abandoned Qumran during the Jewish war with Rome (AD 66-73). Their library was hidden until 1947, when it was discovered by a young Bedouin. The books recovered include portions of the OT (including some Septuagint texts), Apocrypha, Pseudepigrapha, otherwise unknown religious texts, and sectarian texts possibly providing information about the community. Although some claims have been made, there do not appear to be any Christian texts in the collection. It is uncertain whether all the texts represent the beliefs of the community. The value of the Dead Sea Scrolls for Old and New Testament studies is immense. In most cases they provide some of the earliest examples available of this material. They also provide a glimpse into a first-century Jewish community that was in existence at the time Christianity was emerging. Many good English translations are available.[25] One especially helpful for exegesis students is Martínez and Tigchelaar's *The Dead Sea Scrolls Study Edition.*[26] This is a diglot, which includes original language and English translations side by side on facing pages. This edition and most other English translations available do not include the biblical texts.[27]

24. Garden City, N.Y.: Doubleday, 1983-85. This is the present authoritative English translation of this collection and contains a helpful introduction to the corpus and to the individual books.

25. For example, *The Complete Dead Sea Scrolls in English,* rev. ed., trans. and ed. Geza Vermes (London: Penguin, 2004). Older editions of this work can be found used for a few dollars. The word "complete" in these titles is exaggerated; nevertheless, these collections include the most important nonbiblical texts.

26. *The Dead Sea Scrolls Study Edition,* 2nd ed., ed. Florentino García Martínez and Eibert J. C. Tigchelaar, 2 vols. (Leiden: Brill, 2000). Serious work in the scrolls must consult the series *Discoveries in the Judaean Desert* (Oxford: Oxford University Press, 1955-).

27. For an introduction to the Dead Sea Scrolls, see James C. VanderKam and Peter Flint, *The Meaning of the Dead Sea Scrolls: Their Significance for Understanding the Bible, Judaism, Jesus, and Christianity* (San Francisco: HarperSanFrancisco, 2002); Frank Moore Cross, *Ancient Library at Qumran,* 3rd ed. (Sheffield: Sheffield Academic Press, 1995); James C. VanderKam,

Roughly contemporary with the writing of the NT are the two Jewish authors, Philo and Josephus. Born in the late first century BC, **Philo** lived in Alexandria, Egypt, until the middle of the first century of the Christian era (d. approx. AD 50). He had a prolific writing career, which ended just prior to the composition of the first NT documents. Although his writings are highly allegorical and difficult to understand, he represents a Diaspora Jewish voice from the dawn of the ministry of the church. An affordable translation is available by C. D. Yonge[28] but one may wish to consult the twelve-volume set in the Loeb Classical Library series translated by F. H. Colson, G. H. Whitaker, and Ralph Marcus. Ten of the twelve volumes contain both the Greek and the English text in diglot form.[29] **Josephus** was a Palestinian Jew who was a leader in the Jewish War against Rome (AD 66-73). After his capture he became attached to the Flavian family, which soon became the imperial family (Vespasian, Titus, and Domitian ruled Rome from AD 69-96). He wrote late into the first century AD (d. approx. AD 100). His most important contribution is historical. He wrote an account of the unsuccessful Jewish revolt against Rome (*Jewish War*) and most importantly a history of the Jewish people (*Antiquities of the Jews*). The student needs to be aware that there are two numbering systems for Josephus (see the citations below). It is most helpful when both are used. Not only is he a crucial source for Jewish intertestamental and first-century history, but his writing includes other significant information (e.g., his account of the death of Caligula is our best source on this subject [*Antiquities* 19.1-273 = 19.1.1-4.6]). Also of interest to Bible students is his record of the deaths of John the Baptist (*Antiquities* 18.116-119 = 18.5.2; cf. Mark 6:17-28 and parallels), James (*Antiquities* 20.200-203 = 20.9.1), and Herod Agrippa I (*Antiquities* 19.343-351 = 19.8.2; cf. Acts 12:20-23), and his mention of Jesus (*Antiquities* 18.63-64 = 18.3.3).[30] An eighteenth-century translation by William Whiston, slightly corrected and updated by Paul Maier, is affordable and includes additional helps.[31] E. J. Brill is in the process of publishing a

---

The Dead Sea Scrolls Today (Grand Rapids, Mich.: Eerdmans, 1994). For quick access to biblical texts, see Martin G. Abegg, Jr., Peter Flint, and Eugene Ulrich, eds. and trans., *The Dead Sea Scroll Bible: The Oldest Known Bible Translated for the First Time into English* (San Francisco: HarperSanFrancisco, 1999).

28. *The Works of Philo: Complete and Unabridged,* new updated ed., trans. C. D. Yonge (Peabody, Mass.: Hendrickson, 1993).

29. Harvard University Press, 1929-62. For a helpful introduction to Philo, see Kenneth Schenck, *A Brief Guide to Philo* (Louisville: Westminster/John Knox, 2005).

30. For a helpful discussion of this and the James passage, see the excursus by Paul Winter in Schürer, *History of the Jewish People,* 428-41.

31. *The New Complete Works of Josephus,* rev. and expanded ed., trans. William Whiston, updated Paul Maier (Grand Rapids, Mich.: Kregel, 1999). The edition uses both numbering systems. Other editions of Whiston's translation are often found used and inexpensive.

new translation. It is packed with notes and is likely to become the most important English translation of Josephus.[32] Unfortunately, its price will make this work inaccessible to anyone without access to a specialized library. Additionally, as with Philo, the Greek-English diglot edition in the Loeb Classical Library will be helpful to the student who wishes to use his or her Greek.[33] It is interesting to note the similarities between these two men and the NT authors. Philo and Paul were both Diaspora Jews; Josephus and most of the other known NT authors were Palestinian Jews. All wrote in Greek.

In addition to intertestamental and first-century Jewish works which illuminate first-century Judaism and its beliefs, other important categories of literature exist. The large body of **Greco-Roman literature** provides a wealth of information about first-century history, culture, and religion.[34] This material is probably most relevant to Paul, who ministered primarily in areas that would have been more familiar with this information than with the Jewish sources already noted. The Homeric writings (the *Iliad* and *Odyssey*) probably circulated orally for some time before being written down in the second half of the eighth century BC. Although a poor comparison, Homer was probably the closest thing to what we call a Bible for the vast majority of people living in the Roman empire. Additionally, the histories of the classical Greek civilizations (especially Herodotus and Thucydides) were very well known. A number of Greek and Latin historians and biographers (e.g., Tacitus [d. after AD 118], Plutarch [d. after 120]), Suetonius [d. approx. 130], Cassius Dio [d. after 229]) provide information about first-century events and people. These works could not have been read by the writers of the NT; however, they included information that would have been widely known during the period and often form the backbone of our understanding of these times. Additionally, there are many extant works from our approximate period that in addition to providing historical detail would also give us a glimpse into the thought world of the first century (e.g., Virgil [first century BC], Cicero [first century

---

32. *Flavius Josephus: Translation and Commentary*, ed. Steve Mason (Leiden: Brill, 1999-). The set is projected to be ten volumes. This edition is inconsistent in its use of the numbering systems. For example, *Life* uses both but *Antiquities* uses only the first.

33. *Josephus*, trans. Henry St. John Thackeray, Ralph Marcus, Allen Wikgren, and Louis H. Feldman, Loeb Classical Library (Cambridge, Mass.: Harvard University Press, 1926-65). Originally in nine volumes, this set has appeared in eleven and now thirteen volumes without a change in the text. This edition uses both numbering systems.

34. For a helpful introduction to this literature see Loveday C. A. Alexander, "The Relevance of Greco-Roman Literature to New Testament Study," in Green, ed., *Hearing the New Testament*, 109-26. An essential resource for the study of the Greco-Roman world with bibliography is Simon Hornblower and Antony J. S. Spawforth, eds., *The Oxford Classical Dictionary*, 3rd ed. (Oxford: Oxford University Press, 1996).

BC], Seneca [first century AD], Velleius Paterculus [first century AD], and the like). It is unlikely that Paul had read people such as Cicero; however, it seems probable that many of the ideas expressed by these authors would have been familiar to Paul.[35] These authors are easily accessible in the Loeb Classical Library series (English-Greek or Latin diglots)[36] and often in inexpensive series such as the Penguin Classics and/or Oxford World's Classics.[37]

It is necessary to mention one further type of literature in this section. The ancient Greek (romantic) novel cannot really be classified with the more literary works noted above. Its purpose and readership are not certain. It may have been produced by and for the upper classes, people who had the education and time to read them. However, it is also possible that these were a cultural equivalent to Harlequin Romances today. Our earliest extant Greek novel, Chariton's *Callirhoe,* is most likely dated in the middle of the first century AD.[38] This date places it into the same general range as the NT. It is possible that it reflects some popular trends of this time.

There are a number of Jewish sources that post-date the NT. These are often considered *Rabbinic* works because it was the early (post-NT) Rabbis who were responsible for their writing, collection, and preservation.[39] First, the **Targums** are translations or more often paraphrases of the OT in Aramaic.[40] The need for these arose because Jews did not understand Hebrew. These were initially oral, and some form of these

35. F. Gerald Downing, "A bas les aristos: The Relevance of Higher Literature for the Understanding of the Earliest Christian Writing," *NovT* 30 (1988): 212-30.

36. Cambridge, Mass.: Harvard University Press. Loeb volumes do not generally contain critical Greek or Latin texts. For the vast majority of purposes, the Loeb series is sufficient. However, if a specialized study of the Greek or Latin is necessary, one should consult either the Teubner series (Leipzig: Teubner) or the Oxford Classical Texts (Oxford: Oxford University Press). These are critical editions and contain only the Greek or Latin. Both series are in process. As a general principle, the most recent volume of a specific work is the edition of choice. However, both are valuable. Additionally, the Budé series (Paris: Les belles lettres), a French-Greek or Latin diglot, is very helpful.

37. London: Penguin Books, and Oxford: Oxford University Press.

38. A recent translation with a Greek text of this novel is Chariton, *Callirhoe,* trans. and ed. G. P. Goold, Loeb Classical Library (Cambridge, Mass.: Harvard University Press, 1995). A collection of these novels can be found in B. P. Reardon, ed., *Collected Ancient Greek Novels* (Berkeley: University of California Press, 1989). There were also Latin novels. Additionally, *Joseph and Aseneth* from the OT Pseudepigrapha may be classified as a novel, as well as some of the NT Apocryphal works such as *The Acts of Paul and Thecla* (see below concerning the NT Apocrypha).

39. For an introduction to this body of literature (except for the Targums), see Jacob Neusner, *Rabbinic Literature: An Essential Guide* (Nashville: Abingdon, 2005). Neusner is the most important author presently working in this area.

40. The Targums are not usually classified as Rabbinics. They are included here because this is the body of literature among those included in this article that they most closely resemble.

were probably familiar to Jesus and the disciples in the synagogues of Palestine. They began to be written down much later (beginning in the second century) and when used with care (because of the late date) may shed light on first-century understanding of the OT.[41] Additionally, the **Mishnah** is a collection of oral tradition, which is considered the *oral law*. The legend suggests that this was given to Moses on Sinai with the written Law. It generally provides a commentary on the Torah and other issues tied to Jewish practice. It was written down around AD 200 and because of its oral history contains some first-century information.[42] For example, if the capital trial information provided by the Mishnah can be assumed to describe first-century practices, Jesus' trial before the Sanhedrin was riddled with violations. Capital cases were to be tried during the day, a verdict of conviction could not be reached until the following day, and (because guilty verdicts needed a second day) trials could not be held the eve of a Festival day or Sabbath (*m. Sanh.* 4.1).[43] There are two **Talmuds**, Palestinian and Babylonian, the latter being most important. These are much later (completed around AD 400 and AD 600 respectively) and generally provide commentary on the Mishnah.[44] Finally, the **Midrash** (begun to be written down approx. AD 300) is another later collection of writings often providing commentary on (or in some sense rewriting) the OT.[45] These sources contain traditions

41. For an introduction to Targums, see Martin McNamara, *Palestinian Judaism and the New Testament*, Good News Studies 4 (Wilmington, Del.: Glazier, 1983), 205-52. For an English translation see the multivolume series, *The Aramaic Bible*, ed. Martin McNamara et al. (Collegeville, Minn.: Liturgical, 1987-).

42. Jacob Neusner has translated a one-volume English edition, *The Mishnah: A New Translation* (New Haven, Conn.: Yale University Press, 1988). An English-Hebrew diglot edition is *Mishnayoth: Pointed Hebrew Text, English Translation, Introductions, Notes, Supplement, Appendix, Indexes, Addenda, Corrigenda*, 2nd ed. revised, corrected, and enlarged, trans. Philip Blackman, 7 vols. (New York: Judaica, 1963-64).

A related work worth mentioning is the Tosefta (completed approx. AD 300). This is a supplement to the Mishnah (although it is much longer than the Mishnah itself). For an English translation, see *The Tosefta: Translation from the Hebrew, with a New Introduction*, trans. Jacob Neusner, 2 vols. (Peabody, Mass.: Hendrickson, 2002).

43. I was first made aware of this connection by Harold Hoehner in a Ph.D. seminar in NT backgrounds (Fall 1995).

44. For a translation of the Palestinian Talmud, see *Talmud of the Land of Israel: A Preliminary Translation and Explanation*, trans. Jacob Neusner, 35 vols. (Chicago: University of Chicago Press, 1984-93). For the Babylonian Talmud, see *The Babylonian Talmud*, ed. I. Epstein, 18 vols. (London: Soncino, 1948); and/or *The Babylonian Talmud: A Translation and Commentary*, trans. Jacob Neusner, 22 vols. (n.p.: University of South Florida, 1994-99 [under a slightly different name in 36 vols.]; reprint with new introductions, Peabody, Mass.: Hendrickson, 2005).

45. For an important rabbinic collection of Midrash, see *Midrash Rabbah: Translated into English with Notes, Glossary and Indices*, 3rd ed., ed. H. Freedman and M. Simon, 10 vols. (London: Soncino, 1983).

from the first century and earlier. In these cases, the importance for NT studies is immense. Identifying these specific traditions is not always easy. Fortunately, a new series by David Instone-Brewer is attempting to identify traditions that predate AD 70.[46]

A final group of helpful literature is post-NT and generally Christian. Some works of the already mentioned Pseudepigrapha betray at least some Christian influences (e.g., *Sibylline Oracles*). However, here we are concerned with complete and intentional Christian writings. First and most important is the collection of **Apostolic Fathers**.[47] Although one book may have been written before the last NT book (i.e., the *Didache*, often dated as early as the second half of the first century AD), these were written by Christians in the generation or so after the Apostolic Age. They are generally considered orthodox by today's standards, and books such as *1 Clement* seemed to have enjoyed great popularity. Among other important contributions, this collection helps the Bible student to understand how the NT documents were understood by the generations immediately following the apostles. Clement was a Bishop of Rome at the close of the first century and his letter (*1 Clement*) was written to the church at Corinth. Polycarp, who wrote to the Philippians, was a disciple of the apostle John. Two easily accessible editions of this collection are available. First, Bart Ehrman has provided a fresh translation for the Loeb series,[48] and Michael Holmes has revised the classic Lightfoot collection.[49] Both of these are Greek-English diglot editions.

Second, there exists a collection of non-canonical writings called the **New Testament Apocrypha**. These are pseudepigraphal gospels, apocalypses, and the like, which were written after the NT period and provide varying degrees of help for understanding how the NT was used in the early church. They have a dubious history within the early church and often include fanciful stories about Jesus and the apostles. Thus, their

46. The first of six volumes appeared in 2004: *Traditions of the Rabbis from the Era of the New Testament, Volume 1: Prayer and Agriculture* (Grand Rapids, Mich.: Eerdmans, 2004).

47. In addition to the introductions to the collections cited below, for an introduction to this literature see Clayton N. Jefford, *The Apostolic Fathers: An Essential Guide* (Nashville: Abingdon, 2005).

48. *Apostolic Fathers*, trans. and ed. Bart D. Ehrman, 2 vols., Loeb Classical Library (Cambridge, Mass.: Harvard University Press, 2003). This replaces an old edition by Kirsopp Lake. Ehrman's edition includes additional texts, and his translation is up-to-date.

49. *The Apostolic Fathers: Greek Texts and English Translations*, updated ed., trans. and ed. Michael W. Holmes (Grand Rapids, Mich.: Baker, 1999). A new edition of Holmes's English-only volume is forthcoming: *The Apostolic Fathers in English*, 3rd ed. (Grand Rapids, Mich.: Baker, forthcoming, late 2006).

helpfulness for understanding the NT is minimal compared to much of the literature mentioned above.[50]

Finally, **Gnostic Literature** is a collection of material from an early heterodox or heretical sect of Christians. This group apparently flourished in the second and third centuries but was at odds with what is now considered orthodox teaching. There is some overlap here with the NT Apocrypha (e.g., the *Gospel of Thomas* is in both). Much of our extant Gnostic literature was found at Nag Hammadi in Egypt in 1945. Like the NT Apocrypha, this collection does little to illuminate the NT; however, due to the contemporary interest in the nature and composition of the NT canon and the history of the earliest Christianity, it is crucial to be aware of this material, especially the *Gospel of Thomas*.[51] Although Gnostic literature and the NT Apocrypha may be less helpful for NT interpretation, they provide important information for the study of early church history.

7.1.4.2 NONLITERARY SOURCES

There are a number of helpful sources that cannot be classified as literature. Some are essentially linguistic (inscriptions, papyrus, and ostraca), others nonlinguistic (art, architecture, findings of archaeology), and one combines both linguistic and nonlinguistic elements (coins). Although the linguistically oriented sources may contain literature, they served other purposes as well. It is these (nonliterature type) purposes that we will focus on here.

Grouping these sources into a single section is not intended to imply that they are less valuable than literary sources. Many of these are fields of study in their own right. However, they are much less accessible to the student of the Bible. The purpose here will be to give a general overview of the areas and then a means to accessing them.

Inscriptions are anything from a word to a long discourse carved into stone. These were produced to endure time and thus usually were made by authorities or wealthy groups or individuals. Governments used inscriptions to communicate important matters of policy. Authorities as well as others often used inscriptions to inform the public of their great deeds or kindnesses. An advantage of using inscriptions in NT studies is that they

---

50. For introductions and an English translation, see *New Testament Apocrypha,* rev. ed., ed. Wilhelm Schneemelcher and R. McL. Wilson, 2 vols. (Louisville: Westminster/John Knox, 1991-92). For a popular handling of this material, see Darrell L. Bock, *The Missing Gospels: Unearthing the Truth Behind Alternative Christianities* (Nashville: Nelson, 2006).

51. For an introduction to this literature and an English collection, see *The Gnostic Scriptures: A New Translation with Annotations and Introductions,* trans. Bentley Layton (New York: Doubleday, 1987). For a helpful introduction to Gnosticism and the concept of gnosis, see Kurt Rudolph, *Gnosis: The Nature and History of Gnosticism,* trans. P. W. Coxon, K. H. Kuhn, and R. McL. Wilson (Edinburgh: Clark, 1983).

are usually fairly easy to date, and their prominence and longevity make it likely that they were seen by many for years after they were established. Thus, an inscription standing in Ephesus during the time of Paul's visits would certainly have been seen by him and the church there. Nevertheless, they must be used with caution. We can be certain of their presence in an area but we do not know what people thought of them. Many were statements from the ruling authorities that would have contained a significant bias. In this way they are similar to literature. However, their bias may be more easily discernible, making them a helpful tool in our reconstruction of the context (see below).

Although quite different, **papyri** and **ostraca** often contain very informal material such as receipts, letters, lists, and the like. This material provides insight into the common life of the biblical period. A drawback with papyri is that, due to climatic issues, most have been found in or around Egypt. This seems to restrict their informative value to this geographical area only. However, given the relative ease of travel, what has been found in Egypt did not necessarily originate there. It is likely to be more representative of the Roman world than one might suspect.[52]

Coins were an important part of the ancient world. With the absence of modern mass media, coins often served as a means of getting the ruling power's message to a large audience. Coins often included a picture of the ruler (or someone close to him) and a brief message about either the regime or its deeds. For example, after the death of an emperor deemed worthy of deification, it was common for the new ruler (if possible) to include his connection to his divine predecessor (e.g., TI DIVI F AVGVSTVS, "Tiberius son of god Augustus," *RIC* Tib 5).[53] When one considers the prevalence of such a message in the Roman world, one can only imagine the impact the claim that Jesus is the "Son of God" would have had on the Roman people.

Finally, physical remains such as **art**, **architecture**, and the findings from **archaeology** all help to recreate the picture of the ancient world in ways linguistic sources cannot. For example, the conclusion that a prominent building in an important location in Corinth was a temple dedicated to imperial worship during the first century will have implications for the prominence of the emperor and his regime in Corinth at that time.[54] We

52. See Eldon Jay Epp, "The Significance of the Papyri for Determining the Nature of the New Testament Text in the Second Century: A Dynamic View of Textual Transmission," in *Studies in the Theory and Method of New Testament Textual Criticism*, ed. Eldon Jay Epp and Gordon D. Fee, Studies and Documents 45 (Grand Rapids, Mich.: Eerdmans, 1993), 274-97.

53. See note 56 for bibliographic information on *RIC*.

54. C. K. Williams, "A Re-Evaluation of Temple E and the West End of the Forum of Corinth," in *The Greek Renaissance in the Roman Empire: Papers from the Tenth British Museum Classical Colloquium*, ed. S. Walker and A. Cameron (London: University of London Institute for Classical Studies, 1989), 162.

can be confident that the readers of Paul's Corinthian correspondence were well acquainted with this temple.

Unfortunately, with the exception of the use of papyri for text criticism, lexicon, and grammar, this material has not been used extensively in NT research.[55] This is partially due to limited accessibility, either due to language, cost, or the confusion over where to find a specific source.[56] Most will need to be satisfied with secondary access to these sources, whether through the general reference works that will be introduced below or through good commentaries. In addition, sources for lexical terms such as theological dictionaries[57] and lexicons[58] often include references to these materials. Furthermore, a slow moving series called *New Documents*

55. The papyri's usefulness in these areas in some ways falls within the sphere of background studies. However, they are better treated in other areas of the exegetical process.

56. For a brief introduction to this material for NT studies see Evans, *Ancient Texts,* 306-28. The most authoritative collections of inscriptions have no English translation: for Greek: *Inscriptiones Graecae (IG),* 15 vols. (Berlin: de Gruyter, 1903-); however, most of this series covers only Greece. The secondary collections listed below must be consulted for much of the biblical world. For Latin: *Corpus Inscriptionum Latinarum (CIL),* ed. Th. Mommsen et al., 17 vols. (Berlin: de Gruyter, 1863-). The important secondary collections also include no English translation: *Inscriptiones Graecae ad res Romanas pertinentes,* ed. R. Cagnat, vols. 1, 3, 4 (Paris, 1906-27; reprint, Chicago: Ares, 1975); *Orientis Graeci Inscriptiones Selectae,* ed. W. Dittenberger, 2 vols. (Leipzig, 1905; reprint, Chicago: Ares, 2001); *Sylloge Inscriptionum Graecarum,* 3rd ed., ed. W. Dittenberger, 4 vols. (Leipzig, 1915; reprint, Chicago: Ares, 1999); *Inscriptiones Latinae Selectae,* ed. H. Dessau, 3 vols. in 5 (Berlin, 1892-1916; reprint, Chicago: Ares, 1979). These are abbreviated *IGRR* (or *IGR*), *OGIS, SIG³,* and *ILS* respectively. There exist a number of city-specific collections of interest such as Peter Pilhofer, *Philippi: Volume 2: Katalog der Inschriften von Philippi,* WUNT 119 (Tübingen: Mohr Siebeck, 2000). However, these are often difficult to find and use. An essential resource for locating inscriptions by geographic region and topic is François Bérard et al., *Guide de l'epigraphiste: Bibliographie choisie des épigraphies antiques et médiévales,* 3rd ed. (Paris: Éditions Rue d'Ulm, 2000). A major collection of papyri is the ongoing series of Oxyrhynchus papyri (P.Oxy.) in the Egypt Exploration Society's Graeco-Roman Memoirs series: *The Oxyrhynchus Papyri,* ed. B. P. Grenfell et al. (London: Egypt Exploration Society, 1898-). These are generally accessible with English translations; however, there are many other papyri sources that are not easily available. One helpful source of ostraca is the collection edited by Ulrich Wilcken, *Griechische Ostraka aus Aegypten und Nubien,* 2 vols. (Leipzig, 1899; reprint, New York: Arno, 1979). This is one of many and contains Greek with supporting material in German. For coins, the present standard is *The Roman Imperial Coinage (RIC),* ed. H. Mattingly et al., 10 vols. (London: Spink, 1923-). For our purposes, volume 1 is most important, covering Augustus through Vitellius (31 BC–AD 69). This volume was revised in 1984. For the nonliterary material, one should consult various reports and area-specific books on the subject.

57. *Theological Dictionary of the New Testament,* ed. Gerhard Kittel and Gerhard Friedrich, trans. Geoffrey W. Bromiley, 10 vols. (Grand Rapids, Mich.: Eerdmans, 1964-76).

58. See, for example, Walter Bauer, *A Greek-English Lexicon of the New Testament and Other Early Christian Literature,* rev. and ed. Frederick Danker, 3rd ed. (Chicago: University of Chicago Press, 2000); and Henry George Liddell and Robert Scott, *A Greek-English Lexicon,* rev. and aug. Henry Stuart Jones and Roderick McKenzie (Oxford: Clarendon, 1940; revised supplement, 1996), abbreviated BDAG and LJS respectively.

Illustrating Early Christianity, edited originally by G. H. R. Horsley and continued by S. L. Llewelyn, selectively surveys recent inscription and papyri discoveries that impact biblical studies.[59]

7.1.5 Responsible Use of Sources

The presence of sources does not guarantee that we will get a more accurate picture of the NT. Samuel Sandmel warned years ago of the danger of simply finding parallels and assuming that they contribute to biblical studies.[60] Using sources effectively is both a science and an art. One must consider the source as well as its use for a particular purpose. Not all sources are of equal value for every task. Bible students will disagree on the importance of various sources. Nevertheless, there are a few considerations that will lead to responsible use of the sources.

7.1.5.1 PERSPECTIVE: WORKING WITH BIAS

Everyone has a specific perspective on an issue. Creators of sources are no different. All literature reflects personal bias that may result in a limited perspective or inaccuracy, whether intentional or not. Therefore, the critical use of all sources is required. One must always consider who is writing and why. Ideally, a number of diverse sources on a specific issue is preferred. However, this is a luxury rarely afforded the ancient historian or student of the Bible. Nevertheless, this should not discourage the exegete. For our task, whether an event happened exactly as a source has portrayed it is less important than to recognize that the source is revealing what some had thought about the event.[61] If the goal is to reconstruct an ancient event, we must critically consider all evidence and draw appropriate conclusions. However, if the goal is to understand the first-century world, we can take the evidence and attempt to reconstruct the context without being overly concerned whether every detail lines up with our notion of truth.

The exegete must consider why and for what purpose something was written. Most ancient literature was written by socially high-class men. Even the most honest writer is reflecting his own experience and views on the subject. The lack of diverse backgrounds for extant works means that most voices go unheard. We have little material from slaves, women, or other groups of people in the ancient world. The only information on

---

59. Volumes 1-7: Sydney: Macquarie University, 1981-94. The series has been continued under the sole editorship of Llewelyn. Eerdmans began publishing the series in 1997 (vol. 8).

60. "Parallelomania," *JBL* 81 (1962): 1-13. See also, T. L. Donaldson, "Parallels: Use, Misuse and Limitations," *Evangelical Quarterly* 55 (1983): 193-210.

61. It may be worth clarifying that this paragraph is referring to the nonbiblical sources used for understanding the NT.

these subjects comes from elite males. This fact does not make the material useless; rather, it demands that the exegete use the material carefully. Acknowledging bias and attempting to compensate for this (partially by simply noting that certain voices are absent) will result in a responsible use of these sources. Inscriptions and coins often expressed important official policy. We cannot say how people actually responded to these. However, we do know that they communicated something very important for those who created them (few would write something in stone that they deemed unimportant!) and that many people were exposed to them. They were part of their world. The exegete can use this information to help consider how the early Christians would have responded to messages in the NT based on their experiences with inscriptions and coins. A letter on a piece of papyrus may be unique to the individual who wrote it. It may express his concerns and interests. We cannot be certain whether others felt the same way. Nevertheless, it is a piece of evidence from the ancient world of how *one* person thought. This person was real and was there. Only through such evidence can we get back to the ancient world. Depending on the contents, a papyrus letter may represent the views of more than one individual. Conclusions must be made with care, but some conclusions can be made.

7.1.5.2 TIME: CONSIDERING THE DATE OF A SOURCE

One cannot underestimate the importance of considering the time a specific source was created. In the section above concerning literature (7.1.4.1), five types were described. Here we are considering all sources and not merely literature. Most important are sources that were written before the NT. These works were available and may have influenced the writers of the NT. Second, generally contemporaneous works may reflect a shared experience with NT writers. These also may have influenced the NT. However, this is more difficult to prove than the previous category. Although it is unlikely that NT authors read works by men such as Seneca or even Philo, their writings reflect ideas and concepts that were in circulation at the time of NT composition.[62] Additionally, they can give us a clearer picture of NT life. Third, works clearly later than the NT can still reflect a shared experience or even contain traditions dating back to before or during the NT era. However, any claims of earlier tradition which may have influenced the NT must be made only after careful evaluation of the evidence for this conclusion. Additionally, these works, especially later Christian sources, can often reflect an early interpretation. Although not

---

62. Cf. Downing, "A bas les aristos," 212-30. He is primarily arguing that upper-class discourse is relevant. However, this applies to all literature written before and during NT times.

necessarily the best interpretation, these writings reveal an understanding much closer in time to the original than we are today.

A related distinction concerning historical works is also important. Literature that potentially may have influenced the NT must be distinguished from works describing the history of the period. By its very nature, the subject of most historical works is the past. One must recognize that the events described may include as much insight about the period of writing as they do about the subject of the composition.

7.1.5.3 Relevance: Value of Specific Sources

It may seem obvious, but one must always consider how a specific source can be used for a specific task. Some sources are simply more relevant to certain tasks than others. For example, sources with more Greco-Roman influence will be more helpful in understanding the Pauline letters than in understanding the Gospels. Although appropriate for the entire NT, sources of Jewish origin will be more helpful for Gospel work.

7.2 Background Material in Biblical Studies

Essentially, the exegete uses background materials to place himself or herself as close to the experience of the first-century communities as possible. As noted, this lofty goal is impossible to achieve completely. Nevertheless, the more one knows about the period, the closer one is to understanding the text as it would have been written and originally read. There is no easy way to accomplish this. Rather, it is a continual process of learning and refining one's understanding. The process can be divided into three parts. First, gathering potential historical and cultural information. Second, determining its relevance for interpretation. Third, using it in the exegetical process.

As these steps are described, we will apply our findings to a particular issue in NT interpretation. Specifically, what is the significance of *adoption* in Eph 1:5?[63] Thus, we will explore whether an understanding of first-century adoption can add to our interpretation of Ephesians 1:5. The text reads: προορίσας ἡμᾶς εἰς υἱοθεσίαν διὰ᾽Ιησοῦ Χριστοῦ εἰς αὐτόν, κατὰ τὴν εὐδοκίαν τοῦ θελήματος αὐτοῦ ("by predestining us to adoption as sons through Jesus Christ to himself, according to the pleasure of his desire"). There is much that can be explored here. Our focus will be narrow and will utilize only a portion of possible background material.

---

63. The examination of Ephesians also provides the opportunity to interact with Hoehner's impressive commentary on Ephesians (*Ephesians: An Exegetical Commentary* [Grand Rapids, Mich.: Baker, 2002]).

The emphasis will be on certain aspects of the Roman nature of adoption which were likely to have been well known by Paul and his readers.[64]

7.2.1 Gathering Relevant Background Information

I will consider three different approaches to this material. These approaches are not mutually exclusive, and all should be used by serious students of the Bible. As one becomes more experienced, emphasis should move away from the first and move toward the third. Nevertheless, all three approaches should be used.

7.2.1.1 APPROACH 1: NARROW: ISSUE SPECIFIC

In this approach the exegete will look up words and concepts as needed. Any person, place, practice, idea, and the like, that appears in the Bible is a potential subject for background inquiry. It is especially important to pursue background issues when something does not quite seem to make sense in its literary context. However, familiar issues are worth pursuing as well. What seems to be familiar to us may have been quite different in the first century. This is especially true of customs such as marriage, religious rituals, and other social practices. The example discussed in this paper is such an issue. Most modern readers have an understanding of adoption practices in their culture. However, one cannot impose the modern practice on the ancient. Some aspects were the same but others were different; emphases may vary.

The simplest way to surface background material on a passage is to use a specific commentary on NT backgrounds. Craig Keener's *The IVP Bible Background Commentary: New Testament*[65] gives background information in a section-by-section manner in canonical order. One can use this like a commentary. However, it suffers from serious flaws limiting its value for those beyond the most basic level of Bible study. First, although the book is over 800 pages in length, it is far too brief for the task. There are

---

64. This is not to minimize other adoption practices (especially Jewish and Greek). However, there is reason to focus on the Roman material over the Jewish. The word for adoption in Eph 1:5 does not occur in the Septuagint. Nevertheless, we acknowledge a notion of adoption in Jewish tradition, and this certainly needs to be brought into the discussion in a more thorough study. Our focus will be on minimal aspects of Roman adoption that I believe have been overlooked in previous studies. A thorough examination of υἰοθεσία and other words for and traditions of adoption is provided by James M. Scott, *Adoption as Sons of God: An Exegetical Investigation into the Background of* ΥΙΟΘΕΣΙΑ *in the Pauline Corpus*, WUNT 2:48 (Tübingen: Mohr Siebeck, 1992). It is also helpful to read John L. White's work, which interacts with Scott and adds an important perspective to this issue (*The Apostle of God: Paul and the Promise of Abraham* [Peabody, Mass.: Hendrickson, 1999], 179-85). However, Ephesians 1:5 is not a major consideration in either study.

65. Downers Grove, Ill.: InterVarsity Press, 1993.

many areas that are not discussed that would be of interest to the pastor or Bible teacher. Second, none of the background information includes any reference to ancient material. The work is not intended for scholars but, nevertheless, pastors and others may desire to pursue some of the information mentioned. One may wish to do this to verify or understand the points made in context. If one uses this information in preaching or teaching, it is quite possible that someone may ask for the source of the information.[66] More comprehensive is the four-volume set edited by Clinton E. Arnold entitled *The Zondervan Illustrated Bible Backgrounds Commentary*.[67] Finally, good technical commentaries often provide relevant background material as well.[68]

The format of works like Keener's and Arnold's has the advantage of not only providing background material but also using it in the text itself. However, no source can cover all areas of interest. Probably more helpful is to use specific Bible reference works that explain backgrounds in a topical manner. Craig Evans and Stanley Porter have edited a volume for this purpose, *Dictionary of New Testament Background*.[69] The articles in this work were done by various scholars with some measure of expertise in the areas they cover. This helpful and accessible resource provides the exegete with plenty of reliable information in a convenient place. More comprehensive is the *Anchor Bible Dictionary*, edited by David Noel Freedman.[70] This massive six-volume set covers all aspects of biblical studies. Articles on background issues are usually excellent. These sources also include an abbreviation list of ancient material which is essential to making sense of the many abbreviations encountered in the literature. Finally, when background issues are specifically related

---

66. W. Harold Mare has produced a similar work entitled *New Testament Background Commentary: A New Dictionary of Words, Phrases and Situations in Bible Order* (Ross-shire, Scotland: Mentor, 2004). This volume is much shorter than Keener and suffers from the same shortcomings. However, Mare does include some notes to other literature (usually modern works but some ancient literature as well).

67. Grand Rapids, Mich.: Zondervan, 2002.

68. Many commentaries provide helpful background information. The following series, for example, are usually helpful: Anchor Bible (AB; Doubleday); Baker Exegetical Commentary on the New Testament (BECNT; Baker); International Critical Commentary (ICC; Clark [now owned by Continuum]); New International Commentary on the New Testament (NICNT; Eerdmans); New International Greek Testament Commentary (NIGTC; Eerdmans); Word Biblical Commentary (WBC; Thomas Nelson [previously Word]). These series are not always even in their treatment of background issues. Also, there are excellent commentaries for background material in other series as well as independent works. Hoehner's commentary on Ephesians is an example of an independent commentary that includes a wealth of background information.

69. Downers Grove, Ill.: InterVarsity Press, 2000.

70. New York: Doubleday, 1992. Other standard Bible encyclopedias and dictionaries are also helpful. See, for example, *ISBE*.

to words or in some cases concepts, lexical tools such as BDAG, LSJ, and *TDNT* often include many references to ancient texts of interest to the study.

Finally, for advanced study, one should consult special studies or monographs on subject areas. Cited above was the study by James M. Scott. Such works are important because they represent a comprehensive study in relevant background material on a specific subject. Although the analysis in these works may be very helpful, one need not agree with all (or any) of the conclusions of such works. At the very least, they are valuable for their catalogue of relevant texts.

In our study of adoption in Ephesians 1:5, we are interested in learning what adoption practices were occurring in the first century. We are also interested in what people thought about this adoption. When we turn to the sources already noted we discover that Keener's volume does not mention adoption in his discussion of Eph 1:4-5.[71] Other sources are more helpful. Among other insights, we discover that adoption involved a complete break with the previous family, full-membership status as son or daughter in the new family, and was often necessary to continue a family line (related to inheritance). We also learn that many of the Roman emperors were succeeded by adopted sons.[72]

At this stage we are only uncovering facts about adoption and are not ready to decide their impact on the passage.

7.2.1.2 Approach 2: Mid-Range: Book Introduction

One may wish to set aside specific time for research into the background of a specific book at the initial part of one's study. At this time one focuses on all the preliminary issues relevant to the book. These may include authorship, date, and so forth. Additionally, one should pursue any background issues that may be relevant to the entire book. In the case of the letters, this involves specifics about the city(s) to which the letter is

---

71. Keener, *Background Commentary*, 541. Mare, *Background Commentary*, 304-5, does not discuss this passage.

72. See, for example, BDAG, s.v. "υἱοθεσία"; LSJ, s.v. "υἱοθεσία"; P. W. von Martitz and E. Schweizer, "υἱοθεσία," *TDNT*, 8:397-99; Clinton E. Arnold, "Ephesians," in *The Zondervan Illustrated Bible Backgrounds Commentary*, ed. Clinton E. Arnold, vol. 3 (Grand Rapids, Mich.: Zondervan, 2002), 307; Adolf Berger, Barry Nicholas, and Susan M. Treggiari, "Adoption, Roman," in *Oxford Classical Dictionary*, 13; Ernest Best, *A Critical and Exegetical Commentary on Ephesians*, ICC (Edinburgh: Clark, 1998; reprint, London: Clark, 2004), 124-25; Hoehner, *Ephesians*, 194-97; Scott, *Adoption*, 3-120; White, *Apostle of God*, 176-91. Many of these sources also discuss the biblical text, but this is beyond discussion in this step. Arnold and Scott both see 2 Sam 7:14 as an important influence. This seems unlikely (see White). Hoehner provides a nice summary of the possible influences (Jewish, Greek, and Roman) and suggests Roman is most likely.

written. This information is easily accessible in good commentaries and in specific NT Introductions.[73]

This approach serves to orient the student to the book. It helps the exegete to understand the original readers, the purpose(s), and the occasion(s) for writing. It is a necessary step in the study of any NT book and helps prepare the ground for the two other approaches mentioned here. This step contributes little to our specific question in Eph 1:5 except that it emphasizes that the readers were located in a typically Eastern Roman area.[74]

7.2.1.3 APPROACH 3: BROAD: ERA IMMERSION

This final approach is really more of a continual practice than a method. The exegete should continually be attempting to learn more about the ancient world. As one becomes more familiar with material of this period it is likely that specific areas of connection with the biblical text will surface. Connections may not always be obvious, and some may prove illegitimate. The goal is to immerse oneself in the available ancient literature and quality modern material in order to be continually gaining a knowledge of the first-century world. Much of the background material mentioned above was available to the authors and readers of the NT. It could have been read by them or the ideas in the literature may have been representative of the period. This is an ongoing process and can repay huge dividends in the form of fresh insight into the biblical text.

Concerning adoption, one striking feature that is often noted but not emphasized in general sources is the common practice among emperors in the early and middle of the first century to adopt their successor. Thus, succession was accomplished through adoption. Most striking is the example of the first emperor, Octavian (later Augustus; ruled 31 BC–AD 14). He was the adopted son and thus heir of the dictator Julius Caesar, an adoption of which Octavian was unaware until after the dictator's assassination.[75] Octavian was Caesar's nephew. Caesar was apparently impressed with the boy and this resulted in the adoption. Although a

---

73. See, for example, Raymond E. Brown, *Introduction to the New Testament* (New York: Doubleday, 1996); D. A. Carson and Douglas J. Moo, *An Introduction to the New Testament,* 2nd ed. (Grand Rapids, Mich.: Zondervan, 2005); David A. deSilva, *An Introduction to the New Testament: Contexts, Methods and Ministry Formation* (Downers Grove, Ill.: InterVarsity Press, 2004); Donald Guthrie, *New Testament Introduction,* 4th ed. (Downers Grove, Ill.: InterVarsity Press, 1990); Werner Georg Kümmel, *Introduction to the New Testament,* trans. Howard Clark Kee, rev. ed. (Nashville: Abingdon, 1975).

74. There is debate on whether this book was written to Ephesus specifically or as a circular letter to Asia Minor more generally. Conclusions on this issue do not contribute to our specific problem in Eph 1:5.

75. Suetonius, *Augustus,* 9.2; Cassius Dio, 45.1-9.

number of words for adoption existed,[76] υἱοθεσία was used to refer to the adoption of Octavian by Julius Caesar in a Byzantine fragment of a biography of Augustus written by Octavian's contemporary Nicolaus of Damascus *(Life of Caesar, 55)*.[77] Of the remaining four emperors of the Julio-Claudian dynasty (Tiberius through Nero), only Claudius was not adopted by his predecessor. In this case, Claudius was given the position after the assassination of his nephew Caligula. Claudius was the only possible candidate if the dynasty was to continue. The example of the Julio-Claudian dynasty is not intended to suggest that direct descendants were not preferable. Originally, Augustus desired others, including his grandchildren, to succeed him. However, none of these potential heirs survived Augustus. Adopting Tiberius was his only serious option. Of special interest is that Nero, who was the ruling emperor at the time Paul wrote Ephesians, was the adopted son of Claudius despite the presence of a natural heir.[78]

7.2.2 Determining the Relevance of Collected Background Information

The gathering of ancient sources and the existence of parallels does not assure that our understanding of a passage will be enhanced. In fact, there is a danger of adding to the passage that which was not intended. Here it is important to apply the second and third methodological principles introduced in section 7.1.5 above ("Responsible Use of Sources"). We must ask, "How reflective is this information of the first-century context?" Or more specifically, "How likely is it that this information (not necessarily the specific source) was known to the author?" Ideally, sources from earlier than the NT with strong attestation in the first century are best. Such sources are most likely to have been in the thought-world of the author. However, later material and that of apparent restricted circulation can be used with caution. Additionally, if it can be determined, consider the original audience of the biblical book. It is unlikely that an author would write without some knowledge of his readers.

In the case of first-century Roman adoption, it may be questioned whether the family practices of the most elite family of the empire would have any relevance for the common people. Most would not have ex-

---

76. For a survey of adoption terms and the evidence for υἱοθεσία, see Scott, *Adoption*, 13-54. In NT times, υἱοθεσία was common in nonliterary but not literary sources (ibid.).

77. Felix Jacoby, ed., *Die Fragmente der griecheschen Historiker, vol. 2a: Zeitgeschichte: Universalgechichte und Hellenika* (Leiden: Brill, 1961), 401 (no. 90, frag. 130.55).

78. Tacitus, *Annals*, 12.25, 69; Suetonius, *Claudius*, 39.2; *Nero*, 7; Cassius Dio (epitome), 60.33.2; 61.1. Specific reasons for this are not as relevant for our study as the fact that this adoption happened.

perienced such adoptions. However, I suggest it is relevant for two reasons. First, although elite, the reasons for these adoptions were the same reasons as for others, most specifically, to provide an heir. Second, these adoptions were well known. Common people may not have been able to relate entirely, but they would have been aware of imperial adoptions. It is unthinkable that Romans of Paul's time would have been unaware of the adoptive activities of the emperors. What is important for our purposes is that adoption played an important part in Roman policy and thus an important part in the lives of everyone. These adoptions had a direct influence over the policy of the state. They played a dominant role in the thought-world of the NT era.

7.2.3 Using Background Information in Exegesis

We have discussed briefly how to locate potential background material and make some determination of its relevance. With relevant background material in hand, how do we proceed? First, consider and adjust for any apparent bias in our sources and make necessary adjustments to our understanding of the material. Now, the most important consideration is the context of the passage itself. How does our newfound material impact the message? In what way does the knowledge of the background inform our interpretation of the passage? Does it result in exposing misunderstanding due to possible modern conclusions about how things were in the first century? Does it add nuances that were not previously seen? Work any discoveries into a working interpretation of the text. The background material should better focus our understanding of the passage and result in a clearer, more precise reading of the text (this happens in conjunction with other exegetical tools). Essentially, this step is also a skill needing continual refinement.

As already noted, I wish to bring out only one point from the discussion above. My focus is on adoption and not sonship, which could also result in important insights. When one reads Ephesians 1:3-14, we see a number of items in this passage that are relevant for the adoption process. I will focus on two. First, the believer is *chosen* (ἐξελέξατο, Eph 1:4). In Roman adoptions, especially of adults, the choice was not random. There is a reason the person is chosen. It may be due to some merit on the part of the chosen one. Second, the believer *receives benefits and inheritance* from his new father (Eph 1:6-14). The believer becomes part of the family, with all rights and responsibilities associated with the position.

It is possible that readers may have seen this passage and thought of the empire's first family. It is true that some may experience adoption. However, few could experience the adoption that would elevate them into the most important family in their world. Nevertheless, Paul is telling his readers that believers are experiencing an even better adoption. Old (spiritual) family ties are broken, and they are now part of the family of God the Father.

Additionally, Roman adoption was based on choice by the adopting parents (usually the father). The family head chose someone he thought was able to contribute to the family. This at first may seem contrary to the NT teaching concerning grace, in which someone is chosen purely by God without any contribution of works (e.g., Eph 2:8-9). However, Paul qualifies his teaching on adoption. Again the passage states, προορίσας ἡμᾶς εἰς υἱοθεσίαν διὰ Ἰησοῦ Χριστοῦ εἰς αὐτόν, κατὰ τὴν εὐδοκίαν τοῦ θελήματος αὐτου (by predestining us to adoption as sons *through Jesus Christ to himself, according to the pleasure of his desire*). The qualifications highlighted make Christ's role the cause of adoption and remove any question of merit. If this is the case, what does the background have to offer the modern reader on this point? I suggest that this understanding reveals that the believer's adoption is not a random act as is often the case in modern adoptions. Often we desire a child and, within certain limits, any child is acceptable. The believer is known by God beforehand. God does not just want *a* child. God want *you* (yes, *you* the reader), a specific person, to be a part of his family. Again, this is not based on merit, as the Roman adoption of adults may have involved. Nevertheless, it adds a *personal dimension* to the salvation process that might otherwise be overlooked.

7.3 Conclusion

It has been argued that understanding the historical, cultural, social, and other contexts of the first-century world provides an important tool for the exegete to use alongside other tools to better understand the NT. Both tools and approaches have been discussed to help the student pursue these studies in a productive manner. This is not a skill that can be mastered but rather one to be continually developed and refined. We are restricted by an incomplete knowledge of the first-century world. Nevertheless, the more we know, the better we can understand the writers and original readers of our Bible. As we become better acquainted with the people and practices of this time period, we become better acquainted with the text. As we become better acquainted with the NT, we become better acquainted with our God.

7.4 For Further Reading

Barnett, Paul W. *Jesus and the Rise of Early Christianity: A History of New Testament Times.* Downers Grove, Ill.: InterVarsity Press, 1999.

Evans, Craig A. *Ancient Texts for New Testament Studies: A Guide to the Background Literature.* Peabody, Mass.: Hendrickson, 2005.

Evans, Craig A., and Stanley E. Porter, eds. *Dictionary of New Testament Background.* Downers Grove, Ill.: InterVarsity Press, 2000.

Ferguson, Everett. *Backgrounds of Early Christianity.* 3rd ed. Grand Rapids, Mich.: Eerdmans, 2003.

Longenecker, Bruce W. *The Lost Letters of Pergamum: A Story from the New Testament World.* Grand Rapids, Mich.: Baker, 2003.

Schürer, Emil. *The History of the Jewish People in the Age of Jesus Christ (175 B.C.–A.D. 135).* Edited by Geza Vermes, Fergus Millar, Matthew Black, Martin Goodman, and Pamela Vermes. Rev. ed. 3 vols. (in 4 parts). Edinburgh: Clark, 1973-87.

Narrative Genre

8

Studying the Story

MICHAEL H. BURER

8.0 Introduction[1]

"Daddy, tell me a story!"

As any parent of a young child knows, stories have the power to captivate listeners like no other words we might say. It is almost irresistible: when a good storyteller begins to work, the listeners cannot help but be drawn into the world of the story. They imagine themselves in the place of the characters, acting out the plot, feeling the same emotions and drama. The same thing takes place when we read an exceptional story. We are captivated, almost to the point that we cannot put the book down. I have vivid memories of reading through J. R. R. Tolkien's complete *Lord of the Rings* trilogy a few years ago over Christmas break, and the compulsion to read was at times overwhelming. I was driven to follow the characters, to find out what was going to happen, to feel their emotions. Such is the power of story to stir and change us.

---

1. As all who contribute to this volume would attest, I have been greatly influenced by the ministry of Harold Hoehner, both inside and outside the classroom. His dedication to Christian scholarship and ministry have marked my life in many ways, and for that I thank God for him. May his tribe increase!

Fortunately for those who read and cherish the Bible, stories are an important part of its contents. The Bible is filled with narratives about heroes and villains, people whom we cherish and people whom we detest. The Bible is filled with conflict and resolution, twists and turns, all of which create compelling stories. The benefit of the biblical story is that it is not simply given for the purpose of entertainment but for the purpose of changing lives. The end result of a Bible story is not a fun time, but someone who follows the Lord more closely.

It is clear from even a simple perusal of the Bible that narrative[2] is an important part of its contents. Vast portions of both the Old and New Testaments are narrative; because of its power to communicate truth, narrative became a crucial part of the biblical record. Specifically within the NT, the narrative sections are each of the four Gospels and the book of Acts.[3] An exegete who desires to handle the biblical text correctly must be able to handle narrative in these five books.

8.1 Holistic Concerns

8.1.1 Narrative as Genre[4]

One of the first steps that must be taken to understand the Gospels and Acts is to understand the genre to which they belong. Genre is a literary classification that describes the broad contours and features of a particular literary work. There are several represented within the biblical text, including poetry, letters, apocalyptic, proverbs, and psalms. More specifically, the Gospels and Acts are classified as *narrative*.[5] Narrative is essentially a

2. Strictly speaking, there is a technical difference between *narrative* and *story*. Narrative is the more limited term and simply describes what is going on in the text: events are being narrated and described. Story is the more expansive term and implies a host of additional elements: the author intended to communicate a particular meaning; there is plot, characterization, tension, and resolution; the reader is actively involved in the process by thinking about and responding to the story, etc. Practically speaking, however, there is little actual difference in the terms as they are used in discussions about the content of the biblical text.

3. Broadly speaking, the entirety of the NT fits within a narrative framework. Paul's letters, for example, cannot be understood unless they are placed within the larger narrative of his missionary work and church planting efforts. More strictly speaking, though, only the Gospels and Acts represent the *genre* of narrative and are classified as story.

4. The question of how one is to interpret narrative in the Bible has come to the forefront of biblical studies in recent years. For a seminal study see David M. Rhoads and Donald Michie, *Mark as Story: An Introduction to the Narrative of a Gospel* (Philadelphia: Fortress, 1982). For a recent treatment of narrative criticism as an interpretive method, see James L. Resseguie, *Narrative Criticism of the New Testament: An Introduction* (Grand Rapids, Mich.: Baker, 2005).

5. There is a wide-ranging discussion regarding the genre of the Gospels and its relation to Greco-Roman biographies. For a recent, thorough study, see Richard A. Burridge, *What Are*

story: characters are followed through various events that are connected to form a plot with an initial conflict and eventual resolution.[6] Handling the Gospels and Acts requires that the reader know how to handle basic narrative elements common to most every story, the most important of which are characters, plot, and the narrator's perspective.[7]

8.1.1.1 Characters

Central to almost every story are the characters. These are the major players in the story, who are the center of attention. There are different types of characters in most stories. The *protagonist* is the central character in the story, while the *antagonist* is the character who opposes the protagonist in some way. In more complex stories there are a central protagonist and other protagonists besides. Within the Gospels, it is clear that Jesus is the protagonist. He is the central character around whom the entire drama unfolds. There are many lesser characters, however, who in certain situations take on the role of a lesser protagonist. The disciples are very often in situations where they are the major characters around whom the plot unfolds for a time. In the book of Acts, Peter is the protagonist for the first part of the book, but then the narrative mysteriously switches its attention over to Paul, who becomes the central character; in each part of the book, however, the reader receives very clear signs that God is the ultimate protagonist.[8] In a similar vein, many stories have a central antagonist, but if the story is complex, there can be many more.

Finding an antagonist in the Gospels is not as easy as it may seem on the surface. Common opponents to Jesus include the Pharisees and other Jewish leaders of that time, but there are other antagonists lurking in the background, always looking for a chance to act. Satan tempts Jesus, making him clearly an antagonist. Demonic forces oppose Jesus consistently throughout his ministry, thus they are antagonists to him and his work. Recognizing the protagonist and the antagonist is important to knowing how the story works and how the plot will play out. In addition to the major characters, there are other characters who play important roles within the

---

the Gospels? A Comparison with Graeco-Roman Biography, 2nd ed., The Biblical Resource Series (Grand Rapids, Mich.: Eerdmans, 2004).

6. Even more specifically, the Gospels and Acts are *historical* narrative; the genre of narrative retells history, that is, events that occurred and people who lived within space and time.

7. A host of other elements can be examined in studying the narrative genre. Character, plot, and the narrator's perspective are highlighted here as the most fruitful for exegesis of the Scriptures. For an excellent example of literary criticism in use and how extensively it can investigate the biblical text, see Alan Culpepper, *The Anatomy of the Fourth Gospel: A Study in Literary Design* (Philadelphia: Fortress, 1983).

8. So Beverly Roberts Gaventa, *The Acts of the Apostles*, ANTC (Nashville: Abingdon, 2003), 28-31; and Robert L. Brawley, *Centering on God: Method and Message in Luke-Acts*, Literary Currents in Biblical Interpretation (Louisville: Westminster/John Knox, 1990), 107-38.

narrative. These must be examined to determine what they contribute to the narrative, and how they relate to the major characters.

In examining characters, there are many questions to be asked. First, is the character *round* or *flat?* These terms refer to the development the character receives in the narrative. Flat characters are one-sided, one-dimensional, or stereotypical. They embody one character trait, they act only a certain way, or they serve only a single purpose in the narrative. Round characters in contrast are more fully developed in that they are seen from a variety of angles and perspectives. They do not embody only one trait; instead they show a multiplicity of qualities, which makes them more important in the story.[9] Second, how is the character *described?* The way he or she is described by the narrator guides the reader into how the character should be perceived and understood. This involves the words specifically used to describe the character as well as how he or she is introduced and handled in the narrative.[10] Third, what does the character *do* and *say?* The actions and speech of the character must be measured against the other characters and the worldview represented in the story. This allows the reader to assess whether the character is viewed positively or negatively. Fourth, what is the *role* and *function* of the character? Every character is introduced into a narrative for a reason; the author consciously selects all the characters to serve a specific role and function within the narrative. The roles of protagonist and antagonist are usually straightforward, but other characters require some reflection. Does this character help or hinder the protagonist or antagonist? Does the character advance the plot in some fashion? Is he or she meant to be viewed as a foil to another character? Fifth, does the character *change* in any way? Characters are either *dynamic,* in that they exhibit some change during the course of the narrative, or *static,* in that they do not change.[11] As a general rule, round characters are dynamic and flat characters are static, but this is not always the case. If a character changes, what is the nature of the change? Is it positive or negative? Is it an outward change in behavior, or an inward change of attitudes and emotions? Is the change viewed posi-

9. Often in the Gospels the Pharisees as a group are flat; they think and act in one certain way, always in opposition to Jesus. In John 3, Nicodemus becomes a round character because, in spite of the fact that he is a Pharisee, he seeks Jesus out in order to talk with him more carefully about his teaching.

10. Judas Iscariot is clearly a negative character in the Gospels for his betrayal of Jesus, but he is also *described* negatively. In John 12:6 the narrator describes him in a very pointed fashion. In explaining Judas's objection to Mary's anointing of Jesus with the expensive perfume, the narrator states, "Now Judas said this not because he was concerned about the poor, but because he was a thief. As keeper of the money box, he used to steal what was put into it" (NET). The term "thief" is clearly pejorative and is meant to influence the reader's attitude against Judas.

11. So Resseguie, *Narrative Criticism,* 125-26.

tively or negatively from the standpoint of the narrative? Examining these questions helps the reader understand why this character was included and gives some grounds for interpreting characters a certain way.

8.1.1.2 PLOT

Plot refers to a story's movement and usually involves a conflict of some type that finds an eventual resolution. Key to understanding the plot is determining the nature of the conflict, how it gets resolved, and which characters are involved. This will be determined through the interaction of two main elements in the story, the characters and the *events*. Events very simply are what happens to the characters. They can be actions or even states that are represented as singular, non-repeatable events or as representative events that stand for that event itself and other events like it. The responsibility of the reader is to put the characters and events together in such a way that a coherent plot is understood, one which explains the events of the story and provides an appropriate framework for understanding.

There are key questions that can elucidate the shape and function of the plot.[12] What are its constituent parts? In other words, what is its beginning, middle, and end? A common plot to many love stories is the tried and true "boy meets girl, boy loses girl, boy gets girl." These same constituent parts of beginning, middle, and end can be found in biblical narrative, both on a small scale within individual pericopes and on a large scale within entire books. How is causation at work? Plots consist of events linked together by cause and effect; identifying those will illuminate the shape and direction of the plot. Where is the exact point of conflict? Is it external or internal? Is it physical or spiritual? Are any values or ideas in play?

8.1.1.3 NARRATOR'S PERSPECTIVE

When reading a narrative, pay attention to the role of the narrator. In a very real sense, the narrator mediates the story, guiding the reader to understand and interpret characters and events a certain way. The first question to consider is the *point of view* of the narrator. Stated more specifically, is the narrator describing the events in the *first person* or the *third person*? Is the narrator an active participant in the events[13] or detached from them, in some sense viewing them from outside? The second question to consider is the knowledge the narrator has. Is the narrator an *omniscient* observer, able to see many things at once, for example, or able to read people's

---

12. These questions are abstracted from the discussion of plot elements in ibid., 198-203.

13. The best example of this within NT narrative is the "we" sections in the book of Acts (16:10-17; 20:5-15; 21:1-18; 27:1–28:16).

minds? Or is the narrator a *limited* observer, simply describing events as they might be seen by anyone else? Or is the narrator perhaps somewhere in between, able to discern some things another observer would not see but stopping short of showing omniscience? Answering these questions enables the reader to see how the narrator functions in guiding the reader to understand and interpret events. The narrator will frame certain characters and events as important; understanding how the narrator does this helps the reader see the intended end of the story.

8.1.2 Culture as Background

In any story culture is paramount. The reader must understand the culture of the characters and events represented in order to make sense of anything in the story. Culture is loosely defined as the shared beliefs, attitudes, and actions of a particular group. The Gospels and Acts represent different cultures, and these must be understood in order to make sense of the story.

An example will suffice to make the point about the importance of culture. In John 4 Jesus initiates a conversation with a Samaritan woman. She is taken aback by this and questions Jesus about his interaction. To explain this, the narrator includes a parenthetical comment which explains why there was a problem: "For Jews use nothing in common with Samaritans."[14] This comment states the fact but it does not state why this situation existed. By delving into the culture a bit more, the reader learns that Jews as a rule viewed the Samaritans as unclean[15]; if they were to share a drinking utensil, for example, or anything else associated with food, then the Jew would become unclean and would have to go through the necessary purification in order to worship again in the temple.[16] Thus the woman with her challenge to Jesus is expressing a commonly held belief of that culture which impacted the interactions Jews and Samaritans had on a regular basis. The modern reader who does not understand this background will very likely miss the point, and will thus misunderstand how much of a stretch it was for Jesus to reach out to this woman.[17]

14. This translation is from the *NET Bible, New English Translation,* 1st ed. (Dallas: Biblical Studies Press, 2005), available online at http://www.bible.org.

15. The Babylonian Talmud, in the tractate Niddah, states, "The daughters of Samaritans are regarded as menstruants from their cradle" (*b. Niddah* 31b). This would imply a perpetual state of uncleanness for Samaritan women and all who associated with them.

16. In a tractate of the Mishnah, Rabbi Eliezer is reported to have said, "He who eats bread baked by Samaritans is like one who eats the flesh of a pig" (*Shebi'it* 8:10). Even something as wholesome as bread becomes vile to the Jew when it comes from the hand of a Samaritan.

17. This passage at least gives a hint as to the cultural issue underneath the surface. The parable of the Good Samaritan in Luke 10:25-37 is implicitly appealing to this same cultural

In order to benefit from a study of the culture of the biblical text, the reader must first *notice* it. Very often modern readers of the Bible either miss important elements of culture or assume that a particular aspect of the culture is working as we would understand it. Almost every element of the Gospels and Acts can be fruitfully explored, but obviously more central elements should be examined first. Various questions can be asked to help highlight cultural elements. Is there a cultural perspective on which the story seems to hinge? Are there elements that do not make sense from the reader's cultural expectation? Are there repeated elements throughout the Gospels and Acts that serve as important elements? Is there anything that the reader has taken for granted culturally that deserves more investigation?[18] As the reader has time, more elements can be studied for a more fruitful understanding of the biblical world and in turn the biblical text.

The second task in front of the biblical reader is *accessing* the culture of the Gospels and Acts. This requires specialized tools that open up the culture to the modern reader.[19] First and foremost are the primary sources, written by those within the culture, which help the reader understand directly what the culture of the biblical world was like. This includes the Old Testament, the OT Apocrypha, the OT Pseudepigrapha, Josephus, the Dead Sea Scrolls, Philo, the Mishnah, the Targums, the Midrashim, and the Talmud.[20] After these primary sources are secondary works in which the ancient sources are commented on and described. Practically speaking, the easiest way to access the primary material is through secondary sources. A judicious use of these will uncover specific references to primary sources which can then be followed up as necessary. There are three types of secondary sources that deserve special mention. First are

issue but gives no explicit signs that it does so. In fact, it does not need to do so for the issue of culture to be important. The Jews' negative view of Samaritans was a given, an assumed state of affairs, in the cultural understanding of the day. There are two other reasons Jesus might have avoided contact with the Samaritan woman in John 4: the very fact that she was a woman, and the fact that she was sexually promiscuous. Any of the three elements could have kept someone from interacting with her; for Jesus to step over all three cultural boundaries and extend grace to her indicates the extent to which he would go to reach those in need.

18. For example, many aspects of meals and eating are culturally defined. If a reader assumes that sharing a meal with someone in the ancient world is the same as doing that today, a great deal of the meaning and import of that event for the biblical story will be lost.

19. See chapter 7 in this book, on "Background Studies," for detailed treatment of this area of study.

20. The background literature to the New Testament is immense. The best entrée into this material is through Craig A. Evans, *Ancient Texts for New Testament Studies: A Guide to the Background Literature* (Peabody, Mass.: Hendrickson, 2005). This is an excellent text that gives a basic overview of each body of literature, ways in which that literature touches upon interpretation of the NT, and bibliography pointing to standard editions and important studies.

technical commentaries on the biblical text. Many commentaries do an excellent job of providing references to and discussing primary sources that illuminate the biblical text. Using them as a starting point can lead to a focused examination of selected passages in the primary texts. Second are handbooks on culture and history that often give help on specific issues, customs, or passages.[21] Third are Bible encyclopedias and dictionaries that cover a wide range of topics, often with some depth.[22]

8.2 The Gospels

8.2.1 Criticism as Method

When a reader seeks to interpret the Gospels, he is stepping into a stream of study that has been ongoing for two thousand years. In the last two hundred years, specific methods of study have arisen that presently dominate the field. It is worth knowing about these methods of study in brief so the student can understand where the majority of the present interpretive field stands, so he can understand tools that rely on these methods, and so he can use the tools himself in a profitable way.

The first method of study to arise that concerns the modern reader of the Gospels is *source criticism*.[23] Source criticism is simply the study of sources used by an author to create a document. The limit of source criticism is that once these sources are delineated, one cannot delve further to determine how the source itself was compiled. This cul-de-sac gave rise to *form criticism*.[24] Form criticism must be defined carefully, as the term

21. Three books that deserve mention in this regard are Craig S. Keener, *The IVP Bible Background Commentary: New Testament* (Downers Grove, Ill.: InterVarsity Press, 1993); Everett Ferguson, *Backgrounds of Early Christianity*, 3rd ed. (Grand Rapids, Mich.: Eerdmans, 2003); and Albert A. Bell, *Exploring the New Testament World* (Nashville: Nelson, 1998). Keener is especially useful because it is arranged by biblical passage; it does not, however, contain *references* to any ancient sources for additional study.

22. Excellent resources here are *ABD, ISBE, IDB, DJG*, and *DLNT*.

23. Excellent introductions to source criticism, as well as form and redaction criticism, are Robert H. Stein, *Studying the Synoptic Gospels: Origin and Interpretation*, 2nd ed. (Grand Rapids, Mich.: Baker, 2001); and Darrell L. Bock, *Studying the Historical Jesus: A Guide to Sources and Methods* (Grand Rapids, Mich.: Baker, 2002). The term *Synoptic* refers to the first three Gospels—Matthew, Mark, and Luke. This is due to the fact that they share common material and a common order, and thus can be profitably studied when viewed together.

24. The seminal studies on form criticism are Karl Ludwig Schmidt, *Der Rahmen der Geschichte Jesu: Literarkritische Untersuchungen zur ältesten Jesusüberlieferung* (Berlin: Trowitzsch, 1919); Martin Dibelius, *From Tradition to Gospel*, Library of Theological Translations (New York: Scribner, 1971); Rudolf Bultmann, *The History of the Synoptic Tradition*, trans. John Marsh (New York: Harper & Row, 1963); and Vincent Taylor, *The Formation of the Gospel Tradition* (London: Macmillan, 1933).

means one thing generally and another specifically within the history of the discipline. Defined generally, form criticism is the study of the smaller forms and units within the Gospels to determine their proper interpretation and use within the Gospel material. It is a study which recognizes that certain forms aided the transmission of such material when it was first in an oral form by giving similar structure to certain types of accounts. Defined specifically within the discipline by various proponents, form criticism is the study of individual forms and units within the Gospels to determine their use within the early church and then the historical accuracy of the material contained in the form.[25] This method of study eventually gave way to *redaction criticism*.[26] Redaction criticism is the study of similarities and differences between the Gospels based upon determinations of chronological order and editing sequence to determine an individual author's emphasis as an aid to interpretation of his text. Some scholars prefer the discipline of *composition criticism*,[27] the study of such differences for what they tell us about each Gospel's emphases without assuming any particular order or editing sequence.

The importance of understanding this historical sequence is in recognizing that scholars are still using these methods to study the Gospels with valid interpretive results. These will be discussed in order in the following sections and should be understood to be additional methods for studying the Gospels along with issues surrounding narrative and culture as discussed above.

8.2.2 Synopsis: The Primary Tool

The first step in exegeting the Gospels is a careful examination of the biblical text. Most important to note are the similarities and differences between the Gospels, and this has to begin with color-coding a synopsis.

A synopsis is a tool that arranges the Gospel material side by side in parallel columns.[28] The goal is to present the text of the Gospels

---

25. It should be recognized that many proponents of form criticism have challenged the value of historical assessments of this kind virtually from the beginning of the discipline.

26. Key redaction critical studies are Hans Conzelmann, *The Theology of St. Luke*, trans. Geoffrey Buswell (New York: Harper & Row, 1961); Willi Marxsen, *Mark the Evangelist: Studies on the Redaction History of the Gospel*, trans. James Boyce (Nashville: Abingdon, 1969); and Günther Bornkamm, Gerhard Barth, and Heinz Joachim Held, *Tradition and Interpretation in Matthew*, trans. Percy Scott, New Testament Library (London: SCM, 1963).

27. For a discussion of the differences between redaction criticism and composition criticism and some of the implications, see Randall K. J. Tan, "Recent Developments in Redaction Criticism: From Investigation of Textual Prehistory Back to Historical-Grammatical Exegesis?" *JETS* 44 (2001): 599-614.

28. The standard synopsis used in biblical studies is Kurt Aland, ed., *Synopsis of the Four Gospels*, 10th ed. (Stuttgart: German Bible Society, 1993). This is a Greek-English diglot edition.

in such a way that comparisons can be made easily.[29] It is a tool for observation, and color-coding is a useful process for making those observations. This involves coloring the text in such a way that similarities and differences are easily noted. The student can develop a color scheme that is personally useful, or can adopt one that is in common use. Although not every scholar adopts this scheme, the following is somewhat standard in Gospel comparisons: material common to Matthew, Mark, and Luke is colored blue; material common to Matthew and Mark is colored yellow; material common to Matthew and Luke is colored red; and material common to Mark and Luke is colored green.[30] As desired, the scheme can be adapted to account for parallel material in the Gospel of John. The student should also decide whether the words will be highlighted or underlined.[31] The actual process involves examining a unit of the Gospels in the synopsis and coloring similar material. After this process has been completed the student will have an abundance of observations about the biblical text, both in the Gospel under consideration and in the parallel texts. This will form a basis for

The text of the Nestle-Aland 26th edition appears on the left; the 2nd edition of the Revised Standard Version appears on the right. In addition to the text of the Gospels, this synopsis has an index to Gospel passages that shows at a glance the flow of the pericopes in a particular Gospel, leading and following pericopes indicated for each parallel, different typefaces to indicate primary or secondary parallels, and an expanded textual apparatus. The Greek-only version has extensive Patristic citations as well; see Kurt Aland, ed., *Synopsis Quattuor Evangeliorum*, 14th ed. (Stuttgart: Deutsche Bibelgesellschaft, 1995).

29. This type of inter-Gospel comparison is often called a *horizontal* reading, in that the Gospels are compared and contrasted with one another with a goal to determining individual emphases. An intra-Gospel reading, often called a *vertical* reading, is properly a narrative reading, in that a single Gospel is treated as a self-contained unit and examined for its own structure, characteristics, and meaning. Both are necessary for the interpretation of any one Gospel.

30. This is the coloring scheme used in William R. Farmer, ed., *Synopticon: The Verbal Agreement Between the Greek Texts of Matthew, Mark, and Luke Contextually Exhibited* (London: Cambridge University Press, 1969). In this work Farmer uses a mixture of highlighting and underlining to indicate complete and incomplete verbal agreement respectively. For another coloring scheme, see Scot McKnight, *Interpreting the Synoptic Gospels,* Guides to New Testament Exegesis (Grand Rapids, Mich.: Baker, 1988), 40-44.

31. This is usually a matter of personal preference, but there are some important pragmatic considerations. For example, a mistake made with a highlighter on printed paper is almost impossible to correct. I have found colored pencils (commonly available at art supply stores, for example) useful as they can be erased if needed. One very practical recommendation given to me long ago by my teachers was to photocopy several pages and color them first; then, after much practice, color the actual synopsis. Despite the ability of many Bible software programs to color and underline the text easily, I still prefer the printed synopsis. It aligns parallel passages properly with intervening space as necessary so one can quickly compare parallel material; it contains the index to Gospel passages which allows one to see at a glance the flow of the pericopes in a particular Gospel; the leading and following pericopes are indicated for each parallel; and different typefaces are used to indicate primary or secondary parallels.

further study and a springboard for recognition of the unique message of the Gospel text examined.

8.2.3 Sources: The Materials Used

On a broad level, the student must make a determination as to the relationships between the Gospels. This will both inform the student's understanding of any particular Gospel and allow him to use more profitably various tools that depend upon a particular hypothesis.

As a rule, Matthew, Mark, and Luke are considered separately from the Gospel of John; they share much common material and very often the same order of events. For this reason theories specific to their relationship have grown up within biblical studies.[32] There are five major views.[33] The first is the *Oral tradition/independence* hypothesis.[34] This view argues that there is no direct dependence between any of the Gospels; each Gospel author wrote entirely independently of the others. Agreement between the Gospels arises from similar recollection of eyewitness material. The second view is the *Augustinian* hypothesis, so named because this solution was proposed by Augustine.[35] This view argues that the Gospels were written in canonical order, with each subsequently dependent: Matthew wrote first, then Mark who used Matthew, then Luke who used Matthew and Mark. The third view is the *Two Gospel* hypothesis.[36] In this view

32. This refers to what is commonly called the *Synoptic Problem*. Simply described, the Synoptic Problem is the fact that Matthew, Mark, and Luke are at the same time so similar, yet so different, and yet also unique in various ways. Scholars have advanced these solutions as the best ones for this "problem."

33. There are many other solutions proposed by various scholars, but these five are the most widely held. For a listing of many different views, see Stephen C. Carlson's website, "The Synoptic Problem Website," http://www.hypotyposeis.org/synoptic-problem, accessed March 2006.

34. For two recent treatments that argue for this view, see Eta Linnemann, *Is There a Synoptic Problem? Rethinking the Literary Dependence of the First Three Gospels* (Grand Rapids, Mich.: Baker, 1992); and Thomas R. Edgar, "Source Criticism: The Two-Source Theory," in *The Jesus Crisis: The Inroads of Historical Criticism into Evangelical Scholarship,* ed. Robert L. Thomas and F. David Farnell (Grand Rapids, Mich.: Kregel, 1998), 132-57. A more nuanced view, which argues for the shaping of oral tradition still within a largely literary framework, appears in James D. G. Dunn, "Jesus in Oral Memory: The Initial Stages of the Jesus Tradition," in *SBL Seminar Papers, 2000,* vol. 39, Society of Biblical Literature Seminar Papers (Atlanta: Society of Biblical Literature, 2000), 287-326; and James D. G. Dunn, *Jesus Remembered,* Christianity in the Making 1 (Grand Rapids, Mich.: Eerdmans, 2003).

35. For a modern proponent of this view see B. C. Butler, *The Originality of St. Matthew: A Critique of the Two-Document Hypothesis* (Cambridge: Cambridge University Press, 1951).

36. This view is also known as the *Griesbach* hypothesis as it was originally championed by J. J. Griesbach. However, the name "Two Gospel" hypothesis is regarded as more accurate in that it neutrally describes the view. For a modern proponent of this view, see William R. Farmer, *The Synoptic Problem* (Dillsboro, N.C.: Western North Carolina Press, 1976).

two Gospels form the basis for the third: Matthew wrote first, then Luke who used Matthew, then Mark who used both Matthew and Luke. The fourth view is called the *Two Source* hypothesis, so called because there are two sources which form the basis for the Synoptic Gospels. Mark wrote first, and independently of him there was a source called "Q."[37] Both Mark and Q were used independently by Matthew and Luke, who did not know of or use each other's Gospel. Related to this is the *Four Source* hypothesis, which posits that Matthew had access to another source in addition to Mark and Q, usually called "M," and similarly that Luke had access to another source called "L." This theory accounts for the material unique to Matthew and Luke by positing these additional written sources. The fifth view is the *Farrer* hypothesis, so called because it was originally advocated by Austin Farrer.[38] It is similar to the Two and Four Source hypotheses in that Mark was the first Gospel written, but it is different in that there are no sources other than the canonical Gospels. Mark wrote first, then Matthew who used Mark, then Luke who used Mark and Matthew.

Although there are scholars who hold to each of these five major views, they are not all held equally. By and large, most NT scholars hold to the Two Source or Four Source hypothesis, convinced that these hypotheses do the best job explaining all the data.[39] Two examples will suffice.[40] One major category of evidence within the Synoptic Problem can be subsumed under the rubric of *Markan primitivity,* i.e., the Gospel of Mark has primitive characteristics—whether in grammar, style, or theology—which are altered by Matthew or Luke consistently to make a more elegant, natural, or theologically clear presentation. Hypotheses that hold to Markan priority are generally agreed to handle this evidence better than other theories. Another broad example involves the issue of redaction as it relates to Q material. Accounting for the material which Matthew and Luke have in common and the way they each have used it is generally easier with a hypothesis that allows for Q, i.e., the Two Source

---

37. For further discussion, see Darrell L. Bock, "Questions About Q," in *Rethinking the Synoptic Problem,* ed. David Alan Black and David R. Beck (Grand Rapids, Mich.: Baker, 2001), 41-64.

38. A. M. Farrer, "On Dispensing With Q," in *Studies in the Gospels: Essays in Memory of R. H. Lightfoot,* ed. D. E. Nineham (Oxford: Blackwell, 1955), 55-88.

39. This is important not only as an implicit argument for the validity of these hypotheses, based upon the expertise of the scholars who hold these views, but also for understanding the wealth of secondary literature (commentaries, articles, monographs, etc.) that are written on the Gospels. The student should recognize that the vast majority of resources available on the Gospels will follow these more commonly held hypotheses; this helps the reader to understand the resources' viewpoint and presentation.

40. In the interest of space, this assessment must be very brief. See Stein, *Studying the Synoptic Gospels,* 49-96, for a full discussion.

or Four Source hypothesis. Q material which Matthew and Luke share is found in the Gospel of Matthew in the five major discourse sections,[41] while in Luke it is found spread throughout the Gospel primarily as disconnected sayings in a different order. It is much more plausible that Matthew and Luke each used Q in a way that suited them than that Luke took the material neatly arranged in Matthew and spread it around with no easily determinable purpose. When all is said and done, however, the Synoptic Problem is still an open question, and no solution should be treated as a dogmatic answer.

The question of sources for the Gospel of John is a bit different from those for the Synoptic Gospels. There are two questions generally asked: Did John know of the Synoptics; and because this Gospel is so different from the Synoptics, is it historically reliable?[42] There has been a wide range of opinion on this matter in the history of Johannine scholarship. Scholarship has in some ways come full circle. The pre-Enlightenment period as a rule regarded John as the most reliable of the Gospels; it was written by the disciple closest to Jesus and gave the fullest insight about the person and ministry of Jesus. This changed during the Enlightenment, when scholars often created a dichotomy between theology and history; because John is so overtly steeped in theology, its history was immediately called into question. This was augmented by two other viewpoints. First, the cultural background of the Gospel was called into question, with many scholars identifying a Hellenistic background to its thoughts and concepts, implying a later date to its composition.[43] Second, its relationship to the other Gospels was generally regarded as one of *knowledge* and *dependence,* therefore casting doubt upon the historicity of its original material. The pendulum in many respects has swung back in the other direction as many recent scholars argue that John is independent from the Synoptics and contains a more ancient historical tradition.[44]

The task before the student at this point is to examine the theories and determine which one makes the best sense of the biblical data. This is a task that obviously will take some time to complete, and it will of

41. Matthew 5–7, 10, 13, 18, 24–25.

42. A profitable overview of these and other issues related to the interpretation of John is found in Gary M. Burge, "Interpreting the Gospel of John," in *Interpreting the New Testament: Essays on Methods and Issues,* ed. David Alan Black and David S. Dockery (Nashville: Broadman & Holman, 2001), 357-70.

43. The classic commentary that follows this line of reasoning is Rudolf Bultmann, *The Gospel of John: A Commentary*, trans. G. R. Beasley-Murray (Philadelphia: Westminster, 1971).

44. The classic statement of the independence of John from the Synoptics is Percival Gardner-Smith, *Saint John and the Synoptic Gospels* (Cambridge: Cambridge University Press, 1938). A full-orbed presentation of this position and its import upon Gospel studies is John A. T. Robinson, *The Priority of John*, ed. J. F. Coakley (London: SCM, 1985).

necessity be tentative in its conclusions. It is important, however, because the view of sources which one holds determines by default many different conclusions about the Gospels, how they relate, and how one is to determine theology from them. It is certainly a task that is foundational, so it is important for appreciating the historical manner in which all subsequent understanding of the biblical text grows.

8.2.4 Forms: The Shape of the Material

Anytime someone reads something, questions of form are always paramount. What is the shape of this material? How does it begin and end? What are the key structural clues that tell me what I am reading? Answering these questions enables the reader to know better what he is reading and therefore how to interpret it. The very same questions are in play in the Gospels. During the period immediately following the resurrection and ascension of Jesus, the early church began to relate to itself and to those outside information about who Jesus was, what he said and did, how he lived and died, and how he was raised from the dead. In this period of oral transmission, some of the material began to take on a set shape, which enabled the church both to remember it and to retell it anew. Certain types of stories, such as those that told of Jesus' miraculous works, began to be shaped similarly, and certain anthologies comprised of similar material, such as that of Jesus' teaching on various subjects, were developed. This process was essentially the development of form, and understanding the form of the Gospel material is a crucial step in understanding its interpretation.[45]

Most present-day scholars recognize five major forms within the Gospel materials, subject to various subdivisions as appropriate. The first is *pronouncement story*. This material is designed to highlight a saying of Jesus. The narrative itself is generally very brief. The saying routinely comes at the end of the pericope and serves as a sort of "punch line" to drive home the point of the material.[46] This broad category is generally divided into three subcategories. *Controversy dialogues* are so named because the pronouncement comes as the result of a clash between Jesus and opponents.[47] *Scholastic dialogues* focus on a statement of Jesus issued to those favorable to him; it is a prime teaching moment for those who

---

45. Useful material on form criticism includes Darrell L. Bock, "Form Criticism," in Black and Dockery, eds., *Interpreting the New Testament*, 106-27; and Edgar V. McKnight, *What Is Form Criticism?* Guides to Biblical Scholarship: New Testament Series (Philadelphia: Fortress, 1969).

46. E.g., Jesus eating at Levi's home (Mark 2:15-17 and parallels).

47. E.g., the plucking of grain on the Sabbath (Mark 2:23-28 and parallels).

follow him.[48] *Biographical apophthegms* simply describe something that Jesus taught.[49] The second major category of form is *miracle story*. This material is designed to highlight the miraculous works of Jesus. In contrast to pronouncement stories, miracle stories are usually very descriptive, with much detail. The malady or problem is described with great detail, with specific mention of Jesus' actions. Teaching material is usually absent, and often there is strong emphasis on the effects of the miracle and the response of those who see it.[50] Miracle stories are generally subdivided based upon the type of miracle in view. This has led to a multitude of subcategories including exorcism, healing, nature, and gift miracles. The value in recognizing the type of miracle in view is that similar miracles can be compared to see particular emphases in each one. The third major category of form consists of *sayings of Jesus*.[51] This is a very broad category which includes all of Jesus' teaching, from short statements to extended discourses. Understandably this major category has been subdivided into many different categories: maxims, metaphors, parables, commands, and legal sayings are a few. The fourth major category of form is *story about Jesus*. These stories are told to exalt the person of Jesus, but they lack any explicit supernatural elements.[52] The fifth form is *direct supernatural encounter story*.[53] This material contains the explicit presence of super-natural elements, whether good or evil. They show Jesus in connection with the supernatural and thus present him as a divine figure.[54]

The reader of the Gospel material must routinely ask which type of form is in view, as this will help determine how it should be understood. An important caveat is necessary at this point, however, because as stated previously, various proponents of form criticism have used it to make *historical* judgments about the material contained within the Gospels; that is, through a determination of the form, the critic purportedly can state whether the material can be traced back to Jesus or instead to its creation by the early church. The usefulness of form criticism as a historical tool is strongly contested by many, and with good reason: why

48. E.g., Jesus' interaction with the rich man (Mark 10:17-31 and parallels).

49. E.g., Jesus' interaction with Mary and Martha (Luke 10:38-42).

50. E.g., the stilling of the storm (Mark 4:35-41 and parallels).

51. For example, the "I am" sayings of Jesus in the Gospel of John would very naturally fall into this category.

52. E.g., Jesus in the temple as a young man (Luke 2:41-52). These are sometimes called legends, but this can be construed as a prejudgment against historicity and so is not preferred.

53. E.g., Jesus' temptation in the wilderness (Matt 4:1-11; Luke 4:1-13). These are sometimes called myths, but this also is not preferred since it seems to reject historicity a priori.

54. It is often argued that these final two categories are not so much classifications of form as they are classifications of content. This is true, so the student must be prepared to recognize this material in a variety of shapes, but it is still a useful category for discussing an important part of the Jesus material.

should the form of the material over and against other considerations be determinative of historical veracity? Instead, form criticism is useful as a *descriptive* tool which can guide the interpreter to the proper understanding of the material. To that end, the recognition of form can lead to interpretive information. If it is a pronouncement story, the emphasis is on Jesus' final statement; that is where the interpretive weight falls, and anything accompanying the saying should be interpreted in light of it. If it is a miracle story, the details and order of presentation should be examined to see the points of emphasis.[55] If the pericope contains sayings of Jesus, it should be examined in light of appropriate principles. If it is a story about Jesus, it should be examined to see how it explicitly exalts the person of Jesus. If it is a direct supernatural encounter story, it should be examined to see in what way it presents Jesus as a divine figure.

8.2.5 Redaction: The Stamp of the Evangelist

While source criticism examines the sources a particular Gospel author has used and form criticism examines the shape of those sources, redaction criticism examines the particular emphases of the author to determine his unique theological contribution to the Jesus story. This method acknowledges that the Gospel authors were not simply trying to record history; they were writing theology as well through their own choices and selections of the material available to them. This is done both on a macro and a micro scale, as individual changes within a pericope are examined to determine if any trends can be noted throughout the Gospel. Foundational to this investigation is the order of the composition of the Gospels, so redaction criticism must build upon a particular solution to the Synoptic Problem. Even if one wishes to remain agnostic regarding the order of the Gospels, the differences between them can be noticed and understood for their value.[56] Redaction criticism has great strength in that it forces a careful look at the text of each Gospel through an investigation into the similarities and differences between each one and the others. Thus it can both give indications of how each Gospel has contextualized its material and reveal the real force of implications of Jesus' teaching as it is presented in another Gospel. This method has weaknesses, however, in that it is dependent upon a source-critical viewpoint; if that changes, then all results must be reevaluated. In addition, there is danger in reading every change as theologically motivated when it could be attributed to stylistic variation or simple matters of presentation. With appropriate

---

55. For a detailed analysis of miracle stories, see Gerd Theissen, *The Miracle Stories of the Early Christian Tradition,* trans. Francis McDonagh (Philadelphia: Fortress, 1983).

56. This is more properly the approach of composition criticism.

caveats and diligence, though, this method can prove to be the most fruitful way of examining the text of the Gospels.[57]

The first step in redaction criticism is to color the pericope completely in a synopsis. Only when that is done will the student have the raw data needed to make decisions about theological emphases within a particular author. Next the student must choose the best solution for the Synoptic Problem. This solution determines the order of the Gospels and thus the order of any changes between them. Third, the student must look at changes within the pericope under consideration. Are there any variations in wording that are significant? Are there any variations in the order of the events within the pericope? Is there a significant change of emphasis between the accounts as they exist in each Gospel? Answers to these questions will highlight differences that could prove significant in elucidating the meaning of a particular Gospel story. Fourth, the student should look at large-scale differences concerning the pericope under consideration. Is the pericope in the same place in each Gospel? Is there different material before or after? Does the placement of the pericope in the Gospel under consideration give it a different setting than in the other Gospels? Fifth, the student should take the answers from the prior two questions and begin to make some assertions about the Gospel as a whole. Are there particular emphases that recur in this author?[58] Does he emphasize something that the other authors do not? Is there something that he minimizes? Can a structural pattern be recognized that gives clues as to what the author is doing, both within the pericope and within the larger section in which the pericope resides? All of this comes together to create a portrait of the theology of the evangelist, and this theology should be stated and explained to fill out the picture of Jesus that the reader gains from the Gospels.[59]

By way of example, Matthew's use of the word δικαιοσύνη can be illustrative. He uses the term seven times in his Gospel (Matt 3:15; 5:6, 10, 20; 6:1, 33; 21:32). By way of contrast, Mark does not use the term at all, Luke uses it only once (1:75, in Zechariah's hymn of prophecy), and John uses it twice (John 16:8, 10, when Jesus describes the future role of the Spirit). Thus Matthew places distinctive emphasis on the concept of righteousness; it can be regarded as an important theme somewhat

---

57. A helpful resource for the history and method of redaction criticism is Grant R. Osborne, "Redaction Criticism," in Black and Dockery, eds., *Interpreting the New Testament*, 128-49.

58. Concordance work with terms and concepts is key for this step.

59. A recent example of this type of work is Darrell L. Bock, *Jesus According to Scripture: Restoring the Portrait from the Gospels* (Grand Rapids, Mich.: Baker, 2002).

unique to his Gospel.[60] Exactly what he means by the term can then be determined by careful study of its uses in context.

8.3 Acts

The book of Acts, along with the Gospels, reports the history of the early church within a theological framework, all accomplished with the genre of narrative. When one approaches Acts, some of the same questions asked of the Gospels are appropriate. Acts is narrative, and all the questions appropriate to that genre can be asked and answered for a more fruitful understanding. Acts also has its own issues of culture that must be addressed. These can be answered with the appropriate questions and tools as discussed in the prior section. So there are many levels of similarity between Acts and the Gospels that allow for a similar method. There are some important differences from the Gospels, however, that must be addressed in order to understand what the narrative is teaching.

8.3.1 The Canonical Context: Connection to Luke

It has been widely recognized in studies on the book of Acts that it is not meant to be construed as a single-volume work. There are several points of connection between it and the Gospel of Luke which allow most scholars to claim a single author for both books; indeed, the connection is so tight that many scholars regard Acts as a continuation of Luke. This presents the first major issue in interpretation of the book of Acts: it must be interpreted in light of its connection to the Gospel of Luke. This affects many issues of interpretation, most notably the purpose for Acts.

Interpreting any book appropriately requires that issues such as purpose, occasion, and audience be investigated and stated; these inform and limit the interpretive options for any given book. This becomes much more complicated with Luke–Acts because of the seemingly divergent goals for each of these two books. It is a reasonable conclusion that the Gospel of Luke presents the birth, life, ministry, and death of Jesus Christ; it is meant to be informative and motivational. Acts has less unity. There is the growth of the church under the ministries of both Peter and Paul. Is one meant to be primary and the other secondary, or do they complement each other in some way? A major theme of the second half of Acts is Paul's

---

60. If one follows the Two or Four Source hypothesis as a solution to the Synoptic Problem, this emphasis is highlighted further, as Matthew has the term both in unique material and in material common to the other Synoptic Gospels. Thus he has *added* it even to received material (Mark and Q).

travel to Rome to face trial before Caesar, yet the book ends without a resolution to that theme; when we last see Paul he is under house arrest in Rome but is freely sharing the gospel with many visitors. The reader is left hanging in many respects. This has caused many people to argue that Acts serves the purpose of a legal document for Paul's trial, explaining the circumstances around his arrest and showing that Christianity was not a seditious sect. However, this purpose does not necessarily fit when Acts is placed alongside Luke.

The primary problem of the canonical context of the book of Acts is determining an appropriate purpose for the book of Acts which does justice both to its own contents and to the contents of the Gospel of Luke. This in turn provides the proper interpretive framework for understanding the narrative of Acts. It is generally regarded that the purpose of Luke–Acts must be construed quite broadly, but even so there are variations that are important for the reader to comprehend and apply to interpretation of the text.[61]

8.3.2 The Author as Historian

A great deal has been written on Luke as a historian and how that should impact the interpretation of Acts. The student can readily find discussions of this in commentaries and monographs. What is more central to the point of this article is the veracity of the historical material and thus its value for interpretation. It cannot be doubted that Luke desired to connect the growth of Christianity to the larger world stage. His inclusion of particular persons and relating of particular events argues for a sensitivity to the place Christianity had in the world. Thus conflict over the historical value of material in Acts is critical. As a rule, many in the scholarly world have been fairly skeptical of Luke's value as a historian, but certain studies have shown his accuracy in this realm.[62] The student in studying Acts must recognize the value of the history and be able to connect the narrative to the wider historical context. This will require

61. For a succinct overview of five major theories, see Donald Guthrie, *New Testament Introduction,* 4th ed. (Downers Grove, Ill.: InterVarsity Press, 1990), 365-71.

62. Of special note are William Mitchell Ramsay, *The Bearing of Recent Discovery on the Trustworthiness of the New Testament* (London, New York: Hodder & Stoughton, 1915); I. Howard Marshall, *Luke: Historian and Theologian* (Grand Rapids, Mich.: Zondervan, 1971); F. F. Bruce, *The Book of the Acts,* rev. ed., NICNT (Grand Rapids, Mich.: Eerdmans, 1988); Colin J. Hemer, *The Book of Acts in the Setting of Hellenistic History,* ed. Conrad H. Gempf, WUNT 49 (Tübingen: Mohr Siebeck, 1989); Bruce W. Winter, ed., *The Book of Acts in Its First Century Setting,* 5 vols. (Grand Rapids, Mich.: Eerdmans, 1993-96); Ben Witherington, *The Acts of the Apostles: A Socio-Rhetorical Commentary* (Grand Rapids, Mich.: Eerdmans, 1998); and Eckhard J. Schnabel, *Early Christian Mission,* 2 vols. (Downers Grove, Ill.: InterVarsity Press, 2004).

delving into the background with appropriate tools as described above to make those connections.

8.4 Theology from Narrative

The goal of investigation into biblical narrative is not simply to understand a good story or to be entertained. Biblical narrative was written for impact; the biblical authors related events that they knew both had importance for a wider audience and could make a claim for authority and changed lives as a result. Therefore the student must endeavor to understand biblical narrative not simply on the level of story but also on the level of theology. What should the reader understand about God, about the world, and about himself from reading the Gospels and Acts? How should the reader think differently? What should be done in response to this biblical truth? All of these questions can be answered by elucidating the theology of the biblical narrative under consideration.

Understanding the theology of the biblical text is not an easy task, and in some ways narrative complicates the picture because of its many facets. There are three main interlocking elements, however, that provide an appropriate framework for understanding the theology of narrative: *people, events,* and *themes.* Investigating these in turn as a capstone of study, building upon all the prior questions, opens the door to understanding the theology of the story.

8.4.1 People

Central to any narrative, as already stated, are the characters. They are the central focus of the story and provide the most natural connection to the life of the reader. Who are the main characters of the story? For the Gospels and Acts, this question is straightforward. Jesus of Nazareth is the central character of the Gospels; the Gospels tell about his birth, life, ministry, death, and resurrection. The main characters in Acts are Peter and Paul; the narrative describes their ministry of telling Jews and Gentiles about Jesus. Are there other major characters of note? Clearly there are: in the Gospels the disciples are constantly in view, as well as various opponents who set themselves against Jesus. In Acts there are many other characters in the narrative, ranging from compatriots of Peter and Paul to historic figures who interact with them at various points. There are a host of questions that can be asked about the characters that lead to theology. Specifically concerning Jesus, Peter, and Paul, one can ask, Why is this character central? What does the narrative tell me about this character that makes him so special? Concerning other characters, one can ask, Why are these characters included? How do they interact with the main character? Are they viewed positively or negatively? What quality about them is positive or negative? Are they positioned as someone to emulate, someone not to emulate, or perhaps as an example to learn from in some other way?

8.4.2 Events

Narrative is not simply a "who's who" listing of characters and their qualities. Stories are interesting because things happen to the characters. They have adventures that create tension and require resolution. Examining the nature of the events in biblical narrative and how it affects the characters is an important part of the theology. In the Gospels, Jesus is involved in many events, the central ones being the crucifixion and resurrection. In Acts, the events surrounding Peter are quite dramatic, including the coming of the Holy Spirit at Pentecost and the conversion of Cornelius the Gentile. Paul goes on three missionary journeys and then heads to Rome through a complex series of events with irony and plot twists. Even with other less central events, there are profitable questions to ask that help connect the character to the event. Where does this event fit into the larger time line of the narrative? Is it caused by another event, or does it in turn cause another event? Is the event positive for the characters involved or negative? Does it benefit the characters or hurt them? What do the characters do in this event? Does the event reinforce something already understood about the characters, or does it introduce a new aspect to them? How are they interacting with other characters and what can we learn about them from that?

8.4.3 Themes

An investigation into biblical themes strikes more naturally at the heart of the theology of narrative. It cannot be done, however, apart from the characters and events in the narrative. Once those have been thoroughly investigated, the reader can think about the themes and ideas of the text.[63]

There are several major themes presented in the Gospels and Acts. A primary one in the Gospels is the kingdom of God. The term itself is used

---

63. For a discussion of key themes within Jesus' teaching in the Gospels (but not key themes of the Gospels themselves), see Part 4, "A Theological Portrait of Jesus," in Bock, *Jesus According to Scripture*, 559-648. For a discussion of key themes within Acts, see I. Howard Marshall and David Peterson, eds., *Witness to the Gospel: The Theology of Acts* (Grand Rapids, Mich.: Eerdmans, 1998).

frequently by Jesus, and it forms a central aspect of Jesus' teaching and actions. A primary theme in Acts is the preaching of the gospel to those who have not heard, specifically Gentiles, who then join believing Jews in the kingdom of God. There are other lesser themes, though, which can profitably be investigated. There are many questions to ask and answer about these themes. What specifically about the characters and events points to the theme? What is asserted about the theme? It is not enough to say that a major theme of the Gospels is the kingdom of God. What about the kingdom of God is asserted by Jesus in his ministry? Is the theme positive or negative? How does the theme play out throughout the entirety of the book? How does the theme relate to time? What elements make it up? Does a key term for the theme always have the same definition when it is used? Is the theme "closed," in that it is encapsulated within the book itself, or is the theme "open," in that it points to the reality of the world beyond the story? Does the theme indicate that the reader should think or act differently? Does this theme relate to or dovetail with any others in the book?

8.4.4 Putting It Together: Expressing the Theology of Narrative

Once the reader has carefully investigated the people, the events, and the themes of the narrative, he is now in a position to express the theology. A caveat is in order, though: often in expressing theology, truths are stated in a static way. This can be useful to a point, but it should be recognized from the outset that this can be dangerous in that it minimizes the reality of the narrative. Narrative is action, and a theology that does not take that into account in its expression runs the risk of inadequately representing the narrative.

As before, the reader can ask and answer several questions to help formulate and express the theology of the narrative. First and foremost, what does the narrative tell about God and his actions in the world? The Bible as a whole is ultimately a story about God and his ways. The Gospels and Acts tell the story about God working through Jesus, Peter, and Paul. What do these narratives tell about God? What are his concerns? How does he work? What is his character and how is it revealed? Second, what does the narrative tell about humanity and our actions in the world? More specifically, how does humanity react to God and his actions? How does humanity relate to Jesus, Peter, and Paul? Are there differences in the way particular people react? Can these differences be traced to a particular cause, perhaps innate to the person or affecting them from outside? Third, how must humanity react in order to properly relate to God? What requirements does God place upon humanity, and what must be done in response? After asking these questions, the reader should endeavor to formulate an expression of the theology of the narrative. Once this is done, the reader will understand more clearly how narrative speaks to the reader, and how it lays claim to his or her life for change.

8.5 Conclusion

The church in many ways has a hot-and-cold relationship with narrative. We love the stories they tell and the mighty acts of God they describe, but when it comes to learning from narrative and systematically expressing its teachings, we are often on shaky ground. If the reader consistently applies proper method to the Gospels and Acts, he will be able to understand its theology and express that to his own benefit and the benefit of others. In many ways this takes a lifetime of work. The task is so vast that we are always deepening our knowledge of the narrative, but when the subject of our study is the Scriptures, this is a good thing. Narrative is exciting business; read on, and be blessed.

8.6 For Further Reading

Bock, Darrell L. "Form Criticism." In *Interpreting the New Testament: Essays on Methods and Issues,* ed. David Alan Black and David S. Dockery, 106-27. Nashville: Broadman & Holman, 2001.

Bock, Darrell L. *Studying the Historical Jesus: A Guide to Sources and Methods.* Grand Rapids, Mich.: Baker, 2002.

Burge, Gary M. "Interpreting the Gospel of John." In *Interpreting the New Testament: Essays on Methods and Issues,* ed. David Alan Black and David S. Dockery, 357-90. Nashville: Broadman & Holman, 2001.

Marshall, I. Howard. *Luke: Historian and Theologian.* Grand Rapids, Mich.: Zondervan, 1971.

McKnight, Edgar V. *What Is Form Criticism?* Guides to Biblical Scholarship: New Testament Series. Philadelphia: Fortress, 1969.

McKnight, Scot. *Interpreting the Synoptic Gospels.* Guides to New Testament Exegesis. Grand Rapids, Mich.: Baker, 1988.

Osborne, Grant R. "Redaction Criticism." In *Interpreting the New Testament: Essays on Methods and Issues,* ed. David Alan Black and David S. Dockery, 128-49. Nashville: Broadman & Holman, 2001.

Resseguie, James L. *Narrative Criticism of the New Testament: An Introduction.* Grand Rapids, Mich.: Baker, 2005.

Stein, Robert H. *Studying the Synoptic Gospels: Origin and Interpretation.* 2nd ed. Grand Rapids, Mich.: Baker, 2001.

Epistolary Genre   9

Reading Ancient Letters

JOHN D. GRASSMICK

There are many types or genres of literature, and each one has its own characteristics that affect interpretation. New Testament literature has three primary genres: narrative (Gospels and Acts), epistolary (NT epistles or letters), and apocalyptic (Revelation). Within these primary genres are various subgenres, each with its own characteristics and interpretive issues.

The earliest Christian writings known to us are letters. Twenty-one of the twenty-seven books in the New Testament canon are considered "letters," constituting about one-third of the NT. They were written during the first century AD.[1] Thirteen of these letters (Romans through Philemon) name the apostle Paul as the author and are known as the "Pauline cor-

---

1. None of the NT letters gives its date of composition. Because various factors are involved, the dates of many of these letters are debated. For discussion see the relevant sections in Donald Guthrie, *New Testament Introduction*, rev. ed. (Downers Grove, Ill.: InterVarsity Press, 1990); and D. A. Carson and Douglas J. Moo, *An Introduction to the New Testament*, 2nd ed. (Grand Rapids, Mich.: Zondervan, 2005). Harold Hoehner has made a valuable contribution to the study of chronology in the life of Christ and the apostolic era. Based on his Th.D. dissertation, "Chronology of the Apostolic Age" (Dallas Seminary, 1965), he dates James around AD 44-47, the Pauline and Petrine letters between AD 49-67, Hebrews around AD 67-69, Jude about AD 75, and 1, 2, and 3 John between AD 85-95. I offer this chapter in honor of Dr. Hoehner

pus" of letters.[2] The author of Hebrews is anonymous.[3] The remaining seven letters (James through Jude) are known as the "General Epistles." One of them names James, the brother of Jesus, as the author; two bear the name of the apostle Peter (1 and 2 Peter); three are attributed to the apostle John (1, 2, and 3 John); and one bears the name of Jude, the brother of Jesus and James (cf. Mark 6:3; Gal 2:9; Jude 1).[4] In addition, two brief letters are included in Acts (15:23-29; 23:25-30); seven letters appear in Revelation (2:1–3:22), which itself has an epistolary framework (cf. 1:4-5; 22:21); and the use of letters is mentioned elsewhere in the NT (e.g., Acts 9:2; 22:5; 23:25, 33; 1 Cor 5:9; 16:3; 2 Cor 3:1-3; 10:9-11; Col 4:16; 2 Thess 2:2, 15; 2 Pet 3:1, 16). This shows the importance of letters in Christian circles of the first century.

The NT letters share some of the characteristics found in many Greco-Roman letters of the first century AD. In this chapter we will survey key features of Greco-Roman letters and then focus attention on the NT letters in regard to terminology, main characteristics, structural form, and guidelines for interpreting them.

9.1 Greco-Roman Letters

Letter writing reached a high point of development in Greco-Roman times (ca. 300 BC–AD 300), and letters became the main means of writ-

---

as a token of appreciation for his exemplary and salutary influence in my life as a professor, mentor, colleague, and friend.

2. For various reasons, the authorship of six letters in the Pauline corpus—Ephesians, Colossians, 2 Thessalonians, 1 and 2 Timothy, and Titus—is disputed. For discussion and arguments in favor of Pauline authorship, see the relevant chapters on these letters in Guthrie, *Introduction*, and Carson and Moo, *Introduction*. For a masterful defense of the Pauline authorship of Ephesians, see Harold W. Hoehner, *Ephesians: An Exegetical Commentary* (Grand Rapids, Mich.: Baker, 2002), 2-61.

3. Although various suggestions concerning authorship have been made, we do not know who wrote Hebrews. An authorized courier and/or a cover letter may have identified the author to the original readers, verifying the document's authenticity. See Guthrie, *Introduction*, 668-82.

4. The designation "General Epistles" was used originally because most of these letters lacked specific destinations and it was assumed they were intended for Christians everywhere. These epistles are regarded by many NT scholars as pseudonymous writings; that is, they were not written by the person whose name they bear but by another unknown individual at a later time. For discussion and arguments in favor of the author named, see the relevant chapters on these letters in Guthrie, *Introduction*, and Carson and Moo, *Introduction*. An excellent treatment of pseudonymity that argues against its presence in the NT on historical, theological, ethical, and psychological grounds can be found in Terry L. Wilder, "Pseudonymity and the New Testament," in *Interpreting the New Testament: Essays on Method and Issues*, ed. David Alan Black and David S. Dockery (Nashville: Broadman & Holman, 2001), 296-335.

ten communication at every level of society.[5] Latin (Roman) letter writers adopted the epistolary conventions of Greek letter writers before them. A collection of letters written by Roman statesman and orator Marcus Cicero (106-43 BC) had a major influence on letter writing. Soon after, letters in the Greco-Roman world were written not only for private communication but also for public reading. Increasingly the letter form was used for philosophical teaching and moral exhortation, a use found earlier among some Greek philosophers such as Plato (427-348 BC) and Aristotle (384-322 BC). Roman philosopher Lucius Seneca (4 BC–AD 65) wrote many treatises with epistolary features.

Of equal importance were thousands of private letters written on papyri in everyday language. These letters came from a cross section of ancient Greco-Roman life and included legal contracts, business arrangements, family matters, and communication between relatives and friends. The following is an ordinary Hellenistic (Greek) letter from Mystarion, an Egyptian olive-planter, to Stotoëtis, a chief priest, written about AD 50:

> Mystarion to his own Stotoëtis, many greetings! I have sent you my [worker] Blastus for forked sticks for my olive gardens. See then that you stay him not [i.e., detain him]. For you know how I need him every hour. [In another handwriting] Farewell. In year 11 of Tiberius Claudius Caesar Augustus Germanicus Imperator in the month Sebastos 15. [In the first handwriting] To Stotoëtis, chief priest, at the island . . . [final words missing].[6]

This is an example of a private business letter containing the basic formal structure of a Greek letter plus the date, but lacking the usual statements of concern for the recipient's health. It reflects simple grammar, brevity, lack of personal expressions, and the probable use of a secretary or scribe.

Essentially a letter was a substitute for a personal meeting between a sender and recipient who were separated by physical distance. In general, letters served the same purposes as oral communication: (1) to provide

5. The brief overview in this section is based on material presented in William G. Doty, *Letters in Primitive Christianity* (Philadelphia: Fortress, 1973), 1-17; Stanley K. Stowers, *Letter Writing in Greco-Roman Antiquity* (Philadelphia: Westminster, 1986), 27-40; David E. Aune, *The New Testament in Its Literary Environment* (Philadelphia: Westminster, 1987), 160-74; and Abraham J. Malherbe, *Ancient Epistolary Theorists* (Atlanta: Scholars, 1988), 2-14, 21-29.

6. Berliner Griechische Urkunden (BGU), No. 37; reprinted with a photograph in Adolf Deissmann, *Light from the Ancient East: The New Testament Illustrated by Recently Discovered Texts of the Graeco-Roman World*, trans. Lionel R. M. Strachan (London: Hodder & Stoughton, 1927; reprint, Peabody, Mass.: Hendrickson, 1995), 170-72. For access to many Greek papyri letters with translations, see *Select Papyri*, trans. A. S. Hunt and C. C. Edgar, 2 vols., Loeb Classical Library (Harvard University Press, 1932-34). A helpful introduction to papyrus letters, including many translations, is John L. White, *Light from Ancient Letters* (Philadelphia: Fortress, 1986).

information or instruction, (2) to make requests or issue commands, and
(3) to maintain or deepen the relationship between the correspondents.
The same letter may have served more than one of these purposes.[7] Most
Greco-Roman letters have three parts: an opening, a body, and a closing.
The opening and closing sections usually follow a conventional pattern
while the structure of the body depends on the author's purpose and
the message he or she wishes to convey.[8] Some of these letters exhibit
the influence of classical rhetoric since some of its oral features were
adaptable in written correspondence.[9] There were also many different
types of ancient letters, depending on the circumstances related to their
composition and the purposes they served. They have been classified in
various ways such as letters of friendship, official letters, and letter-essays,
to name a few.[10]

In contrast to the large number and variety of Greco-Roman letters,
only a few Jewish letters have survived, and most of these exhibit Hellenistic epistolary traits (cf. 1 Macc 12:6-18; 2 Macc 1:1-10).[11] Similarly,
early Christian writings were influenced more by Greco-Roman than by
Jewish epistolary conventions.

9.2 Terminology: NT Epistles or Letters?

The Greek word used in the NT for a "letter" is ἐπιστολή. Originally
it referred to an oral message delivered by a messenger, but in time it became the usual term for a written message, often in the form of a letter.
Thus in most English translations it is rendered "letter."

The distinction sometimes made between an "epistle" and a "letter"
comes from the literary studies of Adolf Deissmann in the early twentieth
century. In the late nineteenth and early twentieth centuries a large number
of Greek papyrus letters were discovered in Egypt that reflected a wide
cross section of everyday life in the Greco-Roman world. Deissmann

---

7. Victor P. Furnish, "Letters in the New Testament," in *Eerdmans Commentary on the
Bible*, ed. James D. G. Dunn and John Rogerson (Grand Rapids, Mich.: Eerdmans, 2003),
1269.

8. Aune, *Literary Environment*, 162-64; Furnish, "Letters," *ECB*, 1271.

9. Aune, *Literary Environment*, 198-99. For an introduction to Greek rhetoric with
application to NT passages, see George A. Kennedy, *New Testament Interpretation Through
Rhetorical Criticism* (Chapel Hill: University of North Carolina Press, 1984).

10. Stowers, *Letter Writing*, 49-175; Aune, *Literary Environment*, 161-69. Furnish, "Letters," *ECB*, 1271, suggests that students of the NT may find it helpful to think of Greco-Roman
letters in one of three general classes: (1) ordinary letters containing routine information, requests,
or appeals; (2) administrative or official letters; and (3) edifying letters advocating a point of
view or a particular course of action.

11. Aune, *Literary Environment*, 174-80; Furnish, "Letters," *ECB*, 1272.

studied these documents and made a distinction between "epistles" and "letters." In his view "epistles" were artistic literary works written for public reading and future posterity, while "letters" were personal, private messages related to specific situations and not intended for a wider public or posterity. Epistles were well-crafted literary compositions; letters were spontaneous, "occasional" (situational) documents written in everyday language. He compared the NT documents with these papyrus texts and concluded that Paul's writings (except the Pastoral Epistles) as well as 2 and 3 John were "real letters" and the remaining NT letter-form writings were "epistles."[12]

Deissmann's studies were helpful in his day because they focused attention on the historical circumstances and literary features of ordinary letters in the ancient world and revealed many parallels to the NT writings. However, subsequent study has shown that his distinction between epistles and letters is not adequate, especially when applied to the NT. It is no longer employed today, and the terms "epistle" and "letter" tend to be used as synonyms.[13] On one hand, Deissmann overemphasized the similarity between papyrus letters and the Pauline letters, failing to give proper consideration to the well-crafted literary aspects of Paul's letters. On the other hand, he minimized the historical settings of the NT writings he called "epistles." For our purposes, we will use the term "letters" in a nuanced literary sense for the NT writings designated as such, and the adjective "epistolary" will simply mean "associated with a letter or letter writing." Since Deissmann's work, there have been many studies related to the characteristics, forms, and types of letters in the Greco-Roman world, along with comparisons to the NT letters.[14]

9.3 Characteristics of NT Letters

The letters of Greco-Roman antiquity could be placed in two general categories: informal, "nonliterary," private letters; and formal, literary, public letters. The former were part of everyday life and were intended only for the person addressed, while the latter were intended for a public audience. The NT letters occupy a middle ground between these two categories. Some are more informal and personal, such as Philemon, 2 John, and 3 John, while others are more formal and literary, like

12. Deissmann, *Light*, 146-52, 233-51.
13. Aune, *Literary Environment*, 161.
14. Scholars have produced a large amount of literature in this area. See the selected bibliography included at the end of this chapter.

Romans, Ephesians, and Hebrews. At the same time, the latter contain personal elements and the former display literary qualities. The NT letters exhibit several characteristics that reveal many similarities and some differences from other ancient letters. We call attention to four main characteristics.

9.3.1 Authoritative Substitutes for Personal Presence

In the ancient world, as today, a letter served as a substitute for the personal presence of the writer with the reader. It was a substitute for oral, face-to-face communication. In the early church, when an apostle or another leader was not able to address a congregation in person he wrote a letter. The recipients of a letter from Peter, for example, viewed it as a substitute for the personal presence of the apostle himself.

Two additional factors are important for the NT letters. First, Paul, Peter, and John wrote as apostles of Jesus Christ (Gal 1:1; Eph 1:1; 2 Pet 1:1; 1 John 1:1-4 with John 1:14 implied). They were "present" as apostles commissioned by Jesus Christ to those they addressed. Their letters carried authority as Christ's authentic representatives and functioned as authoritative substitutes for their personal presence (cf. 2 Cor 10:8-11). Even the authors who were not apostles were associated with an apostle and were likely viewed as God-appointed leaders by the congregations they addressed. The NT letters, along with the four Gospels, Acts, and Revelation, have been accepted by the church as "canonical." Evangelical Christians receive them as God's revelation, divinely inspired and equal in authority to the Hebrew Scriptures (the OT). At the same time they also affirm that these writings are written by human authors in specific historical situations for specific purposes using literary forms current at that time.[15]

Second, although the NT authors wrote with authority, both the writers and recipients viewed themselves as "one in Christ and equal before God, brothers and sisters within the same family of faith. This accounts for the distinctive tone of the letters, which manifest the warmth and familiarity of correspondence between family members or friends even while they are establishing the absent writer as an authoritative presence with the recipients."[16] Thus from the beginning the NT letters had a normative, authoritative status with a distinctive familial tone.

---

15. Richard N. Longenecker, "On the Form, Function, and Authority of the New Testament Letters," in *Scripture and Truth,* ed. D. A. Carson and John D. Woodbridge (Grand Rapids, Mich.: Zondervan, 1983), 101-14, esp. 101.

16. Furnish, "Letters," *ECB,* 1273.

9.3.2 Addressed to Christian Communities

Most NT letters are addressed to specific church congregations and they usually open and close by invoking God's blessing on those addressed (e.g., 1 Cor 1:3 and 16:23; Jude 2 and 24-25) or by expressing thanks to God for blessings he has bestowed on them (e.g., Rom 1:8-15; 1 Pet 1:3-9). The letters were intended to be read aloud to the congregation for the benefit of everyone (e.g., 1 Thess 5:27; 2 Thess 2:15). They offer instruction, counsel, and encouragement to strengthen the faith and improve the moral and spiritual well-being of each one in the congregation. Apparently some letters were meant to be exchanged with other churches. Accordingly, Paul wanted his letter to the Colossians to be read to the Laodiceans and his letter to the Laodiceans, now lost to us, to be read to the Colossians (Col 4:16).

9.3.3 Careful Composition and Delivery

Most of the NT letters are longer than other Greco-Roman letters. The average length of private Greco-Roman letters was about 87 words, ranging from 18 to 209 words, while the literary letters of Seneca averaged 995 words ranging from 149 to 4,134 words. By comparison, the thirteen Pauline letters average 2,495 words, ranging in length from 335 words (Philemon) to 7,114 words (Romans).[17] The additional length was necessary given the pastoral needs in the various congregations that had to be addressed from a distance.

The process of composing and delivering a letter was somewhat complex.[18] Greco-Roman letters indicate that a trained secretary (amanuensis) was often used to write letters and then in his own handwriting the author/sender would often add personal greetings, a farewell word, and sometimes the date, thereby taking responsibility for what was written. The presence of a secretary is evident either by direct statement, by inference, or by a difference in handwriting style in the letter.[19] The writing skills of secretaries varied, as did the extent of freedom they were given in writing the letter. Nevertheless it was assumed that the author/sender was responsible for everything written.

17. E. Randolph Richards, *The Secretary in the Letters of Paul*, WUNT 2:42 (Tübingen: Mohr Siebeck, 1991), 213.

18. M. Luther Stirewalt, Jr., *Paul, the Letter Writer* (Grand Rapids, Mich.: Eerdmans, 2003), 1-24. Stirewalt discusses the logistics of ancient Greek letter writing and argues that Paul fashioned the logistics for his letters after examples of official rather than personal correspondence. The term *logistics* refers to "the means by which a letter is composed, delivered, and received" (1).

19. See note 6 and the example of a Greco-Roman letter given above.

Even though we possess no original manuscripts of any NT letters, many scholars assume that the authors followed current letter writing practices including the use of secretaries, although they were probably trusted apostolic associates rather than trained scribes. That Paul used a secretary is evident from Rom 16:22, where the secretary identifies himself as Tertius, and from several other letters in which Paul makes reference to a personal subscription in his own handwriting (1 Cor 16:21; Gal 6:11; Col 4:18; 2 Thess 3:17; Phlm 19). It also seems likely that Silvanus served as a secretary in 1 Peter (1 Pet 5:12). Regardless of the amount of freedom a secretary was given in the composition of the letter, the author, not the secretary, was responsible for its final content.[20] Paul's letters as well as the other NT letters show evidence of being composed with care and pastoral concern. They have a literary quality lacking in the papyri letters. Even some of Paul's critics conceded that his letters were "weighty and forceful" (2 Cor 10:10-11).

When a finished copy of a letter was ready to send, it was usually delivered by a trusted friend or associate who was traveling to the destination for some reason. Three men named in 1 Cor 16:17 had apparently brought a letter to Paul from the Corinthian congregation (1 Cor 7:1) so he likely sent 1 Corinthians back with them. Epaphroditus carried Philippians on his return home to Philippi (Phil 2:25). Phoebe was the courier for Romans (Rom 16:1-2), Tychicus for Ephesians (Eph 6:21-22) and Colossians (Col 4:7-9), and Onesimus for Philemon, which was written on his behalf (Phlm 10-17). If a letter was intended for more than one congregation, such as Galatians (Gal 1:2) and probably Ephesians (Eph 1:1) as well as several of the "General Epistles" (e.g., Jas 1:1; 1 Pet 1:1), more than one copy may have been written and more than one courier sent to deliver it. Once delivered to its destination, the letter would be read aloud perhaps initially by the courier to the person who first received it and then to all the members of the congregation at their next meeting. In some cases the courier was expected to provide additional details related to the author or the letter (cf. Eph 6:21-22; Col 4:7-9).

9.3.4 Occasional Writings

Most, if not all, of the NT letters may be considered "occasional" documents. This means they reflect a particular historical situation and were written to address specific issues or problems related to the author or, more often, the readers. The Pauline letters, with some debate about

20. For further discussion, see Richard N. Longenecker, "Ancient Amanuenses and the Pauline Epistles," in *New Dimensions in New Testament Study,* ed. Richard N. Longenecker and Merrill C. Tenney (Grand Rapids, Mich.: Zondervan, 1974), 281-97.

Romans and Ephesians, are pastoral letters in which Paul applies Christian theology to specific issues facing the congregation(s) or individual(s) he addresses.[21] For example, Paul wrote Galatians because some false teachers were opposing him and troubling the Galatian Christians by advocating a return to the Mosaic Law and pressuring them to abandon the gospel of grace he had preached to them (Gal 1:6-9; 5:2-12).

It can be argued that the General Epistles also have a striking local and deeply pastoral character to their teaching and moral exhortation in spite of the fact that several of them lack some epistolary features.[22] The topics they cover and the material the authors use are determined by the particular issues facing the addressees even if we do not know their precise identity. For example, James introduces three themes in chapter 1—trials and temptations, wisdom and speech, and wealth and poverty—and develops them in reverse order in the rest of the letter.[23]

The occasional nature of the NT letters, especially the Pauline letters, indicates several additional things about them. First, they are not treatises of systematic theology, even though they do contain much theology that is pastorally applied to the circumstances faced by those the author addresses.[24] Second, though occasional, the letters are carefully constructed and carry apostolic authority (cf. 1 Cor 14:37; Gal 1:8). Third, because they are occasional, there is historical distance between the first readers and us. The "epistolary situation" must be identified and reconstructed from the letter itself or inferred through appropriate "mirror reading."[25] Some letters provide clear information about their historical situation (e.g., 1 Cor 1:10-15; 16:15-18) while others do not (e.g., 1 John 2:18-19). Some historical situations are easier to reconstruct than others. The

---

21. Some interpreters view Romans and Ephesians as "tractate letters" since they appear to be less "occasional" than other Pauline letters. See Longenecker, "Form, Function, and Authority," 104-6. Others contend that these writings address specific historical situations. On Romans, see Thomas R. Schreiner, *Romans*, BECNT 6 (Grand Rapids, Mich.: Baker, 1998), 10-23. On Ephesians, see Hoehner, *Ephesians*, 69-77, who concludes that "Ephesians is an actual letter with a mixture of genre and styles, such as other Hellenistic and Pauline letters" (77).

22. J. Daryl Charles, "Interpreting the General Epistles," in Black and Dockery, eds., *Interpreting the New Testament*, 433-56, esp. 453 n. 34.

23. This analysis of James as a chiasmus appears in Peter H. Davids, *The Epistle of James*, NIGTC (Grand Rapids, Mich.: Eerdmans, 1982).

24. J. Christiaan Beker, *Paul the Apostle: The Triumph of God in Life and Thought* (Philadelphia: Fortress, 1980), 11-16, uses the terms "contingent" and "coherent" with respect to the Pauline letters. They are "contingent" in that they address specific historical circumstances, but they express a "coherent" theology and theological worldview. For further discussion see Thomas R. Schreiner, "Interpreting the Pauline Epistles," in Black and Dockery, eds., *Interpreting the New Testament*, 412-32, esp. 412-15.

25. On "mirror reading" in the letters, see Schreiner, "Interpreting," 415-21.

"what" (main message) may be clear but the "how" and "why" (various details) may not be. All this has an impact on interpretation, as we shall observe later.

9.4 Structure of NT Letters

Most of the NT letters have the same overall structure and component parts as an ordinary Greco-Roman letter. The standard form consisted of an opening (also called an introduction or prescript), a body or main text of the letter, and a closing (also called a conclusion or postscript). Depending on the purpose and content of the letter, the NT author may modify or vary the length, style, and substance of these formal elements.

9.4.1 The Opening of the Letter

The opening of a NT letter usually has the following four elements: (1) the author/sender (e.g., Paul), (2) the recipients (e.g., "to the churches in Galatia"), (3) the greeting or salutation (e.g., "grace and peace to you . . ."), and (4) an introductory prayer that was usually a thanksgiving (e.g., "I thank my God . . . and this is my prayer," Phil 1:3-11). All the Pauline letters have an opening, as do the non-Pauline letters except Hebrews and 1 John. Careful reading of the opening is important because the author often mentions key ideas or themes that he will develop in the letter.

The NT *author/sender* often designates himself in certain ways and adds details that serve the message of the letter and are significant for interpretation. Paul identifies himself as an "apostle" in all but four of his letters, namely, 1 and 2 Thessalonians, Philippians, and Philemon. He uses the term "slave" (δοῦλος, "bond-servant") in combination with "apostle" in Tit 1:1 and by itself in Philippians 1:1 and the term "prisoner" in Phlm 1. Only the Thessalonian letters have no additional designation. Four times Paul identifies himself with the words "an apostle of Christ Jesus by the will of God" (2 Cor 1:1; Eph 1:1; Col 1:1; 2 Tim 1:1). Romans and Galatians are distinctive (note also Tit 1:1-3). In Rom 1:1-6 Paul elaborates on his apostleship and the gospel he preached in order to introduce himself to his readers in Rome. In Gal 1:1-2a he emphasized the divine origin of his apostleship because his authority as an apostle and his gospel were being questioned by his opponents and the Galatians. Paul also lists various co-senders in his letters such as Timothy (2 Cor 1:1; Phil 1:1; Col 1:1; Phlm 1), Silas and Timothy (1 Thess 1:1; 2 Thess 1:1), Sosthenes (1 Cor 1:1), and "all the brothers with me" (Gal 1:2). Five letters do not mention co-senders (Rom 1:1; Eph 1:1; 1 Tim 1:1; 2 Tim 1:1; Tit 1:1). He names these associates because they participated with him in establishing and caring for these churches. While they had an important supportive role, it is unlikely that they were coauthors in the actual composition of the letters.

Among the non-Pauline NT letters, Peter designates himself as "an apostle of Jesus Christ" (1 Pet 1:1) and "a servant and apostle of Jesus Christ" (2 Pet 1:1). James identifies himself as "a servant of God and of the Lord Jesus Christ" (James 1:1), and Jude calls himself "a servant of Jesus Christ and a brother of James" (Jude 1). The writer of 2 and 3 John simply identifies himself as "the elder," traditionally viewed as the apostle John (2 John 1; 3 John 1).[26]

The *addressees* or recipients of the NT letters are usually Christian congregations in various locations around the northern Mediterranean region. Even when an individual is addressed, such as Timothy, Titus, Philemon, Gaius (3 John 1), or "the chosen lady" (2 John 1), the author has a Christian congregation in view.[27] Except for 3 John, the addressees of the non-Pauline NT letters either are not named directly (i.e., Hebrews, 1 John) or are identified in general terms such as "the twelve tribes scattered among the nations" (James 1:1; note also 1 Pet 1:1; 2 Pet 1:1; Jude 1). More specific identification must be derived from evidence in the letter itself.

In his letters, Paul often refers to his readers with distinctive Christian terms or phrases such as "all in Rome who are loved by God and called to be saints" (Rom 1:7), "To the church of God in Corinth, to those sanctified in Christ Jesus and called to be holy" (1 Cor 1:2), and "To the holy and faithful brothers in Christ at Colossae" (Col 1:2, ESV). In Philippians Paul includes a reference to "the overseers and deacons" (Phil 1:1), the only letter where church leaders are mentioned with the addressees. Significantly, Galatians lacks any descriptive term or phrase (simply "To the churches in Galatia," Gal 1:2).

The *greeting* in a NT letter follows the identification of the author and the addressees. The standard Greek epistolary greeting was χαίρειν ("greetings"). In the NT this simple salutation occurs only in Acts 15:23 and 23:25-26 and in James 1:1. All of Paul's letters have a similar greeting expressed in its simplest form as "Grace and peace to you" (1 Thess 1:1) or expanded with the phrase "from God our Father" (Col 1:2) to make the source explicit, and further amplified to include the words "and our [or, the] Lord Jesus Christ" (Rom 1:7; 1 Cor 1:3; 2 Cor 1:2; Gal 1:3a; Eph 1:2; Phil 1:2; 2 Thess 1:2; Phlm 3), or "Christ Jesus our Savior" (Tit

26. See Guthrie, *Introduction*, 880-86, 891-92. All English translations are from the NIV unless stated otherwise.

27. On the identity of "the chosen lady," see Guthrie, *Introduction*, 886-89.

1:4b). First and Second Timothy have "Grace, mercy and peace from God the Father and Christ Jesus our Lord" (1 Tim 1:2b; 2 Tim 1:2b). Galatians is distinctive because the greeting is expanded into a doxology concluding with "Amen" (Gal 1:3-5). Paul made a wordplay on the usual Greek epistolary word of greeting (χαίρειν) and replaced it with the word "grace" (χάρις), a distinctive element in the Christian gospel, and he added the traditional Hebrew greeting "peace" (shalôm, שָׁלוֹם). The source of both is God the Father and the Lord Jesus Christ. In this way Paul modified the standard letter greeting and gave it a distinctively Christian meaning.

In the non-Pauline NT letters that have a greeting, it occurs in the form of a sincere wish: "May grace and peace be multiplied to you" (Greek optative mood verb, 1 Pet 1:2b, ESV), which is expanded with the words, "through the knowledge of God and of Jesus our Lord" (2 Pet 1:2), and varied with the words, "May mercy, peace, and love be multiplied to you" (Jude 2, ESV). The greeting in 2 John is a promise statement: "Grace, mercy and peace from God the Father and from Jesus Christ, the Father's Son, will be with us in truth and love" (2 John 3).

The final element in the opening of a letter is a *prayer,* usually of thanksgiving to God.[28] Many Greco-Roman letters begin with a health wish and a prayer to the gods for the reader(s). After the greeting, all of Paul's letters, except Galatians and Titus, have a prayer of thanksgiving and petition (e.g., Rom 1:8-17; 1 Cor 1:4-9; Phil 1:3-11; 2 Tim 1:3-7) that begins with the formulaic words, "I thank God . . ." (or an equivalent), or a blessing in the form of a eulogy of praise to God beginning with the words, "Praise be to the God and Father of our Lord Jesus Christ" (2 Cor 1:3-7; and Eph 1:3-14 followed by a thanksgiving prayer, 1:15-23). There is also a prayer eulogy to God in 1 Peter (1:3-12) and a prayer wish for good health in 3 John (v. 2). The other non-Pauline NT letters lack a prayer or thanksgiving following the greeting.

In the opening prayer/thanksgiving section of his letters, Paul often demonstrates his pastoral gratitude and care for his readers and uses this section to introduce important themes that he will develop later in the letter. When distinctive modifications are made, the interpreter should pay close attention. For example, when Paul omits a thanksgiving prayer in Galatians and moves directly from the greeting to strong rebuke, it indicates his deep displeasure with the Galatian Christians for thinking about abandoning the gospel he preached to them.

---

28. For further study of the introductory thanksgiving prayers in Paul's letters, see Peter T. O'Brien, *Introductory Thanksgivings in the Letters of Paul,* NovTSup 49 (Leiden: Brill, 1977).

9.4.2 *The Body of the Letter*

The body of a letter is its center section and is usually the largest part of the letter. It contains the information the author wants to convey to his readers in line with his purpose for writing. In many cases the author addresses specific circumstances or issues facing his readers, but in some cases the "epistolary situation" appears to be more general. The distinct purposes of the authors and the varied circumstances of their readers have produced different kinds of letters in the NT. Though there are similarities, they do not follow a standard format. For this reason formal analysis is difficult, and classifying a NT letter according to a preexisting type is problematic. Most are "multifunctional and have a 'mixed' character, combining elements from two or more epistolary types."[29] Nevertheless it is helpful to investigate the body of NT letters for some common features and influences from letter writing in the Greco-Roman world.

9.4.2.1 TRANSITIONAL FORMULAS

In Greco-Roman letters certain formulaic clauses were often used at the beginning and near the end of the body of the letter as well as in transitions from one section to another within the body. For example, in a letter from the mid-first century AD, the body of the letter begins with a common disclosure formula, "I want you to know" and near the end it has a common transitional formula, "Finally, then."[30]

Several transitional formulas are evident in the body of the Pauline letters. Two letters have a disclosure formula stated positively, "I want you to know, brothers" (Gal 1:11; Phil 1:12); two others have the formula stated negatively, "I do not want you to be unaware, brothers" (Rom 1:13; cf. 2 Cor 1:8); and both statements occur within the body of a letter to introduce another important topic in Paul's discussion (cf. 1 Cor 10:1; 12:1; 15:1; 1 Thess 4:13). The transition to a new section as Paul moves toward his conclusion is sometimes expressed by "Finally, brothers" (e.g., Phil 3:1; 4:8). Several letters contain an appeal formula, "I urge [beseech] you, brothers" (or equivalent), to indicate a change in subject or to introduce a request or exhortation (e.g., Rom 12:1; 15:30; 16:17; 1 Cor 1:10; 1 Thess 4:1b, 10b; 5:12, 14; 2 Thess 2:1; Phlm 9-10). A formulaic expression of confidence, "I am confident in the Lord" (or equivalent), also occurs several times in Paul's letters (e.g., Gal 5:10; 2 Cor 7:4, 16; 2 Thess 3:4; Phlm 21). Even though identifying these transitional formulas is a useful interpretive device, it must be noted that Paul him-

---

29. Aune, *Literary Environment*, 203.
30. Papyrus no. 91 in White, *Light from Ancient Letters*, 143.

self and the other NT authors made literary transitions by other means without using these formulas.

9.4.2.2 Influence of Classical Rhetoric

In recent years scholars have noted that the standard features of classical rhetoric have influenced the type and style of Greco-Roman letters to some extent. There are three major types of rhetoric: (1) judicial (forensic, apologetic), (2) deliberative (hortatory, advisory), and (3) epideictic (demonstrative, laudatory). Judicial rhetoric was designed to persuade an audience about the rightness or wrongness of a past action or event. Accusation and defense were two forms of argument used. Deliberative rhetoric was designed to convince an audience about the benefits of a future course of action. Persuasion and dissuasion were two forms of argument used. Epideictic rhetoric was designed to urge an audience to affirm a point of view or set of values or aspirations in the present. Praise and blame or criticism were two approaches used.[31]

A full-blown, ideal rhetorical speech would have six elements: (1) the *exordium* (or *proem*, introduction) that would capture the attention and goodwill of the audience and give a reason for the speech; (2) the *narratio*, that would contain background and the relevant facts of the case; (3) the *propositio*, the thesis to be proved; (4) the *probatio*, proofs or arguments for the case; (5) the *refutatio*, answers to opposing views or arguments or anticipated objections; and (6) the *peroratio* (or *epilogue*, conclusion) that would summarize the argument and appeal to the audience to make a judgment in the matter. These segments can be subdivided into additional rhetorical categories and/or arranged in another sequence.

In light of these influences, various scholars have applied rhetorical analysis to some of the Pauline letters in an effort to determine the effect that the structure and style of Greco-Roman rhetoric had on early Christian writings. A number of impressive proposals regarding the classification of particular letters has been made, but none has been completely successful.[32] Most NT letters are of "mixed" type and resist attempts to classify them according to specific rhetorical categories. They have been "shaped primarily by the [epistolary] occasion and the writer's specific

---

31. Kennedy, *Rhetorical Criticism*, 19-20; Aune, *Literary Environment*, 198-99.

32. The most well-known example of applying rhetorical analysis to the NT letters is the commentary on Galatians by Hans-Dieter Betz, *A Commentary on Paul's Letter to the Churches in Galatia*, Hermeneia (Philadelphia: Fortress, 1979), 14-25, where he explains the structure of the letter. Betz classifies Galatians as an apologetic letter using judicial rhetoric to defend Paul's past actions and persuade the Galatians to side with him against his opponents. For an evaluation and critique of Betz's view and rhetorical analysis in general, see Schreiner, "Interpreting," 422-23. For other examples including an understanding of Galatians in terms of deliberative rhetoric, see Aune, *Literary Environment*, 206-11.

aims and only secondarily by ancient epistolary conventions."[33] Nevertheless rhetorical analysis has been useful in focusing attention on the well-crafted literary structure and argumentation found in the NT letters, especially the Pauline letters.

Another Greco-Roman discourse style that appears in the NT letters is the *diatribe*. It originated in oral classroom discussion where teachers used it to encourage and enhance learning among their students. Its distinctive feature is its conversational style, a teaching method based on the Socratic method. The teacher anticipates a possible objection to his argument, puts the objection in the words of an imaginary opponent, and refutes it. Paul used diatribe in several places throughout Romans 1–11 (cf. 2:4; 3:1; 9:20), and it is especially evident where he rejects the false conclusion of an objector with the words μὴ γένοιτο, "By no means!" or "Certainly not!" (Rom 3:4; 6:2, 15; 7:7, 13; 9:14; 11:1). Features of a diatribe style also appear in other NT letters (1 Cor 15:29-41; Gal 3:1-9; 19-22; Jas 2:1–3:12; 4:13–5:6).[34]

9.4.2.3 SPECIFIC FORMS WITHIN THE LETTER

The body of various NT letters contains a unique array of embedded literary forms that were shaped and preserved in other settings, usually oral. The flexible nature of the letter format made the inclusion of these literary forms attractive and possible. The following is a survey of some of these forms.

The congregational setting for the initial delivery and reading of most of the NT letters accounts for the inclusion of a variety of forms derived from Christian worship. The closing "Amen" in several letters suggests such a worship setting (Rom 15:33; Gal 6:18; 2 Pet 3:18; Jude 25). *Liturgical forms* found in NT letters include: (1) the "grace" greetings discussed above and "grace" benedictions (e.g., Rom 16:20b; 2 Cor 13:13-14; Phil 4:23; 1 Thess 5:28); (2) blessings in praise of God (e.g., Rom 1:25; 9:5; 2 Cor 1:3-4; 11:31; Eph 1:3-14; 1 Pet 1:3-5); (3) doxologies that ascribe glory to God (e.g., Rom 11:33-36; Phil 4:20; Heb 13:21; 1 Pet 5:11; 2 Pet 3:18; Jude 24-25); (4) poetic hymns or hymn fragments (e.g., Eph 5:14; Phil 2:6-11; Col 1:15-20; 1 Tim 3:16); and (5) confessional statements such as "Jesus is Lord" (1 Cor 12:3) and "Jesus is the Son of God" (Rom 1:4; 1 John 4:15; 5:5); and longer creedal statements related to the death and resurrection of Jesus (e.g., Rom 4:24-25; 1 Cor 15:3-5; Gal 1:4; 1 Pet 3:18). When the NT writers used pre-formed material, they agreed with

---

33. Furnish, "Letters," *ECB*, 1273.

34. For further discussion of Greco-Roman diatribe, see Aune, *Literary Environment*, 200-2.

it, adopted it for their own purposes, and integrated it into the thought-flow of their letters.

Paraenesis (exhortation) is an integral part of most NT letters. Aune makes a helpful distinction between *epistolary paraenesis,* which is found in concluding sections of some NT letters, and *paraenetic style,* which permeates some letters (e.g., 1 Thessalonians).[35] A distinctive feature of Paul's letters is a concluding section of exhortation (e.g., Rom 12:1–15:13; Gal 5:1–6:10; Col 3:1–4:6; 1 Thess 4:1–5:22), and yet exhortations appear elsewhere throughout other letters (e.g., 1 and 2 Corinthians, Philippians, Hebrews, James). Some exhortations are directed to a specific situation faced by the readers while others are more general and could be applied in various situations. In addition, two standard paraenetic forms appear in the NT letters: vice and virtue lists (e.g., Gal 5:19-23; Eph 4:25-32; Tit 1:7-10) and household codes of conduct for wives and husbands, children and parents, slaves and masters (Eph 5:21–6:9; Col 3:18–4:1; 1 Pet 3:1-7, which omits the child-parent relationship).[36] It is important to note that these lists and codes reflect general moral exhortation applicable to all Christians and do not necessarily mean that the Christian community addressed by the letter was having serious problems with the items mentioned. Additional evidence from the letter itself is needed to show that certain items were mentioned because these churches were having problems with them.

9.4.3 The Closing of the Letter

The closing section (postscript) of a Greco-Roman letter usually includes a summary statement or appeal, a final "farewell" (ἔρρωσο/ἔρρωσθε, cf. Acts 15:29), and the date of the writing. The closing of a NT letter has a number of different elements in no set order, and not all of them appear in every letter. Unfortunately, no NT letter has its date of composition at the end. All the Pauline letters have a closing, as do the non-Pauline letters except James and 1 John. Careful reading of the closing is important because the author may summarize key ideas (e.g., Gal 6:11-17) or provide additional information related to the historical situation of the letter (e.g., Col 4:2-17).

The following elements appear in the closing sections of various NT letters: (1) travel plans and/or personal circumstances (e.g., Rom 15:22-29; 1 Cor 16:5-9; 2 Tim 4:9-17); (2) commendation of coworkers (e.g., Rom 16:1-2; 1 Cor 16:10-12); (3) prayer (e.g., 1 Thess 5:23; 2 Thess 3:16;

---

35. Aune, *Literary Environment,* 191.

36. Further treatment of vice and virtue lists and household codes can be found in Aune, *Literary Environment,* 194-96.

Heb 13:20-21); (4) prayer requests (e.g., Rom 15:30-32; Eph 6:18-20; Heb 13:18-19); (5) greetings to others (e.g., Rom 16:3-16, 21-23; Col 4:10-15; Phlm 23-24; 1 Pet 5:13); (6) final instructions and exhortations (e.g., 1 Cor 16:13-18; Gal 6:11-17; 2 Pet 3:14-18a); (7) the holy kiss greeting (e.g., 2 Cor 13:12a; 1 Thess 5:26; 1 Pet 5:14a); (8) the autographed greeting by the author (e.g., Gal 6:11; 2 Thess 3:17; Phlm 19); (9) a grace benediction (e.g., 2 Cor 13:14; Gal 6:18; 1 Thess 5:28; a peace benediction, Eph 6:23; 1 Pet 5:14b); and (10) a doxology (e.g., Rom 16:25-27; 2 Pet 3:18b; Jude 24-25).

9.5 Interpreting NT Letters

At first glance the task of interpreting the letters of the NT may seem relatively easy. And, in some ways it is. But closer analysis reveals complicating factors that make the task more difficult in many places. Alongside other interpretive procedures presented in this volume are several important genre considerations that an interpreter must keep in mind when reading and studying the NT letters. In light of the discussion above, we mention three guidelines.

First, as originally intended (cf. Col 4:16; 1 Thess 5:27), each NT letter should be read as a whole from beginning to end to grasp the full impact and development of the author's thought. Ideally, this should be done several times. This provides an overview of the author's message and helps the interpreter better understand the meaning not only of the whole letter but also of the individual paragraphs and their relationship to the whole. A close reading of the whole letter also reveals any specific details about the author, recipients, or other background information contained in the letter.

Second, as an "occasional" document written in the first century AD, each NT letter, even one with a more "general" character, has its own "epistolary situation." This is essential to remember. Most of our difficulties in interpreting and applying the NT letters is due to their "occasional" nature. The NT author is able to assume certain things that were known to him and his readers but are not articulated in his letter and thus are unknown or not fully known to us.[37] This feature requires an interpreter to observe the purpose of the letter and investigate the specific historical-cultural context of the author and his readers. The interpreter must re-

---

37. The NT author is able to assume certain things such as the identity of Paul's opponents who were causing trouble in Galatia, Corinth, and Colossae; the reason for certain practices ("being baptized on behalf of the dead," 1 Cor 15:29); the identity of certain individuals ("the restrainer," 2 Thess 2:5-7); or the experiences of early Christians ("the painful trial you are suffering," 1 Pet 4:12).

construct the historical context to the extent he or she is able based on information from the letter itself, first and foremost, and supplemented by legitimate, relevant information from outside the letter. A careful, well-supported reconstruction is very important in determining not only the background for the message of the letter but also the extent to which a passage in the letter applies to situations beyond the historical context of the original readers.

In addition, each letter must be read and interpreted on its own terms and in light of its own historical setting first, before another NT letter dealing with the same subject is consulted. In Paul's letters, for example, the interpreter must avoid reading Romans into the interpretation of Galatians, otherwise the distinctive emphasis of Galatians might be obscured or suppressed. And yet, at the same time, one must not keep the two letters separate from each other.[38] The "occasional" nature of the NT letters, which creates historical distance between then and now, also makes proper application of some texts more challenging. Good application rests on good interpretation and takes into consideration the whole of Paul's theology on any issue without ignoring any particular text in the process.

Third, though they are "occasional" in nature, the NT letters have been carefully constructed and exhibit several conventional epistolary patterns. In light of this, the interpreter must observe where and how the author modifies the conventional letter structure and determine the interpretive significance this has for understanding the letter. This is especially applicable to the opening and closing sections. No consistent rhetorical pattern or subgenre occurs in the central body portion of most letters; consequently the interpreter must trace the author's argument carefully, allowing the text itself to disclose the literary structure and any rhetorical features.

9.6 Conclusion

The twenty-one letters of the NT provide information about the life of Christian communities in various places of the Mediterranean world during the first century AD. They serve as authoritative substitutes for the personal presence of the apostles and other church leaders who could not

---

38. The task of "constructing" Paul's theology is difficult because all thirteen of his letters must be studied on their own terms in order to articulate his theology. Thus careful study of each Pauline letter contributes to an understanding of his theology as a whole, and a grasp of his theology as a whole provides the theological context for interpreting each letter. This reflects the *contingent/coherent* formulation set forth by Beker, *Paul the Apostle*, 11-16 (see note 24 above).

be with the letters' recipients in person. Most of these letters were written to address specific issues and meet the practical needs of the readers in various congregations. They were carefully composed and were intended to be read aloud to the congregations, providing them with instruction in Christian theology and practical exhortation.

In discussing epistolary genre, we have noted how it affects interpretation. Proper attention to the "epistolary situation" is crucial. Each letter should be read and studied as a whole on its own terms. Its historical-cultural setting must be given serious consideration, and the author's argument must be carefully traced in its literary context. This provides the basis for proper application to present situations. Most NT letters have an opening with a grace greeting and a closing in which many of them conclude with the fitting words, "Grace be with you. Amen."

9.7 For Further Reading

Aune, David E. *The New Testament in Its Literary Environment.* Library of Early Christianity 8. Philadelphia: Westminster, 1987.

Deissmann, G. Adolf. *Light from the Ancient East: The New Testament Illustrated by Recently Discovered Texts of the Greco-Roman World.* Trans. Lionel R. M. Strachan. London: Hodder & Stoughton, 1927. Reprint, Peabody, Mass.: Hendrickson, 1995.

Kennedy, George A. *New Testament Interpretation Through Rhetorical Criticism.* Chapel Hill: University of North Carolina Press, 1984.

Longenecker, Richard N. "On the Form, Function, and Authority of the New Testament Letters." In *Scripture and Truth,* ed. D. A. Carson and John D. Woodbridge, 101-14. Grand Rapids, Mich.: Zondervan, 1983.

Murphy-O'Conner, Jerome. *Paul the Letter-Writer: His World, His Options, His Skills.* Good News Studies 41. Collegeville, Minn.: Liturgical, 1995.

O'Brien, Peter T. *Introductory Thanksgivings in the Letters of Paul.* NovTSup 49. Leiden: Brill, 1977.

Richards, E. Randolph. *The Secretary in the Letters of Paul.* WUNT 2:42. Tübingen: Mohr Siebeck, 1991.

Stirewalt, M. Luther, Jr. *Paul: The Letter Writer.* Grand Rapids, Mich.: Eerdmans, 2003.

Stowers, Stanley K. *Letter Writing in Greco-Roman Antiquity.* Library of Early Christianity 5. Philadelphia: Westminster, 1986.

Weima, Jeffrey A. D., *Neglected Endings. The Significance of the Pauline Letter Closings.* JSNTSup 101. Sheffield: JSOT Press, 1994.

White, John L. *Light from Ancient Letters.* Foundations and Facets: New Testament. Philadelphia: Fortress, 1986.

Apocalyptic Genre 10

Visions and Symbols

W. HALL HARRIS III

Suppose an intelligent visitor from a distant planet, unfamiliar with the Bible or ancient Near Eastern culture, set out to read the Gospel of Mark or Paul's letter to the Romans. Our otherworldly visitor would be able to understand without a great deal of difficulty the major thrust of the Gospel narrative or the main argument of the letter, though he would certainly not be able to resolve every detail. But if the same visitor were to begin reading the book of Revelation (aside from the letters to the seven churches in chapters 2–3), he would soon be reduced to asking, "What is this all about?" and "How am I to understand all these images?" These problems are not new, nor are they limited to hypothetical extraterrestrial visitors. The same questions have been asked for centuries by ordinary readers, would-be interpreters, and even biblical scholars. Apocalyptic material is perhaps the most difficult genre of literature in the NT to handle from an exegetical perspective. This is true for several reasons (explained further below), but first we must define what we mean by "apocalyptic" since not everyone agrees on a definition. The boundaries between apocalyptic, eschatological, and prophetic literature are also somewhat fuzzy, creating further problems for definition and for exegetical study.

10.1 Attempts to Define Apocalyptic as a Literary Genre

In its broadest sense, apocalyptic is a subset of narrative literature, but its revelatory nature marks it off from other types of narrative. The name itself derives from the Greek noun *apokalypsis,* meaning "making fully known" in the sense of "revelation, disclosure."[1] About twenty-five years ago, in the interest of defining the term "apocalyptic," a study group led by John J. Collins under the auspices of the Society of Biblical Literature (part of the SBL Genres Project) worked through all the texts potentially classifiable as apocalypses dated between 250 BC and AD 250. The group then arrived at a definition that seemed to fit the existing literature, although the scope is admittedly broad and encompasses not only Jewish and early Christian works but Gnostic, Greek, Latin, and even Persian books. The resulting definition has become widely accepted as the standard definition of apocalyptic: "'Apocalypse' is a genre of revelatory literature with a narrative framework, in which a revelation is mediated by an other-worldly being to a human recipient, disclosing a transcendent reality which is both temporal, insofar as it envisages eschatological salvation, and spatial, insofar as it involves another, supernatural world."[2] In simplest terms this could be expressed as "a story viewed through the lens of a heavenly perspective, looking toward the future resolution of cosmic conflict in the end times."

Examined in more detail, the definition involves several key elements. First, apocalyptic is set in a narrative framework (as opposed to poetry, for example). Thus it reads like a story or narrative, and by implication could be expected to possess at least some of the common characteristics of narrative literature such as plot, structure, characterizations, etc. Second, apocalyptic involves an element of supernatural revelation. Third, this revelation is communicated to the human recipient by some otherworldly being like an angel. Fourth, the transcendent reality thus revealed is temporal, in that it looks to ultimate deliverance in the end times, implying temporal progression toward that end. Finally, the transcendent reality in question can also frequently be characterized as spatial in some sense, because both Jewish and Christian apocalypses of the period often involve otherworldly journeys or cosmic and celestial speculations of various kinds (the appearance of the celestial city, the heavenly Jerusalem, at the conclusion of the book of Revelation is also an example of this).

---

1. BDAG, 112.
2. John J. Collins, "Introduction: Towards the Morphology of a Genre," in *Semeia* 14: *Apocalypse: The Morphology of a Genre,* ed. John J. Collins (Missoula, Mont.: Scholars, 1979), 9.

In short, as noted by Mitchell Reddish, "Apocalyptic literature is crisis literature. These writings were produced during a time of perceived crisis to offer hope to oppressed and beleaguered individuals by giving them an alternative picture of reality."[3] D. S. Russell elaborates by pointing out three sets of common circumstances that typically led to the production of apocalyptic literature: (a) a lost world and a corrupt society, (b) the encroachment of Hellenism on Judaism, and (c) experience of persecution and external oppression.[4] Although the definition given by Collins could give the impression that the characteristics of apocalyptic literature are quite rigid, Russell adds a cautionary note: "This literature is of a diverse kind, though it possesses certain fairly well-defined characteristics which mark it off from other literary productions of the same period."[5] We should not make the mistake of assuming too much uniformity among the literary works generally classified as apocalyptic.[6]

10.2 Similarities to OT and Jewish Intertestamental Literature

While most consider the apocalyptic genre to be fully developed by the third to second century BC, there are clearly OT antecedents that have many, if not all, of the formal characteristics of the genre. In Ezek 1:1, for example, the prophet tells the reader "the heavens opened and I saw visions of God." What follows is structurally organized around five visions that concern both future judgment and future salvation. Likewise in Zech 1:1–6:15 various supernatural occurrences are explained to the prophet by an angel as pertaining to future events. The three visions contained in Daniel 7–12 are similarly conveyed by an angelic mediator and, like the material in Ezekiel, concern future judgment and salvation. Some also place Isaiah 24–27 in this genre category as well. If these biblical accounts can be thought of as the beginning of the apocalyptic genre, what follows in the intertestamental period is a veritable flood of apocalyptic. For the study of the NT it is the Jewish apocalypses of the intertestamental period, those composed roughly between 250 BC and AD 150, that are the most significant. These can generally be divided

---

3. Mitchell G. Reddish, *Apocalyptic Literature: A Reader* (Nashville: Abingdon, 1990), 24.

4. D. S. Russell, *Prophecy and the Apocalyptic Dream: Protest and Promise* (Peabody, Mass.: Hendrickson, 1994), 14.

5. D. S. Russell, *The Method and Message of Jewish Apocalyptic* (Philadelphia: Westminster, 1964), 36-37.

6. Most NT scholars will agree that the book of Revelation is, at least for the most part, an example of apocalyptic literature (though some would consider the letters to the seven churches in chapters 2–3 to belong to the epistolary genre). See David E. Aune, *Revelation 1–5*, WBC 52A (Dallas: Word, 1997), lxxii.

into two categories: (1) those which describe some type of otherworldly journey,[7] and (2) those which do not involve a journey but do contain a review of history, usually divided into distinct periods.[8]

Works like *1 Enoch* (especially 1–36; 37–71 [the "Similitudes"], and 72–82), *Testament of Levi* 2–5, *Testament of Abraham* 10–15, the *Apocalypse of Abraham, 3 Apocalypse of Baruch,* the *Apocalypse of Zephaniah,* and *2 Enoch* all are based on the "otherworldly journey" motif. Apocalypses which do not involve journeys but which do tend to divide history into distinct periods include *1 Enoch* 83–90 (the "Animal Apocalypse"), *1 Enoch* 91:12-17; 93 (the "Apocalypse of Weeks"), *Jubilees* 23, *2 Apocalypse of Baruch,* and *4 Ezra.* All of these works are characterized to a greater or lesser degree by supernatural revelations, secret heavenly knowledge, and obscure symbolism. Almost all of them claim as author a well-known OT figure from the distant past, often a hero of the faith (Enoch, Abraham, Levi, Ezra). Since in no case is this likely to be the actual author, these books also belong to the category of pseudepigrapha. They frequently share with other Jewish literature of the intertestamental period a desire for God to intervene in history, rescue and vindicate his people, and restore them to an idealized era of peace, prosperity, and security.[9]

10.3 Apocalyptic and Other Literary Genres

At this point we should pause to distinguish between apocalyptic and prophecy in one major area, that of eschatology.[10] The prophetic escha-

---

7. The motif of an otherworldly journey also appears in many of the works of later rabbinic Judaism. For example, *Pirqe de Rabbi Eliezer* 10 describes a tour of the underworld by Jonah while he was in the belly of the fish.

8. In some cases these distinct periods are quite deterministic in nature—their progression is predestined by God and cannot be changed under any circumstances. Many times the authors of such works saw themselves living at or near the end of the successive periods. In these works repentance, if demanded of the readers, could put one in the right with God individually, but would not prevent the anticipated end from arriving.

9. Often this was associated with Eden in the distant past, or sometimes even with the idyllic situation of Israel under Solomon, prior to the period of the Divided Monarchy.

10. The term *eschatology* is given two definitions by *Merriam-Webster's Collegiate Dictionary*: (1) a branch of theology concerned with the final events in the history of the world or of mankind; (2) a belief concerning death, the end of the world, or the ultimate destiny of mankind; *specifically:* any of various Christian doctrines concerning the Second Coming, the resurrection of the dead, or the Last Judgment (Merriam-Webster, Inc. *Merriam-Webster's Collegiate Dictionary,* 10th ed. [Springfield, Mass.: Merriam-Webster, 1993]). This differs somewhat from the more general definition given by the 1933 edition of the *Oxford English Dictionary,* which defines "eschatology" as a theological term which referred to the four last things: death, judgment, heaven, and hell. The *OED's* definition could be understood to apply to the ultimate destiny of

tology so common in the OT essentially describes the movement to the end (i.e., the "eschaton," from the Greek term *eschatos,* "last") from within human history, with human agents accomplishing the deeds that lead to the ultimate denouement. Apocalyptic eschatology, on the other hand (as exemplified in the book of Revelation) describes movement to the end through the direct intervention of cosmic forces penetrating into human history from outside. Angelic beings are the primary players on stage where apocalyptic is concerned. The escalated role of angels as intermediaries between God and human affairs is characteristic of the intertestamental period, so it is not surprising that they should play an important role in NT apocalyptic.

Another important distinction worth noting exists between the apocalyptic genre as such and writings which, while belonging to other literary genres, nevertheless contain apocalyptic concepts or elements. Up to this point we have focused on apocalyptic as a literary genre. An author may choose to present apocalyptic ideas (e.g., conflict between spiritual forces, direct divine intervention in history, eschatological judgment) but in a different literary genre (e.g., testament, epistle, parable). The parables of Jesus in the Synoptic Gospels offer a good example of this: Their subject matter is frequently the spiritual conflict between good and evil and the judgment that comes at the close of the age (e.g., the parable of the weeds, Matt 13:24-30; the parable of the stewards, Luke 12:42-46), but their literary form is the parable.

10.4 What Makes Interpreting Apocalyptic Literature Difficult

Anyone who wishes to interpret the apocalyptic material in the NT should begin by reading some of the Jewish apocalypses just described. One who has not experienced the extrabiblical expressions of the genre might falsely assume a much higher degree of uniqueness in terms of style, imagery, and emphases on the part of NT apocalyptic than is actually the case. The genre of apocalyptic as found in the NT, while unique in its content, nevertheless reflects many of the literary characteristics of Jewish apocalyptic of the period. Familiarity with the genre helped shape the reader's expectations of what was meant. For the would-be interpreter, this surfaces what may be the central problem in the exegesis of NT apocalyptic: how literally is one to take the often fantastic and sometimes even

---

an individual human being, while the more recent definition by *Merriam-Webster* introduces the notion of the "final events in the history of the world or of mankind," which is the sense in which the word is usually understood in discussions about apocalyptic literature (including the present one). For further discussion of the term *eschatology* and its relationship to time see G. B. Caird, *The Language and Imagery of the Bible* (Philadelphia: Westminster, 1980), 243-71.

grotesque imagery that characterizes the apocalyptic genre? Since many of the other features of the apocalyptic genre are shared with narrative literature in general they can be handled accordingly.

The real difficulty in the exegesis of apocalyptic literature is its use of imagery. Some have viewed the imagery and symbolism of apocalyptic literature as a kind of secret code, conveying information to those who understood it but hiding its message from outsiders.[11] According to this understanding the "code" had to be broken in order to communicate the meaning of the passage. This approach often assumes the intent of apocalyptic was to conceal the true meaning of the visions, probably from hostile or at least unsympathetic opponents.[12]

A somewhat different approach to the use of such imagery regards it as much more open and accessible to the average reader of the day in which it was produced. Speaking of the apocalyptic language in the book of Revelation, George Caird compared the symbolism and imagery to "the conventional symbols of a political cartoon" and suggested the original recipients would have been well versed in comprehending it.[13] This analogy, while often repeated, is not very helpful in practical terms for the exegesis of specific apocalyptic texts. The imagery in political cartoons communicates effectively because the readers are aware, within their culture, of what events or persons are portrayed in such cartoons. These referents are often linked closely to culture and are often quite time-sensitive. A reader from a different culture, or a reader separated in time by only a few years from the events described, may miss most or all of the meaning because the referents are not obvious. Thus to describe the apocalyptic literature of the NT in this way is to imply that, while the original recipients may well have recognized who or what was intended by the symbolism and imagery employed, later readers (including modern ones) will generally find themselves at a loss in attempting to determine the meaning of such texts. This assertion is easy to test, again based on the analogy of the political cartoon: one has only to go back to the editorial page of a newspaper of ten or fifteen years ago and examine the editorial cartoons. One or two may be intelligible, especially if they refer to major historical events or figures still recognizable, but many of these cartoons

11. Support for such an approach is sometimes claimed by pointing out that apocalypses like the book of Revelation often contain within them "decoding instructions" for some of their material.

12. See F. J. Murphy, *The Religious World of Jesus* (Nashville: Abingdon, 1991), 167.

13. G. B. Caird, *A Commentary on the Revelation of St. John the Divine*, HNTC (New York: Harper & Row, 1966), 6. Caird felt the original (Christian) readers possessed this fluency in the language and symbolism of apocalyptic regardless of whether they were formerly Jews or pagans.

will no longer have obvious meaning since the events they described in symbolic form are no longer current.

The proposed analogy of the editorial cartoon illustrates that the problem of determining the referent(s) is the most difficult problem in the exegesis of apocalyptic literature. Standard procedures for lexical (word) studies will help to resolve the meaning of terms (an important contribution), but not necessarily their referents.

10.5 A Starting Point for Interpreting Apocalyptic Literature

Given the number of different hermeneutical approaches to NT apocalyptic, a good starting point is provided by Bernard Ramm's classic *Protestant Biblical Interpretation*. He suggests seven rules to follow in interpreting apocalyptic literature: (1) when interpreting apocalyptic literature all the general rules of interpretation still apply; (2) a completely "literalistic" method of interpretation is impossible when apocalyptic imagery is involved; (3) one should attempt to discover if the symbol had any meaning in the author's culture; (4) one should carefully examine the immediate context to see if the symbol is explained there; (5) one should try to find out if the apocalyptic events have been fulfilled in history—even if this is the case, if the text is a pattern text, fulfillment in one period may not exhaust its meaning; (6) when interpreting NT apocalyptic, intertestamental apocalyptic literature should be examined to see if it is the source of any of the NT symbols; and (7) with reference to the book of Revelation, the OT must be thoroughly examined for clues to the symbols used.[14] These seven guidelines still form a helpful approach to interpreting NT apocalyptic, although it is important to remember that some of these issues are hotly debated (e.g., whether or not the apocalyptic events have been fulfilled in history). It is also important to note that rule (1) presumes the application of standard exegetical method prior to the additional steps that must be taken when dealing with NT literature of the apocalyptic genre.

A somewhat different approach is advocated by Elliott E. Johnson, who focuses on four crucial components of biblical apocalyptic, which he identifies as "(1) theological content, (2) literary function in historical communication, (3) literary structure in composition, and (4) the use of language."[15] Johnson notes the distinction we have mentioned before

---

14. Bernard L. Ramm, *Protestant Biblical Interpretation: A Textbook of Hermeneutics,* 3rd rev. ed. (Grand Rapids, Mich.: Baker, 1970), 268-69.

15. Elliott E. Johnson, "Apocalyptic Genre in Literal Interpretation," in *Essays in Honor of J. Dwight Pentecost,* ed. Stanley D. Toussaint and Charles H. Dyer (Chicago: Moody, 1986), 200.

between prophetic eschatology and apocalyptic eschatology. The former expected the kingdom of God to arise from within history and to exist as a kingdom within history, while the latter expected the kingdom to originate from outside of history. But for Johnson the differences are more a matter of degree rather than kind; from the perspective of theology, differences in hermeneutics between prophetic and apocalyptic literature are essentially nonexistent. The theological content can be treated the same in either case. As for the literary function, this centers on the two primary elements of author and audience present in any communication. Unlike in Jewish apocalyptic literature, the author is not pseudonymous in biblical apocalyptic, so this aspect is not handled differently than in any other literature. Regarding the audience, the intended recipients of apocalyptic literature were oppressed, so the purpose of biblical apocalyptic works like those of Daniel, Ezekiel, John, and Zechariah was "to challenge and encourage" such people.[16] But again, this does not require any special hermeneutics. As for literary structure in composition, Johnson acknowledges the presence of visions in apocalyptic material. But he does not see this as distinguishing apocalyptic literature from prophetic literature, which also contains visionary revelation. The imagery used in the visions might be distinct, but it calls for no special hermeneutics. Finally, the use of language in apocalyptic literature does call for special attention. But although the language may be expressive, it does not by its nature exclude specific reference, and if symbolism is involved, there is no negation of actual and historical reference through the symbol.[17] Ultimately Johnson emphasizes context in the process of interpreting apocalyptic literature.[18] This is the best piece of advice that can be given, since in the final analysis context is determinative for meaning, and the need to observe the context carefully as part of the interpretive process is even greater, not less, when dealing with apocalyptic literature.

10.6 Some Examples from the Book of Revelation

At this point it is helpful to look at a few examples from the book of Revelation. To begin with, we may consider the nature and identity of the locusts described in Rev 9:1-11. At the outset it should be clear that this problem, like so many in apocalyptic literature, is one of identifying the referent. Also involved is the nature of the apocalyptic genre itself: some

16. Ibid., 202.
17. Ibid., 205.
18. Johnson separates this into biblical context on the one hand and historical, cultural, and mythological context on the other (ibid., 207).

have assumed that apocalyptic material works like a motion picture of future events, with the human author describing what he saw (the future) as best he could in terms of first-century terms and concepts. This was necessary because a first-century person would have no words and no frame of reference for what he was seeing in a vision of the future. The creatures described as locusts, for example, might actually be some form of attack helicopters. That such an interpretation can be suggested at all is possible only because some of the characteristics described can be made to fit, at least loosely. The noise ("like the noise of many horse-drawn chariots charging into battle," v. 9) would certainly fit, the "breastplates" might describe armor, the "crowns similar to gold" (v. 8) might describe the pilot's helmets with reflective gold visors, and the "stingers like scorpions" in the tails might describe some sort of weapons installation. If one is willing to grant that this "vision of the future" is the way the apocalyptic genre works, such an interpretation is at least plausible.

However, this approach to apocalyptic material assumes the text is addressing the current time (ca. AD 2000), since this interpretation could not work in AD 1000 or in AD 3000.[19] Furthermore, when the broader context of the passage itself is considered, such an interpretation becomes less attractive and indeed far less likely. The "star" that falls from heaven in v. 1 is almost certainly an angelic being. He is given the key to the "shaft of the abyss," which he opens to release the locusts. The accompanying smoke that comes from the shaft, described as "like smoke from a giant furnace," suggests the underworld (the Pit, hell) as the place of origin for the locusts. The fact that the locusts' "sting" torments people but does not kill them suggests effects different from military weapons. The angel who rules over them is the "angel of the abyss." The entire section is thus framed by references to the "abyss," suggesting that the locusts described in Rev 9:1-11 originate from hell and are demonic in nature.[20] In this case perhaps they are called locusts because of their numbers, the rapidity with which they move, and the havoc they create. Note, however, that while this answers the question of referent, it does not answer the question "Will the locusts described in Revelation 9 actually look like that?" In other words, is the description given in the biblical text "literal" (in the sense that it describes actual external appearance) or is it "figurative" in the sense that the description of the (real) demonic beings is not necessarily literal but is designed to evoke certain emotional (even visceral) responses in the reader by means of the descriptive terms used?

19. Obviously such technology did not exist at the end of the first millennium AD, while a thousand years in the future, helicopters as we know them today will presumably be obsolete.

20. The "abyss" is also the location from which the beast ascends (Rev 11:7; 17:18).

In some instances it may not be possible to answer such a question until the events described actually take place.[21]

A second example is the identification of the city described as "Babylon the Great" (Rev 17:5; 18:2). When initially introduced (17:1-5), "Babylon" is described as "the great prostitute" (17:1) and "a woman sitting on a scarlet beast" (17:3). The beast has seven heads and ten horns, and in 17:9 the seven heads are given not one but two interpretations. The heads are said to be "seven mountains the woman sits on," but they are "also seven kings." In 17:12 the ten horns are also said to be ten kings, but these are kings "who have not yet received a kingdom, but will receive ruling authority as kings with the beast for one hour." Not until the end of the chapter, after the woman's destruction is described (17:16), is the reader told that the woman, the great prostitute, is actually "the great city that has sovereignty over the kings of the earth" (17:18). The destruction of the city is then described in great detail in 18:1-24, where a major city with extensive commercial ties to the rest of the world is clearly in view. Identification of the city is the primary exegetical problem in this passage; once again the difficulty is determining the referent. Interpretations have generally centered around three major possibilities. The first option takes the initial label of the city in 17:5 and 18:2 at face value and identifies it as Babylon, the same city and center of power which appears repeatedly in the OT (including the OT Apocrypha, where it is mentioned over fifty times) and is located in modern Iraq.[22] This interpretation certainly maintains the tightest connection with Babylon as it appears in the OT and the OT Apocrypha. For many students of the Bible it has the additional advantage of being a completely "literal" interpretation.[23]

A second proposed interpretation (which at first may seem highly unlikely) is to identify the city referred to in chapters 17–18 as "Babylon" with the city of Jerusalem. The fact that "the blood of the saints and prophets was found in her" (18:24) might suggest this, although it does not demand it. More significant for this view is Rev 11:8, which refers to the city where the two prophetic witnesses are martyred; their bodies

21. Nevertheless, either approach is quite possible. The descriptions of the beasts in Dan 7:3-7 may originally have been chosen because they reflected characteristics of the nations represented, but over time they came to stand for the nations themselves.

22. The fact that modern Babylon is little more than an archaeological site at present has not hindered this interpretation, and proponents of this view occasionally pointed out that Saddam Hussein, former dictator of Iraq, had extensive plans for the rebuilding of Babylon. These plans suffered a significant setback, however, when Hussein was removed from power following a U.S. invasion of Iraq in 2003.

23. Although interestingly many who would see this as a "literal" interpretation actually take "Babylon" in this passage to refer figuratively not to a city at all, but to the apostate world religious system supported by the Antichrist.

lie "in the street of the great city that is symbolically called Sodom and Egypt, where their Lord was also crucified." Granted there are significant differences with the later mention of Babylon in chapters 17–18: the references to Sodom and Egypt here are specifically referred to as "symbolic," a description not applied anywhere in the book of Revelation to Babylon. Also it is clear that "Egypt" is not a city per se, although it is used along with "Sodom" to describe the city here, presumably to invoke OT associations of these places as locations characterized by godless behavior where the righteous were persecuted and killed. In spite of these differences, mention of the Lord's crucifixion makes a reference to Jerusalem here certain, and the fact that the literal city of Jerusalem can be figuratively referred to by other names ("Sodom" and "Egypt" here) opens the possibility that Babylon could later stand representatively for Jerusalem as well. Furthermore the "beast" who kills the two prophetic witnesses (11:7) is also connected closely with Babylon in 17:8. Thus the possibility that "Babylon" is a reference to Jerusalem is not as unlikely as it might initially seem.

The last major interpretive option for Babylon in Rev 17–18 (and the one preferred by the majority of NT scholars in recent times) is to see it as a reference to Rome.[24] The primary contextual evidence for this, regarded as so compelling by many commentators that no other options are even discussed, is the phrase in Rev 17:9 referring to the seven heads of the beast as "seven mountains the woman sits on," even though a second explanation ("they are also seven kings") is also provided. Rome was widely known in antiquity as "the city of seven hills," even as it is today.[25] The dual explanation given here (seven mountains and seven kings) usually leads interpreters to attempt to identify the seven kings with some combination or sequence of Roman emperors, although this is not easily

---

24. There are some indications that Rome had begun to be associated with Babylon by the first century AD or earlier: (1) mention of the *Kittim* (taken as a reference to the Romans) in the Qumran documents (notably 1QpHab 6:1-4) may have contributed to this association; (2) *2 Baruch* 67:7 describes the destruction of Zion by the "king of Babylon" in a way that may connect Rome with the destruction of Jerusalem toward the end of the war of AD 66-70; (3) some see *Sibylline Oracles* 5:155-178 connecting "Babylon" (5:159) with "the land of Italy" (5:160) and the "city of the Latin land" (5:168) on "the river Tiber" (5:170); (4) a similar connection between Rome and Babylon is suggested by the later *Song of Songs Rabbah* 1.6.4. When these are combined with the contextual evidence from the book of Revelation, many scholars are convinced that Rome is in view in Revelation 17–18.

25. Among many examples are Juvenal, *Satires* 9.130; Propertius, 3.11.57; Horace, *Carmen saeculare* 5; Ovid, *Tristia* 1.5.69; and Pliny, *Historica naturalis* 3.66-67. According to Varro (*De lingua Latina* 5.41-54), the location of Rome was called the *Septimontium* ("Seven Hills"), although his list of the seven differs from others of the period. After Varro this designation became a popular one for Rome; e.g., Virgil (70-19 BC) twice refers to the Seven Hills enclosed by a single wall (*Aeneid* 6.783; *Georgics* 2.535).

and convincingly done. Nevertheless, the last option represents the consensus of scholarly opinion and is probably the most likely. This does not limit the referent, however, to the current city of Rome. It is also possible to see this as a reference to the capital city of Antichrist, wherever that should be. The city, as world capital, will exercise enormous commercial and cultural influence, just as Rome did in John's day. The connection between symbol (Babylon) and referent (future world capital) thus comes not directly but through the intermediate symbolism of Rome and what it represented to the original author and his readers. This last possibility is a "pattern" fulfillment common in the NT's use of the OT, and thus its imagery illustrates some of the complexity involved in determining the referents of symbols in apocalyptic literature.

A third example is the "one thousand years" described in Rev 20:1-6. This passage has long been at the center of debates over premillennialism and the doctrine of an intermediate messianic kingdom prior to the eternal state. Whether or not the book of Revelation involves chronological progression, the immediate issue concerning the exegesis of 20:1-6 involves the specified length of this period as one thousand years. Once again the major exegetical issue is that of referent: is the specified length of the period to be taken literally, or is the number "one thousand" symbolic and thus more representative of a "long period" of time? To begin with, no one has ever demonstrated from any ancient literature that could be relevant to the study of the NT that the number "one thousand" in and of itself has any symbolic significance.[26] When one examines the corresponding Hebrew and Greek terms for "one thousand" in both Old and New Testaments there is no indication of symbolic usage. Likewise the terms for "year" when accompanied by a numeral always appear to designate literal years. Merely asserting that the number must be symbolic here because Revelation is a symbolic book is not sufficient, since many things in the book of Revelation are not symbolic, and there is no contextual evidence supporting an understanding of the one thousand years as symbolic here. Some (e.g., Mathias Rissi) have insisted that the phrase had become a standard expression in rabbinic literature for the messianic age, but this is unwarranted, because there are only a few references prior to the book of Revelation to an intermediate reign of Messiah lasting a thousand years.[27] One of these is in the book of *2 Enoch* (33:1-2, found in the longer recension) and the other is a comment by R. Eliezer ben Hyrcanus (ca. AD 90) in which he inferred a thousand-year reign of Messiah based on

---

26. See Jack S. Deere, "Premillennialism in Revelation 20:4-6," *BSac* 135 (1978): 70. This article surveys well all the major exegetical issues involved with this particular passage.

27. Mathias Rissi, *The Future of the World: An Exegetical Study of Revelation 19:11–22:5* (Naperville, Ill.: Allenson, 1971), 34.

Ps 90:15.[28] Strack regards it as undeniable on chronological grounds that the book of Revelation depends on Jewish tradition for its period of one thousand years, but within rabbinic Judaism other lengths of time for an intermediate kingdom were proposed.[29] For example, 4 Ezra (= 4 Esdras), generally thought to have been written around AD 100, gives the length of the messianic kingdom as four hundred years (7:28).[30] In the absence of any convincing evidence for a stock figure of speech for the messianic age, the only alternative is to accept the number of one thousand years at face value.[31] This is also underscored by the tendency of the apocalyptic genre itself to be deterministic and periodic in its orientation, showing calendrical features as a typical and expected part of the genre that lays out the divine program.[32]

10.7 A Suggested Method for Exegesis of Apocalyptic Literature

When approaching a NT passage that involves apocalyptic material, all the standard techniques for exegesis should be applied first: initial observation to gain an overview of the passage's content and setting, identification of major Greek structural markers to begin to trace the argument flow, leading to construction of an exegetical outline, and the detailed study of key words and phrases at both the lexical and grammatical levels. At some point research in the commentaries should assist in the discovery of significant problems in the passage that require a more detailed study to achieve a solution. Added to these techniques is the identification of symbolism and imagery within the passage, often indicated by an accompanying interpretation in the immediate context. Special attention can then be given to the use of this imagery, beginning with a concordance search for the major elements of the imagery to see if any of them occur elsewhere in the OT or the Septuagint as well as the remainder of the

28. More details can be found in J. W. Bailey, "The Temporary Messianic Reign in the Literature of Early Judaism," *JBL* 53 (1934): 185-86. Bailey refers to 2 *Enoch* as "The Secrets of Enoch" and dates it ca. AD 50. F. I. Andersen dates it more generally to the late first century AD in *OTP*, 1:91.

29. Hermann L. Strack and Paul Billerbeck, *Kommentar zum Neuen Testament aus Talmud und Midrasch,* 6 vols. (Munich: Beck, 1926; 6th unrevised ed. 1974), 3:827.

30. At least in the Latin and one of the Arabic manuscripts; the Syriac manuscript gives "thirty years," while the other Arabic manuscript has "one thousand years." See Charlesworth, *OTP,* 1:537, note f.

31. Such an approach is advocated by John J. Davis, *Biblical Numerology* (Grand Rapids, Mich.: Baker, 1968), 155.

32. Some examples of works that exhibit this tendency to divide history into distinct periods include 1 *Enoch* 83–90 (the "Animal Apocalypse"), 1 *Enoch* 91:12-17; 93 (the "Apocalypse of Weeks"), *Jubilees* 23, 2 *Apocalypse of Baruch,* and 4 Ezra.

NT. Similar imagery can also be sought in the Jewish intertestamental literature, often by tracking down references to this literature found in standard lexical tools like BDAG, *TDNT, EDNT,* and *NIDNTT.* These background searches help to determine if a standard usage is present. After such connections have been fully explored, any remaining issues with the imagery (including uncertainty over the referent) will have to be determined by the context. Again, a survey of the most recent and thorough technical commentaries can be of significant help here. Finally, just as in the exegesis of any other genre of NT literature, an exegetical idea statement should be constructed for the passage which expresses the major movement of thought for the verses under study. This should incorporate any insights the interpreter has gained from the context regarding the identification of the referent(s) of the apocalyptic imagery.

In conclusion, I would like to express my heartfelt gratitude and appreciation to Dr. Harold Hoehner for his extensive contribution to my own exegetical training. This included the privilege of serving under him as a grader and teaching assistant for three of the four years I was a student at Dallas Theological Seminary. Since for many years Dr. Hoehner has offered an elective course in the book of Revelation, it seems particularly appropriate to end this chapter on such a note.

10.8 For Further Reading

Caird, G. B. *The Language and Imagery of the Bible.* Philadelphia: Westminster, 1980.

Johnson, Elliott E. "Apocalyptic Genre in Literal Interpretation." In *Essays in Honor of J. Dwight Pentecost,* ed. Stanley D. Toussaint and Charles H. Dyer, 197-210. Chicago: Moody, 1986.

Luter, Boyd. "Interpreting the Book of Revelation." In *Interpreting the New Testament: Essays on Methods and Issues,* ed. David Alan Black and David S. Dockery, 457-80. Nashville: Broadman & Holman, 2001.

Osborne, Grant R. "Recent Trends in the Study of the Apocalypse." In *The Face of NT Studies: A Survey of Recent Research,* ed. Scot McKnight and Grant R. Osborne, 473-504. Grand Rapids, Mich.: Baker, 2004.

Reddish, Mitchell G. *Apocalyptic Literature: A Reader.* Nashville: Abingdon, 1990.

Scripture Citing Scripture   11

Use of the Old Testament in the New

DARRELL L. BOCK

To think about the use of the Old Testament in the New is to enter one of the most fascinating and complex areas of biblical study.[1] Yet even expressing the subject this way obscures a reality for the earliest Christians. Imagine someone walking up to the apostle Peter two millennia ago and asking him about Jesus' teaching on the use of the OT in the New. He would have looked back at the questioner puzzled. For him the issue would be understanding the promises of the Holy Writings of old: the Law, the Psalms, and the Prophets. It is hard for us to remember or appreciate that the NT did not exist while the books of the NT were being written. Their topic was simply the continuing fulfillment of God's promises. It is the exposition of those promises and what the revelation of Jesus Christ means in their context that brings about "the use of the Old Testament in the New." Thus, this area of study is important to exegetes because it gives major clues as to how the early Christians unified the message of Jesus with the teaching of the old sacred Scriptures. The unity they argued for also formed an apologetic for the fact that Jesus came

---

1. This chapter is an updated version of my "Use of the Old Testament in the New," in *Foundations for Biblical Interpretation,* ed. David S. Dockery, Kenneth A. Mathews, and Robert B. Sloan (Nashville: Broadman & Holman, 1994), 97-114. Used by permission.

in realization of God's promises made long ago. In the ancient world, something with old roots was of value, being time-tested, so the use of these sacred texts to present and explain Jesus showed that God was at work with something he had planned long ago. The Christian faith was a "new" thing, but in its defense it had "old" roots.

Another key observation to make right at the start is the variety of ways in which the OT appears in the New. For example, in the United Bible Societies' first edition of the *Greek New Testament,* the editors note 401 OT quotations or allusions, which they put into bold print. Yet only about half of these (195) have some type of introduction in the biblical text to indicate that the OT is being cited.[2] Sometimes an author quotes the ancient text, sometimes he alludes to it, and sometimes he presents an OT idea without referring to a particular passage. The fulfillment of biblical prophecy also varies. Sometimes the OT text only looked to the future, but more often God made a promise and pictured it in contemporary history first, so that the promise presents a pattern of God's activity in history, which the fulfillment in Jesus only culminates. In other words, God's promises often work throughout history, rather than merely at a moment of time. Such fulfillment shows God's hand in all of history in a way that is more marvelous than merely seeing the Bible as making "crystal ball" promises.[3] All of this means that there is more to the use of the Old Testament in the New than merely lining up OT texts with their NT fulfillments.

Our overview will begin by considering some historical factors of ancient exposition. Then we will consider six key theological presuppositions that influenced how the text was read. Next we will examine the unique issues raised by the text because it has dual authorship and addresses multiple settings at once. Next we will consider how the Bible can be read today, speaking of two ways of reading the text in light of progressive revelation. Finally, the variety of ways in which the NT uses the Old will be examined.

11.1 Historical Factors

It is reasonable to wonder at the outset why in this chapter one should consider historical backgrounds, especially those rooted in Judaism, since

2. Klyne Snodgrass, "The Use of the Old Testament in the New," in *Interpreting the New Testament: Essays on Methods and Issues,* ed. David Alan Black and David S. Dockery (Nashville: Broadman & Holman, 2001), 213.

3. For a theological consideration of the area of biblical typology, see Francis Foulkes, *The Acts of God: A Study in the Basis of Typology in the Old Testament* (London: Tyndale, 1958); and Leonhard Goppelt, *Typos: The Typological Interpretation of the Old Testament in the New,* trans. Donald H. Madvig (Grand Rapids, Mich.: Eerdmans, 1982).

the Christian movement ended up being so opposed to Jewish tradition and religious expression. The argument is that a movement that was so opposed to Jewish tradition would certainly reject its methods of scriptural reasoning and argumentation. But this is to ignore how Scripture in both the OT and NT used and accommodated itself to cultural elements to make its own, often unique points. For example, the Leviathan image in the OT makes use of a popular mythological figure of the surrounding ancient Near Eastern religions, but the imagery was used in a way that showed that Yahweh was the God with whom all must deal. We are going to examine the ways people thought about, reasoned, and argued using the old sacred Scripture. Those forms could lead to solid or poor arguments, but the kind of reasoning they engaged in was common in discussing Scripture. We should not be surprised, then, to find the early Christian writers, most of whom were Jewish, using these common methods to make their case for Jesus. Their audiences were in a position to appreciate the argumentation, and to use their methods to show that Jesus was the promised one of God made their case even stronger. So we consider how the Bible was translated and interpreted before showing what suppositions the early church shared with Judaism and where her suppositions differed. The difference in how Scripture was read was not so much that a different form or method of reading Scripture was used, but that Christians saw the goal of Scripture pointing to Christ, while for Judaism the Law or wisdom was more central.

11.1.1 Language of the Bible

When we speak of the use of the Old Testament in the New, it is important to remember the OT was written in Hebrew and Aramaic, while the entire NT was written in Greek. This means the OT texts had to be translated for the audiences of the NT. In addition, the dominant language used during many of the actual events described in the NT was Aramaic; so in discussions about the OT within these events, the OT likely would have been cited in Aramaic, not Hebrew.[4] This means that using the OT involved a multilingual and multicultural setting (just as the use of our English Bibles also does). Fortunately, the Jews already had a process and a Bible for such purposes.

4. For the issue of what language Jesus spoke, see Joseph A. Fitzmyer, "The Languages of Palestine in the First Century A.D.," *CBQ* 32 (1970): 501-31, reprinted in *A Wandering Aramean: Collected Aramaic Essays* (Missoula, Mont.: Scholars, 1979), 29-56. Jesus probably spoke Aramaic and Greek, and possibly Hebrew as well, but most of his public conversation would have been in Aramaic.

This Bible for Greek-speaking Jews was the Septuagint (LXX), a Greek version of the Hebrew OT. Different OT books were translated into Greek over a long period, starting in about 250 BC. The entire OT was completed before the time of Christ. In some ways, it is better to think of the LXX as a collection of translations rather than one translation.[5] Still, most of the quotations in the NT reflect this OT version, although to differing degrees in different NT books. The translation process for the LXX was one of rendering the Bible into the language of the people for use in synagogue services, since books were not yet printed and collections of texts on papyri were rare. In the ancient world, the biblical text was most often heard, not read, except in the rabbinic centers. The LXX was a highly regarded translation for Jews of the Diaspora, as the *Letter of Aristeas* exalts the quality of the translation to show the respect with which it was held. The Jews of Palestine also had the Targums, or Aramaic renderings of the OT, read in the synagogue. These ran from very literal translations to somewhat paraphrastic renderings, if the later Targums we possess are an indication of earlier practice. *Targum Onqelos,* for example, is a translation comparable to the KJV, NASB, NIV, or RSV in approach. At other times Targums are more interpretive; the *Targum of Neofiti* reminds one of the *Living Bible* in certain sections. The Targums were an important part of Jewish religious involvement, since they put the text in language and wording the people could understand.[6] The Targums as translations into the native tongue made the Bible accessible. The versions that most NT writers would have been familiar with were these Aramaic or Greek editions of the Bible.[7] These "quotations" of the Bible often had

5. On the issues associated with the nature of the Hebrew Scriptures in this period, including the issue of canon, see the article by D. Moody Smith, "The Use of the Old Testament in the New," in *The Use of the Old Testament in the New and Other Essays,* ed. James M. Efrid (Durham, N.C.: Duke University Press, 1972), 3-13.

6. On the nature of the Targums and their function in ancient Judaism, see Daniel Patte, *Early Jewish Hermeneutic in Palestine,* SBLDS 22 (Missoula, Mont.: Scholars, 1975), 55-81; John Bowker, *The Targums and Rabbinic Literature* (Cambridge: Cambridge University Press, 1969), 3-28; Anthony D. York, "The Targum in the Synagogue and in the School," *JSJ* 10 (1979): 74-86.

7. On the diversity of usage of the OT within the NT, see Craig A. Evans, "The Function of the Old Testament in the New," in *Introducing New Testament Interpretation,* ed. Scot McKnight (Grand Rapids, Mich.: Baker, 1989), 163-93; Richard N. Longenecker, *Biblical Exegesis in the Apostolic Period,* 2nd ed. (Grand Rapids, Mich.: Eerdmans, 1999); and D. A. Carson and H. G. M. Williamson, eds., *It Is Written: Scripture Citing Scripture* (Cambridge: Cambridge University Press, 1988). For Jesus' use of Scripture, see R. T. France, *Jesus and the Old Testament* (London: Tyndale, 1971). More historically critical oriented treatments of the NT that are often cited in this discussion include Barnabas Lindars, *New Testament Apologetic* (Philadelphia: Fortress, 1961); and Donald Juel, *Messianic Exegesis: Christological Interpretation of the Old Testament in the New* (Philadelphia: Fortress, 1988). The last two studies overplay the differences between the OT and the New. For an attempt to argue for certain central themes

room to engage in some freedom of rendering as the goal was to bring out the full force of a passage, sometimes in light of larger contexts. The wording of the Greek version was what the original audience of the NT would have recognized as familiar. The NT authors did not ignore this reality. They often cited OT texts in these versions. Even Paul, who as a rabbi knew Hebrew and Aramaic, often chose to quote the version his audience knew (just as a pastor might know Greek and still be content to cite the English version today).[8] So a knowledge of the versions of the Bible and how they worked is important as one studies the use of the old sacred Scripture in the new. Renderings could be somewhat interpretive and free, but in these the NT writers often had in view a larger context of meaning, trying to make clear the full force of the passage.

11.1.2 Midrashic Technique

When it comes to expounding Scripture, the Jews also had common practices. Two Jewish techniques, "midrash" and "pesher," also may have relevance in how the NT presents some OT texts. Midrash refers to scriptural exposition.[9] It is a complex genre, since some Jewish expositions are straightforward while others are rather speculative and fanciful (as sermons today can be). Within the genre came the use of various techniques or forms of argumentation that represented how different passages were brought together to make a theological point. These attempts to "apply the Holy Writings of Old" had certain rules known as the rules of Hillel, which reflect midrashic attempts to expound and apply the Scripture in new settings. Hillel was a Jewish rabbi of the first century BC. He may not have invented the rules, but he received credit for codifying them and

---

emerging from the use of the OT in the New, with their source going back to Jesus, see C. H. Dodd, *According to the Scriptures: The Sub-Structure of New Testament Theology* (New York: Scribner, 1952).

8. The best-known study of Paul's OT interpretation is E. Earle Ellis, *Paul's Use of the Old Testament* (Grand Rapids, Mich.: Eerdmans, 1957), while a more recent treatment of allusions in Paul is Richard B. Hays, *Echoes of Scripture in the Letters of Paul* (New Haven, Conn.: Yale University Press, 1989). His study understates the value of Jewish backgrounds to this question and overstates the difference between the OT meaning and the NT sense.

9. The classic article on midrash is Renée Bloch, "Midrash," trans. Mary Howard Callaway, in *Approaches to Ancient Judaism: Theory and Practice,* ed. William Scott Green (Missoula, Mont.: Scholars, 1978), 29-50, a translation of an article written in 1957. More recent treatments include Bowker, *Targums and Rabbinic Literature;* and Gary Porton, *Understanding Rabbinic Midrash* (Hoboken, N.J.: KTAV, 1985). On ancient Jewish use of the Scripture, see Patte, *Early Jewish Hermeneutic.* For the wide variety of examples of midrash, see Jacob Neusner, *A Midrash Reader* (Minneapolis: Fortress, 1990). For a focused study on Palestinian Judaism and the NT, see Martin McNamara, *Palestinian Judaism and the New Testament* (Wilmington, Del.: Glazier, 1983).

passing them along to later rabbis.[10] Some of these rules merely reflect logic, while others are arguments of a rhetorical type. Seven rules were dominant; three of these rules were most prominent, as noted below:

• *Qal wahomer*, or "the light and the heavy," signified a meaning applied in a less important situation also applies in more important matter. NT texts that make a "how much more argument" reflect this form (Luke 11:9-13; Heb 1:14).

• *Gezerah shawah*, or "an equivalent regulation," meant that where the same words were present in two texts, those texts could be brought together for exposition. Mark 1:2-4 reflects such a textual combination in referring to John the Baptist. A similar combination appears in 1 Pet 2:2-8, around the concept of the stone.

• *Daber halamed me'inyano* is simply "explanation from the context." Numerous NT texts reflect citations that not only deal with the verse cited but summarize arguments in the larger context. Luke 3:6, for example, has a reference to God's salvation that comes not from the verses cited from Isa 40:3-5a but from the theme of the entire context of Isa 40:1-11. Rather than citing the entire passage, which runs for several verses, the summarizing term is inserted to capture the thrust of the larger passage.

Other rules of Hillel also deal with how to relate different texts to one another. Such ways of relating the biblical text show how the text was read, argued for, and understood at this time. To note this background is not to endorse Jewish technique or its conclusions, but the rules do reflect how texts were read and studied. A careful study of Jewish interpretation in this period shows the Jewish community had a sense of which OT texts looked to the future and the end times. (Qumran 4QFlor. [= 4Q174] is a clear example.) The rabbis just debated how to put those many pieces together. So many of the texts the NT uses were already well known in Judaism, though others were not so well known.

11.1.3 Pesher Technique

Pesher is a special type of exposition.[11] It refers to exposition of texts that sees them affirming eschatological fulfillment in the current era. The Qumran community of the Dead Sea is known for reading the OT this way; they thought they were the end-time community of fulfillment. One of the aspects of this type of interpretation is the explanation of mysteries in what is revealed. NT texts similar in flavor to such exposition include

10. For a brief exposition of these rules, see Bowker, *Targums and Rabbinic Literature*, 315-18; and Snodgrass, "Use of the Old Testament in the New," 218-19.

11. The major study is Maurya P. Horgan, *Pesharim: Qumran Interpretation of Biblical Books*, CBQMS 8 (Washington: Catholic Biblical Association of America, 1979).

the mystery parables of Jesus' teaching, which expound the approach of the kingdom and often use and develop OT imagery in the process (Matthew 13), or the explanation of Paul's ministry to the Gentiles as a mystery in Eph 3:4-6, where OT promise and the revelation of Christ to his apostles combine to help explain God's plan.

But if elements of Jewish interpretive technique are similar to that of the early church, then why did the Jews have such a hard time with NT exposition of the OT? To answer this question (and its contemporary equivalent), one has to examine the theological presuppositions about how these texts are read. Some Christian suppositions were shared with Judaism, but the issue of how the suppositions applied was debated.

11.2 Theological Presuppositions

Of the six suppositions we shall note, the first three were shared with Judaism, while the last three were not.[12]

11.2.1 Presuppositions Shared with Judaism

The Bible Is God's Word. First comes the belief that the Bible is God's Word. The implications of this first conviction are significant in three ways: (1) It means the Bible should be read as a unit. The OT may be thirty-nine books, but it ultimately has one Author. This explains why those who utilized Hillel's rules felt comfortable in associating texts that were historically distant from one another in time and setting. (2) It means that what God wrote then still has meaning now. This view of the Bible is crucial, because it means that biblical promises expect fulfillment. This conclusion follows from the third implication: (3) The Bible is true. What it promises will eventually come to pass in full.

The One in the Many. The second conviction is the belief in the one in the many. This means a single member of a community can represent the whole. Biblical illustrations of this concept include how the figure of Adam is used by Paul as a representative of all humanity, just as Christ represents redeemed humanity (Rom 5:12-21; 1 Cor 15:20-23, 45-49). The OT contains this concept as well. The king or a priest would represent the entire nation. An animal sacrificed would bear sins representatively for all the people. A prophet like Hosea pictures a nation's fate as he carries

12. For a discussion of Christian suppositions, see E. Earle Ellis, "How the New Testament Uses the Old," in *New Testament Interpretation,* ed. I. Howard Marshall (Grand Rapids, Mich.: Eerdmans, 1978), 199-219. For a full survey of views about how the Testaments relate to one another, see David L. Baker, *Two Testaments, One Bible,* 2nd ed. (Downers Grove, Ill.: InterVarsity Press, 1991).

out his call. A psalmist can represent anyone who is pious or fears God, even though the exact details of their experiences may differ. This kind of representation is significant because what is said of one figure can then be applied to another who fits within the identity of the group or who serves as its representative.

Pattern in History (Correspondence or Typology). The third conviction is the concept of pattern in history (correspondence or typology). Here the idea is that God works in similar patterns so that one significant event will mirror or pattern another similar event. This would normally be called analogy, except that in biblical thinking the later fulfillment of the pattern usually exceeds the initial event in importance. In other words, it may escalate the pattern, so that the later fulfillment heightens the sense of realization in the promise.

The word *typology* for this phenomenon is used in a special way, not in the way it is often used in popular discussion or popular exposition, which compares each detail of the tabernacle to a NT reality. *Types* in the sense we are using it refers to events or to the functions of an office. The OT tends to apply this imagery to the concept of creation and re-creation or to the theme of Exodus and new Exodus. So when Isaiah spoke of a new Exodus in Isaiah 40, he referred to the redemption of the nation out of exile, and yet his language also applies to what ultimate redemption will be like.

This idea of multiple referents ultimately fulfilled in a unique way is a key to the study of the use of the OT in the New. The NT extends such Creation and Exodus imagery into other categories, such as promises made to righteous sufferers, or promises made to the king, so that when these promises are realized in Jesus, they are realized in him uniquely. In this way, he is the fulfillment of the pattern in a way that is true only of him. This category is probably the least appreciated and yet one of the most significant suppositions for understanding the OT in the New. Here also is where Judaism and the church parted company. What the church saw fulfilled in Christ, Judaism thought was still awaited.

11.2.2 Presuppositions Not Shared with Judaism

These Are the Days of Fulfillment. The fourth conviction is that these are the days of fulfillment. No text declares this as loudly as Acts 2:17-21 (also Luke 4:16-20; Heb 1:1-4). In fact, when Peter cited the text from Joel in Acts 2, he inserted (as one would in an explanatory targum) the phrase "in the last days" to make the point that the pouring out of the Spirit showed that the fulfillment of last days expectation had come. In Luke–Acts, this note of fulfillment is underscored at a narrative level by recalling a theme that goes back to Luke 3:15-17 and John the Baptist's prediction that the way to know the Christ had come was when he baptized with the Spirit and fire—something Luke 24:49 and Acts 1:4-5 also lead us to anticipate by the time Acts 2:17 comes along. Paul's reference to the coming of the New Covenant expounds and contrasts the Old Covenant of the Mosaic Law with the New Covenant (2 Corinthians 3). The point in all of this is that the time of fulfillment had started in the early church. God's attestation of Jesus in the midst of his ministry (Luke 7:18-23) and the reality of Jesus' resurrection (Luke 24:43-47) gave ample basis for the earliest church to have this conviction.

Now and Not Yet. Yet in regard to fulfillment, a fifth, corollary conviction also existed. It was that this fulfillment, though inaugurated, was both now and not yet. This meant God's promises, though initially fulfilled in Christ, still had elements yet to be fulfilled. That such a view of the process of salvation could exist with some fulfillment or partial fulfillment now and more coming later should not be surprising. Our personal salvation is seen similarly. Our justification is already fulfilled, but glorification that is part of the same salvation is not yet. For the early church, salvation was part of a process, and the last days had begun with Jesus but were far from over. What Judaism expected to come all at once, Christians split into phases of a divine process. Thus, in expounding the promise of the subjection of all things to Jesus in 1 Cor 15:25-27, Paul used Ps 110:1 and Ps 8:6-7 and affirmed both Christ's present rule and the future decisive subjection of all things to him. In Phil 2:11, Paul used Isa 45:23 (LXX) to look forward to the eventual recognition of Jesus by all creation. In the Acts 2 example already noted, Peter pointed to the present fulfillment of the outpouring of the Spirit while anticipating the yet-to-be-fulfilled arrival of the Day of the Lord. This was the basis for his call to the audience to believe in Jesus and miss the judgment that would come with the arrival of that Day. This means that some OT texts when cited as fulfilled may be only *initially* fulfilled, as opposed to being fulfilled in a consummative sense. Fulfillment *can* be *inaugurated* without being *consummated;* in some cases fulfillment is partial, not exhaustive. The use of Joel in Acts is an example of this, since the decisive judgment of God is still awaited, even though the outpouring of God's Spirit has come.

Jesus Is the Christ. These five convictions, which were framed by Scripture in union with events in Jesus' ministry, led to a final conviction and conclusion: *Jesus is the Christ and represents fulfillment par excellence of God's promises.* When the church says all of the Scriptures speak of Christ, this is what is meant. He is the goal and culmination of the promises of God. In saying this, it must be noted that the OT's use in the New is not limited to affirming prophetic fulfillment, whether it be in pattern or direct prophecy. Other uses also exist. We shall look at these in our final section, but before getting there, we need to examine some special issues.

11.2.3 Unique Issues

Dual Authorship. The issue of dual authorship raises unique problems.[13] Although God inspired the authors who wrote the books, these human authors did not understand all they had written. 1 Pet 1:10-12 indicates the human authors did not understand the time or circumstances of all they predicted. Dan 12:5-13 makes it clear Daniel did not understand everything revealed and recorded in his visions. Some have espoused the concept of *sensus plenior* ("fuller sense") to explain the difference in understanding between the human author and the divine.[14] God knew the fuller sense (i.e., the *sensus plenior*) of what he revealed, even if the prophet did not. God could have multiple referents and time frames in mind, even if the prophet may not have known all the constituent details. This concept is not a bad one, provided one makes it clear what the human author did say and that whatever more God says through him has a relationship in sense to what the human author originally said. But the fact is that often *sensus plenior* is used simply to avoid such detailed examination. One claims *sensus plenior* and does not make any more analysis of the relationship between the uses. Used in this merely descriptive way, *sensus*

13. For a full discussion of the variations of approach to this question within evangelicalism, see Darrell L. Bock, "Evangelicals and the Use of the Old Testament in the New: Parts 1 and 2," *BSac* 142 (1985): 209-23, 306-19. Little has changed in the character of the four basic schools discussed in this article or in the issues evangelicals are concerned about in this area. However, many evangelicals have contributed an array of technical studies on specific aspects of the use of the OT in the NT that fit within the view that pays careful attention to the use of the OT in its first-century Jewish context. Among these studies are Robert Horton Gundry, *The Use of the Old Testament in St. Matthew's Gospel: With Special Reference to the Messianic Hope*, NovTSup 18 (Leiden: Brill, 1975); Douglas J. Moo, *The Old Testament in the Gospel Passion Narratives* (Sheffield: Almond, 1983); Darrell L. Bock, *Proclamation from Prophecy and Pattern: Lucan Old Testament Christology*, JSNTSup 12 (Sheffield: Sheffield Academic Press, 1987); Mark L. Strauss, *The Davidic Messiah in Luke-Acts: The Promise and Its Fulfillment in Lukan Christology*, JSNTSup 110 (Sheffield: Sheffield Academic Press, 1995); Rikki E. Watts, *Isaiah's New Exodus and Mark*, WUNT 2:88 (Tübingen: Mohr Siebeck 1997); David W. Pao, *Acts and the Isaianic New Exodus*, WUNT 2.130 (Tübingen: Mohr Siebeck, 2000). Any of these studies provides a good example of method in working with the OT in the NT. For Pauline materials a key work is Ellis, *Paul's Use of the Old Testament.*

14. For an evangelical assessment of *sensus plenior,* see Douglas J. Moo, "The Problem of *Sensus Plenior,*" in *Hermeneutics, Authority, and Canon,* ed. D. A. Carson and John D. Woodbridge (Grand Rapids, Mich.: Zondervan, 1986), 179-211, 397-405. For a Catholic treatment of this theme, see Raymond E. Brown, "Hermeneutics," *Jerome Bible Commentary* (Englewood Cliffs, N.J.: Prentice Hall, 1968), 605-23. For a vigorous argument against this approach, see Walter C. Kaiser, Jr., *The Uses of the Old Testament in the New* (Chicago: Moody, 1985), though aspects of this argument are overstated, as Moo's essay indicates.

plenior is of little help as an exegetical concept. The question is, How does the *sensus plenior* actually work between a set of texts? Dual authorship and the issue of a "deeper sense" raises two key related issues: language referent issues and the concept of the progress of revelation.

Because of the presence of typological pattern in history, it is possible to address two or more events in the same utterance. The flexibility within language allows this as well, if the descriptions are kept generic enough. To illustrate this point, some definition and review is needed about how words work.[15] Those who study words often speak of a word having three elements that contribute to meaning (besides the context of the utterance, which is a crucial factor). They are (1) symbols, (2) sense, and (3) referent.

Let us take the word *paraclete* in John 14 as an example. The *symbols* are the alphabetic signs that make up the word. In our example each letter of the word *p-a-r-a-c-l-e-t-e* comprises the symbols of what makes it up. (If the original Greek were used, the symbols would be the Greek letters for this word, παράκλητος, which is merely transliterated into English in our Bible to get the English word *paraclete*.) The *sense* is the dictionary definition of the word, its generic meaning in the context. Here that would be "comforter" or "encourager." This sense-level meaning is likely the term one would see in a translation. But most important for specific interpretation is the specific thing, person, object, or concept referred to by the term in the context. This is the *referent*. (When preaching on a text is vague, often it is because the preacher has not made clear what the referent in the passage is.) In John 14, it is important to know that the referent is the Holy Spirit. Jesus has a specific one in mind when he discusses a comforter.

But what happens when a text discusses a typological pattern, as opposed to one event only? The sense becomes key in the text, and the referents in the passage become multiple as each context or time frame is addressed. We have already discussed how, in Isaiah 40, a summary text introduces all the topics of Isaiah 40–66. Now it can refer both to the short-term situation (Israel's rescue from exile through Cyrus) and to the long-term one (the eventual complete salvation) at one time. This is a simple example of the language-referent process. Salvation in the short-term setting merely refers in terms of its referent to "deliverance from exile"; but in the long-term view of the NT the referent is "salvation in Christ" or "eternal life." Such a distinction reflects biblical typology and the progress of revelation, where the event escalates in its later fulfillment. This type of pattern fulfillment may mean that though the sense of a term is maintained at one level in all the fulfillments, the referent is

---

15. This concept is also discussed in the chapter on word studies in this volume.

heightened to a new level of realization in the later fulfillment because of the escalation of scope within the new context.[16]

Let me illustrate this possibility with a potentially more controversial example, Isa 7:14. For the sake of discussion and illustration, if this passage were read typologically, this is how the language-referent, multiple-context situation would work. In the short term, the referent must be one that Ahaz could experience about a sign child. Isa 7:15-17 appears to give timing for the original promise that ties it to the defeat and judgment of Ahaz, although assuring that the Davidic house will still be preserved, keeping an element of futurity to the promise. So Isaiah points to a woman who is currently a virgin (referent: some unidentified woman in the court) who will give birth to a child. That child's arrival is the sign, represents "God with us," and starts the clock ticking on Ahaz's judgment. The child contextually would probably be Maher-Shalal-Hash-Baz (Isa 8:1-4), although the exact initial referent is debated among exegetes of Isaiah. But the text as a potential pattern text points to a "type" of sign child that has a second, escalated realization in Jesus. With the type's arrival in history comes the escalation to point to the unique culminating fulfillment. So now the woman (referent: Mary) who gives birth *is* a virgin *at the child's birth* (here is the escalation—the anticipated birth from a current virgin has escalated to become a virgin birth), and yet the child still represents *and is* (a second escalation) "God with us." Note how the language of the text has not changed, since Isa 7:14 is cited here. The referents and their force have shifted slightly (to reveal the escalation). Both women were virgins at the time of the prediction, but in the escalation, the second has a virgin birth. The relationship to the original pattern and its language is still clear. God did judge the Davidic line in Ahaz and yet preserved it for the future, as Jesus' coming shows. This kind of interaction is how language-referent and multiple settings can combine to allow God to develop the force of a text in the progress of revelation through a pattern fulfillment. In doing so, God's design within history is highlighted even more than in a direct prediction, for now his hand is present in at least two settings, showing his sovereignty over history at a variety of points.

The mention of the progress of revelation introduces an idea that also is a special feature of the concept of dual authorship. It is that God gradually reveals his plan, so that the revelation of his plan progresses. This means that the force and specific referents of earlier passages in God's plan as revealed in the OT become clearer or can be developed along fresher lines as more about the plan is revealed in later texts on the same topic.

---

16. For a fuller treatment of this typological-prophetic category, along with numerous examples in Luke–Acts, see Bock, *Proclamation from Prophecy and Pattern*, 47-51.

This leads naturally into the issue of two ways to read the Bible. It also raises the topic of the progress of revelation. But before turning to those topics, one illustration of referent expansion because of the progress of revelation is needed. It is important to appreciate the variety of ways in which the NT uses the OT and how sometimes the explicit meaning that the NT surfaces works within the scope of the OT meaning but does so in a surprising direction.

In Acts 4:25-27, the church prayed. They appealed to Psalm 2:1 as an example text for the nations raging and the peoples plotting against the anointed one of Israel. Every Jew reading that psalm in its OT context would have assumed the enemies gathered against the Messiah and his Lord would be comprised only of the nations, of Gentiles. Yet when the church prayed that prayer, the enemies opposed to Messiah included seemingly pious Jews who nevertheless had rejected Jesus alongside Gentiles like Pilate. What produced this change in referent? It simply emerged as the psalm was read in a fresh context in light of the progress of divine events. The central idea, or sense, of the psalm was that many people stood opposed to God and his Messiah. So whoever opposed Messiah came under the heading of enemy in the psalm, whether that person was Jew or Gentile. Until the Jewish rejection of Jesus, most Jews would have interpreted this text as a word of comfort because God stands with his anointed, on whose side they also stand. However, now in Acts the Jewish Christians use this text as a rebuke to much of Israel because she has failed to recognize the Messiah, just as the text notes that people often oppose God's chosen one. Here is a wonderful example where the sense of a passage is fixed, but referents shift in surprising (but in scripturally anticipated) directions as a result of the progress of divine events.

Use of the Septuagint in the New Testament. Before discussing the progress of revelation in more detail, one other special feature of the use of the OT needs brief attention. We briefly alluded above to the issue of the use of the LXX in the NT. When the OT is cited in the New, often the wording does not exactly match that of the Hebrew OT.[17] This is because of the multilingual setting of these texts. This difference need not be significant, since concepts can be rendered in various ways. An examination of NT use of the OT shows that this happens frequently. Authors are often selecting texts with which their audience is most familiar. Some of these differences reflect the fact that the text is being rendered interpretively to bring out its full force according to targumic style (Isa 61:1 in Luke

---

17. For a work that lists such differences, but without reference to technical editions of the LXX and without a full discussion of the historical options, see Gleason L. Archer and Gregory Chirichigno, *Old Testament Quotations in the New Testament: A Complete Survey* (Chicago: Moody, 1983).

4:16-20). In other instances, a summary of the larger context or other texts and concepts may be brought into the citation to compact the discussion (Ps 68 in Eph 4:7-10; Isa 42:1 and Ps 2:7 in Luke 3:22). At times pattern is invoked, and the shift shows the escalation in the pattern (Ps 40:6-8 in Heb 10:5-10). Though what exactly is happening in particular cases often is hotly debated and can be complex, the factors mentioned above usually enter into the wording differences between the Hebrew and the NT cited text. It is the case that sometimes the point made in the LXX is clearer than the expression as it appears in the Hebrew and this may have impacted the choice as well. But the relationship between the meanings is often worth considering, both in the original Hebrew context and how that OT text was read within Judaism as indicated by the LXX, even though only one version is actually cited in the NT.

11.3 Ways of Reading Scripture and the Progress of Revelation

Much debate rages around the use of the OT in the New. Often it is because the exegete or theologian is reading the text in two distinct ways and the claim is made that the interpreter is forced to make a choice that indicates a preference for one of the two readings. However, a recognition of the nature of dual authorship, the progress of revelation, and the use of pattern often makes this either/or choice unnecessary, since a both/and approach often is appropriate.[18]

11.3.1 Complementary Ways to Read Individual Texts

Two ways to read the text are the "historical-exegetical" reading and the "theological-canonical" reading. These terms are not altogether adequate ones. Exegesis is theological, and theology should be exegetical. Still, the terms are chosen because they summarize the central concern in each type of reading. A historical-exegetical reading is primarily concerned with discussing a text in its original historical setting in terms of the human author's understanding and message for his original audience. A theological-canonical reading views the text in light of subsequent revelation and the full force the passage comes to have because of that additional revelation.

---

18. The categories of discussion raised in this section are a decidedly theologically conservative way to state the question. Many critics will simply pit the historical reading of a text in the OT against the reading of the NT without trying to probe the theological relationship between the two sets of text. For another, differently stated breakdown of this question attempting to deal with the same issue, see Vern Poythress, "Divine Meaning of Scripture," *WTJ* 48 (1986): 241-79.

In such a reading the progress of revelation may "refract" on an earlier passage so that the force of the earlier passage is clarified or developed beyond what the original author could have grasped. How this is done is debated among evangelicals and divides into three broad views. (1) Some argue that the later NT meaning tells us what the OT meant (even though at the time of the OT revelation that meaning was not very transparent). (2) Others argue that the OT revelation determines the meaning and defines the limits of the concept in a way that fixes that meaning, so the NT must mean what the OT meant or else the resultant NT meaning is distinct from the OT text and should not be directly connected to it. (3) Others argue that the NT meaning can develop or complement what the OT meant, but never in a way that ends up denying what the OT originally affirmed.[19]

Again an illustration may suffice. Let us take a famous text, Gen 3:15. Here is a promise that the serpent will bruise (i.e., "nip at") the heel of the child ("seed") of Eve, while the child will crush the serpent's head. In Christian circles, this is known as the *protoevangelium*, the first revelation of the gospel. This approach reads the text theologically-canonically, especially when it identifies the seed as Jesus Christ and the serpent as Satan. When Genesis was written, the human author could not have named Jesus. That understanding is "refracted" onto the passage in light of the progress of revelation.

But is there more here? In the context of Genesis, and reading historically-exegetically, one could argue that the major thrust is that enmity is introduced within the creation.[20] The near context is certainly one emphasizing the judgment God brings into the creation because of Adam's disobedience. Nature and man are at odds with one another, where harmony had existed. Since the snake is condemned to the ground in Genesis 3:14, a battle between a man and a snake (enmity) now takes place (v. 15a) with the snake lunging at the man's most vulnerable target that the now grounded snake can reach, the heel, while the man seeks to kill the lunging snake by crushing his head. In short, historically-exegetically the passage illustrates the devastating effects of the Fall, as do the other parts of God's remarks in response to Adam's sin (3:14-19). The point in Genesis 3 alone is that, after sin, the creation becomes more hostile to man. This certainly is a central point being made in Genesis 3.

19. The author prefers this third option as being most consistent with how language works and with a belief that Scripture is designed to have a clear sense from the time it is given. The three options often reflect the difference between a reformed amillennial approach (view 1), a traditional dispensational approach (view 2), and a progressive dispensational approach, which some historic premillenarians might also share (view 3).

20. Josephus, *Biblical Antiquities* 1.1.4.40-51, reads the text this way. He is one of the earliest commentators on this text.

However, the issue is *not forcing a choice* between the interpretations about Jesus as the seed of Eve and the introduction of hostility into the creation because of Adam's sin. Both are legitimate readings of the text, but it is a matter of which type of reading and how much context is being drawn into the reading that allows one to make either point. Subsequent revelation makes it clear that Jesus is a son of Adam (Luke 3:38), meaning that Jesus is the Second Adam (Rom 5:12-21). Subsequent revelation also appears to compare Satan to one who is crushed by God through Jesus (Rom 16:20). The key in thinking through interpretations related to the use of the OT in the New is understanding how the NT text is reading the OT text. Which of the two levels of reading is being applied? It is often the case that the NT is reading these OT texts more canonically than exegetically. The same rule applies to our exposition of these passages in teaching the texts. Which level of legitimate reading is being made? Is one interested in discussing a historical-exegetical reading or a theological-canonical one, or both? In most cases where a Christological point is being made in the NT, a theological-canonical reading is being given, where the factors of additional OT revelation and the ministry of Christ have helped to clarify the existence of patterns and the presence of fulfillment through escalation.

Such readings are not limited to issues tied to Christology. When Isaiah 65–66 is related to the future, specifically with reference to either the new heavens and the new earth or the millennium, it is subsequent revelation (namely Revelation 20–22) and a theological-canonical reading that makes such specific identification or a distinction between them possible. In the OT alone, one can see that Isaiah describes the consummative kingdom to come, even calling it a new heaven and new earth. However, the specifics of Rev 20:1-6 also suggest that a millennium is a part of what Isaiah describes. After we read Revelation, our understanding of Isaiah is impacted by Revelation's additional detail. In fact, we often read the OT through such full revelatory glasses, and at a canonical reading level, this is entirely appropriate.

The benefit of understanding the possibility of a dual reading is that a text has a full range of meaning, depending on the contextual limits placed upon the reading. Usually there is more in the text than we look for at any one level of reading. Some short-circuit the short-term message by leaping immediately to its larger, canonical significance. Others cut short God's development of the imagery by limiting themselves only to the short-term, historical context. The exegete of the Bible should be aware of the possibilities and know which is the concern of study. Of course, the student may want to be sensitive to both readings as the text is studied. The point is that the text can yield meaning at either level and the meaning of the two readings can be related, as our illustrations below shall seek to show.

11.3.2 Types of Usage

We have now laid sufficient background to turn our attention to specific types of usage.[21] The use of the OT extends beyond fulfillment about Jesus. The first few categories will deal with prophetic kinds of fulfillment, and then we will move to more illustrative and explanatory categories.

Prophetic Fulfillment. Some texts reflect *directly prophetic* fulfillments. In such cases, the human author and the divine author share the expectation, and only one event or series of events is in view. The NT fulfillment of Dan 7:13-14 is an example of such a fulfillment (among many such uses, see Luke 21:27). Here the issue is the granting of authority to one like a Son of Man by the Ancient of Days (God). It pictures the vice-regent and representative authority that the Son of Man has for God's people. In this passage, the concept of the "one and the many" applies as well, since in Dan 7:27 the Son of Man is associated with the vindication of the saints, the people of the Most High. Now the picture of the Son of Man is an image Jesus picked up and used for Himself. It was his favorite self-designation (Mark 14:62; Luke 22:69). He chose it because it beautifully weaves together his divinely bestowed authority with his representative role on behalf of God's people. In this case what the NT sees as fulfilled is all that was ever in view, the decisive vindication of God's people through a representative figure who receives total authority from God.

Typological-Prophetic. Other texts are *typological-prophetic* in their fulfillment. This means that pattern and promise are present, so that a short-term event pictures and mirrors (or "patterns") a long-term fulfillment. This category is frequently present in Christological readings of the OT. It is often debated whether it is a prophetic category in the strict sense of the term, since often the pattern is not identifiable until the ultimate fulfillment is seen. In this category and in light of this observation about realization, it is best to distinguish two types of typological-prophetic fulfillment.

The first is *typological-PROPHETIC* fulfillment. In these texts, there is a short-term historical referent, and yet the promise's initial fulfillment is such that an expectation remains that more of the pattern needs "filling up" to be completely fulfilled. The passage begs for and demands additional fulfillment (because God's Word is true). In fact, such expectation

---

21. Moo, "Problem of *Sensus Plenior,*" is right to make the point that there is a variety of ways the NT uses the Old. His article contains numerous helpful references to periodical discussions on this theme.

usually already existed among Jewish readers of these texts, showing the expectation that the text naturally generated. A non-Christological example is Isaiah 65–66, where the descriptions of victory over the enemies are so idyllically portrayed as a new creation that the expectation arose of a greater, ultimate fulfillment. This fulfillment looked for the total restoration of peace on earth, a type of "golden age." Although this is expressed most explicitly in Revelation 21–22, the expectation was a part of Jewish thinking on the end times as well (*1 Enoch* 6–36; 90). Another way in which these passages might be fulfilled in this way is for a promise to be made, which is only partially realized in the short term, so that the expectation of its completion continues into the future. A typical pattern image in the OT is the image of the "day of the Lord," which predicts catastrophic judgment. Although "day of the Lord imagery" is fulfilled in certain events within the OT (e.g., parts of Joel 2), the nature of that fulfillment looks forward to the decisive period of such fulfillment (the "day *par excellence*"). In all of these examples, the imagery is such that an aspect of the passage demands fulfillment beyond the short-term event and thus points to the presence of pattern. The prophetic character of the text resides in this "needs to be fulfilled" feature in the pattern.

Perhaps the best Christological example of this category is the Servant figure of Isaiah (Isa 42:1-9; 49:1-13; 50:4-11; 52:13–53:12). In Isa 49:3, this figure is explicitly called "Israel." Even Jewish hope saw a future for a glorified servant figure, viewed in terms of the nation; but they did not know how to integrate his suffering into the image or how to deal with the individuality of the expression in Isaiah 52–53. The issue of pattern and "one in the many" was not sufficiently taken into account. It is the decidedly individual nature of the language in Isaiah 52–53 that serves as the major clue that both pattern and "one in the many" are invoked. Interestingly, the NT application of the Servant image shows similar ambiguity. In Luke 1:54, Israel is called the Servant. But in Acts 13:47, servant imagery using Isa 49:6 is applied not to Jesus but to Paul and Barnabas. Other texts apply the image to Jesus (Acts 8:32-35). Thus, the image reflects a certain type of relationship to God in being his representative and experiencing suffering. Yet it is uniquely true of Jesus. But, according to the pattern, it also is true of others as well. Other OT texts that belong in this category include Ps 110:1 and 118.

The second typological-prophetic category is better called TYPOLOGICAL-*prophetic*. Here the pattern is not anticipated by the language, but is seen once the decisive pattern occurs. Only then does the connection of design become clear. It is still a prophetic category because God has designed the correspondence. But it works differently from the previous category in that the pattern is not anticipated or looked for until the fulfillment makes the working out of a pattern apparent. Perhaps the outstanding illustration here is the use of Hos 11:1 in Matt 2:15 ("Out of Egypt I have called my Son."). In Hosea, when the book is read historically-exegetically, this remark applies to Israel as she was called out in the Exodus. Everything about Hos 11:1-4 looks to the past, although it is important to observe that Hos 11:8-11 does not give up hope for Israel. So the review of history is set in a larger context that does remind the nation that God's care for her will not end, despite her past unfaithfulness in the face of his faithfulness. Jesus' reenactment of the nation's Exodus experience invokes the pattern of God working for his people again. So, the TYPOLOGICAL-*prophetic* connection can be made when one recognizes that the Exodus itself is a "pattern" image for salvation and that Jesus as King (and as the "one in the many") is able to represent (and thus recapitulate) the nation's history.

Numerous righteous-sufferer psalms and other regal psalms applied to Jesus also belong to this class of usage (Ps 16, 22, 45, 69). These righteous-sufferer texts are used in the Passion accounts. In their historical-exegetical use, they described the plight of an innocent sufferer, usually an OT saint or king, who is persecuted for identifying with God. But they are uniquely true of Jesus Christ. So when the NT points to their fulfillment in him, they emphasize the uniqueness of the way he fulfills them. Psalm 45 is a beautiful illustration, since it is a wedding psalm, complete with reference to the queen who is marrying the king. Jesus never married a queen, but the "regal" tie allows the connection, so that what is said of the king in the psalm in terms of his position before God is also true of the subsequent and decisive king, Jesus. So the language of that portion of the psalm can be applied to him as well in Heb 1:8-9, with the heightened sense that fits this category. Another possible example in this category is the use of Jer 31:15 in Matt 2:18, where the text and event are associated because of the pattern of suffering and the "one in the many" connection between Jesus and the nation.

Authoritative Illustration. A final category that appeals to pattern or analogy can be called *authoritative illustration* or, simply, *typology.* The term itself is reflected in the example of the Exodus used by Paul in 1 Cor 10:1-13, where Paul explicitly spoke of Exodus events as "types" (v. 6; the Greek term in *typos;* in the NIV, the term is translated "examples"). Here the goal is not a prophetic use but one of exhortation. The Corinthians are to learn from a past example about behavior to avoid, namely, associating closely with activities related to idolatry. The use simply points to the lessons of the past. Such illustrative and exhortative use of the OT is very common.

In a variation on such usage, the OT is appealed to because a *principle* of spiritual life is in view. The text is cited because it states a truth to be applied to living or appeals to an event to contemplate its (usually ethical) significance. Jesus' multiple use of Deuteronomy during his temptation is a good example of this usage. The use of Deut 5:16 in Eph 6:2-3 is another example, as is the appeal to Abraham and Rahab in Jas 2:20-26. Sometimes it is the analogy between the two situations that allows for the connection and calls for reflection.

Ideas or Summaries. Another use of the OT simply appeals to the use of ideas or summaries. Here no specific text is cited, but the teaching of the OT is summarized and stated in fresh words in a proposition. An example is Luke 24:44-47, where the OT is said to teach about Christ's death and resurrection and the promise that repentance shall be preached to all the nations in Jesus' name. No texts are cited explicitly, but one senses that all the texts Luke uses in Luke–Acts stand behind the remark. Another possible example is the debated sentence of Jas 4:5, which may be nothing more than a freshly worded summary of OT teaching that God is a jealous God.

A variation of this last use is the appeal to OT language, where no specific passage or context is in view, just the use of an OT image. Paul's remarks in 1 Cor 4:6 may appeal to the general tone of OT teaching about pride.

11.4 Studying the Use of the Old Testament in the New

So how does an exegete study the use of the Old Testament in the New? We have room in this chapter only to overview the steps (for specific examples, consult the studies listed in note 13 above as well as chapter 18 in this book, and observe their use of key aspects of the method this chapter describes).

First, examine the passage in its OT context for both its wording and message in the original context. This is the exegetical-historical reading we noted above. The goal is to determine the meaning in the book in which the passage appears.

Second, as much as is possible, study how this text was read in its historical Jewish context. Be careful to distinguish readings that predate or are contemporary to the NT era as compared with those that come later, since much evidence in Jewish materials for these readings is from later material.[22] Nevertheless a full study is valuable for examining whether a given reading became established or whether there were features about

22. This means that readings from the Apocrypha, some OT Pseudepigraphical texts, the Dead Sea Scrolls, Josephus, and Philo will be most important. Still, though they are later texts, the midrashim and targumic evidence may give some of the best clues of what Jews were doing with specific passages, especially if those readings parallel what shows up in the earlier collections.

the passage that were debated among the Jews. Not everything one finds here will be relevant, and it may well be that the NT usage will stand in contrast to that of Judaism. In other cases it can be seen that the NT reading may parallel what Judaism was also reading. Such a study gives some context to what the NT is doing with a text. It may be that moves made in the NT were already set up by how Jews were reading these texts.

Third, pay attention to the NT use of the text. Start with the wording of the citation and how it is like or unlike the MT and LXX textual traditions. Keep in mind both how the NT words the passage and the variations of wording for the text that may have existed in the MT and LXX traditions. Examine these differences to see if the differences may reflect a different translation base of wording for the LXX or NT, whether the difference is merely stylistic, whether an application is being developed, or whether a specific theological point is being emphasized in the difference. But to really decide these questions, the next step is needed.

Fourth, examine the NT usage of the OT in its NT context to see specifically what use the NT author makes of the passage. Is there an introductory formula tied to the usage? What theological or ethical point does the OT text make in its larger NT context? What OT themes are being pursued?

Finally, consider the type of usage the author is making. Is it predictive, one of the typological uses, analogy, illustration, the use of OT language or concept, or a summary of OT ideas? It is here that the hermeneutical use of the OT is explicitly considered. It is also in examining any differences between the OT and NT citations that hermeneutical clues can appear: How is the OT text being read canonically? Is the change one the NT author makes or one he inherited from the textual tradition he drew upon in citing the text? This area of study is extremely complex and often involves judgments working with small pieces of evidence. The student works in the area realizing the complexity of the study and the questions being pursued. Guidance can often come from monographs that have addressed these questions fully with a competency beginning students often do not have.

This complexity can also appear in the study of allusions, where a text is not being cited but only a few words or maybe even just a term is being appealed to for a point. Sometimes it is hard to be sure whether an allusion is present.[23] However, when one is able to determine the allusion, it often opens up the passage in fresh ways. For example, the hymns of Luke's infancy material are full of allusive references to the OT. A study

---

23. For one attempt to define standards for determining when an allusion is present, see Hays, *Echoes of Scripture*, especially his opening chapter.

of these allusions shows the depth of Luke's portrayal of Jesus as the one who fulfills God's promise.

The study of the OT in the NT is not easy, but it can be rewarding for it often gives major textual clues to what the NT author is saying about his topic, establishing connections to what God had already revealed and said he would do.

11.5 Conclusion

The use of the OT in the New involves a very complex interaction between hermeneutics, history, and theological-canonical concerns. It is a rich area of study and reflection. The OT's use in the New also has a variety of functions: it points to God's design, reassures, instructs, and encourages. As the NT was being written, the ancient Scriptures of Genesis through Malachi served as the "Holy Book." That book was synthesized and mined for information about God's promises, and the mine was full of gold. Different pieces emerged through different means, as authors used different kinds of "picks and shovels." Some tools used were old, drawn from study of the Scripture whose roots extended into Judaism; others were freshly forged as a result of events in Jesus' life. Together they produced a set of convictions about how the Holy Writings of old should be read. With those convictions formed through Scripture and events, the church preached a Jesus of fulfillment. As the Christ and the Son of God, Jesus fulfills God's promises and, in accordance with God's plan, reveals the way into everlasting relationship with the God of promise, the God of Abraham, Isaac, and Jacob.

11.6 For Further Reading

Beale, G. K., ed. *The Right Doctrine from the Wrong Texts? Essays on the Use of the Old Testament in the New.* Grand Rapids, Mich.: Baker, 1994.

Dodd, C. H. *According to the Scriptures: The Sub-Structure of New Testament Theology.* New York: Scribner's, 1952.

Evans, Craig A. "The Old Testament in the New." In *The Face of NT Studies: A Survey of Recent Research,* ed. Scot McKnight and Grant R. Osborne, 130-45. Grand Rapids, Mich.: Baker, 2004.

Longenecker, Richard N. *Biblical Exegesis in the Apostolic Period.* 2nd ed. Grand Rapids, Mich.: Eerdmans, 1999.

Snodgrass, Klyne. "The Use of the Old Testament in the New." In *Interpreting the New Testament: Essays on Methods and Issues,* ed. David Alan Black and David S. Dockery, 209-29. Nashville: Broadman & Holman, 2001.

Theological Analysis   12

Building Biblical Theology

BUIST M. FANNING

The book of Hebrews grabs our attention in its opening verses with a striking contrast: "In the past God spoke to our forefathers through the prophets at many times and in various ways, but in these last days he has spoken to us by his Son" (Heb 1:1-2a, NIV). These verses encourage us to look at the broad sweep of God's revelation and see lines of continuity and discontinuity in its different eras and portions. This is based on the fact that the same God who spoke in former times through his prophets has now spoken ultimately in the good news about his son Jesus Christ. Features of universality, particularity, and development are inherent in the revelation of God and his ways to mankind.

This reminds us that faithful, competent exegesis of the Bible itself depends on a solid grasp of the nature of Scripture as a divine and human book. This is how the Bible presents itself and what orthodox Christian theology has always affirmed: it is God's word communicated through human writers in their particular historical and cultural situation (cf. Matt 2:15; Mark 12:26, 36; Acts 3:18; 4:25; 28:25; 2 Tim 3:16-17; 2 Pet 1:20-21). What this means for interpretation is that we must pay attention to both sides of this duality without allowing either one to deny or eclipse the true nature of the other. We read the Bible as God's abiding and inerrant revelation to his people, and we must submit to its authority and allow its message to judge us rather than vice versa. But we must understand it in terms of the particular language, history, culture, conceptual background, and literary style of the human writers through whom God has chosen to reveal his truth.

This is readily seen and practiced in regard to language and history. Inspiration of Scripture should not be understood as *dictation,* that is, the Holy Spirit so dominating the human writers that their language, style, conceptual background, and so forth are eclipsed and their history and culture overridden. The evidence of Scripture itself is that the writers were not passive automatons, empty instruments through whom God spoke. Instead inspiration is seen as *concursive,* the divine superintending of the human such that God speaks in the midst of a real human situation and by means of the particular idiom and culture that is characteristic of the person through whom he speaks.[1] So we seek a grammatical, historical approach to interpretation, trying to be honest with the human side of Scripture in this way. Much of this book emphasizes components of interpretation required by this approach (e.g., chapters on grammar, backgrounds, lexical study). It is easy to see, also, that literary genre is another component to give attention to for the same reason. It is a normal part of human communication to read some types of literature differently than others (e.g., narrative, parable, epistle). Some of the chapters in this book explore the importance of genre for interpretation.

The point of this chapter is that biblical theology is a significant component of interpretation for the same reason. Because the Bible is a divine and human book, we must study the theology of the Bible in regard to both its divine character (i.e., its unity and truthfulness) and its human character (i.e., its address initially to a particular time and place). The definition of biblical theology must be seen in light of this rationale.

12.1 Definition of Biblical Theology

Ryrie has defined biblical theology as "that branch of theological science which deals systematically with the historically conditioned progress of

---

1. See Benjamin B. Warfield, "The Divine and Human in the Bible [1894]," in *Selected Shorter Writings of Benjamin B. Warfield,* ed. John E. Meeter, 2 vols. (Nutley, N.J.: Presbyterian & Reformed, 1973), 2:546-47; and D. A. Carson, "Recent Developments in the Doctrine of Scripture," in *Hermeneutics, Authority, and Canon,* ed. D. A. Carson and John D. Woodbridge (Grand Rapids, Mich.: Zondervan, 1986), 5-48. Carson defines concursive inspiration as follows: "God in His sovereignty so superintended the freely composed human writings we call the Scriptures that the result was nothing less than God's words and, therefore, entirely truthful" (45; cf. 29).

the self-revelation of God as deposited in the Bible."[2] Several important components appear in this definition. The foundational one is that God has revealed himself progressively. He has chosen to unveil his truth not all at once in full and complete form but in stages of increasing disclosure. This can be seen clearly in God's dealings with humanity across the centuries of OT history (e.g., God's promises as given in the succession of biblical covenants: the Noahic, Abrahamic, Mosaic, Davidic, and New covenants), in the change from OT to NT (e.g., the change from promise and anticipation to inauguration of fulfillment), and even within the NT itself (e.g., the growing understanding of Christology, the inclusion of Gentiles in the Christian community). What Adam and Noah and Abraham knew of God was not the same as what Moses and David and Isaiah knew. And their knowledge is not the same as Peter's or Paul's or John's. A number of biblical passages indicate this clearly (e.g., Isa 8:16-17; 29:11-12; Dan 12:4, 9; John 14:25-26; 16:12-14; Heb 1:1-4; 1 Pet 1:10-12).

And just as the stages of theological insight differ over the centuries, so individual writers even within the NT era reflect different lines of emphasis, distinctive ways of representing God's truth, and unique developments of ideas as God reveals his ways in their diverse situations. This is what Ladd brings out in his definition: "biblical theology has the task of expounding the theology found in the Bible in its own historical setting, and its own terms, categories, and thought forms."[3] So we find God's saving work described, for example, by John as "new birth," by Paul as "justification," and by Hebrews as "purification." While "justification" seems important to Paul, he refers to it hardly at all in 1 Corinthians, Ephesians, Philippians, Colossians, 1 and 2 Thessalonians, the Pastorals, and Philemon. The Synoptics speak much of the "kingdom of God," while John emphasizes "eternal life." The Gospels and Acts often refer to Jesus as "Son of Man," a title that almost never occurs in the rest of the NT, while the title "Lord" is used of Jesus often in the Epistles but much less commonly in the Gospels. The value of biblical theology is to pay attention to this diverse texture of ideas and assess its development and significance rather than allow it to be flattened out too quickly in a broad amalgam of "Christian theology."

The other dimension of Ladd's definition is significant as well: biblical theology seeks to articulate the theology of various biblical books, periods, or the Bible as a whole "in its own terms, categories, and thought

---

2. Charles Caldwell Ryrie, *Biblical Theology of the New Testament* (Chicago: Moody, 1959), 12. See a similar definition in Geerhardus Vos, *Biblical Theology: Old and New Testaments* (Grand Rapids, Mich.: Eerdmans, 1948), 5.

3. George Eldon Ladd, *A Theology of the New Testament*, rev. ed., ed. Donald A. Hagner (Grand Rapids, Mich.: Eerdmans, 1993), 20.

forms." What we look for are the lines of connection and emphasis that are natural to the biblical material itself rather than imposed upon it from traditional dogmatics or from contemporary issues. It can be distorting to ask the text to answer our questions or to structure its answers according to our framework. We must try to proceed as inductively as we can and discover its own theological teaching in the categories and imagery of the text itself. Later we can make the transition to contemporary relevance. Sometimes the theological themes of the text are quite coherent with the questions of Christology, soteriology, and so forth that we are used to asking.[4] Nevertheless, we must patiently allow the biblical passages to set the agenda, and we will often discover insights about God and his purposes we would otherwise have overlooked. For example, wealth and poverty is a central, characteristic theme in two of the books of the NT, Luke and James, where it is intricately woven into the larger theological-ethical fabric of the text. How does God relate to rich people and poor people and vice versa? How should God's people relate to wealth and poverty? Yet often we move right past these themes because they are not on our list of questions—or worse, we evade what the text commands because of our own context.

Alongside the diversity and particularity described above, an essential component of biblical theology is the unity of God's revelation in the Bible. As Carson says, "biblical theology . . . seeks to uncover and articulate the unity of *all* the biblical texts taken together, resorting primarily to the categories of those texts themselves. . . . On the one hand, biblical theology will try to preserve the glorious diversity of the biblical documents; on the other hand, it will try to uncover all that holds them together, sacrificing neither historical particularity nor the unifying sweep of redemptive history."[5] This is a feature of the Bible's divine character: it is the self-revelation of *one* God in spite of the many human authors and situations reflected in it, and it is the record of the saving purpose of that one God being worked out in history and eternity. So we can expect the range of ideas in different periods and through different writers to have an underlying coherence. We must try to see how the individual portions fit into the big picture of what the Bible is about without effacing their historical specificity.

---

4. As D. A. Carson, "New Testament Theology," in *DLNT*, 805, says, "NT theology is above all theology: i.e., it is discourse about God. For Christians this means it is discourse about the God and Father of our Lord Jesus Christ, about his character, nature, self-disclosure; about his acts of creation, providence and redemption; about his people, their origin, circumstances, salvation, destination."

5. D. A. Carson, "Systematic Theology and Biblical Theology," in *New Dictionary of Biblical Theology*, ed. T. Desmond Alexander and Brian S. Rosner (Downers Grove, Ill.: Inter-Varsity Press, 2000), 100-1.

12.2 Relationship of Biblical Theology to Exegesis and Systematics

To understand biblical theology clearly is to understand how it interacts with related disciplines, especially exegesis on the one hand and systematic theology, ethics, preaching, and wider application to Christian living on the other.

Biblical theology relates to exegesis in an interdependent or dialogical way.[6] On the one hand, exegesis is the *basis* for biblical theology. What the biblical text itself says is the primary "stuff," the building blocks of biblical theology, and we must do the hard work of interpretation as laid out in the different chapters of this book to allow the text to speak. We are seeking to discover inductively the meaning of the author as expressed in the biblical text, not to impose our preferred meanings on it. This gives us access to the truths of Scripture that we seek to pull together in formulating biblical theology.

On the other hand, biblical theology is the *framework* within which exegesis is synthesized, and so the two are interdependent. This is simply an extension of the principle of contextual interpretation (i.e., understanding the parts in light of the whole). Exegesis by itself can become overly analytical and atomistic. Biblical theology forces us to reflect on what the features of the text mean in synthesis with the theological ideas of the larger book, of other writings by the same author, and of the Testament or Bible as a whole. Tying together the theological strands from individual passages in a thematic unity helps to clarify the sense of the whole, and this in turn gives greater insight into the contribution of the individual parts. So exegesis and biblical theology function in dialogue with each other.

An example of this is the interpretation of "sinning willfully after receiving the knowledge of the truth" in Heb 10:26, for which the text says there is no further sacrifice available. On the face of it this seems to be a general reference to any sin committed in an arrogant or defiant way after conversion, since the verse itself does not specify the type of sin any further. It clearly alludes to the "sin with a high hand" described in Num 15:30-36 and elsewhere in the OT, but does it mean any deliberate post-conversion sin? This must be rejected in light of the wider theology of Hebrews. The statement that "there no longer remains a sacrifice for sins" in the context of Hebrews does not mean merely that such a sin cannot be forgiven. Instead it invokes the larger argument of Hebrews

---

6. For further discussion of this point, see Grant R. Osborne, *The Hermeneutical Spiral: A Comprehensive Introduction to Biblical Interpretation* (Downers Grove, Ill.: InterVarsity Press, 1991), 263-77; and K. J. Vanhoozer, "Exegesis and Hermeneutics," in *New Dictionary of Biblical Theology*, 55.

that Christ's sacrifice is God's full and final provision for sin. Hence the hopelessness of anyone who knowingly rejects that sacrifice. So it makes much more sense to see that the general point of 10:26 (willful sin) is filled out in detail a few verses later in 10:29 (defiant rejection of the sacrifice of the Son of God). The same thing occurs in Heb 6:4-6, where there is a general reference to "falling away" or "trespassing" (6:6a), for which there can be no renewal to repentance. This is then immediately specified by 6:6b, where it is described as "crucifying the Son of God again and subjecting him to contempt." Thus the issue in these verses is insolent rejection of the value of Christ's high priestly work.[7]

In a wider dimension, biblical theology is interdependent with exegesis in the sense that "Scripture interprets Scripture," a long-standing principle of Protestant biblical interpretation. But we must be clear what this means, since it frequently seems to justify imposing "what I have always believed" on passages that actually teach something different. The principle assumes rightly that Scripture presents a unified (though not necessarily uniform) teaching on all matters on which it speaks.[8] Thus obscure or single statements that seem to contradict the broad teaching of a number of passages in the Bible ought to be examined further. Perhaps the seemingly contradictory verses are actually speaking about something different. Perhaps that reading of them will prove to be superficial and invalid when looked at more carefully. Conversely, perhaps our synthesis of the "broad teaching of the Bible" needs to be revised in light of the passage at hand. We must remember to give a fair hearing to all the biblical texts on a given topic and not be guilty of having our own "canon within the canon," that is, verses to which we give more weight simply because they agree with our preconceptions.[9] If some passages are taken as more central to a given teaching than others, we should be prepared to defend the criteria and rationale for this from the text itself.

A classic illustration of Scripture interpreting Scripture is Jas 2:14-26 in comparison with Romans 3–4 and Galatians 2–3. Both writers use the same key words (faith, works, justification) and the same OT illustration (Abraham), but they seem to assert exactly opposite truths about salvation! James draws the conclusion, "a person is justified by works and not by faith alone" (2:24). Paul declares, "a person is justified by faith apart from the works of the law" (Rom 3:28; cf. Gal 2:16). In the Protestant

---

7. It is not the sort of struggle with sin and temptation that is the common plight of God's people. According to Hebrews, Christ as merciful High Priest stands ready to provide mercy and grace for this kind of weakness (2:17-18; 4:14-16).

8. This is of course ultimately rooted in the divine authorship of Scripture, as laid out earlier in this chapter.

9. See the helpful discussion of these issues in Osborne, *Hermeneutical Spiral*, 11, 273-74; also 307-9.

tradition Paul's conclusion is usually regarded as normative and James 2 as the passage seemingly out of step "with the broad teaching of Scripture." This is certainly the case, but there is always a danger of making even Paul "a canon within the canon" to the detriment of our ability to listen to the true teaching of the rest of Scripture.

The broad Protestant tradition has listened to both Paul and James on this issue and has concluded that they provide a complementary, not contradictory, teaching. The situations they address seem to be quite different, as indicated in the wider contexts of Galatians and Romans on the one hand and James on the other. Paul is combating a misunderstanding of the Law's purpose and cites Abraham as the paradigmatic example of how God declares people righteous by faith not by obedience to the Law. James warns against claims to Christian faith that ring hollow due to partiality, injustice, arrogance, and lack of charity. He uses Abraham as an example of true faith demonstrated or vindicated by real obedience when tested. The fact that the two are complementary comes out clearly when we look at the wider teaching of both: Paul also calls for godly living as the expression of true faith (Rom 6:22; Gal 5:6; Eph 2:8-10; Phil 1:11), and James for his part attributes salvation to God's gracious initiative in the lives of people, not to their merit (1:17-18; 2:5, 12-13).[10]

But it cannot be stressed enough that an unnatural reading must not be imposed on a certain passage because it seems to disagree with passages in other biblical books or authors. It is wrong to say, "This cannot mean what it plainly says because the rest of Scripture teaches otherwise." We must give the apparently idiosyncratic text the right to speak on its own, even if this means refining and adjusting our previous understanding of the larger theological synthesis in ways we did not envision before. Or it may become evident that our initial grasp of that text was superficial, and on further reflection we can see a more complementary relation to the other passages, as the example from James illustrates.

Biblical theology is interdependent with exegesis and serves as part of the culminating and synthesizing stage of exegetical study proper. It relates the specifics of an individual passage to the larger teaching of the Bible as a whole in a dialogical way. As such it also serves as a *bridge* toward assessing the wider significance of the passage for the church today. Systematic theology, ethics, preaching, counseling, and wider application of the Bible to Christian living require a keen grasp of the present-day situation in all of its cultural, social, and personal characteristics. Skilled theologians or preachers must bring together these two worlds: the world of the biblical text and the contemporary world they are called to serve in

---

10. Leonhard Goppelt, *Theology of the New Testament,* trans. John E. Alsup, ed. Jürgen Roloff, 2 vols. (Grand Rapids, Mich.: Eerdmans, 1982), 2:209-10.

Christ's name. Biblical theology is a significant component drawn from the world of the text to aid in bringing these together faithfully.[11]

But how does biblical theology serve as a bridge to systematic theology, for example? First, we must clear up a possible misunderstanding of terms. To compare biblical theology and systematic theology does not imply that systematics is unbiblical or that biblical theology is not systematic. The Bible has a significant place in systematic theology, but biblical content is not its only concern. Likewise, biblical theology seeks to systematize the teaching of the Bible regarding God and his ways, but the organizing principles are different. Systematic theology consciously attempts to express the truth of God in ways relevant to and understandable by the contemporary culture. The categories and thought forms of biblical theology are often not readily grasped by present-day audiences. The job of systematics (and preaching, counseling, etc.) is to recast biblical ideas about God and his ways in terms that communicate these truths faithfully in today's world and call people to respond in faith and obedience.[12]

Another misconception to dispel concerns division of labor. Many discussions of the relation of biblical theology to systematic theology and so forth conjure up images of academic specialization or "closed-shop" manufacturing. One expert in biblical studies operates in his or her esoteric discipline and then hands off the results to a specialist in another department. Or the "product" moves through a succession of steps, each of which requires a union card for any who participate. It discourages any normal pastor or counselor from thinking that he or she has the credentials for doing such work at any stage! But as a matter of fact, the process works best when we are engaged with every step along the way, since insights tend to go back and forth between stages. Of course, we should utilize specialized contributions from experts in one field or another (e.g., commentators, theologians, observers of contemporary Christianity and culture, etc.). These are "conversation partners" to aid us in our biblical, theological, and pastoral reflection. But the actual reflection and then ministry to those in our care is what God has called each of us to do, and we must not shy away from it.

11. Osborne, *Hermeneutical Spiral*, 263-69, 284.

12. Ibid., 309-10. Richard Lints, *The Fabric of Theology: A Prolegomenon to Evangelical Theology* (Grand Rapids, Mich.: Eerdmans, 1993), 112, captures this well: "The primary cultural task of the theologian is to clothe the entire counsel of God in a conceptuality that is intelligible to the modern community. The goal is to facilitate the communication of the gospel in a language that modern people will understand and be able to apply to their lives. . . . we must begin with redemptive-historical exegesis and then proceed to translate that framework into a conceptuality that informs the reality of our social structures and applies to the dominant patterns of contemporary life."

Biblical theology serves as a bridge between exegesis and such contemporary use primarily in that it pulls together the Bible's particular teachings into a coherent whole. Exegesis by itself is prone to focus on the individual pieces of a text. Even if it can trace the flow of ideas in textual order, it often leaves significant concepts unconnected from passage to passage, book to book, and so forth. Yet to bridge from the world of the text to the present-day world requires a full-orbed view of the biblical teaching in a given area coupled with a grasp of the larger sweep of biblical truth, without sacrificing the specific exegetical considerations that feed into these syntheses. Various theological-ethical issues, some longstanding, some brand-new, require understanding and action on the part of contemporary Christians: issues like divine sovereignty and human responsibility; suffering and divine goodness; the relationship of Christians to society; personal and corporate worship; gender issues in ministry and society; overcoming addictions; marriage, divorce, and remarriage; homosexuality; use of financial and environmental resources; use and abuse of power; care for the sick and aged; the clash of cultures and religions. Such issues are not easy to resolve in any case, but how inadequate it would be to base our responses on the study of one or two isolated passages of Scripture that touch on these topics.

In this vein, one of the most important tasks that biblical theology performs in the service of systematics and wider application is that it helps to avoid proof-texting. Proof-texting is taking verses out of context in support of a theological or pastoral point, stringing together verses that seem to pertain to an issue without regard for the larger complex of ideas operating in the biblical passages. Biblical theology on the other hand is rooted in exegesis, so it should flow from the necessary work of grammatical, historical, contextual, and literary analysis important to interpretation. Since it takes into account particular features of history, setting, genre, figurative language, and so forth as well as the wider sweep of theological development, biblical theology can provide a more solid bridge between the text and its significance for today.[13]

Finally, just as we argued that exegesis and biblical theology are interdependent or dialogical in relationship, so in turn exegesis and biblical theology taken together are interdependent with systematic theology and application.[14] It is easy to see how one dimension of this interaction

13. See chapter 13 in this book on "Application, Ethics and Preaching" for the way in which biblical theology is an aid to preaching. See also P. J. H. Adam, "Preaching and Biblical Theology," in *New Dictionary of Biblical Theology,* 104-12.

14. For further reading on this point, see Carson, "Systematic and Biblical Theology," in *New Dictionary of Biblical Theology,* 89-104; and idem, "Unity and Diversity in the New Testament: The Possibility of Systematic Theology," in *Scripture and Truth,* ed. D. A. Carson and John D. Woodbridge (Grand Rapids, Mich.: Zondervan, 1983), 77-95.

should work: exegesis and biblical theology ought to be the source and basis for our theology and ethics. If this is not so, they should serve as a corrective to existing theological convictions and ethical practice. Our current grasp of Christian truth should never be regarded as infallible. Theological models and systems by their very nature can be too many levels removed from their supposed biblical base and in need of specific or even wholesale refinement. Because of custom or traditional loyalties they can gain a permanence and a status beyond what they deserve.[15] They may also become so ingrained that we are oblivious to how much they color our interpretation of Scripture. The only solution to this is to have the grace to hold our convictions with humility and teachability. Exposure to the ideas of others is essential to give us perspective on our current conclusions: either to confirm and broaden our understanding when they agree or to challenge and perhaps correct us when they disagree. This is where the use of a range of commentaries, dictionaries, theologies, sermons, and so forth is invaluable. It is comfortable but potentially dangerous to read only those who reinforce our preconceptions. The goal that we all seek is to see with increasing clarity what the Scripture says and to allow it to judge and amend our theology and conduct.

But there is the other dimension of this interaction: our existing theology and ethical practice always provide the framework in which we interpret Scripture. However much some may claim it, no one is a purely neutral and objective reader of the Bible. We all come to the text with a certain point of view, as the first chapter in this book explains. At issue is how sympathetic our point of view is toward that of the text and how honest we will be in allowing our "framework" to be genuinely influenced by what we read. If we are hostile to the Bible's ideas about God and resistant to its instructions for living (however difficult those are to interpret) or even just indifferent to them, we are less likely to come to a true understanding. The goal is for our preconceptions and the text to be mutually informing, the perspective that we bring to the text helping us to see it in the right light and the text correcting and clarifying our perspective and view of the whole. The image of the hermeneutical *spiral* is a helpful picture to capture what is needed: the continuous interaction of the two over time bringing us to greater and greater comprehension of God and his ways.[16]

15. Osborne, *Hermeneutical Spiral*, 304, writes, "The basic problem of theological models is the tendency of their adherents to give them an absolute or permanent status that often becomes more powerful than Scripture itself. This is demonstrated in the tendency of all traditions to interpret Scripture on the basis of their beliefs rather than to examine their systems and alter them as needed on the basis of the scriptural evidence."

16. Ibid., 12-15, 304.

12.3 How to Do Biblical Theology

Practical steps for doing biblical theology are difficult to lay out, since it pervades the whole process of exegesis in some sense. But we could break it down into two broad stages, the analytical and the synthetic. In the analytical stage we are probing and exploring the text's theological significance and coherence throughout the exegetical process. We must keep theological questions in mind at every step: textual criticism, background studies, grammar, overview and flow of the argument, lexical studies, use of OT in NT, genre considerations, and validation. Theological meaning, coherence, and development should be a central focus especially in working with word studies, use of the OT, and validation (as discussed in those chapters in this book).

The synthetic stage begins toward the end of the process of studying individual passages or books, as a part of the larger process of synthesizing the results of exegetical analysis. Here the goal is to construct a biblical theology of an individual passage or book, or even the theology of the author in general (e.g., of Paul or Luke) or eventually of the NT as a whole.[17]

In both stages the basic process is to focus on key terms or phrases or on wider themes (there may not be a single word to capture the theme). Just as with lexical study, trace the treatment of these key terms or themes in concentric circles: in the passage itself, in the book as a whole, in other books by this author, in the Testament or Bible in general. Treatment of the topic in extrabiblical sources is also valuable, not because they have canonical authority but because they may give insight into historical and conceptual development in a wider way. Of course, we are not looking at words in isolation (e.g., what does "call" mean?) but at the propositions and paragraphs using those words and the theological ideas expressed in them (e.g., how does Paul describe God's work of "calling," its reasons, process, effects, etc.?). Often tracing a theme via one key term leads into a study of a cluster of related terms. For example, "call" in Pauline usage connects also with "choice," "foreordination," "foreknowledge," "ap-

---

17. Or we could trace a theme across various authors in the NT or the Bible. The strength of this approach is that it forces us to pay more attention to the features that unify biblical theology across the whole NT or Bible. Examples of this approach are: Donald Guthrie, *New Testament Theology* (Downers Grove, Ill.: InterVarsity Press, 1981); and G. B. Caird, *New Testament Theology*, completed and edited by L. D. Hurst (Oxford: Clarendon, 1994). The advantage of the approach mentioned in the text above is seeing the distinctive themes and coherence of individual writers on their own terms. Examples of this approach are: Ladd, *Theology of the New Testament*; Roy B. Zuck and Darrell L. Bock, eds., *A Biblical Theology of the New Testament* (Chicago: Moody, 1994); and I. Howard Marshall, *New Testament Theology: Many Witnesses, One Gospel* (Downers Grove, Ill.: InterVarsity Press, 2004). Marshall, however, does a nice job of bringing together both emphases.

pointment," "purpose," "will," "counsel," "good pleasure," "grace," "gift," "love," and so forth. This is due not only to the obvious conceptual connection of many of these terms but also to their usage together in the statements of many passages (Rom 8:28-30; 1 Cor 1:26-31; Eph 1:3-14; 2 Tim 1:9-11). In studying key terms it is, of course, helpful to compare your own conclusions about the theological sense with the relevant entries in the standard NT theological dictionaries.[18]

As you trace these themes, look for coherence, distinctiveness, and development of ideas. How does a key theme connect with related ideas both within a given book and across several books or authors? What is distinctive about a theological point in this author as over against other authors? What is the central theme (or themes) to which other ideas all seem to connect?[19] How do the theological ideas show development or change in understanding or progress of revelation compared to other biblical material, especially OT concepts? In the process we must remember that silence about a specific matter does not necessarily mean indifference or opposition to it. Luke, for example, does not extensively develop the atoning significance of Christ's death, especially in comparison to Paul or even Peter. But the few explicit statements he does include (e.g., Luke 22:20; Acts 20:28) indicate that he is not out of step with them and certainly not in disagreement with them in regard to atonement. Luke's focus on the resurrection-exaltation of Jesus as the source of God's saving blessings seems to include the death of Christ with it as part of the larger package.

In looking for these larger relationships it is important to take into account the redemptive era, individual situation, and particular characteristics of each book or author. Where does the book fit in the progress of redemptive history? Does it present a more limited picture of God's dealings with mankind even though it may anticipate later developments? Is the teaching quite occasional (focused on particular issues) or is it clearly intended to speak more universally? These are not easy questions, since even occasional teachings (as most of the epistles, for example, are!) can be abstracted to yield broader principles. Other questions pertain to genre or other matters of literary form: Is figurative language used? Are there important allusions to note? How does the genre affect interpretation? And so forth.

Many of these points can be illustrated by one final example. The references to Jesus being "begotten" as God's Son and as the "firstborn"

18. See the works cited in chapter 5 of this book on "Studies in Words."

19. For a nice example of this focus in Hebrews, see David J. MacLeod, "The Doctrinal Center of the Book of Hebrews," *BSac* 146 (1989): 291-300. I follow his ideas with some refinements in Buist M. Fanning, "A Theology of Hebrews," in Zuck and Bock, eds., *A Biblical Theology of the New Testament*, 369-415.

in Heb 1:5-6 are sometimes taken to denote his "eternal generation from the Father" in the Trinitarian terms hammered out in the Council of Constantinople (AD 381).[20] But in examining the verses, we discover that this language comes from a quotation of Ps 2:7 (connected with one from 2 Sam 7:14) and an allusion to Ps 89:27. The statement in Ps 2:7 "You are my son! Today I have begotten you" in its original setting is celebrating the coronation of Israel's king in Jerusalem as Yahweh's anointed representative on earth (see 2:6). This human king in the OT setting has a special relationship and status as the Lord's vice-regent on earth, the one through whom divine rule is expressed. This is pictured figuratively as "sonship," drawing from the promise about the Davidic dynasty in 2 Sam 7:14 (cf. 1 Chr 17:13), "I will become a father to him and he will become a son to me." The same imagery is reflected in Ps 89:26-27 (explicitly based on the Davidic promise; cf. 89:3-4), "He will cry to me, 'You are my father, my God, the rock of my salvation.' I will appoint him my firstborn, the most exalted of the kings of the earth." In this context "firstborn" is also figurative, a reference to the status of being the privileged heir, one in the position of greatest authority. Taken in this way, these OT verses do not refer exclusively or solely to Jesus in a purely messianic prophecy of his coming. But in light of the broader perspective of canonical Scripture, we see that they (and the Davidic promise they reflect) anticipate Christ's first and second comings when he fulfills this role and these promises in the ultimate way.

This is the sense Hebrews intends in citing these OT verses about divine sonship. In chapter 1 and throughout the book Hebrews portrays Jesus actually in three stages of "sonship."[21] He is the preexistent, eternal son, sharing fully in God's divine nature and activity (1:2b-3a; 7:3, 16); he is the incarnate, earthly son, who entered into our humanity in every way and submitted to the costly obedience of a sacrificial death (1:3b; 2:9-18; 5:8); and he is the exalted son, who now sits in God's heavenly presence as the king-priest of a new order having accomplished all that is necessary for our redemption (1:3b-5; 7:28). Heb 1:5-6 refers then to Jesus' entrance into this third stage of sonship when he was exalted to God's right hand (note that 1:4 says he *became* superior in inheriting the name "Son," so it cannot refer exclusively to a status he had from all eternity). His exaltation is indicated also by the citations in 1:3 and 1:13

---

20. Ryrie, *Biblical Theology*, 236; Hugh Montefiore, *A Commentary on the Epistle to the Hebrews*, HNTC (San Francisco: Harper & Row, 1964), 44-45; and Guthrie, *New Testament Theology*, 362.

21. Cf. George Milligan, *The Theology of the Epistle to the Hebrews with a Critical Introduction* (Edinburgh: Clark, 1899), 74-88; Mikeal C. Parsons, "Son and High Priest: A Study in the Christology of Hebrews," *Evangelical Quarterly* 60 (1988): 200-208; and Fanning, "A Theology of Hebrews," 370-88.

of Ps 110:1, which, along with 110:4, is central in all of the theology of Hebrews. This interpretation makes more sense in the near and broad context of Hebrews than a reference to "eternal generation."[22]

But although this seems to provide less support for the Trinitarian conclusions of the later church councils, in the idiom and theology of Hebrews these verses and others are the basis for a very high Christology. One of the widely acknowledged distinctives of Hebrews' theology is its "how much more" argument, that is, the way it traces the relationship of OT to NT by means of typological escalation. The book repeatedly cites OT people, forms, and institutions that in God's plan anticipate the fulfillment of his salvation through Christ. But the relationship between the two always displays an intensification or escalation in the NT counterpart when compared with the OT. This heightening is consistently profound, as shown by examples like Heb 3:3 (the glory of Moses vs. the glory of Jesus the exalted high priest); 7:3 (Melchizedek vs. the Son of God as "without beginning of days or end of life"); 7:16, 23-24 (a priestly succession according to physical descent and limited by physical death vs. one that continues forever by the power of an indestructible life); 9:10, 13-14 (sacrifices for physical, outward cleansing vs. one that cleanses the conscience and renews inwardly); 9:11, 23-24 (an earthly, man-made sanctuary vs. a heavenly one); 10:3-4, 10-14 (blood of animals that remind of sin each year vs. the body of Jesus Christ as the eternally effective sacrifice); 12:18-24 (assembly at Mt. Sinai vs. in the heavenly Jerusalem); 12:25-26 (one who warns from earth and shakes the earth vs. one who warns from heaven and shakes both earth and heaven). In each of these the correspondence is clear, but the typological escalation produces a profound significance regarding the person of Jesus Christ and his saving work with its effects on those who benefit from it. In many of these the pattern on the OT side is only superficially or figuratively true, while the NT fulfillment is profoundly true (e.g., Melchizedek's "eternality," sacrifices that "cleanse" and "forgive," a sanctuary with "access" to God) or it is a true earthly and human expression but pales in significance compared to the heavenly and divine counterpart yet to come (e.g., Moses' "glory," Melchizedek as "king-priest," a priesthood that "continues," the "holy assembly" on Sinai).

The typology in Heb 1:5-6 shares these characteristics: the human Davidic king as God's "son" corresponding to Jesus as God's "Son." The typology in 1:8 is the same: the human king in Jerusalem addressed as "God" versus Jesus addressed as "God." In both cases there is a metaphorical, beggarly sense in which the OT descendent of David could be seen as God's "son" and addressed as "God," since he represented God's

22. Ps 2:7 is cited in Acts 13:33 also as a reference to Jesus' resurrection-exaltation.

rule and authority on earth. But the writer of Hebrews indicates that Jesus can be seen as God's Son and addressed as God in the most profound and true sense. His roles as exalted Son and earthly Son are both rooted in who he always has been as the eternal Son who shares in the essence of God and embodies God's ultimate revelation (1:1-4).

12.4 Conclusion

It is vital for students of the NT to understand how biblical theology functions in relation to exegesis, systematic theology, and wider uses of the Bible in the life of the church. This helps us to see the theological texture and development that is true to the Scripture itself. We are prone to flatten it out based on our theological tradition and our efforts to think synthetically at the wrong stage in the process. It helps us to look for larger connections—across the whole NT and the whole canon—for the exegetical decisions we must make. We are prone to stop with analysis of individual units. It helps us not to ask the wrong theological questions of a passage. We are prone to assume too easily that the passage's answers are direct responses to our contemporary concerns. Above all, biblical theology is a tool to guide us in reading the Scripture according to its true nature as a divine and human book.

12.5 For Further Reading

Alexander, T. Desmond, and Brian S. Rosner, eds. *New Dictionary of Biblical Theology*. Downers Grove, Ill.: InterVarsity Press, 2000.

Caird, G. B. *New Testament Theology*. Completed and edited by L. D. Hurst. Oxford: Clarendon, 1994.

Ladd, George Eldon. *A Theology of the New Testament*. Rev. ed. Edited by Donald A. Hagner. Grand Rapids, Mich.: Eerdmans, 1993.

Marshall, I. Howard. *New Testament Theology: Many Witnesses, One Gospel*. Downers Grove, Ill.: InterVarsity Press, 2004.

Osborne, Grant R. *The Hermeneutical Spiral: A Comprehensive Introduction to Biblical Interpretation*. Downers Grove, Ill.: InterVarsity Press, 1991.

Zuck, Roy B., and Darrell L. Bock, eds. *A Biblical Theology of the New Testament*. Chicago: Moody, 1994.

Showing the Relevance   13

Application, Ethics, and Preaching

TIMOTHY J. RALSTON

With all the tools available today, the average student can discover the basic meaning of a biblical text.[1] The more advanced exegete learns to discover the nuances of each passage in its original language and summarize it into a coherent whole. Now looms a final challenge: to discover how this ancient text speaks to the needs of modern listeners, then to present the mandate of obedience for the glory of God. If the apostle Paul taught the universal profitability of the Scriptures for Christian ethics (1 Tim 3:16-17) and the danger of information without action (1 Cor 8:1), then those who ignore this final interpretive task encourage spiritual dysfunction. Ultimately they have failed in the ministry of the Word.

In this role preachers and teachers present a wide spectrum. Some emphasize relevance. They massage their listeners with action strategies, often sacrificing the biblical text. Others bombard listeners with textual details, linguistic minutiae, and historical discussions with little audience significance, abandoning relevance to the listeners' intuition. Between

---

1. This brief essay bears tribute to Dr. Harold Hoehner's passionate emphasis on legitimate application born directly from the exegete's proper understanding of the biblical text. Thank you, Dr. Hoehner, for teaching and modeling the connection between the Word of God and the works of his people.

these two extremes many serve up exegesis and application without a clear connection between them. This scenario leads one prominent evangelical to conclude, "More heresy is preached in application than in Bible exegesis."[2]

Exegesis seeks the text's meaning as heard by its original audience. Application explores how an audience in a new context should hear the same truth. But it is not enough to tell them what it means or even what to do. Application is not complete until the new audience has adopted these attitudes and behaviors.

13.1 Approaches to Application

After investing hours studying a passage, it can be easy to overemphasize the exegetical product. Students' first sermons resemble lectures filled with textual details, peppered with Christian jargon, and spiced with sentimental stories. Such speakers leave their listeners to find their way as best they can, without landmarks by which to apply the information. Sometimes well-intentioned exegetical mentors have consciously belittled application.[3] Some object that explicit application by the preacher is unnecessary, since this implies the irrelevance of the Bible. Others argue that application is the Holy Spirit's prerogative due to the limitations of the expositor, the listener, and the culture. Some believe application is inevitable if the text has been understood by the listener and the Holy Spirit provides the listener divine empowerment.[4] All these assumptions misrepresent the purpose of application, overlooking the implicit mandate of behavioral learning.[5] They also ignore the obvious: few modern listeners possess the exegetical and theological controls to guide them to an appropriate application. Most listeners will avoid the work altogether.

Other approaches to application may have their own pitfalls. One method merges exegesis with application, the former said by definition to pose the question of contemporary significance.[6] The meaning is sur-

2. Haddon Robinson, "The Heresy of Application," *Leadership* 18, no. 4 (Fall 1997): 21.

3. For a general survey see Roy B. Zuck, "Application in Biblical Hermeneutics and Exposition," in *Walvoord: A Tribute*, ed. Donald K. Campbell (Chicago: Moody, 1982), 16-19.

4. This philosophy of application as the exclusive prerogative of the Holy Spirit can be inferred from the method proposed by the contributors to *Rediscovering Expository Preaching*, ed. Richard Mayhue (Dallas: Word, 1992).

5. Zuck, "Application," 24-25.

6. Reginald Fuller notes that "The disciples of Bultmann, following Karl Barth, insist that exegesis itself already poses the question: What does the text mean today? . . . until one has heard it speak to the contemporary situation, one has not heard the text." See Reginald Fuller, *Preaching the Lectionary: The Word of God for the Church Today*, rev. ed. (Collegeville, Minn.:

faced by the exegete's questions of the passage. This approach, typical of recent trends in hermeneutics, obscures the distinctions between the ancient text and its modern interpreter. He does not share the exact circumstances or characteristics of the original audience. Further, his questions may be prejudiced by his own circumstances and imagination. Consider, for example, Jesus' first miracle at Cana (John 2:1-11). The interpreter who blurs the horizons may interpret the context (a wedding festival) and the miracle (the creation of even more wine to allow the reveling to continue) as Jesus' reckless endorsement of alcoholism. For biblical injunctions dealing with social relationships, the same interpreter may argue that modern social or scientific viewpoints invalidate biblical statements dealing with hierarchical relationships (e.g., master-slave, husband-wife) or certain sexual prohibitions (such as homosexuality). These approaches diminish the integrity of the text in its own context. A good Bible student must be able to identify the differences between the world of the text and the world of the audience and then build a bridge between these two worlds so that the message heard by its original audience is heard by the new audience with all of the same authority and implications.[7]

Another typical application strategy emphasizes application through the text's form rather than its meaning, imitating an action from the text without reference to its significance. Observing an exegetical detail, the preacher draws a direct behavioral correspondence between an individual in the passage and the modern listener. For example, sermons drawn from the Pauline prayers in the Pauline epistles urge "Pray like Paul prayed." While Paul's prayers are excellent examples of OT *hadoyah*,[8] mere imitation obscures the unique theological emphasis of each prayer. Similarly the "What Would Jesus Do" paradigm[9] has obvious limits, otherwise preachers would urge listeners to raise the dead, command

Liturgical, 1984), xvii. See also Stephen Neill and Tom Wright, *The Interpretation of the New Testament 1861-1986*, 2nd ed. (Oxford: Oxford University Press, 1988), 93-94; Leander E. Keck and Gene M. Tucker, "Exegesis," in *The Interpreter's Dictionary of the Bible*, Supplementary Volume (Nashville: Abingdon, 1976), 296-303.

7. John R. W. Stott, *Between Two Worlds: The Art of Preaching in the Twentieth Century* (Grand Rapids, Mich.: Eerdmans, 1982), 135-50.

8. Paul Bradshaw, *Two Ways of Praying* (Nashville: Abingdon, 1995), 51-55, notes that, while the NT contains examples of the Hebrew *berakah* form of Jewish prayer ("Blessed be . . ."), the *hadoyah* form ("I acknowledge/give thanks . . .") is preferred.

9. This particular way of approaching application has been practiced throughout the church's history, often in popular religiosity. Consider Thomas à Kempis, *de Imitatione Christi* (first printed in Latin at Augsburg, 1472, the year after his death); or Charles Monroe Sheldon's *In His Steps* (Chicago: American, 1897), whose most recent editions (1988 through 1998) often bear the subtitle, *What Would Jesus Do?*

meteorological changes, and multiply church supper stocks.[10] Such actions alone, however, are rarely universal norms. Hermeneutically, the passage's "do" forms part of the author's historical-grammatical-literary-contextual communication. The character's actions contribute to the text's meaning. Focusing on one "do" obscures the larger context of the act, resulting in interpretive error. The "do" may fall within the bounds of acceptable practice or theological orthodoxy, but becomes exemplary only when the individual involved appears explicitly as a Christian norm or model. For example, Paul's injunctions to Timothy and Titus as followers of Christ concerning paradigms of Christian maturity can be applied generally since all Christians share this goal.[11] But there are obvious limits. When behaviors could be fulfilled only by the original audience, they are not normative.[12] Application by imitation has limits.

A third strategy looks for momentary, coincidental points of correspondence between the modern audience and the first recipients, without observing sociocultural implications. Atomistic points of correspondence become applications. They often ignore the broader implications. For example, an exposition of 1 Cor 6:12-20 that focuses only on prohibiting explicit sexual immorality, ignores how sexuality functioned in the Corinthian temples as an act of spiritual syncretism, so that the apostle's warning goes beyond mere sexual immorality to a more general principle that prohibits associations that threaten one's singular allegiance to Christ. An exposition of 1 Corinthians 13 that focuses only on the abstraction of "love" ignores the apostle's emphasis concerning the community and ministry functions within the context of Christian community.

10. This problem becomes more acute as historical and theological distance between text and audience increases. Examples abound in OT sermons. Jephthah becomes an example of godly parenting because he kept his promise, despite the obvious facts that the promise keeping emanated from a rash vow, was preserved through familial ignorance of Torah, killed his only child, and thereby forfeited participation in the covenant (Judg 11:29-40). Naaman's servant girl teaches the priority of sending youth into missions, while ignoring the warfare and capture by which she entered her servitude (2 Kgs 5:1-3). Gideon's actions with the fleece becomes an example of how God can reveal his will in a miraculous way, disregarding the actual circumstances, in which Gideon's actions represented his consistent desire to avoid obedience to the already clear direction of God (Judg 6:36-40).

11. Paul repeatedly commands Timothy as a disciple with whom he shares his aspirations for Christian maturity (1 Tim 6:11; 2 Tim 1:2; 2:1-2) and to whom he gives responsibility for orthodox proclamation and discipleship (1 Tim 1:3, 18; 3:15; 6:17; 2 Tim 2:2). Similarly Paul commissions Titus his apostolic legate to establish church order in Crete according to Paul's paradigm (Tit 1:5) and teach Christian orthodoxy (Tit 2:1).

12. Paul exhorts Timothy to "remain at Ephesus" (1 Tim 1:3), "come to me soon" (2 Tim 4:9) "before winter" (2 Tim 4:19), "bring the cloak which I left at Troas" (2 Tim 4:13); and he exhorts Titus to come to Nicopolis (Tit 3:12). Obedience would be possible only for the original recipients of these requests. Therefore, some other method must be found to apply these texts if they are to have relevance to a different audience.

A fourth strategy draws application from the preacher's imagination without (or in contradiction to) a textual validation. For example, preachers sometimes preach that Jesus' self-revelation to his disciples at Emmaus (Luke 24:30) occurred through the visible scars from his crucifixion. Nothing in the passage supports this. Instead Jesus' self-revelation follows a verbal recapitulation of the Passover event (cf. Luke 22:14-22 with 24:30), which is reinforced by the disciples' report (24:35), emphasizing the significance of the rite and increasing the reader's appreciation of the new covenant meal.[13]

In each of these methods the text disappears under the weight of the expositor's assumptions,[14] whether the "do" of the passage, a detail from the passage, or a sentimental reading into the text. Something outside the text determines its meaning and application. These strategies will always favor the expositor's theological prejudices. Only the theological orthodoxy of the expositor precludes interpretive and behavioral error. But further danger awaits.

13.2 A Quest for Authority

Improper application of the Scriptures will lead inevitably to incorrect theology—the homiletic extension of lex orandi, lex credendi ("the law of worship, the law of belief").[15] People integrate new information within existing frameworks of knowledge and experience. Exegetical and theological discussions are abstract. They demand a listener's intense focus.

13. This summary is further complicated by the popular method of application that directs one to look for "an example to follow, . . . a command to obey, . . . an error to avoid, . . . a sin to forsake, . . . a promise to claim, . . . a new thought about God Himself" (Zuck, "Application," 33). Obviously this approach is insufficient. Some biblical commands and promises are specific to certain persons or situations. Actions designated as covenant violations (sins) in one text (e.g., wearing varied fabrics, eating certain foods) are not treated similarly in other contexts. Many recognize these distinctions and do not extrapolate the requirement across the audiences. Therefore, intuitively expositors use a method that filters out inappropriate applications.

14. Historically this form of biblical application was permitted by the church as lectio divina/sacra ("sacred reading," the intuitive application of a text). Applications of this type might prove individually beneficial but were not authoritative for the community or its members. Only application derived through lectio continua ("continuous reading," the contextual exposition of the text) or lectio selecta ("selected reading," as a theological exposition of coordinated texts) possessed such authority. See Michael Casey, Sacred Reading: The Ancient Art of Lectio Divina (Ligouri, Mo.: Ligouri/Triumph, 1996); Mariano Magrassi, Praying the Bible: An Introduction to Lectio Divina (Collegeville, Minn.: Liturgical, 1998).

15. The Latin phrase, a shorthand for the ancient theological principle expressed by Prosper of Aquitaine, ut legem credendi lex statuat supplicandi, describes how worship praxis, while incarnating Christian beliefs, forms the beliefs themselves for the worshiper. See Kevin W. Irwin, Context and Text: Method in Liturgical Theology (Collegeville, Minn.: Liturgical, 1994), 4-6.

So the listener grasps for what can be most easily understood as the message proceeds. Concrete examples of truth applied (application) tempt the listener to exchange the effort of processing abstractions for the more easily grasped images. Extrapolating the application backwards to the text, the listener infers the text's meaning through its application. Application that cannot demonstrate congruence with the passage on which it is based teaches methodological errors in exegesis—or worse, a heretical theology. Only an orthodox theology as the preexisting framework over such application guards the listener from the intrusion of heresy through improper application.

How does one apply the ancient statements to a modern world with the same authority as when it was delivered? How can the expositor be sure that what is uttered from pulpit or lectern can be prefaced with confidence by "thus saith the Lord"? The real issue in biblical application is authority.

Not all applications have equal textual justification and, therefore, equal authority. The message of a biblical passage is inferred from an accurate synthesis of the passage details. The degree of congruence between the exegetical synthesis and the exegetical particulars determines the accuracy of the expositor's presentation. Similarly the stated application of a passage must not violate other elements in the passage. When this happens, the application loses its claim to biblical authority.

Classical rhetoric identified three sources of authority: *pathos,* the appeal to the emotional attachments or sentiments of the audience; *ethos,* the appeal to the authority of the speaker in the eyes of the audience (which may be due to the speaker's education, maturity, or experience); and *logos,* the appeal to the coherence between evidence and inference within the speaker's argument.[16] Tragically too many preachers depend on *pathos* or *ethos.* Biblically, *logos* takes precedence.[17] Unfortunately *logos* can often be prostituted to an individual's theological presuppositions and systematic formulations.[18] The challenge for authoritative relevance is a

16. Aristotle, *Rhetoric,* I.2.3-6. Consider the ancient means for determining the orthodoxy of belief: *pathos* corresponding to the biblical canon bearing witness to the Christ as the object of Christian affection and aspiration; *ethos* corresponding to the office of the bishop and his imprimatur; and *logos* corresponding to the formulation of the ancient creedal distillations of theological thought and argument. Despite the good intentions and orthodox belief of many expositors, too many messages rely on the authority of their advocates and lack intrinsic authority derived from the text before them.

17. For example, Paul affirmed the Berean Christians, who would not trust his *pathos* or *ethos* but tested his *logos* (Acts 17:11).

18. *Ethos* and *pathos* are still relevant. A speaker has greater difficulty persuading his audience (regardless of the form or substance of his argument) if he is known to misrepresent either the truth or his authority to address the subject (lacking *ethos*) or if he addresses his audience in a way that suggests disinterest or disbelief in what he proposes (lacking *pathos*).

message in which *logos* represents accurately the theological argument of the biblical passage and its relevance.

From the beginning biblical teachers have searched for relevance and debated the legitimacy of applications. The Ancient Near Eastern world divided all reality into the seen and the unseen, then extended this into literature and mythology. Every text and story had a twofold meaning, the literal (seen or obvious) and the spiritual (unseen or less obvious). Each storyteller's task included the retelling of both meanings. After the destruction of Solomon's temple and their loss of the theocratic framework for OT covenant stipulations, Israelite storytellers adopted this twofold hermeneutic. Teachers reinterpreted OT events and requirements in their new socio-political context to produce targumim and rabbinical allegory. Christians inherited and adopted this twofold approach, strengthened by Jesus' apparent endorsement of it (Luke 24:25-27). Post-apostolic writers continued the tradition.[19] Patristic methods for moving beyond the literal sense became more complex in an attempt to bridge the literal meaning of a biblical text and its significance for a new audience.[20] In Christian worship the sermon represented the climax of an application matrix beginning with the OT as God's record of covenant faithfulness, a Psalm expressing anticipating the fulfillment of God's work, an Epistle providing insight on the new work undertaken through Christ, and a Gospel as the climax of God's work through the incarnate Word.[21] All these attempted to develop

---

Even a weak argument delivered by a highly trusted speaker is more convincing than a strong argument delivered well by someone unknown to or mistrusted by his audience. See the studies referenced by Donald Sunukjian, "The Credibility of the Preacher," *BSac* 139 (1982): 255-66. Hence, Aristotle proposed that a speaker's integrity may be the most significant aspect of interpersonal communication (ibid.).

19. Boniface Ramsey, *Beginning to Read the Fathers* (New York: Paulist, 1985), 33, writes that, "For the most part, however, the Fathers simply occupied themselves with two senses, the literal and the spiritual, without making further distinctions. Taken most broadly, the patristic approach to these senses may be resolved into three schools—one that gives overwhelming weight to the spiritual sense, often to the detriment of the literal; one that holds a more or less middle position; and one that gives overwhelming weight to the literal sense, often to the detriment of the spiritual, although without denying the existence of the spiritual."

20. For example: Origen (*De princ.*, 4.2.4) spoke of the moral/ascetical (soul) and spiritual/mystical (spirit); Ambrose (*Exp. Evang. sec. Luc.*, prol. 2) classified these as the natural (natural ethics), moral (Christian ethics), and mystical/rational (corresponding to the truly spiritual mind); Augustine (*De util. cred.* 3.5) argued for the aetiological (explanation of cause), analogical (unity between Old and New Testaments), and allegorical (meaning of things not to be taken literally); Augustine's contemporary, Cassian (*Conlat.*, 14.8) divided them into the tropological (moral sense dealing with life in general), allegorical (mysteries of the New Covenant hidden/prefigured within historical events), and anagogical (sublime secrets of heaven itself). Cassian's categories came to dominate exegesis through the Middle Ages.

21. Liturgically a congregation recited an ecumenical creed (Nicea or its derivatives) as the functional litmus test of the truth taught, affirming their unity with the entire community

a systematic and authoritative means to present the text's significance beyond its original context. Most models portray a single move between exegesis and exposition. Respected preachers intuit the latter from the former without a clear bridge. Preaching becomes both science (exegesis) and art (application). This masks the complexity of the process.

13.3 The Challenge of Meaning (Exegesis)

Recently homileticians have begun to reexamine exposition as a three-stage process: exegesis, theology, and application. Each stage presents a distinct challenge for the expositor.[22] The first stage (exegesis) challenges the expositor to accurately recover the text's meaning as understood by its first recipients.[23] It gathers the passage's linguistic, grammatical, and theological details, and then synthesizes a whole that accommodates them. Proper exegesis seeks to "grasp the meaning of the original text untainted by the influence of either a more fully developed theology or any contemporary cultural significance."[24] The exegete employs "hermeneutical bracketing," suspending all judgment of the text's meaning that might be imposed by theological systems or urgent inquiry.[25] He attempts to insulate his exegesis from his beliefs, prejudices, and questions (as well as those of his prospective audience) outside of the text under scrutiny.[26]

---

of faith in its teaching. Some modern communities use the Apostles' Creed for its simplicity, but neither its ecumenicity nor its antiquity has been proved.

22. Timothy S. Warren, "A Paradigm for Preaching," *BSac* 148 (1991): 463-86. Traina taught a more complex four-step process of Observation-Interpretation (two steps in exegesis), Evaluation (theological congruence), and Application (modern significance) that anticipated Warren. See Robert A. Traina, *Methodical Bible Study: A New Approach to Hermeneutics* (Asbury, Ky.: Asbury Theological Seminary, 1952), 203-13.

23. Litfin identifies ten "challenges" to the exegete posed by the NT literature itself: absent textual dividers, mistaken textual dividers, exegetical ambiguities, NT citations of the OT (text form, theology, and role in the argument), unique genres (synoptic and epistolary), the presence of secondary voices (as in narrative), imprecise textual purpose, absence of explicit central ideas (thesis statements), long grammatical constructions, and lists of exhortations (apparently unrelated). See Duane Litfin, "New Testament Challenges to Big Idea Preaching," in *The Big Idea of Biblical Preaching: Connecting the Bible to People,* ed. Keith Willhite and Scott M. Gibson (Grand Rapids, Mich.: Baker, 1998), 53-66. Inasmuch as the previous chapters in this volume have attempted to describe this process in some detail, further comment here is superfluous.

24. Warren, "Paradigm for Preaching," 475 n. 54.

25. A complete hermeneutical bracketing as described is philosophically impossible. No interpreter can approach a text without a preunderstanding. The bracketing ideal, however, sustains the search for objectivity in interpretation in order to allow the text to speak for itself (and not merely reinforce the reader's prejudice). This attitude lies behind modern advances in biblical scholarship and our renewed understanding of the text's significance for our circumstance.

26. See David Stewart and Algis Mickunas, *Exploring Phenomenology* (Chicago: American Library Association, 1974), 23-27, 45-48.

One can perform a practical test of one's exegetical understanding by writing a single declarative statement of the passage's meaning—the exegetical proposition of the passage.[27] This sentence (including subordinate clauses) must possess a single subject (or theme) that defines the issue of the text and one or more complements that provide the text's answer to the issue. This summary is a heuristic tool that forces one from the safety of textual ambiguity.[28]

The exegetical summary statement reflects the extent of the passage. The summary of an entire book is supported by exegetical statements for each major section. These in turn are supported by summary statements of each paragraph. These in turn are supported by a summary of each whole sentence and then by each independent and dependent clause. The same phenomenon occurs in narrative literature with a new twist: the meaning of a single pericope can be properly understood only when placed within the larger context (structure) of the book as a whole and the subsection within which the pericope lies.

Exegetical summary statements often contain two common mistakes. Both avoid interpretation. One repeats the exegetical summary with the same words as used in the biblical text (that is, the translation used by the exegete).[29] Obviously where symbols or figures are involved, this shows that the exegete does not fully understand the concept—or at least does not understand it in such a way as to communicate the meaning clearly. There are places where a single English term does not capture the nuance of the word in the original language. If the summary just repeats the En-

27. This construction has been described as a "central thought" (H. Grady Davis, *Design for Preaching* [Philadelphia: Fortress, 1958], 20-21); "main idea" (Haddon W. Robinson, *Biblical Preaching: The Development and Delivery of Expository Messages,* 2nd ed. [Grand Rapids, Mich.: Baker, 2001], 33-50); "big idea" (Willhite and Gibson, *The Big Idea of Biblical Preaching,* passim); "central proposition" (Warren, "Paradigm for Preaching," 475; Ramesh Richard, *Scripture Sculpture* [Grand Rapids, Mich.: Baker, 1995], 67-78, 87-97; Allen P. Ross, *Creation and Blessing: A Guide to the Study and Exposition of the Book of Genesis* [Grand Rapids, Mich.: Baker, 1988], 45-46); "propositional statement" (Reg Grant and John Reed, *The Power Sermon: Countdown to Quality Messages for Maximum Impact* [Grand Rapids, Mich.: Baker, 1993], 25-26); "controlling purpose or 'big idea'" (John D. Grassmick, *Principles and Practice of Greek Exegesis,* rev. ed. [Dallas: Dallas Theological Seminary, 1976], 15, 190-91); or "central idea" (Donald G. McDougall, "Central Ideas, Outlines, and Titles," in Mayhue, ed., *Rediscovering Expository Preaching,* 225-41).

28. This is distinct from the method of formulating "principles" from the text whose significances are then extrapolated to situations within the experience of the modern audience. "Principalizing" as a bridge for application usually occurs with fewer exegetical controls and greater theological dependence for its legitimacy, with a greater potential for error or merely the reinforcement of one's predispositions about the text and its ethics.

29. For example, an exegetical summary of Eph 4:17 must not repeat the textual expression "walking as Gentiles walk," but must interpret it as "following a non-Christian manner of life."

glish translation, an audience may miss its significance. Or, some words appear so often that their nuance is no longer vivid enough to prevent the listener from importing another meaning into them.[30] Using appropriate synonyms for biblical terminology forms a test of the exegete's full understanding of the passage.

The other error appears when summary statements describe the text's actions rather than summarize their contextual significance. "Paul prays for the Ephesians" describes what is happening but not the content of his prayer, the point of the passage. This problem grows larger in biblical narrative where the rhetorical contribution of a pericope (its point within the broader context of the book) can be quite distinct from a mere descriptive summary of individual events or actions. Avoiding these two mistakes will crystallize the exegete's understanding and presentation of textual meaning.

13.4 The Challenge of Significance (Theology)

Having defined what the passage meant in one specific cultural context (exegesis), the second step on the path to authoritative application requires a theological correlation between the original audience and the new context. This step has been addressed in two different ways. Richard proposes a biblical-theological "purpose bridge" correlation between textual message and modern audience.[31] Such a process, however, can leave the expositor without a precise understanding of the specific theological correspondence between the two audiences that permits the application of the original message to the new audience. On the other hand Warren encourages the formulation of the universal, noncontextualized statement of the passage, a single declarative summary sentence.[32] This statement of transcendent significance identifies the text's message when its cultural dress is removed. The passage now speaks as a consistent theological truth that can be discerned across the biblical canon, the abstract truth true for all audiences.

In both models "theology" does not refer to the historical and systematic disciplines that answer historical and philosophical questions. It

---

30. For example, the NT often identifies the means of salvation as "the blood [of Jesus]," an expression that contributed to the misrepresentation of the gospel by modern Liberals who did not represent it properly as "the atonement provided by the substitutionary death [of Jesus]."

31. See, for example, Richard, *Scripture Sculpture*, 79-85.

32. See, for example, Warren, "Paradigm for Preaching," 477-78; Grant and Reed, *Power Sermon*, 31-41; Bruce L. Shelley, "The Big Idea and Biblical Typology's Grand Theme," in *The Big Idea of Biblical Preaching*, ed. Willhite and Gibson, 95-107. Recently the theological process has emerged as the new locus of discussion in homiletical literature. See Timothy Warren, "The Theological Process in Sermon Preparation," *BSac* 156 (1999): 336.

refers to *biblical* theology, but larger than the themes within a specific biblical book, author, or literary genre. The term here refers to broader motifs developed across the Bible that link together the entire canon in a theological matrix. These themes form bridges between the Old and New Testaments by which later biblical authors appropriated earlier biblical statements and applied them to their own circumstances.

Some biblical-theological themes are self-evident: the formation, prerequisites, and ethical obligations of biblical covenant and community; the nature, requirement, and justification of holiness; the righteous remnant, appearing in the NT appropriation of OT texts, strengthened by the NT theology of promise-fulfillment and the church as a community representing the inbreaking of the eschaton. Some themes require an even higher level of abstraction, such as sanctuary, the place where God's Spirit chooses to dwell among humanity, both historically (Eden, tabernacle, temple), eschatologically (the temples of Ezekiel and Revelation), and existentially in both individual believers and the Christian community (since the Holy Spirit chooses to be resident within both). With this theme one can make theological correlations between the symbolism of the many temples in Scripture and the modern Christian or church, and such comprehensive themes are the most helpful due to their specific referents.

The theological challenge grows in direct proportion to the distance between the text and its new audience. The smallest gap usually exists between the NT epistles and the modern Christian audience. They share the same theological assumptions, and their message is dominated by logical argument followed by ethical admonition. They may even share certain social, cultural, and theological presuppositions that significantly narrow or almost eliminate the distance between the two audiences.[33]

Even here small gaps remain. First, as does most of the Bible, the epistles often express themselves in figurative terms, symbols, and connotations (e.g., "the cross," representative of death and atonement; "blood," denoting "life"). Second, they assume or address specific cultural situations and practices. If one does not understand the practice, the application will only reflect the superficial actions described by the epistle. Consider, for example, the Corinthian situation's temple prostitution (1 Cor 6:12-20) or buying meat offered to idols (1 Cor 8:1-13; 10:23-33). In each case the issue involves more than sexual immorality or mere grocery shopping; it involves the question of religious syncretism suggested by each act. In the first case, Paul argues that since this prostitution represents a pagan worship practice, participation represents a defection from the faith and should be avoided. In the second case, Paul notes that the purchase and

33. See Ramesh Richard, "Application Theory in Relation to the New Testament," *BSac* 143 (1986): 205-17.

consumption of such food in the context of the marketplace does not represent syncretism and is permissible (as long as this does not impose an undue burden on the Christian confidence of another believer whose immature faith only sees it as a defection).

With NT narrative the situation becomes more complex. Jesus lived within the OT framework of first-century Judaism. This increases the theological and cultural distance slightly. The significance of the narrative appears through its rhetorical context. In NT apocalyptic literature (Revelation), the presence of theological images complicates the exegesis, the symbolism often assuming knowledge of OT themes.

13.5 The Challenge of Relevance (Application)

Having clearly stated the biblical-theological significance of the passage, one scholar assumes, "It should be a relatively simple matter to move from the exegetically derived theological statement to the application."[34] This third step, however, can prove quite difficult because now we "deal with things about which we deliberate, but for which we have no systematic rules."[35]

First, one must distinguish between relevance and application. The term *application* is usually limited to an explicit statement of behavioral response to the passage.[36] The audience must understand the text's meaning, then its significance; the application appears at the message's end. This approach confuses message structure (introduction, body, conclusion) with its argument and reduces application to a structural afterthought. Often it produces a disproportionate emphasis on information over behavior, a *de facto* devaluation of preaching's goal that contributes to the functional malaise. Christian maturity becomes biblical knowledge rather than godly character.

"Relevance" describes a broader approach. The speaker frames the entire message in the audience's frame of reference. The introduction focuses the issue from the audience's frame of reference. The body similarly develops the message, offering explicit direction for action as the argument progresses. The conclusion summarizes and reinforces the practical direction already stated. Relevance defines a speaker's rhetorical stance toward the audience from the opening sentence through to the conclusion. The expositor functions with a specific audience in view from the message beginning, crafting all the message's parts in the audience's terms. The

---

34. Ross, *Creation and Blessing*, 47.
35. Aristotle, *Rhetoric* I.2.12.
36. Note the definitions provided by Zuck, "Application," 19.

message is text-centered but remains audience focused. Relevance assumes a specific audience to which this text (and its theological message) will be preached at this moment, exploring how the text's biblical-theological truth should be actualized by people whose life circumstances were not explicitly envisioned by the biblical author.

Having already determined the exegetical proposition and the theological proposition for the text, relevance determines the audience's position with respect to the biblical-theological summary.[37] Imagine an ideal world and ask how a contemporary listener would act if he or she were doing all that this truth demanded. What is the key behavior that would demonstrate obedience to this truth? The greatest distance between each ideal behavior and reality generates the primary statement of relevance for the message. Now the effective preacher asks, "Why isn't my audience living this way?"

In terms of rhetoric, people do not act as they should because of one (or more) of the following reasons: they do not know what to do (lack of information); they do not believe it is appropriate for them (lack of validation); or they do not know how to do it (lack of direction). These reasons can be phrased as questions,[38] sometimes called "developmental (or diagnostic) questions" to emphasize their role for developing the sermon's primary emphasis, structural argument, and persuasive elements,[39] or "focusing questions" for their role in forming the sermon's purpose.[40] Others speak more generally of a sermon's "purpose," "intent," "aim," or "objective" with or without specific reference to one or more of these questions.[41] All affirm, however, that determining the purpose for a spe-

37. A speaker's rhetorical stance must include the context in which the message must be delivered and the audience's position toward the speaker as an authority. Both of these issues, however, are outside the scope of this essay.

38. These three questions can be framed in the following ways: "What does this mean?" (information); "Why should I believe this is true?" (validation); and "How does this influence my daily conduct?" (application).

39. See, for example, John A. Broadus, *On the Preparation and Delivery of Sermons*, 4th ed., rev. Vernon Latrelle Stanfield (San Francisco: Harper & Row, 1979), 128-98; Robinson, *Preaching*, 81-96; Warren, "Paradigm for Preaching," 479-80; Davis, *Design for Preaching*, 81 (who refers to them as "functional questions").

40. See, for example, Grant and Reed, *Power Sermon*, 50.

41. See, for example, H. C. Brown, Jr., H. Gordon Clinard, Jesse J. Northcutt, and Al Fasol, *Steps to the Sermon: An Eight-Step Plan for Preaching with Confidence*, rev. ed. (Nashville: Broadman & Holman, 1996), 67-76; Harold T. Bryson, *Expository Preaching: The Art of Preaching Through a Book of the Bible* (Nashville: Broadman, 1995), 322-25; James W. Cox, *Preaching* (New York: Harper & Row, 1985), 83-87; Richard, *Scripture Sculpture*, 111. For many writers the destination is a structural emphasis (outline) rather than an explicit audience and rhetorical purpose. See, for example, Donald L. Hamilton, *Homiletical Handbook* (Nashville: Broadman, 1992), 22-23; David L. Larsen, *The Anatomy of Preaching: Identifying the Issues in Preaching Today* (Grand Rapids, Mich.: Baker, 1989), 64. Such a message becomes a discourse on the

cific audience precedes the development of the sermon's main thrust and argument structure by consciously exposing the differences between the world of the Bible and the world of his audience.

These questions also provide a check on the accuracy of the whole process to this point. An inability to answer the first question (explanation and understanding) with any degree of simplicity that does not use the words of the biblical text (or even the technical theological language of the seminary classroom) indicates a problem carried over from the exegetical stage. The expositor has failed to explore, develop, or integrate some aspect of the text or its understanding into the exegetical summary and from there into the theological principle (or perhaps has merely used theological language and generalizations while lacking a full appreciation of their significance and relationship to this text).

The speaker must determine the audience's understanding of, attitudes toward, and capabilities for the application of the proposition. The speaker then develops the message to answer the audience's initial problem (understanding, belief, or direction) and moves up through the remaining levels to end with a clear behavioral direction, a single sentence phrased in language appropriate to the audience. This sentence is best stated as an imperative (rather than a declarative) sentence in order to focus the application for the audience. Such a statement forms the homiletical proposition, and the entire message grows as an argument for this application statement. The expositor carefully selects (a) appropriate textual details to validate the exegetical meaning of the text, (b) biblical-theological correlations to validate the universal truth, and (c) specific situations appropriate to the audience in which the proposed action would appear.[42]

13.6 An Example from Didactic Literature

Didactic literature communicates primarily through grammatical relationships and lexical-historical referents. The exegetical proposition follows and summarizes the structure of the passage. In Eph 3:1-7 Paul described the means and content of his message concerning the unity of Jew and Gentile in the church. Now in Eph 3:8-13 he discusses the significance of his ministry. The exegetical proposition of this passage can be phrased as follows: "The reason that the apostle Paul encouraged the Ephesians to regard the opposition he received during his ministry as an

passage's exegetical or biblical-theological aspects without apparent significance for a specific (and ever-changing) audience. Only the preacher's intuition produces relevance.

42. The expositor must decide how to eliminate as many of the audience's barriers to textual and theological understanding and belief as appropriate within the available time.

honor, not a discouragement, was that his apostolic ministry concerning the church as a Jew-Gentile community united in Jesus Christ represented a cosmic display of God's wisdom." (Someone might protest that Paul's ministry is the issue in this section, not the encouragement of the Ephesians, producing a different exegetical summary statement. This would be true only if the last sentence [3:13] were eliminated. Taking, however, the entire paragraph as a single unit of thought, Paul's ministry becomes a subpoint in the argument's larger development.)

To formulate the theological proposition for this passage, one must first identify how Paul functions in this illustration. His concern for the church's nature as one people, a unified community in Jesus Christ, lies at the heart of the NT message, and Paul's teaching concerning Christian attitudes toward ministry opposition is paradigmatic. In this paragraph, however, the Ephesian Christians and their encouragement are the focus of his discussion. Therefore, after stripping away the time-specific referents, the theological proposition of the passage could be phrased in this way: "Those who encourage the divinely created unity displaying God's wisdom consider opposition an honor." From the beginning, unity in community has been the evidence of a righteous people under God, whether in ancient Israel, in the church, or in a future eschaton. Therefore, the theological statement reflects the broader biblical-theological concept of community.

What about the modern audience? Few churches around the world struggle with the problem of Jew-Gentile unity. Therefore, to preach a direct correspondence between ancient text and modern audience would make little difference. Most churches will loudly affirm they believe in and practice biblical unity. Considering the linguistic, cultural, economic, and social homogeneity of most congregations, they might be right. But if the group's members are challenged to accept, affirm, or even promote someone or some group not possessing their characteristics, their concept of unity can be threatened. The challenge becomes acute if the meetings require cooperation with an ethnic group or social class they would culturally reject. Often Christian unity becomes the first casualty.

The Holy Spirit did not create a cluster of clones. Every local community of believers draws from a cross section of the larger society, gathering and delighting in common access to God's grace through faith in a common Savior. Therefore, the potential for division exists in every church, and the message of unity must be preached in each context. Those who teach such a radical, countercultural concept will face opposition. It may come from within the congregation (and in a world where such divisions define identity, opposition will certainly come from the surrounding society). Therefore, the homiletical proposition will argue: "Accept the struggle for unity as God's medal of honor for your priorities." The application will assert how in a truly unified community under Christ the only allowed discrimination must be based on maturity, on the degree of one's obedience to God's expectations. This application will point out where discrimination appears, describe the inevitability of struggle, and offer encouragement that the opposition distinguishes those who know God's grace from those who do not.

13.7 An Example from Narrative Literature

Narrative communicates its point implicitly, primarily through structural relationships within the broader context that inform the significance of its internal events. In order to state an accurate exegetical summary statement for a narrative text, one must include the rhetorical significance of the pericope. In Mark's Gospel the three passion prediction cycles (Mark 8:27–10:45) focus on presentation of Jesus' identity and the correction of his disciples' misunderstanding of his mission. Two healings of the blind bracket the section. Before the cycles, a blind man requires a two-stage healing, the first having left him unable to identify properly what he sees, after which Jesus acts a second time and sends him home directly with instructions to avoid the village (Mark 8:22-26). After the cycles, blind Bartimaeus properly identifies Jesus, is healed, and follows Jesus immediately (Mark 10:46-52). Each story emphasizes the degree of knowing necessary for discipleship. Therefore, the exegetical main idea for this story can be stated as follows: "The ability of Bartimaeus to follow Jesus immediately upon his healing by Jesus in response to his proper identification of Jesus by faith demonstrates that a proper appreciation of Jesus' servant identity and mission is a prerequisite to Christian discipleship."

This long statement may sound cumbersome, but in this form it carefully places each element of the text in its proper relationship to the other elements. This helps avoid an inappropriate focus for the text's significance by an explicit statement of significance (application). At this point pedantry is a virtue.

The primary theological significance of the pericope will reflect the narrative significance. By eliminating the specific exegetical circumstances and abstracting the circumstantial referents in the significance, a biblical-canonical theological statement can be stated: "The prerequisite for obedience to God's way for his people is a proper appreciation of the identity and mission of his chosen representative." Without the limitations imposed by the language of the passage, the statement becomes simpler in its construction.

When one surveys the Old and New Testaments, many events reflect this theological principle. This can confirm that the concept represents the primary theological idea behind Mark's use of the story. Since the NT and the modern audience share the same theological matrix, the homiletical move adopts the same Christ-centered language, phrased in several ways, but generally, "To follow Jesus, give everything with a single focus." The issue of application becomes the identification of what the modern audience must assume as a commitment to Jesus and what the listeners will sacrifice in order to follow Jesus' direction. The application calls the listeners to know who Jesus is; if they know who he is, to commit themselves fully to follow him; if they are committed, to follow through on that commitment. The application points out what each listener might hold more important than following Jesus.

13.8 Summary

While many Bible students propose applications, the search is for a method that preserves the integrity of the entire text's original meaning in its context. Only an application of this type possesses intrinsic authority commensurate with the intended meaning for the original audience. When broken down into its constituent parts, the method moves between three products. First, the expositor must synthesize the exegetical message of the text as a single proposition. Second, knowing the biblical factors that make this exegetical message peculiar to its own time and audience, one can eliminate them to identify the primary biblical-theological focus of the passage as a single proposition in language that possesses no specific temporal referents. This biblical-theological proposition exists as a universal statement of truth as presented in the passage without the peculiar aspects of the original context (culture, expectation, biblical theology, canonical theology) that are unique to and nuance the meaning of the exegetical situation to which the text is addressed.[43] Third, the expositor identifies how specific listeners would incarnate this biblical-theological truth, comparing it with this actual behavior and determining whether the cause for this discrepancy lies with their lack of knowledge of the truth, their lack of belief in the truth, or their lack of clear direction for living congruent with the truth. Application identifies this incongruence and proposes specific actions to bring the listeners' understanding, belief, and behavior into conformity with the truth while justifying how it was derived from the text. Such a method ensures that the listener understands both the application and the process by which it was derived from the passage, preserving the authority of the Bible for the new generation.

43. This process is described by Ross, *Creation and Blessing*, 44-45.

13.9 For Further Reading

Richard, Ramesh. *Scripture Sculpture*. Grand Rapids, Mich.: Baker, 1995.

Robinson, Haddon W. *Biblical Preaching: The Development and Delivery of Expository Messages*. 2nd ed. Grand Rapids, Mich.: Baker, 2001.

Stott, John R. W. *Between Two Worlds: The Art of Preaching in the Twentieth Century*. Grand Rapids, Mich.: Eerdmans, 1982.

Willhite, Keith, and Scott M. Gibson, eds., *The Big Idea of Biblical Preaching: Connecting the Bible to People*. Grand Rapids, Mich.: Baker, 1998.

PART TWO

Exegetical Examples and Reflections

Mark 1:1-13

Introducing the Gospel of Mark

14

I. HOWARD MARSHALL

> Focus on the opening verses of Mark's Gospel, reflecting on important areas to investigate and questions of method.

Over the past few years one of my regular duties has been to teach a class on exegesis of selected portions of the Gospel of Mark. At the opening meeting of the class I have begun by saying something like this:

> I am conscious that this is in some ways the most difficult and significant hour that I spend with you. For on it depends whether or not I fire you with enthusiasm to actually read and study the New Testament and specifically this Gospel. The whole process is bound to be imperfect because we have only a very limited number of class sessions to cover a short book (just over 11,000 words in the Greek text) but one of tremendous fascination and difficulty.
>
> It is staggering that a modern entertainer, Alec McCowan, could put on a performance that consisted simply in a one-man recitation of this Gospel on the stage of a London theatre. Maybe I should simply do the same and read the Gospel to you instead of talking about it, but then there must have been something about his reading that I cannot imitate. I want you, or rather us, to read and understand this book. It is difficult to reduce understanding to a method or set of rules, and therefore I hope that we can learn the "how" by doing the job, by learning to ask the right questions, and in this way learning how to listen to what the text is saying to us and to hear its questions.

There had been nothing like the Gospel of Mark published before, so far as our evidence goes.[1] So what is it?

Clearly it is intended to be based on history, because it describes events that the writer believed happened in the real world, even if some of them may seem fantastic. It looks like a biography, because it is entirely about one person, but it plunges into the story of an adult, rather than beginning with childhood. It covers a short period of time, and it devotes something like a third of the space to the last, fatal week of his life. Most remarkably—at least for readers of the other Gospels—it concludes with a very brief account of his burial, followed by a visit to his tomb by a small group of women who find it empty and see what sober-minded people would call an apparition: terror seizes them, and they run away without saying anything to anybody. End of story. We do not know whether that is the intended end of the story, or whether the last page or so has been lost.

And it is a book that says extraordinary things. The most odd is in 14:28. The longest section describing what Jesus said is chapter 13, a remarkably pessimistic description of the future.[2] In other places Jesus says things that are almost unintelligible: what do you make, for instance, of 9:49-50? And some of what he said was difficult to understand even at the time (e.g., some of the parables; see 4:13).

I do not know whether we can solve all the puzzles, or whether we are even meant to. Mark is like a piece of art, with the capacity to engender new experiences.

And there is the danger that by dissecting Mark we shall ruin it, cutting up a living body and reducing it to a specimen on an anatomy table—great if you like anatomy, but hopeless if you want a personal relationship with the subject. But analysis can help understanding: art critics probably understand and appreciate pictures better than an untutored person like me.

So we take the plunge into the text.

From this brief summary it will be apparent that the main thing I want to do is to convey the fascination and mystery of this book, so that students will want to read it and get to the bottom of it. But to do so, they must learn to ask questions of the text, and therefore the secondary purpose in what I am doing is to use the text inductively as a means of learning what is involved in exegesis (I do not know any other way of teaching exegesis than by actually doing it).

So after we have read and talked about the opening section of Mark, I stop and have a post mortem on what we have been doing, and what I now share with you is a summary of the conclusions about method that I draw at this point. I offer it as a help to teachers who want to know how

1. Here I am assuming that Mark is the earliest Gospel. The class had discussed such matters in an earlier course.

2. I was exaggerating to make my point. There are some hopeful accents in Mark 13, but there is an awful lot of tribulation that I would prefer to miss out on!

to deal with exegesis and as a guide to students to help them recognize what is going on in an exegesis class. I make no claim to originality or completeness. I suggest, then, that there are about ten things that arise in a study of the opening verses of the Gospel.

(1) The first task is to carry out a rough structural analysis, which will establish whether we can determine meaningful self-contained sense units and what their mutual relationships are.

It is common to think of the opening verses of Mark as the introduction to the Gospel. But where does the introduction end? Does it end, or does it flow smoothly into the rest of the story that follows? The NRSV has a major break at 1:15/16, but the NIV has two sections, 1:1-8 and 1:9-13, with 1:14-15 as part of a third section (1:14-20). What justification is there for regarding either 1:1-13 or 1:1-15 (or an even longer passage) as "the introduction"? What difference does it make to our understanding of the section if we label it "introduction" or "prologue"?

The two translations I have consulted suggest that, if there is an introduction, it contains some subsections.[3] There is not too much difficulty in recognizing 1:1-8 as a unified piece that gives a general picture of the activity of John, culminating in the prophecy of the coming of the stronger one. "This prophecy is partially fulfilled immediately afterwards in the appearance of Jesus on the scene in 1:9-11; he comes as "the stronger one," but the fulfillment of the prophecy is only partial in that baptism by him with the Holy Spirit does not yet happen. Instead Jesus himself receives the Spirit and is commissioned for his work. So the activity of John links the two sections together. Then 1:12-13 follows as the next item in chronological order. At this point there is clearly a temporal gap during which John's activity is terminated (presumably after some further activity beyond that recorded here) by his imprisonment, and then we have a fresh start with Jesus preaching independently and announcing what looks like a new beginning (1:14-15). So the temporal break at 1:13/14, the appearance of Jesus acting by himself, and his statement that now the time is fulfilled strongly suggests that 1:1-13 is preliminary or introductory and 1:14 is the commencement of the real action.

(2) A second question concerns the place of this passage in the Gospel, looking especially at its function for the readers. What was Mark trying to do with the passage? Here we need to ask questions about the kinds

---

3. The reason for choosing the NIV and the NRSV for primary use in study is that they are both fairly literal in their rendering of the Greek text, avoiding the interpretation found in some translations and the freedom to recast the text found in others. I once had to write a commentary based on one of these other versions of a NT book, and I found that time and again I was writing: "The translation says this, but the Greek really means that." For study purposes it is better to have the next best thing to the Greek text; but for reading to the unchurched youth and indeed for wider use generally, give me the Good News Bible!

of things that introductions do. Their task is to transport readers out of the world that they are already in, into the "world" of the text, to make a transition between their situation and that of the text, to entice them to read further, and to encourage them to interact with the story.

Mark does something of this kind right at the very beginning with his title "The beginning of the gospel about Jesus Christ, the Son of God." (Here we note in passing the puzzling fact that some early copies of the Gospel do not have the words "the Son of God" and recognize that there is a problem of textual criticism.)

One of the most popular of twentieth-century genres of fiction is the detective story, which usually presents the readers with a mystery or puzzle and leads them through a series of pieces of evidence and argumentation from which they may be able to deduce who committed the murder.[4] Occasionally you may get a detective story of a different kind that tells you at the outset what happened or who committed the crime and then takes you through what happened either from the point of view of the perpetrator of the murder or through the workings of the mind of the investigator. So the detective story may be a puzzle till you get to the last page, or the author may let the cat out of the bag very early on. The latter procedure resembles that of many ancient Greek dramas, where the audience knew what would happen at the end of the play and the interest and excitement lay in the fresh way in which the dramatist took them to the denouement.

Which kind of story does Mark's Gospel resemble? It could be said that the Gospel falls into two parts, in the first of which the other people in the story are facing the question "Who is Jesus?" and the correct answer is given by Peter, "You are the Christ" (8:29). Then in the second part of the story Jesus both explains that (against all expectation) the Christ must suffer and actually does suffer. So far as the first part of the Gospel is concerned, it plainly falls into the second category of detective stories: the readers already know what the actors in the story do not know, that Jesus is the Christ; only in the second half does the Gospel resemble the first category of detective stories in that there is a surprise ending (but perhaps not so surprising, since the readers would probably be well aware of the death of Jesus).

Here, then, we see something of what the introduction to the Gospel achieves so far as the readers are concerned. It puts them into a privileged position over against the actors in the story and so gives them something of the agenda for what is to follow.

4. It is an interesting fact that whereas the greatest of mystery writers, Arthur Conan Doyle, wrote about all kinds of puzzles faced by Sherlock Holmes, for contemporary writers there is only one kind of puzzle, murder.

(3) We cannot read very far in 1:1-13 before we find material that cannot be explained simply from within the text. We need to look for background material that helps us to understand the passage.

One example of this is the description of John's diet, locusts and wild honey (1:6). It was sometimes suggested by early Christian writers that the locusts were some kind of vegetable matter that could be found in the desert. Never very likely in itself, the suggestion is refuted by the fact that in the Dead Sea Scrolls, which are from the same general period and whose milieu is the desert surrounding the River Jordan and the Dead Sea, there are explicit instructions about the eating of the insect of that name.

Even earlier, in 1:2-3 we have what is identified as a quotation from the Old Testament; the quotation is allegedly from Isaiah but in fact also contains some wording from Malachi. But in addition to this, Mark describes the clothing of John using phraseology that is paralleled in the OT (2 Kgs 1:8), and similarly the wording of the voice from heaven has parallels in Psalm 2 and Isaiah 42. In the one case Mark has signposted what was happening for his readers by using a citation formula, but in the other cases there are no signposts, and so the readers may need to be constantly on the alert in order to pick up the allusions. The modern reader may be helped to do so by looking up words in a concordance and seeing where else they occur, but the ancient reader had to rely on a familiarity with the texts.

It is interesting that the authors of the Dead Sea Scrolls also cite the passage from Isaiah with regard to their own activity, and we know that they practiced ceremonial actions involving washing with water. What light does this shed on what John was doing? What was his relationship to this contemporary or near-contemporary group of fellow-countrymen?

(4) The use of the Old Testament here demonstrates at the very least some artistic skill at work in the use of language that was evocative of other texts. This alerts us to the fact that many statements may have an allusive force that can be very important. The description of John's clothing is reminiscent of that used about the prophet Elijah; when we bear in mind that the future messenger of Mal 3:1 was understood to be the prophet Elijah (Mal 4:5-6), the question arises whether John is understood by Mark (and other early Christians) to be the fulfillment of that prophecy.

But the language may also have links forward, as well as backwards. It may link not only with the language of other books (inter-textual links) but with other passages in the same book (intra-textual links). Key words may recur later in the narrative. Thus there is a discussion about the coming of Elijah later on, and an express statement that by that point Elijah had already come and people had done to him whatever they pleased, as was written about him (9:11-13). Again, in the story of Jesus being baptized, he is addressed by the heavenly voice (clearly God's voice) as "my Son"; this identification, already made (if the words are original to Mark) in the cat-out-of-the-bag description in 1:1, will be repeated later in the Gospel (9:7; 13:32; 15:39) and forms a significant thread running through the Gospel. Here, then, are two strands woven into the narrative of the Gospel, both of which are adumbrated in the introduction. Again we see how the use of specific words and phrases functions to enable one passage to throw light on another.

(5) Particular details of the narrative cause problems of understanding for us. Sometimes it is a question of syntax, how phrases are tied together. Does the quotation in 1:2-3 belong to 1:1 or is it tied rather to 1:4? Within the quotation the words "in the desert" are tied to "crying out," but in the original text in Isaiah they are tied to "prepare the way of the Lord."

Or the puzzle may be one of linguistics. The most conspicuous problem of this kind is just outside our passage in 1:15, where the Greek verb translated "has come near" is ambiguous: does it mean "has arrived" or "has come into the vicinity"? A decision on that point is of crucial importance in determining whether Jesus and the Evangelists regarded the kingdom of God as something that had actually come into effect there and then or as something that was now very imminent but not yet quite there.

Sometimes it is a matter of understanding cryptic statements in the story. What is the force of the comparison between the Spirit and a dove? What were the wild beasts doing in the desert? Were they a menace to Jesus, or were they friendly?

In these examples we may be dealing both with matters that are obscure to us but were not so to the original readers (who understood the contemporary scene and the Greek language better than we do) and with matters that may have been obscure to them as well as to us.

(6) Another type of problem may arise from trying to relate the passage to our general theological understanding, which itself may be drawn from elsewhere in the New Testament. According to the writer of the Letter to the Hebrews Jesus was "tempted in every way, just as we are—yet was without sin" (Heb 4:15, NIV), and other writers refer to his being righteous (2 Cor 5:21; 1 Pet 3:18; 1 John 2:1). Here, however, Mark tells about John proclaiming a baptism for the forgiveness of sins and describes how people came to be baptized, confessing their sins, and then Jesus himself comes and shares in this baptism. Does this mean that he was conscious of sins that he had committed and came to be forgiven? What other explanation might there be?[5] This might lead us to explore

---

5. This is not the same problem as the one faced in Matthew's version of the story, where John protests that he needs baptism from Jesus rather than vice versa; the point there is more

whether baptism might be something more than an act of cleansing from sin. Might the cleansing from sin be a part of a more inclusive action, such as total commitment of oneself to God, in which case Jesus might have been publicly dedicating himself to the positive way of life proclaimed by John without having to confess any past failure to do so?

A further question of the same sort would be: what is envisaged by the prophecy of the stronger one baptizing with the Holy Spirit? The Gospel does not apparently relate the fulfillment of this prophecy: how did Mark understand it? These points indicate how theological problems cannot be avoided in our study of the text.

(7) Earlier in our discussion we came across language that was allusive. But there is another possible use of language which needs investigation also. This is the problem of language that may not be meant literally but rather symbolically. In 1:10 it is related that Jesus saw the heavens torn open and saw the Spirit come on him like a dove, and heard a heavenly voice. It is not stated whether other people present saw and heard these things. Did the things described happen literally, in the sense that any other observer present would have witnessed them? Or were they private to Jesus? And what exactly was happening? For some ancient people the sky may have been thought of as a solid dome, and a miraculous splitting of it (followed by a restoration to its original state) could have been a possibility. For others the sky is a vast emptiness stretching for light-years, and the idea of it splitting open seems unreal. So did Mark intend to record a visionary experience, a communication from God to Jesus expressed by using this realistic language? And what about the experience in the desert? No problem about the wild animals being there, but what about the angels waiting on Jesus? Is this symbolical language again for divine strengthening? What are we to make of angels?

Some of this language can be categorized as "apocalyptic," which does not really explain anything but simply says that it is language about massive, supernatural things occurring in the world of nature as well as of people.[6] Or it may be categorized as "mythological," which means that it is language about God or other spiritual beings intervening in the day-to-day life of the world like ordinary people, only with enormous power and the ability to do things that ordinary people cannot do (like splitting the heavens open or walking on water). Did such things happen just as they are described, or are we again dealing with some kind of symbolical use of language?

---

the sense of unworthiness felt by John.

6. It is so called because it is typical of the kind of literature called "apocalypse." See, for example, Rev 6:14.

(8) Some of the points already mentioned raise the question whether things actually happened literally as they are told, and the examples produced so far have to do with things that might be regarded as highly unusual if not impossible in the world as we know it (even as we know it as Christians). But the same question may arise on a more ordinary level. It is the question of historicity. Does Mark's story rest on facts? Did Jesus actually come and submit to John's baptism? Did John really prophesy the baptism with the Holy Spirit? There are not wanting skeptics who ask for some kind of confirmation that these things happened. How do we know that Mark was not simply telling a tall story?

For many people, of course, the fact that these incidents are recorded in Scripture is sufficient evidence that they actually happened. But, as we have seen already, acceptance of Scripture as entirely adequate for its God-given purpose[7] does not allow us to duck questions about precisely what it is that Scripture regards as having happened—were the angels figures that Jesus could see and touch in the desert or were they spiritual, unseen, heavenly sources of strength?

To be sure, we are probably on firm historical ground in this section of Mark. It has often been observed that the baptism of Jesus is not a story that early Christians are likely to have invented in view of the kind of misunderstandings that have already been mentioned. Moreover, the whole story of John fits in so well with the Jewish background of the time as to be quite credible. There were presumably no witnesses of Jesus' conflict in the wilderness, but may he not have shared such an experience subsequently with his close friends? Considerations such as these indicate that historical criticism is not necessarily negative in its conclusions. It cannot produce cast-iron, knock-down arguments for historicity (or against historicity), but it can produce arguments giving greater or lesser degrees of probability for individual incidents.

(9) Most of the above discussion has been carried out on the basis of understanding Mark in its own light but also in the light of all appropriate background material. One area that has scarcely been mentioned so far is that of the parallel material in the three other Gospels (with the occasional parallel also in some of the later, apocryphal Gospels). Matthew and Luke in particular cover the same ground as Mark, and there are such close resemblances between the three Gospels as to raise the question whether any of the Gospel writers was acquainted with the work of any of the others or with earlier sources and traditions that were also known to any

---

7. I hasten to reassure any readers who feel the need for reassurance that I share with my good friend, the honoree of this volume, in accepting "the divine inspiration and infallibility of Holy Scripture, as originally given, and its supreme authority in all matters of faith and conduct." But that acceptance is not meant to stop us from asking questions and seeking answers.

of the others. For myself, I have yet to be persuaded that any theory is superior to the one that Matthew and Luke each knew and reproduced in their own characteristic way the account in Mark together with other material (the so-called "Q" traditions). Whatever view we take of the relationships between the Gospels and their sources, it remains the case that the characteristic qualities of Mark's story stand out all the more clearly when we compare it with the other versions.[8] So far as getting at Mark's meaning is concerned, it is important not to assume that he was trying to convey exactly the same truths as the other Gospel writers; this is particularly true, for example, of the much shorter temptation narrative in Mark. We may compare how different preachers may draw different lessons out of the same text, not necessarily disagreeing with one another but each seeing facets of the truth not perceived by the others and not seeing some of the facets that the others saw. To be sure, in trying to get at a full picture of the original incident and its significance, it would be necessary to take all the Gospels into account, and the ultimate goal of Gospel study is surely to shed as much light on the life and teaching of Jesus as possible. But it is an important first step to let each account shine in its own light.

(10) Having asked all these questions and entered these different areas of investigation, we still have a task of synthesis. We have to use the material we have collected in this way to write out an exegesis of the passage. What, then, is an exegesis? Exegesis is (and must always remain) the servant of the text, and is no substitute for it. It is the attempt to explain to subsequent readers what the original text was intended to say to its original readers. It is necessary because we are not the original readers. So exegesis will bring out the message of the text, especially explaining the difficulties in understanding it. It should enable the readers to understand what was in danger of being misunderstood or not fully understood. There may, of course, also be the discussion of things that do not seem to have been problematic to the original readers (or perhaps not even to the author). For example, the question about the sinlessness of Jesus may not have been a problem to Mark or his readers. Again, the question of whether the heavens can be literally split open probably is not one that would have occurred to them.

It is not within the scope of this short article to attempt a synthetic understanding of this passage. Our concern has been rather with the

---

8. Where we possess a document and its sources, it is perfectly proper to see what light can be shed on the document by observing the way in which it has utilized its sources, i.e., by redaction criticism. If my statement above is correct, then in the case of Mark we do not possess the sources that he was using for the story of Jesus, although we might still ask redaction-critical questions about (for example) his use of Old Testament texts (see point 3 above).

preparatory tasks that must be included in exegesis. We have listed a number of questions to be asked and procedures to be followed, all of which were relevant to this passage, but which are not necessarily all appropriate with every passage.[9]

It is a joy to share in the tribute rendered by this book to a friend of many years' standing who has contributed so solidly to the study of the background and chronology of the Gospels and, more than that, has given us such a fine example of how to do exegesis of the Epistles in his superb commentary on Ephesians.

9. A Gospel narrative may require different treatment from a doctrinal instruction in an Epistle.

Mark 1:1-15

15

The Paradox of Authority and Servanthood

NARRY F. SANTOS

Exploration of the literary technique of paradox in Mark 1:1-15, using elements of reader-response criticism, narrative criticism, and rhetorical criticism.

The prologue of Mark 1:1-15[1] is a crucial introduction to the entire Markan narrative.[2] The prologue gives readers the necessary back-

---

1. There are differences of opinion as to how far the prologue extends. Some scholars hold that the extension of the prologue is to 1:8, others to 1:11, others to 1:13, and others to 1:15. This study takes the prologue to 1:15 in light of two framings within this section. The outermost framing (1:1 and 1:15) is bracketed by a ring composition (i.e., about Jesus and his gospel) which is further closed by the repeated word "gospel" (εὐαγγελίου in 1:1; εὐαγγελίῳ in 1:15). The inner framing of inclusio relates to what occurs to John the Baptist. The beginning of John's ministry is presented in 1:2-8, while the end of his ministry (i.e., being taken into custody) is mentioned in 1:14a. In addition, 1:14b-15 forms an important link to 1:1-13 in light of the alternating focus of attention between Jesus and John. The pattern is thus: Jesus (1:1), John (1:2-8), Jesus (1:9-13), John (1:14a), and Jesus (1:14b-15). For arguments for and against extending the prologue to 1:15, see Frank Matera, "The Prologue as the Interpretative Key to Mark's Gospel," *JSNT* 34 (October 1988): 3-20; M. Eugene Boring, "Mark 1:1-15 and the Beginning of the Gospel," *Semeia* 52 (1990): 53-59; R. T. France, "The Beginning of Mark," *RTR* 49 (1990): 11-19; and Scaria Kuthirakkattel, *The Beginning of Jesus' Ministry According to Mark's Gospel (1:14–3:6): A Redaction Critical Study,* AnBib 123 (Rome: Editrice Pontificio Istituto Biblico, 1990), 3-25.

This essay is adapted from my dissertation now published as *Slave of All: The Paradox of Authority and Servanthood in the Gospel of Mark,* JSNTSup 237 (Sheffield: Sheffield Academic Press, 2003).

I thank God for Dr. Hoehner, a faithful man of God, whose diligence in the study and teaching of the Word inspires me in my own study and teaching of the Word in the Philippines.

2. Morna D. Hooker, *The Message of Mark* (London: Epworth, 1983), 16. She writes, "These first few verses are a kind of theological commentary on the rest of the narrative. . . .

ground material for a clear understanding of the narrative.[3] As Matera states, "Few things are more essential to appreciating a story than understanding the manner in which the narrator begins."[4]

The way Mark begins his narrative is essential for readers in two ways. First, Mark provides them inside or privileged information, which is unknown to the characters of the story.[5] He lets them into secrets that remain hidden, throughout most of the drama, from the great majority of the characters in the story.[6] According to R. T. France, Mark allows readers to see a glimpse behind the scenes, a clue to enable them to understand the story that follows in a way that is not granted to those who will observe the public aspect of Jesus' ministry.[7] Second, Mark's prologue is essential to his readers in the sense that it prepares them for the story that follows.[8] Mark prepares his readers by orienting them to the characterization of Jesus and John the Baptist, and to the main themes in the narrative,[9] the authority and servanthood themes held in paradoxical tension. Thus, in relation to readers, the experience of reading Mark 1:1-15[10] brings out

---

Mark has allowed us to see Jesus from God's angle." For more about the Markan prologue, see Robert C. Tannehill, "Beginning to Study 'How Gospels Begin,'" *Semeia* 52 (1990): 185-92; Joanna Dewey, *Markan Public Debate: Literary Technique, Concentric Structure, and Theology in Mark 2:1–3:6*, SBLDS 48 (Missoula, Mont.: Scholars, 1980), 144-47; Vernon K. Robbins, *Jesus the Teacher: A Socio-Rhetorical Interpretation of Mark* (Philadelphia: Fortress, 1984), 76-82; Mary Ann Tolbert, *Sowing the Gospel: Mark's World in Literary-Historical Perspective* (Minneapolis: Fortress, 1989), 239-44; Augustine Stock, *The Method and Message of Mark* (Wilmington, Del.: Glazier, 1989), 43-57; Kuthirakkattel, *Beginning of Jesus' Ministry*, 3-22; John Drury, "Mark 1:1-15: An Interpretation," in *Alternative Approaches to New Testament Study*, ed. A. E. Harvey (London: SPCK, 1985), 25-36; and Robert A. Guelich, "'The Beginning of the Gospel' Mark 1:1-15," *Biblical Research* 27 (1982): 5-15.

3. Meir Sternberg, *Expositional Modes and Temporal Ordering in Fiction* (Baltimore: Johns Hopkins University, 1978), 1.

4. Matera, "Prologue as Interpretative Key," 3.

5. Benoît Standaert, *L'Evangile selon Marc* (Paris: Cerf, 1983), 42.

6. Hooker, *Mark*, 6.

7. France, "Beginning of Mark," 16.

8. William L. Lane, *The Gospel of Mark*, NICNT (Grand Rapids, Mich.: Eerdmans, 1974), 39-40; cf. Leander E. Keck, "The Introduction to Mark's Gospel," *NTS* 12 (1965/66): 352-70; J. M. Robinson, *The Problem of History in Mark and Other Marcan Studies* (Philadelphia: Fortress, 1982). Lane argues that the prologue suggests the general plan of the work by anticipating the crucial points in the history he relates (Lane, *Mark*, 39).

9. Boring, "Mark 1:1-15 and the Beginning of the Gospel," 63-64. Boring contends that Mark's prologue has five themes under Christology; namely: (1) the power of the Christ who is the manifestation of the power of God; (2) the story of the Christ as the key, climactic segment of history as the mighty acts of God; (3) the weakness of the Christ who is a representation of the weakness and victimization of humanity; (4) the secrecy of the Christ as Mark's literary means of holding divine power and human weakness together in one narrative; and (5) the disciples of the Christ as the messianic people of God.

10. John Drury, "Mark," in *The Literary Guide to the Bible*, eds. Robert Alter and Frank Kermode (Cambridge, Mass.: Harvard University Press, 1987), 407. Drury uses the metaphor of

the prologue's twofold essential nature: (1) to provide readers inside information, and (2) to prepare them for the story that follows.

The purpose of this study is to demonstrate how the prologue of Mark 1:1-15 evinces its twofold nature with regard to the paradox of authority and servanthood, a prominent theme in the Markan narrative.

The Paradox of Authority and Servanthood in the Gospel of Mark

As used in this study, paradox is taken in terms of its twofold nuance: (1) a statement that departs from accepted opinion (which is the etymological nuance), and (2) an apparently self-contradictory or absurd statement (which is the derivational nuance). Thus, the term *paradox* refers to an unusual and apparently self-contradictory rhetorical statement or concept that departs dramatically from accepted opinion.

In Mark, paradox is a rhetorical device used throughout the narrative to surprise and challenge readers to depart from the accepted opinion that servanthood is incompatible with authority. Initially, Mark presents the person of Jesus in tension; that is, Jesus, the "authoritative one," is the one who serves. The paradox extends later in the narrative to the characterization[11] of the disciples, who are the delegated recipients of Jesus' authority and are called to become the "serving ones."

In other words, the Markan Christological concept of authority (i.e., that of Jesus and that which he delegates to his disciples) needs to be reflected in the Markan discipleship concept of servanthood (i.e., that of serving Jesus and his community of faithful ones). This reflection of authority in servanthood dramatically teaches Mark's readers that true authority in the community of faith is genuinely authenticated by servanthood.[12]

---

a symphony overture to describe his experience of reading Mark's prologue. He writes, "Mark 1:1-15 is the overture which keys our mind into an atmosphere, the tabulation of the codes and ciphers used in the rest of the book."

11. Characterization extends throughout the narrative to those characters who had authority and yet served Jesus (e.g., John the Baptist, Joseph of Arimathea), to those characters who did not have authority but still served Jesus (e.g., Bartimaeus, the woman who anointed Jesus), to those characters who had authority but did not serve Jesus (e.g., the religious leaders, the rich man, Judas Iscariot), and to those characters who had authority but struggled to serve Jesus and others (e.g., the disciples).

12. As used in this study, "authority" refers to the Markan Christological motif of power and rule that is exercised by Jesus and later delegated to the disciples by virtue of Jesus' high position and relationship with the heavenly Father. Moreover "servanthood" refers to the Markan discipleship motif of renouncing domineering power and exercising service on behalf of others.

Method in the Study of the Paradox

This study proposes an eclectic literary approach in investigating the paradox of authority and servanthood in the Gospel of Mark. A combination of three text-based and reader-focused methods will be used, namely, reader-response criticism, narrative criticism, and rhetorical criticism.

Reader-Response Criticism

The practice of reader-response criticism that addresses paradox is that of Robert M. Fowler, as seen in his book *Let the Reader Understand: Reader Response Criticism and the Gospel of Mark*. Fowler observes the impact of the paradox on the readers at the discourse level, not at the story level. The term *discourse* refers to Mark's means of narrative rhetoric or how he presented the content of the narrative in order to address the readers. It is the "how" of the narrative (i.e., how the narrative is told), including how the settings, characters, happenings, and actions are expressed or narrated by the author.

On the other hand, "story" is the "what" of the narrative (i.e., what the narrative is about), including its settings, characters, happenings, and actions. Story refers to the characters and events that make up the content of the narrative.[13] In light of the Gospel of Mark, Fowler sees paradox in the Gospel of Mark as primarily occurring at the level of discourse, where Mark seeks to influence the readers about the importance of paradox and its significance in their own lives.

The relevant tools of reader-response criticism method (e.g., anticipation, retrospection) enable us to see how Mark addresses the readers at critical sections where the paradox is present. Moreover, this method equips us to distinguish between the dramatic (i.e., through events and characters) and verbal instances (i.e., through paradoxical sayings) of the authority/servanthood paradox.

Narrative Criticism

Aside from reader-response criticism, the eclectic approach includes narrative criticism. With the help of narrative criticism, this study will investigate Mark's characterization of certain figures in the narrative in terms of the authority and servanthood motifs. Characters and characterization in the Gospel of Mark play a key role in indicating the pres-

---

13. Robert M. Fowler, *Let the Reader Understand: Reader Response Criticism and the Gospel of Mark* (Minneapolis: Fortress, 1991), 116.

ence of paradox. Characterization is the process through which Mark provides the readers with what is necessary to reconstruct a character from the narrative,[14] whereas characters[15] are Mark's constructs, created to fulfill a particular role.[16] The constructs regarding characters consist of an analysis of the actions, words, and traits of the characters themselves.[17]

In the Gospel of Mark, the characters can be analyzed through character indicators distributed within the text. These indicators include direct description by Mark, other characters' responses, individuals' words and thoughts, and self-characterization.[18] Such means of characterization are applied to the method of tracing within the narrative the instances where characters who have (or do not have) authority actually serve (or do not serve). Tracing such instances by means of characterization puts into focus Mark's plea for the readers to emulate the ways of the ones who serve, and to shun the ways of those who do not. These instances also emphasize to the readers that the reality of the paradox can best be understood through the examples of characters in the story who, despite their authority, are exhibiting acts of servanthood. Closely associated with characterization in the Markan narrative is the motif of conflict. In narrative criticism, conflict works as the pivot on which the plot of Mark's story turns.

Rhetorical Criticism

Along with reader-response and narrative criticisms, rhetorical criticism forms part of the eclectic literary approach of this study. Rhetorical criti-

---

14. Mark Allan Powell, *What Is Narrative Criticism?* (Minneapolis: Fortress, 1990), 52.

15. On characters, check Seymour Chatman, *Story and Discourse: Narrative Structure in Fiction and Film* (Ithaca, N.Y.: Cornell University Press, 1978), 107-38; W. J. Harvey, *Character and the Novel* (Ithaca, N.Y.: Cornell University Press, 1966); Baruch Hochman, *Character in Literature* (Ithaca, N.Y.: Cornell University Press, 1985), 13-40; and James Garvey, "Characterization in Narrative," *Poetics* 7 (1978): 72-73. In this study "characters" means the portrait of people formed by the way the evangelist describes and selects details about them.

16. E. M. Forster, *Aspects of the Novel* (New York: Harcourt Brace, 1927), 103-18; Jerry Camery-Hoggatt, *Irony in Mark's Gospel: Text and Subtext*, SNTSMS 72 (Cambridge: Cambridge University Press, 1992), 50. Camery-Hoggat describes characters as "round" (i.e., complex or subtle), "flat" (i.e., two-dimensional, less complex and more predictable), or "stock" (i.e., one-dimensional, with a single predictable trait).

17. Seymour Chatman, "On the Formalist-Structuralist Theory of Character," *Journal of Literary Semantics* 1 (1972): 57-79; and idem, *Story and Discourse*, 107-38. Chatman defines character as a "paradigm of traits," which is composed of personal qualities of a character that persist over a part or the whole of the story (*Story and Discourse*, 121, 125-26).

18. These means of characterization in the Gospel of Mark appear in more detailed form in Joel F. Williams, *Other Followers of Jesus: Minor Characters as Major Figures in Mark's Gospel*, JSNTSup 102 (Sheffield: JSOT Press, 1994), 54-67.

cism deals with the use of rhetoric, which is basically the communicator's intentional use of language and other symbols to influence or persuade selected receivers to act, believe, or feel the way the communicator desires in problematic situations.

According to George Kennedy, rhetoric and rhetorical criticism aim to take the text as the readers have it, and to look at it from the point of view of the "author's intent," the unified results, and how it would be perceived by the "audience of near contemporaries."[19] In light of the present study, the "author's intent" is reflected in the discourse of the narrative as revealed by Mark to the readers. Moreover, the "audience of near contemporaries" refers to the readers of the narrative in NT times.

With the help of rhetorical criticism, the reader experiences firsthand the benefit of spotting key rhetorical techniques (e.g., inclusion; chiasm; repetition). In addition, this study adds the rhetorical technique of juxtaposition (i.e., the intentional placing of two related words, phrases, or concepts side by side in order to highlight their similar or tensive relationship). These rhetorical indicators cue the readers on the existence of the paradox of authority and servanthood. These devices also cause them to reflect on the significance of the paradox and its relevance in their lives.

Application of the Eclectic Approach to the Markan Prologue

Having laid out the eclectic literary approach to paradox of reader-response criticism, narrative criticism, and rhetorical criticism, this study now seeks to briefly apply the method to the Markan prologue. Why choose the Markan prologue? As cited earlier, there are two reasons for the choice: (1) the prologue of Mark (1:1-15) is a crucial introduction to the entire Markan narrative; and (2) the prologue gives the readers the necessary background material for a clear understanding of the narrative.

The prologue opens the narrative with an immediate presentation of this paradox of authority and servanthood. The paradox is seen in four juxtapositions of authority and servanthood motifs and through the parallel characterizations of Jesus and John. These paradoxical juxtapositions and parallel patterns prepare readers for key themes to be developed throughout the narrative.

---

19. George A. Kennedy, *New Testament Interpretation Through Rhetorical Criticism* (Chapel Hill: University of North Carolina Press, 1984), 4.

The Gospel's Title: Authority of Jesus (1:1)

Readers immediately gain access to privileged information[20] about who Jesus is: "The beginning of the gospel of Jesus Christ, the Son of God" (1:1). Through this concise title in Mark 1:1,[21] they see Mark's evaluative description of Jesus as the central figure in both story and discourse. They immediately understand that Jesus is a character of unique and lofty authority: the Christ and Son of God.[22] Though Mark does not elaborate the full significance of these titles in the prologue, readers are left to anticipate how Mark would use the rest of the narrative to put full meaning into the authoritative designation of Jesus as God's agent. Matera discusses this key point:

> As in all good narratives, the narrator does not reveal everything to the readers at the beginning. The information given in the prologue tells who Jesus is (the Son of God), but does not disclose the full significance of his person through this title. This information must be supplemented by what is told in the rest of the narrative. Thus by the end of the narrative the readers discover that they must integrate their knowledge of Jesus learned in the prologue with their knowledge of him learned in the light of the cross and resurrection.[23]

The Authority and Servanthood of John the Baptist (1:2-8)

As readers continue reading the prologue, they observe that aside from Jesus (1:1), Mark presents John the Baptist as another figure of authority (1:2-6). He presents John's authority in four instances of commentary. The

20. Drury, "Mark," 405. Drury stresses the privileged information given in the narrative's title: "Mark 1:1 gives divine knowledge to the readers. It is all-important."

21. Boring sees Mark 1:1 as a title for the whole narrative, not the heading for a particular subsection, the introduction ("Mark 1:1-15," 50). Similarly, Fowler argues that this first verse of the Gospel functions as a "kind of descriptive title for the entire work" (Fowler, *Let the Reader Understand,* 87). Cf. Stock, *Method and Message,* 44; Detlev Dormeyer, "Die Kompositionsmetapher 'Evangelium Jesu Christi, des Sohnes Gottes' Mk 1.1: Ihre theologische und literarische Aufgabe in der Jesus-Biographie des Markus," *NTS* 33 (1987): 452-68; Mark Errol Glasswell, "The Beginning of the Gospel: A Study of St. Mark's Gospel with Regard to Its First Verse," in *New Testament Christianity for Africa and the World: Essays in Honor of Harry Sawyer,* ed. E. W. Fashole (London: SPCK, 1974), 36-43.

22. The phrase υἱοῦ θεοῦ is to be taken as originally part of 1:1. It reappears in important portions of the narrative (i.e., 1:11; 3:11; 5:7; 9:7; 12:6; 13:32; 14:61; 15:39). For external and internal evidence favoring the inclusion of this phrase, see Bruce M. Metzger, *A Textual Commentary on the Greek New Testament,* 2nd ed. (Stuttgart: Deutsche Bibelgesellschaft, 1994), 62; Lane, *Mark,* 41, n.7.

23. Matera, "Prologue as Interpretive Key," 4. Cf. Werner H. Kelber, *Mark's Story of Jesus* (Philadelphia: Fortress, 1979), 17; Jack Dean Kingsbury, *Conflict in Mark: Jesus, Authorities, Disciples* (Minneapolis: Fortress, 1989), 32; idem, *The Christology of Mark's Gospel* (Philadelphia: Fortress, 1983), 56.

first instance uses a scriptural quotation attributed to Isaiah (1:2-3).[24] By means of this form of explicit commentary,[25] Mark considers John as the messenger, who prepares the way of the Lord (1:2), and the voice of one crying in the wilderness (1:3a), who announces the message of readiness and straightening of paths (1:3b). The function of the scriptural quotation is to identify who John is: the messenger of God's covenant and the eschatological prophet foretold by Isaiah.[26] The task of John is to prepare the way of the Lord for the final act of salvation found in Jesus.

The second instance that shows John's authority is the Markan inclusion of John's message (1:4). Readers observe that before Mark presents John's message, he first volunteers the information that "John the Baptist appeared in the wilderness" (1:4a). The appearance of John's name for the first time in Mark 1:4a affirms that he is the "voice in the wilderness"[27] of Mark 1:3a with a distinct message. His message in the wilderness is to proclaim a "baptism of repentance for the forgiveness of sins" (1:4b). The importance of this message hinges on the "repentance" and "forgiveness of sins" it offers to the people who have turned their backs on God.

John's authority is further reinforced in the third instance when Mark includes in the prologue the overwhelmingly positive result of John's proclamation: "all the country of Judea and all the people of Jerusalem" congregate around him (1:5a). Readers see Mark's repetition in Greek chiastic order of the word "all" at the beginning and end of 1:5a.[28] This repetition rhetorically helps them recognize John's great popularity[29] and impact on the people.[30] The impact of his authority and proclamation is further seen in the people's resultant confession of sins and actual baptism (1:5b).

Having read up to Mark 1:5, readers further notice how the characterization of John in Mark 1:4-5 matches with the description of the "mes-

24. Though 1:2-3 is attributed to Isaiah, 1:2 is a mixed quotation from Exod 23:20 and Mal 3:1, while 1:3 comes from Isa 40:3. Fowler lays out the significance of this "epigraph" in Fowler, *Let the Reader Understand*, 87-89.

25. Ibid., 89, 111.

26. Matera, "Prologue as Interpretative Key," 6.

27. For discussion of the significance of the phrase "in the wilderness," see Ulrich Mauser, *Christ in the Wilderness*, SBT 39 (Naperville, Ill.: Allenson, 1963), 77-102; J. M. Robinson, *The Problem of History in Mark*, SBT 21 (Naperville, Ill.: Allenson, 1957), 24-26; C. C. McCown, "The Scene of John's Ministry," *JBL* 59 (1940): 113-131; Robert W. Funk, "The Wilderness," *JBL* 78 (1959): 205-14.

28. Mark uses "all" in 1:5 as a figure, not in the literal sense that everybody in Judea and Jerusalem went to see John the Baptist. The hyperbolic use emphasizes the immensity of the crowds so that it looks as if all Judea and all Jerusalem were literally present with John at the Jordan.

29. James A. Brooks, *Mark*, NAC 23 (Nashville: Broadman, 1991), 41.

30. Robert A. Guelich, *Mark 1–8:26*, WBC 34A (Dallas: Word, 1989), 20.

senger" in Mark 1:2-3. Gundry details such match-ups between John (as described in 1:4-5) and the "messenger" (as described in 1:2-3):

> John's appearance on the scene . . . matches the sending of God's messenger (v 2). John's activity of baptizing matches the messenger's preparing the way of the Lord (i.e. of Jesus—v 2). The location "in the wilderness" matches the location of "one crying in the wilderness" (v 3). John's preaching matches the crying out of the voice (v 3). The "baptism of repentance," which starts with confession of sins . . . and ends in their forgiveness, matches the making ready of the Lord's way and making straight of his paths (v 3).[31]

Through these match-ups, Mark reinforces his point that the "voice," along with the message proclaimed by that "voice," appears for the first time in the narrative with great authority through the person of John the Baptist.

The fourth instance that demonstrates John's authority is found in the Markan description of John's appearance (1:6). The Markan characterization of John (i.e., his being clothed with camel hair and being girded with a leather belt around the waist) appeals to his readers' knowledge of the Old Testament.[32] John's garb associates him with the prophetic order[33] and particularly with the prophet Elijah[34] (2 Kgs 1:8), who is similarly garbed with leather belt.[35] Thus, Mark associates John's garb with the authoritative prophet Elijah.

---

31. Robert H. Gundry, *Mark: A Commentary on His Apology for the Cross* (Grand Rapids, Mich.: Eerdmans, 1993), 36.

32. Larry W. Hurtado, *Mark*, NIBC 2 (Peabody, Mass.: Hendrickson, 1989), 16. Hurtado lays out the OT connection: "The passage from Malachi 3:1 (quoted in Mark 1:2) seems to have been understood by many ancient Jews and Christians as predicting a prophet-like figure of the end time, and this figure was understood, in the context of Malachi 4:5-6, like Elijah, the OT prophet (see 1 Kings 17-21; 2 Kings 1-2). Mark's description of John's attire seems intended to recall for his readers the image of Elijah, who is similarly attired in the OT (2 Kings 1:8)."

33. Vincent Taylor, *The Gospel According to St. Mark*, 2nd ed. (London: Macmillan, 1966), 156; Brooks, *Mark*, 41; R. A. Cole, *The Gospel According to St. Mark: An Introduction and Commentary*, TNTC (Grand Rapids, Mich.: Eerdmans, 1961), 57-58; William Hendriksen, *Exposition of the Gospel According to Mark*, NTC (Grand Rapids, Mich.: Baker, 1976), 39. Cole describes John the Baptist in relation to Mark 1:6: "Dress and food and dwelling-place alike marked him out as being in the rugged tradition of Elijah and the other desert prophets, as did his eschatological and 'forward-looking' preaching" (Cole, *St. Mark*, 57-58). Hendriksen also affirms, "Such rugged apparel may have been regarded as symbolic of the prophetic office. Zechariah 13:4 (cf. 1 Samuel 28:14) seems to point in that direction" (Hendriksen, *Mark*, 39).

34. The coming of Elijah is foretold in Mal 3:1; 4:5ff.; cf. Mark 9:9-13. For information on the belief that Elijah is precursor of the Christ, see George Foot Moore, *Judaism* (Cambridge, Mass.: Harvard University Press, 1927-30), i-iii.

35. Morna D. Hooker, *A Commentary on the Gospel According to St. Mark*, BNTC (London: Black, 1991), 37; Daryl D. Schmidt, *The Gospel of Mark: With Introduction, Notes, and Original Text Featuring the New Scholars Version Translation*, The Scholars Bible (Sonoma,

The four instances of commentary in Mark 1:2-6 clearly indicate to readers that, aside from Jesus, John is also a man of authority in the narrative. He fulfills a scriptural promise in Isaiah (1:2-3); he delivers God's authoritative message of baptism and repentance (1:4); he gathers overwhelming response and harvest from Judeans and Jerusalemites (1:5); and he is associated with Elijah, the prophet of great authority (1:6).

However, what dramatically surprises readers is what immediately follows the presentation of John's authority. Mark 1:7-8 quotes the surprising proclamation by John: "After me One is coming who is mightier than I, and I am not fit to stoop down and untie the thong of His sandals. I baptize you with water; but He will baptize you with the Holy Spirit" (NASB).

The juxtaposition of John's authority in Mark 1:2-6 with his humility and servanthood in Mark 1:7-8 shocks readers. John, the prophet of great authority (1:2-3), is suddenly pictured as a person who is really not that authoritative or mighty (1:7a). John, the popular preacher to whom throngs of people come to be baptized (1:4-5a), is quickly presented as a lowly slave who is unfit to stoop down and untie someone else's sandals[36] (1:7b). John, the famous baptizer with water at the Jordan (1:5b), is instantly downplayed by someone else's baptism with the Holy Spirit (1:8).

This juxtaposition of John's authority and servanthood is the first occurrence in the Markan narrative of the surprising paradox of authority and servanthood. Right in the middle of the prologue (1:7-8), readers are introduced to the importance of putting both authority and servanthood in tension. Through this early introduction of the paradox, Mark is implicitly addressing his readers to follow the example of John the Baptist, and to reflect on the significance of his example in their own lives.

The Authority and Servanthood of Jesus (1:9-15)

As readers move on to Mark 1:9-11, they again experience the presence of the authority/servanthood paradox, beginning with their encounter of the "authority" side of the paradox. They figure out for themselves that Jesus, who has come from Nazareth in Galilee, is the authoritative, "coming mightier one" foretold by John in Mark 1:7-8. Gundry supports

---

Calif.: Polebridge, 1990), 44. Hooker writes, "The reference to the leather belt is an almost exact echo of the description of Elijah in 2 Kgs. 1:8: the details of John's clothing, therefore, suggest again that he is seen as 'Elijah the prophet' who is sent to call the nation to repent 'before the great and terrible day of the Lord' (Mal. 4:5f.; cf. Mark 9:12f.)."

36. Gundry, *Mark*, 38; Hooker, *St. Mark*, 38. Hooker affirms, "The action of unfastening sandals was regarded by the Jews as the most menial of all the tasks performed by a slave. It was a demeaning task."

this by observing the following Markan rhetorical indicators that relate John's prophecy to Jesus:

> "And it came to pass" prepares for the bringing of Jesus on stage. "In those days" alludes to the beginning of the good news about him in John's prediction: "The one stronger than I is coming after me". . . . "Jesus came" notes the quick fulfillment of that prediction and identifies the stronger one as Jesus. Mark does not explicitly state fulfillment. It is not his style to do so; rather, he narrates the fulfillment so as to let his audience discover it for themselves. Leaving no doubt about it are the textual juxtaposition of vv 9-11 with vv 1-8, the solemn Semitism "and it came to pass," the temporal clamping of vv 9-11 together with vv 1-8 by means of "in those days" (cf. 8:1), the repetition of the verb ἔρχομαι, "come," the naming of Jesus after John's prediction concerning the stronger one, [and] the verbal interrelating of vv 9-11 with vv 1-8.[37]

Thus, the entry of Jesus into the narrative in Mark 1:9a marks him out as the man of greater authority, who is mightier than John (1:7a), whose sandal thongs John is unworthy to untie (1:7b), and who will baptize with the Spirit (1:8). In the minds of readers, they have already identified this Jesus of Nazareth as "the Christ, the Son of God" in Mark 1:1.

However, they are again surprised upon reading Mark 1:9b, "And Jesus was baptized by John in the Jordan." What surprises them is that this Jesus, who has been consistently presented as the mightier one of authority, is submitting himself to be baptized by John,[38] who himself recognizes his inferiority of might (compared to Jesus). This Jesus, who is to baptize others with the Holy Spirit, allows himself to stoop down before John as the latter baptizes him with water. As France observes, "Jesus, the 'stronger one' who is to come with a baptism in the Holy Spirit, comes, paradoxically not yet himself dispensing baptism, but rather receiving it as one of the restored community of God's people."[39]

This instance of dramatic paradox in Mark 1:9 implicitly challenges Mark's readers to follow the model of Jesus. In the manner that Mark has urged them to follow the model of John in Mark 1:7-8, he is again encouraging them to follow the exemplary model of the one mightier than John.

In Mark 1:10-11, readers meet another instance of this paradox. These verses present the extraordinary events of Jesus' baptism. France comments on the private nature of this declaration: "What Jesus knows as a result of this experience, and what we, the readers, are privileged to

---

37. Gundry, *Mark*, 47.

38. Lane, *Mark*, 55. Lane describes Jesus in relation to his baptism in 1:9 as the one "in whom true submission to God was perfectly embodied."

39. France, "Beginning of Mark," 15.

share in, remains a secret to all other characters in the story."[40] In this private declaration of Mark 1:10-11a, Mark gives a double attestation[41] of Jesus' authority. The attestation comes from the descent of the Spirit in the form of a dove (1:10b), and from the first part of the testimony of a voice from heaven (1:11a).

The descent of the Spirit, along with the splitting of the heavens (1:10a), affirms the heavenly source of Jesus' power.[42] Moreover, just as the "voice" in the scriptural quotation of Mark 1:2-3 authenticates the authority of John the Baptist, so the heavenly "voice" of Mark 1:11a validates the authority of Jesus. Particularly, the first portion of the voice's testimony addresses Jesus as God's unique Son:[43] "You are my beloved Son" (1:11a). This unique Son identified in Mark 1:11 is linked[44] by Mark to the Son of God in Mark 1:1; that is, Jesus, the Son of God, is the authoritative one who has a unique relationship with God.

Thus, the double attestation of Jesus' source of power and his unique relationship with God again informs readers about the correct interpretation of Jesus' authority.[45] However, when readers arrive at the second part of the voice's testimony in Mark 1:11b, they do not find the same attestation of authority that has been emphasized in the previous two verses. They find that the testimony quickly shifts from the authority of Jesus to his servanthood. In fact, they hear[46] the servanthood aspect of Jesus' character in these words: "In you I am well pleased" (1:11b). These words inform readers, as well as Jesus, that God considers Jesus an obedient son.[47] In encountering Jesus' obedience and submission, readers again struggle to understand how a man of authority, who deserves obedience, can be described by Mark as someone who is submissively obedient and well-pleasing to the voice from heaven.

40. Ibid.

41. Gundry, *Mark*, 46. Gundry's term "double attestation" refers to the Spirit's enduement of power in 1:10 and to God's testimony in 1:11.

42. Ibid., 48. For two other interpretations for the descent of the Holy Spirit, see Lane, *Mark*, 56-57; and Rudolf Bultmann, *The History of the Synoptic Tradition* (Oxford: Blackwell, 1963), 248-50.

43. Lane, *Mark*, 57. It must be noted that the use of the two participles, ἀναβαίνων ("coming up") from the water by Jesus, and καταβαίνων ("coming down") of the Spirit from the heavens, at the beginning and the end of 1:10, highlights the attestation that Jesus' power is derived from on high.

44. This link between 1:1 and 1:11 is made through the use of the term "Son," which occurs in both verses.

45. Gundry, *Mark*, 49.

46. Guelich, *Mark*, 35. Guelich observes, "The reader permitted to share in this private audience with Jesus expectantly listens to the voice from heaven."

47. Gundry, *Mark*, 50; Hendriksen, *Mark*, 43. Hendriksen contends that in the context of Jesus' baptism, the obedience is seen in the willingness of the Son to submit to this baptismal rite (Hendriksen, *Mark*, 43).

The sense of authority and submission conveyed by the voice from heaven regarding Jesus, which Guelich calls a "mixed signal" of Jesus' royal sonship and servant motif coming from the Old Testament,[48] is the third occurrence of the paradox of authority and servanthood in the prologue. This instance again reinforces early in the narrative the way Jesus needs to be viewed by readers: the authoritative Son, who pleases God with his obedience and submission.

In Mark 1:12-13, the narrator further exemplifies this motif of submission in the person of Jesus: "And immediately the Spirit impelled Him to go out into the wilderness" (1:12, NASB). Jesus' obedience to the Spirit is affirmed and sustained in the former's wilderness experience for forty days (1:13a), being tempted by Satan in the company of wild beasts (1:13b). Lane describes this submission motif:

> The aspect of humiliation in Jesus' mission is not yet terminated in spite of the declaration that he is the beloved Son. Jesus must remain submissive: the Spirit does not allow him to abandon the wilderness after his baptism. The function of verse 13 is to clarify the consequences of this submission: confrontation by Satan and temptation, exposure to the wild beasts, and reception of the ministry of the angels.[49]

Thus, in the temptation scene of Mark 1:12-13, the narrator stresses that Jesus' submission to God leads him to confrontation and conflict with the enemies of God (i.e., Satan and his allies, pictured as the wild beasts[50]). Mark does not report the end of the temptation scene[51] nor its result[52]

48. Guelich, *Mark*, 35. According to Guelich, this mixed signal "begins with a royal messianic designation of sonship drawn from Ps 2:7 and concludes with the servant motif of Isa 42:1. . . . But the tension continues throughout Mark's narrative. Both the royal messianic sonship and the servant figure persist. . . . Therefore, we should not be surprised that this tension should appear explicitly at the scene of Jesus' introduction in Mark."

49. Lane, *Mark*, 59-60.

50. Though the inclusion of the information about the wild animals has been taken by some scholars (e.g., Joachim Jeremias, "Ἀδάμ," in *TDNT*, 1:141; Erich Fascher, "Jesus und die Tiere," *TLZ* 90 [1965]: 561-70) as an element in the paradise motif (i.e., the restoration in which man is at peace with the animals), it seems more likely that the affinity is with the realm of Satan (Lane, *Mark*, 61).

51. France, "Beginning of Mark," 17.

52. For the view that Mark implies that Jesus is victorious during his temptation, see Keck, "Introduction to Mark's Gospel," 362; C. S. Mann, *Mark*, AB 27 (Garden City, N.Y.: Doubleday, 1986), 194. Keck argues that the Son of God has not failed during this period of testing, for he returns from the wilderness with the gospel of God (1:14). Keck writes, "Mark's Jesus is the victorious Son of God who returns from the testing-ground with the εὐαγγέλιον." Mann also affirms that "it is only when the eschatological conflict between the Tempter and Jesus has been joined and decided that any ministry of proclamation is possible" (193).

because for him, what is important at the prologue of the narrative is simply the introduction of the confrontation itself.[53]

With his succinct presentation of Jesus' confrontation with Satan, Mark prompts readers to expect more conflicts with Satan and all his spiritual and human forces in the remainder of the narrative.[54] This brief account also warns readers that the way ahead will not be easy for Jesus, and that there are issues at stake that will bring Jesus into confrontation with supernatural opposition. Though readers know that Jesus is indeed the Son of God, and that he comes with the direction and power of the Spirit, they are also made to know that there are other forces in the unseen worlds and in the story of Jesus that could ignite a series of conflicts of eternal dimensions in the narrative.[55]

Aside from recognizing Mark's clue of sustained conflict throughout the narrative, readers also observe the importance of the angels' serving ministry, as stated in Mark 1:13b, "And the angels were ministering to him." Mark did not indicate whether the angels had attended to or ministered to Jesus during or after the temptation, or whether they had helped him resist temptation, fed him, or witnessed what he had done.[56] What is important for Mark is to emphasize the fact that Jesus' spiritual allies had served him.

It is important to note at this point that Mark uses the verb διακονέω ("to serve") for the first time in the narrative (1:13b). He uses the verb at a time when Jesus, the obedient Son, is submissively serving God in the wilderness, at a time when Satan persistently seeks to get Jesus to disobey God, and at a time when the angels align themselves with Jesus as his servants from God.[57]

What intrigues readers about the service of the angels is that Jesus, who is viewed as the submissive and obedient servant during his temptation days, is in turn served by God's allies, the ministering angels. In the context of spiritual conflict with Satan, this servant is again presented as one having authority, since he is the recipient of the services by the ministering angels.

In reading the first thirteen verses of the prologue, readers have already encountered four juxtapositions of the authority and servanthood motifs which are found in Mark 1:2-8, 9, 10-11, and 12-13. The first juxtaposition refers to the authority and servanthood of John the Baptist,

53. Lane, *Mark*, 61.

54. Brooks, *Mark*, 44. Brooks argues that the reason Mark did not state whether Jesus was victorious or not is "perhaps he looks upon Jesus' entire life as a continuing struggle with Satan."

55. France, "Beginning of Mark," 17.

56. Ibid.

57. Lane, *Mark*, 62.

while the last three refer to the authority and servanthood of Jesus. These four, staccato-like juxtapositions present the paradox of authority and servanthood.

Going further in the prologue, readers are once more surprised with another piece of information that Mark offers: "And after John had been taken into custody . . ." (1:14a). When they recall what the narrator has written in Mark 1:2-6, they remember how Mark presents the great authority of John and the overwhelmingly positive response to his ministry. They expect a favorable treatment toward this authoritative prophet and baptizer. So it is surprising for them to read of John's arrest. They are surprised by this sudden twist in the story line of John.

Furthermore, they are made to wonder whether there will be a similar twist in Jesus' story line. They are led to ask about Jesus' future as well because of the way Mark has presented John and Jesus in a parallel pattern.[58] This parallel pattern of presentation is observed by Eugene Boring in his outline of Mark 1:1-15[59]:

Title		1:1
John		1:2-8
	Identified by off-stage transcendent voice	1:2-4
	John in the wilderness: baptizing	1:5-6
	Preaching: repentance/ in terms of promise	1:7-8
Jesus		1:9-15
	Identified by off-stage transcendent voice	1:9-11
	Jesus in the wilderness: testing/being tested	1:12-13
	Preaching: repentance/in terms of fulfillment	1:14-15[60]

58. Boring, "Mark 1:1-15," 63.

59. Ibid., 60-61. Boring sees the introduction (1:2-15) in two parts, "the first (2-8) featuring John and the second (9-15) featuring Jesus. John is brought on the stage with ἐγένετο in 1:4, while Jesus is introduced into the narrative with καὶ ἐγένετο in 1:9. . . . Each part identifies the character, places him in the wilderness, and describes his preaching" (59).

60. See also Drury, "Mark," 408; J. Ramsey Michaels, *Servant and Son* (Atlanta: John Knox, 1981), 44; Dewey, *Markan Public Debate*, 144-47. Drury similarly sees a parallel, chiastic pattern in the presentation of John and Jesus. He presents this pattern thus: "The first to be announced, Jesus the Son of God, is the last to arrive. The second announced, John the herald, appears penultimately; the structure is ABBA. The effect is to rouse us to the possibility that something momentous is happening in 1:1-15—something to do with John that brings Jesus into the lead" (Drury, "Mark," 408). As a further development of this pattern, Ramsey also suggests that 1:1-15 is designed in a deliberately chiastic form (Michaels, *Son and Servant*, 44), as follows:

a. the gospel of Jesus Christ (1:1)
  b. John the Baptist in the desert, in fulfillment of Scripture (1:2-4)
    c. John baptizing in the Jordan (1:5-8)

As readers proceed to the end of the prologue (1:15), they see this parallel pattern at work. They observe that after Mark tells about John's custody in Mark 1:14a, he immediately presents what Jesus has done in light of what has happened to John: "Jesus came into Galilee, preaching the gospel of God" (1:14b). Like his presentation of John as a preacher of repentance (1:4), Mark also characterizes Jesus as the proclaimer of the people's need to repent (1:14-15).

Having observed the prologue's parallel pattern of presentation, readers also wonder what kind of response Jesus would receive regarding his proclamation of God's gospel[61] (1:14b), the nearness of the kingdom (1:15a), and the need for repentance and belief in the gospel (1:15b). They ask within themselves whether Jesus, like John, will initially have a large following, only to be taken into custody later in the narrative. Though they see no explicit response from Jesus' hearers about their question, they anticipate the possibility that something drastic may happen to Jesus as a result of his proclamation of God's message.

They entertain this possibility because of Mark's parallel pattern of presentation: John, the authoritative proclaimer of God's message, is put in custody; so also Jesus, the more authoritative proclaimer of God's gospel, is expected to suffer some casualty in the narrative. In addition, the Markan emphasis on conflict during Jesus' temptation scene in Mark 1:12-13 further reinforces the possibility of how difficult Jesus' early ministry might be in the narrative despite readers' early recognition of his divine authority in the prologue.

Conclusion

In summary, the prologue of Mark's Gospel can be described as paradoxical. This can be seen in Mark's use of four juxtapositions of material (1:2-8, 9, 10-11, and 12-13) that show the presence of the dramatic authority/servanthood paradox. The paradox is also observed through the use of parallel patterns in the characterization of John and Jesus. Mark

---

      c. Jesus is baptized in the Jordan (1:9-11)

     b. Jesus in the desert (1:12-13)

   a. the gospel of God (1:14-15)

Similarly, Dewey presents a structural layout of 1:1-8 with symmetrical rhythm. She argues for a concentric and chiastic ordering of materials in 1:1-5 as well (Dewey, *Markan Public Debate*, 144-47).

    61. Drury, "Mark," 407. Drury discusses the importance of this gospel rhetorically: "Jesus' gospel is announced in 1:1a just before the story begins, and in 1:14-15 Jesus comes into Galilee preaching it. Between those two pointed occurrences of the word 'gospel' lie the events that form the starting motor of the whole gospel narrative."

presents John and Jesus as people of authority who serve and submit to God. His paradoxical merger of the two motifs of authority and servant-hood in the prologue surprises readers with the question: Why are these people of authority pictured as those who serve? As people of authority, are they not the ones who are to receive service? This surprising paradox prepares readers to recognize the importance of authority and servant-hood at the outset of the narrative, and to see how Mark develops it fully throughout the discourse.

Mark 7:27

Jesus' Puzzling Statement

16

JOEL F. WILLIAMS

An illustration of how to tackle an exegetical problem in narrative material, using insights from the character of narration itself and from Mark's narrative technique.

In Mark 7:27, Jesus makes a statement to the Syrophoenician woman that is difficult to understand in light of the broader narrative of Mark's Gospel. In response to the woman's request for her daughter's deliverance, Jesus states, "Let the children be satisfied first, for it is not good to take the children's bread and throw it to the dogs." The response appears to be a refusal to heal the Syrophoenician woman's daughter because of her status as a Gentile. The problem posed by Jesus' statement is contextual in nature. How do Jesus' words fit within the context of Mark's Gospel as a whole? Jesus never refuses a request for healing elsewhere in the narrative. Earlier, Jesus spoke to a great multitude and healed many, showing his authority over demons (3:7-12). According to Mark, some of the people in that crowd were from Tyre, the same region where Jesus met the Syrophoenician woman. Moreover, Jesus delivered the Gerasene demoniac, who was a man from the Decapolis and apparently a Gentile (5:1-20). Just prior to Jesus' encounter with the Syrophoenician woman, Jesus argued that people should not be judged by outward defilements but by matters of the heart (7:14-23). So why would Jesus refuse this woman? The problem is significant because it touches on the nature and proper recipients of God's mercy available through Jesus.

The purpose of this essay is to evaluate the common approaches for solving the puzzle of Mark 7:27. The conclusion offered here builds on the viewpoint that Jesus' statement is a test to determine the extent of the woman's understanding and faith. The essay expands on this solution by exploring how Jesus' puzzling statement functions within the narrated story. Mark's Gospel is a narrative, that is, a narration of a series of events, and in narratives, ambiguous statements may be useful for producing a desired effect. Therefore, this essay is an exercise in exegetical problem solving or validation, an attempt to make sense of Jesus' statement in the context of Mark's narrative as a whole.

A Problem of Time

Interpreters generally explain Mark 7:24-30 and Jesus' puzzling statement in that passage in one of three ways. One view is that Jesus' response is unrelated to the Gentile status of the woman. Instead, Jesus rejects the woman initially because she is interrupting his time with the disciples and his rest away from the demands of the crowd.[1] For example, Robert H. Gundry argues that Jesus' statement in Mark 7:27 sets up a contrast between Jesus' teaching of his disciples and his meeting the needs of children. It is not good to take the bread of the children (the time and effort needed by Jesus to teach his disciples) and throw it to the little dogs (to Gentile children like the woman's daughter).[2] According to Gundry, Jesus retreated to Tyre away from the crowd (7:24) for the same reason he sought solitude in Mark 9:30-31, because he wanted to teach his disciples. Jesus is against "depriving the disciples of the attention that teaching them demands and giving it instead to the woman's daughter and other Gentile

---

1. John D. Grassmick, "Mark," *Bible Knowledge Commentary: New Testament,* ed. John F. Walvoord and Roy B. Zuck (Wheaton, Ill.: Victor, 1983), 135-36; Walter Grundmann, *Das Evangelium nach Markus,* 3rd ed., THKNT 2 (Berlin: Evangelische, 1965), 152-155; Robert H. Gundry, *Mark: A Commentary on His Apology for the Cross* (Grand Rapids, Mich.: Eerdmans, 1993), 371-75; John Paul Heil, *The Gospel of Mark as a Model for Action: A Reader-Response Commentary* (New York: Paulist, 1992), 159-62; Kenzo Tagawa, *Miracles et Évangile: La Pensée personnelle de L'Évangéliste Marc,* Études d'Histoire et de Philosophie Religieuses 62 (Paris: Presses Universitaires de France, 1966), 117-121. According to William L. Lane (*The Gospel of Mark,* NICNT [Grand Rapids, Mich.: Eerdmans, 1974], 261-62), Jesus' statement operates on different levels, at least one of which would have communicated to the woman that her request was an intrusion upon Jesus' rest and time with his disciples.

2. Gundry, *Mark,* 373.

children in her train." [3] The tension is not between the needs of Jews and those of Gentiles in general, but between the needs of Jesus' disciples and those of one Gentile child in particular. Jesus changes his course of action because of the Syrophoenician woman's clever remark, which shows that her little dog can receive a small crumb of Jesus' mighty power at the same time his disciples are enjoying their full portion. [4]

This viewpoint faces a number of problems. The first difficulty is the lack of any reference to the disciples in the passage. Jesus retreats to the region of Tyre and enters a house, hoping to remain unrecognized (7:24). It is not clear that the disciples are even with Jesus at this point. If the main purpose for Jesus' refusal in Mark 7:27 is in order to spend uninterrupted time with his disciples, then it would not be unrealistic to expect the disciples and Jesus' teaching activity to figure more prominently in the passage or at least to be mentioned. Next, in Mark 7:26 the woman's status as a Gentile is stressed, since she is described as Greek by way of culture and Syrophoenician by way of nationality. It is difficult to explain the presence of this emphasis if it is unrelated to Jesus' objection to the woman in the next verse. Gundry apparently attempts to deal with this difficulty by arguing that Mark included the information as a way of capturing the interest of his mainly Gentile audience. [5] A further problem is that the time necessary to care for the woman's daughter is not an issue in the story. Jesus stays where he is and simply informs the woman of her daughter's deliverance (7:29). It takes less time for Jesus to heal the daughter than to refuse and engage the mother in a dialogue. Finally, this viewpoint presents a picture of Jesus that is strangely inconsistent with the portrayal of Jesus in Mark 10:13-16. There Jesus is indignant with his disciples for believing that he should not be bothered with children.

A Change of Mind

A second option for explaining Jesus' response to the woman is that Jesus himself was uncertain about the scope of his ministry. His remark to the woman is a hesitant affirmation on his part that the extent of his ministry ought to be limited to the Jews. The woman's answer helps Jesus to see that he has a responsibility also to the Gentiles. [6] According to

3. Ibid.
4. Ibid., 375.
5. Ibid., 372.
6. Benjamin Wisner Bacon, *The Beginnings of Gospel Story* (New Haven, Conn.: Yale University Press, 1909), 90-91; B. Harvie Branscomb, *The Gospel of Mark*, MNTC (London: Hodder & Stoughton, 1937), 128-33; Hisako Kinukawa, *Women and Jesus in Mark: A Japanese Feminist Perspective* (Maryknoll, N.Y.: Orbis, 1994), 51-61; Sherman E. Johnson, *The Gospel*

Vincent Taylor, Jesus probably sought privacy in Tyre in order to reflect upon the scope and course of his ministry.[7] There Jesus encounters the Syrophoenician woman, who brings her request to him. In Taylor's view, Jesus' reply is not a test of the woman's faith, since the subject of faith is never explicitly mentioned in the context. Instead, Jesus' answer to the woman expresses the tension that Jesus has in his own mind concerning the boundaries of his mission. His words are directed to himself as well as to the woman.[8] The Syrophoenician woman, quick to perceive Jesus' hesitation, does not reject his metaphor but carries it a stage further so that it becomes clear to him that his ministry can extend to the Gentiles without any harm to the Jews. In a similar way, Sherman E. Johnson concludes that this occasion involves "an actual development of Jesus' understanding of his mission; now it is clear that he must not restrict the Good News to his own nation."[9]

The major problem with this view is that it depends on a change of mind by Jesus, which implies that Jesus was mistaken when he first spoke to the woman. Nothing in the preceding narrative of Mark's Gospel prepares the reader for confusion on the part of Jesus, and nothing in the following narrative confirms it.[10] Throughout Mark's Gospel, Jesus is the authoritative and reliable teacher of God's message.[11] Jesus, the Son of God, preaches the gospel of God from the very beginning of his ministry (1:1, 11, 14-15). Jesus teaches as one having authority and not as the scribes (1:22). In contrast to others, Jesus sets his mind on God's interests, not human interests (8:31-33), and God himself demands that Jesus' teaching should be heeded (9:7). Heaven and earth will pass away, but Jesus' words will never pass away (13:31). The idea that Jesus' teaching on the scope

According to St. Mark, HNTC (Peabody, Mass.: Hendrickson, 1972), 135-38; C. S. Mann, *Mark,* AB 27 (Garden City, N.Y.: Doubleday, 1986), 318-21; David Rhoads, "Jesus and the Syrophoenician Woman in Mark: A Narrative-Critical Study," *JAAR* 62 (1994): 361-63; Vincent Taylor, *The Gospel According to St. Mark,* 2nd ed. (London: Macmillan, 1966), 348-51.

7. Taylor, *St. Mark,* 349.

8. Ibid., 350.

9. Johnson, *St. Mark,* 137.

10. For a similar criticism of Taylor's position, see T. A. Burkill, "Mark 6:31-8:26: The Context of the Story of the Syrophoenician Woman," in *The Classical Tradition: Literary and Historical Studies in Honor of Harry Caplan,* ed. Luitpold Wallach (Ithaca, N.Y.: Cornell University Press, 1966), 343-44; idem, "The Historical Development of the Story of the Syrophoenician Woman (Mark vii:24-31)," *NovT* 9 (1967): 171-72.

11. For a discussion of Jesus as a reliable character in Mark's narrative, see Robert M. Fowler, *Let the Reader Understand: Reader-Response Criticism and the Gospel of Mark* (Minneapolis: Fortress, 1991), 61, 127; Jack Dean Kingsbury, *The Christology of Mark's Gospel* (Philadelphia: Fortress, 1983), 47-50; David Rhoads, Joanna Dewey, and Donald Michie, *Mark as Story: An Introduction to the Narrative of a Gospel,* 2nd ed. (Minneapolis: Fortress, 1999), 44; Robert C. Tannehill, "The Disciples in Mark: The Function of a Narrative Role," *JR* 57 (1977): 391.

of his ministry needed to be corrected is impossible to reconcile with the presentation of Jesus' teaching in the rest of Mark's Gospel.

A further difficulty is that there is no distinct change in the pattern of Jesus' ministry after this encounter with the Syrophoenician woman.[12] Jesus continues to travel in and around Galilee and then into Judea. He directs his ministry primarily to the people of Israel, although he responds positively toward Gentiles who come to him in faith, just as earlier in the narrative. There is no consistent, intentional outreach in Gentile territories. Instead, Jesus foresees the task of preaching the gospel to the nations as the future responsibility of his followers (13:9-13).

A Test of Faith

A third alternative for dealing with Jesus' statement in Mark 7:27 is that Jesus is testing the persistence of the woman's faith by putting an obstacle in her path. Jesus' metaphorical reply becomes a barrier to the woman because it indicates that as a Gentile she cannot expect to receive help from Israel's messiah.[13] A representative of this view is C. E. B. Cranfield. He points out that the purpose for Jesus' journey into Tyre is not recorded, but the most apparent purpose is that Jesus is seeking privacy.[14] Yet privacy proves impossible, because of the interruption by the Syrophoenician woman. Mark describes the woman in a way that emphasizes her non-Jewish character, setting the stage for her dialogue with Jesus. According to Cranfield, Jesus responds to the woman's request for help by pointing out the distinction between Jews and Gentiles and the divinely appointed privilege of the Jews. Yet Jesus does not intend to extinguish the woman's faith but to encourage it. Jesus shuts the door on her not to exclude her altogether but to move her to exercise her faith

---

12. For a similar point, see C. E. B. Cranfield, *The Gospel According to Saint Mark*, 4th ed., CGTC (Cambridge: Cambridge University Press, 1972), 249; David E. Garland, *Mark*, NIVAC (Grand Rapids, Mich.: Zondervan, 1996), 291.

13. James A. Brooks, *Mark*, NAC 23 (Nashville: Broadman, 1991), 120-21; John Calvin, *Calvin's New Testament Commentaries*, trans. T. H. L. Parker, 12 vols. (Grand Rapids, Mich.: Eerdmans, 1972), 2:165-71; R. Alan Cole, *Mark*, 2nd ed., TNTC (Grand Rapids, Mich.: Eerdmans, 1989), 187-90; Cranfield, *Saint Mark*, 245-49; D. Edmond Hiebert, *Mark: A Portrait of the Servant* (Chicago: Moody, 1974), 183-86; Craig S. Keener, *The IVP Bible Background Commentary: New Testament* (Downers Grove, Ill.: InterVarsity Press, 1993), 154; Joel Marcus, *Mark 1-8*, AB 27 (New York: Doubleday, 2000), 468-70; Rudolf Schnackenburg, *The Gospel According to St. Mark*, trans. Werner Kruppe, 2 vols. (London: Sheed & Ward, 1971), 1:128-30; Ben Witherington III, *Women in the Ministry of Jesus*, SNTSMS 51 (Cambridge: Cambridge University Press, 1984), 63-66; idem, *The Gospel of Mark: A Socio-Rhetorical Commentary* (Grand Rapids, Mich.: Eerdmans, 2001), 231-33.

14. Cranfield, *Saint Mark*, 246.

with greater effort.[15] James A. Brooks summarizes the view by stating that "the seeming harshness could have served to test the woman's faith."[16]

This viewpoint seems to fit best within the context of Mark's Gospel. It is the only approach that gives an adequate explanation for why Jesus would alter his course from an apparent refusal to a fulfillment of the woman's request for healing. He changes because his initial statement served to test the extent of the woman's understanding and faith. Since she passes the exam, he delivers her daughter from the unclean spirit. Jesus' actions are not inconsistent but rather responsive to the persistent faith of the woman.

Another support for this explanation is that other healing stories in Mark's Gospel include an obstacle that must be overcome by the suppliant's persevering faith. Those who want to bring the paralytic to Jesus make a hole in the roof in order to bypass the crowd and reach Jesus with their friend (2:1-5). Jairus needs to continue in his faith even after he learns of his daughter's death (5:35-36). The hemorrhaging woman must overcome the press of the crowd and the complicating factor of her ceremonial uncleanness in order to touch Jesus' garment (5:24-29). The man with the demon-possessed boy must hold out hope for Jesus' help after the initial failure of the disciples (9:14-27). Bartimaeus continues to call out for Jesus' attention even though many others try to quiet him (10:46-52). In Mark 7:24-30, Jesus himself sets up the obstacle, but through her reply the Syrophoenician woman shows her continuing trust in God's provision through Jesus.

Some interpreters expand on this third view by arguing that, although Jesus tests the woman with his statement in Mark 7:27, we ought not think that Jesus is expressing his own viewpoint. Jesus' words are said in jest, reflecting a common feeling among Jews at that time but not his own attitude. Jesus wants to see how the woman will respond.[17] For example, according to Jerry Camery-Hoggatt, Jesus' saying on the inappropriateness of throwing the children's bread to the dogs should not be taken at face value. His saying is a special kind of irony that presents a verbal

15. Ibid., 248-49.

16. Brooks, *Mark,* 121.

17. William Barclay, *The Gospel of Mark,* 2nd ed., Daily Study Bible Series (Philadelphia: Westminster, 1975), 176-79; F. F. Bruce, *The Hard Sayings of Jesus* (Downers Grove, Ill.: InterVarsity Press, 1983), 110-11; R. T. France, *The Gospel of Mark,* NIGTC (Grand Rapids, Mich.: Eerdmans, 2002), 295-99; Ezra P. Gould, *A Critical and Exegetical Commentary on the Gospel According to St. Mark,* ICC (Edinburgh: Clark, 1897), 133-37; Royce Gordon Gruenler, "Mark," *Evangelical Commentary on the Bible,* ed. Walter A. Elwell (Grand Rapids, Mich.: Baker, 1989), 779; Jerry Camery-Hoggatt, *Irony in Mark's Gospel: Text and Subtext,* SNTSMS 72 (Cambridge: Cambridge University Press, 1992), 149-51; A. E. J. Rawlinson, *St. Mark,* 3rd ed., Westminster Commentaries (London: Methuen, 1931), 97-100.

challenge intended to test the other's response. It is a riddle to be solved, not an expression of his true intentions.[18]

A significant stumbling block for the view that Jesus' words should be understood as ironic is that the Syrophoenician woman takes his words at face value. Her answer accepts the truth of Jesus' parabolic statement and builds on it. She humbly accepts the distinction between the children and the dogs, between Jews and Gentiles, between those who can expect to receive messianic blessings and those who cannot. She acknowledges the prior claims of the people of Israel. Here, then, is the real puzzle: How can Jesus' words be true and at the same time not indicate a complete rejection of the Gentile woman? How can the blessings of God's kingdom available in Jesus be given to the people of Israel without excluding Gentiles who come in faith? Any answer which suggests that Jesus is mistaken or only pretends to give priority to the Jewish people overlooks God's sovereign choice of Israel within his plan of redemption. Such approaches "result from a failure to reckon seriously enough with the mystery of God's election of Israel."[19] The Syrophoenician woman's solution to the puzzle must be allowed to stand. After all, Jesus rewards the woman for her response by healing her daughter. She accepts that she cannot demand the children's bread; she asks only for a small crumb that may fall from the table. Her solution to the puzzle points to the abundance of God's grace in Jesus, which is able not only to satisfy the children but also to spill over the edges to meet the needs of believing Gentiles. She is convinced God's power in Jesus is so great that a small crumb is sufficient to meet her need. In this way, the Syrophoenician woman displays her humility and understanding and thereby passes the test of faith. The answer of the Syrophoenician woman also helps to make sense of Jesus' care for Gentiles elsewhere in Mark's Gospel. His compassion toward them grows out of the extent of God's mercy. Jesus foresees a time when the blessings of God will be directed toward the Gentiles. That is why he says in Mark 7:27 that the children must be satisfied first. However, during his own ministry, the people of Israel take priority. He cares for believing Gentiles who cross his path as a manifestation of the abundance of God's grace.

The narrative drives the reader to accept the Syrophoenician woman's answer to the test of her faith, and therefore it is worth reflecting on how the narrative works in order to highlight the wisdom of the Syrophoenician woman.[20] Sometimes we forget that the narrator controls the amount of

18. Camery-Hoggatt, *Irony in Mark's Gospel*, 150-51.

19. Cranfield, *Saint Mark*, 246.

20. For introductions to how Gospel narratives work, see Elizabeth Struthers Malbon, "Narrative Criticism: How Does the Story Mean?" in *Mark and Method: New Approaches in Biblical Studies*, ed. Janice Capel Anderson and Stephen D. Moore (Minneapolis: Fortress, 1992), 23-49; Mark Allan Powell, *What Is Narrative Criticism?* (Minneapolis: Fortress, 1990).

information the reader receives.[21] The narrator can tell the story in such a way that the reader knows more than some or all of the characters in the story or less than some or all the characters in the story. Also, a narrator can highlight the ignorance of a particular character in the story and then control the information so that the reader knows just as little. Ambiguous statements, which may be unacceptable in a tightly reasoned theological treatise, can be useful in a narrative for controlling information and influencing the reader.[22]

So, for example, some of the most difficult and ambiguous statements in Mark's Gospel occur in contexts in which the disciples are being criticized for their lack of understanding. In Mark 6:51-52, the narrator criticizes the disciples because they respond with astonishment when Jesus walks on the water and calms the wind. For Mark, their response shows the hardness of their hearts and their lack of insight into "the loaves." Mark as the narrator does not clarify how "the loaves" in the preceding episode (the feeding of the five thousand) should have prepared the disciples to see their master walk on water. In Mark 8:14-21, Jesus criticizes the disciples because of their lack of understanding and the hardness of their hearts. They have eyes but do not see and ears but do not hear. Jesus then asks about the number of baskets left over from the feeding of the five thousand and the feeding of the four thousand. The disciples answer that in the first instance, the leftovers filled twelve baskets and in the second, seven baskets. Certainly, the main point cannot be missed: Jesus is more than able to meet the physical needs of his followers. However, Jesus specifically inquires about the number of leftover baskets in each case, and Mark never clarifies the exact significance of the numbers twelve and seven. He leaves the reader with some of the same confusion that the disciples must have felt.

Mark also controls the amount of information that the reader has and the way in which further information is given in the passage under study in this essay. In Mark 7:27, Jesus offers a puzzling statement and acts in a way that seems to contradict his activity elsewhere in the narrative. Mark could have stepped in and explained Jesus' words and apparent refusal of the woman's request. Instead, he gives the necessary information for making sense of Jesus' statement by presenting the wise response of the Syrophoenician woman. Jesus then commends her answer and heals her

21. Just as a narrative implies a picture of its author, so a narrative implies a picture of its ideal reader, an individual who responds appropriately to the rhetorical features of the text and accepts the values and perspectives of the author. For a further discussion of the implied reader in Mark's narrative, see Joel F. Williams, *Other Followers of Jesus: Minor Characters as Major Figures in Mark's Gospel*, JSNTSup 102 (Sheffield: Sheffield Academic Press, 1994): 67-88.

22. For further information on the use of ambiguity in Mark's narrative, see Fowler, *Let the Reader Understand*, 195-209.

daughter. The narrator informs the reader through the exemplary response of the Syrophoenician woman. The point is that any solution to the interpretive problem of Jesus' statement in Mark 7:27 that detracts from the response of the Syrophoenician woman or claims to have information that the woman did not understand misses the force of the narrative. The narrative works to highlight the wisdom of the woman's answer. Since the woman takes Jesus seriously, the reader must do so as well.

Conclusion

The Syrophoenician woman accepts that the people of Israel have priority in receiving the blessings of God's kingdom available through Jesus' ministry. She has the humility to recognize her own unworthiness. Her solution to Jesus' puzzling statement in Mark 7:27 is to trust in the abundance of God's mercy, to hope that a small but sufficient crumb might fall her way. Indeed, it does. The Syrophoenician woman serves as an example of humility, wisdom, and persevering faith. In conclusion, it is worth noting that she is also exemplary as an exegete. She is an insightful interpreter of the words of Jesus. When confronted with a difficult saying, she discerns its meaning and its significance for her life. In learning exegesis, students are normally taught methods of study and encouraged to develop important skills. The example of the Syrophoenician woman is a reminder that understanding the Word of God depends not only on one's skill but also on one's character. The woman is able to grasp Jesus' message because she has the humility to welcome it. She is open to the teaching of Jesus because she has confidence in the abundance of God's grace toward her through Jesus. Unfortunately, students can learn the skills of biblical exegesis with an attitude of self-reliance and self-interest. Yet, it takes humility to welcome and accept the true message of God. It also takes God's grace to interpret God's Word. The good news is that in Jesus the grace of God spills over all barriers to reach the unworthy—even unworthy exegetes.

Acts 8:26-40 17

Why the Ethiopian Eunuch Was Not from Ethiopia[1]

EDWIN M. YAMAUCHI

A study in a wide range of background materials to illuminate the
NT text.

To understand the New Testament properly we need to broaden our
vision to encompass not only chronological and historical but also
geographical data, inasmuch as names over time come to refer to different places.[2] As a historian of the ancient world I find that many New
Testament scholars are confined by tunnel vision to the immediate text,
with little awareness of its broader background. Let us take the text of
the "Ethiopian Eunuch" in Acts 8:26-40 as an example.

1. This essay is a revision of chapter 6 in Edwin M. Yamauchi, *Africa and the Bible* (Grand
Rapids, Mich.: Baker, 2004). Used by permission.
2. For example, the designation "Asia," which is derived from Hittite Assuwa, once designated the area around Ephesus (Acts 19:10). Later, in the phrase "Asia Minor," it corresponded
to Turkey; today it refers to countries such as China and Japan. See Edwin M. Yamauchi, *The
Archaeology of New Testament Cities in Western Asia Minor* (Grand Rapids, Mich.: Baker,
1980), 15.

The Belief That the Ethiopian Eunuch Was from Ethiopia

Ethiopian Orthodox Christians themselves view the conversion of the eunuch as the foundation of their church.[3] In a major reference work, an Ethiopian scholar states, "The local cultural situation of the first century, identified by Aksum, then the country's capital, does not conflict—what little evidence exists is, in fact, in harmony—with the story of the Ethiopian eunuch's conversion by the apostle Philip (Acts 8)."[4]

The medieval Ethiopian epic *The Kebra Negast* not only claimed that the Queen of Sheba, who visited Solomon, was from Ethiopia, but also identified this queen with Candace, ignoring the chronological distance of the episodes, and thus associated the envoy of the latter with Ethiopia.[5]

Modern Ethiopia Was Until Recently Abyssinia

Though some later church fathers may have referred to the kingdom of Aksum as Aithiopia,[6] this area was generally known as Abyssinia[7] from the fourth century until after the Second World War[8] after the Arabic designation of the country as al-ḥabaša.[9] Aksumite coins from the fourth century bear the legend, "king of the Habashat,"[10] and medieval texts speak of the "queen of the Habasha."[11] King Menelik II (d. 1913) laid the groundwork for the modern country of Ethiopia by expanding his control southward and establishing the new capital of Addis Ababa.[12] It was his great nephew

3. Ephraim Isaac, *The Ethiopian Church* (Boston: Sawyer, 1968), 18.

4. Getatchew Haile, "Ethiopian Orthodox Church," in *Encyclopedia of Africa South of the Sahara*, ed. John Middleton (New York: Scribner, 1997), 1:77.

5. Edward Ullendorf, "Candace (Acts VIII.27) and the Queen of Sheba," *NTS* 2 (1955/56): 53-54; idem, *Ethiopia and the Bible* (London: Oxford University Press, 1968), 9.

6. The first Greek writer to designate the Kingdom of Axum as "Aithiopia" was the church historian Philostorgius (d. ca. 440), according to Erich Dinkler, "Philippus und der ANHP AI-ΘΙΟΨ (Apg. 8, 26-40)," in *Jesus und Paulus*, ed. E. Earle Ellis and Erich Grässer (Göttingen: Vandenhoeck & Ruprecht, 1975), 90.

7. Cf. David Buxton, *The Abyssinians* (London: Thames & Hudson, 1970).

8. Raymond A. Silverman, "Ethiopia," in *Encyclopedia of Africa South of the Sahara*, 75: "Ethiopia was known to the Western world through classical literature as Abyssinia until the end of World War II."

9. Hans Wehr, *A Dictionary of Modern Written Arabic* (Ithaca, N.Y.: Cornell University Press, 1961), 154.

10. S. Munro-Hay, *Aksum: An African Civilisation of Late Antiquity* (Edinburgh: Edinburgh University Press, 1991), 81.

11. Knud Tage Andersen, "The Queen of the Habasha in Ethiopian History, Tradition and Chronology," *Bulletin of the School of Oriental and African Studies* 63, no. 1 (2000): 31-63.

12. Harold G. Marcus, *The Life and Times of Menelik II, Ethiopia 1844-1913* (Oxford: Clarendon, 1975).

Tafari Makonnen, the Ras or "chief" of the province of Harar, who in 1928 assumed the name of Haile Selassie ("Might of the Trinity")[13] and who was crowned Negus ("Emperor") in 1930, only to see his country invaded by the Italians in 1934 under the order of Mussolini.[14]

Different Toponyms for Areas of Africa

The Egyptians called the area to the south of them between the First and Second Cataracts *Wawat*. The area further south they called Kush/Cush, a word that was borrowed into Hebrew as כוש (Kûsh).[15] The Greek word Αἰθίοψ (*Aithiops*), "sun-burned face," originally meant dark or black-skinned people.[16] In some texts such as in Homer's *Odyssey* (1.22-24) and in Herodotus (7.70), Aithiopians designated black-skinned people in the East in India and the Mauretanians in the West, according to the later interpretations of Posidonius and Strabo.[17] But after the fifth century BC for the most part Αἰθίοψ (Latin *Aethiops*) meant for Greeks and the later Romans an inhabitant of the region south of Egypt. Scholars call this area *Nubia*, after a tribe called the Nuba/Noba, who still live in the area.[18] Today the country is called Sudan, after the Arabic phrase *Bilad as-Sudan*, "The Land of the Blacks" (see Fig. 17.1).

Afrocentric Bibles

With the laudable aim of interesting African-Americans in recognizing the presence of Africans in the Bible, two Bibles have recently been published under the influence of Afrocentric scholars:[19] *The Original African Heritage Study Bible* (1993), edited by Cain Hope Felder, and *The Holy*

---

13. An influential Caribbean movement, known as the Rastafarians, regarded Haile Selassie as God, much to his displeasure. See William D. Spencer, *Dread Jesus* (London: SPCK, 1999).

14. Frank Hardie, *The Abyssinian Crisis* (London: Batsford, 1974). For a comprehensive history, see Richard Pankhurst, *The Ethiopians* (Oxford: Blackwell, 1998).

15. John N. Oswalt, "כוש (Kûsh) Ethiopia, Cush, Ethiopians," in *Theological Wordbook of the Old Testament*, ed. R. Laird Harris, Gleason L. Archer, and Bruce K. Waltke (Chicago: Moody, 1980), 1:435.

16. Frank M. Snowden, Jr., *Blacks in Antiquity: Ethiopians in the Greco-Roman Experience* (Cambridge, Mass.: Harvard University Press, 1970), 3-5.

17. J. Y. Nadeau, "Ethiopians," *Classical Quarterly* 20 (1970): 339-41.

18. O. and H. Luz, "Proud Primitives, the Nuba People," *National Geographic* 130, no. 5 (1966): 673-99.

19. Afrocentrism tends to exaggerate the black presence in Africa, so that every inhabitant of the continent including Cyrenians and Egyptians are viewed as black. See Edwin M. Yamauchi, "Afrocentric Biblical Interpretation," *JETS* 39 (1996): 397-409; idem, "The Archaeology of Biblical Africa: Cyrene in Libya," *Archaeology in the Biblical World* 2 (1992): 6-18.

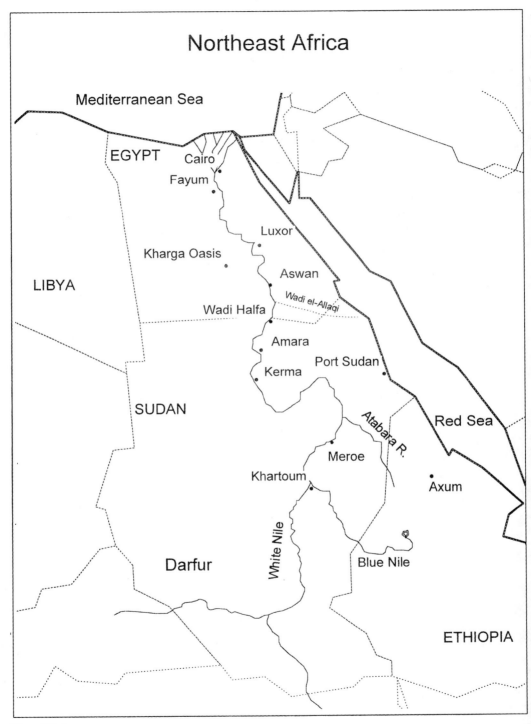

Fig. 17.1

Bible: African American Jubilee Edition (1999), published by the American Bible Society with the assistance of Felder and other scholars.[20] Rather surprisingly, these reference Bibles do very little to enlighten their readers as to the location and nature of the "Ethiopia" mentioned in Acts.

The Original African Heritage Study Bible contains a rather polemical note on Acts 8:27:

> This is the longest passage in the New Testament that explicitly and unambiguously deals with black Africa in relation to the Holy Land in the New Testament. In some ways it has been a thorn in the flesh of those interpreters who have harbored a definite racial bias against blacks. Some of them have refused to accept the idea that Ethiopians are to be considered black people and have gone as far as locating biblical Ethiopia as far away as in Mesopotamia.[21]

The Original African Heritage Study Bible also contains an essay by Maggie S. Peebles, "African Edenic Women and the Scriptures," in which she makes this unfounded statement about Candace: "She is credited for bringing Christianity to her country by sending her high treasurer the Eunuch to Jerusalem to seek information concerning the teaching of Christ."[22] It also reprints a long sermon by Edward W. Blyden delivered in 1882 on "Philip and the Eunuch," in which the preacher asserted: "The eunuch returned to his country . . . and became the founder, it is believed, of the Abyssinian Church, which through various trying vicissitudes, continues to this day."[23] *The Holy Bible: African American Jubilee Edition* fails in any note on Acts 8 or in two essays to inform its readers about the location and background of the Ethiopia mentioned in this passage.[24]

New Testament Scholars on Acts 8:26-40

Contrary to the diatribe on Acts 8 found in *The Original African Heritage Study Bible*, biblical scholars have for a long time recognized that the reference to Candace identified Aithiopia as the kingdom of Meroë. (I will use the transliteration *Aithiopia* to distinguish it from modern Ethiopia.) All the studies and the score of commentaries on Acts that I

20. Cain Hope Felder, ed., *The Original African Heritage Study Bible* (Nashville: Winston, 1993); and idem et al., *The Holy Bible: African American Jubilee Edition* (New York: American Bible Society, 1999).

21. Felder, ed., *Original African Heritage Study Bible*.

22. Ibid., 1811.

23. Ibid., 1835.

24. Prince Vayani Ntintili, "The Presence and Role of Africans in the Bible," *Holy Bible: African American Jubilee Edition*, 106; Cain Hope Felder, "The Presence of Blacks in Biblical Antiquity," *Holy Bible: African American Jubilee Edition*, 122.

have examined correctly recognize that Candace was the title of one who ruled over the "black" kingdom of Meroë. Most of them cite well-known classical references to this kingdom.[25] But what is rather striking is that with few exceptions[26] there is little awareness of the growing body of scholarship on Meroë.[27]

The Location of Meroë

Martin perceptively notes one major reason for the ignorance of most Bible readers about the location of Aithiopia (Meroë), as follows: "Of the useful atlases recommended by Joseph A. Fitzmyer in his excellent reference work, *An Introductory Bibliography for the Study of Scripture*, the majority do not include Meroë (or Nubia) in their maps of the world of the New Testament."[28]

What is little appreciated is the enormous distance the eunuch traveled, and the formidable obstacles he had to overcome. Meroë lies nearly one thousand miles south of the Mediterranean coast. Travel within Egypt proper was facilitated by two factors: in traveling from south to north, one could float down the Nile; in traveling in the reverse direction, one

25. These classical references were known a long time ago. Cf. E. Grohmann, "Kandake," *Paulys Realencyclopädie der classischen Altertumswissenschaft,* 20 Halbband (Stuttgart: Alfred Druckenmüller, 1858, reprint 1919), 1858-59; and were already exploited by S. Lösch, "Der Kämmerer der Königin Kandake (Apg. 8, 27)," *Theologische Quartalschrift* 111 (1930): 477-519; for a more recent exposition see F. F. Bruce, "Philip and the Ethiopian," *JSS* 34 (1989): 377-86.

26. Exceptions are: Clarice J. Martin, *The Function of Acts 8:26-40 Within the Narrative Structure of the Book of Acts: The Significance of the Eunuch's Provenance for Acts 1:8c* (Ann Arbor, Mich.: University Microfilms, 1990; Duke University Ph.D. Dissertation, 1985); idem, "A Chamberlain's Journey and the Challenge of Interpretation for Liberation," *Semeia* 47 (1989): 105-35; T. Piers Crocker, "The City of Meroe and the Ethiopian Eunuch," *Buried History* 22 (1986): 53-66; Abraham Smith, "'Do You Understand What You Are Reading?': A Literary Critical Reading of the Ethiopian (Kushite) Episode (Acts 8:26-40)," *Journal of the Interdenominational Theological Center* 22 (1994): 48-70. But even these studies hardly do justice to the scholarship on Meroë that is available.

27. Even articles in the comprehensive *ABD* by Ben Witherington III on "Candace" (1:837), and by Beverly Roberts Gaventa, "Ethiopian Eunuch" (2:667), show little awareness of Meroitic studies. For general introductions, see: P. L. Shinnie, *Meroe: A Civilization of the Sudan* (London: Thames & Hudson, 1967); Fritz and Ursula Hintze, *Civilizations of the Old Sudan: Kerma, Kush, Christian Nubia* (Amsterdam: Grüner, 1968); Fritz Hintze, "The Kingdom of Kush: The Meroitic Period," in *Africa in Antiquity,* ed. S. Hochfield and E. Fiefstahl (New York: Brooklyn Museum, 1978), 1:89-105; S. M. Burstein, ed. *Ancient African Civilizations: Kush and Axum* (Princeton, N.J.: Wiener, 1998); idem, "The Kingdom of Meroe," in *Africa and Africans in Antiquity,* ed. E. M. Yamauchi (East Lansing: Michigan State University Press, 2001), chapter 4; D. A. Welsby, *The Kingdom of Kush: The Napatan and Merotic Empires* (Princeton, N.J.: Wiener, 1998).

28. Martin, "A Chamberlain's Journey," 121.

would be aided by the prevailing winds. But once one reached Aswan the traveler encountered a formidable series of cataracts, granite outcroppings which created rapids in the rivers, beginning with the First Cataract and proceeding upstream to the Sixth Cataract (see Fig. 17.2).[29]

The Sixth Cataract is forty-five miles north (downstream) from the modern capital of the Sudan, Khartoum, where the Blue Nile from Ethiopia joins the White Nile from central Africa. Meroë is located seventy-five miles northeast of Khartoum. The triangle formed between the White Nile, the Blue Nile and the Atbara River was the so-called "Island of Meroë" known to classical authors.

Ptolemaic Relations with Kush/Aithiopia

Ptolemy I marched against Aithiopia in 319-18 BC, as did Ptolemy II in 274. Thereafter peaceful relations developed for nearly a century, as attested by the presence of Greek luxury goods in Meroitic tombs. A Meroitic king, Ergamenes I, who was a contemporary of Ptolemy II, received a Greek education according to Diodorus (3.6). Burstein comments, "Greeks of all sorts—diplomats, intellectuals, artisans, and most important, Ptolemaic elephant hunters—travelled freely throughout Meroitic territory."[30] Kendall notes, "One Simonides was said to have lived there five years and to have written a book about his adventures."[31] An inscribed drum with the Greek alphabet was found at Meroë.[32] All of these indications would freely explain why the Aithiopian eunuch could read Isaiah in the Septuagint version.

Roman Relations with Meroë[33]

After his victory over the forces of Antony and Cleopatra at Actium in 32 BC, Octavian pursued his defeated foes to Egypt. After their suicide in

29. Hermann Kees, *Ancient Egypt: A Geographical History of the Nile* (Chicago: University of Chicago Press, 1961), chapters 12–13; John Baines and Jaromir Málek, *Atlas of Ancient Egypt* (New York: Facts on File, 1980); Claude Vandersleyen, "Des obstacles que constituent les cataracts du Nil," *Bulletin de l'Institut d'archaeologie orientale du Caire* 69 (1969): 253-66.

30. Stanley M. Burstein, *Agatharchides of Cindus: On the Erythraean Sea* (London: Hakluyt Society, 1989), 7.

31. Timothy Kendall, *Kush: Lost Kingdom of the Nile* (Brockton: Brockton Art Museum, 1982), 12.

32. Stanley M. Burstein, *Graeco-Africana: Studies in the History of Greek Relations with Egypt and Nubia* (New Rochelle, N.Y.: Caratzas, 1995), 111-13.

33. See Jehan Desanges, "Les relations de l'Empire romain avec l'Afrique nilotique et érythréenne, d'Auguste à Probus," *ANRW* II.10 (1988), 3-43.

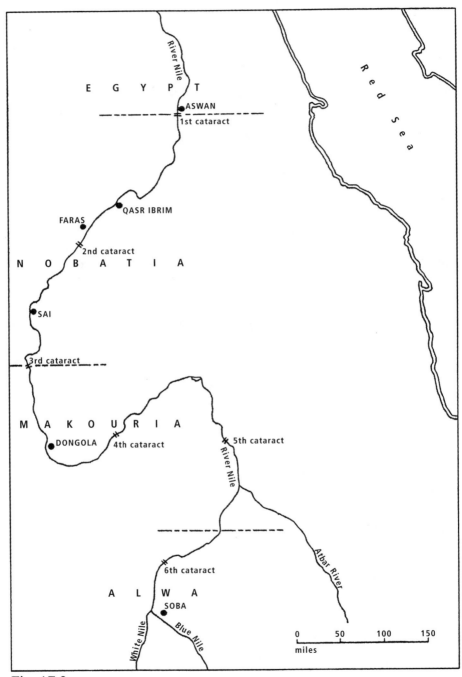

Fig. 17.2

30, Octavian (known after 27 as Augustus) became master of Egypt.[34] He installed as his first prefect or governor, Cornelius Gallus.[35] By 28 Gallus had succeeded in conquering Upper Egypt as far as Aswan. He met the Meroitic envoys at Philae and set up a trilingual inscription (Latin, Greek, Egyptian) in the temple of Augustus there,[36] which declared the kingdom of Meroë a Roman protectorate, subject to an annual tribute. A governor, answerable to Rome, was to take charge of a stretch of the Nile south of Philae, called the Triakonteschoinos (30 schoinoi equal 320 km. or about 200 miles).

After the suicide of Cornelius, Aelius Gallus, the second prefect was ordered by Augustus to conquer Arabia and Aethiopia. Taking advantage of his absence in the campaign against Arabia, in 24 the Candace of Meroë, Amanirenas, and the crown prince Akinidad,[37] defeated the Roman cohorts at Syene (Aswan), Philae, and Elephantine, and returned with prisoners and booty, which included several statues of Augustus.[38] In Strabo's detailed account (17.53-54) of these events, Candace is described as a brave, masculine woman, blind in one eye. Dio Cassius (54. 5, 4ff.) reported that she herself led the army.

A magnificent bronze head of Augustus, now in the British Museum, was found buried in a temple at Meroë. Scholars believe that it was one of those taken in this campaign.[39] A wall painting in this temple depicted several prisoners including a light-skinned Roman.[40]

But two years later a Roman army advanced as far south as Napata, and Augustus boasted in his *Res Gestae* (26): "Ethiopia was penetrated as

34. Eleanor G. Huzar, "Augustus, Heir of the Ptolemies," *ANRW* II.10.1 (1988), 343-82.

35. Stanley M. Burstein, "Cornelius Gallus and Aethiopia," *Ancient History Bulletin* 2 (1988): 16-20.

36. Another temple of Augustus at Dendur to the south was sent to the U.S. by Egypt in gratitude for its aid in the survey and salvage of monuments before the Aswan Dam flooded Nubia. It is housed in a special wing of the Metropolitan Museum in New York. See Cyril Aldred, *The Temple of Dendur* (New York: Metropolitan Museum of Art, 1978).

37. The king, Teriteqas, must have died shortly before the conflict with the Romans. See Inge Hofmann, *Beiträge zur meroitischen Chronologie* (St. Augustin bei Bonn: Anthropos-Institut, 1978), 93. Akinidad bore the titles *pqr* and *peseto,* indicating that he was the "Viceroy" of Lower Nubia.

38. Shelagh Jameson, "Chronology of the Campaigns of Aelius Gallus and C. Petronius," *Journal of Roman Studies* 58 (1986): 71-84.

39. Inge Hofmann, "Der Feldzug des C. Petronius nach Nubien und seine Bedeutung für die meroitische Chronologie," in *Ägypten und Kusch,* ed. E. Endesfleder et al. (Berlin: Akademie, 1977), 200, has expressed doubts about this association. She further doubts that Petronius reached as far south as Napata as the distance was too great for the time involved.

40. P. L. Shinnie and R. J. Bradley, "The Murals from the Augustus Temple, Meroe," in *Studies in Ancient Egypt, the Aegean, and the Sudan,* ed. W. K. Simpson and W. M. Davis (Boston: Museum of Fine Arts, 1981), 167-72.

far as the town of Nabata, which adjoins Meroë" (*In Aethiopiam usque ad oppidum Nabata perventum est, cui proxima est Meroe*).[41] The Romans left a garrison at the mountain fortress of Primis (Qasr Ibrim).[42] The queen had to send to Augustus, in the winter of 21-20 BC, envoys who traveled all the way to the island of Samos to sue for peace.

Quite generously Augustus remitted the tribute, and peaceful relations were established between Rome and Meroë. This enabled Meroë to prosper. According to Shinnie, "The amount of building shows that the first century AD was one of wealth and power in the Meroitic kingdom, but, after the early part of the century, we have very little information other than the names of rulers."[43] It was this Pax Romana and Meroitic prosperity that enabled the so-called Ethiopian eunuch to travel to Judea.

Diplomatic and Cultural Exchanges

Meroë's strategic position commanded trade routes into inner Africa, which gave access to such highly desirable objects as ivory and ebony.[44] In the excavation at Wad ben Naga, by Jean Vercoutter from 1958 to 1960, a great store of ivory and ebony was found.[45] The Meroites also had gold,[46] slaves, leopard skins, and incense to offer. Despite the great distances involved, archaeological finds at Meroitic burial sites, even after the inevitable looting by tomb robbers, indicate the presence of fine imported jewelry; vases; wine from Rhodes, the west coast of Asia Minor, and southern France; as well as olive oil from north Africa.[47] These objects came from diplomatic and trade missions.[48]

---

41. P. A. Brunt and J. M. Moore, eds., *Res Gestae Divi Augustus: The Achievements of the Divine Augustus* (London: Oxford University Press, 1967), 32-33.

42. The waters of Lake Nasser have transformed Qasr Ibrim into an island. See Michael P. Speidel, "Nubia's Roman Garrison," *ANRW* II.10.1 (1988), 768-98.

43. Shinnie, *Meroe*, 116. See George A. Reisner, "The Pyramids of Meroe and the Candaces of Ethiopia," *Museum of Fine Arts Bulletin* 21 (1923): 12-27. The results were later published in Dows Dunham, *The Royal Cemeteries of Kush*, 5 vols. (Cambridge, Mass.: Harvard University Press, 1950-63).

44. L .P. Kirwan, *Rome Beyond the Southern Egyptian Frontier* (London: British Academy, 1978), 17.

45. Jean Vercoutter, "Un palais des 'Candace,' contemporain d'Auguste (Fouilles à Wad-ban-Naga 1958-1960)," *Syria* 39 (1962): 262-99.

46. Karl-Heinz Priese, *The Gold of Meroe* (New York: Metropolitan Museum of Art, 1993).

47. Inge Hofmann, "Der Wein- und Ölimport im Meroitischen Reich," in *Egypt and Africa: Nubia from Prehistory to Islam*, ed. W. V. Davies (London: British Museum, 1991), 234-35.

48. László Török, *Economic Offices and Officials in Meroitic Nubia* (Budapest: L'Université Laránd Lötwös, 1979).

As Snowden observes, "Ethiopian diplomats were not uncommon, since Ethiopian relations with the Ptolemies and Romans involved diplomatic exchanges. Diodorus (3.11.3) interviewed Ethiopian ambassadors resident in Egypt."[49] We have many inscriptions of individuals containing the titles in Meroitic *apote-leb Arome-li-s* (envoys to Rome) or *apote qor-s* (ambassador of the king).[50] The eunuch had, no doubt, been in Alexandria, where he would have learned about Judaism from the large Jewish population there. I suggest that he may have traveled to Judea to establish economic and diplomatic ties with Herod Agrippa I, the new King of the Jews (AD 37-44).[51] Like many other foreign tourists he would have wanted to see Herod's magnificently rebuilt temple.

Meroitic Inscriptions

For a long time the Kushites simply used Egyptian hieroglyphs for their monumental inscriptions. In the late second century BC a distinctive Meroitic script, based on Egyptian, was introduced.[52] The twenty-three Meroitic hieroglyphic signs were borrowed from Egyptian hieroglyphs; the twenty-three Meroitic cursive signs are related to Egyptian hieratic (including fifteen consonantal signs, four syllabic signs, and four vowel signs). Many of the inscriptions are funerary texts.[53] Since Griffith's decipherment of the phonetic values in 1911, almost no further progress has been made. This means that we can read the names of the kings and queens, but we know the meaning of only twenty-six words such as *wi* (brother), *sem* (wife), *kdi* (woman), *mk* (deity), *qore* (ruler). The variants *kdke, ktke, kdwe,* which became the basis of Greek *Kandake* (Candace), may have originally meant king's sister.[54]

49. Frank M. Snowden, Jr., "Ethiopians and the Graeco-Roman World," in *The African Diaspora: Interpretive Essays,* ed. Martin L. Kilson and Robert I. Rotberg (Cambridge, Mass.: Harvard University Press, 1976), 27.

50. László Török, *The Kingdom of Kush: Handbook of the Napatan-Meroitic Civilization* (Leiden: Brill, 1997), 65.

51. See S. Perowne, *The Later Herods* (London: Hodder & Stoughton, 1958), chapter 10. The Bible focuses on religious matters to the exclusion of political and economic interests, as in the case of the Queen of Sheba's visit to Solomon, and the message sent by Merodach-baladan to Hezekiah.

52. Török, *Kingdom of Kush,* 62.

53. F. L. Griffith, *Meroitic Inscriptions: Napata to Philae and Miscellaneous, part 2* (London: Egyptian Exploration Fund, 1912; reprint Warminster: Aris & Phillips, 1976).

54. Török, *Kingdom of Kush,* 63.

Meroitic Chronology

The remarkable Aithiopian kingdoms of Napata and Meroë extended about 1,100 years (from 750 BC to AD 350).[55] The chronology of the first kings, the so-called XXVth Dynasty, is well established by Egyptian data, as these rulers temporarily conquered and occupied Egypt.[56] Among their most famous rulers was Tirhakah (Taharqa), who is mentioned in 2 Kgs 19:9/Isa 37:9 during the invasion by Sennacherib of Palestine in 701 BC. After the invasion into Kush by Psammetichus II of the XXVIth Dynasty in 593 BC, the capital was shifted from Napata by the Fourth Cataract to Meroë by the Sixth Cataract, about 400 miles upstream.

The relative chronology of about 70 kings was established by George A. Reisner, who between 1916 and 1925 dug at the cemeteries near Napata (Kuru, Nuri, and Gebel Barkal) and at Meroë (Begrawiyeh North and South).[57] Reisner divided pyramids into groups and then assigned each one the name of a king or queen known from inscriptions.[58]

The uncertainties of the details of this chronology are underlined by Hintze:

> We know only a few fixed points for a period of more than 600 years, and some of these points are not fully reliable. The succession of the pyramids within the groups established by Reisner on the basis of archaeological traits is in many instances still rather uncertain; most of the pyramids have no names so that it is hypothetical and often problematical to associate them with certain rulers. On the other hand, we know many names of kings without being able safely to associate certain pyramids with them. Besides, some pyramids were destroyed or pulled down. . . . Another uncertain factor in reconstructing the Meroitic chronology is the respective length of reign of individual rulers, which can be estimated only in terms of the size and decoration of the pyramids.[59]

55. David O'Connor, *Ancient Nubia: Egypt's Rival in Africa* (Philadelphia: University Museum, 1993).

56. D. M. Dixon, "The Origin of the Kingdom of Kush (Napata-Meroë)," *Journal of Egyptian Archaeology* 50 (1964): 121-32; K. A. Kitchen, *The Third Intermediate Period in Egypt* (Warminster: Aris & Phillips, 1973).

57. The earliest cemetery is Kurru, eight miles downstream from Gebel Barkal; six miles upstream from Gebel Barkal is Nuri. The cemeteries at Meroë come from the village of Begarawlya (abbreviated Beg.) Gebel Barkal is the sacred mountain of the Kushites/Meroites. See Timothy Kendall, "The Kingdom of Kush," *National Geographic* 178 (November 1990): 96-125.

58. George A. Reisner, "The Meroitic Kingdom of Ethiopia: A Chronological Outline," *Journal of Egyptian Archaeology* 9 (1923): 34-79, 157-60.

59. Fritz Hintze, "Meroitic Chronology: Problems and Prospects," *Meroitica I: Sudan im Altertum*, ed. Fritz Hintze (Berlin: Akademie, 1973), 142. See also Fawze F. Gadallah, "Meroitic Problems and a Comprehensive Meroitic Bibliography," *Kush* 11 (1963): 196-216.

Candace as a Title

After the third century BC we see the remains of large pyramids and buildings bearing the names of queens exclusively, who seem to have ruled in their own right. The title Candace is first mentioned by Bion in book 1 of his *Aithiopika*. Most scholars believe that the word Candace is a title for the Queen Mother.[60]

According to Burstein, "Candace was the title of the mother of the Meroitic king. During the late first century B.C.E. and first half of the first century C.E. several Candaces appear to have functioned as ruling queens."[61] The practice of naming such figures Candace comes to an end after the kings Natakamani, Amenitere, and Sherakarer in the first half of the first century.

Adams notes complicating factors in reconciling classical sources with Meroitic inscriptions:

> It must have been the prestige and behind-the-scenes power enjoyed by the Nubian queens which gave rise to the Roman tradition that Kush was governed by a hereditary line of female rulers, all named Candace. The name seems in fact to be a corruption of a Meroitic title (*kdke*) which was borne by all the royal consorts or queen-mothers of Kush; it does not specify a queen-regnant. There were indeed at least five queens regnant during the later centuries of the Kushite dynasty, but no two of them reigned in succession, and it is not certain that they bore the title *kdke*.[62]

Only four queens used the Meroitic title *qore* (ruler): Amanirenas, Amanishakheto, Amanitore, and Nawidemak.

1. Queen Amanirenas ruled during the last third of the first century BC; she is called both *qore* (ruler) and *kdwe* (Candace). Her burial may be in the Barkal pyramid 4.
2. Queen Amanishakheto ruled in the late first century BC and early first century AD. She is also called *qore* and *kdke*. According to Török, "The prosperity of her reign is indicated by her building

---

60. Hintze, "The Kingdom of Kush: The Meroitic Period," 98; Welsby, *The Kingdom of Kush*, 26. See also Bruce G. Trigger, "La Candace, personage mystérieux," *Archeologia* 77 (December 1974): 10-17. Inge Hofmann, "Cleopatra-Kandake," *Göttinger Miszellanen* 52 (1981): 34, comments: "Ich möchte an dieser Stelle nicht wieder darauf eingehen, dass wir für eine Interpretation Kandake = Königsmutter keinen einzigen Beleg haben und dass ich deshalb das meroitische kdke, ktke, kdwe für den Titel halte, den die neben dem König fungierende Frau (kdi) trägt."

61. Burstein, *Ancient African Civilizations: Kush and Axum*, 140 n. 17.

62. William Y. Adams, *Nubia: Corridor to Africa* (Princeton, N.J.: Princeton University Press, 1984), 260.

activity at Kawa and Wad ben Naqa, and attested to by the splendid collection of jewels discovered by Ferlini (1837) in a recess on the front side of the pyramid of Beg[rawiyeh] N[orth] 6."[63]

3. Queen Amanitore was coregent with King Natakamani in the middle of the first century AD. She is buried in Beg[rawiyeh] N[orth] 1. Earlier scholars had identified the Candace of Acts 8 as Amanitore, whose reign was dated by Dows Dunham to AD 25-41, but her reign has now been dated to 12 BC–AD 12 by Hintze.

4. Queen Nawidemak ruled in the first half of the first century AD; she is called *qore*. Her burial is in Bar. 6. She is probably the Candace mentioned in Acts 8.[64]

According to Kendall, Meroitic queens are portrayed as "powerful figures, enormously fat, covered with jewels and ornament and elaborate fringed and tasseled robes. Their huge frames tower over their diminutive foes, whom they are shown grasping brutally by the hair with one hand and to whom they deal the *coup de grace* with the other."[65] He also observes, "By Meroitic times, with the decline of Egyptian influence, extreme corpulence had again become the fashion in the Sudan, at least among the ladies at court, and a remarkable succession of massive queens and princesses appears in monumental art from the third century B.C. to the fourth century A.D."[66]

Christianity in Aithiopia (Nubia)

The Ethiopian eunuch eventually went home and presumably testified about his newfound faith. According to Irenaeus, in *Adv. Haer.* 3.12.8, written about AD 180, he was "sent into the regions of Ethiopia, to preach what he had himself believed." According to Eusebius's *History of the Church* (2.1.13-14), written in the early fourth century AD:

Tradition says that he, who was the first of the Gentiles to receive from Philip by revelation the mysteries of the divine word, and was the first-fruits of the faithful through the world, was also the first to return to his native land and

63. Török, *Kingdom of Kush*, 456.

64. The dating of these queens is based on the latest determinations by Török in his 1997 summary (*Kingdom of Kush*). An earlier study by Stefan Wenig, "Bemerkungen zur Chronologie des Reiches von Meroe," *Mitteilungen des Instituts für Orientforschung* 13 (1967): 43, had dated this queen to 70 to 60 BC, and the Amanitore to around AD 20.

65. Kendall, *Kush: Lost Kingdom of the Nile*, 14.

66. Timothy Kendall, "Ethnoarchaeology in Meroitic Studies," *Studia Meroitica, 1984*, ed. S. Donadoni and S. Wenig (Berlin: Akademie, 1989), 655.

preach the Gospel of the knowledge of the God of the universe and the sojourn of our Saviour which gives life to men, so that by him was actually fulfilled the prophecy which says, "Ethiopia shall stretch out her hand to God" [Ps. 68:31].

Unfortunately, we have no evidence of Christianity taking root in that region until centuries later. The official conversion of Nubia following the mission of Julian to Nobatia came in the 540s, though individual conversions may have occurred earlier.[67]

---

67. Bruce M. Metzger, "The Christianization of Nubia and the Old Nubian Version of the New Testament," in *Historical and Literary Studies* (London: Brill, 1968), 111-22; David N. Edwards, "Post-Meroitic ('X-Group') and Christian Burials at Sesibi, Sudanese Nubia. The Excavations of 1937," *Journal of Egyptian Archaeology* 80 (1994): 159-77.

Romans 15:9b-12 18

Gentiles as the Culminative Focus of Salvation History

DON N. HOWELL, JR.

An analysis of OT quotations in the NT and their contribution to a significant theme in biblical theology.

Introduction[1]

The magisterial letter to the Romans has been well described as *the* missionary charter of the apostle Paul. The inclusio of passages that spell out Paul's missionary agenda (1:1-15; 15:14-33) frame the articulation of his gospel, which is the constitution of his mission.[2] Further, both at the outset and at the conclusion of the letter Paul specifies the objective of his mission: to lead the Gentiles to "the obedience of faith" (1:5; 16:26).[3]

---

1. Dr. Harold Hoehner combines a scholar's erudition, a pastor's warmth, and a missionary's concern for lost people in his teaching ministry. Such a rare combination was deeply appreciated by this former student.

2. Lucien Legrand, *Unity and Plurality: Mission in the Bible,* trans. Robert B. Barr (Maryknoll, N.Y.: Orbis, 1990), 115-24.

3. The consensus view of commentators is that the doxology of 16:25-27 is post-Pauline, a later scribal attempt to round off what seemed an incomplete ending. Larry W. Hurtado ("The Doxology at the End of Romans," in *New Testament Textual Criticism: Essays in Honour of Bruce M. Metzger,* eds. Eldon J. Epp and Gordon D. Fee [Oxford: Clarendon, 1981], 185-99) effectively disputes several traditional arguments against Pauline authorship and concludes that

This phrase captures the full-orbed character of Paul's ministry: to bring the Gentiles to the kind of faith that produces a life of obedience to Christ as Savior and Lord.[4]

Paul's intentionality in targeting the non-Jewish peoples for evangelism and discipleship is evident throughout Romans. The "Gentiles" (ἔθνη) are: the scope of his calling (1:5, 13); a people in whose conscience the law of God is planted (2:13), but who blaspheme God due to Israel's disobedience (2:24); accountable to the one Creator-God (3:29); included in the covenantal promises to Abraham (4:17-18); privileged to enter the covenant community through the principle of faith (9:24, 30); the means by which Israel is provoked to jealousy to seek salvation (10:19; 11:11-13, 25); the culminative focus of God's salvation-historical program (15:9-12, 27); the crowning offering of worship which Paul brings to God (15:18).

Their desperate spiritual need, their relationship to Israel, and their access by faith into the riches of salvation, then, comprise the bedrock convictions that drive Paul to prosecute his ministry to the Gentiles. Nowhere is this missiological intent clearer than in Rom 15:9b-12, where God's program for Gentile salvation is established by a series of four OT quotations. The quotations, joined by the motif of "Gentiles,"[5] follow a theological declaration that the incarnate Christ became a servant of the Jewish people on behalf of truth, that is, God's covenant faithfulness, in order to confirm the patriarchal promises (15:8). This confirmation reaches its final intent with the Gentiles glorifying God for his mercy (15:9a).[6] The entire statement (15:8-9a, γάρ) supports the ethical imperative to receive one another (15:7): the "weak" Jewish believer should not judge one who

---

the apostle's composition of the doxology remains a viable option. External manuscript evidence is impressive in support of its authenticity and location at the end of the epistle (P61, ℵ, B, C, D, 81, 1739, vg, eth, Clement).

4. Douglas J. Moo, *The Epistle to the Romans*, NICNT (Grand Rapids, Mich.: Eerdmans, 1996), 51-53. πίστεως is thus taken as both an epexegetic and a subjective genitive.

5. This is the chain quotation or חרז method that was a common style of rabbinical exposition of the OT in the synagogues. See E. Earle Ellis, *Paul's Use of the Old Testament* (Grand Rapids, Mich.: Baker, 1957), 49-51.

6. The syntax of vv. 8-9 is difficult. It is possible with Moo (*Romans*, 876-77) to take the two aorist infinitives βεβαιῶσαι and δοξάσαι as parallel in dependence on εἰς τό, thus creating two parallel purpose expressions (see KJV, Amplified, NASB, NRSV, NLT). But two factors make us hesitate to adopt this arrangement: (1) there is a change in the subject governing the infinitives from Christ to the Gentiles; (2) the conjunction δέ, not καί, joins the clauses and may take on a slightly transitional ("moreover," "in the next place") rather than a purely adjunctive ("and") sense. We view the infinitival phrase of v. 9a as subordinate to the preceding infinitival purpose phrase in v. 8b: the ultimate intent of Christ's becoming a servant of the Jews in order to confirm the patriarchal promises is that the Gentiles might glorify God (see NIV); or, alternatively, v. 9a spells out the specific promise of the Abrahamic covenant which encompasses the Gentiles (δοξάσαι epexegetic to τάς ἐπαγγελίας).

is incorporated in such a climactic way into the Abrahamic covenant (Gen 12:3b (NIV): "and all peoples on earth will be blessed through you"); nor should the "strong" Gentile believer despise one from whom one's spiritual ancestry is drawn.

The four quotations either support v. 9a alone, God's glorification by the Gentiles, or, more likely, undergird vv. 8-9a as a whole, in which case they point toward the union of Jews (v. 8) and Gentiles (v. 9a) in the believing community of praise. In the analysis of the quotations we follow a functional approach with three steps that answer the following questions: (a) What OT text is cited or alluded to? If the text does not follow the MT or the LXX is there a substantive reason for the modification or is it incidental? (b) What is the meaning of the passage in its OT setting? How does Paul's handling of the OT passage reflect his grasp of its original context?[7] (c) How does the OT passage cited function in the argument of the epistle? What point is the apostle making by this citation?[8]

1. Psalm 18:49 (LXX 17:50) = 2 Samuel 22:50

(a) Identity of the Text Cited in Romans 15:9b

Paul quotes a slightly adapted form of the Septuagint, which itself is a careful rendering of the Masoretic Text. The only change is the omission of the vocative κύριε, which translates the Hebrew tetragrammaton.

(b) Old Testament Context

The title identifies Psalm 18 as a song of David, the servant of the Lord, celebrating deliverance from enemies, chief among whom was King Saul. In the prelude God is declared to be his servant's rock, fortress, deliverer, refuge, horn, and stronghold (18:1-3). In the direst of circumstances, then, God alone is the source of security and strength. As David calls out, the Lord hears (18:4-6) and descends with wrath against his foes, rescuing David from mortal danger poetically depicted in the language of the threatening waters of the Red Sea at Israel's exodus (18:7-19). David's righteousness, that is, his integrity of heart in aligning the nation with

---

7. We begin with the presupposition that the apostle Paul is sensitive to the OT context and does not distort its original sense, though he may at times transcend it. For a similar approach see M. Silva, "Old Testament in Paul," in *DPL*, 630-42.

8. This is a simplified form of the methodology proposed and exemplified in Richard B. Hays and Joel B. Green, "The Use of the Old Testament by New Testament Writers," in *Hearing the New Testament: Strategies for Interpretation*, ed. Joel B. Green (Grand Rapids, Mich.: Eerdmans, 1995), 232-36.

God's covenant demands, is rewarded (18:20-24) by the faithful and holy One who lifts up the humble (18:25-29). By the favor of the Lord his servant prospers and goes forth to subdue all his enemies to become the "head of the nations" (v. 43; 18:30-45).

The verse cited falls in the concluding doxology, where the psalmist praises God for his unfailing loyal love to his anointed one and his descendants forever (18:46-50). He calls out, "Therefore I will praise you among the nations, O LORD; I will sing praises to your name" (v. 49, NIV). He who has been exalted as head of the non-Jewish peoples surrounding Israel (vv. 43-45) vows to declare God's excellence to those without that knowledge.

(c) Function of the OT Passage in Its NT Context

The major difficulty is, whom does Paul understand as the "I" of Ps 18:49 in its present context of Rom 15:9b? Perhaps Paul understands himself as the one who, as the antitype of David, fulfills the role of declaring God's praises to the Gentiles. This is plausible, since in the following paragraph he exults in his priestly ministry of bringing the Gentiles as a spiritual offering to God (15:16-18). More likely, however, Paul sees this messianically: the greater David, suffering and now exalted (18:48), brings praise to God in the midst of the nations he has redeemed. The voices of the Redeemer and the redeemed of the nations (the next two quotations) will combine to bring great glory to God for his mercy. The Christological motif that precedes this series of quotations (15:3, 5, 6, 7, 8) lends weight to this interpretation.

2. Deuteronomy 32:43

(a) Identity of the Text Cited in Romans 15:10

The quotation is an exact reproduction of the third line of this verse in the Septuagint. This corresponds in sense (see NIV) to the first line of Deut 32:43 in the Masoretic text, but this third line of the LXX is missing from the MT. The Septuagint may translate a different Hebrew Vorlage which is attested in the Qumran scroll 4QDeut.[9]

(b) OT Context

The citation from the Song of David (Psalm 18) in v. 9b is followed in v. 10 by a brief excerpt from the Song of Testimony (Deut 32:43), where

9. Joseph A. Fitzmyer, *Romans*, AB 33 (New York: Doubleday, 1993), 707.

Moses summons heaven and earth to hear his declaration of God's greatness to the assembly of Israel poised on the plains of Moab to enter the Promised Land (Deut 32:1-3). The Lord's faithfulness contrasts markedly with the faithlessness of his people (32:4-9). Both in Egypt and during the desert sojourn God's fatherly care of Israel was quickly forgotten (32:10-18). Therefore the holy wrath of Yahweh was poured out in judgment during the wilderness period on a nation without spiritual discernment (32:19-33). But his compassion will triumph even as he must righteously judge his people for their idolatry (32:34-38).

In the final paragraph God speaks as the one who will assuredly heal those he has wounded, making atonement for both his land and people (32:39-43). The promise of redemption elicits the summons, "Rejoice, O nations, with his people."

(c) Function of the OT Passage in Its NT Context

In summoning the non-Jewish nations to rejoice together with God's covenant people, Israel, does Paul see here a prophecy of the combination of Jew and Gentile in the redeemed community? Even as the greater David vows to praise God among the Gentiles (Rom 15:9b) so the greater Moses summons the new people of God, formed of Gentile and Jew, to rejoice. Typology and direct messianic prophecy coalesce in such quotations. The term *rejoice* points toward joyful worship of the faithful Lord and the happiness of participating in the eschatological harvest of redeemed people.[10]

3. Psalm 117:1 (LXX 116:1)

(a) Identity of the Text Cited in Romans 15:11

Paul quotes the Septuagint (which is a verbatim rendering of the MT with two second person plural imperatives) with some slight revisions: πάντα τὰ ἔθνη is thrust forward to stress the universality of the praise; and the second command, linked to the first with καί, is a third person plural imperative ἐπαινεσάτωσαν (rather than second plural ἐπαινέσατε) to perhaps underscore the willing response of the Gentiles to the summons to praise the Lord.

---

10. The verb εὐφραίνω is commonly used in the LXX to express the joyful experience of participation in the worshiping community (cf. Lev 23:40; Deut 12:7, 12, 18; 26:11; 33:18). One remarkably analogous occurrence of this verb is in Isa 54:1, which Paul quotes in Gal 4:27 to refer to the jubilance felt by the citizens, both Jew and Gentile, of the heavenly city of God, the Jerusalem above.

(b) OT Context

Psalm 117, the shortest chapter in the Bible, provides this command or summons to the Gentile peoples of the world to join Israel in praising the Lord. The following verse (117:2) confirms ("for") the summons to worship by reminding Israel ("toward us") of her Lord's ever-enduring covenant faithfulness. As in the previous quotation (Deut 32:43), the psalmist's call is for all nations and peoples to join the worshiping community. It is the universality of Gentile inclusion in extolling God's worth that the author anticipates ("all . . . all").

(c) Function of the OT Passage in Its NT Context

Romans 11 has earlier developed the biblical theme that the spiritual destiny of the Gentile nations flows directly out of the salvation-historical stream that begins with Abraham (esp. 11:11-24). The climactic promise of the Abrahamic covenant is that all the nations of the earth will be blessed through him (Gen 12:3b). The promise stretches forth into a family that produces a nation, Israel, which brings forth the Messiah. The redemptive work of Messiah then reaches its culmination in the apostolic proclamation of the gospel to the Gentiles and the incorporation by faith of those heretofore ignorant peoples into the covenant community.

4. Isaiah 11:10

(a) Identity of the Text Cited in Romans 15:12

This is a characteristic quotation from the Septuagint, which bears conceptual, but not exact linguistic, correspondence to the Masoretic text. Paul's minor revision of the LXX involves omission of the phrase ἡμέρᾳ ἐκείνῃ, which perhaps arises from his view of the realized eschaton (no longer a purely future anticipation) in the finished work of Christ. The MT is rendered in the NIV: "In that day the Root of Jesse will stand as a banner for the peoples; the nations will rally to him, and his place of rest will be glorious."[11] A banner placed on a

---

11. The LXX creates two coordinate sentences by inserting καί and adding the definite article to make the participle substantival (ὁ ἀνιστάμενος); neither insertion is justified by the Hebrew construction of a present participle עֹמֵד following the waw-consecutive וְהָיָה. Further, to render the Hebrew term for banner or ensign, נֵס, by the Greek verb "rule over" (ἄρχω) is at best an imprecise paraphrase. It is not unusual for Paul and the other NT authors, however, to depend upon the Septuagint even when it differs appreciably from the Masoretic text. See the listing of twenty-two such cases (Category D) in Gleason L. Archer and Gregory Chirichigno, *Old Testament Quotations in the New Testament* (Chicago: Moody, 1983), xxvi-xxviii.

pole was a visible sign for military troops to gather (Isa 5:26; 13:2; Jer 4:6, 21) or, symbolically, a call for Israel and the nations to unite under Messiah's protection (Isa 11:10, 12; 49:22; 62:10). The LXX conveys the same idea, though with the language of ruling and hoping, that Israel and the nations find their salvation by streaming to the "root of Jesse."

(b) OT Context

Isaiah 11 opens with the prediction that the dynasty of David, called the chopped but still vital "stump" and "roots" of Jesse, in the aftermath of Assyria's near annihilation of Judah, will be restored in a new "shoot" or "branch" (11:1). The root of Jesse will arise "in that day" to rule over the Gentiles who in turn place their hope in him (11:10). Once more we see the poles of particularism and universality coming together as the non-Jewish peoples rally to the Davidic Messiah.

What is this eschatological "day" when a greater David comes to rule the Gentiles who place their hope in him? The Isaianic description focuses on the character of the ruler and the security of the messianic age: he is endowed with the Spirit of wisdom and understanding to know and fear the Lord (11:2-3a); he judges righteously, vindicating the oppressed and destroying the wicked (11:3b-5); peace and safety reign in this age as little children play unharmed by formerly dangerous animals; natural adversaries in the animal world (wolf and lamb, leopard and goat, lion and ox) dwell in harmony (11:6-9a); ignorance of God is removed, "for the earth will be full of the knowledge of the LORD as the waters cover the sea" (11:9b, NIV).

The day when Messiah arises to rule over the nations (11:10) is coterminous with the time when he regathers the scattered remnant of Israel from both the northern (Ephraim) and southern (Judah) kingdoms (11:11-14). As he parted the Red Sea to enable his people to pass safely through, so the Lord will make a highway across the Euphrates back to the land of their heritage (11:15-16).

The historical reference to the return of exiles from Assyrian and Babylonian exile (11:11-16), following as it does the idyllic portrait of perfect peace and safety in a transformed created order (11:6-9), brings together near and more distant events that are common to the prophetic perspective. If the reigns of such righteous kings as Hezekiah and Josiah and the returns from exile under Zerubbabel and Ezra are the immediate focus of the prophet, they serve as adumbrations for the coming of the greater

Davidic ruler, Messiah, to whom not only Israel but also the Gentile nations will come.[12]

(c) Function of the OT Passage in Its NT Context

Paul sees a magnificent eschatological drama unfolding before his very eyes as Gentile churches have been planted in the space of ten years in the major metropolitan areas of four Roman provinces (cf. Rom 15:15-22 and the quotation of Isa 52:15 in v. 21). Through the work of his own missionary team these "millennial" passages of the OT are finding *initial* fulfillment. This is why Paul glories in his ministry (15:17). Jesus Messiah has come to inaugurate his rule over Gentiles and a remnant of Jews, but it will ultimately encompass the whole Jewish nation (cf. 11:25-27).

Conclusion

During his winter "sabbatical" in Corinth the apostle reflects on what God has accomplished through him among the Gentiles during the past two decades of ministry in the eastern Mediterranean (Rom 15:18-19). Set to deliver the voluntary monetary offerings of his Gentile churches to the impoverished brothers in Jerusalem (15:25-28a, 31), he will also bring to the holy city a representative group of Gentile converts as a spiritual offering to God (15:16). Though they had been judged unworthy by Paul's Judaizing opponents, Paul knew these Gentile converts were justified by faith and sanctified by the indwelling Spirit and "were thus fitted to be a 'pure offering' to that God whose name, through the Gentile mission, had now become 'great among the nations' as another Hebrew prophet had put it."[13] In the inspired declarations of lawgiver (Deut 32:43), poet (Ps 18:49; 117:1), and prophet (Isa 11:10), Paul sees Gentile salvation as the culminative focus of salvation history. And this is no mere academic interest—he is driven to make new plans to evangelize the unreached province of Spain after establishing Rome as his new sending base (15:23-24, 28b-29).

Theologians have long argued that the unifying theme of Holy Scripture is the progress of divine redemption. Missiologists respond that it is not

---

12. John N. Oswalt, *The Book of Isaiah. Chapters 1–39*, NICNT (Grand Rapids, Mich.: Eerdmans, 1986), 277-78, 286-89. Oswalt draws the connection between Isaiah 11 and Romans 11, where the great final ingathering of Israel is anticipated. But it is the rallying of the Gentile nations, along with Israel, to Messiah that both Isaiah (11:10) and Paul (11:11-32) eagerly await.

13. F. F. Bruce, *Paul: Apostle of the Heart Set Free* (Grand Rapids, Mich.: Eerdmans, 1977), 323.

redemption accomplished but redemption proclaimed to the nations that is the burden of Christ and his apostles. Both are correct. But perhaps what integrates the theological and missiological dimensions of Scripture is an even greater ultimate concern—the doxological. "That the Gentiles might glorify God for his mercy" (15:9a, NIV) is the stated purpose of redemption accomplished and proclaimed. Even as it is man's chief end to glorify God and enjoy him forever, so it is God's chief end to glorify himself through the redeemed worshiping community.[14] The glory of God—such was the energizing incentive behind Paul's superlative missionary endeavors. May it be ours as well.

14. John Piper, *Let the Nations Be Glad! The Supremacy of God in Missions* (Grand Rapids, Mich.: Baker, 1993), 11-40.

Galatians 3:10-13   19

Crucifixion Curse and Resurrection Freedom

DAVID CATCHPOLE

Exegesis of Gal 3:10-13 tracing its theological implications and correlation with 2 Cor 5:21.

I n the Church of the Holy Trinity in Cambridge there is a memorial tablet to the great evangelical divine of the late eighteenth and early nineteenth century, Charles Simeon. Erected by the congregation of that parish, it reads:

In memory of
The Rev. Charles Simeon, M.A.,
Senior Fellow of King's College,
And fifty four years Vicar of this Parish,
who whether as the ground of his own hopes,
or as the subject of all his ministrations
determined to know nothing but
Jesus Christ and Him Crucified, 1 Cor 2:2.

Knowing Harold Hoehner's appreciation of King's as his own *alma mater,* and, even more important, the conviction he shares with Charles Simeon concerning the centrality of the cross in Christian faith and life, this seems the place to begin an essay contributed with warm regard and friendship to his Festschrift. In what follows the aim will be to provide an exegesis of Gal 3:10-13, on any showing one of the most testing of all the texts that spell out the meaning of the great motif of "Jesus Christ and him crucified."

The most controversial of Pauline statements, that "Christ redeemed us from the curse of the law by becoming a curse for us . . ." (Gal 3:13) arguably points toward an understanding of Christian life as modeled on the Spirit-endowed experience of the risen Christ; in short, it implicitly warns against an isolation of the cross from the resurrection and gift of the Spirit. But before that inference can be secured, a series of exegetical moves needs to be made, moves designed first to clarify the religious and social context in which the Galatians find themselves, then to expose the significance of Gal 3:13 in its immediate context in 3:1-14.

First, the problems in Galatia should be understood in terms of social identity theory.[1] The Jewish community is split between those who do not acknowledge the crucified Christ and those who do. The first group is persecuting the second group, and the ostensible reason for persecution (at least as far as Paul is concerned) is "the cross of Christ" (6:12). It is clear that "the cross of Christ" means in this setting an interpretation of the cross which threatens Jewish identity, an interpretation which Paul believes the Christian Jews wish to abandon, or at least not to press. They are currently sharing table fellowship with Gentiles on the basis of faith in Christ, a practice that flouts the principle that Jews do not eat with Gentiles, in itself a principle that protects Jewish social identity.[2] Their practice of eating meals, including passing around and sharing the one loaf and the one cup of eucharistic fellowship (cf. 1 Cor 10:16-17), undermines that social identity which circumcision fundamentally embodies. The first group, the non-Christian Jews, doubtless with the encouragement of the theological conservatives in Jerusalem, is therefore bringing pressure to bear on the Christian Jews either to withdraw from fellowship with Gentile fellow-Christians (cf. Gal 2:12) or to solve the problem by persuading their Gentile fellow-Christians to accept circumcision. If they do the latter, there is no problem about table fellowship, nor is there a problem about social identity, for the Gentiles, once persuaded to be circumcised, will have become Jews. That implies that the definition of "the people of God" as the Jewish people will have been restored. Harmony within the Jewish community will bring a cessation of "persecution." The Christian community as a distinct entity over against the synagogue community will have ceased to be. The death of Christ as a community-founding event might as well not have happened (cf. 2:21).

1. Philip F. Esler, *Galatians* (London: Routledge, 1998), 37-57.
2. Ibid., 82-116.

Second, Paul's criticism of the wavering Christian Jews in Galatia is severe indeed. He is aware of an ad hominem charge that he himself had been a promoter of circumcision, and therefore should not object (5:11). Hence, "why am I still being persecuted if I am still preaching circumcision?" Against the suggestion that the preacher of circumcision is the pre-Christian Paul,[3] it would be better to envisage a period of the Christian Paul's missionary activity during which this was the case: (1) the debate between Paul and his Galatian converts is about a matter of *Christian* theology, and to this issue any allusion to Paul's pre-Christian position would be irrelevant; (2) the debate about whether Gentiles should be circumcised would have broken out a good deal earlier than the conference of Gal 2:1-10 if for any considerable period beforehand a circumcision-free Christian gospel had been presented to Gentiles; (3) in spite of Esler's argument,[4] it is extremely difficult to envisage such a gospel being presented to Gentiles in Jerusalem at such a time as to provoke the pre-Christian pro-circumcision Paul into his campaign of persecution of what has on this basis to be regarded as already a sectarian community. It is the Paul who has abandoned the requirement of circumcision for Gentile converts, the Paul who had himself been a persecutor and then had been arrested by the vision of the heavenly Son of God (1:16) who is presently being persecuted, in just the same way as the waverers in Galatia are being persecuted.

Paul's criticism is also distinctly ad hominem: Peter represents the thread connecting the three episodes described in 1:18-24; 2:1-10, 11-14, and he is subjected to searing criticism. First, he was the person in authority who, after fifteen days of consultation with Paul, was able to confirm that the erstwhile persecutor had become a genuine promoter of the faith (1:22-24). Second, he was a key figure in the conference that brought reconciliation and gave formal ratification to the circumcision-free Gentile mission, a mission that was itself recognized as on a par with the Petrine pro-circumcision mission to the Jewish people (2:7-8). Third, subsequently in Antioch Peter had abandoned "the truth of the gospel" (2:14),[5] which had already been threatened prior to the Jerusalem conference (2:4-5) and then had been affirmed at that conference. In other words, if someone is guilty of inconsistency, that someone is Peter. Peter, along with the other two "pillars," had abandoned the requirement that Gentile Christians should be circumcised, and had resisted the objections to unrestricted

---

3. Ibid., 74.

4. Ibid., 123-26.

5. Ibid., 119. Esler is surely correct in his interpretation of this phrase, which occurs nowhere else in the Pauline letters, as "the freedom with which his Israelite and Gentile converts can be members of the same congregation without having their 'freedom' replaced with the demands of the Mosaic law."

Jew/Gentile eucharistic table fellowship—and then under pressure from the leading "pillar" he had reinstated the two-in-one requirement that circumcision should happen and Jew/Gentile table fellowship not happen. He had reverted from an understanding of the people of God as the community brought into being without qualification by the death of Christ and entered by faith in him, and he had resumed his earlier belief that the people of God are the Jewish people, and that table fellowship with non-Jews should be abandoned. In short, he was requiring circumcision, and his conduct was providing grist to the mill of his fellow-Christians in Galatia who required the same.

It is in this context that the argument in Gal 3:1-14 needs to be set. And to achieve an accurate exegesis *of what* is being said, it will be important to note *how* it is being said—in a word, to attend to the structure of the passage.

First, Gal 3:1-5 focuses on the experience of the Spirit (vv. 2, 3, 4) and the context in which that once-for-all experience has become available, i.e., the hearing of faith rather than works of law.[6] The presence here of the phrase "by works of law" (ἐξ ἔργων νόμου) is a deliberate echo of the same phrase in Gal 2:16, where two alternative routes into the people of God are contrasted, two routes that represent the sharply contrasting definitions of the people of God, as we have already noted. "Works of law" constitute any or all acts of obedience to the law: in traditional Jewish terms they are inseparable from "righteousness."[7] In this context they are, as already noted, concentrated in, though the generic phrase suggests that they are not confined to, the so-called boundary markers, i.e., circumcision, food laws, and sabbath.[8] They are equivalent to, and the encapsulation of, the law as a whole: how otherwise could Paul insist that acceptance of circumcision implies acceptance of the requirement to keep the law *in toto* (Gal 5:3), and how otherwise can being ἐξ ἔργων νόμου be equivalent to "remaining in all those things written in the book of the law to do them" (Gal 3:10)? Naturally, those "works of law" or boundary markers are an issue at the point of entry to the people of God (most obviously circumcision), but they also define and determine the life of those who have so entered (most notably food laws and sabbath, which do not belong to the "rite of passage" into the community). For

6. By "works of law" Paul almost certainly means the "boundary markers" that defined the frontier between membership and non-membership of the Jewish people, i.e., circumcision and observance of Sabbath and food laws. Cf. J. D. G. Dunn, *The Epistle to the Galatians,* BNTC (London: Black, 1993), 154-55. By labeling them "flesh," Paul mounts a critique of any tendency to equate Christian identity with religious and ethnic identity as understood in Judaism.

7. Esler, *Galatians*, 181-84.

8. See Dieter Luhrmann, *Galatians* (Minneapolis: Fortress, 1992), 46; J. D. G. Dunn, *The Theology of Paul the Apostle* (Grand Rapids, Mich.: Eerdmans, 1998), 354-59.

this reason a certain stereotyping can occur, so that those who maintain the traditional Jewish understanding of the people of God, its admission conditions and its continuing commitments, can be labeled synonymously as οἱ ἐκ περιτομῆς in Gal 2:12 and (of) ἐξ ἔργων νόμου in Gal 3:10. They are, in the strictest sense of the term, law people: that, from their (internal) point of view, is their glory, and that, from the Pauline (external) point of view, is their undoing.

To return to the theme of the Spirit, experienced overwhelmingly and incontrovertibly at the moment of the Galatians' Christian initiation, we note that after v. 5 there is no further reference to the Spirit in this passage until v. 14 is reached.

Second, Gal 3:6-9 focuses on the experience of Abraham. That experience is the prototype of the experience described in vv. 1-5, for the word καθώς, with the Genesis 15:6 LXX citation attached, causes v. 6 to lean on what precedes. It is also an experience that anticipates what happens when the gospel is preached in the form of a promise and received by faith: that was how it was for Abraham in the past, and that is how it is working out right now. The promise is a promise of blessing for all nations (Gentiles as well as Jews, therefore the Genesis 12:3/18:18 citation) through Abraham: it could not be realized except with the involvement of Gentiles as well as Jews. Logically, that involvement of Gentiles could be achieved in either of two ways: by their incorporation into the Jewish people (so, Peter prior to the conference and now again after the Antioch incident; Paul himself prior to a moment of theological transformation in the course of his mission; and now Paul's opponents in Galatia), or by their coming to faith in Abraham's God by some other means (so, Paul now and ever since that moment of theological transformation). For Paul, involvement in the Abrahamic promise is conditional upon replication of Abrahamic faith. As far as the structure of this passage is concerned, we note that after v. 9 there is no reference to Abraham, the promise, or the Gentiles until we reach v. 14. There all three reappear.

Third, the incidence of the themes of Spirit, Abraham, promise, and Gentiles in vv. 1-9, 14 serves to isolate vv. 10-13 as a separate unit of argument. In those four verses none of the four themes is mentioned. This separateness is further confirmed by its internal arrangement: four statements by Paul supported by four OT quotations. Moreover, the four quotations form a chiastic *gezerah shawah*, with the two quotations in vv. 10, 13 (Deut 27:26; 21:23) sharing the phrase ἐπικατάραρος πᾶς . . . , and the two quotations in vv. 11, 12 (Hab 2:4; Lev 18:5) sharing the word ζήσεται. This suggests that the logic of the argument requires that an inference first be drawn from vv. 11, 12 together, and that the required inference will depend on interpreting accurately the shared term ζήσεται. The logic then requires that an inference be drawn from vv. 10,

(11-12), and 13 together, and that this time the required inference will depend on interpreting accurately the shared term ἐπικατάρατος. The combination of those two inferences finally permits the argument from vv. 1-9 to move to its climax in v. 14.

The first inference arising from vv. 11-12 is that the experience of righteousness by faith—cf. v. 6, Abraham "believed God, and it was counted to him for righteousness"—does not occur in the sphere of law, for the text that encapsulates the gospel and speaks of faith does not mention law, and the text that encapsulates the law speaks not about faith but about doing. The upshot is that there are two theoretically possible routes to the achievement of life (ζήσεται), but the only one that counts is the non-law route. In the process it is clear that the experience of living, as defined by the non-law route, involves a new beginning; i.e., it is not just a matter of consecutive human existence, it has a beginning; and the moment when life begins is the moment when righteousness happens.

The second inference arising from vv. 10, 13 is that the law, far from being the means of life, is in fact the encapsulation of a problem it cannot solve. To take one's stand on the law implies a commitment to total obedience, or else the curse defined by law is imposed by law.[9] This observation needs to be defended against an alternative interpretation proposed by James Dunn. Arguing that for a Jew, first, obedience to the law was not the means to the achievement of righteousness, and, second, incomplete obedience was covered by the provision of the sacrificial system, he then exploits the Pauline affirmation of blameless conformity to the law in Philippians 3 as an indication that complete obedience was not required. Contrary to (1) the repeated insistence of Deuteronomy that complete obedience *was* required,[10] and (2) the thrust of many righteousness-texts that the term righteousness *does* stand for unrestricted and unqualified obedience to the demands of the law,[11] and (3) the insistence of Gal 5:3 in this same letter that being circumcised means automatically being obligated to perform the *whole* law (ὅλον τὸν νόμον ποιῆσαι), and (4) the argument in Rom 7:13-25 that the Adamic Jewish person's release through Christ

9. Paul's omission of the phrase ὑπὸ θεοῦ from the citation of Deut 21:23 is no coincidence. It shows an instinctive recognition that the definitive action of God takes place apart from law. The same position is indicated by the use of the traditional Jewish view of angels as the divine agents who brought the law: Gal 3:19b-20 holds against the law that non-immediacy of its origin, as against the promise which was spoken personally by God himself and without mediation. See Esler, *Galatians*, 198-200.

10. See, for example, Deut 26:13; 27:1; 28:1, 14, 58; 30:8.

11. Full weight should be given here to Paul's earlier adoption of the cry of the person oppressed by a sense of universal human shortcoming in Ps 143:2 οὐ δικαιωθήσεται ἐνώπιόν σου πᾶς ζῶν in Gal 2:16 and his adaptation of that text by the insertion of the loaded phrase ἐξ ἔργων νόμου and the change from πᾶς ζῶν to πᾶσα σάρξ.

and the Spirit (cf. Rom 8:3-4) is release from the frustration of inability to keep the law,[12] Dunn argues that the curse of Gal 3:10 is imposed on those who hold a certain *view*. It is not primarily what they *do*, or do not do, that is the problem. It is what they *believe* or stress, namely that the covenant requires a clear-cut distinction between Jews and non-Jews. By "resisting the manifest will of God in the gospel . . . their understanding and practice of the law was deficient" and they were therefore under the curse pronounced by Deut 27:26.[13] Dunn's view arguably assigns to the law a position that the law did not maintain but the Pauline gospel did. To see a divine curse falling on those who maintained faithfully and with conviction the covenant-based Jew/Gentile distinction *that the law itself maintained* is profoundly problematic. The law's curse stands over οἱ ἐξ ἔργων νόμου, that is, those who adopt, live by, and persuade others of, the traditional law-based understanding of the people of God, not because they believe what they believe but because they, in Paul's view, *cannot* and *do not* succeed in living according to the law's contents. Identifying with the law, ironically, they are undermined by the law. They need the gospel to rescue them but, in Paul's view, they have reneged from it. Theirs is an "old age" theology; Paul's gospel is a "new age" theology. To state the matter as clearly as possible, his conviction is that a curse stands over all persons who are ἐξ ἔργων νόμου (cf. vv. 2, 5), that is, all persons who *define* the people of God on the basis of law, believe they *belong to* the people of God on the basis of law, and insist that *living* as the people of God is a matter of living according to law. Their problem? Failure to keep the law in its entirety. But of what then does the curse consist? The answer is provided by v. 13: the curse is the experience of death, imposed by law on law-breakers, which in the particular experience of Christ took the form of crucifixion (cf. v. 1). But his death was our death (cf. ὑπὲρ ἡμῶν). Therefore we have died. Therefore the curse imposed by the law upon us has been experienced by us. Therefore all that the law laid down has been respected and provided.[14] Therefore, having passed through

---

12. In Rom 7:13-25 the argument moves on from the assertion that Adamic humankind under the law *does not* keep the law to the claim that such persons *cannot* do so. Dunn, *Theology*, 361, uses Rom 8:4; 13:8-10 (every commandment) and Gal 5:14 ("the whole law") to establish, *together with* Phil 3:6, that obedience was considered practicable, whereas, on the contrary, those passages should be *distinguished from* Phil 3:6 as characterizations of what is freshly, under the influence of the Spirit, possible for the members of the Christian community. In any case, the particular intention of Phil 3:6 should be defined with reference to the context of conflict in which it is written: it should not be extracted from that context and given a dispassionate objectivity that it cannot sustain.

13. Dunn, *Theology*, 362.

14. Cf. Esler, *Galatians*, 188, who writes: "By becoming a curse for our sakes, Christ has saved us from the curse; he has suppressed the effects of the Sinaitic curse so as to allow antecedent blessings to come into effect. By dying, he has destroyed the death which threatened

death, we are participants in a new order of existence. Therefore we are free (ἐξηγόρασεν ἐκ . . .) and alive (ζήσεται), with death behind us. The people of God are freshly defined as resurrection people!

Fourth, with this rich and profound pair of inferences duly established, the way is clear for the argument in vv. 1-5, 6-9 to proceed to its conclusion in v. 14. By virtue of participation in Christ, the solidarity-representation-involvement concept that stands at the heart of Pauline theology, the undefined content of the blessing promised to Abraham can now be defined in *pesher-style* as the Spirit, and experienced as such by the whole of believing humankind. The death of Christ is a death with which law-breaking Jewish people (ἡμεῖς) as well as Gentiles outside the sphere of law can identify. The event in which he became a curse (γενόμενος . . . κατάρα) was the event in which he was a cursed person, that is, he came under the authority of the law, indeed identified with law-breakers, and died their death. It was an event that belonged to the old era, while certainly concluding that era: it prepared the ground for, but did not initiate or establish the new era. Only the resurrection *could* do that—and *did* do that!

The accuracy of this exegesis can be tested by returning to the Corinthian correspondence and, in particular, to that summary statement of the Pauline gospel which has always been recognized as intimately related to the thought of Gal 3:10-13. The statement in question is 2 Cor 5:21: "He made him . . . to be sin for us, so that in him we might become the righteousness of God."

This statement, which in principle might need to be located in its social and community setting, in practice turns out to be a free-standing tradition applicable in any and every setting. This follows from its literary distinctness from what precedes it in 2 Corinthians 5: (1) in the immediate context (v. 20; cf. 6:1) "we" stands for the proclaimers of the Christian gospel, whereas in v. 21 "we" stands for all those who participate in Christ; (2) the context is dominated by the language of "ministry" and "reconciliation" while neither term appears in v. 21; (3) v. 21 works by means of a polarization of sin/righteousness, neither of which terms appears in the context. We can, moreover, go further than that. There is a certain symmetry between the main clause (v. 21a) and the subordinate clause (v. 21b): (1) Sin in the one is matched by righteousness in the other, the two being the opposing powers set over against one another, as in Rom 6:13, 16, 18. (2) Solidarity language is used in each, "for us (ὑπὲρ ἡμῶν) . . . in him (ἐν αὐτῷ)," the two phrases being equivalent, and the

---

from Sinai, so that he might allow us access to life promised earlier to Abraham." I agree with the emphasis on Sinai as the source of the curse, but would prefer to replace both "suppressed" and "destroyed" with "experienced."

use of the one rather than the other deriving simply from the identity of the subject of the sentence in question. So we appear to have here a discrete summary of the Pauline gospel, shaped poetically and attached to 2 Corinthians 5:11-20 because it is felt to be particularly appropriate as an amplification of what has just been said, but nevertheless a summary that is detachable and meaningful in its own right.

The process of interpretation engages the exegete with the meaning of a trio of problematic phrases: (1) "he knew no sin," (2) "he made him to be sin," and (3) "that we might become . . . the righteousness of God."

The first phrase is the least difficult: to "know Sin" is to be in a personal relationship with, and in this case to be under the sway of, the authoritative being, Sin. Knowledge means relatedness, and not being in such a relationship means being entirely sinless and perfect, even though unreservedly human. The second phrase, "he made him to be Sin" is much more difficult, and is best interpreted in the light of our findings in respect of the very similar language in Gal 3:13. To "become Sin" and to "become a curse" mean in each case to "come under the authority of . . ." In both cases, "coming under the authority of . . ." means experiencing that death which the law/Sin imposes. The third problematic phrase in 2 Cor 5:21 can now be freed of all ambiguity and uncertainty. "Becoming" righteousness equals coming into the sphere controlled by righteousness. This is the sphere where the rule of Sin is not present, and it is the sphere in which there live those with whom Christ identified (ὑπὲρ ἡμῶν) and who have identified with him (ἐν αὐτῷ), the one who died *and now has passed beyond death in resurrection.* This surely is the heart of the matter. The gospel of 2 Corinthians 5 is the same as the gospel of Galatians 3: the people of God, defined by faith and belonging to Christ, have come through his death into his life. Their experience of righteousness is their experience of resurrection. They are "new age people," resurrection people!

Ephesians 2:19-22

The Temple Motif

20

SCOTT S. CUNNINGHAM

An analysis of three distinct problems in a unit, involving syntactical, lexical, and theological issues.

Consequently, you are no longer foreigners and aliens, but fellow citizens with God's people and members of God's household, built on the foundation of the apostles and prophets, with Christ Jesus himself as the chief cornerstone. In him the whole building is joined together and rises to become a holy temple in the Lord. And in him you too are being built together to become a dwelling in which God lives by his Spirit (Eph 2:19-22, NIV).

This passage comes as the climax to Eph 2:11-22,[1] which as a whole has been called "the key and high point of the whole epistle."[2] Having described in 2:1-10 the sinful human condition and the work of grace that brings humanity from spiritual death to spiritual life, Paul now describes the outcome of that divine work: through the cross the Gentiles are brought

---

1. Dr. Hoehner's magisterial commentary on Ephesians (*Ephesians: An Exegetical Commentary* [Grand Rapids, Mich.: Baker, 2002]) appeared after the writing of this article and hence was not available for use in my own study. However, a comparison of this article with his commentary on the same passage reveals my indebtedness to his exegetical method, an observation I am grateful to acknowledge.

2. Markus Barth, *Ephesians: Introduction, Translation and Commentary on Chapters 1–3*, AB 34 (Garden City, N.Y.: Doubleday, 1974), 3.

into a new relationship with the Jews and to God. This reconciliation is discussed in three respects: the fact (2:11-13), its means (2:14-18), and its result (2:19-22). The result of this reconciliation between Jew and Gentile is the formation of a new entity described metaphorically as the temple of God.

While its broader context is clear, to a large extent the reader's interpretation of this passage is determined by three major exegetical decisions. First, what is the meaning of "the foundation of the apostles and prophets" (ἐπὶ τῷ θεμελίῳ τῶν ἀποστόλων καὶ προφητῶν)? What precisely is the foundation, and who are the apostles and prophets? Second, what is the lexical reference of ἀκρογωνιαίου? Should this word be understood to signify a "cornerstone" or a "capstone"? And, third, how should the reader understand the phrase πᾶσα οἰκοδομή (if that is the correct reading)? Does the grammar allow for "the whole building," or should it be translated "every building," understanding multiple structures?

The Nature of the Foundation

The Jews and the Gentiles together, in Paul's description, are built upon "the foundation of the apostles and prophets" (ἐπὶ τῷ θεμελίῳ τῶν ἀποστόλων καὶ προφητῶν).

The first issue in understanding the nature of this foundation is to determine the relationship between the foundation, on the one hand, and the apostles and prophets, on the other. This is decided by examining the use of the genitive case present in the phrase. There are three plausible alternatives[3]: (a) genitive of possession: "the foundation *which belongs to* the apostles and prophets"; that is, Christ[4]; (b) subjective genitive: "the foundation *which is laid by* the apostles and prophets"; that is, their teaching[5]; or (c) genitive of apposition: "the foundation *which consists of* the apostles and prophets."[6]

---

3. For the syntactical categories of the genitive case I have followed Wallace's treatment in *ExSyn*, 78-136. See especially p. 100 for his brief discussion of the classification of this genitive.

4. Henry Alford, *The Greek Testament*, vol. 3, *Galatians—Philemon*, rev. Everett F. Harrison (Chicago: Moody, 1958), 100.

5. John Eadie, *Commentary on the Epistle to the Ephesians*, Classic Commentary Library (Edinburgh: Clark, 1813; reprint, Grand Rapids, Mich.: Zondervan, n.d.), 197. So NEB: "the foundation laid by the apostles and prophets."

6. T. K. Abbott, *Commentary on the Epistles to the Ephesians and Colossians*, ICC (Edinburgh: Clark, 1897), 71; Barth, *Ephesians*, 271; William Hendriksen, *Exposition of Ephesians*, NTC (Grand Rapids, Mich.: Baker, 1967), 142. So JB: "a building that has the apostles and prophets for its foundations."

The fault with the first alternative is that it leads to a confusion of the metaphor. Paul is describing three distinct parts of the building: the superstructure, the foundation, and the cornerstone. It is unlikely that Christ is both the foundation and the cornerstone.

The second alternative is much closer to the idea. Here the genitive has the idea of agency, where the apostles and prophets have laid the foundation through their teaching. The primary support for this interpretive option is the parallel imagery in 1 Corinthians 3:10-17, where Paul speaks of *laying* a foundation through his preaching of Christ, but not himself as *being* the foundation. Against this interpretation, however, the architectural metaphor in Ephesians 2 seems to call for persons to be the foundation, since in the immediate context believers are pictured as the building blocks and Christ is the cornerstone.

Following from this, it is likely that the genitive should be understood in such a way that the foundation of the church consists of the apostles and prophets themselves. It is acknowledged that here Paul's use of the foundation imagery differs from that of 1 Corinthians 3. But this is neither contradictory nor inconsistent, and the different contexts allow for varied uses of the same metaphorical images.[7] As the subsequent pericope (3:1-6) makes clear, the apostles and prophets can themselves be described as the θεμέλιος inasmuch as this foundation comes to men through their proclamation of the divine mystery of Christ and his body.[8]

The nature of the foundation is also dependent upon the precise relationship between and identification of "the apostles and prophets" (τῶν ἀποστόλων καὶ προφητῶν). It can be generally stated that when two nouns are joined by καί and the article precedes only the first, there is a close connection between the two.[9] If the Granville Sharp Rule applied, then the "prophets" would refer to the same persons as the "apostles." However, the Rule does not admit to constructions using plural nouns.[10] Wallace suggests that for personal plural substantives in this construction

---

7. There are several other "foundation" texts in the NT (cf. Matt 16:18; 1 Cor 3:10-11; Rev 21:14). There is no basis for insisting that the imagery in all must be identical; rather each must be interpreted within its own context. Cf. Klyne Snodgrass, *Ephesians*, NIVAC (Grand Rapids, Mich.: Zondervan, 1996), 137. Nor can the differences in imagery between 1 Corinthians 3 and Ephesians 2 be used as evidence for assigning different authors to these texts (*pace* Andrew T. Lincoln, *Ephesians*, WBC 42 [Dallas: Word, 1990] 154).

8. J. Blunck, "θεμέλιος," *NIDNTT*, 1:662. As Lincoln comments, "The apostles and prophets are foundational in the sense of being primary and authoritative recipients and proclaimers of revelation" (*Ephesians*, 153).

9. "Sometimes groups more or less distinct are treated as one for the purpose in hand, and hence use only one article" (A. T. Robertson, *A Grammar of the Greek New Testament in the Light of Historical Research*, 4th ed. [Nashville: Broadman, 1923], 787).

10. On the first Granville Sharp Rule specifically, and the article-substantive-καὶ-substantive construction in general, see *ExSyn*, 270-90.

there are five semantic possibilities: (a) distinct groups, though united; (b) overlapping groups; (c) first group is a subset of the second; (d) second group is a subset of the first; or (e) the two groups are identical.

Largely due to the work of Wayne Grudem, this particular text has become the focus of debate. In Grudem's view, while in other NT texts apostles and prophets are to be understood as two distinct groups, *in this particular passage* where they are together said to be the foundation of the church, the apostles and prophets are identical.[11] Grudem supports this contention by noting similar article-substantive-καί-substantive constructions where the reference of the first and second substantives is identical. However, as Wallace counters, for examples in NT Greek where the substantives are plural *nouns,* it is much more likely that either the two groups are distinct or that the first group is a subset of the second, there being no clear NT examples where plural nouns refer to identical groups. Wallace himself believes that the ἀπόστολοι are a subset of the προφῆται so that the phrase may be translated, "the apostles and [other] prophets."[12]

Wallace's observations clearly weaken any perspective viewing the apostles and prophets as identical. However, in view of the two other instances in Ephesians where ἀπόστολοι and προφῆται are proximate, it may be preferable to understand them in this passage as distinct yet united for the purpose at hand, rather than one as a subset of the other. In Eph 4:11 Paul writes, "It was he who gave some to be apostles, some to be prophets [τοὺς μὲν ἀποστόλους, τοὺς δὲ προφήτας], some to be evangelists, and some to be pastors and teachers [τοὺς δὲ ποιμένας καὶ διδασκάλους] . . ." (NIV). It would seem that if Paul meant to indicate that the apostles were a subset of the prophets, in Eph 4:11 he also would have used one article to govern both nouns. Instead he distinguishes them by placing definite articles before both. This is particularly striking since in the same breath, he groups "pastors and teachers" together with the article-substantive-καί-substantive construction. The other occurrence of "apostles" and "prophets" together in Ephesians is a few verses later at 3:5, where Paul uses a similar construction. Here he speaks of "[the

---

11. For Wayne Grudem's discussion of Eph 2:20 see his *The Gift of Prophecy in 1 Corinthians* (Washington, D.C.: University Press of America, 1982), 82-105. As Wallace points out, Grudem's view of this passage is necessary to his understanding of NT prophecy, which admits to non-apostolic, non-inerrant prophets both in the early church and today. "If in Eph 2:20 the Church is built on the foundation of apostles and *other* prophets, then it would seem that Grudem either has to deny inerrancy or affirm that non-apostolic prophets only spoke truth (and were thus on par with OT prophets)" (*ExSyn,* 285). For a sound critique of Grudem's interpretation of "apostles and prophets" in this passage, cf. Peter T. O'Brien, *The Letter to the Ephesians,* Pillar New Testament Commentary (Grand Rapids, Mich.: Eerdmans, 1999), 214-16.

12. *ExSyn,* 284-86.

mystery of Christ] which was not made known to men in other generations as it has now been revealed by the Spirit to God's holy apostles and
prophets" (τοῖς ἁγίοις ἀποστόλοις αὐτοῦ καὶ προφήταις). The apparent reason the apostles and prophets are grouped in Eph 2:20 and 3:5 is
that in Paul's mind the apostles and prophets together are those through
whom God has revealed the mystery of Christ and the unity of his body,
thereby forming the foundation of the church.

Who then are the "apostles" who together with the prophets form
the foundation of the church? There is considerable uncertainty as to the
origin, criteria, and character of the apostolate, and the Pauline conception of its scope is only somewhat more defined. However, it seems fairly
certain that "Paul never applies the title of apostle to the Twelve as a
definite group."[13] Rather, based on the credal formula of 1 Corinthians
15:5-9, it is likely that the Pauline conception of the "apostles" included
the "Twelve," a larger group of apostles ("then to all the apostles"),
and, third, Paul himself ("the least of the apostles"). There is no reason
why this same Pauline conception should not also be understood in Eph
2:20. Clearly Paul would have considered himself as one of the apostles
who made up the foundation, as he numbers himself among the apostles
and prophets who are the recipients of the revelation of the mystery of
Christ (3:1-5).

With respect to the identification of the "prophets," the issue is whether
Paul was referring to the prophets of Israel or the prophets of the early
church. There are a few modern commentators who believe that Paul is
referring to Israel's prophets.[14] Habeck believes several factors support
this identification.[15] First, it is said that the history of the church does
not give such a prominent role to the NT prophets.[16] And, second, the

---

13. D. Müller, "ἀποστέλλω," *NIDNTT* 1:130. Besides Müller's article and the literature
cited there, for a general overview of the Pauline conception of the apostolate, see P. W. Barnett,
"Apostle," *DPL*, 45-51.

14. This interpretation was seemingly more common among the church fathers, such as
in Origen and Ambrosiaster. Cf. citations in *Ancient Christian Commentary on Scripture*, vol.
8, *Galatians, Ephesians, Philippians*, ed. Mark J. Edwards (Downers Grove, Ill.: InterVarsity
Press, 1999), 143. This interpretation would be consistent with an ecclesiology that sees the
church having its beginning in the Old Testament people of God.

15. Irwin J. Habeck, "Who Are the Prophets of Ephesians 2:20?" *Wisconsin Lutheran
Quarterly* 71 (1974): 121-25.

16. In support Lenski writes, "What we know of them places them far below the great
Old Testament prophets as well as below the apostles. Their function was only incidental, their
revelations only occasional, they were few in number" (R. C. H. Lenski, *The Interpretation
of St. Paul's Epistles to the Galatians, to the Ephesians, and to the Philippians*, Commentary
on the New Testament [Minneapolis: Augsburg, 1937], 451). Against this, Paul seems to give
special prominence to prophecy, listing the gift second in order only to apostleship on several
occasions (1 Cor 12:28; Eph 3:5; 4:11).

OT prophets played an important role in the preaching of Paul and thus in grounding the faith of the Gentiles.

However, it appears likely that the "prophets" of Eph 2:20 refer to those of the early church. (a) If OT prophets were intended, it would seem somewhat unnatural for them to have been mentioned second in order, after the apostles. (b) In all three occurrences of προφήτης in Ephesians the word is used in conjunction with ἀπόστολος, and in both 3:5 ("the mystery has now been revealed to his holy apostles and prophets") and 4:11 the prophets are unambiguously prophets of the early church. The similarity of expression, the proximity, and the relevance of 3:5 are particularly compelling, for what qualifies the apostles and prophets to be the foundation of the church is that *it is precisely to them that the mystery of Christ has now been revealed.* (c) Paul's building metaphor may imply a conceptual framework in which the cornerstone, foundation, and superstructure are placed in chronological order. In this case, any mention of OT prophets as being in the same foundation as the apostles and as coming after Christ the cornerstone would seem anachronistic.

The Interpretation of the "Cornerstone"

What is meant by the "cornerstone"? Much of the doubt lies in the fact that the word ἀκρογωνιαῖος is found only rarely in the extant Greek literature, and without any known use in Classical Greek. Its earliest certain appearance is in the LXX of Isa 28:16.[17] The word may be of biblical coinage,[18] being formed by joining the two words ἄκρος (= extreme, outermost, at the end) and γωνία (= corner, angle) with the combination meaning "lying at the extreme corner."[19] Besides Eph 2:20 the only other NT occurrence is in 1 Pet 2:6, where it appears in a fairly close quotation of the Isaiah passage and which, like Ephesians, also interprets ἀκρογωνιαῖος Christologically.

Traditionally, ἀκρογωνιαῖος has been thought to refer to a stone located in one of the corner extremities of the foundation of a building, hence the English translation "cornerstone." However, initially due to the

---

17. LXX Isa 28:16: ἐγὼ ἐμβαλῶ εἰς τὰ θεμέλια Σιων λίθον πολυτελῆ ἐκλεκτὸν ἀκρογωνιαῖον ἔντιμον εἰς τὰ θεμέλια αὐτῆς, "I am laying for the foundations of Zion a stone—costly, choice, a corner [stone], precious—for its foundations."

18. Cf. "ἀκρογωνιαῖος," MM, 19.

19. Thus, ἀκρογωνιαῖος is actually an adjective, but often the substantive which it naturally qualifies (λίθος, stone) is not present and needs to be supplied in the translation.

influence of J. Jeremias,[20] a number of prominent scholars[21] have been persuaded that ἀκρογωνιαῖος, at least in some passages, refers instead to a stone that crowns a building by being placed at its topmost angle or point as a capstone.

Jeremias marshals a number of texts that support the interpretation of ἀκρογωνιαῖος as "capstone" or "final stone," the most important of which is from the *Testament of Solomon*. The passage describes how Solomon, in completing the building of the Jerusalem temple, has the ἀκρογωνιαῖος placed at the top of the building: "And Jerusalem had been built and the temple was being completed (συνεπληροῦτο). And there was a great cornerstone (λίθος ἀκρογωνιαῖος) which I wished to put at the head of the corner crowning the temple of God (εἰς κεφαλὴν γωνίας τῆς πληρώσεως τοῦ ναοῦ τοῦ θεοῦ, 22:7)." The stone was carried up the staircase and placed at the extremity of the entrance of the temple (εἰς τὴν ἄκραν τῆς εἰσόδου τοῦ ναοῦ, 23:3).

While the LXX uses ἀκρογωνιαῖος only in Isaiah 28:16, its two uses in the later Greek translation of the OT by Symmachus are also frequently cited in confirmation of this view. In 2 Kings (LXX 4 Kingdoms) 25:17 it is used of a capital of a column, and in Psalm 118:22 (LXX 117:22) it replaces the LXX translation κεφαλὴν γωνίας.

It is argued that the understanding of ἀκρογωνιαῖος as "final stone" or "capstone" is similarly preferable in Eph 2:20.[22] First, it is argued the unique position of Christ would be emphasized so that he is not just one of the stones of the foundation in common with the apostles and prophets. Second, it is suggested that a "final stone" would better portray the unification Christ brings to the church. And third, it is said this understanding corresponds more naturally with the main Pauline image of the church in Ephesians, that of the Head and the body (4:12-16), in which Christ is given an exalted position. As Christ is the κεφαλή of the σῶμα, so he is the ἀκρογωνιαῖος of the οἰκοδομή. If the growth of the body is "to the head" (4:15), then the growth of the building should also be expected to be toward a final stone, rather than from a cornerstone.

However, it is not at all certain that Jeremias should be followed in this understanding of ἀκρογωνιαῖος. At best he has demonstrated that

20. Most accessible is J. Jeremias, "ἀκρογωνιαῖος," *TDNT*, 1:792.
21. Cf. Barth, *Ephesians*, 319; F. F. Bruce, *The Epistle to the Colossians, to Philemon, and to the Ephesians*, NICNT (Grand Rapids, Mich.: Eerdmans, 1984), 304-5; Lincoln, *Ephesians*, 154-56; H. G. Stigers, "Cornerstone, Corner Stone," *ZPEB*, 1:979-80. For support of the translation "cornerstone," cf. R. J. McKelvey, "Christ the Cornerstone," *NTS* 8 (1962): 352-9 (McKelvey's article is a sustained rejoinder to Jeremias's position); H. Krämer, "γωνία," *EDNT*, 1:267-69; W. Mundle, "γωνία," *NIDNTT*, 3:388-90.
22. Cf. Stig Hanson, *The Unity of the Church in the New Testament: Colossians and Ephesians* (Uppsala: Almquist & Wiksell, 1946), 131-32.

ἀκρογωνιαῖος *may* be used to refer to a final stone or capstone. It should first be noted that none of the evidence for the use of ἀκρογωνιαῖος as final stone is found in literature composed before or contemporaneous with the NT and thus this evidence is of doubtful value in establishing the range of lexical meaning in NT texts. Symmachus's Greek translation of the OT is dated between the second and third centuries AD,[23] and the *Testament of Solomon,* a Christian apocryphal document, originated in perhaps the third century AD.[24]

The OT background of Eph 2:20 should weigh heavily in the interpretation of Paul's use of ἀκρογωνιαῖος. With the confluence of "foundation" and "cornerstone" in Eph 2:20, it appears certain the apostle had Isa 28:16 in mind.[25] And, in the Isaiah passage the identification of ἀκρογωνιαῖος as part of the foundation is certain, being made doubly explicit in the Greek text from which Paul draws: ἐμβαλῶ εἰς τὰ θεμέλια . . . ἀκρογωνιαῖον . . . εἰς τὰ θεμέλια, "I lay for its foundations . . . a cornerstone . . . for its foundations." Jeremias actually admits that the LXX identifies ἀκρογωνιαῖος with the foundation stone in the Isaiah passage, but then makes the claim that "this usage is not found except in LXX Is 28.16 and quotations from it."[26] But Eph 2:20 is, in all likelihood, an allusion to Isa 28:16, and thus Jeremias's admission should have led him to conclude that ἀκρογωνιαῖος refers to a foundation stone in the Ephesians passage as well.[27]

Given the fact that ἀκρογωνιαῖος can refer to a cornerstone, the question is whether in fact it does so in Eph 2:20. There are several features in the context that point in the affirmative.[28] First, the close proximity of

23. Cf. Leonard Greenspoon, "Symmachus, Symmachus's Version," *ABD,* 6:251.

24. The dating of *T. Sol.* is uncertain. Cf. D. C. Duling, "Testament of Solomon," in *OTP,* 1:940-43.

25. That a Christological interpretation of Isa 28:16 was known to Paul is certain (cf. Rom 9:33; 10:11). It is possible that the origin of its use in the early church as a *testimonium* should be located in Jesus' own messianic use of Ps 118:22 (LXX 117:22) (cf. Matt 21:42 = Mark 12:10-11 = Luke 20:17; Acts 4:11), to which Isa 28:16 was then related through the cornerstone imagery (cf. 1 Pet 2:4-7, where Isa 28:16 and Ps 118:22 are juxtaposed). This would be consistent with the messianic and eschatological interpretations of Isa 28:16 already current in certain sectors of Judaism. (Cf. Snodgrass, *Ephesians,* 138).

26. Jeremias, *TDNT,* 1:792. Longenecker notes that Jeremias's qualification is "much too reserved" (Richard N. Longenecker, *The Christology of Early Jewish Christianity* [Naperville, Ill.: Allenson, 1970], 52).

27. Bruce admits that the wording of Eph 2:20 is from Isa 28:16, which refers to a foundation in both the Hebrew and Greek versions. In order to circumvent the obvious conclusion that ἀκρογωνιαινος thus refers to a cornerstone in the foundation, in a case of special pleading, Bruce claims that with ἀκρογωνιαῖος the Septuagint translator chose "an unsuitable designation for a foundation stone," since ἀκρογωνιαῖος "does not mean a cornerstone" (*Ephesians,* 305-6).

28. Although the evidence is slender and fairly evenly balanced, I am not as pessimistic as Ernest Best, who believes "the problem is insoluble," given our present state of knowledge (*A Critical and Exegetical Commentary on Ephesians,* ICC [Edinburgh: Clark, 1998], 286).

the words ἀκρογωνιαῖος and θεμέλιος, precisely as in Isaiah 28:16, would indicate that Paul is thinking of the lower part of the building and thus a cornerstone. Second, the texts that Jeremias produces have little to do with the context of Eph 2:20. The subject of the context of the passage is the unity of the church produced by Christ's death. As McKelvey notes, "If, however, we follow Jeremias the crucial unifying function attributed to Christ is jettisoned completely, for the stone mentioned in II Kings xxviii. 17 and Test. Sol. xxii. 7ff. was placed on the top of the two pillars . . . at the entrance of the temple simply for decorative purposes."[29] Third, the passage speaks of the dynamic process in the growth of the structure, a process not yet completed. This is the syntactical significance of the two present tense indicative verbs (αὔξει, "rises"; συνοικοδομεῖσθε, "are being built together") preceded by the present tense participle (συναρμολογουμένη, "is joined together"). Just as the body grows from the head (ἐξ οὗ, 4:16), so the building grows upward in relation to the cornerstone (ἐν ᾧ, 2:21). If the final stone were already in place, this would seem to destroy one of the primary features of the metaphor: the building is still under construction. Fourth, Jeremias's interpretation would lead to the unnatural image of a building rising to meet a topstone suspended in the air. And finally, the building metaphor appears to assume a chronological framework in which the ἀκρογωνιαῖος (Christ as cornerstone) is placed first, followed by the laying of the foundation (the apostles and NT prophets), and then the building of the superstructure (Gentile and Jewish believers) upon this foundation.

If the ἀκρογωνιαῖος can be identified as a cornerstone, what is the significance of this image? First, the cornerstone conveys a sense of primacy. It is the first stone laid in the building; it is important, necessary, and unique. This sense of Christ's primacy seems to be at the forefront of Paul's thinking throughout the immediate context. Beginning in 2:14 Paul notes that, "He *himself* [noting the emphatic position of αὐτός] is our peace." The enmity was destroyed in *his* flesh. In *himself* he has created one new man (2:15). Through *him* we have access to the Father (2:18). And most significant, Paul emphasizes the primacy of Christ in relation to the church in the phrase "Christ Jesus *himself* is the cornerstone," understanding αὐτοῦ intensively.[30] Finally, the primacy of Christ (or at least

29. McKelvey, "Christ the Cornerstone," 357.

30. In the genitive absolute, ὄντος ἀκρογωνιαίου αὐτοῦ Χριστοῦ Ἰησοῦ, the pronoun αὐτοῦ can be (a) taken, as I have done, in the predicate position in relation to Χριστοῦ Ἰησοῦ, that is, "Christ Jesus *himself*," in contrast to the apostles and prophets. (b) Or, αὐτοῦ may be related to the predicate genitive ἀκρογωνιαίου as "the cornerstone *itself*," i.e., "the essential, decisive part of the foundation (cf. 1 Cor 3:11, which contrasts the true foundation with all others)" (Krämer, "γωνία," *EDNT*, 1:268). (c) Or, least likely, αὐτοῦ may be functioning as a possessive pronoun, "the cornerstone *of it* (i.e., the foundation)."

his distinctiveness) is supported by Paul's use of a genitive absolute clause in his identification of Christ as the cornerstone, a grammatical feature that "serves to distinguish Christ from the apostles and prophets," and "draws attention to his standing and special function."[31]

Second, the cornerstone imparts harmony to the structure. As the building is constructed, the angle of the cornerstone governs all of its lines, bearings, and other angles, resulting in symmetry, coherence, and integration.[32] This idea may find support in the OT background of this passage, for in the Hebrew text of Isaiah 28:16 the "stone of testing" can be understood in the active sense.[33] Hence, "a stone may well be called *a stone of testing* if every other stone has to be laid in a line determined by it, is laid rightly or wrongly according as it is or is not true to this primary, standard stone."[34] Thus, in the same way that a cornerstone determines the lie and character of the building, so also Christ governs the growth of the church. This idea is germane to the context, for in the following phrase Paul will say that in Christ the building is being fitted together (συναρμολογουμένη) into a holy temple, also conveying the idea of harmony in the growth of the church.[35]

The metaphor of the cornerstone has a third point of significance: just as the cornerstone is the source of unity in the building, so the church is united in Christ. Indeed, this is one of the main points of the building metaphor as a whole, and the wider context as well (2:11-22). As a result of the reconciling work of Christ, the Gentile Christian has been brought into the one people of God, joining his fellow Jewish believer in the "new man," a community of fellowship in which God dwells. Lexically, this unity of the church is emphasized through repetition of "one" in the immediately preceding context[36] as well as the three-fold use of the prefix συν- in the surrounding four verses.[37]

31. O'Brien, *Ephesians*, 216.

32. W. W. Lloyd is frequently cited in support of this point: "The acrogoniaios here is the primary foundation-stone at the angle of the structure by which the architect fixes a standard for the bearing of the walls and crosswalls throughout" ("Eph. II. 20-22," *Classical Review* 3 [1889]: 419).

33. So Bruce, *Ephesians*, 305. Alternatively, the "stone of testing" may mean one that is tested and found true.

34. G. H. Whitaker, "The Chief Corner-stone," *Expositor,* eighth series 22 (1921): 471.

35. Later in Ephesians Paul will use the same word (συναρμολογούμενον, 4:16) to describe the harmony in the growth of the church sourced in Christ, here within the metaphor of the head and the body.

36. 2:14: "he has made us both one"; 2:15: "that he might create in himself one new man in place of the two"; 2:16: "reconcile us both to God in one body through the cross."

37. 2:19: συμπολῖται, "fellow citizens"; 2:21: συναρμολογουμένη, "being fitted together"; 2:22: συνοικοδομεῖσθε, "being built together."

The Interpretation of the "Building"

The third major exegetical focus in this passage relates to the phrase πᾶσα οἰκοδομή, located in 2:21: "In him *the whole building* is joined together and rises to become a holy temple in the Lord" (NIV). This translation depends on the interpreter's answer to three interrelated questions. There is a textual problem that concerns the presence of a definite article; a grammatical problem that concerns the translation of πᾶς with a singular, anarthrous noun; and a lexical problem concerning the meaning of οἰκοδομή.

While the large majority of interpreters follow the text πᾶσα οἰκοδομή,[38] a noteworthy alternative reading exists, πᾶσα ἡ οἰκοδομή (with the definite article).[39] The anarthrous variant is favored by a preponderance of the external evidence including its early date, as well as the character and wide geographical distribution of the supporting manuscripts. On internal grounds the anarthrous reading is also to be preferred. It is both the more difficult reading,[40] and the reading which best explains the origin of the other.[41]

Having decided upon the original text, the problem arises as to how this expression, πᾶσα οἰκοδομή, should be understood. The general rule of grammar would indicate that where πᾶς is followed by a singular noun without the article, the translation should be "each" or "every."[42] Following this normal pattern, the verse would be translated: "In him each several building, being fit together, grows into a holy temple in the Lord," by which Paul might be referring to a plurality of local congregations making up the universal church, just as many buildings made up the Jewish temple.[43]

---

38. πᾶσα οἰκοδομή is read by the uncials ℵ*, B, D, G, K, and Ψ as well as the minuscules 33, 181, 1739*, and the Byzantine tradition.

39. πᾶσα ἡ οἰκοδομή is read by the first corrector of ℵ, A, C, P, 81, 1739 (corrected), 1881 and others.

40. It is harder because πᾶς before a singular, anarthrous noun is usually translated as "every," implying a multiplicity of buildings in this passage. However, the context seems to imply that only one building is in view and not several. Thus, the tendency would be for a copyist to insert the article according to the sense, "the whole building" or "all the building" (which was likely the motivation behind the scribal "corrections" in ℵ and 1739).

41. While it would have been possible for the definite article to have been accidentally omitted due to a confusion of the sounds (itacism) of ἡ and the following diphthong οἰ, it is more likely that it was absent in the original but added in an attempt to clarify the sense (cf. Bruce M. Metzger, *A Textual Commentary on the Greek New Testament*, 2nd ed. [Stuttgart: Deutsche Bibelgesellschaft, 1994], 534).

42. Robertson, *Grammar*, 771.

43. For this minority position, cf. Fenton John Anthony Hort, *The Christian Ecclesia* (London: Macmillan, 1908), 164; P. W. Comfort, "Temple," *DPL*, 925; JB: "As every structure is aligned on him." It is sometimes said that this picture would nicely fit the theory that Ephesians was

However, the context would seem to demand that only one building be in view and not many, the imagery focusing on the totality rather than the detail. Thus Abbott argues:

> For to speak of the several local churches, or of the Jews and Gentiles as so many several buildings, would not be in accordance with the figure in ver. 20, or with St. Paul's language elsewhere. Moreover, he has just used a forcible figure to express the unity of the whole Church, and it would be strange if he now weakened it by speaking of several buildings.[44]

While Paul speaks of local churches elsewhere in his writings, in Ephesians there appears to be no expression of the church universal as made up of many congregations. Thus, any translation which implies a plurality of churches, such as "each several building," should be suspect due to the strength of the idea of unity in this passage, in its context, and in the letter as a whole.

Is it possible that πᾶσα οἰκοδομή can be understood, then, as referring to "the whole building" or "all the building," even without the definite article? In fact, grammarians point out that there are several classes of nouns that form an exception to the general rule[45] including proper names,[46] monadic nouns,[47] and abstract nouns.[48] In such cases, πᾶς may still mean "all" or the "whole" though not followed by the definite article. Taking a different tack, Lincoln argues that πᾶσα οἰκοδομή can be translated "all the building" due to a Hebraism that has affected Koine usage.[49] Further, it is possible that there are sufficient exceptions in biblical Greek where the anarthrous construction means "all/the whole [noun]," and thus the translation of "all the building" in Eph 2:21 is permitted simply on the force of the context.[50]

---

intended as an encyclical to churches in the cities of Asia Minor. On the other hand, this interpretation would be more plausible if Paul had in mind multiple structures growing into a ἱερόν (temple complex), but here he speaks of the shrine or sanctuary of the temple using ναός.

44. Abbott, *Ephesians and Colossians*, 74-75.

45. Cf. Robertson, *Grammar*, 771-72; C. F. D. Moule, *An Idiom Book of New Testament Greek*, 2nd ed. (Cambridge: Cambridge University Press, 1959), 94-95.

46. E.g., πᾶσα Ἱεροσόλυμα (Matt 2:3); πᾶς Ἰσραήλ (Rom 11:26).

47. Monadic nouns are "one-of-a-kind" nouns, such as "sun" or "earth." Cf. G. B. Winer, *A Treatise on the Grammar of New Testament Greek*, trans. and rev. W. F. Moulton, 3rd ed. (Edinburgh: Clark, 1882), 149-50 for examples.

48. E.g., πᾶσαν δικαιοσύνην (Matt 3:15); πᾶσα ἐξουσία (Matt 28:18).

49. Lincoln, *Ephesians*, 156. In this Lincoln is following a suggestion of Moule, *Idiom Book*, 95. But neither Moule nor Lincoln makes it clear why the grammatical form of πᾶσα οἰκοδομή in this passage should be affected by Hebraistic usage.

50. *ExSyn*, 253. A few of Wallace's examples appear to be genuine exceptions (i.e., they are not proper names nor monadic nor abstract nouns): πάσης ἐκκλησίας κυρίου, "all the assembly of the Lord" (LXX 1 Chr 28:8); πάσης φυλῆς, "the whole family" (LXX Amos 3:1); παντὶ χρόνῳ, "all the time" (Acts 1:21).

There is, however, a third related issue in the translation of πᾶσα οἰκοδομή. Should οἰκοδομή be understood as referring to a structure? Or should it be understood more abstractly, focusing on the act or process of building up? Lexically, either force is possible,[51] a distinction that roughly corresponds to the difference in English between "edifice" and "edification." If the former sense is taken, Paul's focus would be on the structure itself as it grows into a temple. For the more abstract sense, Robinson suggests the following translation: "all that is builded" or "all building that is done." He continues, "But this hardly differs from 'all the building' when we keep before our minds the thought of the building in process, as opposed to the completed edifice."[52]

It is the more abstract rendering which likely expresses Paul's intention. While not determinative, it should first be noted that οἰκοδομή is overwhelmingly used in Paul's writings with this force. Of his fourteen uses (besides the one in question), Paul uses the concrete sense at most only twice.[53] In Ephesians the word is used on three other occasions (4:12, 16, 29), and in all three instances it is used abstractly. Second, this interpretation more readily explains the absence of the definite article in the phrase, πᾶσα οἰκοδομή, noting that with abstract nouns the definite article is not essential to express the "all/the whole [noun]" idea. And, third, this view fits the context well. As Robinson explains: "St. Paul is speaking not of the building as completed, i.e. 'the edifice', but of the building as still 'growing' towards completion. The whole edifice could not be said to 'grow': but such an expression is legitimate enough if used of the word in process."[54]

Summary and Conclusion

These three interpretative problems have been chosen, first, for their illustrative benefit. In the space of a brief passage the NT exegete is presented with opportunities to use his or her skills in textual criticism, lexicography, grammar, syntax, inter-textuality (here, the use of the OT

---

51. The ambiguity of οἰκοδομή is similar to that of the English words "building" and "construction," both of which can be used of either the process itself or the result of the process.

52. J. Armitage Robinson, *Commentary on Ephesians,* 2nd ed. (London: Macmillan, 1904; reprint, Grand Rapids, Mich.: Kregel, 1979), 70-71. The abstract sense is also supported by Barth, *Ephesians,* 272, and Abbott, *Ephesians and Colossians,* 73-75.

53. The fourteen occurrences are: Rom 14:19; 15:2; 1 Cor 3:9; 14:3, 5, 12, 26; 2 Cor 5:1; 10:8; 12:19; 13:10; Eph 4:12, 16, 29. Only in 1 Cor 3:9 and 2 Cor 5:1 may it possibly have the meaning of "a building" (but cf. L&N, "οἰκοδομή," 514). In all the other uses, it has a verbal force and is consistently translated by the KJV as "edification" or "edifying." Cf. J. Goetzmann, "οἰκοδομέω," *NIDNTT,* 2:252.

54. Robinson, *Commentary on Ephesians,* 164.

in the NT), and use of context. Second, these problems are difficult, notoriously so in the cases of determining the reference of ἀκρογωνιαῖος (where respected commentators are divided), and of resolving the grammatical-lexical problem attached to the absence of the article in πᾶσα οἰκοδομή. And, third, these are exegetically significant problems, their outcome critically affecting the reader's understanding of the entire passage. While respectfully acknowledging the differing conclusions of others, we understand Paul to be speaking in this passage of a church with a foundation consisting of the apostles and prophets of the early church and with Christ as its cornerstone. The whole building, viewed as a result of an ongoing process of growth, is becoming a holy temple and divine habitation.

Ephesians 5:26

The Baptismal Metaphor and Jewish Ritual Baths

21

HELGE STADELMANN

Treatment of an exegetical-theological issue that requires careful syntactical analysis as well as research into the historical-cultural background of the passage.

Doing exegesis within the framework of historical-grammatical interpretation often requires us to study the meanings of linguistic expressions, taking into account both the syntactic and the historical contexts in which they are used by the New Testament author in question. Both of these two aspects are essential for determining the meaning of the much debated verse Eph 5:26. In the context husbands are admonished, according to the phrasing of the NIV, to love their wives *"(25b) just as Christ loved the church and gave himself up for her (26) to make her holy, cleansing her by the washing with water through the word, (27) and to present her to himself as a radiant church, without stain or wrinkle or any other blemish, but holy and blameless."*

The Syntactic Context

The purpose of Christ sacrificing himself for the church (v. 25) is unfolded in two ἵνα clauses, of which v. 26 is the first; the second (v. 27a-b) is subordinate to the participial construction of v. 26b.[1] The main verb of this first clause ([ἵνα αὐτὴν] ἁγιάσῃ / [in order] to make [her] holy) is modified by a modal participle (καθαρίσας / by cleansing [her]).[2] Thus, putting the church into a holy state is what is intended and made possible by the sacrifice of Christ (v. 25) and brought about or applied in an act of cleansing as described in v. 26.

So far, so good. We start running into difficulties, however, as soon as we try to relate the two phrases of v. 26b (τῷ λουτρῷ τοῦ ὕδατος / ἐν ῥήματι) to v. 26a. Schnackenburg leaves the question undecided as to whether ἐν ῥήματι is to be linked syntactically to the main verb (ἁγιάσῃ) or to the phrase τῷ λουτρῷ τοῦ ὕδατος.[3] Ewald, on the other hand, almost a century ago argued convincingly that the phrase "by [the] word"—being anarthrous and being placed at the very end of the verse—carries so much semantic weight of its own that it is hardly meant to be linked back to the main verb at the beginning of v. 26.[4] The expression *"by the washing of [or: with] water,"* on the other hand, is to be connected to the participle *"by cleansing,"* as its position and content make clear. But in what sense exactly is it used? And where does the phrase "through [or: in] [the] word" fit in syntactically?

Linking ἐν ῥήματι exclusively to τοῦ ὕδατος, giving it an epexegetical force (*"the water which consists of the word"*) would—according to Pjotr Pokorny—be a serious option only if it were preceded by the article (τοῦ ἐν ῥήματι), which is not the case.[5] Though this seems to be an overstatement,[6] it is true that this combination would not suggest itself as the first choice on grammatical grounds. Others have linked ἐν ῥήματι to the whole of the

---

1. A third ἵνα in v. 27c does not introduce a third clause parallel to the preceding ἵνα clauses, but is used instead of a participle construction parallel to the ἵνα clause of v. 27b (v. 27b presenting the negative aspect and v. 27c the positive aspect within the intended contrast). In substance v. 27c brings us back to the point already implied in the main verb in v. 26a (the *making holy* of the church).

2. It is rather unlikely that the aorist participle is used with a temporal nuance here. The action referred to (*"cleansing"*) is probably to be viewed as simultaneous to the main verb action *"making holy,"* though both are expressed by aorist forms.

3. Rudolf Schnackenburg, *Der Brief an die Epheser*, EKKNT 10 (Neukirchen-Vluyn: Neukirchener, 1982), 255.

4. Paul Ewald, *Die Briefe des Paulus an die Epheser, Kolosser und Philemon*, Kommentar zum Neuen Testament 10 (Leipzig: Deichert, 1905), 241. Ewald himself links the *"word"* with the *"washing of water"*: ". . . das unter Anwendung von Wort sich vollziehende Wasserbad" (ibid).

5. Pjotr Pokorny, *Der Brief des Paulus an die Epheser*, THKNT 10/2 (Berlin: Evangelische, 1992), 224 n. 48.

6. For an analogous example of an epexegetically used phrase introduced by ἐν, also without the article, see BDAG under ἐν 4.c. Concerning the use of the article there are too many exceptions, so that it would not be advisable to exclude an attributive force of the phrase ἐν ῥήματι solely on the basis of the article missing (cf. 2:11-15; 4:1; 6:12).

phrase τῷ λουτρῷ τοῦ ὕδατος. Taking *"the washing of water"* as referring to Christian baptism—and rightly so![7]—they then interpret the whole phrase as a short explanation of the "sacramental" character of baptism: water plus word (understood as either the baptismal formula[8] or as the confession of faith at baptism) together are supposed to constitute the "sacrament."[9] But if the intention of the text was to express such a combination of "water" and "word," would this not more likely have been expressed by the phrase μετὰ ῥήματος than by ἐν ῥήματι? Thus syntactically the best option would seem to be to link ἐν ῥήματι (with instrumental force) to the participle καθαρίσας.[10] In this case, the meaning would be that the *"cleansing"* is accomplished *"by the word"*[11] at the occasion of baptism (τῷ λουτρῷ . . . as a locative dative of time): *"(26) to make her holy, cleansing her at the washing of water by the Word."* How this fits into the historical and theological framework of the letter needs now to be discussed.

The Historical Context

Historically, the one Christian baptism (Eph 4:5) in New Testament times was conversion baptism (Acts 2:38ff.; 8:36-37; 9:18; 10:47-48; 16:14-15, 31ff.; etc.). In the immediate context of conversion, people who had heard and been reached by the gospel were baptized in faith in an act full of symbolism,[12] denoting the dividing line between their pre-Christian and Christian life by the immediate realization of the things symbolized as a result of God's gracious working through his Spirit.[13] So

7. Cf. Andrew T. Lincoln, *Ephesians*, WBC 42 (Dallas: Word, 1990), 375: "The definite article (lit. '*the* washing in water') may well indicate a specific event, and the readers are scarcely likely to have taken this as anything other than a reference to their experience of baptism . . ."

8. "I baptize you in the name of the Father, of the Son, and of the Holy Spirit." Through this formula or word baptism is thought to acquire its cleansing power, cf. Schnackenburg, 255, taking reference to the famous explanation of Augustine, *In Joh Ev Tract* 80.3: "Detrahe verbum, et quid est aqua nisi aqua? Accedit verbum ad elementum, et fit sacramentum, etiam ipsum tamquam visibile verbum."

9. Cf. Joachim Gnilka, *Der Epheserbrief*, HTKNT 10/2, 3rd ed. (Freiburg: Herder, 1982), 281f.

10. So T. K. Abbott, *Epistles to the Ephesians and to the Colossians*, ICC (Edinburgh: Clark, 1897), 168.

11. How this is to be understood will be explained below in the final section ("The Intended Meaning").

12. E.g., the burying of the pre-Christian life and rising out of that grave to a new Christian existence (Rom 6:3ff.); the water as a symbol of the washing away of sins (Acts 22:16; 1 Pet 3:21); the baptismal formula proclaiming the Lordship of the triune God over the new convert (Matt 28:19).

13. Cf. Roland Gebauer, "Taufe und Ekklesiologie," *Bausteine zur Erneuerung der Kirche*, ed. Helge Stadelmann (Giessen: Brunnen, 1998), 152-62, who explains conversion baptism on

it is not surprising to find an allusion to Christian baptism in a context that speaks of the life-transforming consequences of Christ's sacrifice as in Eph 4:25ff.

But this allusion to the baptismal "water bath" deserves to be explored in more detail, as this will lead us to a better grasp of the particular aspect of early Christian baptism expressed in this verse. What traditio-historical background may help us to interpret it meaningfully in terms of its own time, rather than anachronistically reading back later Christian baptismal views into this apostolic text? Quite a number of exegetes think that the author alludes here to Jewish (or even Hellenistic) bridal baths as a cleansing rite forming an analogy to Christian baptism.[14] More specifically they view Ezek 16:8-14 as the background for the setting of this text, where the marriage between Yahweh and his unfaithful wife Israel is metaphorically described, mentioning also the cleansing of the bride. But this washing is only a minor and incidental aspect in Ezekiel 16, and it is not described as a means to become pure, blameless, and holy. The emphasis is laid on the beauty of the wife used as a means for adultery. So there is only a superficial resemblance between this imagery and the one in the context of Eph 4:26. Lindemann also points out that in the Ancient Near East bridal baths certainly were not conducted by the bridegroom, whereas in Ephesians it is emphasized that it is Christ who purifies his church.[15] So, perhaps another background for the baptismal metaphor in Eph 4:26 is more fitting.

Several commentators have mentioned that in early Judaism, and especially in Qumran, holiness, cleansing, and ritual washing occasionally were linked (1QS 3:9f; 1QH 11:10ff.).[16] But it is surprising that no one seriously traced Jewish ritual baths as the most likely background to a Christian baptismal theology as expressed in Eph 4:26 (and, in fact, baptism as represented in Acts, cf. 22:16).[17] The fact that the *washing of*

---

the one hand as a human act of faith, and at the same time on the other hand as the occasion of God's giving of salvation. If baptism is not practiced as conversion baptism, these human and divine aspects may fall apart; but in NT conversion baptism they coincide.

14. So, e.g., Abbott, *Ephesians and Colossians,* 168; Gnilka, *Epheserbrief,* 280; Lincoln, *Ephesians,* 375, sees this only as "a secondary connotation."

15. Andreas Lindemann, *Der Epheserbrief,* ZBK 8 (Zurich: Theologisher, 1985), 103f.

16. Gnilka, *Epheserbrief,* 281; Lincoln, *Ephesians,* 375; Franz Mussner, *Der Brief an die Epheser,* ÖTKNT 10 (Gütersloh: Gütersloher, 1982), 158.

17. A notable exception is the informative essay by William Sanford LaSor, "Discovering What Jewish Miqvaoth Can Tell Us About Christian Baptism," *Biblical Archaeology Review* 13, no. 1 (January/February 1987): 52-59; cf. Bryant G. Wood, "To Dip or to Sprinkle? The Qumran Cisterns in Perspective," *Bulletin of American Schools of Oriental Research* 256 (Fall 1984): 45-60. Perhaps the fact that George Foot Moore, *Judaism in the First Centuries of the Christian Era,* vol. 1 (Cambridge, Mass.: Harvard University Press, 1927), 332ff., claimed a fundamental difference between Jewish proselyte baptism and baths of purification (not yet

water" here marks the occasion at which *"cleansing"* takes place could
have suggested such a background, because καθαρίζειν in the NT normally
is used denoting cleansing from ritual contamination or impurity (Matt
8:3; John 3:25; Acts 10:15; Heb 9:13).[18] The fact that Paul takes up this
term in Eph 4:26 does not necessarily mean that he literally viewed baptism as cleansing from ritual impurity (acquired through "unclean" body
liquids, contact with a menstruant woman or a corpse, etc.). By NT times
the spiritualization of Jewish cultic concepts, as well as the metaphorical
identification of religious concepts with certain (spiritualized) terms out of
the cultic realm, already had a long history; and originally cultic or ritual
features often had been transferred into the realm of ethical concepts.[19]
The idea of describing baptism in (transposed) terms of Jewish ritual
bathing suggested itself readily on two grounds: (a) ritual bathing had
nothing to do with outward cleansing, but rather with making a defiled
person acceptable in the presence of a holy God; and (b) ritual bathing
was widespread in first-century Judaism, as we know today, and therefore could easily become a pattern by which to describe certain aspects
of Christian baptism.

As Roland Deines has proven by an exhaustive analysis of the archaeological evidence of Jewish stone vessels used for purification rites,
by NT times the interest in ritual purity acquired by ritual bathing (cf.
Leviticus 11–15) was no longer to be found only in priestly circles in
the context of their temple service, but spread as part of Pharisaic piety
through the many local synagogues to wider Jewish circles.[20] Therefore it
is not surprising to find the Jewish ritual baths or Miqvaoth of this time,
not only around the Jerusalem temple, but also in the Herodian quarter
and near the Essene gate on Mount Zion, in the Hasmonean palaces
at Jericho, the palaces of Herod the Great, and in many rural villages

---

knowing the evidence of more recent archaeological findings and the Qumran writings) may
have led exegetes to see only points of difference between ritual baths and baptism, instead of
also considering traditio-historical links between the two.

18. L&N, 535.

19. See Hans-Jürgen Hermisson, *Sprache und Ritus im altisraelitischen Kult: Zur 'Spiritual-
isierung' der Kultbegriffe im AT* (Neukirchen-Vluyn: Neukirchener, 1965); Hans Wenschkewitz,
Die Spiritualisation der Kultusbegriffe Tempel, Priester und Opfer im Neuen Testament (Leipzig:
Pfeiffer, 1932); cf. Helge Stadelmann, *Ben Sira als Schriftgelehrter*, WUNT 2:6 (Tübingen: Mohr
Siebeck, 1980), 99-112.

20. Roland Deines, *Jüdische Steingefässe und pharisäische Frömmigkeit*, WUNT 2:52 (Tübingen: Mohr Siebeck, 1993), 4ff., 17, 96, 140, 166ff., 197, 244. According to Rabbi Shimeon
ben Eleazar "purity broke into Israel" in the times of Hillel (*t. Shabb.* 1.14 et par.). Living a
holy life in the presence of a holy God required the exclusion of (ritual) impurity (Lev 11:44).
Therefore ritual bathing was a must for priests—and became seminal for all who wanted to
share priestly purity.

with synagogues.[21] Even if not all the stepped pools excavated during the last fifty years were official ritual baths,[22] there can be no doubt about the Essene idea of priestly living even for the laity. Along with this the Pharisaic "holiness movement," with its widespread practices of washing and bathing to achieve ritual purity and holy living in combination with obedience to the word of the law, set a pattern on which the Christian teaching on baptism could draw in certain respects. Behind Jewish ritual baths there was no "sacramental" idea of a holy rite conveying *ex opere operato* spiritual goods. As the Qumran texts show, cleansing from sin in connection with the "water of purity" requires both the expiatory working of the Spirit of God and a human spirit of humility, righteousness, obedience, and submission under the commandments of God. Without this attitude, it would even be unacceptable to take such a bath of purification (1QS 2:25f; 3:3-9).[23] The Miqvaoth, with their steps on which the impure person went down on the one side of a small dividing wall into the water, immersing the whole body with a desire to be made clean by God, and then stepping out of the water on the other side of the dividing wall, thus symbolically making clear the intention to live a pure life, easily could become an example for what happens in the once-and-for-all bathing of Christian baptism: the repentant sinner being washed by God and henceforth living a sanctified life in the presence of a holy God.

Certain features of such a Christian reinterpretation of Jewish purification rites can already be seen in the Gospel of John. The Jewish concern for purification is repeatedly mentioned there (John 2:6; 3:26ff.; 11:55; 18:28). But in the context of the washing of the feet of his disciples, Jesus

21. Temple mount: Meir Ben-Dov, *In the Shadow of the Temple: The Discovery of Ancient Jerusalem* (New York: Harper & Row, 1985), 150ff. Herodian Quarter: Nahman Avigad, *The Herodian Quarter in Jerusalem* (Jerusalem: Keter, 1991), 19f. Essene Quarter: Rainer Riesner, *Essener und Urgemeinde in Jerusalem*, 2nd ed. (Giessen: Brunnen, 1998 [reprint from *ANRW II 26/2*, ed. W. Haase (Berlin: de Gruyter, 1995)]), 1811ff. Hasmonean and Herodian Palaces: Ehud Netzer, *Die Paläste der Hasmonäer und Herodes des Grossen* (Mainz: Zabern, 1999), 9ff., 25, 28, 30-33, 64, 79, 103, 107. Other: Ronny Reich, "The Great Mikveh Debate," *Biblical Archaeology Review* 19, no. 2 (March/April 1993): 52, speaks of 300 stepped or immersion pools identified so far; cf. Deines, *Jüdische Steingefässe*, 4ff., 72 (Gamla), 112 (Bethany), 140 (Samaria). According to *m. Miqw.* 1.1.4.6ff. a valid Miqveh needed to hold forty Seah (about 527 liters) of ritually clean water.

22. While Ronny Reich in his (Hebrew) Ph.D. dissertation takes the maximalist position, identifying 300 excavated stepped pools as Miqvaoth (*Miqvaoth in the Second Temple Period and the Period of the Mishnah and Talmud* [Jerusalem: Hebrew University, 1990]), Benjamin G. Wright III takes the minimalist position, doubting on the basis of the relatively few instances in which Miqvaoth were mentioned in ancient Jewish literature that most of those pools actually served ritual purposes ("Jewish Ritual Baths—Interpreting the Digs and the Texts," in *The Archaeology of Israel*, ed. Neil Asher Silberman and David Small [Sheffield: Sheffield Academic Press, 1997], 190-214).

23. Cf. Helge Stadelmann, *Epheserbrief* (Neuhausen-Stuttgart: Hänssler, 1993), 238f.

tells them that they are already καθαροί (13:10); the deeper reason for this is not some ritual bathing, but being cleansed by the word of Jesus: ἤδη ὑμεῖς καθαροί ἐστε διὰ τὸν λόγον ὃν λελάληκα ὑμῖν (15:3).[24]

The Intended Meaning

Based on this background, the intended meaning of Paul in Eph 5:26 can now be described in the following way: The loving self-sacrifice of Christ on behalf of his church (v. 25b) had the purpose of making her holy, with holiness being used quite often in Ephesians as an attribute of the people set apart for God (1:1, 15, 18; 2:19; 3:18; 4:12 in a positional sense; 1:4; 5:3 in an ethical sense). This (positional) "setting apart" Christ brought about by cleansing his people (καθαρίσας = modal participle). It took place in the context of Christian baptism, which is analogous to the Jewish ritual baths, picturing a bathing in water with a cleansing effect before God. Being reinterpreted in a Christian sense, it is not the obedient bathing that conveys ritual cleansing, but Christ alone on the basis of his death (v. 25; Tit 2:14).[25] The instrument of this cleansing was the word (v. 26b; John 13:10; 15:3), which is best understood as the word of the gospel proclamation, which conveys to the believer what it proclaims (cf. 1:12-14; 6:19).[26] Thus, if one wants to retain sacramental terminology, it would be possible to speak of the "sacramental" character of the word of the gospel in the life of the believer; but it seems to be anachronistic to interpret baptism in Eph 5:26 in sacramental terms. The baptismal metaphor here seems best to be understood against the background of Jewish ritual baths, interpreted in the Christian context in non-ritual Christ-centered terms.

---

24. Cf. Deines, *Jüdische Steingefässe*, 251-57.

25. Thus the cleansing power of the blood of Christ is mentioned repeatedly (1:6; cf. 1 Pet 1:2; Heb 9:14, 22-23). The ritual baths under the Old Testament order in themselves could not yet accomplish this (cf. Heb 6:2; 9:10).

26. In other instances in the NT the means of this cleansing before God is the shed blood of Christ (Heb 9:14; 1 John 1:7, 9).

Philippians 2:6-7

22

The Image of God and the Cross of Christ

TIMOTHY B. SAVAGE

Exegetical and devotional insights gained from tracing a key biblical theme.

For insight into what it means to be human, few concepts are as important as the image of God. According to the Holy Scriptures, it is this image that distinguishes men and women from all other living beings. We are created in God's image.

But how should we view this distinction? What does it mean to be created in the image of God? The question has prompted much speculation—so much that at least one commentator believes the notion of God's image has been grossly over-interpreted.[1]

For this reason, it is important to confine our inquiry to what the biblical text explicitly says about God's image. Remarkably, it says very little. In the first chapter of Genesis, where we find the fullest account of the bequest of the divine image, there is only the slightest elucidation of the term—namely, that to be created in God's "image" means to share in his

---

1. Thus James Barr, "The Image of God in the Book of Genesis—A Study of Terminology," *BJRL* 51 (1968): 24.

"likeness" (Gen 1:26). Human beings are in some sense *like God!*[2] This is a stunning revelation, but it raises the question, "In what sense?"

The near context offers only oblique clues. The image of God is a possession shared equally between male and female (Gen 1:27). It qualifies human beings to rule over creation (vv. 26 and 28). It is related to the command to multiply and fill the earth (v. 28). These are enticing tidbits, but hardly sufficient to provide a satisfactory understanding of the divine image. Little is added in the rest of Genesis or, for that matter, in the Old Testament as a whole. On a subject of such strategic importance as the investiture of God's own image, the Hebrew Scriptures are surprisingly silent.

Doubtless this explains why the matter of God's image became a topic of debate among later Jewish exegetes. An interpretive gap needed to be filled. Beginning with the most valuable clue, that bearing God's image meant in some sense to be like God, the rabbis argued that human beings must possess the attribute most closely associated with the Almighty: his irradiating glory. When Rabbi Bana'ah came to the cave of Machpelah (where, according to tradition, Adam was buried), he heard the voice of God saying, "You have beheld the likeness of my likeness"—an experience that prompted Bana'ah to declare, "I have discerned Adam's two heels, and they were like two orbs of the sun" (*b.B.Bat.* 58a). Similarly, Rabbi Levi: "The ball of Adam's heel outshone the sun . . . how much more the beauty of his face" (*Qoh.Rab.* VIII. 1.2).[3] Made in God's likeness, Adam naturally radiated his glory.

The connection between the image and the glory of God is comparatively late in the rabbinical writings, but it does represent a form of exegesis present in the first century AD. The former Pharisee Paul repeatedly made the link between divine image and glory, and in contexts where Adam is at least implicit.[4] But by far the most profound of Paul's insights is the direct connection he forged between the glorious image of God and the person of Jesus Christ. The disclosure reaches its apogee in the fourth chapter of 2 Corinthians, where the now converted rabbi reveals his conviction that the bedazzling glory of God received its sharpest definition in "the face of Jesus Christ," who *is* "the image of God" (2 Cor 4:4 and 6).[5]

---

2. The word "likeness" in Gen 1:26 defines and limits the meaning of "image."

3. Cf. *Lev.Rab.* XX.2 and *Pesiq.Rab.Kah.* 36b; for other refs. see Jacob Jervell, *Imago Dei: Gen 1, 26f. im Spätjudentum, in der Gnosis und in den paulinischen Briefen* (Göttingen: Vandenhoeck & Ruprecht, 1960), 100-1.

4. See Rom 1:21-23; 8:29-30; 1 Cor 11:7; 15:40-49; and 2 Cor 3:18–4:6.

5. Cf. Col 1:15; and see Timothy B. Savage, *Power Through Weakness: Paul's Understanding of the Christian Ministry in 2 Corinthians*, SNTSMS 86 (Cambridge: Cambridge University Press, 1996), 127-29.

Undoubtedly it was on the Damascus road that this reality hit home to Paul.[6] Formerly, he had abominated the very name of Jesus. He persecuted Christians.[7] But on that fateful day, when confronted by divine glory and moved to inquire into the identity of the heavenly apparition—"Who are you, Lord?"—the pharisaic zealot received the astonishing reply, "I am Jesus" (Acts 9:5). It is astonishing because it exposed the hitherto unthinkable anomaly that the glory of God could be expressed in a person who was accursed by God.[8] Or to put it more sharply: it was above all in the broken body of a crucified carpenter that one discovers what it means to be like God.

The full extent of this discovery is unraveled in one of the most breath-taking compilations of words ever committed to writing. In the second chapter of his letter to the Philippians, Paul opens a penetrating window on the very nature of God. It is in Jesus Christ, writes the apostle, that we behold "the form of God" (Phil 2:6). The term μορφῇ θεοῦ is the near equivalent of εἰκὼν θεοῦ.[9] Existing in the form of God, Jesus naturally radiates the image of God. He is one in being with the Lord of the universe. He is "equal to God" (ἴσα θεῷ, v. 6).

But the apostle is not interested in mere ontological identities. He wishes to regale his readers with the *implications* of this dramatic union of Jesus and God. How does the divine image work out in practice? To answer this question, we need look only at Jesus. In him the image receives both a radical and a paradoxical expression. Radical, because Jesus never uses the divine image for personal gain. According to Philippians 2, he refuses to exploit his lofty position to win human applause through eye-popping exploits or dramatic feats of power.[10] Paradoxically, because he interprets it as a call to do just the opposite—to empty himself (ἑαυτὸν ἐκένωσεν, Phil 2:7), to pour himself out on a Roman gibbet (θανάτου δὲ σταυροῦ, v. 8), to endure a form of execution reserved for hardened criminals and

6. Cf. Seyoon Kim, *The Origin of Paul's Gospel,* 2nd ed. WUNT 2:4 (Tübingen: Mohr Siebeck, 1984).

7. Cf. Acts 8:3; 1 Cor 15:9; Gal 1:13; and Phil 3:6.

8. Cf. Deut 21:23 with Acts 5:30 and Gal 3:13; and see discussion of the curse of crucifixion in Savage, *Power Through Weakness,* 131-33.

9. So Ralph P. Martin, *Carmen Christi: Philippians ii. 5-11 in Recent Interpretation and in the Setting of Early Christian Worship,* SNTSMS 4 (Cambridge: Cambridge University Press, 1967), 99-120.

10. Thus interpreting ἁρπαγμός in Phil 2:6 to mean "the act of snatching," and especially snatching for personal gain; cf. C. F. D. Moule, "Further Reflexions on Philippians 2:5-11," in *Apostolic History and the Gospel: Biblical and Historical Essays presented to F. F. Bruce on his 60th Birthday,* ed. W. Ward Gasque and Ralph P. Martin (Exeter: Paternoster, 1970), 266-68, 271-76; Roy W. Hoover, "The Harpagmos Enigma: A Philological Solution," *HTR* 64 (1971): 118; and N. T. Wright, "ἁρπαγμός and the Meaning of Philippians 2:5-11," *JTS* 37 (1986): 339-44.

rebellious slaves.[11] For Jesus, to exist in "the form of God" means to take on "the form of a slave."[12]

The descent of our Lord to an ignoble cross must not be viewed as an abdication of divine prerogatives.[13] Rather, it is the perfect expression of those prerogatives.[14] At Golgotha, we receive the quintessential portrait of what it means to be like God. We behold the glory of God in the face of Jesus Christ. We see the very image of God. We see *the humility of self-emptying love*.[15]

Here is a truth whose relevance to humanity is incalculably precious. By radiating the unblemished image of God, Jesus provides a paradigm of what every human ought to be like. Humanity's distinguishing mark should be its capacity for self-giving love.

No wonder we were created male *and* female (Gen 1:27). Without this plurality, the divine image could never be expressed. In the Godhead, as well as in humanity, there must be at least two beings, one to lavish self-emptying love and another to receive it.

This also explains why the bequest of God's image was accompanied by the command to multiply and fill the earth (Gen 1:28). What could bring God greater glory than the dissemination of his self-giving image to every corner of the planet? Such a project would be accomplished through the far-flung migrations of his image bearers.

Nor is it surprising that it is specifically humans who are enjoined to rule over creation (Gen 1:26 and 28). Those whose hands have been anointed with the unique capacity of sacrificial service will inevitably cultivate a terrestrial paradise.

Yet the great tragedy of the human race is that this image of self-giving love so quickly and universally degenerates into self-grasping greed. When offered the fruit of personal glory and exaltation, we readily take and eat (cf. Gen 3:6). But we eat to our impoverishment. By seeking to be more like God, by seeking a position as high as his, we actually fall away from

---

11. So Martin Hengel, *Crucifixion in the Ancient World and the Folly of the Message of the Cross* (London: SCM, 1977), 1-10.

12. Note the intended antithetical interplay between μορφὴν δούλου in Phil 2:6 and 7; cf. the interpretation of N. T. Wright, "Adam in Pauline Christology," in *Society of Biblical Literature 1983 Seminar Papers*, ed. Kent Harold Richards (Chico, Calif.: Scholars, 1983), 379-81. The phrase ὃς ἐν μορφῇ θεοῦ ὑπάρχων in v. 6 should be taken causally, not concessively: "*because* he existed in the form of God . . ." (so C. F. D. Moule, "The Manhood of Jesus in the New Testament," in *Christ, Faith and History: Cambridge Studies in Christology*, ed. S. W. Sykes and J. P. Clayton [Cambridge: Cambridge University Press, 1972], 97).

13. *Pace* many commentators on Philippians: Calvin, Lightfoot, Bruce, Collange.

14. Cf. Morna Hooker, "Philippians 2:6-11," in *Jesus und Paulus: Festschrift für Werner Georg Kümmel zum 70. Geburtstag*, ed. E. Earle Ellis and Erich Grässer (Göttingen: Vandenhoeck & Ruprecht, 1975), 163-64.

15. Thus Phil 2:8 ἐταπείνωσεν ἑαυτόν.

him. We exchange his glory for a darkened image. We turn his image into an idol. We use what was intended for God's glory, his image in us, for personal aggrandizement. We become worshipers of ourselves (cf. Rom 1:21-23).[16] This idolatry of self plunges humanity into the darkness of a living death (cf. Rom 1:24-32) and subjects creation to the agonizing groans and pain of childbirth (Rom 8:18-22).

But the travails of childbirth always come with a promise. And for humans it is the hope of a new creation, borne in the arms of the ultimate Self-Giving One. He who resisted the allure of self-worship, and thereby vanquished the power of sin; he who absorbed in his own body the hideous entailments of self-worship, the separation from God that is our death, and thereby paid the penalty for our sin—he it is who, if we put our trust in him, can renew us according to the image of the One who created us (cf. Col 3:10). To every man or woman who has eyes to see the glory of God radiating in the face of Jesus Christ comes the blessed assurance of transformation into that same self-giving image, from one level of glory to another (2 Cor 3:18).[17]

The restoration of the image of God in the people of God, exhibited in sin-defying expressions of self-giving love, is a beacon of hope to a dark world. Just one person demonstrating the love of Christ can cause the praise of many to redound to our matchless Creator. One such person, in whom we have witnessed a consistent manifestation of the image and glory of God, is the friend and teacher in whose honor the essays of this book have been compiled. For giving us reason to extol the grace of God, we offer these thoughts with deepest gratitude.

---

16. The word εἰκών in Rom 1:23 has a double meaning. By worshiping themselves people make *idols* of God's *image!* Cf. A. J. M. Wedderburn, "Adam in Paul's Letter to the Romans," in *Studia Biblica 1978*, vol. 3, *Papers on Paul and Other New Testament Authors,* ed. E. A. Livingstone, JSNTSup 3 (Sheffield: JSOT, 1980), 417-19.

17. See the discussion in Savage, *Power Through Weakness,* 145-54.

Colossians 1:12-20

23

Christus Creator, Christus Salvator

E. EARLE ELLIS

Analysis of a passage for exposition, moving from historical background and literary structure to basic themes for preaching.

Prerequisite to a good expository sermon is a study of the historical background and literary structure of the particular biblical text. In that light the inspired teaching of the passage will be best received and expounded.

The Historical Setting of Colossians

The letter "to the holy and faithful brothers[1] in Christ at Colossae" is attributed to "Paul, apostle of Christ Jesus . . . and Timothy the brother,"

---

1. This probable translation of τοῖς ἐν Κολοσσαῖς ἁγίοις καὶ πιστοῖς ἀδελφοῖς (Moule) indicates that the letter's immediate recipients are Paul's coworkers, i.e., the brothers (Ellis), who are then to read and explain it to the whole congregation. Cf. Col 3:16; 4:16; C. F. D. Moule, *The Epistles of Paul the Apostle to the Colossians and to Philemon*, Cambridge: Cambridge University Press, 1957, 45f.; E. Earle Ellis, "Paul and His Co-Workers Revisited," in *History and Interpretation in New Testament Perspective* (Leiden: Brill, 2001), 85-97; idem, "Paul and His Co-Workers," *Prophecy and Hermeneutic in Early Christianity,* WUNT 18 (Tübingen: Mohr Siebeck, 1978), 17f. The precise translation of the masculine gender and the occasional generic masculines in the essay reflect my theological understanding and a commitment to hear and to read the text within its historical and theological meaning.

i.e., coworker.[2] In accordance with good historical method one "tests the genuineness and demonstrates the non-genuineness" of one's sources.[3] Colossians is attested as Paul's letter in the canon of Marcion[4] at about AD 140[5] and was being cited as such in the later second century by writers from Gaul,[6] Italy,[7] North Africa,[8] and Egypt.[9] Its genuineness was never questioned in the patristic period, but in F. C. Baur's nineteenth-century Hegelian reconstruction of early Christianity[10] Colossians was rejected on internal grounds. It was declared to be pseudo-Pauline because it reflected "the period of Gnosticism," which in Baur's view began only in the second century,[11] and because it had a vocabulary, style, and theological themes different from the letters that Baur accepted.[12] The first objection was short-lived since gnosticizing elements were shown to be present in the false teaching opposed by first-century Christian writers.[13]

It is a pleasure to dedicate this article to Harold Hoehner, a Christian brother, friend, and NT colleague for over thirty years.

2. Cf. Markus Barth and Helmut Blanke, *Colossians*, trans. Astrid B. Beck, AB 34B (New York: Doubleday, 1994), 138f.; Ellis, *Prophecy*, 17f.

3. Ernst Bernheim, *Lehrbuch der historischen Methode und der Geschichtsphilosophie* (Leipzig: Duncker & Humblot, 1914; reprint, New York: Franklin, 1970), 332.

4. Tertullian, *Against Marcion* 5, 19; cf. Tertullian, *Adversum Marcionem*, ed. Ernest Evans (Oxford: Clarendon, 1972), 629-37, 646. Cf. John Knox, *Marcion and the New Testament* (Chicago: University of Chicago Press, 1942), 40.

5. So, Adolf von Harnack, *Marcion: The Gospel of the Alien God*, trans. John E. Steely and Lyle D. Bierma (Durham, N.C.: Labyrinth, 1990), 17f. = GT: 25-29, cf. 121*-24* (Harnack's reconstruction of Marcion's mutilated text of Colossians).

6. Irenaeus, *Against Heresies* 3.14.1 (ca. AD 180).

7. The Muratorian Canon (ca. AD 170).

8. Tertullian, *Prescription against Heretics* 7, middle (ca. AD 200).

9. Clement of Alexandria, *Stromata* 1.1, end (ca. AD 194).

10. F. C. Baur, "Die Christuspartei in der korinthischen Gemeinde . . . ," *Tübinger Zeitschrift für Theologie* 4 (1831): 61-206, 76, 136, 205f. = idem, *Ausgewählte Werke*, ed. Klaus Scholder, 5 vols. (Stuttgart: Frommann, 1963-75), 1:1-46, 16, 76, 145f. Cf. E. Earle Ellis, *The Making of the New Testament Documents*, Biblical Interpretation Series 39 (Leiden: Brill, 1999), 441f.

11. F. C. Baur, *Paul*, 2nd ed., 2 vols. (Peabody, Mass.: Hendrickson, 2003 [1845]), 2:7-32 = GT: 2:11-36. Baur (2:35 = GT: 2:39) followed E. T. Mayerhoff, and he gave less attention to differences of style and vocabulary. But others who accepted Baur's conclusions about authorship have increasingly relied on these factors. Cf. Werner Georg Kümmel, *Introduction to the New Testament*, rev. ed., trans. Howard Clark Kee (Nashville: Abingdon, 1975), 340ff.

12. Baur, *Paul*, 2:106-111 = GT: 2:116-122, regarded as genuine only four Pauline letters—Romans, 1—2 Corinthians, and Galatians. A. Hilgenfeld (*Einleitung in das Neue Testament* [Leipzig: Fues, 1875], 236-47, 328-48), a member of Baur's school, extended the genuine letters to include Philippians, 1 Thessalonians, and Philemon. These seven letters are those "undisputed" by contemporary followers of the Baur tradition.

13. E.g., by J. B. Lightfoot, "The Colossian Heresy," *St. Paul's Epistles to the Colossians and to Philemon*, 2nd ed. (London: Macmillan, 1879; reprint, Grand Rapids, Mich.: Zondervan, 1974), 73-113, whose views received striking confirmation with the discovery of the Dead Sea Scrolls. Cf. Pierre Benoit, "Qumran and the New Testament," *Paul and Qumran*, ed. J. Murphy-

Objections to Paul's authorship on the basis of a vocabulary, style, and theology absent from the Apostle's earlier letters continued throughout the twentieth century.[14] But they were undermined, if not discredited, by two decisive developments in the research, the recognition of the role of the secretary[15] and the identification of numerous preformed traditions, many non-Pauline, in virtually all of Paul's letters.[16] The Apostle of necessity used a secretary, and preformed traditions in Colossians total at least 42 percent of the letter.[17] In the light of these developments there are today no adequate reasons, literary or historical, for rejecting the attributed authorship when the author of the letter is recognized to be not necessarily the one who penned it or who dictated it verbatim but the one under whose direction and authority the letter was composed and sent.[18]

Colossians is one of five prison letters of Paul.[19] Imprisonment was used in the Roman world not as a punishment but only for disorderly conduct, protective custody, and detention for trial or for execution.[20] Such detentions known to us in the Apostle's ministry that were long enough for writing letters were one in Caesarea, Palestine (AD 58-60), and two in Rome (AD 61-63 and 67-?68).[21]

O'Connor (Chicago: Priory, 1968, 16f.); E. Earle Ellis, "The Opposition Common to the [Apostolic] Missions," *Making*, 314-18; idem, "Paul and his Opponents," *Prophecy*, 80-101, 112f.; Peter T. O'Brien, *Colossians, Philemon*, WBC 44 (Waco, Tex.: Word, 1982), xxx-xxxviii.

14. E.g., Victor Paul Furnish, "Colossians," *ABD*, 1:1092ff.; cf. Eduard Lohse, *Colossians and Philemon* (Philadelphia: Fortress, 1971), 90f., 181ff. = GT: 138ff., 255ff. But see George E. Cannon, *The Use of Traditional Materials in Colossians* (Macon, Ga.: Mercer University Press, 1983), 175ff., 196-229. Also affirming the genuineness of Colossians and recognizing "the weight of traditional materials" in it are Barth and Blanke, *Colossians*, 64-72, 114-126. Cf. also O'Brien, *Colossians, Philemon*, xli-xlix.

15. Otto Roller, *Das Formular der paulinischen Briefe* (Stuttgart: Kohlhammer, 1933), 17-20; E. Randolph Richards, *The Secretary in the Letters of Paul*, WUNT 2:42 (Tübingen: Mohr Siebeck, 1991), 23-67, who show that the secretary in antiquity often influenced the vocabulary and style of a letter, even to the extent of becoming the coauthor of it. Cf. Ellis, *Making*, 115n, 305n, 326f.

16. Cf. Ellis, *Making*, 69-117, 139, 407-18, and the literature cited; for Colossians cf. Barth and Blanke, *Colossians*, 64-72; Cannon, *Traditional Materials*, 11-49 (confessions and hymns), 54-65, 82-94 (vice and virtue lists), 95-131 (household code), who concludes that Colossians is so permeated with traditional materials that literary analysis "has little value in determining authorship" (177).

17. Cf. Ellis, *Making*, 108-11, 116f., 326f.

18. Cf. Barth and Blanke, *Colossians*, 72: "the test of an author's originality and creativity lies not in the scarce or abundant endorsements of other people's words, formulations, and ideas, but in what he makes of given materials."

19. Cf. Eph 6:20; Phil 1:10, 13, 17; Col 4:3, 18; 2 Tim 1:8; 2:9; Phlm 9, 23.

20. Ellis, *Making*, 267ff. It was used domestically as a punishment for slaves.

21. Acts 23:23f.; 24:27; 28:16, 30; 2 Tim 1:8, 16f.; 4:6ff. Cf. 1 Clem 5:7; *Apocryphal Acts of Paul* 11:1-5; Ellis, *Making*, 267f., 283f. But see 2 Cor 11:23. A detention in Ephesus has been inferred from 1 Cor 15:32, but the "beasts" there very probably refer to Paul's opponents. See Ellis, *Making*, 268f.; Gordon D. Fee, *The First Epistle to the Corinthians*, NICNT (Grand

Colossians, along with Ephesians and Philemon, was very likely composed and sent from Caesarea[22] although traditionally it has been given a Roman provenance during Paul's first imprisonment there.[23] Favoring Caesarea are (1) Paul's plans to go to Spain (Rom 15:24), later qualified to fit in an intervening visit to Colossae (Phlm 22); the qualifier is quite compatible with a journey from Caesarea after his expected release from prison there, but it is difficult to understand if the visit were undertaken from Rome, over 1000 miles to the west of Colossae. The plans to go to Spain were not canceled at Rome but, as the evidence shows,[24] were carried out.

(2) If Ephesians, Colossians, and Philemon were carried to the recipients at the same time by Tychicus,[25] as is probable, the omission of Onesimus from the circular letter of Ephesians is understandable on a westward overland journey from Caesarea: Onesimus was left at Colossae (Phlm 10ff.; cf. Col 4:9). It is passing strange on an eastward journey from Rome. (3) The mention of several of the same coworkers both in the letters and in Paul's collection visit to Jerusalem, preceding the Caesarean imprisonment, also supports a Caesarean provenance for the letters.[26] (4) The number of preformed traditions in Ephesians and Colossians that have a Semitic-Greek idiom and style[27] are a secondary support for a Caesarean provenance although they would, of course, be fully compatible with a Pauline letter from Rome.[28]

The Literary Form of Colossians 1:12-20

The passage incorporates a confession (1:12ff.) and a following hymn (1:15-20). That the confession goes with the hymn and not with the

Rapids, Mich.: Eerdmans, 1987), 700f.; Archibald Robertson and Alfred Plummer, *First Epistle of St. Paul to the Corinthians,* 2nd ed., ICC (Edinburgh: Clark, 1914), 361f. For the (unsuccessful) hypothesis of an Ephesian imprisonment cf. George Simpson Duncan, *St. Paul's Ephesian Ministry* (London: Hodder & Stoughton, 1929), 66-123, 111-14.

22. Ellis, *Making,* 266-75, and the literature cited; cf. Kümmel, *Introduction,* 346ff.; Bo Reicke, "The Historical Setting of Colossians," *RevExp* 70 (1973), 429-38; already, H. A. W. Meyer, *Philippians and Colossians and . . . Philemon* (New York: Funk & Wagnalls, 1885), 198; idem, *Epistle to the Ephesians* (New York: Funk & Wagnalls, 1884), 299ff.

23. E.g., Codices A B¹ K P; cf. O'Brien, *Colossians, Philemon,* l-li.

24. 1 Clem 5:6f.; *Acts of Peter (Vercelli)* I.1-3; Muratorian Canon, middle; cf. Ellis, *Making,* 278-83; idem, "'The End of the Earth' (Acts 1:8)," in *History,* 53-63.

25. Cf. Eph 6:21; Col 4:7.

26. I.e., Aristarchus, Luke, Timothy, Tychicus. Cf. Acts 20:4, 6 ("we"); Eph 6:21; Col 1:1; 4:7, 14; Phlm 1, 24; Ellis, *Making,* 271-75. Only Luke and Aristarchus accompanied Paul to Rome (Acts 27:1f.).

27. E.g., Eph 1:3-14; 4:25–5:14; Col 1:12-20; 3:18–4:1. Cf. Ellis, *Making,* 105-10, and the literature cited. See below, notes 30, 35, 61, 62.

28. E.g., Phil 2:6-11; cf. Ellis, *Making,* 275ff.; idem, "Preformed Traditions and Their Implications for the Origins of Pauline Christology," in *History,* 133-50.

preceding prayer (1:9-11c)[29] is supported by two indicators: (1) There is an opening imperatival participle, μετὰ χαρᾶς εὐχαριστοῦντες (1:12), which in common Jewish usage began a confessional statement.[30] (2) The change from the second to the first person plural, although not unusual in Paul's writings, points to a shift from the Apostle's intercession for the Colossians (1:9ff.) to a common thanksgiving of the church (1:12ff.)[31]:

> 12 With joy giving thanks to the Father
> Who made us fit for a share of the appointed lot of the saints in light
> 13 Who delivered us from the power of darkness and transferred us into the kingdom of his beloved Son
> 14 In whom we have redemption, the forgiveness of sins.

The thanksgiving opens with a participial clause introducing three relative clauses. This liturgical and poetic style, suited to congregational usage,[32] and the words and idiom unusual or unique in Paul's letters[33] make probable that this is a preformed non-Pauline piece employed in the worship of Paul's churches before he incorporated it into his letter. Col 1:13b-14 marks a transition from the work of the Father (1:12-14) to the cosmic and redemptive work of the Son, *Christus Creator* and *Christus Salvator* (1:15-20).[34]

The literary form of 1:15-20 also has the markers of poetic structure, that is, "the typical distinguishing features of the (oriental) hymnic style . . ."[35] It contains three major divisions: the middle stanza opens with the

---

29. So, Lohse, *Colossians and Philemon*, 34 = GT: 68f.; Ralph P. Martin, *Colossians and Philemon*, NCB (London: Oliphants, 1974), 53; Cannon, *Traditional Materials*, 12-19; cf. Eduard Norden, *Agnostos Theos: Untersuchungen zur Formengeschichte religiöser Rede* (Berlin: Teubner, 1913; reprint, Darmstadt, 1956), 250-54. Otherwise and traditionally: O'Brien, *Colossians, Philemon*, 18f.; Barth and Blanke, *Colossians*, 172f.; J. D. G. Dunn, *The Epistles to the Colossians and to Philemon*, NIGTC (Grand Rapids, Mich.: Eerdmans, 1996), 67f.; Lightfoot, *Colossians*, 140.

30. Cf. Lohse, *Colossians and Philemon*, 34f. = GT: 68f.; David Daube, "Participle and Imperative in I Peter," in Edward Gordon Selwyn, *The First Epistle of Peter*, 2nd ed. (London: Macmillan, 1947; reprint, Grand Rapids, Mich.: Baker, 1981), 467-88, esp. 471-80. The editors of the Greek text place the phrase "with joy" in v. 11.

31. Col 1:12, ἡμᾶς A C D F G M lat syr bo, 13; 1:14, ἔχομεν. The ὑμᾶς at 1:12 ℵ B is, then, probably an assimilation to 1:9 (ὑμῶν).

32. Cf. Cannon, *Traditional Materials*, 14f.; Norden, *Agnostos Theos*, 250-54.

33. E.g., κλῆρος ("lot"); ἀπολύτρωσις, identified here and in the preformed hymn at Eph 1:3-14 as "the forgiveness of sins"; the phrases "saints in light," and "kingdom of his beloved Son." Cf. Lohse, *Colossians and Philemon*, 32f., 39; Ellis, *Making*, 107f.; Cannon, *Traditional Materials*, 15; Norden, *Agnostos Theos*, 250-54.

34. Cf. Meyer, *Philippians and Colossians*, 233. It may be that Paul himself coupled the two pieces when he composed the letter.

35. Barth and Blanke, *Colossians*, 228, first detailed, apparently, by Norden, *Agnostos Theos*, 141-276, 380-87, 250-54. Further, cf. Reinhard Deichgräber, *Gotteshymnus und Chris-*

emphatic αὐτός (1:17); the first and last begin with relative clauses (1:15, 18b: ὅς ἐστιν), each followed by two causal clauses (1:16, 19: ὅτι) that are elaborated in a rhythmic succession of phrases:[36]

> 15   Who is the image of the invisible God, the firstborn (πρωτότοκος) before
>   all creation[37]
> 16   Because in him all things were created in the heavens and on the earth
>   The visible and the invisible
>   Whether thrones or lordships
>   Or rulerships or authorities.
>   All things have been created through him and for him.
> 17   And he is before all things
>   And all things subsist in him
> 18   And he is the head of the body, the church.
>   Who is the beginning, the firstborn from out of the dead bodies (νεκρῶν)
>   In order that he might continue to be first (γένηται πρωτεύων) in all
>   things
> 19   Because *it* pleased *the Father for* all the fulness to dwell in him
> 20   And through him to reconcile all things to himself[38]
>   Having made peace through the blood of his cross
>   Through him, whether the things on the earth
>   or the things in the heavens.

Whether or not the hymn has been slightly reworked to fit it more closely to the concerns of the letter,[39] it generally reflects a preformed character.[40] Its similarities with an earlier non-Pauline preformed pas-

---

tushymnus in der frühen Christenheit (Göttingen: Vandenhhoeck & Ruprecht, 1967), 143-55; Klaus Wengst, *Christologische Formeln und Lieder des Urchristentums*, Gütersloh 1972, 170-80; Jean Noël Aletti, *Colossiens 1, 15-20*, AnBib 91 (Rome: Biblical Institute Press, 1981).

36. Cf. Norden, *Agnostos Theos*, 252ff.; Cannon, *Traditional Materials*, 20. For literature on the passage cf. Michael Wolter, *Der Brief an die Kolosser. Der Brief an Philemon* (Gütersloh: Gütersloher, 1993), 70f.

37. The preposition "before" is required both by the subsequent assertion that "all things have been created through him" (Col 1:16d) and by the meaning of πρωτότοκος. Cf. F. F. Bruce, *The Epistles to the Colossians, to Philemon, and to the Ephesians*, NICNT (Grand Rapids, Mich.: Eerdmans, 1984), 58f.; Lohse, *Colossians and Philemon*, 44, 46, 48f. = GT: 82, 84f., 87f.; Lightfoot, *Colossians*, 146-150, 154f. Otherwise: Dunn, *Colossians*, 88f., 91. On πρωτότοκος cf. Barth and Blanke, *Colossians*, 246ff.

38. Reading αὐτόν = ἑαυτόν and referring to God the Father. Cf. Bruce, *Colossians*, 74n.

39. E. g., perhaps adding Col 1:18. Cf. the repetition of certain key words of Col 1:18 in Col 1:22, 24; 2:11, 17ff. (σῶμα); 1:24 (ἐκκλησία); 2:10, 19 (κεφαλή).

40. Col 1:15-20 is a distinct and independent pericope, moving from a thanksgiving to the Father (Col 1:12-14) to a hymn to the Son (1:15-20), from the first person (1:12-14) to the third (1:15-20). Col 1:21f. shifts to the second person (introduced by the Pauline idiom, "then . . . but now," ποτέ . . . νυνί; cf. Gal 4:8f.; Rom 6:21f.; 11:30) and from the cosmic perspective of the hymn to the interpretation and application of it to the Colossians. Cf. Ellis, *Making*, 108f.

sage, 1 Cor 8:6,[41] as well as the presence of vocabulary[42] and idiom[43] unusual or unexampled in the Pauline letters, argue also that this hymn was not created by the Apostle.[44] It was clearly composed by a highly gifted pneumatic, most probably an apostle of Jesus Christ, within the Pauline mission or in an allied mission.[45] In the light of affinities with 1 Cor 8:6, it may have been used in Pauline congregations before the Apostle's detention in Caesarea, although a Caesarean provenance for the hymn cannot be excluded.

The Teaching of Colossians 1:12-20

An expository sermon on Col 1:12-20 could not expound every teaching in the text (and should not attempt to). Using a traditional three-point outline, plus an introduction and conclusion, it can bring out important aspects of the Apostle's teaching. Supplemented with illustrations at appropriate intervals, it can apply the passage to the theological instruction and to the practical needs of the particular congregation.

Each preacher will choose aspects of the passage that he (or she) wishes to include in the sermon, and each will find illustrations suitable to them. The following will summarize, without illustrations, teachings of the passage that to my mind are significant and that fit into a unified theme for exposition and for preaching.

41. Like 1 Cor 8:6, Col 1:16f. presents the Son as one "through whom and for whom all things have been created" (16) and reconciled (20). Cf. Ellis, *Making*, 87-90; idem, "Preformed Traditions and Their Implications for the Origins of Pauline Christology," 133-150. But contrast Rom 11:36.

42. I.e., the hapaxes ὁρατός (16), θρόνος (16), πρωτεύειν (18), ἀρχή (18, as a title for Christ), ἀποκαταλλάσσειν (20, except in another non-Pauline preformed piece, Eph 2:16), εἰρηνοποιεῖν (20). Cf. Ellis, *Making*, 105f., 108f.; Lohse, *Colossians and Philemon,* 42 = GT: 78f.

43. E.g., "the visible and the invisible" (16), "blood of his cross" (20). Cf. Lohse, *Colossians and Philemon,* 42 = GT: 78f.

44. So Wolter, *Der Brief an die Kolosser,* 71f.; Lohse, *Colossians and Philemon,* 41f.; Bruce, *Colossians;* Martin, *Colossians,* 65. Otherwise: Seyoon Kim, *The Origin of Paul's Gospel,* 2nd ed. WUNT 2:4 (Tübingen: Mohr Siebeck, 1984), 144-49; Dunn, *Colossians,* 84ff.; Moule, *Colossians,* 60ff. Of course, the hymn *becomes* Pauline in that the Apostle incorporates, reworks, and affirms it in his letter.

45. Cf. Ellis, *Making*, 311-314; idem, *History,* 138-141. Hypotheses of a pre-Christian or non-Christian origin of (parts of) the hymn are not convincing since they fail to show that Paul's more likely sources, i.e., Christian pneumatics, could not have produced it. "Preformed" does not necessarily nor ordinarily mean "pre-Pauline." Some writers are prone to confuse the two terms.

Introduction

In Colossians 1:12-20 the apostle Paul combines a thanksgiving to God the Father (1:12-14) with a hymn to the Son (1:15-20) to teach their respective roles in the deliverance and redemption, that is, the salvation[46] of those who have been brought to faith in Christ (1:4, ἐν Χριστῷ) and who have continued steadfast in their faith toward Christ (2:5, εἰς Χριστόν). He presents the Father as the one who has, already in the past, accomplished this salvation; and the Son, who is the visible "image of the invisible God" (1:15), as the one through whom God the Father has brought it to pass.[47] But how is this deliverance and redemption already a present reality and how does it remain future? What is the nature of the Son, that is, Jesus Christ, that qualifies him to be the mediator of the Father's act of salvation? Let us see how the passage before us deals with these questions.

I. God's Gracious Action of Salvation (Col 1:12-14)

The saving action of God presupposes that man has need of it. That need is central to Paul's teaching and is expressed elsewhere in terms of the condition of the whole human race as it is descended from our first parents, Adam and Eve, and as our race exists "in Adam": "All in Adam die and all in Christ shall be made alive."[48] More explicitly, Paul teaches that,

> Just as through one man sin entered into the world
> And death through sin
> So also death came upon all men
> Because[49] all had sinned.[50]

46. The term "salvation" (σωτηρία) does not appear in Colossians, but it encompasses both the terms "to deliver" (1:13, ῥύεσθαι) and "redemption" (1:14, ἀπολύτρωσις). Cf. Luke 1:71; Acts 7:25; Matt 1:21; Acts 2:38ff.

47. The Holy Spirit appears in Col 1:8, where the fruit of the Spirit, i.e., love, is expressed as "your love in the Spirit." Cf. Gal 5:22. But he is not in view in the present passage.

48. 1 Cor 15:22. This translation reflects what the next verse, 1 Cor 15:23, makes clear: the "all" in Adam is not identical with the "all" in Christ.

49. The phrase ἐφ᾽ ᾧ was taken as a relative and in the Old Latin text and in Jerome's Latin Vulgate was translated "in quo" = "in whom" (cf. Bonifatius Fischer et al., eds., *Biblia Sacra iuxta Vulgatum Versionem*, 2 vols. [Stuttgart: Deutsche Bibelgesellschaft, 1969]). Augustine used this translation to support the doctrine of original sin. It is probably better translated as a causal conjunction, as it is in Phil 3:12; cf. 4:10, but also like those passages the past tense of the verb of the subordinate clause (ἥμαρτον) is antecedent to the past-tense action of the main verb (διῆλθεν). Consequently, although Augustine (or better, the Latin translation) probably mistook the force of the ἐφ᾽ ᾧ, he was correct in expounding the text to teach original sin, i.e., that all men had sinned in Adam's act. See below, note 50.

50. I.e., in the Garden. On the use of the aorist for the English pluperfect cf. Ernest DeW. Burton, *Syntax of the Moods and Tenses in New Testament Greek*, 3rd ed. (Edinburgh: Clark, 1898), 22-28. Further, note the discussion and the literature cited in David A. Sapp, "An Introduction to

> ... For just as through the disobedience of one man
> The many were constituted sinners
> So also through the obedience of one *man*
> The many will be constituted righteous.[51]

That is, Paul declares that all, that is, "the many" who belong to Adam by descent, are condemned to death for his sin because they all existed corporately in Adam,[52] all participated corporately in that sin, and all corporately died in Adam (Gen 3:19; 1 Cor 15:22).[53] In the following verses of Romans 6 he says similarly that "God's chosen ones" (Rom 8:33; Col 3:12), those who "by grace through faith" belong to Christ, also corporately were put to death with Christ in AD 33[54]:

> Our old man [Adam] was crucified with him. . . .
> So also reckon yourselves to be dead in *the sphere of* sin
> And living with God in Christ Jesus.[55]

This past corporate participation of believers in Christ's AD 33 death and resurrection, particularly in his resurrection, Paul expresses more fully in Eph 2:5f.:

Adam Christology in Paul [Rom 5:12-21]," (Ph.D. diss., Southwestern Baptist Theological Seminary, 1990), 225-31: "[A pluperfect sense] is the required meaning when [as in Rom 5:12d] the subordinate clause denotes an action antecedent to the past action of the main clause" (228).

51. Rom 5:12, 19. Just as the all in Adam are not identical with the all in Christ (1 Cor 15:22), so also the many constituted sinners are not identical with the many constituted righteous (cf. Rom 5:17).

52. This corporate solidarity in Adam's sin and in Christ's righteousness is best understood in terms of the corporate nature of their persons. Cf. E. Earle Ellis, *Paul's Use of the Old Testament* (Grand Rapids, Mich.: Eerdmans, 1957; reprint, Eugene, Ore.: Wipf & Stock, 2003), 58ff.; idem, "Corporate Personality," *The Old Testament in Early Christianity*, WUNT 54 (Tübingen: Mohr Siebeck, 1991; reprint, Eugene, Ore.: Wipf & Stock, 2003), 110-16, and the literature cited; idem, "The Corporate Dimension of Human Existence," *Pauline Theology: Ministry and Society* (Grand Rapids, Mich.: Eerdmans, 1989; reprint, Lanham, Md.: University Press of America, 1998), 8-17; idem, "The Believer's Corporate Existence in Christ," *Christ and the Future in New Testament History*, NovTSup 97 (Leiden: Brill, 2000), 148-64, 171ff.; Sang-Won [Aaron] Son, *Corporate Elements in Pauline Anthropology*, AnBib 148 (Rome: Pontificio Istituto Biblico, 2001); and the literature cited.

53. Eph 2:8; Rom 3:22ff.

54. Cf. also Gal 2:19f.; Rom 7:4: "You were put to death *by God* (ἐθανατώθητε) in the sphere of the law through the body of Christ. . . ." The passive very probably implies a reference to God. Cf. C. E. B. Cranfield, *The Epistle to the Romans*, 2 vols., ICC (Edinburgh: Clark, 1975, 1979), 1:335f.; Thomas R. Schreiner, *Romans*, BECNT 6 (Grand Rapids, Mich.: Baker, 1998), 349f.; J. D. G. Dunn, *Romans*, 2 vols., WBC 38A-B (Dallas: Word, 1988), 1:361f.; J. B. Lightfoot, *Notes on the Epistles of Paul* (London: Macmillan, 1895), 301. That is, the penalty of God's law has been executed on Christ's individual and corporate body.

55. Rom 6:6, 11, bringing out the force of the dative-locative. Cf. Ellis, *Pauline Theology*, 12f.

[God] made us alive together with Christ (συνεζωοποίησεν τῷ
Χριστῷ) . . .
And raised us up with him
And made us sit with him in the heavenly places in Christ Jesus.

It is expressed even more sweepingly in Rom 8:29-30:

> For those whom [God] foreknew
> He also predestined *to be* conformed to the image of his Son . . .
> And whom [God] predestined, these he also called
> And whom he called, these he also justified
> And whom he justified, these he also glorified.

Col 1:12-14 sets forth the same present eschatology, but it does this
not, as in Romans 5–8 and in Ephesians 2, in terms of a corporate inclusion of all God's chosen ones in Christ's death, resurrection, and exaltation in AD 33, but in terms of an individual incorporation into him at
one's conversion.[56] It proclaims a deliverance from the sphere of darkness
and a transference into the domain of the kingdom of God's beloved
Son (1:13) as a three-fold act of God the Father: God made us fit, or
worthy; he rescued us; and he transferred us into Christ's kingdom.[57] In
God's gracious purpose the individual actualization, although temporally
separated, does not exclude the prior corporate reality. Nor is the prior
corporate reality independent of the later individual actualization. Both
are complementary parts of one inseparable whole whose fulfillment is
as certain as the character and the word of God himself.

In the realm of Christ's kingdom, that is, "in Christ" (1:14, ἐν ᾧ),[58]
believers now possess the redemption (ἀπολύτρωσις). This redemption
implies, as we have seen above, a previous bondage from which they
have been ransomed,[59] and it is strikingly apparent in, although it is not
limited to, the forgiveness of sins.

56. So, O'Brien, *Colossians, Philemon*, 27. Cf. Rom 8:1.
57. Already, H. Alford, *The Greek Testament*, 3rd ed., 4 vols. (London: Rivingtons, 1856-
61), 3:192. Cf. Lohse, *Colossians and Philemon*, 36 = GT: 72; O'Brien, *Colossians, Philemon*,
27f.
58. For the demonstration of the locative force of this idiom cf. Adolf Diessmann, *Die
neutestamentliche Formel "in Christo Jesu"* (Marburg: Elwert, 1892).
59. So B. B. Warfield, "The New Testament Terminology of Redemption," *The Person and
Work of Christ* (Philadelphia: Presbyterian & Reformed, 1950), 429-475, 440ff.; Leon Morris,
"Redemption," in *The Apostolic Preaching of the Cross*, 3rd ed. (Grand Rapids, Mich.: Eerdmans, 1965), 11-64, esp. 40-51. Otherwise: David Hill, *Greek Words and Hebrew Meanings*,
SNTSMS 5 (Cambridge: Cambridge University Press, 1967), 49-81, 73ff.; F. Büchsel, "ἀπολύτρωσις," *TDNT*, 4 (1967), 351-356, 354f. That ἀπολύτρωσις has at least the implication
of a paid ransom (Morris, Warfield) and not only liberation (Büchsel, Hill) must be left for
another discussion.

It also involves a sharp contrast and a spiritual conflict that is expressed elsewhere[60] as a deeply Jewish ethical dualism between darkness and light, a dualism that is perhaps most dramatically elaborated in the Qumran tractate 1QM on the war of the sons of light against the sons of darkness.[61] The redemption that is corporately a present reality points to an individual actualization in "the redemption of our bodies" at the future resurrection of the dead and in the life of the world to come.[62] But who is the One through whom and for whom God the Father has accomplished this great redemption? Who is the Son into whose kingdom believers have been incorporated? A hymn to Christ in the next six verses addresses these questions.

II. Christ: The Head of Creation, the Head of the Church (Col 1:15-20)

This is a stupendous hymn to the person and work of Christ. With reference to his person it presents him as "the image of the invisible God"[63] and the "firstborn" (πρωτότοκος) who is "prior to and supreme over" the whole creation.[64] The term "firstborn" can have both connotations as well as the meaning, the first in a series. It was given the latter interpretation, that is, Christ as the first creature, by the Arians in the fourth century[65] and by Jehovah's Witnesses today. But it cannot have that significance in Col 1:15 since the hymn goes on to teach that "he is before all things" (1:17) and that "all things," that is, the whole creation was created "in him," "through him" and "for him" (1:16). The hymn gives this staggering ascription to a man who had been ignominiously executed about twenty-five years before Colossians was composed, and it had been used even earlier in the congregations of the Pauline and probably of other

60. Matt 4:16; 6:23; Rom 2:19; 13:12; 2 Cor 4:6; 6:14; Eph 5:8; 6:12; 1 Pet 2:9; 1 John 1:5-8; cf. Luke 16:8; 2 Pet 2:17.

61. 1QS 3:13, 20f.; 1QM 1:1; 13:5, 10ff., passim. Cf. Florentino García Martínez, *The Dead Sea Scrolls Translated* (Leiden: Brill, 1994); idem and Eibert J. C. Tigchelaar, *The Dead Sea Scrolls Study Edition*, 2nd ed., 2 vols. (Leiden: Brill, 2000); Yigael Yadin, *The Scroll of the War of the Sons of Light Against the Sons of Darkness*, Oxford 1962; K. G. Kuhn, "The Epistle to the Ephesians in the Light of the Qumran Texts," in *Paul and Qumran*, ed. Jerome Murphy-O'Connor (Chicago: Priory, 1968), 115-31 = GT: *NTS* 7 (1960-61), 334-46. Otherwise: Hans Conzelmann, "φῶς," *TDNT*, 9 (1974), 325f., 347f.

62. Cf. Rom 8:23; 1 Cor 15:42-49.

63. Col 1:15; cf. Rom 8:29.

64. Col 1:15. Cf. Moule, *Colossians*, 64f.; see above, note 37.

65. Cf. Bernard J. F. Lonergan, *The Way to Nicea* (Philadelphia: Westminster, 1976), 68-87; F. L. Cross and E. A. Livingstone, ed., *The Oxford Dictionary of the Christian Church*, 3rd ed. (New York: Oxford University Press, 1997), 99f. (Arianism).

apostolic missions.[66] What was the basis and background for an early Christian pneumatic to compose such an exalted acclamation to Jesus and for the apostle Paul to affirm it and to include it in his letter to the Colossians?

The primary basis for the ascriptions given to Christ in Col 1:15-19 was in all likelihood the author's own experience of the resurrected Lord. It was this that according to John's Gospel evoked from the skeptical apostle Thomas the confession, "my Lord and my God,"[67] that prompted the apostle John to call Jesus "the only begotten God,"[68] and that caused the apostle Paul to refer on occasion to Christ as "God over all things, blessed forever,"[69] as "our great God and Savior Jesus Christ"[70] and as "the image of God,"[71] and to regularly apply to Christ Old Testament passages referring to Yahweh.[72] The conscious recognition among the apostles of Christ that their Lord was indeed the incarnate manifestation of Yahweh came as an explosive revelatory experience in his resurrection appearances; it was not a slowly developing idea. It was brought to literary expression over time as they expounded the Old Testament in the light of that revelation. For Col 1:15-17 it involved an application to Christ of Old Testament teachings on divine wisdom.

The "history of religions" school,[73] apparently, led some to speak of "wisdom" Christology in Col 1:15-20 as rooted in "Hellenistic" Judaism over against "Palestinian" Judaism. But this geographical dichotomy has, in fact, no historical basis. In both Palestine and the diaspora some Jews were "Hellenists," that is, lax in their observance of the ritual Law, and some were "Hebraists" = "the circumcision party," that is, strictly

66. On the preformed character of the piece see above, note 40.

67. John 20:24-28. Cf. Herman N. Ridderbos, *The Gospel According to John*, trans. John Vriend (Grand Rapids, Mich.: Eerdmans, 1997), 647f.

68. John 1:18. Cf. Brooke Foss Westcott, *The Gospel According to John*, 2 vols. (London: Murray, 1908; reprint in 1 vol., Grand Rapids, Mich.: Baker, 1980), 1:28, 66ff. Otherwise: Ridderbos, *John*, 58f.

69. Rom 9:5. Cf. Cranfield, *Romans*, 2:464-70. Otherwise: Ernst Käsemann, *Commentary on Romans*, trans. Geoffrey W. Bromiley (Grand Rapids, Mich.: Eerdmans, 1980), 259f. = GT¹: 247f.

70. Tit 2:13. Cf. I. Howard Marshall, *The Pastoral Epistles*, ICC (Edinburgh: Clark, 1999), 279-82.

71. 2 Cor 4:4. Cf. Kim, *Origin of Paul's Gospel*, 229-33, passim.

72. E.g., Rom 10:9, 13; 2 Cor 3:16ff.; Phil 2:9ff. Cf. David B. Capes, *Old Testament Yahweh Texts in Paul's Christology*, WUNT 2:47 (Tübingen: Mohr Siebeck, 1992).

73. E.g., Wilhelm Bousset, *Kyrios Christos* (Nashville: Abingdon, 1970 [1913]), 31-60 = GT: 1-26, passim, who had an Enlightenment, essentially Epicurean, worldview as a confessional presupposition, had to explain how a human and nonmiraculous Jesus that fitted his worldview could become the divine/human figure presented in the New Testament. He used, among other things, an alleged dichotomy between "Palestinian" and "Hellenistic" Judaism to create his revisionist history.

observant.[74] But after more than 300 years under Greek culture, all Judaism was conceptually influenced in some measure and form by Greek thought: "From the third century B.C. . . . a new world of ideas forced its way into the complex of Jewish wisdom," especially in the areas of anthropology, soteriology, and eschatology.[75]

The hymn in Col 1:15-20 is utilized by Paul to present Christ as the hypostasis of the divine wisdom in whom, through whom, and for whom the whole universe was brought into being. It does this, as do other New Testament writings,[76] by interpreting the Old Testament Creation and Fall passages[77] Christologically. In this case it does so by interpreting the creation accounts of Genesis by the eulogy to a personified divine wisdom in Prov 8:22-31.[78] The hymn may also reflect descriptions of God's wisdom that had come to expression in other biblical interpretations and in elaborations of intertestamental Judaism.[79] In this way it set forth a Christological interpretation of Old Testament thought that both countered and transformed Greek conceptions of divine wisdom ($\sigma o\phi i\alpha$/ חכמה).[80] In this respect Col 1:15-20 is similar to the midrash on Gen 1:1-5 in the Prologue of the Gospel of John that also offered a Christological alternative to Stoic conceptions of the divine word ($\lambda o\gamma os$/דבר).[81] What

---

74. E.g., Acts 6:1; cf. Ellis, *Making*, 287f., 315; idem, "The Circumcision Party and the Early Christian Mission," *Prophecy*, 116-128. Somewhat differently: Oscar Cullmann, "The Significance of the Qumran Texts for Research into the Beginnings of Christianity," *The Scrolls and the New Testament*, ed. Krister Stendahl (New York: Harper, 1957), 25-32.

75. Rudolf Meyer, "φαρισαῖος," *TDNT*, 9 (1974), 11-35, 21; idem, "Σαδδουχαῖος," "σάρξ" *TDNT*, 7 (1971), 35-54, 46, 117ff.; Erik Sjoberg, "πνεῦμα," *TDNT* 6 (1968), 377ff., showed the influence of Hellenistic conceptions on even the strictest Judaism of the period. Cf. David Daube, *New Testament Judaism* (Berkeley: University of California Press, 2000), 5: Col 1:15-18 "is good rabbinic doctrine—once it is granted that Jesus is the Messiah."

76. Luke 3:38; 23:43; John 1:1-5; Rom 5:12-21; 1 Cor 11:7ff.; 15:22, 45; 2 Cor 11:3; 1 Tim 2:8–3:1a; Heb 1:2. Cf. 1 Cor 1:24.

77. E.g., Gen 1–3; Ps 8:3-8; 33:6; Prov 8:22-31.

78. So, C. F. Burney, "Christ as the ΑΡΧΗ of Creation," *JTS* 27 (1925-26), 160-177; W. D. Davies, *Paul and Rabbinic Judaism,* 2nd ed. (London: SPCK, 1955), 150ff., 172; cf. N. T. Wright, "Poetry and Theology in Colossians 1. 15-20," *NTS* 86 (1990), 455-58. But see Barth and Blanke, *Colossians,* 238f.; Lohse, *Colossians and Philemon,* 46f. = GT: 85, whose own preference for a "Hellenistic," i.e., diaspora Jewish background also has problems (see above, note 75).

79. E.g., Ben Sira = Sirach = Ecclesiasticus 1:4, 9; 24:1-7; Wisdom 7:27; Philo, *On the Sacrifices of Abel and Cain* 8 (III); *Allegorical Interpretation* I, 43 (on Gen 2:8): The "heavenly wisdom is of many names; for [Moses] calls it 'beginning' and 'image' and 'vision of God'. . . ." Cf. Ellis, "Wisdom and Knowledge in 1 Corinthians," *Prophecy*, 48f.; idem, *Making*, 88ff.

80. Cf. Ulrich Wilckens, "σοφία," *TDNT* 7 (1971), 473: "[The Stoic ideal of] σοφία as knowledge is the διάθεσις ["disposition"] which corresponds to the λόγος that constitutes the unity of the cosmos, . . ." The Stoic Emperor Marcus Aurelius (AD 161-80) so speaks of the cosmos: "From you are all things, in you are all things, for you are all things" (*Meditations* 4, 23).

81. John 1:1-5. Cf. Ellis, *Making*, 166f.

Stoic philosophy ascribed to a kind of pantheistic divine wisdom Paul, by this hymn, attributes to Jesus Christ, both as the Creator of the present world and also as the supreme head, the beginning (ἀρχή, 1:18),[82] of the world to come.

The section's final chord (1:20) returns to the soteriological theme of its opening (1:12-14).[83] It again presents God the Father as the initiator and the Son as his agent "to reconcile all things" (ἀποκαταλλάξαι τά παντα).[84] The reconciliation that removes the hostility and pacifies the enmity between God and his rebellious creatures has two aspects and produces two outcomes. The first aspect is that man in his sin, in his egocentrism is hostile toward God, and the second is that God in his fixed and righteous wrath toward all evil is hostile toward sinners.[85] Yet God in his love for sinners has taken the initiative to effect a reconciliation.

To "reconcile" an enemy means to remove the hostile situation. For those who persist in rebellion against God, the hostility will be removed by their own death.[86] But for elect believers, God's chosen ones, it was removed, from God's side, by "the blood of his cross" (1:20), in which Christ paid the death penalty for sin[87]; from the human side the reconciliation is accomplished and is still being accomplished by the gospel proclamation through which man is brought back into a loving and righteous relationship with God. Col 1:12-20 is intended to celebrate this gracious redemption and the glorious possessions and prospects of the people of God.

82. In the Greek Old Testament and in the New Testament ἀρχή may denote supremacy or temporal priority. In Col 1:18 it appears to include both aspects. Cf. Gerhard Delling, "ἀρχή," *TDNT* 1 (1964), 481-84.

83. Cf. Lohse, *Colossians and Philemon*, 61 = GT: 103: The "right understanding of the cosmological statements of the first part of the hymn is disclosed only by the soteriological statements of the second strophe [of the hymn]."

84. The term occurs in the New Testament only at Col 1:20f. and Eph 2:16. But the cognate, καταλλάσσειν, is used by Paul in Rom 5:10; 1 Cor 7:11; 2 Cor 5:18ff.

85. Cf. John R. W. Stott, *The Cross of Christ* (Leicester: Inter-Varsity, 1986), 195-202.

86. Cf. Ellis, "New Testament Teaching on Hell," *Christ*, 179-99, 180n. E.g., Rom 2:8f.; 6:23; Phil 3:18f.; 2 Thess 1:7ff.; 2:8-11.

87. Cf. Leon Morris, "Reconciliation," in *The Apostolic Preaching of the Cross*, 3rd ed. (Grand Rapids, Mich.: Eerdmans, 1965), 186-223.

James 1:19-27

24

Anger in the Congregation

DONALD J. VERSEPUT

A study of James 1:19-27 within its first-century context to show that it is a connected argument, not a collection of unrelated proverbs.

I t would not be an overstatement to suggest that Jas 1:19-27 is uniquely important for understanding the epistle attributed to James, the brother of Jesus. As we shall soon see, this much-neglected pericope marks a major transition in James's letter. With the introduction of the three-part admonition in 1:19, the author abruptly shifts the addressees' attention from the potentialities of their situation to the appropriate action in view of their identity as a "reborn" community. By thus standing at the head of the letter body, the instruction of Jas 1:19-27 signals the reader as to the prevailing tenor of the subsequent injunctions. For this reason alone the passage warrants scrupulous investigation.

Unfortunately, the coherence of Jas 1:19-27 has been occasionally obscured by competing conceptions of the document's literary character. The magisterial commentary of Martin Dibelius, published in 1921, has proven especially influential in this regard. It was Dibelius's contention that since the superscription in Jas 1:1 is the only epistolary component in

the entire composition, it is "impossible to consider Jas an actual letter."[1]
Instead, he read the text as a collection "of unconnected sayings which
have no real relationship to one another" and concluded that "the entire
document lacks continuity in thought."[2] Not unexpectedly, he found in
1:19-27 a complex web of individual sayings loosely attached around
the general theme of hearing the word.[3] The three-part aphorism in 1:19
together with its appendix in 1:20 was thought to have been included
by the ancient author for its urgent appeal to "be quick to hear." To this
traditional maxim, vv. 21-25 were then added as an elaboration about
hearing and doing. Next, v. 26 was joined to the expanding unit for its
affinity to the second part of the introductory triplet, "be slow to speak."
And, finally, v. 27 was appended to the whole by means of a catchword
in order to conclude on the very note with which the author had begun,
that of doing and not just hearing. Thus, for Dibelius, the entire section
consisted of a series of sayings concerning the proper response to the word,
among which the matter of speech was merely an incidental element.

But a half century after the publication of Dibelius's work, new winds
began to blow. First one, then another scholar challenged Dibelius's reading
of James's document.[4] The combined effect was compelling. The infatua-
tion with the process of textual composition that characterized Dibelius's
work slowly gave way to a search for the meaning in the completed text.
Nor was the lack of a continuity that might be immediately apparent to
the modern reader deemed sufficient to stigmatize a work as hopelessly
incoherent. As a result, a fresh effort is currently underway to locate the
inner cohesion of James's writing.

In the light of these developments, it is certainly advisable to take
another look at the crucial text of Jas 1:19-27. Rather than accepting
Dibelius's skepticism regarding the epistolary genre of James's composition, we shall proceed from the conviction that the text we have before
us was intended to be read as a letter and not as an unreflected collection
of traditional sayings material. Already in 1930, H. Windisch helpfully
observed that the opening address "to the twelve tribes of the Diaspora"

1. Martin Dibelius, *James*, rev. Heinrich Greeven, trans. Michael A. Williams, Hermeneia
(Philadelphia: Fortress, 1976), 2.
2. Ibid., 2, 3.
3. Ibid., 108-9.
4. Key voices in the discussion of the 1970s and 80s were: Fred O. Francis, "The Form
and Function of the Opening and Closing Paragraphs of James and I John," *ZNW* 61 (1970):
110-27; Gottfried Schille, "Wider die Gespaltenheit des Glaubens: Beobachtungen am Jakobusbrief," *Theologische Versuche IX*, ed. J. Rogge and G. Schille (Berlin: Evangelische, 1977), 71-89;
Leo G. Perdue, "Paraenesis and the Epistle of James," *ZNW* 72 (1981): 241-56; Wiard Popkes,
Adressaten, Situation und Form des Jakobusbriefes (Stuttgart: Katholisches Bibelwerk, 1986);
Hubert Frankemölle, "Das semantische Netz des Jakobusbriefes: Zur Einheit eines umstrittenen
Briefes," *Biblische Zeitschrift* 34 (1990): 161-97.

associated James with a family of letters to the Diaspora exemplified by, among others, Jeremiah 29 and *2 Bar* 78–87.[5] Such epistles typically consoled the scattered people of God with the assurance that, despite their current afflictions, God would indeed triumphantly fulfill his promises. At the same time, they exhorted their audience on how to live in the interim. Adopting this pattern, James appropriately begins with a note of encouragement to the readers in the face of their situation (1:2-18), before moving on to matters of instruction in the letter body of 1:19–5:11. Moreover, given this generic identification, an important clue for reading the work is conveniently provided: the proper setting in which to encounter the epistle is its oral performance before a gathered congregation.

Receiving the Word in Gentleness (James 1:19-25)

The transition from the exordium (1:2-18) to the new segment of James's letter is punctuated by a brief interjection, ἴστε, ἀδελφοί μου ἀγαπητοί. While some interpreters would like to read the verb, ἴστε, as an imperative calling attention to what the author is about to say, the δέ which introduces the following injunctions makes such a connection improbable. Whether the verb is read as an imperative or an indicative, its elided object is to be found in what precedes. Thus, after having assured the addressees in vv. 13-18 that God was not the source of their current struggle but had instead "given us birth by the word of truth that we might be a kind of first fruits among his creatures," James hastily interposes, "you may be assured [of this], my dear brothers and sisters," before moving on to his exhortation regarding the proper response to the word of truth.

The ensuing text is easily divided into two parts. The first seven verses form a cohesive unit, moving smoothly forward by means of logical connectives. In contrast, the final two verses, vv. 26-27, are not only asyndetic, that is, appended without aid of conjunctions, they also abruptly transpose the author's language from the "reception of the word" (v. 21) to that of the veneration of God or θρησκεία. Nonetheless, despite this sudden shift in expression, the continuity between the two segments is assured. Underlying both is a common distinction between an unacceptable piety

---

5. H. Windisch, *Die katholischen Briefe,* 2nd ed., HNT 15 (Tübingen: Mohr Siebeck, 1930), 4. In more recent times, the "Diaspora letter" genre of the James epistle has been explored by numerous authors: Manabu Tsuji, *Glaube zwischen Vollkommmenheit und Verweltlichung,* WUNT 2:93 (Tübingen: Mohr Siebeck, 1997), 5-50; Karl-Wilhelm Niebuhr, "Der Jakobusbrief im Licht frühjüdischer Diasporabriefe," *NTS* 44 (1998): 420-43; Donald J. Verseput, "Wisdom, 4Q185, and the Epistle of James," *JBL* 117 (1998): 691-707; idem, "Genre and Story: The Community Setting of the Epistle of James," *CBQ* 62 (2000): 96-110; Richard Bauckham, *James,* New Testament Readings (London: Routledge, 1999), 11-28.

that lacks the appropriate behavior on the one hand and an active devotion that elicits God's blessing on the other. The former is consistently depicted as a self-deception, a worthless sacrifice stained with impurity, while the latter is seen as being a pure and blameless offering to God. The significance of James's appropriation of sacrificial language as well as the essential unity of the two segments will become clearer as we proceed.

It should not be denied that James's rhythmic, tripartite admonition in v. 19 resembles an aphoristic saying of conventional wisdom. Indeed, parallels are not hard to find. Sir 5:11("Be quick to hear, but deliberate in answering"), 1QH 10.37 ("Be slow to anger and do not despise . . .") and Plutarch, *On Listening to Lectures* 39b ("skillful educators . . . teach them to hear much and speak little") all illustrate not only a widespread respect for restraint in speech and aversion to anger, but also the ancient propensity for terse and epigrammatic language. Nevertheless, James's pithy, almost sententious style should not obscure the relevance of his words within their immediate context. After having reminded his audience of their rebirth by "the word of truth," James now adds, "but be quick to hear, slow to speak, slow to anger." The opening colon, standing as it does immediately after v. 18 and parallel to the injunction on how to "receive the inborn word" in v. 21, is most naturally taken in reference to the hearing of the divine message by which the community was given "birth." But if that is the case, to what do the ensuing cola refer? To whom is one to be "slow to speak, slow to anger"? This question has not only been a frequent stumbling block to interpreters, it is an important key to comprehending the point of the entire passage.

In the small congregations of the first-century house churches, tensions between the gathered believers sometimes spilled over into angry and abusive speech in the assembly. On this score, the early Christian congregations were not unlike their Jewish or pagan counterparts, whether it be a Jewish sect in the desert or a Hellenistic cult organization gathered in an urban temple precinct. Indeed, so frequently did the problem occur and so sensitive were ancient groups to the shame that a major altercation might cause, that the statutes of these various communities often endeavored to impose penalties on the offenders. Regulations of this sort can be found, for example, in a charter of a late Ptolemaic (69-58 BC) guild of Zeus Hypsistos, in which it is forbidden for the members "to abuse one another at the banquet or to chatter or to indict or accuse another," or in the nomoi of a guild from the reign of Tiberius wherein a monetary penalty is assessed "if anyone speak against or slander another."[6]

---

6. P.Lond. 2710 and P.Mich. 243, 7-8. For a translation and discussion of P.Lond. 2710, see Colin Roberts, Theodore C. Skeat, and Arthur Darby Nock, "The Gild of Zeus Hypsistos," *HTR* 29 (1936): 39-87. Helpful information on the statutes of these ancient guilds can be found

Similarly, in the *Rule of the Community* discovered at Qumran, we read:

> One must not speak to his fellow with anger or with a snarl or with a [stiff] neck [or in a jealous spirit] of wickedness. And he must not hate him [in the fores]k[in] of his heart, for he shall admonish him on the very same day lest he bear iniquity because of him. And also let no man accuse his companion before the Many without a confrontation before witnesses, and they shall eat in unity, say benedictions in unity, and give counsel in unity.[7]

This same concern for mutual harmony and the prevention of angry speech in the communal assembly reoccurs with regularity in the New Testament. It was not only the Corinthian church that needed to be admonished on the maintenance of order (1 Cor 14:26-40). In 1 Timothy 2, for example, we find pointed instructions on how one ought to conduct oneself in the house of God: the men, gathered in common assembly, are to pray with hands unstained by "wrath and dissension," while women are to adorn themselves with the social virtues of αἰδώς ("a sense of restraint based upon respect for proper boundaries") and σωφροσύνη ("self-control"), both cases expressing a warning against discord within the congregation. Similarly, in 1 Peter 2, on the heels of an exhortation to "fervently love one another from the heart," the readers are admonished to lay aside all unloving behavior and "like newly born babes yearn for the unadulterated milk of God's word"—an injunction to attend to the communal message without strife and conflict. Such, then, is the thought in Jas 1:19. The assembled members of the Christian congregation to whom the letter is addressed, knowing that they have been brought into being by the "word of truth," are to respond to that word without giving way to hasty, angry speech in the communal gathering, "for human anger does not accomplish the righteousness which God requires."

What follows is intimately connected to the warning of Jas 1:19-20. Both the inferential particle, διό, and the substance of the command in v. 21b continue the thought established by the admonition against verbal abuse. Because angry speech does not bring about the righteousness which God approves, "on this account, laying aside all filth and surpassing wickedness, with gentleness receive the inborn word which is able to save you." Brushing aside the participium coniunctum for the moment, let us concentrate our attention upon the main thought: ἐν πραΰτητι, δέξασθε τὸν ἔμφυτον λόγον. The phrase ἐν πραΰτητι describes the manner of the

in A. E. Boak, "The Organization of Gilds in Greco-Roman Egypt," *Transactions and Proceedings of the American Philological Association* 68 (1937): 212-20.

7. 1QS v.25–vi.3

desired reception of the "inborn word."[8] But if, as we have already noted, this "inborn word" is the same "word" by which the readers were "given birth" in 1:18, to what does ἐν πραΰτητι refer? Lacking a sensitivity to the congregational context of James's message, the NIV, NASB, and the NJB have preferred to translate πραΰτης as "humility," assuming that it describes a humble, trusting attitude toward God. Indeed, it might be fairly pointed out that the Septuagint uses πραΰς twelve times to translate the Hebrew words עָנוּ or עָנִי, words which depict those who are poor and needy, in a position of servanthood or subjection. In the Psalms, in particular, the term πραεῖς (עֲנָוִים) describes those who look to God for deliverance and experience his merciful intervention. But it cannot be argued on this basis that in the present context of James's letter πραΰτης has lost its ethical sense and become a religious term. On the contrary, the logic of Jas 1:19-21 leaves little room for ambiguity. The phrase ἐν πραΰτητι stands in conspicuous antithesis to the ὀργή of v. 20. After admonishing the congregation to listen to the "word" without anger or vituperative speech, James concludes that the gathered community should receive the message by which they had been born "in gentleness," that is, with the affable mildness of one who scrupulously avoids communal conflicts.

The contrast between πραΰτης ("gentleness") and ὀργή ("anger") is not only apparent within the text, it was axiomatic in Greco-Roman moral reflection. Already in the classical period, Aristotle placed gentleness (πραότης) as the proper mean between irascibility (ὀργιλότης) and spiritlessness (ἀοργησία) in his discussion of anger (ὀργή).[9] From this noble beginning, the propensity to view gentleness in opposition to anger and harshness spread throughout the ancient world. Thus—to name but a few examples—the Alexandrian doxographer, Arius Didymus, philosophical teacher of Augustus, epitomized Stoic sentiment by defining gentleness as "not being carried into anger in any matter."[10] Similarly, Plutarch, the middle Platonist philosopher and biographer from Chaeronea in Greece (ca. AD 50-120), wrote a charming little essay *On the Control of Anger*, in which "gentleness" is the coveted solution to anger, "the most hated and despised of the passions." Indeed, so natural and ordinary was the contrast between anger and gentleness that we find it reoccurring with consistent regularity in the language of a broad variety of first-century authors such

---

8. The most frequent usage of ἔμφυτος indicates that which is a result of birth in contrast to what is acquired (cf. e.g., Plutarch, *Mor.* 746D; 1026D). There is, however, no justification for perceiving a Stoic influence in either content or expression (cf. Epictetus 2.11.3; Cicero, *Leg.* 1.18-19); the metaphor of God's word as σπέρμα by which the community is brought forth in Jas 1:18 (cf. 1 Pet 1:23-25) is sufficient to account for the τὸν ἔμφυτον λόγον in 1:21.

9. *Nicomachean Ethics* 2.7.1108.

10. *Arius Didymus: Epitome of Stoic Ethics*, ed. Arthur J. Pomeroy, Text and Translations 44 (Atlanta: Society of Biblical Literature, 1999), 98.

as Philo, Josephus, Dio of Prusa, and Dionysius of Halicarnassus.[11] Given this ancient antithesis, there is no reason to question the ethical nature of James's injunction. Rather than responding to the constitutive word of the community with an attitude of anger and acrimony toward fellow believers, James admonishes his audience to lay aside all defiling moral filthiness and receive the message with a spirit of calm restraint that demonstrates mildness and congeniality in the face of quarrels.

This call to "hear" or "receive the word" with a gracious demeanor, eschewing anger or discord, leads directly to the urgent warning in vv. 22-25. At this point, however, special care must be taken to grasp the nature of James's admonition. The δέ of v. 22 does not present a new injunction; rather, it has an explanatory force best translated by "indeed" or "and at that." So perceived, it introduces a carefully crafted caution to the congregation which underscores the imperative to "receive in gentleness" by offering divine blessing to those who obey.[12] Two observations support this contention. In the first case, the language the author uses to describe the proper response to the communal message admits no progression of thought from vv. 19-21 to vv. 22-25. Already the opening injunction "be quick to hear" goes beyond mere external hearing, since in the biblical tradition "hearing" the word of the Lord is indistinguishable from obedience.[13] Moreover, the corresponding mandate in v. 21, to "receive the inborn word which has the power to save you," is no less a call to actively respond to the word, for once it has been received it is said to accomplish the receiver's eschatological salvation. Hence, James's charge in v. 22 to "be doers of the word and not hearers only" is not intended to advance the thought, but to clarify what has already been said about the reception of the word in gentleness.

The author's elucidation of v. 22 in the succeeding verses confirms this conclusion. Despite superficial appearances, the one who is pejoratively labeled a "hearer only" is not one who has "heard" or "received" the word in the sense presented by vv. 19-21, but is, rather, one who abandons what has been initially received. James employs a common figure for moral instruction in the ancient world, the metaphor of a mirror, to illustrate his point.[14] The one who only listens without doing the word, we are told, is like an individual who looks in a mirror and then "goes away and forgets." In contrast, the doer of the word peers at the perfect law of liberty and "remains," not being a "forgetful hearer" but a doer

---

11. Philo, *Mos.* 2.279; Josephus, *Ant.* 19.334; Dio Chrysostom 11.126; Dionysius of Halicarnassus, *Ant.* 4.41.4; 7.2.4.

12. Cf. e.g., Rom 3:22; Phil 2:8; 1 Cor 10:29.

13. E.g., Deut 8:20; 11:25-27; 28:1, 2, 13, 15; 30:10. James's usage of ταχύς in 1:19 makes the implication of obedience in "hearing" certain.

14. Plutarch, *Mor.* 14A; 42A-B; 85A; P.Oxy. 31.2603.

of deed. The key distinction between the "forgetting" and "remaining" echoes traditional biblical language wherein to "forget" God and his law was a regular expression for turning aside from the divine statutes to walk stubbornly according to one's own way.[15] Having urged his audience to be characterized by gentleness or meekness in their assemblies where the word is taught, James now underscores his message by reiterating, "indeed, be doers of the word" rather than like the wicked who "go away and forget." Only those who by their gentle behavior "remain" with the perfect law of liberty are "blessed in their doing."

The first segment of our text reveals, thus, a coherent message. The central theme is not the proper response to the word, as Dibelius supposed, but deportment in the gathered assembly. James is primarily concerned with the problem of anger and divisive behavior within the congregation, a matter that bothered other ancient writers and communities as well. To avert the problem, he admonishes his audience to be "quick to hear" the divine word and "slow" to react against one another in angry speech. The reason he gives is simple but persuasive: "for human anger does not accomplish the righteousness which God requires." Because of this, the Christian congregation should "receive the word in gentleness," the calm and tranquil spirit that was typically perceived to be the opposite of anger. That is to say, James adds, the community members are to be "doers of the word and not hearers only," for those who turn aside from the divine way "deceive themselves," but those who remain with the word by putting it into practice are "blessed in their doing."

Pure and Undefiled Worship (James 1:26-27)

But what about the final two verses of the chapter? For Dibelius, these verses were originally independent sayings, the first being inserted by the author to do justice to the admonition to "be slow to speak" while the second returned the readers' attention immediately to the real subject, that of doing. Admittedly, there is, once again, a traditional sound to James's message. The logic of the text is scarcely original to our epistle. But we should not therefore reduce these verses to the role of a crudely attached appendix. The coherence of Jas 1:26-27 to what precedes is not only exceptionally strong, these verses are demonstrably the culmination of the entire segment.

But first, let us review the threads that fasten vv. 26-27 to the foregoing text. The distinction between doing and "forgetting" introduced by

15. E.g., Deut 6:12; 8:11, 14, 19; Ps 11:16; 61; 83; 93; Jer 3:21; 1 Macc 1:49; Bar 4:8; 1Q22 ii.4; 4Q216 f1 ii.16; 4Q390 f1.8; 4Q436 f1 i.5; 4Q427 f2 i.6; *T. Dan* 7:3; *T. Naph.* 4:4.

vv. 22-25 is neatly continued in the language of pure versus vain worship in vv. 26-27. Moreover, those who find themselves on the wrong side of this distinction are once again said to be engaged in self-deception much as was the case in v. 22. Nor may we dismiss the reference to bridling the tongue in v. 26 as peripheral to the author's main concern quite as easily as did Dibelius. Indeed, James's hasty return to the theme of verbal restraint after his warning in vv. 22-25 confirms our conjecture that the admonition to replace anger with gentleness is central to the passage. Given these tight connections with the preceding, the asyndetic juncture at v. 26 does not indicate a fresh start but introduces, instead, a weighty climax to what has gone before. In the closing verses of chapter 1, James recasts the preceding mandate on deportment within the community in terms of a familiar prophetic topos, thereby reinforcing his message with the persuasive clout of an ancient truism.

The most obvious feature of Jas 1:26-27 is the sudden shift in terminology from the language of hearing or receiving the word to the context of communal worship. The noun θρησκεία was typically used in one of two closely associated senses: (1) of the practice of obligations arising from the veneration of a supernatural being, whether of individual religious rites or of the entire religious system by which the deity was honored[16]; or (2) of a personal proclivity for the diligent practice of such obligations.[17] In the present context, the former sense is clearly intended. The logic of these verses is as simple as it was prevalent among ancient writers. Since classical times, Greco-Roman philosophers had continuously reaffirmed the need for purity of life to accompany the offering of cultic service to the deity.[18] The same can be said of Jewish theologians. Already numerous passages from the Hebrew Bible taught the priority of ethical requirements over cultic obligations—whether by proclaiming the divine rejection of sacrifice unaccompanied by obedience (Prov 15:8; Isa 1:10-17; Jer 6:20; 7:21-23; Hos 8:13; Mal 1:10-14) or by suggesting that obedience is equal to or better than cultic service (1 Sam 15:22; Ps 69:30-31; Prov 21:3; Hos 6:6; Amos 5:20-25). And subsequent Jewish teachers did not fail to capitalize on this biblical theme. Of the many extant references, two brief examples must suffice. The first is drawn from the wisdom of Jesus Sirach:

16. E.g., Acts 26:5; Col 2:18; Dionysius Halicarnassus, *Ant. Rom.* 2.63.2; Philo, *Spec. Laws.* 1.315; Josephus, *Ant.* 4.306; 12.271; 19.284; *J.W.* 1.146; 2.198; 4.324; 7.45; *1 Clem.* 62.1; Lucian, *Sacr.* 10; Sextus, *Pyrr.* 3.220, 222, 226. The adjective θρησκός is so far unknown in the Greek language before James.

17. E.g., Chariton, *Chaer.* 7.6.6; Josephus, *Ant.* 1.223-24, 234; 6.18; 8.279; 13.244.

18. Note e.g., Xenophon, *Mem.* 1.3.3; Plato, *Leg.* 4.716E; Isocrates, *Or.* 2.20; Diodorus Siculus, 12.20.2; Dio Chrysostom 3.52-53; Seneca, *Ben.* 1.6.3.

34:23 The Most High approves not the gifts of the godless,
   nor for their many sacrifices does he forgive their sins . . .
35:1 To keep the Law is a great oblation,
   2 and whoever observes the commandments sacrifices a peace offering.
3 In works of charity one offers fine flour,
   4 and when he gives alms he presents his sacrifice of praise.
5 To refrain from evil pleases the Lord,
   and to avoid injustice is an atonement.

The second comes from the first-century Alexandrian exegete and philosopher Philo, who writes in *Spec. Leg.* 1.271:

> To such a one [i.e., the unholy] I would say, "Sir, God does not rejoice in sacrifices even if one offer hecatombs, . . . but he rejoices in the will to love Him and in men that practice holiness and from these He accepts plain meal or barley. . . . And indeed though the worshipers bring nothing else, in bringing themselves they offer the best of sacrifices. . . ."

It is scarcely a coincidence that in both of the above texts a pattern very similar to Jas 1:26-27 emerges. God does not approve of the service of those who stubbornly refuse to walk in his way, we are told. And then, with a rhetorical tour de force, both authors insist true worship is purity of life. Applying the same paradigm to the experience of the Christian congregations, James writes: "If anyone thinks themselves to be a person who worships God but does not bridle the tongue, thus deceiving themselves, this person's worship is futile." Then, completing the thought in a manner appropriate to the pattern, he adds: "The worship that is pure and undefiled before God the Father is this: to look after orphans and widows in their distress, to keep oneself unstained by the world." With this appeal to a familiar Jewish axiom, James points an accusing finger at the incongruity of verbal abuse in the context of the communal assembly and at the same time identifies the nature of true and acceptable worship. The ideal that he holds up to the community in v. 27 deliberately echoes the stern voice of the Hebrew prophets, most nearly that of Isa 1:15-17:

> 15 When you stretch out your hands in prayer,
> I will hide my eyes from you . . .
> Your hands are full of blood;
> 16 wash and make yourselves clean . . .
> Take your evil deeds out of my sight!
> Stop doing wrong, 17 learn to do right!
> Seek justice, encourage the oppressed.
> Defend the cause of the fatherless,
> Plead the case of the widow.

For James, dissension and division in the community was something that rendered the community unclean, its worship unacceptable. True worship, he tells his readers, was to offer to God with hands unstained by strife the righteous deeds of which the prophets had spoken.

Conclusion

Far from being a loose mosaic of traditional thoughts on doing rather than hearing the word of the community, Jas 1:19-27 addresses a problem endemic to ancient associations: conflict control within the assembly. James begins with a series of injunctions reminiscent of ancient conventional wisdom, urging his audience to be quick to hear and to respond to the word of God, but slow to engage in angry speech "because human anger does not accomplish the righteousness which God requires." On this basis, he encourages the believers to receive the communal word "with a gentle demeanor," reacting to provocation with restraint and tranquility rather than with anger. "Indeed," he explains, "be doers of the word" and not those who go away and forget the perfect law of liberty. Then, borrowing from the prophetic pattern of declaring purity to be a necessary accompaniment to sacrifice, he applies this principle metaphorically to the Christian community. To worship God without controlling the tongue is futile; pure and undefiled worship is the obedience required by the prophets, that is, to look after the widows and the orphans, and to keep oneself unstained by the world. James's message is therefore not primarily concerned with instructing his readers on how to cope with life nor with exhorting them on the proper response to the word. The primary issue on the author's mind is the behavior of the gathered community, and that is precisely the theme that leads him forward into the next chapter.

1 Peter 2:2a

Nourishment for Growth in Faith and Love

25

W. EDWARD GLENNY

A detailed exegetical discussion of a key phrase, illustrating the value of careful lexical work.

The first clause in 1 Pet 2:2, ὡς ἀρτιγέννητα βρέφη τὸ λογικὸν ἄδολον γάλα ἐπιποθήσατε, is one of the most important and controversial clauses in the letter, containing what is sometimes called the work's central imperative.[1] My goal in this brief study is to offer an interpretation of this clause, especially the two most debated words in the clause, λογικός and γάλα, based on the context and the hermeneutic Peter describes in 1:10-12 and demonstrates in 2:4-10.

The author of 1 Peter combines exhortation to Christian growth, good works, and faithfulness with supporting attestation that the gospel message, which the recipients had believed and which is contained in 1 Peter, is the "true grace of God" (5:12).[2] The main body (1:13–5:11) divides

---

1. Peter H. Davids, *The First Epistle of Peter*, NICNT (Grand Rapids, Mich.: Eerdmans, 1990), 81-82; Klyne R. Snodgrass, "1 Peter II. 1-10: Its Formation and Literary Affinities," *NTS* 24 (1977): 97; John H. Elliott, *The Elect and the Holy* (Leiden: Brill, 1966), 200-1, 215-7.

I offer this essay to Harold Hoehner as a token of my appreciation for his good and godly influence in my life as a professor, mentor, and friend.

2. Peter is presented as the author in the letter and will be referred to as such in this chapter.

into three main sections, which attest to three different dimensions of the
Christian experience of the recipients and in which the author exhorts
them from those three different perspectives: 1:13–2:10, "As children of
God, grow"; 2:11–4:11, "As strangers and sojourners, do good"; and
4:12–5:11, "As Christians, be faithful in suffering."[3]

1 Peter 2:2 is near the end of the first main exhortation section, 1:13–2:3,
which is followed by the main indicative statement of the letter, 2:4-10,
attesting to the truthfulness of the gospel, and supporting all of 1:1–2:3.
In 1:13–2:3 Peter exhorts his readers to "grow" (2:2) from their present
status ("faith" and "love," 1:8) to mature hope ("hope completely in
the grace of God," 1:13-21) and to consistent, steadfast love ("love one
another fervently," 1:22–2:3). The unhypocritical love, which should
consistently characterize the recipients' relationships with one another,
is possible because of the incorruptible "seed" of the divine nature by
which they have been begotten anew through the word that has been
preached to them, which here must be the gospel (1:23; cf. 1:25).[4] In vv.
24-25a Peter supports the exhortation to consistent love with the truth
from Isaiah 40 that the word of God is eternal ("living and abiding" and
thus "incorruptible"), and then in v. 25b he confirms that this "living
and abiding word of God" described in Isaiah 40 is the very same "word
about the Lord" (1:25a) that was preached as the gospel to them.[5]

On the basis of the "truth" of 1:22-25, in 2:1 Peter continues the
exhortation to grow in love (1:8, 22) by urging the recipients to refrain
from antisocial behavior (2:1), which is inconsistent with love for one
another (1:22) and dulls their appetite for the Christian nourishment de-

---

3. The phrase "as newborn babes" in 2:2 is one example of the use of the imagery and
language of childhood in the first section (cf. 1:14, 17, 23). I have described the argument of
the letter more fully in "The Hermeneutics of the Use of the Old Testament in 1 Peter" (Th.D.
diss., Dallas Theological Seminary, 1987), 312-42.

4. I take the "incorruptible seed" in 1:23 to represent the Spirit of God, whose presence
is the means of the new birth of believers through the Word of God. Through the eternal and
imperishable gospel the divine nature of God has been implanted in them in the person of the
Holy Spirit ("you are a spiritual house" 2:5; cf. 1:12; 4:14), and they have been purified and set
apart (cf. the sanctifying work of the Spirit in 1:2) to offer spiritual service ("to offer spiritual
sacrifices" 2:5), which consists especially of loving one another without hypocrisy (2:22; cf.
4:8). That this "incorruptible seed" is the basis of love also suggests the Spirit is the seed (Gal
5:22). See also 1 John 3:9.

5. The genitive, "of the Lord," in 1:25a is further defined as "the word that was preached
as the gospel to you" (εὐαγγελισθέν), a phrase that hearkens the reader back to the same verb
in 1:12 and the message of Christ's sufferings and glory from the OT that is now being preached
to Peter's recipients (cf. 1:10-11). This fact, along with the change that Peter makes in the LXX
text from "of God" to "of the Lord" in 1:25a, indicates that in 1 Peter 1:25 the genitive refers to
Christ, the content of the "word" of the gospel preached to the recipients of 1 Peter. (See 1:12,
where the OT revelation about Christ is for Christians, not for the OT saints.)

scribed in 2:2.[6] The main statement and command of 2:1-3, which is the focus of this study, exhorts the recipients to desire spiritual nourishment as newborn babes desire milk, so that by means of this nourishment they may grow toward their final salvation (2:2).[7] V. 3, "If you have tasted that the Lord is good," is certainly a motivation for the readers to feast on the spiritual nourishment described in v. 2 in order to grow to final salvation, but the motivation is given in the form of a condition, and the force of the condition should not be blunted.[8] The condition indicates that only those who have tasted "the goodness of the Lord [Jesus]" are expected to desire the nourishment necessary for growth.[9] Vv. 4-10 conclude the first main section with the main indicative statement of the letter, in which the author attests and confirms from the OT the election and honor of the Lord Jesus Christ and, by virtue of their belief in him, the election and honor of Christians.

The phrase τὸ λογικὸν ἄδολον γάλα is the object of the command ἐπι-ποθήσατε ("crave"), which describes an intense desire. Peter may have chosen this verb because the desire of which it speaks is often instinctive, thus communicating an inborn or natural tendency to behave in a characteristic way.[10] When he writes that his recipients are to crave milk

6. See T. J. Ryan, "The Word of God in 1 Peter: A Critical Study in 1 Peter 2:1-3" (Ph D. diss., Catholic University of America, 1973), 278-84, for a helpful development of the old lifestyle described in v. 1.

7. See J. Ramsey Michaels, *1 Peter*, Word Biblical Themes (Dallas: Word, 1989), 67-68, for a helpful discussion of "salvation" in 1 Peter.

8. Peter changes the double command in the Hebrew and LXX, "taste and see," to the condition in 2:2, adapting the message to his metaphor and adding the conditional element. On the force of the condition in 2:3, see Thomas R. Schreiner, *1, 2 Peter, Jude*, NAC 37 (Nashville: Broadman & Holman, 2003), 101, who summarizes contra the NIV rendering, "now that you have tasted," "Peter did not write 'if' [first class condition] to sow doubts in the minds of the readers, but neither should 'if' be confused with 'since.'" Psalm 34, David's declarative psalm of praise, invites others to experience the same goodness of the Lord he has experienced; in 2:2 Peter uses the psalm to motivate those with past experience of the Lord's goodness to crave further nourishment. On the importance of Psalm 34 for 1 Peter, see W. Bornemann, "Der erste Petrusbriefe—eine Taufrede des Silvanus?" *ZNW* 19 (1919/20): 143-65; Snodgrass, "1 Peter II, 1-10," 97-106, esp. 103; William L. Schutter, *Hermeneutic and Composition in 1 Peter*, WUNT 2:30 (Tübingen: Mohr Siebeck, 1989), 44-49; and Karen H. Jobes, "Got Milk? Septuagint Psalm 33 and the Interpretation of 1 Peter 2:1-3" *WTJ* 64 (2002): 1-14, esp. 9-12.

9. The one who has been begotten again by this imperishable seed has a capacity for un-hypocritical love of the brethren (1:22); has been made a partaker of a new, imperishable realm of existence (1:23-25); has tasted the goodness of the Lord (2:3); and, by implication from the OT passages used to support this section in 2:6-10, has the capacity to understand and accept the message of Christ, as found in the OT Scriptures.

10. Ceslas Spicq, *Theological Lexicon of the New Testament*, 3 vols., trans. and ed. James D. Ernest (Peabody, Mass.: Hendrickson, 1994), 1:59. It describes a deer's craving for water (Ps 42 [41]:1), the lusting of God's Spirit to possess believers (Jas 4:5), and Paul's ardent desire to see those he loves (1 Thess 3:6).

"as new born infants" he does not mean that they are new believers, a situation that would be impossible in light of the scope of his audience (1:1).[11] The metaphor means that they are always to have a craving for and dependence on their spiritual nourishment as newborns crave milk so that they may grow.

The adjective ἄδολον is the least controversial word in the phrase τὸ λογικὸν ἄδολον γάλα. It means "pure" or "unadulterated."[12] It is the negative form of the second vice ("guile" or "deceit," δόλος) in v. 1, and the contrast between the two words emphasizes that the exhortation in v. 1 is the negative dimension of the positive command in v. 2. The rejection of "deceit" (2:1) complements the pursuit of "pure" nourishment (2:2).[13]

There is no question about the translation of the noun "milk" (γάλα); the question with this metaphor involves its referent. There are three main views. First, many believe the "milk" refers to the Word of God.[14] These interpreters base their understanding of "milk" on the references to the "word," which the preceding context indicates was preached to the recipients of the letter (2:23-25). Second, several interpreters believe the "milk" in 2:2 refers to "God's life-sustaining grace in Christ,"[15] "the sustaining life of God,"[16] "spiritual nourishment,"[17] or a similar idea.[18]

---

11. The particle "as" (ὡς), as often in 1 Peter, introduces the perspective from which the recipients or subjects are to be viewed or understood (BDAG, 1104-5; Elliott, *Elect*, 36 n. 2). If the recipients have all recently been begotten spiritually, this expression is an allegory; it is better understood to be a metaphor, teaching that throughout their spiritual lives Christians are to be like physically "newborn infants," in the sense that they crave the "milk" that is the source of their growth (2:2).

12. MM, 10. In this context the pureness of the milk is not a result of its separation from what is false (i.e., false teaching), but rather an inherent quality of the milk.

13. Cf. also 2:22; no "guile" (δόλος) was found in Christ's mouth.

14. Paul J. Achtemeier, *1 Peter*, Hermeneia (Minneapolis: Fortress, 1996), 145-47; Wayne A. Grudem, *1 Peter: An Introduction and Commentary*, TNTC (Grand Rapids, Mich.: Eerdmans, 1988), 95-96; Norman Hillyer, *1 and 2 Peter, Jude*, NIBC 16 (Peabody, Mass.: Hendrickson, 1992), 56-57; Dan G. McCartney, "λογικός in 1 Peter 2:2," ZNW 82 (1991): 128-32; Bo Reicke, *The Epistles of James, Peter, and Jude*, AB 37 (Garden City, N.Y.: Doubleday, 1982), 90; and Schreiner, *1, 2 Peter, Jude*, 100-1.

15. Jobes, "Got Milk?" 14; Jobes claims that her view goes back to John Calvin, *Commentaries on the Catholic Epistles*, trans. and ed. John Owen (Grand Rapids, Mich.: Eerdmans, 1948), 62. However, Calvin is not as supportive of Jobes as she suggests; he describes the milk that is to be craved as a way of life. It is "not elementary doctrine," but rather "a mode of living which has the savor of the new birth, when we surrender ourselves to be brought up by God" (63).

16. J. Ramsey Michaels, *1 Peter*, WBC 49 (Waco, Tex.: Word, 1988), 89.

17. Ernest Best, *1 Peter*, NCB (Grand Rapids, Mich.: Eerdmans, 1971), 97. He writes that for the Christian, "there can be no food beyond Christ."

18. Fenton John Anthony Hort, *The First Epistle of St. Peter I.1–II.17* (London: Macmillan, 1898; reprint, Minneapolis: Klock and Klock, 1976), 101-2, suggests the milk is "a Divine

Jobes, a recent proponent of this view, supports it with the following arguments, which address primarily the previous interpretation: (1) "The metaphorical incoherence between milk [2:2] and seed [1:22]" makes it unlikely that the word of God is the referent of both metaphors[19]; (2) Since the Word of God is not mentioned in Psalm 34 (LXX Ps. 33), which Peter quotes in 2:3, it is likely he has moved on to a new concern in 2:1-3[20]; (3) "This wider view is appropriate to Peter's goal of redefining his reader's self-identity in light of the new reality into which they have come through new birth."[21] Although Jobes's first two arguments are not convincing,[22] her third touches on a foundational purpose in 1 Peter. In this letter Peter is redefining the self-identity of his readers in light of the perspective that the Christ event brings to the OT Scriptures.[23] This new identity is, of course, a result of their new birth, as Jobes suggests, but they were born again through the preaching of Christ from the OT Scriptures, the gospel message, and their understanding of their identity is based upon that message.

Another, and I believe the best, understanding of the "milk" in 2:2, is the gospel of Christ, which was preached to the recipients from the OT Scriptures.[24] The distinction Peter makes between the OT Scripture

---

grace or spirit coming directly from above." Jobes, "Got Milk?" 14, cites Hort (*First Epistle of St. Peter*, 100) as support for her view, but the support is not strong. Ryan, "Word of God in 1 Peter," 287-89, concludes that the "milk" refers to Christ and his message, an interpretation that overlaps with the next option.

19. Jobes, "Got Milk?" 3. I will also differentiate the referents of "seed" (1:23) and "milk" (2:2).

20. Ibid., 12.

21. Ibid., 14.

22. See Schreiner, *1, 2 Peter, Jude*, 100 n. 195 for a response to Jobes's first argument; he believes that the "seed" (1:23) and the "milk" (2:2) both refer to the Word of God (95, 100-1). Jobes's second argument misses the fact that the connection between the "seed" by which believers are begotten and "milk" by which they grow is that they both relate to the controlling metaphor of 1:13–2:10, the description of the recipients from the perspective of "children of God."

23. This is clear from 1:9-12 and 2:4-10.

24. This view combines elements of the other two. It is not simply the OT Scriptures; nor is it simply the message of Christ. Some who hold this view are Stephen Richard Bechtler, *Following in His Steps: Suffering, Community, and Christology in 1 Peter*, SBLDS 162 (Atlanta: Scholars, 1998), 150; Davids, *First Epistle of Peter*, 83; John H. Elliott, *1 Peter*, AB 37B (New York: Doubleday, 2000), 399; Leonhard Goppelt, *A Commentary on 1 Peter*, ed. Ferdinand Hahn, trans. John E. Alsup (Grand Rapids, Mich.: Eerdmans, 1993), 128-29; J. N. D. Kelly, *A Commentary on the Epistles of Peter and Jude*, HNTC (New York: Harper & Row, 1969), 85-86; Troy W. Martin, *Metaphor and Composition in 1 Peter*, SBLDS 131 (Atlanta: Scholars, 1992), 56, 174; Edward Gordon Selwyn, *The First Epistle of St. Peter*, 2nd ed. (London: Macmillan, 1946), 154; and Lauri Thurén, *Argument and Theology in 1 Peter*, JSNTSup 114 (Sheffield: Sheffield Academic Press, 1995), 124. Jobes ("Got Milk?" 10) cites Selwyn ("milk" is "the divinely given nourishment supplied by the Gospel," 154) as a representative of the second view, which she holds. He may be, but I would want to differentiate what he says from her view, on the basis of

(γραφή, 2:6) and the gospel message (λόγος, ῥῆμα), which is not simply
the OT Scriptures but is "contained in Scripture," (2:6) is foundational
to this understanding of the "milk" in 2:2.[25] "The disobedient" stumble
over the "word" (2:8, λόγος) and are "disobedient" to the "gospel"
(4:17, εὐαγγέλιον).[26] The gospel, the message of Christ's sufferings and
glory prophesied in the OT, is the message announced to believers in this
age (1:11-12, εὐαγγελίζω) and the word about Christ ("of the Lord")
preached to Peter's recipients (1:25; cf. 4:6).[27] Thus the gospel preached
to the recipients is not simply the OT text, but it is also not simply the
message of Christ without foundation. The eternal word of God (1:23b),
the message of Christ ("the Lord") found in OT Scripture (1:24-25a), is
the gospel preached to them (1:25b).[28]

This "milk" of 2:2 is the means ("by it") by which the recipients are
to "grow to [final] salvation" (2:2). Since they were "begotten again"
by the gospel (1:23), and they were "begotten again" for final salvation
(1:3-5), and in 2:2 "milk" is the means of growth to final "salvation,"
the "milk" is apparently the same gospel message.[29] Understanding the
"milk" in 2:2 as the message of Christ found in and preached from the
(OT) Scriptures when they are rightly understood combines the other two
options, both of which are inadequate in and of themselves.[30]

The last word to be considered, λογικόν,[31] is commonly translated
"spiritual," signaling the metaphor in 2:2.[32] Other interpreters translate

the fact that in the NT the gospel is clearly tied to and seen as the fulfillment of OT Scripture
(Acts 13:32; 1 Cor 15:2-5; and esp. 1 Pet 1:10-12), and therefore more related to Scripture than
she explains or seems to mean in her understanding of the referent of "milk."

25. This is the only occurrence of γραφή in 1 Peter. Schreiner writes, "We can be almost
certain . . . Peter used the term 'word' (λόγος) to refer to the gospel" (*1, 2 Peter, Jude*, 95).

26. The same verb is translated "disobedient" in both verses. The verses connect the
"word" with the "gospel."

27. The change to ῥῆμα in 1:25 is because it is in the LXX text quoted; it does not signal
any change in meaning from λόγος in 1:23 (Achtemeier, *1 Peter*, 142). This λόγος, by which
they were born again (1:23), would be natural for newborn babes to crave (2:2). The use of
λόγος in 3:1 (2x) also seems to refer to the gospel. In 3:15 and 4:5 it is a verbal "answer" or
"account."

28. Cf. 1 Thess 2:13, where the Thessalonians are commended for receiving the gospel (2:4,
8, 9) preached to them as the "word of God." The "gospel" (cf. 1 Pet 1:12, 25; 4:17) is described
in the NT as the message of Christ, which fulfills OT Scripture (1 Cor 15:2-5; Acts 13:32).

29. The description of the recipients as "newborn babes" (2:2) makes the connection even
clearer between 1:3-5, 1:22, and 2:2.

30. The essence of the gospel is illustrated by the message concerning Christ and its implications for the recipients that Peter develops from the OT Scripture in the following context,
2:4-10.

31. It does not occur in the LXX and, elsewhere in the NT, only in Rom 12:1.

32. ASV, NRSV, NIV, TNIV, NET, NLT, ESV. Cf. Michaels, *1 Peter*, 87; Davids, *First Epistle
of Peter*, 82; Goppelt, *1 Peter*, 131; Selwyn, *First Epistle of St. Peter*, 154-55; Best, *1 Peter*, 98;

it "of the word," referring to the "word" in 1:22-25.[33] Third, going back to the basic meaning of the word, some understand it to have the idea of "rational" or "reasonable."[34] McCartney, realizing that this third view represents the most usual rendering of the Greek term λογικός, writes that the problem with this translation "lies in explaining what 'rational' milk might be."[35] I have argued that this "milk" represents the gospel of Christ, which the early church found in and preached from the OT. This "milk" is "reasonable" or "rational" because it is the interpretation of γραφή intended by the Holy Spirit (1:11), which Spirit-led ministers preach in this age (1:12), and the minds of members of God's "spiritual house" (2:5) that he is building in this age are able to grasp the force of the evidence and proof for this gospel found in γραφή.[36] Peter describes the rational nature of the gospel and his Christological hermeneutic in 1:9-12, and he demonstrates both in the following verses, 2:4-10, for which he is preparing his recipients in 2:2.[37] This understanding of λογικός is also consistent with the emphasis on the mind in 1 Peter.[38] Finally, for "children of God" (the perspective from which the recipients are addressed in 1:13–2:10), who have obeyed "the truth" (1:22), have been born again by "incorruptible seed" through the gospel (1:23) and have tasted the goodness of the Lord (2:3), the recognition of and appetite for

---

Grudem, *1 Peter*, 95, favors the translation "figurative." In response, one wonders why any further indication of the metaphor is necessary in this context.

33. KJV, NASB. Cf. Reicke, *Epistles of James, Peter, and Jude*, 88; Elliott, *1 Peter*, 400-401; Achtemeier, *1 Peter*, 145-47; McCartney, "λογικός in 1 Peter 2:2," 132, who bases his translation on the connection of the basic idea of λογικός, "rational," with the facility of speech and on the use of λόγος in the context. Hort, *First Epistle of St. Peter*, 100, adamantly rejects this interpretation.

34. Vulgate, *rationale*; Tyndale, "reasonable"; Calvin, *Catholic Epistles*, 62; Hort, *First Epistle of St. Peter*, 100-2; Schreiner, *1, 2 Peter, Jude*, 100; Jobes, "Got Milk?" 13, "true"; McCartney, "λογικός in 1 Peter 2:2," 132, allows that Hort's understanding of "rational" is valid as well as his own.

35. McCartney, "λογικός in 1 Peter 2:2," 128 n. 3. See the helpful discussions of the meaning of λογικός in McCartney and in Hort, *First Epistle of St. Peter*, 100-2.

36. "True" (Jobes, "Got Milk?" 7) is not the best understanding of λογικόν in 2:2; that understanding of it would repeat the basic idea of ἄδολον, adding little if anything to the phrase.

37. Cf. also 1:24-25 and the other OT references in 1 Peter. Elliott, *Elect*, 16-23, demonstrates the logical interrelationship and connection between 2:4-5 and 2:6-10. The OT references in 2:6-10 support the important theological statements in 2:4-5. The "disobedient" stumble over Christ because they cannot see the reasonableness and preciousness of the gospel (2:6-8); even though it is the objectively correct interpretation of γραφή, they do not have the subjective capacity to see it.

38. Cf. "minds," 1:13; "ignorance," 1:14; "truth," 1:22; "same mind," 4:1. See also 3:15. Peter contrasts the recipients' former "lusts" in their "ignorance" (1:14, ἄγνοια; cf. 1:18) and the "craving" for the "rational" milk (2:2, λογικός), as he contrasts "deceit" (δόλος, 2:1) and "pure" milk (ἄδολος, 2:2).

this gospel message and its implications as found in γραφή is as natural, instinctive, and reasonable as desire for milk is for newborn babes (2:2).[39]

Peter's purpose in this letter is to exhort his readers and to attest that in Christ they truly are recipients of the grace of God (5:12). This grace has come to them in the gospel of Christ found in the (OT) Scriptures. They are to crave that gospel (γάλα) because it is inherently "rational" (λογικόν), the demonstrably correct interpretation of the Scriptures that produces hope (1:13, 21; cf. 3:15), and because it is inherently "pure" (ἄδολον), the source of the incorruptible seed that produces love (1:22-23; 2:1).

---

39. See, for example, W. J. Wainwright, *Reason and the Heart* (Ithaca, N.Y.: Cornell University Press, 1995), whose thesis is, "mature religious belief can, and perhaps should, be based on evidence but that the evidence can be accurately assessed only by men and women who possess the proper moral and spiritual qualifications" (3).

3 John

26

Tracing the Flow of Thought

HERBERT W. BATEMAN IV

An illustration of how to use syntactical features to trace the flow of thought and main ideas of an epistle.

A n awareness of any biblical author's flow of thought is not only critical to biblical interpretation, it is fundamental for communicating God's Word rightly. A structural outline is one hermeneutical technique that enables us to isolate a biblical author's flow of thought and his main point. The brevity of 3 John (39 clauses, 219 words) qualifies it to exemplify the structural outline process for this brief essay. Although seldom read and rarely preached, 3 John not only reveals several concerns of the early church, it confronts us with a significant obligation—people who travel and proclaim the message of Christ Jesus merit Christian support.

In the structural outline below, 3 John's flow of thought and main idea are determined by reproducing the exact word order of the text according to its major clauses. Three essential steps are taken to visualize 3 John's structure. First, all independent clauses (the main thought) are placed farthest to the left. Second, dependent clause(s) that directly modify a word or concept of an independent clause are indented and positioned under that word or concept for easy identification. Finally, all *important* structural markers or signposts that help isolate significant clauses, as well as highlight the main points of a clause, are underlined. (For convenience, verses are grouped into conceptual units and exegetical issues are in the notes.[1])

Salutation

Ὁ πρεσβύτερος Γαΐῳ τῷ ἀγαπητῷ, ---
[1a]The Presbyter, to Gaius the beloved,

ὃν ἐγὼ ἀγαπῶ ἐν ἀληθείᾳ.
[1b]whom I love in truth.

Ἀγαπητέ, περὶ πάντων εὔχομαί σε εὐοδοῦσθαι καὶ ὑγιαίνειν,
[2a]Beloved, in all respects I pray that you are prospering and that you are well,

καθὼς εὐοδοῦταί σου ἡ ψυχή.
[2b]just as your soul is prospering.

In a manner typical of first-century letter writers, vv. 1 and 2 serve as the opening greeting for 3 John. The author, however, adapts the conventional first-century greeting for his own purposes via four clauses, one independent and three dependent clauses. Despite the anonymity of the author and the structure of v. 1,[2] the independent clause contains the main thought of these verses, a prayer (εὔχομαι) for Gaius (v. 2).[3] Thus the clause is placed to the far left and the important structural marker, "I pray" (εὔχομαι), is underlined for easy identification. The content of the prayer concerns Gaius's prosperity (εὐοδοῦσθαι) and physical health (ὑγιαίνειν).

The dependent clause (καθὼς εὐοδοῦταί σου ἡ ψυχή) is placed directly under the concepts modified (εὐοδοῦσθαι καὶ ὑγιαίνειν), and

---

1. Structural outlines display the *results* of the fundamental grammatical and syntactical work already completed.

2. Due to the fact that salutations are not intended to be sentences, ὁ πρεσβύτερος is a nominative absolute, and thus, it has no verb. The use of the article, ὁ, points out that the πρεσβύτερος is a well-known person. Although little evidence exists that *demands* authorship to be by someone other than the apostle John, some suggest the author to be an unnamed elder, John the Elder, a group of church elders, or John and a second-generation redactor. I refer to the composer as "the author."

3. The recipient of the letter, Γάϊος, is unknown. The commonality of the name makes it unlikely that he was associated with Paul (1 Cor 1:14; Rom 16:23; Acts 19:29, 20:4). Gaius, in 3 John, is well known to the author (vv. 1-2), he is a valuable ally in providing support for traveling Christian workers (vv. 3, 5-8), and he is apparently a friend to the author. Although the *Apostolic Constitutions* 7.46.9 (ca. AD 370) states that John the apostle ordained a person by the name of Gaius as bishop of Pergamum, the connection with the Gaius of 3 John seems dubious.

the important structural marker, καθώς plus the verb εὐοδοῦται, is underlined for easy identification. Thus speaking comparatively (καθώς), the author prays that the physical health of beloved (ἀγαπητέ, cf. ὃν ἐγὼ ἀγαπῶ, v. 1) Gaius be in keeping with his spiritual health (vv. 1-2). After this opening salutation and prayer, the author proceeds with two statements of joy.

Statements of Joy

<u>ἐχάρην</u> γὰρ λίαν
^{3a}For I rejoiced greatly

    <u>ἐρχομένων</u> ἀδελφῶν καὶ <u>μαρτυρούντων</u> σου τῇ ἀληθείᾳ,
    ^{3b}when the brothers came and testified to your truth,

        <u>καθὼς</u> σὺ ἐν ἀληθείᾳ <u>περιπατεῖς</u>.
        ^{3c}even as you are walking in truth

μειζοτέραν τούτων οὐκ <u>ἔχω</u> χαράν,
^{4a}I have no greater joy than this,

    <u>ἵνα ἀκούω</u> τὰ ἐμὰ τέκνα ἐν τῇ ἀληθείᾳ περιπατοῦντα.
    ^{4b}namely, that I hear my children are *continually* walking in the truth.

Although vv. 3 and 4 embody two sentences, they express the same concept, one of joy (ἐχάρην . . . λίαν; ἔχω χαράν). Of the five isolated clauses, two are independent (placed to the far left), and three are dependent (two are positioned directly under the verbs they modify and the third is in apposition to τούτων and placed accordingly). The stress of these sentences, however, does not revolve around the independent but around the dependent clauses.

Unlike v. 4, v. 3 is more complex because of its two dependent clauses. The first describes the arrival of traveling Christian workers (ἀδελφῶν)[4] who have testified about Gaius. From the structural outline, two points are clear. (1) The position of ἐρχομένων directly under ἐχάρην indicates that the clause belongs to the main verb (ἐχάρην) in the independent clause. (2) The underlined participles ἐρχομένων and μαρτυρούντων tell us when the author rejoiced.[5] The second dependent clause, καθὼς σὺ ἐν

---

4. Although ἀδελφοί usually refers to Christian believers in general (esp. in Paul), Johannine usage indicates that ἀδελφῶν (lit. "of the brothers") refers to traveling or itinerant Christian workers. The use of προπέμπω and ὑπὲρ . . . τοῦ ὀνόματος in 3 John 7 supports contextually the reason why "the brothers" mentioned in vv. 3, 5, 6, 7, 8 (and possibly 12) are traveling Christian workers who proclaim the message of Christ Jesus.

5. Although ἐρχομένων and μαρτυρούντων are unconnected with the rest of the sentence, they are dependent verbals to the main clause. These genitive absolute participles are temporal

ἀληθείᾳ περιπατεῖς (placed directly under μαρτυρούντων),[6] informs us that the testimony about the "truth of Gaius's lifestyle" *matches* what the author knows to be true about Gaius's life (ἐν ἀληθείᾳ περιπατεῖς).[7] Thus the author's joy ensued when Gaius's Christlike deeds were reported to him (v. 3).

The final clause in this group of verses is another dependent clause. The appositional relationship of ἵνα ἀκούω . . . περιπατοῦντα is clearly observed in the position of ἵνα directly under τούτων. The author's joy is not limited to hearing of Gaius's Christlike behavior. He experiences similar joy whenever he hears of people under his spiritual authority (τὰ ἐμὰ τέκνα) behaving in a Christlike manner (v. 4).[8] Thus vv. 3 and 4 tell us that joy ensues when saints make it a practice to behave in a Christlike manner. Gaius's Christlike behavior, however, not only brings joy; his example also serves as a transition to a universal solicitation of all Christians.

---

in that they answer *when*. Nevertheless, the temporal nuance may convey a secondary notion indicating *why*. Thus they may describe both *when* (primary notion) and *why* (secondary notion) the author rejoiced.

6. Two renderings exist for this καθώς clause. On the one hand, καθώς could introduce an indirect discourse because it follows a verb of saying (μαρτυρέω, "I testify"). Thus καθώς may be translated *"namely, how* you walk in the truth" (Acts 15:14; cf. BAGD, 391c 5; BDAG, 493c 5), or *"that is, how* you walk in the truth" (NASB), or "as exemplified by the fact that." Thus, the clause informs us what was regularly testified, namely, how Gaius behaved in a Christlike manner (ἐν ἀληθείᾳ περιπατεῖς). Yet the difficulty with this view is that the governing verb μαρτυρέω appears already to be modified by σου τῇ ἀληθείᾳ. On the other hand, καθώς could modify μαρτυρούντων as a comparison and thereby evidence a structural parallel to the previous καθώς clause in v. 2. A comparative force would be translated "as indeed" (RSV, Stephen S. Smalley, *1, 2, 3 John*, WBC 51 [Waco, Tex.: Word, 1984], 347), "even as" (KJV), or "just as" (NET). Obviously both are evidenced in contemporary versions.

7. The phrase ἐν ἀληθείᾳ περιπατεῖς in this clause literally means, "you are walking in truth." Ἀλήθεια occurs twice in 3 John 3. In the Johannine letters, the term may refer to Christological belief (1 John 2:21-23; 4:2, 6; 5:10, 20; 2 John 7) or ethical behavior (1 John 1:6; 2:4; 3:18-19; 4:20). Here, the emphasis is on behavior. Christian workers commend Gaius for his actual "living in the truth" or "living faithfully" (v. 3), particularly as it pertains to Gaius providing for their needs (v. 5). Thus the phrase emphasizes Gaius's behavior. Cf. Brooke Foss Westcott, *The Epistles of John: The Greek Text with Notes*, 3rd ed. (London: Macmillan, 1892; reprint, Grand Rapids, Mich.: Eerdmans, 1966), 236; Raymond E. Brown, *The Epistles of John*, AB 30 (Garden City, N.Y.: Doubleday, 1982), 705-6; NET.

8. Somewhat idiomatic of Johannine literature (John 17:3; 1 John 3:11, 23; 4:21; 5:3; 2 John 6), the substantival ἵνα clause is appositional (cf. *ExSyn*, 475-76). The use of τέκνα in this clause does not imply that Gaius himself is one of the author's converts (contra to Pauline usage: 1 Cor 4:14-15; Gal 4:19; Phlm 10). Since it is plural, τέκνα is best understood as a general statement on the part of the author, who regards all those under his spiritual authority as his "children"; this is also consistent with his use of "Presbyter" as a self-designation in both 2 and 3 John.

Solicitation of All Christians

Ἀγαπητέ, πιστὸν <u>ποιεῖς</u>
^{5a}Beloved, you *continually* demonstrate faithfulness

ὃ ἐὰν ἐργάσῃ εἰς τοὺς ἀδελφοὺς καὶ τοῦτο ξένους,
^{5b}in whatever you do for the brothers, and strangers at that,

οἳ <u>ἐμαρτύρησάν</u> σου τῇ ἀγάπῃ ἐνώπιον ἐκκλησίας,
^{6a}who have testified to your love before the church,

οὓς καλῶς <u>ποιήσεις</u> προπέμψας ἀξίως τοῦ θεοῦ·
^{6b}whom you will do well by sending on their way in a manner worthy of God;

ὑπὲρ <u>γὰρ</u> τοῦ ὀνόματος <u>ἐξῆλθον</u>
^{7a}for they have gone forth on behalf of "The Name,"

μηδὲν <u>λαμβάνοντες</u> ἀπὸ τῶν ἐθνικῶν.
^{7b}while accepting nothing from the pagans.

ἡμεῖς <u>οὖν ὀφείλομεν ὑπολαμβάνειν</u> τοὺς τοιούτους,
^{8a}Therefore, we ought to support such people,

ἵνα συνεργοὶ <u>γινώμεθα</u> τῇ ἀληθείᾳ.
^{8b}so that we might become coworkers with *them* in the truth.

The central message of 3 John is found in these eight clauses. The first independent clause (placed to the far left) states a fact about Gaius: he continually demonstrates Christlike behavior (πιστὸν ποιεῖς).[9] The dependent relative clause, ὃ ἐὰν ἐργάσῃ (positioned directly under πιστὸν ποιεῖς), tells us that Gaius exhibited Christlike behavior in various works of service (particularly but not necessarily limited to acts of hospitality) for itinerant preachers, people whom Gaius did not know personally.[10]

9. Although πιστὸν ποιεῖς has no parallels in the NT, it is equivalent to ἐν ἀληθείᾳ περιπατεῖς in 3 John 3. Since the author is about to ask Gaius for additional help (v. 6b), he once again commends Gaius by restating what was acknowledged and what he knows to be true (vv. 3, 5). Perhaps the phrase is an intentional expansion of the common use of πιστός (cf. Matt 25:21; Luke 12:42; 1 Cor 4:17; Eph 6:21; Col 1:7), which has been described as "an attribute or epithet of Christian" (Judith Lieu, *The Second and Third Epistles of John,* Studies in the New Testament and Its World [Edinburgh: Clark, 1986], 105). The present tense indicates the habitual nature of his behavior. Thus Gaius is once again praised for his habitual Christlike behavior.

10. Ὃ ἐὰν ἐργάσῃ is an indefinite relative clause. Although it has no antecedent, the clause refers to the variety of faithful services offered by Gaius. Thus ὃ ἐὰν ἐργάσῃ may be translated "in whatever you do." The concluding phrase of the clause, καὶ τοῦτο ξένους, is an unusual expression. In fact, some witnesses read "καὶ εἰς τούς" in an attempt to ease the

Gaius's commendation for supporting itinerant workers (v. 5) did
not go unannounced. The two dependent relative clauses in v. 6 (οἳ
ἐμαρτύρησαν . . . and οὓς καλῶς ποιήσεις . . . positioned directly
under εἰς τοὺς ἀδελφούς) describe their antecedent, τοὺς ἀδελφούς.
The first tells us that Christian workers reported Gaius's acts of love
regularly to those who attended the author's church (v. 6a). The second
clause (v. 6b), when translated literally, is rendered "whom you will
do well having sent them forward." Yet translations reconstruct the
clause as an independent clause because it is a subtle form of persuasion typical of letter writing during the first century.[11] Although οὓς
καλῶς ποιήσεις is positioned under its antecedent, the author's assertion is clear: Christian workers merit support in a manner worthy
of God (v. 6b).[12]

The explanatory γάρ in the clauses of v. 7 (positioned under ποιήσεις)
is critical because it provides the reason they merit such support. First,
they proclaim Jesus (v. 7a).[13] Second, they reject support from nonbeliev-

difficulty of the phrase. However, the better reading, καὶ τοῦτο, may be translated as "and
at that" or "and especially" (BDF § 290 [5] and 442 [9]; cf. 1 Cor 6:6). In addition, we could
translate καὶ τοῦτο ξένους in apposition to εἰς τοὺς ἀδελφοὺς ("in whatever you do for the
brothers—and strangers at that!"; cf. Westcott, *Epistles of John,* 238). Thus Gaius's faithfulness
is elevated because those whom he helped (those in v. 3 as well) were strangers to him; he did
not know them personally.

11. KJV, NASB, NRSV, NIV, NET render the clause: "You will do well to send them on
their way in a manner worthy of God." The phrase καλῶς ποιήσεις is a mitigated exhortation, which softens the author's command so as to make it more palatable to the listener or
reader (Martin M. Culy, *1, 2, 3 John: A Handbook on the Greek Text* [Waco, Tex.: Baylor
University Press, 2004], xvii-xx, 161). More specifically, Brown identifies καλῶς ποιήσεις
"as a standard way in Epistolary Format for introducing the request that embodies the whole
purpose of the letter" (*Epistles,* 710). Thus this grammatically dependent relative clause takes
on significant force, which issues a subtle expectation and thereby is rendered in English as
an independent clause.

12. Προπέμψας is an aorist adverbial participle of means which means to "help on one's
journey with food, money, by arranging for companions, means of travel, etc., send on one's
way" (cf. BAGD, 709b 2; BDAG, 873c 2). Προπέμπω is frequently used in the NT in the sense
of providing Christian workers with supplies to enable them to continue their journey to the
next stopping place (Acts 15:3; Rom 15:24; 1 Cor 16:6, 11; 2 Cor 1:16; and Tit 3:13). Thus
προπέμπω is virtually a technical term for supporting Christian workers.

13. The verb ἐξέρχομαι is used of Paul's travels in Acts 14:20 and 15:40. Thus ὑπὲρ
. . . τοῦ ὀνόματος seems to refer to some form of missionary activity. Within Rabbinic
Literature, "The Name" is a frequent substitute for the Tetragrammaton *Yahweh.* Within the
broader Christian community, however, it referred to the title "Lord" for Jesus (Rom 1:9;
1 Cor 12:3; Phil 2:9-11; etc.). Within the community of Johannine Christians the Tetragrammaton or "I AM" was used to refer to Jesus. Here in 3 John 7, "the Name" could refer to
God's name, but there is no inconsistency in using this designation for Jesus also. Paul uses
a similar phrase in Rom 1:5, and in 1 John 2:12 the author wrote, "your sins are forgiven
on account of his [Christ's] name." John's Gospel also makes reference to believing "in the

ers (v. 7b).[14] (We might say the converse is true: Traveling servants who proclaim Jesus *depend on Christian support*.)

The second independent clause in v. 8 (placed to the far left) concludes (οὖν) this section with a specific yet universal solicitation and duty: Christians everywhere are obligated (ὀφείλομεν) to support traveling Christian workers who proclaim Jesus (v. 8a).[15] The dependent clause (ἵνα συνεργοὶ γινώμεθα τῇ ἀληθείᾳ, positioned directly under ὀφείλομεν), however, conveys a significant theological perspective about Christians who support such traveling servants: they become partners with them and their work (v. 8b).[16] Thus vv. 5-8 identify the reasoned duty of all followers of Jesus: Christians are to support missionaries because they preach Christ to unbelievers and thereby depend upon Christian support. The author quickly follows with an intentional benefit to all who support missionaries, namely they become partners with them and their ministry. Despite this expectation and intentional benefit, the author identifies an individual who impedes the support of God's traveling servants.

---

name of Jesus" (cp. 1:12, 3:18). Brown, *Epistles*, 711-12; Lieu, *Second and Third Epistles of John*, 198; NET.

14. Although I render λαμβάνοντες as an adverbial participle with a temporal force, it might also be means ("by accepting"). Attendant circumstance is another good alternative because it coordinates with the finite verb, ἐξῆλθον (cf. *ExSyn*, 640-46). Brown argues that λαμβάνοντες serves to "confirm" the finite verb (*Epistles*, 712; NLT). Thus λαμβάνοντες would be translated as a finite verb, connected to the main verb by *and* ("they have gone forth . . . and have accepted nothing . . ."), providing a second reason why traveling Christian workers merit support. Most translations, however, acknowledge the participle's adverbial relationship with ἐξῆλθον (KJV, NASB, NIV, NRSV, NET; cp. Smalley, *1, 2, 3 John*, 341; Lieu, *Second and Third Epistles of John*, 108; John Painter, *1, 2, and 3 John*, SP 18 [Collegeville, Minn.: Liturgical, 2002], 370).

15. The inferential conj. οὖν, gives a deduction, conclusion, or summary to vv. 5-7. In addition, the author gives emphasis to ἡμεῖς in this clause when he says ἡμεῖς οὖν ὀφείλομεν ὑπολαμβάνειν τοὺς τοιούτους. He does not refer to himself alone. Ἡμεῖς is first person plural construction inclusive of all true Christians. Thus ἡμεῖς is an inclusive "we." The term ὑπολαμβάνειν (a complementary infinitive completing the thought of ὀφείλω, "I ought"), according to Delling, is not limited to hospitality but extends even to protecting those who are persecuted (s.v. "ὑπολαμβάνω," *TDNT*, 4:15; cp. BAGD, 845b 2; BDAG, 1038c 2). Thus believers are to offer various kinds of support to those who proclaim the Lord—Jesus.

16. The dependent adverbial ἵνα clause is purpose because it reflects the author's intention. It might appear difficult to become coworkers (corresponding to the συν-prefix of the noun modified) with an abstract concept like "truth." Yet "truth" is personified in Johannine literature (cp. John 8:32, "the truth will make you free"; in 1 John 4:6 the Holy Spirit is "the Spirit of Truth," a characterization repeated in 1 John 5:6, NET). Thus the "truth" at work here in 3 John could be the Holy Spirit, and thereby support of a traveling Christian worker results in becoming a coworker with the Spirit of God. Nevertheless a more straightforward understanding is simply this: Christians are to support itinerant missionaries so that they may be coworkers with them. Thus τῇ ἀληθείᾳ serves as a complement of συνεργοί with an implied αὐτός and thereby translated "fellow-workers *with them* in the truth" or "partners *with them* for the truth" (NLT).

Stubbornness of Diotrephes

Ἔγραψά τι τῇ ἐκκλησίᾳ·
^{9a}I wrote something to the church;

ἀλλ' ὁ φιλοπρωτεύων αὐτῶν Διοτρέφης οὐκ ἐπιδέχεται ἡμᾶς.
^{9b}but Diotrephes, namely, the one who loves to be first among them, does not acknowledge us.

διὰ τοῦτο, ἐὰν ἔλθω,
^{10a}Therefore, if I come,

ὑπομνήσω αὐτοῦ τὰ ἔργα - - - ⌐
^{10b}I will bring up his deeds,   │
┌ - - - - - - - - - - - - - - - - - - - ┘
│

ἃ ποιεῖ λόγοις πονηροῖς φλυαρῶν ἡμᾶς,
^{10c} which he is *continually* doing, by talking nonsense about us with evil words.

καὶ μὴ ἀρκούμενος ἐπὶ τούτοις
^{10d}And not being content with that (lit. "these things"),

οὔτε αὐτὸς ἐπιδέχεται τοὺς ἀδελφοὺς
^{10e}he himself refuses to welcome the traveling servants of God.

καὶ τοὺς βουλομένους κωλύει
^{10f}Furthermore, he hinders the people who want *to welcome these servants*

καὶ ἐκ τῆς ἐκκλησίας ἐκβάλλει.
^{10g}and he throws them out of the church.

These nine clauses reveal Diotrephes' multifaceted acts of stubbornness. On the one hand, his stubbornness is directed at the author and Gaius (first two independent clauses placed to the far left). Despite (ἀλλά, contrast. conj.) the author's letter to the church, Diotrephes has rejected the author's authority as well as Gaius's (οὐκ ἐπιδέχεται ἡμᾶς) concerning the support of God's traveling servants (v. 9).

On the other hand, his stubbornness is also directed toward people in his church who support such workers (last two independent clauses placed to the far left). The dependent clause καὶ μὴ ἀρκούμενος ἐπὶ τούτοις (positioned directly above ἐπιδέχεται) serves to introduce the continuation (καί, coord. conj.) of Diotrephes' stubbornness introduced in v. 9 and elaborated on in 10c. Thus because he is not content (adv. ptc. of cause, ἀρκούμενος), God's traveling servants are not received by Diotrephes (οὔτε αὐτὸς ἐπιδέχεται, v. 10e). Furthermore, the people in his congregation are forbidden to help them (κωλύει, v. 10f), and those who do so are expelled from the church (ἐκβάλλει, v. 10g).[17]

Sandwiched between Diotrephes' stubborn acts of resistance are the author's intentions expressed in three clauses, one independent (v. 10b) and two dependent (v. 10a, c). Although the first dependent clause exhibits some uncertainty (ἐὰν ἔλθω, positioned directly above ὑπομνήσω), the author speaks of visiting Diotrephes' church (v. 10a).[18] Based (διὰ τοῦτο) upon Diotrephes' rejection of authority mentioned in v. 9b, the third independent clause explains the author's intention to publicly reprimand (ὑπομνήσω) Diotrephes' habitual acts of resistance that undermine his authority (v. 10b).[19] The dependent relative clause (ἃ ποιεῖ . . .) defines the nature of Diotrephes' resistance—he gossips maliciously against those in authority

17. Ὁ φιλοπρωτεύων (v. 9) suggests that Diotrephes is an arrogant leader in his church. Perhaps he rose to prominence through his own enterprising efforts (Brown, *Epistles*, 743). Regardless of how he rose to prominence, the three present tense verbs in vv. 9b-10 indicate Diotrephes' continual policy of resistance against those who serve Christ. Each clause is linked together with the coord. conj, καί. (1) Ἐπιδέχεται in the phrase "He himself does not receive *them*" (οὔτε αὐτὸς ἐπιδέχεται), is an outward manifestation of Diotrephes' rejection of the author's authority. He not only rejects the author's proposal (v. 9a; cp. P.Petr. 3.32), he acts out his rejection with his denial of support for traveling servants (v. 10d; cp. P.Oxy. 2.271-72; cp. BAGD, 292a or BDAG, 370c with Brown, *Epistles,* 718). (2) Whereas the KJV and NASB translate κωλύει as "forbids," the RSV and NIV translate it as "stop." Which translation is correct? Κωλύει has several nuances of meaning: "stop" (Acts 27:43; P.Oxy. 3.147-51), "prevent" (Exod 36:6: 1 Kgs 25:6: Acts 8:36), and "forbid" (Num 11:28; 2 Kgs 13:13; 1 Tim 4:3; Jos. *Ant.* 11. 3. 8; P.Oxy. 8.166-68). "Forbid" may be the better rendering for at least two reasons: (a) it shows the gradually increasing severity of Diotrephes' actions (he does not receive, he forbids, he expels); and (b) if Diotrephes was successful in stopping people in his congregation, there would be no need to expel them. (3) Ἐκβάλλει (lit. "he throws out") is a term typically used of divorce ("nor to put her away," MM, 191), of the Essenes who expelled people from their community ("those who are convicted of serious crimes they expel for the order," Jos. *War* 2. 8. 8), and of synagogue expulsion (John 9:34-35). It seems that Diotrephes as a leader in this church convinced the community to institute a policy of forbidding people to support traveling Christian workers and expelled those who disobeyed that policy. The church mentioned in vv. 9 and 10 (i.e., Diotrephes' church) is not the same one mentioned in v. 6 (i.e., Gaius's church) because of αὐτῶν. If Gaius's church is intended, it would have been more natural to use a second person pronoun: "Diotrephes, who loves to be first among you [ὑμῶν]." Thus Gaius seems to belong to (or is in charge of) one local church while Diotrephes belongs to another.

18. Διὰ τοῦτο refers to what precedes (typical Johannine usage: 1:31; 6:65; 7:21-22; 9:23; 12:27; 13:11; 15:19; 16:15; 19:11; 1 John 4:5; 3 John 10; Brown, *Epistles*, 391-92). Although Smalley translates ἐὰν ἔλθω as a temporal intention: "When I come" (*1, 2, 3 John,* 357), the third-class condition (ἐὰν ἔλθω) probably indicates real uncertainty on the author's part as to whether he will visit Diotrephes' church (Brown, *Epistles,* 718).

19. Ὑπομνήσω from ὑπομιμνήσκω, (lit. "bring up"), may be either positive (of Herod before the Roman Senate, Jos. *Ant* 14. 14. 4) or negative (of Cretans, Herodotus 7.171; Wis 12:2; 2 Tim 2:14). Here in this clause it is negative. The author intends to expose publicly Diotrephes' malicious acts that will require congregational disciplinary action (perhaps expulsion—certainly removal from leadership). Ὑπομνήσω is a predictive future, thereby expressing what will take place or come to pass if John should visit Diotrephes' church.

(φλυαρῶν ἡμᾶς) (v. 10c).[20] Thus vv. 9-10 tell us that stubborn resistance against and malicious gossip about church leaders, which undermines their authority (particularly but not exclusively as it concerns supporting Christian workers), are grounds for public reprimand. The author does not, however, end his letter with Diotrephes' negative example. Rather, he shifts attention to a positive model, a person who is to be imitated as well as supported.

Sponsor for Demetrius

Ἀγαπητέ, μὴ μιμοῦ τὸ κακὸν ἀλλὰ τὸ ἀγαθόν.
[11a]Beloved, do not imitate that which is bad but that which is good.

ὁ ἀγαθοποιῶν ἐκ τοῦ θεοῦ ἐστιν·
[11b]The one who does well is of God;

ὁ κακοποιῶν οὐχ ἑώρακεν τὸν θεόν.
[11c]the one who does what is bad has not seen God.

Δημητρίῳ μεμαρτύρηται ὑπὸ πάντων καὶ ὑπὸ αὐτῆς τῆς ἀληθείας·
[12a]Demetrius has been testified to by all, even by the truth itself;

καὶ ἡμεῖς δὲ μαρτυροῦμεν,
[12b]and we also testify to him,

καὶ οἶδας ὅτι ἡ μαρτυρία ἡμῶν ἀληθής ἐστιν.
[12c]and you know that our testimony is true.

Collectively, these six clauses (placed to the far left) serve to vouch for Demetrius as one who merits the support spoken of in 6b and 8. In typical Johannine style, the author presents an antithetical structure in v. 11 that differentiates Diotrephes (τὸ κακόν) from Demetrius (τὸ ἀγαθόν).[21] The author appeals to Gaius not to imitate the bad (μὴ μιμοῦ τὸ κακόν, 11a)

---

20. The adverbial participle (φλυαρῶν) to the verb in the relative clause (ἃ ποιεῖ) explains the means by which Diotrephes does evil works. The *hapax legomenon* φλυαρέω is generally translated as "talk nonsense (about)" or may speak of one who is "an idle babbler" or of one who "brings unjustified charges against" another. The noun φλύαρος occurs in 1 Tim 5:13 and is translated "gossipy" or "foolish" (MM, 673; BAGD, 862b; BDAG, 1060c). Thus Diotrephes talks nonsense or gossips. He apparently does so with hostility ("evil words" λόγοις πονηροῖς), or as Smalley translates it, "with a malicious tongue" (*1, 2, 3 John*, 356). Thus the relative clause can be translated "which he is doing, by talking nonsense about us maliciously" or perhaps "gossiping maliciously about us."

21. Demetrius may have been the leader of a delegation of traveling Christian workers and perhaps the bearer of this letter to Gaius. Letters of introduction are attested in Paul's writings, cf. 1 Cor 16:3; 2 Cor 3:1; Col 4:7-9; perhaps Rom 16:1-2 (though Lieu, *Second and Third Epistles of John*, 118-19 disagrees). We know very little about Demetrius, but he comes to Gaius with the highest of recommendations.

of those whose behavior calls into question their relationship with God (11c), namely Diotrephes. Rather (ἀλλά, contrast. conj.), he should imitate the good (11a) of those whose behavior demonstrates their relationship with God (11b).[22] Thus the appeal is not to follow negative examples but to do what is right (v. 11), specifically as it pertains to imitating godly Christian workers.

The last three clauses are progressive in nature to introduce Demetrius as a Christian worker worthy of support (v. 12). As his sponsor, the author begins with a well-known fact about Demetrius: he has received a good testimony from others (μεμαρτύρηται ὑπὸ πάντων) concerning both his belief and his practice (12a). The author adds (καί, coord. conj.) to this fact with his own testimonial about him (v. 12b), a testimonial Gaius can rely upon as dependable (12c). Thus vv. 11-12 tell us which traveling Christian workers merit support: (1) those whose good behavior merits imitation, (2) those whose behavior identifies a relationship with God, and (3) those whose commitment to Christ Jesus is verified by other believers. Having expressed his concern for Christ's itinerant teachers, the author proceeds to end his letter.

Summation

Πολλὰ <u>εἶχον γράψαι</u> σοι
[13a]I had many *more things* to write to you,

<u>ἀλλ᾽</u> οὐ <u>θέλω</u> διὰ μέλανος καὶ καλάμου σοι <u>γράφειν·</u>
[13b]but I do not wish to write *it out* to you by means of ink and pen;

[14] <u>ἐλπίζω</u> δὲ εὐθέως σε <u>ἰδεῖν</u>,
[14a]Rather, I hope to see you immediately,

<u>καὶ</u> στόμα πρὸς στόμα <u>λαλήσομεν</u>.
[14b]and we will speak face to face.

22. When a conjunctive word or phrase introduces an independent clause like "the one who does what is bad has not seen God," the phenomenon is known as asyndeton (a construction "not bound together"). Asyndeton is a vivid stylistic feature that occurs often for emphasis, solemnity, or rhetorical value (staccato effect), or when there is an abrupt change in topic (*ExSyn*, 658). Thus the abrupt introduction of "the one who does good is of God . . ." adds emphasis. In addition, Brown views the parallels in v. 11 (good/bad) as reflecting a chiastic Semitic literary pattern (*Epistles*, 720). The emphasis, then, is on 11b & 11c. Finally, the statement reiterates the common Johannine theme of behavior as an indication of genuine faith (cf. John 3:17-21; 1 John 3:6, 10, 4:7; 4:20). Thus the use of the phrase "has not seen God" calls into question the genuineness of Diotrephes' faith because he has obviously done "what is bad" (vv. 9-10). Granted, the author does not describe Diotrephes as an antichrist, a secessionist, a false prophet, or one who denies that Jesus Christ has come in the flesh (cf. 1 John 2:18-23; 4:1-2; 2 John 7), but the genuineness of Diotrephes' faith is questioned.

εἰρήνη σοι.
[15a]Peace *be* to you.

ἀσπάζονταί σε οἱ φίλοι.
[15b]The friends [here] greet you.

ἀσπάζου τοὺς φίλους κατ᾽ ὄνομα.
[15c]Greet the friends [there] by name.

Like the previous seven clauses, these are also independent. The first four (vv. 13-14) reveal the author's personal desire. Although (ἀλλά, contrast. conj.) other matters need to be discussed (πολλὰ εἶχον γράψαι), the author wishes to communicate with Gaius in a way other than a letter (οὐ . . . διὰ μέλανος καὶ καλάμου).[23] Rather (δέ, contrast. conj.) than communicating further by letter, he desires (ἐλπίζω) to visit Gaius (σε ἰδεῖν) and (καί, coord. conj.) have a heart-to-heart discussion (στόμα πρὸς στόμα λαλήσομεν).[24] The last three clauses conclude the letter in a typical Jewish manner (εἰρήνη σοι), followed by two summary salutations. One offers greetings from friends (ἀσπάζονταί σε οἱ φίλοι), the other, greetings to friends (ἀσπάζου τοὺς φίλους).[25] Thus vv. 13-15 express the author's desire to visit and communicate with Gaius in person and offer his concluding greetings.

In conclusion, the foremost concern of 3 John is the obligation that every Christian has to support those (like Demetrius) who travel and proclaim the message about Jesus who is the Christ, come in the flesh (1 John 4:2-3; 2 John 7). Such people merit Christian support. Some (like

23. The phrase οὐ θέλω διὰ μέλανος καὶ καλάμου σοι γράφειν parallels 2 John 12, but it is a bit more elegantly stated (Brown, *Epistles*, 725). Perhaps both letters were written at approximately the same time. Regardless, the author tells Gaius that he has more to say (πολλὰ εἶχον γράψαι σοι). Whereas γράψαι is an epexegetical infinitive that clarifies the "many more things" (πολλά, v. 13a), γράφειν is a complementary infinitive completing the thought of the verb θέλω (v. 13b). Thus γράφειν is underlined. Like γράφειν (v. 13b), ἰδεῖν is also a complementary infinitive completing ἐλπίζω and is underlined.

24. The phrase "by means (διά) of paper and ink" simply means that John wishes to communicate with Gaius in a more personal way, heart to heart (στόμα πρὸς στόμα λαλήσομεν, lit. "we will speak mouth to mouth," v. 14) (Brown, *Epistles*, 677). The author appears to anticipate a personal visit to Gaius's church in the very near future. This may be the same visit mentioned in connection with Diotrephes in v. 10. Perhaps the churches were in the same city, or in neighboring towns, so that the author anticipated visiting both on the same journey.

25. On the one hand, the φίλοι may indicate that these are personal friends of Gaius. But if this is the case it is somewhat surprising that their names are not mentioned. On the other hand, φίλοι may be an alternative to ἀδελφοί, especially within the Johannine community. It may have arisen in the Johannine community from Jesus' teaching in the Gospel of John 15:13-15, "you are my friends if you do what I command you" (Brown, *Epistles*, 726; Lieu, *Second and Third Epistles of John*, 121-22). Thus the articles that accompany φίλος (οἱ φίλοι and τοὺς φίλους) are perhaps individualizing articles (cf. *ExSyn*, 216-31).

Gaius and his church) excel in their support of Christ's servants. Others (like Diotrephes and his church) stumble. In both cases, their reputations precede them. What reputation precedes your church concerning the support of God's servants?

Harold, though I will always hold you in high regard as a serious scholar, one who has contributed to my ability to interpret the New Testament and to understand the world in which it was written, my cherished memory of you will always be your commitment to your family and your sense of humor. Thank you for contributing to my life both in and outside the classroom.

Scripture Index

General Index